Newham London

ADULTS

E 10/14	
24/03/14	

D0533332

24 hour automated telephone renewal line
0115 929 3388
Or online at www.newham.gov.uk

This book must be returned (or its issue renewed)
on or before the date stamped above

NEWHAM LIBRARIES

90800100038843

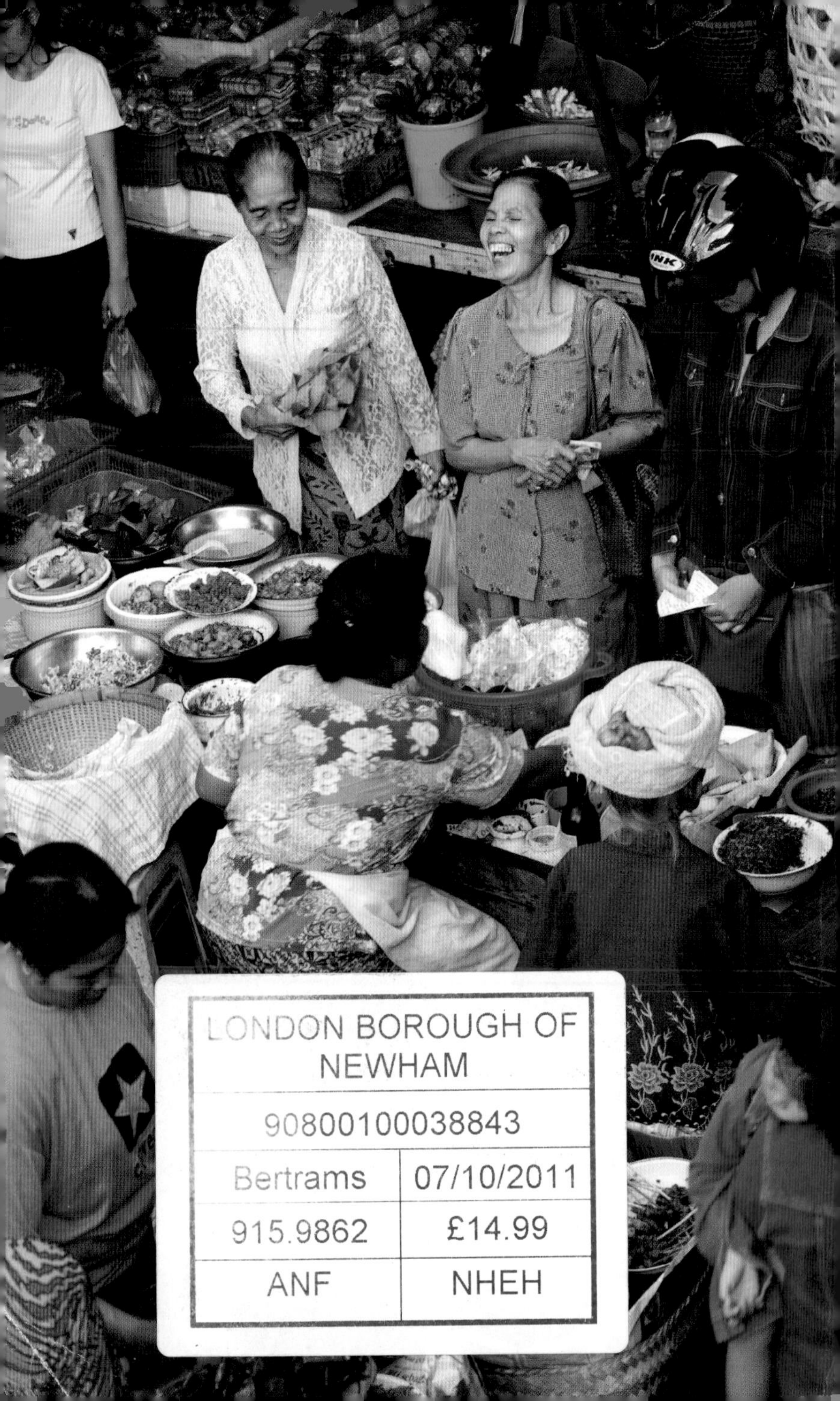
INK

Contents

The crafts of Bali and Lombok colour section following p.184

Volcanoes and rice-fields colour section following p.284

3

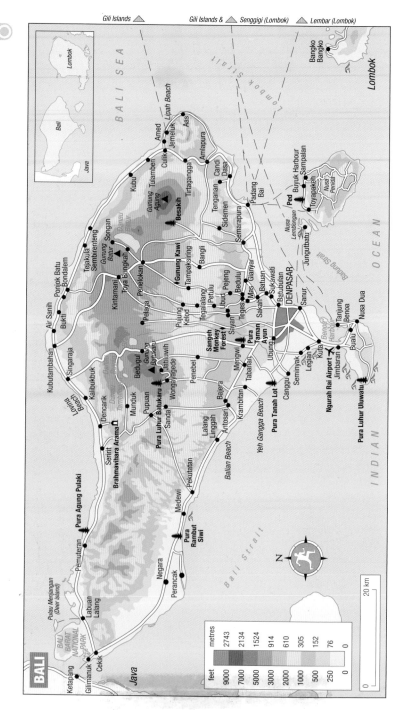

Gili Islands ▲   Gili Islands & ▲ Senggigi (Lombok)   ▲ Lembar (Lombok)

BALI

4

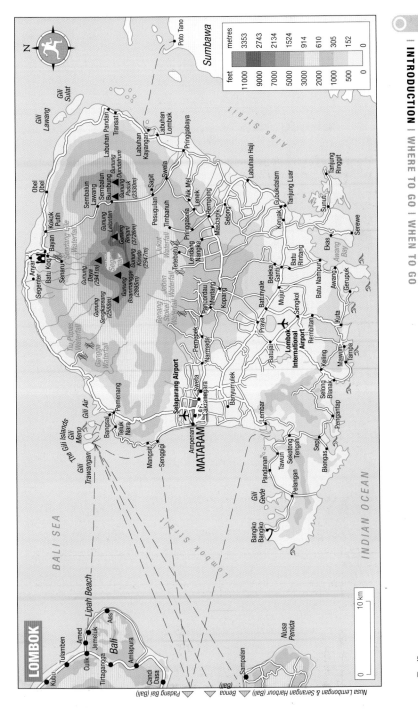

LOMBOK

Bali

Kubu
Tulamben
Amed
Culik
Jemeluk
Lipah Beach
Aas
Tirtagangga
Amlapura
Candi
Dasa

BALI SEA

The Gili Islands
Gili Trawangan
Gili Meno
Gili Air
Bangsal
Teluk Nara
Pemenang

Mangsit
Senggigi

Lombok Strait

Nusa Penida

Sampalan

INDIAN OCEAN

Bangko Bangko

Gili Gede

Pelangan
Tawun
Sekotong Tengah
Pandanan
Blongas
Sepi
Pengantap
Selong Blanak

Lembar

Banyumulek

AMPENAN
MATARAM
Cakranegara
Sweta
Selaparang Airport

Segenter
Anyar
Batu Koq
Senaru
Bayan
Kokok Putih
Obel Obel

Sendang Gile Waterfall

Tiu Pupus Waterfall

Gangga Waterfall

Gunung Sengkaraang (2568m)
Gunung Daya (2941m)
Seg... Nat.
Gunung Rinjani (3726m)
Gunung Leuenten (2885m)
Gunung Kondo (2947m)
Gunung Buanmangge (2895m)

Sembalun Lawang
Sembalun Bumbung
Gunung Dundartum
Gunung Pusuk (2330m)

Labuhan Pandan
Transat
Labuhan Lombok
Labuhan Kayangan

Pringgabaya

Swela
Sapit
Pesugulan
Timbanuh
Aik Mel
Lenek
Rempung
Masbagik
Sembung
Selong
Labuhan Haj

Pringgasela
Loyok
Benang Stokel Waterfall
Jukut Waterfall
Joben Waterfall
Tetebatu
Lenidang
Nangka
Mantang
Kopang
Praya
Lombok International Airport
Rembitan
Keling
Mawun
Tampa
Kuta
Awang
Gerupuk
Batu Nampur

Pemepek
Narmada
Batujai
Pengordau
Sakra
Batnyale
Mujur
Sengkol
Sukarara

Batu Rintang
Beleka
Ganti
Keruak
Tanjung Luar

Gubukdalam
Sunil
Serewe
Tanjung Ringgit

Awang Bay

Ekas

Alas Strait

Poto Tano

Sumbawa

Gili Sulat
Gili Lawang

feet	metres
11000	3353
9000	2743
7000	2134
5000	1524
3000	914
2000	610
1000	305
500	152
0	0

10 km

Nusa Lembongan & Serangan Harbour (Bali) • Padang Bai (Bali) • Benoa • Padang Bai (Bali)

Introduction to

Bali &
Lombok

**The islands of Bali and Lombok are part of the Indonesian
archipelago, a 5200km-long string of over thirteen
thousand islands, stretching between Malaysia in the
west and Australia in the east. Sandy beaches punctuate
the dramatically rugged coastlines, and world-class surf
pounds both shorelines.**

Both islands are small – Bali extends less than 150km at
its widest point, Lombok a mere 80km – and both are
volcanic, graced with swathes of extremely fertile land,
much of it sculpted into terraced rice paddies. Culturally,
however, Bali and Lombok could hardly be more different.
Bali remains the only **Hindu** society in Southeast Asia, and
religious observance permeates every aspect of modern
Balinese life; the Sasak people of Lombok, on the other hand, are **Muslim**,
like the vast majority of other Indonesians.

With a tourist industry that dates back ninety years, the tiny island of
Bali (population 3.8 million) has become very much a mainstream destination, offering all the comforts and facilities expected by better-off tourists,
and suffering the predictable problems of congestion, commercialization
and breakneck Westernization. However, its original charm is still much in
evidence, its distinctive temples and elaborate festivals set off by the lush
landscape of the interior. Although tourist arrivals plummeted after the

▲ Fishing in the sea

Fact file

• Bali and Lombok are part of the **Republic of Indonesia**, an ethnically diverse democracy of 237 million people. Everyone over the age of 17 is eligible to vote in the national **elections**, held at least every five years. The electorate votes first for the 560 members of the House of Representatives (DPR), and subsequently for the **president** and vice-president.

• As one of 33 self-contained provinces (*propinsi*) of Indonesia, **Bali** is overseen by a governor who is elected by Bali's Regional House of Representatives (DPRD) for a five-year term. The province is divided into one city or *kota*, Denpasar, and eight districts, or *kabupaten*. The *kabupaten* reflect the borders of the old regencies and are named after them: Badung, Bangli, Buleleng, Gianyar, Jembrana, Karangasem, Klungkung and Tabanan.

• **Lombok** and its eastern neighbour, Sumbawa, together form the province of Nusa Tenggara Barat (NTB or West Nusa Tenggara). Lombok has four districts – North, South, East and West Lombok – and one municipality, Mataram, the seat of the provincial government.

• Both islands are **volcanic**; the highest peak in Bali's spine of volcanoes is **Gunung Agung** (3142m). Lombok's highest point is the summit of **Gunung Rinjani** (3726m), one of the tallest mountains in Indonesia. Separating the two islands is the **Lombok Strait** – just 35km wide, but 1300m deep in places.

bombs of 2002 and 2005, visitors are returning in their previously high numbers (nearly 2.5 million in 2010). Meanwhile, **Lombok** (population 3.1 million) plays host to far fewer foreign visitors and boasts only a handful of burgeoning tourist resorts, retaining its reputation as a more adventurous destination than its neighbour, with plenty of unspoilt beaches and forested mountain slopes.

Until the nineteenth century, both Bali and Lombok were divided into small **kingdoms**, each domain ruled by a succession of rajas whose territories fluctuated so much that, at times, parts of eastern Bali and western Lombok were joined under a single ruler. More recently, both islands endured years of colonial rule under the Dutch East Indies government, which only ended with hard-won

Sanur beach

independence for Indonesia in 1949. Since then, the Jakarta-based government of Indonesia has tried hard to foster a sense of national identity among its extraordinarily diverse islands, both by implementing a unifying five-point political philosophy, the Pancasila, and through the mandatory introduction of Bahasa Indonesia, now the lingua franca for the whole archipelago. Politically, Bali is administered as a province in its own right, while Lombok is the most westerly island of Nusa Tenggara, a chain of islands stretching east as far as Timor, which is divided into two provinces, West Nusa Tenggara and East Nusa Tenggara.

Where to go

Bali's best-known resort is the **Kuta-Legian-Seminyak** strip, an eight-kilometre sweep of golden sand whose international reputation as a hangout for weekending Australian surfers is enhanced by fashionable restaurants and chic designer shops. Travellers seeking more relaxed alternatives generally head north to the beaches around and beyond Canggu, across the southern peninsula to **Sanur** or offshore to **Nusa Lembongan**; to sedate **Candi Dasa** or **Amed** further east; or to the black volcanic sands of **Lovina** on the north coast. Quieter, upmarket seaside options can be found at **Jimbaran** in the south and **Pemuteran** in the northwest. On Lombok, the trio of white-sand **Gili Islands** draw the biggest crowds; there are quieter islands off the **Sekotong** peninsula, a wide range of resort accommodation around **Senggigi** and a series of extraordinarily beautiful beaches near **Kuta** in the south. All these resorts make comfortable bases for **divers** and **snorkellers** and are within easy reach of the islands' many reefs. **Surfers** have countless swells to choose from, including the famously challenging Uluwatu on Bali and Desert Point on Lombok, as well as many more novice-friendly breaks.

Swimming with mola mola

The waters around Nusa Lembongan and Nusa Penida from July to October each year are the best chance most people will ever have of spotting a **mola mola** (a.k.a. oceanic sunfish), one of the most elusive and startling of underwater creatures. The heaviest bony fish in the world, it has an average weight of 1000kg. Some specimens weigh more than double that and grow up to 3m long, making it roughly the size of a small car. *Mola* is Latin for millstone, which it resembles in being huge, grey, rough and rounded in shape – it has no tail. Fortunately it is docile and no danger to divers, as it eats jellyfish and other gelatinous marine life. Much remains unknown about this gentle giant but it is thought to spend most of its life well below 200m.

For some reason the annual shift of ocean currents brings it up to shallower waters for a few months each year, which is when enthusiasts and the merely curious head to the seas around these two small islands in the hope of spotting one.

▲ *Munduk Moding, Asah Gobleg*

Most visitors also venture inland to experience more traditional island life. On Bali, the once-tiny village of **Ubud** has become a hugely popular cultural centre, still charming but undeniably commercialized, where traditional dances are staged every night and the streets are full of craft shops and purveyors of alternative therapies. **Tetebatu** on Lombok occupies a similarly cool position in the foothills, although, like the island as a whole, it lacks the artistic heritage of Bali. In general, the villages on both islands are far more appealing than the towns, but Bali's capital, **Denpasar**, the historic

▲ *Monkey at Pura Luhur Uluwatu*

district capital of **Semarapura**, and Lombok's **Mataram** conurbation are all worth a day-trip for their museums, markets and temples.

Bali's other big draw is its proliferation of elegant Hindu **temples**, particularly the island temple of **Tanah Lot**, the dramatically located **Uluwatu** at the southern tip of the island and the extensive **Besakih** complex on the slopes of Gunung Agung. Temple **festivals** are also well worth attending: held throughout the island and at frequent intervals during the year, most are open to tourists.

Both islands hold a number of **hiking** possibilities, many of them up **volcanoes**. The best is undoubtedly the climb to the summit of Lombok's **Gunung Rinjani** – one of the highest peaks in Indonesia. The ascent of Bali's **Gunung Agung** is shorter and less arduous although still pretty challenging. The climb up **Gunung Batur** is much less taxing and therefore more popular. Bali's sole **national park**, Bali Barat, has relatively few interesting trails, but can be rewarding for **bird-watching**, as is the area around **Danau Bratan** in the centre of the island. Even if you don't want to

Traditional dress

It is customary for Balinese men and women to wear **traditional dress** whenever they attend temple festivals, cremations, weddings, birth rites and other important rituals; men also wear temple dress if playing in a gamelan orchestra and occasionally for *banjar* meetings too.

The traditional outfit for **women** is a lacy, close-fitting, long-sleeved blouse (*kebaya*) and a tightly wound sarong (*kain kamben*), set off by the all-important sash (*selempot*), which symbolically contains the body and its physical appetites. It's currently fashionable to wear a vividly coloured bustier under the *kebaya*, and some women don flamboyant hair-pieces as well. For some big festivals, women from the same community will all wear the same-coloured *kebaya* to give their group a recognizable identity.

Men also wear a type of sarong (*kamben sarung*), a knee-length hip-cloth (*saput*), and a formal, collared shirt (generally white but sometimes batik) or a starched jacket-like shirt. The distinctive headcloth (*udeng*) can be tied according to personal taste, but generally with a triangular crest on top (shops sell ready-tied *udeng*). As with the sash, the *udeng* symbolically concentrates the mental energies and directs the thoughts heavenwards, via the perky cockscomb at the front.

go hiking, it's worth considering a trip to an inland village for the change of scenery (often with some lovely rice terrace views) and refreshing temperatures; the villages of **Sidemen, Tirtagangga, Sarinbuana** and **Munduk** are all good bases.

When to go

ocated in the **tropics**, just eight degrees south of the equator, Bali and Lombok enjoy fairly constant year-round temperatures, averaging 27°C in coastal areas and the hills around Ubud and 22°C in the central volcanoes around Kintamani. Both islands are hit by an annual **monsoon**, which brings rain, wind and a sometimes unbearable 97 percent humidity from October through to March.

The **best time to visit** is outside the monsoon season, from May to September, though monsoons are, like many other events in Indonesia, notoriously unpunctual, and you should be prepared to get rained on in Ubud at any time of year. However, the prospect of a daily rainstorm shouldn't put you off: you're far more likely to get an hour-long downpour than day-long drizzle; mountain-climbing, though, is both unrewarding and dangerous

◀ Women carrying religious offerings

at this time of year. You should also be aware of the peak **tourist seasons**: resorts on both islands get packed out between mid-June and mid-September and again over the Christmas–New Year period, when prices rocket and rooms can be fully booked for weeks in advance.

Average monthly temperatures and rainfall

	Jan	Feb	Mar	Apr	May	Jun	Jul	Aug	Sep	Oct	Nov	Dec
Kintamani												
°C	22	22	22	22	22	21	21	21	22	22	22	22
mm	444	405	248	174	72	43	30	21	35	50	166	257
Kuta												
°C	28	28	28	28	27	27	26	26	27	27	28	28
mm	394	311	208	115	79	67	57	31	43	95	176	268
Mataram												
°C	27	27	26	26	26	25	25	25	26	27	27	27
mm	253	254	209	155	84	67	38	21	36	168	250	209
Singaraja												
°C	27	27	27	27	28	28	27	27	28	29	28	28
mm	318	318	201	123	57	36	31	7	21	54	115	180
Ubud												
°C	27	27	27	27	27	26	26	26	26	27	27	27
mm	412	489	274	224	101	172	128	132	142	350	374	398

30

things not to miss

It's not possible to see everything that Bali and Lombok have to offer in a single trip – and we don't suggest you try. What follows is a selective and subjective taste of the islands' highlights: memorable places to stay, outstanding beaches and spectacular hikes. They're arranged in five colour-coded categories, so you can browse through the very best things to see, do, buy and experience. All highlights have a page reference to take you straight into the Guide, where you can find out more.

01 Gamelan music Page 375 • The frenetic syncopations of the Balinese xylophone provide the island's national soundtrack.

02 Bali Museum, Denpasar
Page **119** • Traditional architecture and a good ethnological introduction to the island.

03 Temple festivals Page **372** • Every one of Bali's twenty thousand Hindu temples holds at least one annual festival to entertain the gods with processions and offerings.

04 Cocktails at sunset
Page **94** • Seminyak is the place for sundowners on the beach and sophisticated DJ-bars, while Kuta is famous for its boisterous Aussie pubs.

05 Tirtagangga Page **223** • Admire the aquatic follies of the Water Palace then take off for a hike through the encircling paddyfields.

06 **Sunrise from Gunung Batur** Page **242** • Climb this ancient volcano before dawn and you'll be rewarded with the most extraordinary panoramas.

07 **Pura Meduwe Karang** Page **266** • A wonderfully exuberant example of north Bali's ornate temple architecture.

08 Diving and snorkelling
Page **45** • Wreck dives, submerged canyons and visiting oceanic sunfish are just a few of the islands' underwater attractions.

10 Nusa Penida's south coast
Page **141** • Stunning limestone cliffs rise sheer from the ocean on this handsome, rugged island.

09 Classical Kamasan Art
Page **199** • At its best on the ceiling of the historic Kerta Gosa and in the exceptional Nyoman Gunarsa Museum nearby.

11 Spas
Page **47** • Pamper yourself with some of the local beauty treatments, including the famous *mandi lulur* turmeric scrub.

12 **Tanah Lot** Page **275** • Bali's most photographed temple sits serenely atop its own tiny island.

13 **Climbing Rinjani** Page **342** • The most challenging and rewarding climb on the islands takes in a dramatic crater lake with its own volcano rising from the waters.

14 **Fine dining** Page **38** • Splash out on creative gourmet cuisine at ultra-chic restaurants on both Bali and Lombok.

15 **Gili Islands** Page **324** • Dazzlingly white sand, limpid turquoise waters and a great choice of hotels and restaurants draw hordes of visitors to these three lovely little islands.

16 **Ubud** Page **152** • The arty heart of Bali has it all: beautifully sited accommodation, great restaurants, masses of craft shops and ricefields in every direction.

17 **Sekumpul Falls** Page **265** • Hike through a valley full of coconut, coffee and cacao plantations to reach these seven majestic cascades.

19 **Seminyak shopping** Page **96** • Imaginative but inexpensive design infuses everything from luscious silk drapes and unusual homewares to sassy fashion and accessories.

18 **Neka Art Museum, Ubud** Page **166** • A breathtaking selection of the finest paintings in Bali, from seventeenth-century narratives to 1960s expressionism and contemporary abstracts.

20 **West Bali beaches** Pages **88**, **279**, **284** & **285** • The wilder, less-visited beaches on Bali's west coast, from Canggu along to Medewi, offer great surfing and striking coastal landscapes.

21 **Surfing** Page **45** • Awesome, challenging breaks at Uluwatu, Padang Padang and Desert Point; beginners' waves at Kuta (Bali), around Kuta (Lombok) and at Medewi.

22 **Seafood barbecues, Jimbaran** Page **102** • Enjoy fresh fish grilled to order at candlelit tables on the beach.

23 **Pemuteran** Page **294** • Appealingly low-key beach haven on Bali's northwest coast, close to the spectacular Menjangan reefs.

24 **Amed** Page **226** • Exceptional diving and snorkelling close to shore and a breathtakingly dramatic coastline.

25 Nusa Lembongan Page **134** • Laidback island life, breathtaking coastal scenery and good surfing, diving and snorkelling are all just a short boat ride from the mainland.

26 The foothills of Gunung Batukaru Page **280** • Awesome mountain views, a garden temple and charming accommodation at Wongayagede, Munduk Lumbung and Sarinbuana.

27 Sekotong and the Secret Islands Page **314** • The pace of life is seductively slow on this quiet Lombok peninsula and its enticing offshore islands.

28 Kecak dance Page **379** • Unforgettable spectacle featuring an a cappella chorus of at least fifty men.

29 Sidemen guest houses Page **208** • Stay in this quiet upland village for exhilarating ricefield views and tranquility in abundance.

30 South Lombok beaches Page **353** • The wild and glorious Kuta coastline has some of the most beautiful white-sand bays on the islands.

Basics

Basics

Getting there

There's no shortage of international and domestic flights to Bali's only airport, Ngurah Rai Airport – officially referred to as being in Denpasar (DPS), though it's actually 3km south of Kuta and 11km south of Denpasar (see p.78 for full details). The only international airline currently serving Lombok's Selaparang Airport, in Mataram (see p.306), is the Singapore Airlines subsidiary Silk Air, but Lombok is on several domestic routes. International connections are set to increase enormously, however, when the new Lombok International Airport opens, possibly by 2012, in the south of the island.

The most expensive times to fly to Bali and Lombok are during **high season**, which on most airlines runs from the beginning of July through to the middle or end of August and also includes most of December and the first half of January. During these peak periods flights should be reserved several weeks in advance.

Flights from the UK and Ireland

There are no nonstop flights **from the UK or Ireland** to Bali. Singapore Airlines and Malaysia Airlines offer some of the fastest London–Denpasar flights; both require a brief transfer in Singapore or Kuala Lumpur, but can get you to Bali in as little as seventeen hours. They are often competitively priced against the other major airlines that serve Bali, most of which require longer transit times and can take up to 22 hours. From London and Manchester low-season **fares** rarely cost less than £600 including tax, up to £900 in high season. Flying from Ireland, you'll need to add on the return fare to London.

To Lombok

When Lombok's new international airport finally opens (perhaps by 2012) there should be plenty of direct long-haul flights **to Lombok**. Until then, the most convenient way of getting to Lombok is to fly nonstop London–Singapore with Singapore Airlines and then change on to their subsidiary carrier, Silk Air, for the nonstop flight to Mataram (3 weekly; 2hr 45min); the entire trip can be done in seventeen hours. The complete return journey from London, with taxes, costs around £680 in low season, £820 at peak times. You can buy the return Singapore–Mataram flight direct from the Silk Air website for about £185 inclusive, but it's hard to find a London–Singapore flight for under £500. Alternatively, take the cheapest available flight to Bali, from where a one-way flight to Mataram costs about £20, a tourist boat £11 or a ferry less than £3. For full details on getting from Bali to Lombok, see p.306.

Flights from the US and Canada

There's a big choice of flights to Bali **from North America**, although none goes direct. Flights leaving from the **west coast** cross the Pacific to Asian hubs such as Taipei, Seoul, Tokyo, Hong Kong, Singapore or Kuala Lumpur, with connections on to Bali. The best journey times are around 24 hours (crossing the Pacific in one hop), although considerably more than this is not unusual; slower journeys touch down midway, perhaps in Honolulu and/or Guam, while some schedules involve overnighting en route. From the **east coast**, airlines take a northern trajectory "over the top"; for example, New York–Tokyo is typically fourteen hours' flying time, New York–Bangkok is seventeen hours. Best journey times are also around 24 hours. Typically you'll be looking at a **fare** of US$1000-plus in low season and US$1700 or more in high season from either starting point.

RTW or Circle Asia multi-stop **tickets** put together by consolidators can cost little more than the return prices quoted above. Another possibility, which could also work out cheaper, is Cathay Pacific's **"All Asia Pass"**, which typically offers extremely good value for flights from North America to Hong Kong with stops in all or some of 23 cities over 21 days.

To **Lombok** the route is from Denpasar on a local airline, or to Singapore and then connecting with the three-hour flight to Mataram on Silk Air.

Flights from Australia, New Zealand and South Africa

Scores of flights operate every day **from Australia to Bali**, with the best deals on low-cost carriers such as Jetstar, Pacific Blue, Indonesia AirAsia and Strategic Airlines; Garuda also flies major routes.

Return fares from Western Australia and the Northern Territory, including Perth (4hr), Port Headland (2hr 10min) and Darwin (2hr 30min), start at Aus$500 including tax, or Aus$600 in high season. Flights from Sydney (5hr 30min), Melbourne (6hr), Adelaide (5hr), Brisbane (6hr) and Townsville (5hr 30min) start at Aus$600/700.

There are no nonstop flights **from New Zealand** to Bali, but Pacific Blue offer good deals and fast connection times via Brisbane, Sydney or Melbourne. This can be done in twelve hours from Auckland or eleven hours from Christchurch, with through-fares starting from NZ$1200 inclusive in low season, NZ$1400 in high season. Alternatively, shop around for the cheapest Sydney flight then change on to one of the budget airlines listed above.

There are no direct **flights to Lombok** from either country, so you'll either need to change in Bali on to a half-hour domestic

---

Six steps to a better kind of travel

At Rough Guides we are passionately committed to travel. We feel strongly that only through travelling do we truly come to understand the world we live in and the people we share it with – plus tourism has brought a great deal of **benefit** to developing economies around the world over the last few decades. But the extraordinary growth in tourism has also damaged some places irreparably, and of course **climate change** is exacerbated by most forms of transport, especially flying. This means that now more than ever it's important to **travel thoughtfully** and **responsibly**, with respect for the cultures you're visiting – not only to derive the most benefit from your trip but also to preserve the best bits of the planet for everyone to enjoy. At Rough Guides we feel there are six main areas in which you can make a difference:

- Consider what you're contributing to the **local economy**, and how much the services you use do the same, whether it's through employing local workers and guides or sourcing locally grown produce and local services.
- Consider the **environment** on holiday as well as at home. Water is scarce in many developing destinations, and the biodiversity of local flora and fauna can be adversely affected by tourism. Try to patronize businesses that take account of this.
- Travel with a purpose, not just to tick off experiences. Consider **spending longer** in a place, and getting to know it and its people.
- Give thought to how often you **fly**. Try to avoid short hops by air and more harmful night flights.
- Consider **alternatives to flying**, travelling instead by bus, train, boat and even by bike or on foot where possible.
- Make your trips **"climate neutral"** via a reputable carbon offset scheme. All Rough Guide flights are offset, and every year we donate money to a variety of charities devoted to combating the effects of climate change.

Tying the knot

If you fancy the idea of getting married in Bali the options are mind-boggling. Many hotels will organize the whole thing for you, as will any number of wedding planners. They will also advise on the paperwork and formalities, which are significant, so start planning early. Prices vary enormously and its important to check exactly what is included. It's also a good idea to check out postings on travel forums for locations and planners. Characterful **boutique hotels** that host weddings include *Desa Seni* (see p.88) and *Mick's Place* (see p.105), or *Puri Taman Sari* (p.275).

Denpasar–Mataram flight (cheapest if booked online; see p.79 for details of domestic airlines) or take one of the cheaper ferry routes, as described on p.306.

There are no nonstop flights **from South Africa** to Bali or Lombok but there are reasonably fast connections on to Denpasar with Malaysia Airlines via Kuala Lumpur, Singapore Airlines via Singapore and Cathay Pacific via Hong Kong; minimum travel time is sixteen hours. Choose Singapore Airlines for flights to Lombok via Singapore. Return fares on all routes start from R6500.

Airlines, agents and operators

For specialist diving and surfing tours it can work out cheaper to contact Bali- and Lombok-based operators direct; see p.128, p.132, p.227, p.232, p.331 and p.351 for dive operators and p.91 for surfing packages.

Airlines

Air Asia ⓦ www.airasia.com
British Airways ⓦ www.ba.com
Cathay Pacific ⓦ www.cathaypacific.com
China Airlines ⓦ www.china-airlines.com
Etihad ⓦ www.etihadairways.com
EVA Air ⓦ www.evaair.com
Garuda Indonesia ⓦ www.garuda-indonesia.com
Hong Kong Airlines ⓦ www.hkairlines.com
Jetstar ⓦ www.jetstar.com
KLM (Royal Dutch Airlines) ⓦ www.klm.com
Korean Air ⓦ www.koreanair.com
Malaysia Airlines ⓦ www.malaysia-airlines.com
Pacific Blue Airlines ⓦ www.flypacificblue.co.nz
Qantas Airways ⓦ www.qantas.com
Qatar Airways ⓦ www.qatarairways.com
Silk Air ⓦ www.silkair.com
Singapore Airlines ⓦ www.singaporeair.com

Strategic Airlines ⓦ www.flystrategic.com.au
Thai Airways ⓦ www.thaiair.com

Agents and operators

Adventure Center US ☎ 1-800/228-8747, ⓦ www.adventure-center.com. Adventure specialists offering overland trips including trekking.
Airtreks US ☎ 1-877/AIRTREKS, ⓦ www.airtreks.com. Low fares and the website links to travel blogs.
Asian Pacific Adventures US ☎ 1-800/825-1680, ⓦ www.asianpacificadventures.com. Small-group tours including "Bali: Through an Artist's Eye", fourteen days based mostly in Ubud concentrating on art, music and culture.
Backroads US ☎ 1-800/462-2848, ⓦ www.backroads.com. Adventure tours including the nine-day "Bali Biking", which includes cycling, snorkelling and whitewater rafting.
ebookers UK ☎ 0203/320 3320, ⓦ www.ebookers.com; Republic of Ireland ☎ 01/4311 311, ⓦ www.ebookers.ie. Low fares.
Flight Centre US ☎ 1- 877 992 4732, Canada ☎ 1-877/967-5302, UK ☎ 0870/499 0040, Australia ☎ 13 31 33, New Zealand ☎ 0800/243 544, South Africa ☎ 0860 400 727; ⓦ www.flightcentre.com. Guarantee to offer the lowest air fares; also sell package holidays and adventure tours.
Harvey World Travel Australia ☎ 1300/855492, ⓦ www.harveyworld.com.au. Sells flights and package tours with all the big operators.
Imaginative Traveller UK ☎ 0845/077 8802, ⓦ www.imaginative-traveller.com; Australia ☎ 1300/135 088, ⓦ www.imaginative-traveller.com.au. Small-group adventure tours to Bali and Lombok, including treks to the crater rim on Rinjani.
Intrepid Travel US ☎ 1-800/970-7299, Canada ☎ 1-866/915-1511, UK and Ireland ☎ 0203/147 7777, Australia ☎ 1300/364 512, New Zealand ☎ 0800/600 610; ⓦ www.intrepidtravel.com. Well-regarded, small-group adventure tour operator that favours local transport

and travellers'-style accommodation; destinations include Ubud, Sidemen, Pualau Menjangan, Gili Air and Rinjani.

North South Travel UK ☎01245/608 291, ⊛www.northsouthtravel.co.uk. Travel agency whose profits support projects in the developing world.

STA Travel UK ☎0871/2300 040, US ☎1-800/781-4040, Australia ☎134 782, New Zealand ☎0800/474 400, South Africa ☎0861/781 781; ⊛www.statravel.co.uk. Worldwide specialists in independent travel; good discounts for students and under-26s.

Sunda Trails Lombok, Indonesia ☎+62 (0)370/647390, ⊛www.sundatrails.com. Highly regarded Dutch-run tour operator based in Mataram on Lombok. Offers tours of Lombok, Bali and Nusa Tenggara on foot, by bicycle or motorbike as well as diving and trekking packages.

Surf Travel Company Australia ☎02/9222 8870, ⊛www.surftravel.com.au. Flights and accommodation packages – resort-based or on yachts – to the best surf spots in Bali and Lombok.

Symbiosis Expedition Planning UK ☎0845/123 2844, ⊛www.symbiosis -travel.com. Unusual tailor-made holidays plus small-group specialist trips to Bali and Java focusing on arts and crafts.

Trailfinders UK ☎0845/058 5858, Ireland ☎01/677 7888, Australia ☎1300/780 212; ⊛www.trailfinders.com. One of the best-informed agents for independent travellers.

Travel CUTS Canada ☎1-866/246-9762, US ☎1-800/592-2887; ⊛www.travelcuts.com. Budget travel specialist.

USIT Ireland ☎01/602 1906, Northern Ireland ☎028/9032 7111; ⊛www.usit.ie. Discounted and student fares.

Getting around

Bali and Lombok are both small enough to traverse in a few hours by road (there's no rail transport on either island), although the lack of road or route numbers can make things confusing if you are driving yourself. The major roads are good, carrying at least two-way traffic, and are fairly well maintained, although they see a lot of large trucks. On less-frequented routes, the roads are narrow and more likely to be potholed, while off the beaten track they may be no more than rough tracks.

The state of the road is a reasonable indication of the frequency of **public transport**, which is generally cheap, but offers little space or comfort. In addition to the public transport system, **tourist shuttle buses** operate between major destinations on Bali and Lombok, and although these are more expensive, they are convenient. If you prefer to drive yourself, bicycles, motorbikes, cars and jeeps are available to rent throughout the islands, or you can rent cars or motorbikes with a driver.

Getting **between Bali and Lombok** is easy by plane or boat. For details, see p.306.

Bemos and buses

On both Bali and Lombok, public transport predominantly consists of buses and bemos. **Bemos** are minibuses of varying sizes: tiny ones scurry around local routes, while larger versions travel further afield. **Buses** operate long-distance routes such as Denpasar to Singaraja, Denpasar to Amlapura, and Mataram to Labuhan Lombok. Because of the rise in motorbike ownership, bemos are declining on the islands year on year making public transport ever more time-consuming.

You can pick up a bus or bemo from the **terminal** in bigger towns or flag one down

Journey through lost kingdoms and discover the hidden history of Asia - let Asian Trails be your guide!

CAMBODIA

Asian Trails Ltd. (Phnom Penh Office)

No. 22, Street 294, Sangkat Boeng Keng Kong I

Khan Chamkarmorn, P.O. Box 621, Phnom Penh, Cambodia

Tel: (855 23) 216 555 Fax: (855 23) 216 591

E-mail: res@asiantrails.com.kh

CHINA

Asian Trails China

Rm. 1001, Scitech Tower, No. 22 Jianguomenwai Avenue

Beijing 100004, P.R. China

Tel: (86 10) 6515 9259 & 9279 & 9260 Fax: (86 10) 6515 9293

E-mail: kris.vangoethem@asiantrailschina.com

INDONESIA

P.T. Asian Trails Indonesia

Jl. By Pass Ngurah Rai No. 260 Sanur

Denpasar 80228, Bali, Indonesia

Tel: (62 361) 285 771 Fax: (62 361) 281 515

E-mail: info@asiantrailsbali.com

LAOS

Asian Trails Laos (AT Lao Co., Ltd.)

P.O. Box 5422, Unit 10, Ban Khounta Thong

Sikhottabong District, Vientiane, Lao P.D.R.

Tel: (856 21) 263 936 Fax: (856 21) 262 956

E-mail: vte@asiantrailslaos.com

MALAYSIA

Asian Trails (M) Sdn. Bhd.

11-2-B Jalan Manau off Jalan Kg. Attap 50460

Kuala Lumpur, Malaysia

Tel: (60 3) 2274 9488 Fax: (60 3) 2274 9588

E-mail: res@asiantrails.com.my

MYANMAR

Asian Trails Tour Ltd.

73 Pyay Road, Dagon Township, Yangon, Myanmar

Tel: (95 1) 211 212, 223 262 Fax: (95 1) 211 670

E-mail: res@asiantrails.com.mm

THAILAND

Asian Trails Ltd.

9th Floor, SG Tower, 161/1 Soi Mahadlek Luang 3, Rajdamri Road

Lumpini, Pathumwan, Bangkok 10330

Tel: (66 2) 626 2000 Fax: (66 2) 651 8111

E-mail: res@asiantrails.org

VIETNAM

Asian Trails Co., Ltd.

5th Floor, 21 Nguyen Trung Ngan Street, District 1

Ho Chi Minh City, Vietnam

Tel: (84 8) 3 910 2871 Fax: (84 8) 3 910 2874

E-mail: vietnam@asiantrails.com.vn

CONTACT

Contact us for our brochure or log into

www.asiantrails.info   www.asiantrails.travel

on the road. Fares are paid to the driver or conductor, if there is one. You can't buy tickets in advance – except for inter-island trips, such as from Bali to Java or Lombok.

No local person negotiates a **fare**. When they want to get off they yell "Stoppa", hop out and pay the fixed fare. This system has variable accessibility to tourists. Some bemo drivers insist on agreeing the price beforehand; tourists are usually charged several times the local fare. At a few of the main terminals on the islands there are fare charts of prices to major destinations, but it can be hard to find them. There's no substitute for asking a few local people what the fare should be. It's useful to carry small notes so you can pay the exact fare. If you sit with your luggage on your knees, you should not be charged extra for it but bulky rucksacks will entail a supplement of around Rp5000.

Tourist shuttle buses

The most established **tourist shuttle bus operator** is Perama (ⓦwww.peramatour .com), serving all major tourist destinations. Fares generally work out at least double that of public transport, but the big advantage is that their service is usually direct, while bemo routes often require connections; also there's room for luggage, wheelchairs, baby buggies and surfboards. For example, fares from Kuta are Rp50,000 to Ubud and Rp125,000 to Lovina; from Ubud Rp50,000 to Candi Dasa or Padang Bai; and from Mataram to Kuta (Lombok) Rp125,000. You should try to book the day before, but you can sometimes get a seat the same day. Hotel pick-ups and drop-offs are sometimes available for an extra Rp10,000. The "Travel details" section at the end of every Guide chapter, lists routes.

There are several **rival companies** operating on both Bali and Lombok who advertise throughout tourist areas and offer a similar service, but are not as high profile. These are worth checking out if, for example, the Perama office is inconveniently far from the town centre (as in Lovina and Ubud): a rival company may drop you more centrally. They can also make for a calmer arrival: every hotel tout

on Bali and Lombok knows when and where the Perama bus arrives and waits to entice passengers to their lodging. This has advantages when beds are limited but a crowd of touts gathering to accost new arrivals can be an unpleasant entrance anywhere. Smaller companies attract less notice.

Ferries and boats

Huge inter-island **ferries** connect Bali and Lombok with the islands on either side, from Gilimanuk to Java (see p.288), from Padang Bai to Lembar on Lombok (see p.211) and from Labuhan Lombok to Sumbawa (see p.348). They run frequently and regularly, day and night.

Small, expensive **fast boats** connect the Balinese mainland with the islands of Nusa Lembongan and Gili Trawangan; there are also smaller, slower boat services to Lembongan from Bali and from mainland Lombok to all three Gili Islands. A regular ferry runs from Padang Bai on Bali to Nusa Penida.

Taxis

Metered **taxis** – with a "Taxi" sign on the roof – cruise for business in Kuta, Sanur, Nusa Dua, Jimbaran and Denpasar on Bali, and Ampenan-Mataram-Cakranegara-Sweta, Lembar and Senggigi on Lombok. They are not expensive: on Bali there is an initial pick-up charge of Rp5000 (on Lombok Rp4700), and then Rp4000 per kilometre day or night. It's usual to round the fare up to the nearest Rp5000 when paying.

On Bali, there are several companies, the most common being the light-blue Blue Bird Bali Taksi (ⓣ0361/701111, ⓦwww .bluebirdgroup.com). Always check that the meter is turned on when you get in. As an example of fares, to get from Jalan Arjuna in Legian down to the *Hard Rock Hotel* in Kuta will cost you around Rp20,000.

On Lombok, the light-blue Blue Bird Lombok Taksi (ⓣ0370/627000, ⓦwww .bluebirdgroup.com) have similar charges: to get from Mataram to central Senggigi costs around Rp50,000.

As an alternative, you can simply flag down an empty bemo and charter it like a taxi, although you'll have to bargain hard before you get in.

Dokar/cidomo

The traditional form of transport on the islands is horse and cart. Called **dokar** on Bali and **cidomo** on Lombok, they usually ply the back routes, often transporting heavy loads. They are the only form of public transport on the Gili Islands. Negotiate a price before you get in.

Rental vehicles

There's a big selection of vehicles available for rental on the islands; think about your itinerary before you decide what you need. In the mountains, you need power for the slopes and on rougher terrain clearance is vital.

Renters must produce an **international drivers' licence**. On major public holidays (like Galungan and Nyepi) vehicles are snapped up quickly by Balinese, so make arrangements in advance. Rental vehicles need to have both Balinese and Lombok registration to travel on both islands, so you must tell the rental agency if you intend to take the vehicle between the islands, and check with them exactly what paperwork is required.

The multinational **rental agency** Avis (Ⓦwww.avisworld.com) has two Bali offices, although with their prices at $265 per day it's far more economical to rent a car locally after you arrive; for outlets, see the "Listings" sections for the major resorts in the Guide chapters, or enquire at your hotel. Typical daily **rates** are Rp150,000 for a Suzuki Jimny, Rp180,000 for a Kijang or Isuzu Panther and Rp200,000 for a Feroza. Discounts are available for longer rentals.

Some outfits offer partial **insurance** as part of the fee; typically, the maximum you'll end up paying in the event of any accident will be $150–500. The conditions of insurance policies vary considerably and you should make certain you know what you're signing. Bear in mind that under this system, if there is minor damage – for example if you smash a light – you'll end up paying the whole cost of it.

Before you take a vehicle, **check** it thoroughly and record any damage that has already been done, or you may end up being blamed for it. Most vehicle rental agencies keep your passport as security, so you don't have a lot of bargaining power in the case of any dispute. Wherever you get the vehicle from, take an emergency telephone number to contact if your car breaks down.

On the road

Traffic in Indonesia drives **on the left**. There's a maximum speed limit of 70kph. Fuel costs Rp4500 a litre, but may well rise.

Foreign drivers need to carry an **international driving licence** and the **registration documents** of the vehicle or you're liable to a fine. Seatbelts must be used. The police carry out regular spot checks and you'll be fined for any infringements.

In recent years, there have been reports of police stopping foreign drivers for supposed infringements and "fining" them on the spot – accepting only foreign currency – in what is essentially an extortion racket. Official clean-up campaigns have followed; if it happens to you, the best advice is to keep calm and have some easily accessible notes well away from your main stash of cash if you have to hand some over.

It's worth driving extremely defensively. **Accidents** are always unpleasant, disagreements over the insurance situation and any repairs can be lengthy, and many local people have a straightforward attitude to accidents involving tourists – the visitor must be to blame. Don't drive at **night** unless you absolutely have to, largely because pedestrians, cyclists, food carts and horse carts all use the roadway without any lights. There are also plenty of roadside ditches.

Hiring a driver

Hundreds of drivers in tourist areas offer **chartered transport** – this means you rent their vehicle with them as the driver. Most have cars or jeeps, but you can usually find somebody with a motorbike. You're expected to pay for the driver's meals on all trips and accommodation if the trip takes more than a day, and you must be very clear about who is paying for fuel, where you want to go and stop, and how many people will be travelling. With somebody driving who knows the roads, you've got plenty of time to look around and fewer potential problems to worry about, but it's very difficult to guarantee the quality of the driving. If you're hiring a driver just for the day, you'll pay Rp350,000–550,000 for the vehicle, driver and fuel, but you'll need to bargain. Try to get a personal recommendation of reliable drivers – we've listed our recommendations in Kuta (see p.81), Ubud (see p.159), Candi Dasa (see p.219), Lovina (see p.259) and Senggigi (see p.322). Alternatively, check the Bali and Lombok Travel Forum (W www .travelforum.org/bali) or Lombok Lovers Forum (W lomboklovers.aforumfree.com).

Motorbike and bicycle rental

Motorbikes available for rent vary from scooters through small 100cc jobs to more robust trail-bikes. Prices start at Rp50,000 per day without insurance, with discounts for longer rentals. You'll need to show an international motorcycle licence. Conditions on Bali and Lombok are not suitable for inexperienced drivers, with heavy traffic on major routes, steep hills and difficult driving off the beaten track. There are increasing numbers of accidents involving tourists, so don't take risks. All motorcyclists, both drivers and passengers, must wear a helmet; these will be provided by the rental outlet, but most aren't up to much.

In most tourist areas, it's possible to rent a **bicycle** for around Rp25,000 a day;

check its condition before you set off and carry plenty of water. Helmets, puncture repair kits and locks may or may not be provided so, if you intend to cycle a lot, it would be wise to take your own. There is occasional bag-snatching from bicycles in less populated areas, so attach your bag securely to yourself or the bike. Ubud is a popular area for cycling day-trips and guided rides (see p.157) and they are available in Lombok (see p.322); on the Gili Islands cycling is the only way to get around, other than walking. If you're planning to tour by bike, bear in mind that, should you get tired or stranded, bemos will be extremely reluctant to pick you and your bike up.

Planes

Bali's domestic terminal is adjacent to the international one at Ngurah Rai Airport, 3km south of Kuta; **Lombok's** domestic arrivals share the Selaparang Airport runway in Mataram with the handful of international flights. Domestic airlines have ticket sales counters in the domestic terminal at Ngurah Rai Airport, at Selaparang Airport and/or offices in nearby cities (see p.79 & p.306 for details). Fares depend on the airline and the conditions of the ticket but typical fares between Bali and Lombok are from Rp265,000 and between Bali and Jakarta or Yogyakarta from Rp530,000.

Accommodation

Whatever your budget, the overall standard of accommodation in Bali and Lombok is high. Even the most inexpensive lodgings are enticing, nearly always set in a tropical garden and with outdoor seating. Interiors can be a bit sparse – and dimly lit – but the verandas encourage you to do as local people do and spend your waking hours outdoors.

The majority of cheap places to stay are classed as **losmen**, a term that literally means homestay but most commonly

describes any small-scale and inexpensive accommodation (generally **❶**–**❸**). Some offer the option of hot water and

Online booking agents

Asia Hotels ⓦ www.asiahotels.com
Bali Hotels ⓦ www.balihotels.com
Bali Online Hotels ⓦ www.indo.com
/hotels
Gili Hotels ⓦ www.gili-hotels.com
Lombok Hotels ⓦ www
.lombokhotels.com
Travelethos ⓦ www.travelethos.com

air-conditioning, and many include **breakfast** (*makan pagi*) in the price of the room. Very few losmen offer **single rooms** (*kamar untuk satu orang*), so lone travellers will normally be given a double room at 75–100 percent of the full price.

Nearly all other accommodation falls into the **hotels** category, most of which offer air-conditioning and a swimming pool. Rooms in both losmen and hotels are often in "**cottages**" (sometimes known as "**bungalows**"), which can be anything from terraced concrete cubes to detached rice-barn-style chalets (*lumbung*). Bali in particular does **boutique hotels** very well: small, intimate places, often with gorgeous rural views and tasteful Balinese furnishings. The islands' **super-luxury hotels** ($300–800) tend to give you more for your money than similarly priced hotels in the West,

especially when suites come with private plunge pools and living areas.

Villas are luxurious private holiday homes (*rumah*) with pools and kitchens; they're especially good for families, and some sleep up to twelve. They can be rented by the day or the week and often include the services of a housekeeper and cook. Be aware though that a growing number of villas operate illegally, without government licences, which means they could get closed down at any time; you may be able to check a villa's licence online, and licences must be displayed prominently on the premises. Online villa-rental **agencies** include ⓦ www.balion.com, www.bali-tropical-villas.com and www.balivillas.com.

There are so many cheap losmen near almost every decent beach on Bali and Lombok that it's hardly worth lugging a tent and sleeping bag all the way around the islands. It's not easy to get permission to **camp** in Bali Barat National Park and it's considered inappropriate to camp on the slopes of Bali's most sacred mountains, although camping on Lombok's Gunung Rinjani is normal practice and tents and sleeping bags can be rented for the climb.

Room rates in all classes of accommodation can vary considerably according to demand. During **low season** (Feb–June and

Accommodation price codes

All the accommodation listed in this book has been given one of the following price codes, corresponding to the **least expensive double room** in high season if booked via the hotel website, where available, and excluding tax. Rates in low season may be up to fifty percent lower and booking via online agencies at any time may give you significant discounts. Nearly all losmen and hotels quote their rates exclusive of government **tax** (ten or eleven percent); many of the more expensive hotels add an extra ten percent **service charge** (in hotel-speak, these supplements are usually referred to as "plus-plus").

The most upmarket hotels quote their rates in **US dollars**, or sometimes in **euros**, and usually accept cash, travellers' cheques or credit cards, but will also convert to rupiah.

❶ Rp135,000 and under; US$15 and under
❷ Rp136,000–195,000; US$16–22
❸ Rp196,000–295,000; US$23–34
❹ Rp296,000–445,000; US$35–51
❺ Rp446,000–600,000; US$51–64
❻ Rp601,000–850,000; US$65–95
❼ US$96–200
❽ US$201–310
❾ US$311 and over

Bathrooms

The vast majority of losmen and all hotel rooms have en-suite **bathrooms** (*kamar mandi*). **Toilets** (*wc*, pronounced *way say*) are usually Western style, though flushing is sometimes done manually, with water scooped from an adjacent pail. The same pail and scoop is used by Indonesians to wash themselves after going to the toilet (using the left hand, never the right, which is for eating), but most tourist bathrooms also have toilet paper.

Many Balinese and Sasak people still **bathe** in rivers, but indoor bathing is traditionally done by means of the scoop and slosh method, or **mandi**, using water that's stored in a huge basin. This basin is not a bath, so never get in it; all washing is done outside it and the basin should not be contaminated by soap or shampoo. Many losmen and all hotels in the bigger resort areas provide showers as well as *mandi*. Outside the bigger resorts, the very cheapest rooms may not have hot water (*air panas*).

In the more stylish places, bathrooms can be delightful, particularly if they are designed with open roofs and bedecked with plants. These "**garden bathrooms**" often have showers and *mandi* fed by water piped through sculpted flues and floors covered in a carpet of smooth, rounded pebbles. However, they're not to everyone's taste, especially as they can also attract squadrons of bloodthirsty mosquitoes.

Sept–Nov) many moderate and expensive hotels also offer good discounts on walk-in rates. In **peak season** (July, Aug & the Christmas holidays), however, rates can rise dramatically, especially in Amed and on the Gili Islands; rooms are at a premium during these months so it's advisable to **reserve** ahead. **Check-out time** in losmen and hotels is usually noon.

Food and drink

If you come to Bali or Lombok expecting the range and exuberance of the cooking elsewhere in Southeast Asia, you'll be disappointed. Somehow the ingenuity and panache don't seem to have reached this far, or maybe they've been elbowed out of the way by Japanese, Mexican and even Russian food. However, there's an impressive array of food available. Ironically, the most elusive cuisines on the islands are the native Balinese and Sasak.

At the inexpensive end of the scale, you can get a bowl of *bakso ayam* (chicken noodle soup) for Rp5000 from one of the **carts** (*kaki lima*) on the streets, at bus stations during the day and at night markets after dark. Slightly more upmarket are **warung** or *rumah makan* (eating houses), ranging from a few tables and chairs in a kitchen to fully fledged restaurants. There's usually a menu, but in the simplest places it's just rice or noodle dishes on offer. Most places that call themselves **restaurants** cater for a broader range of tastes, offering Western, Indonesian and Chinese food, while others specialize in a particular cuisine such as Mexican, Japanese or Italian. The multinational fast-food chains have also arrived in the tourist and city areas.

Vegetarians get a good deal, with tofu (*tahu*) and *tempeh*, a fermented soybean cake, alongside plenty of fresh vegetables.

Restaurant **etiquette** is pretty much the same as in the West, with waiter service the norm. If you're eating with friends, don't count on everyone's meal arriving together; there may be just one gas burner in the kitchen.

Prices vary dramatically depending on the location rather than the quality of the meals. In the humblest local *rumah makan*, a simple rice dish such as *nasi campur* is about Rp10,000–15,000, while basic tourist restaurant prices start at Rp20,000 for their version of the same dish with the sky the limit in the plushest location. If you choose non-Indonesian food such as pizza, pasta and steak, prices start at around Rp40,000 in tourist restaurants and again become stratospheric for imported steaks with all the trimmings in swanky locations. Bear in mind that restaurants with more expensive food also have pricier drinks and, in addition, most places add anything up to 21 percent to the bill for tax and service.

See p.406 for a menu reader of dishes and common terms.

Styles of cooking

Throughout Bali and Lombok the most widely available food is **Indonesian** rice- and noodle-based meals, followed closely by **Chinese** (essentially Cantonese) food, as well as a vast array of other Asian (Thai and Japanese especially) and **Western** food in the resorts. Native Balinese food on Bali, and Sasak food on Lombok, is something you'll need to search out. Should you wish to learn more about local food, cookery schools for visitors are available; see p.55.

Indonesian food

Based on rice (*nasi*) or noodles (*mie* or *bakmi*), with vegetables, fish or meat, **Indonesian food** is flavoured with chillies, soy sauce (*kecup*), garlic, ginger, cinnamon, turmeric and lemongrass. You'll also find chilli sauce (*sambal*) everywhere.

One dish available in even the simplest warung is **nasi campur**, which is boiled rice with small amounts of vegetables, meat and fish, often served with *krupuk* (huge prawn crackers). The accompanying dishes vary from day to day, depending on what's available. Other staples are **nasi goreng** and **mie goreng**, fried rice or noodles with vegetables, meat or fish, often with fried egg and *krupuk*. The other mainstays of the Indonesian menu are **gado-gado**, steamed vegetables served with a spicy peanut sauce, and **sate**, small kebabs of beef, pork, chicken, goat or fish, barbecued on a bamboo stick and served with spicy peanut sauce.

Fish is widely available; grilled, kebabed, baked in banana leaves or in curries. However, although tasty, by Western standards a lot of it is overcooked.

Inexpensive, authentic and traditionally fiery **Padang** fare is sold in *rumah makan Padang*, in every sizeable town. Padang food is cold and displayed on platters. There are no menus; when you enter you either select your composite meal by pointing to the dishes on display, or just sit down and the staff will bring you a selection – you pay by the number of plates you have eaten from at the end. Dishes include *kangkung* (water spinach), *tempeh*, fried aubergine, curried eggs, fried fish, meat curry, fish curry, potato cakes, beef brain curry and fried cow's lung.

Balinese food

The everyday **Balinese** diet is a couple of rice-based meals, essentially *nasi campur*, eaten whenever people feel hungry, supplemented with snacks such as *krupuk*. The full magnificence of Balinese cooking is reserved for ceremonies. One of the best dishes is **babi guling**, spit-roasted pig, served with *lawar*, a spicy blood mash. Another speciality is **betutu bebek**, smoked duck, cooked very slowly – this has to be ordered in advance from restaurants.

The Balinese rarely eat desserts but, *bubuh injin*, **black rice pudding**, named after the colour of the rice husk, is available in tourist spots. The rice is served with a sweet coconut-milk sauce, fruit and grated coconut. Rice cakes (*jaja*) play a major part in ceremonial offerings but are also a daily food.

Sasak food

According to some sources, the name "Lombok" translates as "chilli pepper" – highly appropriate considering the savage heat of traditional **Sasak food**. It's not easy to track down, however, and you'll find Indonesian and Chinese food far more widely available on Lombok. Traditional Sasak food uses rice as the staple, together with a wide variety of vegetables, a little meat (although no pork), and some fish, served in various sauces, often with a dish of **chilli sauce** on the side in case it isn't hot enough already. Anything with *pelecing* in the name is served with **chilli sauce**. Taliwang dishes, originally from Sumbawa, are also available on Lombok, consisting of grilled or fried food with, you've guessed it, a chilli sauce. All parts of the animals are eaten, and you'll find plenty of offal on the menu.

Fine dining

Just as it's possible to get by spending a dollar or less for a meal in Bali or Lombok, you can also enjoy some superb **fine dining** experiences on the islands. Plenty of innovative chefs, some Western, some Asian, have imported and adapted modern international gourmet cooking. They offer menus that are creative and imaginative and, best of all, taste great. Restaurants serving this food are invariably stylish, with excellent service, charging $50 or more per head. This can seem a lot in the context of Indonesian prices, but when compared with restaurants of a similar standard in London or New York, it's decidedly good value. Top choices include *The Damai* in Lovina (see p.258),

Sardine in Seminyak (p.94), *Mozaic* in Ubud (p.176), *Seasalt* in Candi Dasa (p.218), *Kokomo* on Gili Trawangan (p.331) and *Kokok Pletok* at Lombok's *Tugu* hotel (see p.339).

Fresh fruit

The range of **fresh fruit** available on Bali and Lombok is startling. You'll see **bananas**, **coconuts** and **papaya** growing all year round, and **pineapples** and **watermelons** are always in the markets. Of the citrus fruits, the giant **pomelo** is the most unusual to visitors – larger than a grapefruit and sweeter. **Guavas**, **avocados** (served as a sweet fruit juice with condensed milk), **passion fruit**, **mangoes**, **soursops** and their close relative, the **custard apple**, are all common. Less familiar are seasonal **mangosteens** with a purple skin and sweet white flesh; hairy **rambutans**, closely related to the lychee; **salak** or **snakefruit**, named after its brown scaly skin; and **starfruit**, which is crunchy but rather flavourless. **Jackfruit**, which usually weighs 10–20kg, has firm yellow segments around a large stone inside its green bobbly skin. This is not to be confused with the **durian**, also large but with a spiky skin and a pungent, sometimes almost rotten, odour. Some airlines and hotels ban it because of the smell, but devoted fans travel large distances and pay high prices for good-quality durian fruit.

Drinks

Bottled water is widely available throughout the islands (Rp3000–4000 for 1.5 litres in supermarkets), as are international brands of **soft drinks**; you'll pay higher prices in

Betel

One habit that you'll notice in Bali and Lombok, and throughout Southeast Asia, predominantly among older people, is the chewing of **betel**. Small parcels, made up of three ingredients – areca nut wrapped in betel leaf that has been smeared with lime – are lodged inside the cheek. When mixed with saliva, these are a stimulant as well as producing an abundance of bright red saliva, which is regularly spat out on the ground and eventually stains the lips and teeth red. Other ingredients can be added according to taste, including tobacco, cloves, cinnamon, cardamom, turmeric and nutmeg. You may also come across decorated boxes used to store the ingredients on display in museums.

restaurants. There are also delicious **fruit juices** although many restaurants automatically add sugar to their juices so you'll need to specify if you don't want that. Inexpensive tourist restaurants charge from Rp7000 for juice drinks, excluding tax and service.

Indonesians are great **coffee** (*kopi*) and **tea** (*teh*) drinkers. Locally grown coffee (*kopi Bali* or *kopi Lombok*) is drunk black, sweet and strong. The coffee isn't filtered, so the grounds settle in the bottom of the glass. If you want milk added or you don't want sugar, you'll have to ask (see p.406). Increasing numbers of espresso machines have arrived in the swisher tourist restaurants along with imported coffee, and Nescafé instant coffee is also available.

Alcohol

Locally produced **beer** includes Bintang, a light, reasonably palatable lager. Expect to pay around Rp20,000 for a 620ml bottle from a supermarket and Rp25,000 upwards in a restaurant. Draught beer is available in some places. There are four varieties of locally brewed organic Storm beer from the palest (like a British bitter ale) to the darkest (a stout).

Many tourist restaurants and bars offer an extensive list of **cocktails** (Rp40,000 upwards) and imported spirits; the cheaper cocktails are invariably made with local alcohol.

Locally produced **wine** is available on Bali, made from grapes grown in the north of the island by Hatten Wines or from imported Australian grapes by L'Artisan or Two Islands (Rp175,000 upwards per bottle) – the Two Islands shiraz and chardonnay both hit the spot, as does the L'Artisan chardonnay, while Hatten's rosé and sparkling wines get the best reports. Imported spirits are available in major tourist areas, where wines from Australia and New Zealand, California, Europe and South America are also available. However, huge increases in duty (now more than 300 percent) have caused prices to sky-rocket: expect to pay Rp50,000–80,000 upwards for a glass and Rp350,000 upwards for a bottle. Local brews include *brem*, a type of rice wine, *tuak*, palm beer brewed from palm-tree sap, and powerful *arak*, a palm or rice spirit that is often incorporated into highly potent local cocktails.

Look out for **happy hours** in tourist areas – the most generous last all evening.

Health

Most travellers to Bali and Lombok end up with nothing more serious than a bout of traveller's diarrhoea ("Bali belly"). However, illness and accidents (including motorbike accidents and surfers' mishaps) can't be ruled out. In the event of serious illness or accident, you'll need private health care and possibly medical evacuation, so it is vital to have adequate health insurance (see p.60).

Discuss your trip with your **doctor** or a specialist travel clinic (see p.42) as early as possible to allow time to complete courses of **inoculations**. If you've come directly from a country with yellow fever, you'll need to be immunized and you should carry the immunization certificate. Apart from this no inoculations are legally required for Indonesia. However, inoculations against the following should be discussed with your medical adviser: diphtheria, hepatitis A, hepatitis B, Japanese encephalitis, polio, rabies, tetanus, typhoid, tuberculosis (see the sources of information on p.42 or *The Rough Guide to Travel Health*).

If you have any medical conditions, are pregnant or are travelling with children, it is especially important to get advice. If you need regular medication, carry it in your hand baggage and carry a certificate/letter from your doctor detailing your condition and the drugs – it can be handy for overzealous customs officials. It's also wise to get a dental check-up before you leave home.

Treatment in Bali and Lombok

You'll find **pharmacies** (*apotik*), village **health clinics** (*klinik*) and **doctors** across the islands and **public hospitals** in each district capital and in Denpasar, supplemented by **specialist tourist clinics** in the main tourist areas. In local facilities the prevalence of English-speaking staff and their ability to tackle accidents and common tourist ailments varies from area to area. Most Balinese use local facilities together with traditional healers (*balian*) as they believe that physical symptoms are a sign of spiritual illness (see p.390 for more on this).

If you need an **English-speaking doctor**, seek advice at your hotel (some of the luxury ones have in-house doctors). For more serious problems, you'll want to access private **clinics** in the main resorts. A couple of places on the outskirts of Kuta have good reputations for dealing with expat emergencies: Bali International Medical Centre (BIMC) and International SOS (see p.99) offer consultations (from $63) at the clinic, doctor call-out ($180–230) and ambulance and call-out ($300–450); prices depend on the time of day or night and distance from the clinic. The only **recompression chamber** on Bali is located in Denpasar (see p.122) and there is another on Lombok (see p.312). For details of local medical facilities including **dentists** (*doctor gigi*), see the "Listings" section of each city account.

Major diseases

Bali and Lombok are home to a range of diseases endemic to tropical Southeast Asia, most of which are not a threat in travellers' home countries. Inoculations are therefore strongly advised.

Most Western travellers will have had inoculations against **polio, tetanus, diphtheria and tuberculosis during childhood**. Travellers should check that they are still covered against them and have booster injections if necessary.

Typhoid can be lethal and is passed through contaminated food or water. It produces an extremely high fever, abdominal pains, headaches, diarrhoea and red spots on the body. Dehydration is the danger here as with all intestinal problems, so take rehydration salts and get medical help urgently. Inoculation and personal hygiene measures (see p.41) offer the best protection.

Avoid contact with all animals, no matter how cute. **Rabies** is spread via the saliva of infected animals, most commonly cats, dogs or monkeys; it is endemic throughout Asia and all visitors to Bali should be aware of the disease. Between late 2008 and February 2011, 124 people on Bali died from the disease. A major culling and vaccination programme is underway as the government has promised that Bali will be rabies free by 2013. If you get bitten, wash the wound immediately with antiseptic and get medical help. Treatment involves a course of injections, but you won't need all of them if you have had a course of pre-departure jabs.

Japanese encephalitis is a serious viral illness causing inflammation of the brain. It is endemic across Asia and is transmitted from infected birds and animals via mosquitoes. Inoculation is available for those planning extended periods in rural areas who are most at risk, although it is rare among travellers. The symptoms are variable but flu-like headache, fever and vomiting are common and the best advice is to seek medical help immediately if you develop these.

There are several strains of **hepatitis** (caused by viral infections) and vaccines can offer some protection against some. Symptoms in all of them are a yellow colouring of the skin and eyes, extreme exhaustion, fever and diarrhoea. It's one of the most common illnesses that afflicts travellers to Asia and can last for months and also lead to chronic illness. Hepatitis A is transmitted via contaminated food and water or saliva. Hepatitis B is more serious and is transmitted via sexual contact or by contaminated blood, needles or syringes, which means that medical treatment itself can pose a risk if sterilization procedures are not up to scratch.

Malaria

Both Bali and Lombok are within **malarial zones** and information regarding the prevalence, prevention and treatment of malaria is being constantly updated so you must seek medical advice at least a couple of weeks before you travel. Current advice seems to be that there is little risk of malaria in the major resorts on Bali but be sure to let your health adviser know if you're visiting other parts of Indonesia or Asia, even in transit. The latest information shows an increase in the most serious form of malaria across Asia and there are reports of resistance to certain drug treatments by some strains. Pregnant women and children need specialist advice.

Malaria, which can be fatal, is passed into humans in mosquito bites (one is all it takes). The appropriate prophylactic drug depends on your destination but all are taken to a strict timetable beginning before you enter the malarious area and continuing after leaving. If you don't follow instructions precisely, you're in danger of developing the illness. The symptoms are fever, headache and shivering, similar to a severe dose of flu and often coming in cycles, but a lot of people have additional symptoms. Don't delay seeking help: malaria progresses quickly. If you develop flu-like symptoms any time up to a year after returning home, you should inform a doctor of your travels and ask for a blood test.

However, none of the anti-malarial drugs are one hundred percent effective and it is vital to try to stop the mosquitoes biting you: sleep under a **mosquito net** – preferably one impregnated with an insecticide especially suited to the task – burn mosquito coils, and use **repellent** on exposed skin. The most powerful repellents should be brought from home; DEET is effective but can be an irritant and natural alternatives are available containing citronella, eucalyptus oil or neem oil.

Dengue fever

Another reason to avoid mosquito bites is **dengue fever**, caused by a virus carried by a different species of mosquito, which bites during the day. There is no vaccine or tablet available to prevent the illness – which causes fever, headache and joint and muscle pains among the least serious symptoms, and internal bleeding and circulatory system failure among the most serious – and no specific drug to cure it. Outbreaks occur across Indonesia throughout the year. It is vital to get an early medical diagnosis and obtain treatment to relieve symptoms.

AIDS/HIV

Bali has the fifth-highest rate of HIV/AIDS cases in Indonesia behind West and East Java, Jakarta and Papua; bear in mind, as well, that other travellers may also be infected. Many people with HIV are also infected with hepatitis. **Condoms** can be bought on both islands, but it's as well to bring your own.

General precautions

Precautions while you are travelling can reduce your chances of getting ill. Personal hygiene is vital and it pays to use some discretion about choosing where to eat – if the bits you can see are filthy, imagine the state of the kitchen which you can't. Avoid **food** that has sat around in the heat in favour of freshly cooked meals; food prepared in fancy tourist places is just as likely to be suspect as that from simple streetside stalls. **Ice** is supposedly prepared under regulated conditions in Indonesia, but it's impossible to be sure how it has been transported or stored once leaving the factory. If you're being really careful, avoid ice in your drinks – a lot easier said than done in the heat. Treat even small cuts or scrapes with antiseptic. Wear flip-flops or thongs in the bathroom rather than walk around barefoot.

Water hygiene

Do not drink untreated tap **water** on Bali or Lombok, as it is likely to contain disease-causing microorganisms. **Bottled water** is available everywhere and there are several methods of treating either tap water or natural ground water to make it safe for drinking (and this also avoids creating mountains of waste with your empty plastic water bottles); the most traditional method is boiling, although this isn't practical when you're travelling. However, **water purifying tablets**, **water filters** and **water purifiers** are all available in travel clinics (see below) and specialist outdoor-equipment retailers.

Heat and skin problems

Travellers are at risk of **sunburn** and **dehydration**. Limit exposure to the sun in the hours around midday, use high-factor sunscreen and wear sunglasses and hat. Make sure that you drink enough as you'll be sweating mightily in the heat. If you're urinating very little or your urine turns dark (this can also indicate hepatitis), increase your fluid intake. When you sweat you lose salt, so add some extra to your food or take oral rehydration salts (see below).

A more serious result of the heat is **heatstroke**, indicated by high temperature, dry skin and a fast, erratic pulse. As an emergency measure, try to cool the patient off by covering them in sheets or sarongs soaked in cold water and turn the fan on them; they may need to go to hospital, though.

Heat rashes, **prickly heat** and fungal infections are also common; wear loose cotton clothing, dry yourself carefully after bathing and use medicated talcum powder or anti-fungal powder if you fall victim.

Intestinal trouble

The priority with an **upset stomach** is to prevent dehydration. Start drinking **rehydration solution** as soon as the attack starts, even if you're vomiting as well, and worry about a diagnosis later. Rehydration salts (such as Oralit and Pharolit) are widely available in pharmacies but it makes sense to carry some with you. The home-made form of these is eight teaspoons of sugar and half a teaspoon of salt dissolved in a litre of clean water.

Stomach upsets can either be a reaction to a change of diet, or can signal something more serious. You should seek medical advice if the attack is particularly severe, lasts more than a couple of days or is accompanied by constant, severe abdominal pain or fever, blood or mucus in your diarrhoea or smelly farts and burps.

Drugs such as Lomotil and Imodium, which stop diarrhoea, should only be used if you get taken ill on a journey or must travel while ill; they are not a cure, and simply paralyse your gut, temporarily plugging you up, at a time when your insides need to get rid of the toxins causing the problem.

Cuts, bites and stings

Divers should familiarize themselves with potential **underwater hazards** and the appropriate first-aid, although you're probably more at risk from the cold and scrapes from coral than from tangling with sharks, sea snakes, stingrays or jellyfish. All cuts should be cleansed and disinfected immediately, covered and kept dry until healed.

On the land, there are poisonous **snakes** on both Bali and Lombok, although they're only likely to attack if you step on them – they are most often encountered in ricefields, so if you are exploring these look where you're stepping. In jungle areas wear long thick socks to protect your legs when trekking and walk noisily. If you're bitten, try to remember what the snake looked like, move as little as you can and send someone for medical help. Under no circumstances do anything heroic with a Swiss army knife. There are also a few poisonous **spiders** in Bali and Lombok, and if you're bitten by one you should also immobilize the limb and get medical help. If you get **leeches** attached to you while trekking in the jungle in the rainy season, use a dab of salt, suntan oil, or a cigarette to persuade them to let go, rather than just pulling them off.

Medical resources for travellers

UK and Ireland

Hospital for Tropical Diseases Travel Clinic
☎020/7388 9600, ⑩www.thehtd.org.

MASTA (Medical Advisory Service for Travellers Abroad) ℡ www.masta.org for the nearest clinic.
Tropical Medical Bureau ℡ 1850/487 674, ℡ www.tmb.ie. Travel advice and clinics across Ireland.

US and Canada

Canadian Society for International Health ℡ 613/241-5785, ℡ www.csih.org. Extensive list of travel health centres.
CDC ℡ 1-800/232 4636, ℡ www.cdc.gov /travel. Official US government travel health site.

International Society for Travel Medicine ℡ 1-404/373-8282, ℡ www.istm.org. Has a full list of travel health clinics.

Australia, New Zealand and South Africa

Travellers' Medical and Vaccination Centres ℡ 1300/658 844, ℡ www.tmvc.com.au. Lists travel clinics in Australia, New Zealand and South Africa.

Festivals and events

Religious ceremonies and festivals remain central to Balinese life and anyone spending more than a few days on the island is likely to spot local people heading to or from temples. Visitors are welcome as long as they follow the guidelines suggested on p.48. Hindus on Lombok adhere to the same customs. On top of these, an array of non-religious festivals are equally appealing.

Balinese festivals

Bali has a complex timetable of religious ceremonies and festivals both local and island-wide, made even more complicated by Bali having two **traditional calendars**; the *saka* calendar, with 354–356 days, is divided into twelve months and runs eighty years behind the Gregorian year, while the *wuku* calendar is based on a 210-day lunar cycle. One of the biggest is **Galungan**, an annual event in the *wuku* calendar. This ten-day festival (see box below, for dates) celebrates the victory of good over evil and the ancestral souls are thought to visit earth. Elaborate preparations take place: *penjor* – bamboo poles hung with offerings – arch over the road. Galungan day itself is spent with the family. The final and most important day is **Kuningan**, when families once again get together, pray and make offerings as the souls of the ancestors return to heaven.

The main festival of the *saka* year is New Year, **Nyepi**, generally in March or April, the major purification ritual of the year. The night before Nyepi the evil spirits are frightened away with drums, gongs, cymbals, firecrackers and huge **papier-mâché monsters** (*ogah-ogah*). On the day itself, everyone sits quietly at home to persuade any remaining evil spirits that Bali is completely deserted. Visitors are expected to stay quietly in their hotels.

Every temple has an annual **odalan**, an anniversary and purification ceremony. The majority of these are small, local affairs, but the celebrations at the large directional temples draw large crowds (see p.371). There are also local temple festivals related to the moon, some associated with full moon and some with the night of complete darkness.

> **Galungan** Feb 1, 2012; Mar 27, 2013; Oct 23, 2013; May 21, 2013.
> **Kuningan** Feb 11, 2012; Apr 6, 2013; Nov 2, 2013; May 31, 2014.

Another annual event, **Saraswati**, in honour of the goddess of knowledge (see p.370), takes place on the last day of the *wuku* year. Books are particularly venerated and the faithful are not supposed to read, while students attend special ceremonies to pray for academic success. Other annual festivals are **Tumpek Kandang**, when all animals are blessed, and **Tumpek Landep**, a day of devotion to all things made of metal, including tools, motorbikes, cars and buses.

Nonreligious anniversaries that are celebrated in Bali include April 21, **Kartini Day**, commemorating the birthday in 1879 of Raden Ajeng Kartini, an early Indonesian nationalist and the first female emancipationist. Parades, lectures and social events are attended by women, while the men and children take over their duties for the day. September 20, the anniversary of the **Badung puputan** in Denpasar in 1906 (see p.363), is commemorated each year by a fair in Alun-alun Puputan. November 20 is **Heroes Day** in Bali, in remembrance of the defeat of the nationalist forces led by Ngurah Rai at Marga in 1946 (see p.365).

The huge month-long **Arts Festival** (ⓦwww.baliartsfestival.com) celebrates all Balinese arts and is held annually at Denpasar's Taman Werdi Budaya Arts Centre, usually from mid-June. Watersports competitions and parades are the highlights of the **Kuta Karnival** (ⓦwww.kutakarnival .com) which runs for a week, usually in September. Up in Ubud, there's the **Bali Spirit Festival** of world music, dance and yoga every March (ⓦwww.balispiritfestival .com) and the **Ubud Writers and Readers literary festival** (ⓦwww.ubudwriters festival.com), with talks and workshops

from an international cast of writers, every October.

Lombok festivals

In **Lombok**, festivals are a mixture of Hindu, Muslim and local folk festivals. **Ciwaratri** (in Jan) is celebrated by Hindus in West Lombok, where followers meditate without sleeping or eating for 24 hours to redeem their sins. A far more public occasion is **Nyale** (see p.352) which takes place every February or March near Kuta and along the south coast, attracting thousands of people to witness the first appearance of the sea worms. **The Anniversary of West Lombok**, a formal government event, takes place on April 17. **Harvest festival** is celebrated by Balinese Hindus in March/April at Gunung Pengsong, when they give thanks for the harvest by the ritual slaughter of a buffalo. **Lebaran Topat** occurs seven days after Ramadan, when Sasak people visit family graves and the grave of Loang Baloq on the edge of Mataram.

In November or December comes **Perang Topat**, informally known as the **Ketupat War** (see p.313), a riotous and spectacular public rice-throwing battle between local Hindus and Wetu Telu followers that takes place at Pura Lingsar in Mataram. Also around this time, offerings are made at Gunung Rinjani's crater lake, Segara Anak, to ask for blessings, known as **Pekelem**, and the **Pujawali** celebration is held at Pura Kalasa temple at Narmada, at Pura Lingsar and at Pura Meru in Mataram. December 17 marks the anniversary of the political **founding of West Nusa Tenggara**. Finally, **Chinese New Year** (Imlek) sees many Chinese-run businesses closing for two days in January or February.

Outdoor activities

The sea and the mountains are the two great focuses of outdoor activities in Bali and Lombok. Bali in particular is renowned for its world-class surf breaks, and both islands offer excellent diving as well as several spectacular volcano hikes.

Surfing

Bali's volcanic reef-fringed coastline has made this island one of the great **surfing** centres of the world, with a reputation for producing an unusually high number of perfect and consistent tubes, and waves that regularly top 5m. There are also plenty of gentler beach breaks, which are ideal for beginners.

From April to October, the southeast trade winds blow offshore, fanning the waves off **Bali**'s southwest coast and off Nusa Lembongan, and making this both the best time of year for surf, and the pleasantest, as it's also the dry season. The most famous and challenging of the southwestern breaks are around **Uluwatu** on the Bukit peninsula – at **Balangan** (see p.104), **Dreamland** (p.104), **Bingin** (p.105), **Padang Padang** (p.105) and **Suluban** (p.106). These are tough, world-class breaks and get very crowded, particularly from June to August; small, surfer-oriented resorts have grown up around each one. **Nusa Lembongan**'s breaks can be less busy but are also challenging (see p.132). Novice and less confident surfers generally start with the breaks around **Kuta** (see p.89), **Canggu** (p.87) and **Medewi** (p.285). From November to March, the winds blow from the northwest, bringing rain to Bali's main beach breaks, though the lesser breaks off eastern Bali, around **Sanur** (see p.127) and **Nusa Dua** (p.111), are still surfable at this time of year.

On **Lombok**, Bangko Bangko's **Desert Point** (see p.317) is rated as one of the world's top breaks, but there are plenty of other good breaks for all levels of experience around **Kuta** on the south coast (see p.352), including at **Gerupuk**, **Mawi**, **Ekas** and **Selong Blanak**.

Bali and Lombok have so many different breaks that it's worth doing your homework and being selective if you're a novice; even pros find the tougher breaks very challenging.

Equipment, lessons and information

The main **surf centres** are Kuta, Bali and Kuta, Lombok. In both these resorts you'll find shops that rent **boards** from Rp50,000 per day, sell new boards (from about $700) and international-brand equipment, and repair boards. Some also run **surf schools**, offering lessons from $45 per half-day, and even **kite surfing** lessons; there is also a women-only luxury surf camp, *Surf Goddess Retreats* (@www .surfgoddessretreats.com), in Seminyak. For detailed reviews of surf breaks, see the **book** *Indo Surf and Lingo*, available from @www.indosurf.com.au and from surfshops and bookshops in Bali; the Bali Waves website (@www.baliwaves.com) is also useful.

Many **airlines** will take boards in the hold for free so long as your total luggage weight doesn't exceed 20kg, but call to check if they require special insurance. Board bags with straps are a good idea, as some breaks are only accessible by motorbike. Some **tourist shuttle buses** on Bali and Lombok refuse to carry boards, though Perama buses will take them for an extra Rp15,000 per board. You may be best off renting a car or a motorbike to get to the breaks. In the main centres, it's fairly easy to rent **motorbikes** with special surfboard clips already attached.

Diving and snorkelling

Bali and Lombok are encircled by reefs that offer excellent and varied year-round **diving**

45

and **snorkelling**; see p.292 for more about reefs and reef fish. The main **dive resorts on Bali** are at Amed (p.227), Candi Dasa (p.217), Nusa Lembongan (p.132), Padang Bai (p.212), Pemuteran (p.296) and Tulamben (p.232); the beach resort of Sanur (see p.128) also has many dive operators but is further from the best dive sites. On **Lombok** the Gili Islands (see p.328), Kuta (see p.351) and the Sekotong peninsula (see p.316) all have very good diving nearby. Most of these dive resorts are also rewarding for **snorkelling**, though obviously the shallowest reefs are best. Many hotels and boat captains offer dedicated snorkelling trips from about Rp100,000 per person, including gear. Some dive centres will also take accompanying snorkellers for a reduced rate.

Dive centres and courses

There are dozens of **dive centres** on Bali and Lombok. If possible, get recommendations from other divers as well, and check the centre's PADI (ⓦwww.padi.com) or SSI (ⓦwww.divessi.com) accreditation. Some dive operators in Bali and Lombok do fake their PADI credentials; others are not PADI dive centres, though their staff may be individually certified. Technical diving using gases other than compressed air is gaining in popularity in Bali and Lombok; the relevant associations are Technical Diving International (ⓦwww.tdisdi.com) and IANTD (ⓦwww.iantd.com). Avoid **booking** ahead over the internet without knowing anything else about the dive centre, and be wary of any operation offering extremely cheap courses: maintaining diving equipment is an expensive business in Indonesia, so any place offering unusually good rates will probably be compromising your safety. Ask to meet your instructor or dive leader, look at their qualifications, find out how many people there'll be in your group (four divers to one dive master is a good ratio) and whether they're a similar level to you, and look over the equipment, checking the quality of the air in the tanks yourself and also ensuring there's an oxygen cylinder on board.

Most dive centres charge similar **rates** for dives and courses. One-day **dive trips** featuring two dives usually cost $66–90 including equipment, and two- to five-day safaris cost $135–200 per day all-inclusive. Equipment is generally rented at $5 per item.

All dive centres offer a range of internationally certified **diving courses**, generally with time spent in the classroom and at a hotel pool as well as out on the reef. Sample prices include three- or four-day PADI Open Water courses for $350–415 (dive shops must include the dive manual and exam papers in this price) and two-day PADI Advanced Open Water courses for around $275–345. Most dive centres also run PADI's introductory Discover Scuba course for novices, and Scuba Review for those needing a refresher.

Safety and information

When planning your trip, note that as you shouldn't go anywhere that's more than **300m above sea level** for eighteen hours following a dive, you'll have to be careful neither to fly straight after your dive, nor to go into the highlands of Bali or Lombok. Specifically that means the Kintamani (Batur) region, Wongayagede and Sanda are all temporarily out of bounds on Bali, as are Senaru and Rinjani on Lombok.

Bali's **recompression chamber** is at Sanglah Public Hospital (see p.122) but any reputable dive centre should organize treatment for you in the very unlikely event that you need it. There is also a recompression chamber on Lombok (see p.312). Make sure your travel insurance covers you, as treatment costs about $4000.

See "Books" on p.398 for a recommended diving **book** on Bali and Lombok.

Hiking

The most challenging **hikes** on Bali and Lombok take you up the islands' towering volcanoes, but there are also lots of gentler treks through ricefields in the interior. The biggest undertaking is the ascent of Lombok's **Gunung Rinjani** (see p.342), which involves at least one night on the mountain, several more if you want to reach the summit as well as the crater lake; guides are obligatory for this. Bali's holiest peak, **Gunung Agung** (see p.205), also involves a very strenuous guided climb, but the ascent and descent can be managed in one day. **Gunung Batur** (see p.242), also on Bali, is a much easier proposition and by far the most popular of the volcano walks; don't be put off by this, though, as the sunrise from the top is glorious. **Gunung Batukaru** is less commonly hiked but guides are available at the several start-points (see p.281).

The most popular centre for **ricefield treks** is Ubud (see p.165), but arguably more rewarding are the smaller and far less busy tourist centres on Bali at Sidemen (p.209), Candi Dasa (p.217), Tirtagangga (see p.225), Munduk (see p.250), Wongayagede (see p.283), Sarinbuana (see p.283) and Sanda (see p.299), and on Lombok at Senaru (p.344) and Tetebatu (p.346).

Rafting, kayaking and horseriding

Whitewater rafting on Bali's rivers ranges from Class 2 to Class 4, so there are routes for first-timers as well as the more experienced; you can book trips in all the major coastal resorts as well as in Ubud. It's also possible to go **kayaking** on the gentler rivers, as well as on Danau Tamblingan and off Gili Trawangan; overnight kayak trips can be arranged from Senggigi.

There's **horseriding** in Kerobokan near Seminyak, at Yeh Gangga, in Kuta (Lombok) and on Gili Trawangan.

Spas, traditional beauty treatments and yoga

Herbal medicines or *jamu* (see p.180) and massages using oils and pastes made from locally grown plants have long played an important role in traditional Indonesian health care. In the last few years, this resource has been adapted for the tourist market, with dozens of spas and salons now offering traditional beauty treatments to visitors.

The biggest concentrations of hotel **spas** and **traditional beauty salons** are in Seminyak/Petitenget (see p.98), Ubud (p.179) and Nusa Dua (see p.112) but there are many more across Bali and Lombok: browse Bali Spa Guide (ⓦ www .balispaguide.com) for a comprehensive database.

Treatments

The most famous traditional treatment is the Javanese exfoliation rub, **mandi lulur**, in which you're painted and then massaged with a turmeric-based paste. Such is its apparent power to beautify, that Javanese brides are said to have a *lulur* treatment every day for the forty days before their

---

Yoga and holistic therapies

Ubud-based Bali Spirit (ⓦ www.balispirit.com; see p.179) is an excellent resource for all things **holistic** in Bali, and the website carries a detailed programme of all upcoming yoga retreats. Regular **yoga sessions and courses** for all levels are held in Canggu (see p.99), Nusa Lembongan (see p.136), Ubud (see p.179), Candi Dasa (see p.214), Alas Tunggal (see p.207), Amed (see p.230), Lovina (see p.259), Tejakula (see p.267), Wongayagede (see p.281), Ume Anyar (see p.298), Gili Gede (see p.317) and Gili Trawangan (see p.331).

wedding ceremonies. Another popular body wrap is the **Balinese boreh**, a warming blend of cloves, pepper and cardamom that improves circulation and invigorates muscles. Most scrub treatments include a gentle Balinese-style massage and a moisturizing "milk bath"; prices vary from Rp150,000 to $150, depending on the poshness of the venue. Prices for a simple massage start at Rp30,000 for a half-hour rub on the beach but may cost $50 or more at a top hotel. Some massage centres in Seminyak (see p.98) and Ubud (see p.179) also run massage **courses**.

Culture and etiquette

The people of Bali and Lombok are extremely generous about opening up their homes, temples and festivals to the ever-growing crowd of interested tourists but, though they're long-suffering and rarely show obvious displeasure, they do take great offence at certain aspects of Western behaviour. The most sensitive issues on the islands are Westerners' clothing – or lack of it – and the code of practice that's required when visiting holy places.

Religious etiquette

Anyone entering a **Balinese temple** (*pura*) is required to show **respect** to the gods by treating their shrines with due deference (not climbing on them or placing themselves in a higher position) and by **dressing modestly**: skimpy clothing, bare shoulders and shorts are all unacceptable, and in many temples you'll be required to wear a sarong (usually provided at the gate of the most-visited temples). In addition, you should wear a **ceremonial sash** around your waist whenever you visit a temple: these can be bought cheaply at most shops selling sarongs, and can be of any style (the Balinese sometimes make do with a rolled-up sarong wrapped around their waist or even a towel); they too are provided for visitors to popular temples.

When attending special **temple ceremonies**, cremations and other village festivals, you should try to dress up as formally as possible: sarongs and sashes are obligatory, and shirts with buttons are preferable to T-shirts. Don't walk in front of anyone who's praying, or take their photo, and try not to sit higher than the priest or the table of offerings. Never use a flash.

At temples, you'll be expected to give a **donation** towards upkeep (Rp10,000 is an acceptable amount) and to sign the donation book. There's no need to be prompted into larger sums when you read how much the previous visitor donated – extra noughts are quite easy to add.

Because the shedding of blood is considered to make someone **ritually unclean** (*sebel*) in Balinese Hinduism, women are not allowed to enter a temple, or to attend any religious ceremonies, during **menstruation**, and the same applies to anyone bearing a fresh wound. Under the same precepts, new mothers and their babies are also considered to be *sebel* for the first 42 days after the birth (new fathers are unclean for three days), and anyone who has been recently bereaved is *sebel* until three days after burial or cremation. These restrictions apply to non-Balinese as well, and are sometimes detailed on English-language notices outside the temple.

Mosques

On the whole, the **mosques** of Lombok and Bali don't hold much cultural or architectural interest for tourists, but should you have occasion to visit one, it's as well to be aware of certain Islamic practices. Everyone is required to take off their shoes before entering, and to wear long sleeves and long trousers; women should cover their shoulders and may also be asked to cover their heads (bring your own scarf or shawl). Men and women always pray in separate parts of the mosque, though there are unlikely to be signs telling you where to go. Women are forbidden to engage in certain religious activities during menstruation, and this includes entering a mosque.

During the month of **Ramadan** (see p.65 for more), devout Muslims neither eat, drink nor smoke in daylight hours. If visiting Lombok during this time, you should be sensitive to this, although you'll certainly be able to find places to eat. Adherence varies across the island at this time: it is most apparent in the south and the east, but something you might not even notice in Senggigi.

The body

Despite tolerating skimpy **dress** in the beach resorts, most Indonesians are extremely offended by topless and nude bathing, and by immodest attire in their towns and villages. You'll command a great deal more respect if you keep your shortest shorts, vests and bare shoulders for the seaside.

Balinese caste and names

Balinese society is structured around a hereditary **caste system**, which, while far more relaxed than its Indian counterpart, does nonetheless carry certain restrictions and rules of etiquette, as ordained in the Balinese Hindu scriptures. Of these, the one that travellers are most likely to encounter is the practice of **naming** a person according to their caste.

At the top of the tree is the **Brahman** caste, whose men are honoured with the title **Ida Bagus** and whose women are generally named **Ida Ayu**, sometimes shortened to **Dayu**. Traditionally revered as the most scholarly members of society, only Brahmans are allowed to become high priests (*pedanda*).

Satriya (sometimes spelt Ksatriya) form the second strata of Balinese society, and these families are descendants of warriors and rulers. The Balinese rajas were all Satriya and their offspring continue to bear telltale names: **Cokorda**, **Anak Agung**, **Ratu** and **Prebagus** for men, and **Anak Agung Isti** or **Dewa Ayu** for women. The merchants or **Wesia** occupy the third most important rank, the men distinguished by the title **I Gusti** or **Pregusti**, the women by the name **I Gusti Ayu**.

At the bottom of the heap comes the **Sudra** caste, the caste of the common people, which accounts for over ninety percent of the population. Sudra children are named according to their position in the family order, with no distinction made between male and female offspring. Thus, a first-born Sudra is always known as **Wayan** or, increasingly commonly, **Putu**, or **Gede** (male) or **Ilu** (female); the second-born is **Made** (or **Kadek**, or **Nengah**); the third **Nyoman** (or **Komang**) and the fourth **Ketut**. Should a fifth child be born, the naming system begins all over again with Wayan/Putu, and so it goes on. In order to distinguish between the sexes, Sudra caste names are often prefaced by "**I**" for males and "**Ni**" for females, for example I Wayan. Some Wayans and Mades prefer to be known by their second names, and many have distinctive nicknames, but you will come across many more Wayans than any other name in Bali.

Unlike their counterparts in the far more rigid Indian caste system, the Sudra are not looked down upon or denied access to specific professions (except that of *pedanda*), and a high-caste background guarantees neither a high income nor a direct line to political power.

This is especially true in central and eastern Lombok, where Sasaks do not subscribe to the relatively relaxed attitudes of their compatriots in Senggigi and the Gili Islands.

The Balinese and Sasak people themselves regularly expose their own bodies in public when **bathing** in rivers and public bathing pools, but they are always treated as invisible by other bathers and passers-by. As a tourist you should do the same: to photograph a bathing Balinese would be very rude indeed. If you bathe alongside them, do as they do – nearly all Balinese women wash with their sarongs wrapped around them – and take note of the segregated areas: in public pools, the men's and women's sections are usually clearly defined, but in rivers the borders are less tangible.

According to Hindu beliefs, a person's body is a microcosm of the universe: the **head** is the most sacred part of the body and the feet the most unclean. This means that you should on no account touch a Balinese person's head – not even to pat a small child's head or to ruffle someone's hair in affection; nor should you lean over someone's head or place your body in a higher position than their head without apologizing. You should never sit with your **feet** pointed at a sacred image (best to sit with them tucked underneath you) or use them to indicate someone or something. Balinese people will never walk under a **clothes line** (for fear of their head coming into contact with underclothes), so you should try not to hang your washing in public areas, and definitely don't sling wet clothes over a temple wall or other holy building. The **left hand** is used for washing after defecating, so the Balinese will never eat with it or use it to pass or receive things or to shake hands.

Social conventions

As elsewhere in Asia, Indonesians dislike **confrontational behaviour** and will rarely show anger or irritation. Tourists who lose their cool and get visibly rattled tend to be looked down on rather than feared. A major source of irritation for foreigners is the rather vague notion of **time-keeping** in Indonesia: lack of punctuality is such a national institution that there is even a word for it – *jam karet*, or rubber time.

Since the downfall of Suharto in 1998, and the subsequent democratic elections, Indonesian people seem to have become much more confident about discussing **political issues** and voicing critical opinions of the state. This is mirrored by a more open press. Religious beliefs, however, are a much more sensitive issue, and it would be bad form to instigate a debate that questions a Balinese person's faith.

You will probably find Balinese and Sasak people only too eager to find out about your **personal life** and habits. It's considered quite normal to ask "Are you married?" and to then express sorrow if you say that you aren't, and the same applies to questions about children: marriage and parenthood are essential stages in the life of most Balinese and Sasaks.

Public **displays of affection** are subdued – you're more likely to see affectionate hand-holding and hugging between friends of the same sex than between heterosexual lovers.

Tipping

It's becoming increasingly common to **tip** on Bali or Lombok, generally about ten percent to waiters (if no service charge is added to the bill), drivers and tour guides; a few thousand rupiah to bellboys and chambermaids in mid-range and upmarket hotels; and a round-up to the nearest Rp5000 for metered-taxi drivers.

Photography

While Bali and Lombok are both incredibly photogenic, not all local people want to be the subject of visitors' holiday snaps; always ask by word or gesture whether it is OK to take a photograph, and respect the answer. Be especially sensitive during religious events such as cremations and take care never to get in the way of worshippers.

Shopping

Shopping can easily become an all-consuming pastime in Bali: the range and quality of artefacts is phenomenal, and although the export trade has dulled the novelty, the bargain prices are irresistible. Bali also has a well-deserved reputation for its elegant modern designs in everything from fashion to tableware, much of it dreamt up by expat designers and best sourced in Seminyak and Ubud. On Lombok, Senggigi has the widest choice of shops, but the real pleasure is visiting the island's pottery and textile villages.

Remember that touts, guides and drivers often get as much as fifty percent **commission** on any item sold to one of their customers – not only at the customer's expense, but also the vendor's. Many shops will organize **shipping**, but be prepared for a huge bill; the minimum container size is one cubic metre, which will set you back at least $140, even to Australia. For parcels weighing under 10kg, use the postal system, as detailed on p.61.

Arts and crafts

Locally produced arts and crafts include traditional and modern **paintings**, **pottery**, **textiles**, **basketware**, **stone sculptures** and **woodcarvings**. Though the big resorts stock a wide range of all these artefacts, there's much fun and better bargains to be had, at least on the high-quality versions, at the craft-producing **villages** themselves. For a round-up of where to buy what, see the box on p.52, and for an introduction to the crafts and their producers, see the colour section *The crafts of Bali and Lombok*.

There are a couple of practical points to note when choosing **woodcarvings**. Be warned that not all "sandalwood" (*cendana*), which is an extremely expensive material, is what it seems as the aroma can be **faked** with real sandalwood sawdust or oil. In either case, the smell doesn't last that long, so either buy from an established outlet or assume that it's faked and reduce your price accordingly. **Ebony** is also commonly faked; compare its weight with any other wood: ebony is very dense and will sink in water. Most tropical woods **crack** when exported to a less humid climate: some carvers obviate this by drying the wood in kilns, while others use polyethylene glycol (PEG) to fill the cracks before they widen. Always check for cracks before buying.

Some **stonecarvings** are also not what they seem, though shops rarely make a secret of this. Specifically, the cheapest lava-stone *paras* sculptures are usually mass-produced from moulded lava-stone paste rather than hand-carved. They're sometimes referred to as "**concrete**" statues but can still be very attractive.

Soft furnishings, clothing and jewellery

Designers make delicious use of the sumptuous local fabrics for luxurious and unusual **soft furnishings**, including cushions, bedspreads, sheets, curtains, drapes and tablecloths. Seminyak, Legian, Sanur and Ubud have the best outlets.

Bali also produces some great **clothes**. Kuta–Legian–Seminyak have the classiest and most original boutiques, along with countless stalls selling beachwear. Brand-name surfwear and urban sportswear is also good value here, as are custom-made leather shoes, boots and jackets.

Bali's small but thriving **silver** and **gold** industry is based in the village of Celuk, where silversmiths sell to the public from their workshops. For more unusual jewellery, you're better off scouring the jewellery shops in Kuta, Ubud, Lovina and Candi Dasa, where designs tend to be more innovative and prices similar, if not lower. Lombok is known for its bargain-priced

Where to shop

Basketware On Lombok: Sayang-Sayang. On Bali: Tenganan; Pengosekan.

Beaded bags, necklaces, shoes Penestanan; Kuta; Ubud.

Books Ubud.

Ceramics Pejaten; Jimbaran.

Fashion Kuta–Legian–Seminyak.

Furniture Modern furniture in Kerobokan. Repro antique furniture from Batubulan, Mas, Seminyak and Senggigi.

Interior decor and soft furnishings Seminyak; Legian; Ubud; Tegalalang–Pujung road.

Jewellery and silver Celuk is Bali's main silver-producing village; shops in Kuta, Seminyak, Ubud, Lovina and Candi Dasa. Gold shops on Jl Hasanudin, Denpasar. Freshwater and South Sea pearls in Mataram and Senggigi, Lombok.

Leather shoes and jackets Kuta.

Markets and pasar seni On Bali in Sukawati, Ubud and Denpasar. On Lombok in Mataram and Senggigi.

Masks Mas; Singapadu.

Paintings Ubud area; Batuan; Kamasan.

Pottery On Lombok in Mataram; Senggigi; Banyumulek; Gili Meno; Penakak.

Puppets Sukawati.

Stone sculptures Batubulan.

Textiles Traditional *ikat* in Tenganan, Gianyar, Sidemen and Singaraja on Bali; and in Mataram and Sukarara on Lombok. Traditional Sumba and Flores textiles in Kuta, Ubud and Candi Dasa. Batik and dress fabrics in Denpasar, especially Jl Sulawesi. Mass-produced and hand-printed batik sarongs in *pasar seni* and tourist shops in Kuta, Sukawati, Ubud, Lovina, Candi Dasa and Senggigi.

Woodcarvings Unpainted figurines from Mas, Ubud and Nyuhkuning. Painted wooden artefacts from villages along the Tegalalang–Pujung road.

imported freshwater **pearls**, and for its home-grown South Sea pearls; shops in Mataram are best for the latter, while Senggigi vendors sell the imports.

Furniture

Several shops in Bali and Lombok advertise, quite ingenuously, "Antiques made to order". The **antiques** in question generally either come from Java or are **reproductions** of mostly Javanese items, chiefly **furniture**, screens, carved panels, window shutters and doors. Weather worn or fashionably distressed, most of the furniture is heavy, made from teak to a Dutch-inspired design, but carved with typical Indonesian grace and whimsy. Check items for rot and termite damage (genuine teak is resistant to termites), as well as for shoddy restoration work.

There is an increasing demand for interesting **modern furniture** on Bali and aside from a few outlets in Seminyak the best places to browse are out of the main centres, for example, north of Seminyak in Kerobokan.

Travelling with children

The Balinese make a great fuss of their own and other people's children, and permit them to go pretty much anywhere.

One peculiar cultural convention you might encounter, though, is that the Balinese abhor young children crawling on the ground – a practice that's considered far too animal-like for young humans – and so in their early months kids are **carried** everywhere, either on the hip or in slings made from sarongs. Don't be surprised if your child gets scooped off the ground for the same reason.

Activities for kids

There's plenty on Bali and Lombok to appeal to children. Aside from the beach and other water-based activities in the southern resorts, Waterbom Park is fun for all ages (see p.89). Many **dive centres** will teach the PADI children's scuba courses on request: their Bubblemaker programme is open to 8-year-olds and the Junior Open Water course is designed for anyone over 10. Active children may also enjoy **learning to surf**, **mountain-biking**, **whitewater rafting** and **horseriding** (see box, p.90), **swinging through the trees** at the Bali Treetop Adventure Park in Bedugul (see p.248) and **wildlife attractions** such as the Elephant Safari Park at Taro (see p.187), the Bird and Reptile parks in Batubulan (see p.148) and the Bali Safari and Marine Park in Gianyar (see p.197). **Ubud** (see p.152) is especially child friendly, with a huge amount on offer that they will love, including chances to try their hand at jewellery-making, batik, gamelan and dancing, and a multilingual kids' library. The colour and dynamism of the **dance and music shows** could almost be tailor-made for children – from the beauty and grace of Legong to the drama of the Barong. Older, more fashion-conscious children will relish the varieties of brand-name **clothing** on offer and the endless offers to "plait your hair", while parents will appreciate the bargains to be had in the children's sections of department stores in Kuta and Denpasar and the specialist children's clothing stores.

Practicalities

Many upmarket **hotels** provide extra beds for one or two under-12s sharing a room with their parents and the best ones have a kids' club as well, and may also offer babysitting services. The Tuban area of south Kuta is particularly strong on family-oriented hotels, many of which have grounds that run right down to the sea: the *Holiday Inn Resort* runs a programme of kids' activities (see p.84). In Sanur, the mid-range *Swastika* is one of several family-friendly options, complete with children's swimming pool (see p.126). Up near Ubud, in the village of Mas, *Taman Harum Cottages* gets rave reviews from families, not least because of all its activities (see p.161); *Klub Kokos*, also near Ubud, has a kids' playroom and special family unit (see p.162). On Lombok several hotels in Senggigi have kids' play areas and pools and a few restaurants advertise special children's menus; hotels on Gili Trawangan are also increasingly family friendly. A growing number of **losmen**, particularly in Kuta and Ubud, have a family bungalow available for rent, usually with at least two bedrooms and sometimes a kitchenette as well. Others offer adjoining rooms. **Villas** are the obvious top-notch alternative.

On the whole, children who occupy their own seat on **buses** and **bemos** are expected to pay full fare. Most **domestic flight** operators charge two-thirds of the adult fare for children under 14, and ten percent for infants.

Although you can buy **disposable nappies** (diapers) in the supermarkets of Kuta, Sanur, Denpasar and Ubud, the Balinese don't use them, so prices are inflated. Bring a **changing mat**, as there are precious few public toilets in Bali and

Lombok, let alone ones with special baby facilities (though posh hotels are always a useful option). For touring, child-carrier **backpacks** are ideal. Opinions are divided on whether or not it's worth bringing a **buggy** or three-wheeled **stroller** – pavements are bumpy at best, and there's an almost total absence of ramps; sand is especially difficult for buggies, though less so for three-wheelers. Buggies and strollers do, however, come in handy for feeding and even bedding small children, as highchairs and cots are only provided in the most upmarket hotels. Taxis and car-rental companies never provide baby seats, but you can rent **baby car seats**, backpacks and cots through Bali Family Holidays (ⓦ www.balifamilyholidays.com). A child-sized **mosquito net** might be useful. **Powdered milk** is available in every major tourist centre, but sterilizing bottles is a far more laborious process in Indonesian hotels and restaurants than it is back home.

Food on Bali and Lombok is generally quite palatable to children – not much spice and hardly any unfamiliar textures – but, as always, avoid unwashed fruit and salads, and dishes that have been left uncovered. Some restaurants offer special kids' menus. The other main hazards are thundering traffic, huge waves and strong currents, and the **sun** – not least because the islands' main beaches offer almost no shade at all. Sun hats, sunblock and waterproof suntan lotions are essential, and can be bought in the major resorts. You should also make sure, if possible, that your child is aware of the dangers of rabies (see p.40); keep children away from animals, especially dogs and monkeys, and ask your doctor about rabies jabs.

Information and advice

The Bali for Families **website** (ⓦ www .baliforfamilies.com) is run by parents who have lots of first-hand experience of travelling in Bali; as well as child-friendly recommendations, there's also a travellers' forum. The more commercial Bali Family Holidays website (ⓦ www.balifamilyholidays .com) is another good resource.

Charities and volunteer projects

Despite the glossy tourist veneer, Bali and Lombok are part of a poor country with limited resources to provide good-quality education and health care to its citizens, whose opportunities, quality of life and very survival are compromised as a result. Below are some suggestions for charities that welcome help from visitors; most of their websites include information on volunteer work.

AdoptA ⓦ www.adoptaschool.org.au. Established as a dressmaking cooperative run by and for women who were widowed by the 2002 Kuta bomb, with a small shop in Candikuning, Bedugul (see p.247), the organization also administers the sponsorship of pupils at underprivileged schools in Bali and links with schools in Western Australia.

Bali Hati Foundation ⓦ www.balihati.org. Promotes access to education for all, provides student scholarships and sponsorship, offers community education and health care and runs an acclaimed school in Mas. Their spa centre, Spa Hati, in Ubud (see p.180), helps fund the work.

BAWA Jl Monkey Forest 100X, Ubud ⓦ www .bawabali.com Working to improve all aspects of animal welfare on Bali including the vaccination, as opposed to culling, of dogs as a response to rabies on the island.

Crisis Care Foundation ☏ 0812/377 4649, ⓦ balicrisiscare.org. Provides free health care for local people both in the clinic in Lovina and as outreach and is run on charitable donations, which are always needed. The driving force is an Englishwoman, Gloria, and visitors are welcome to see the work. There's more information and a Wish List on the website. If you can't make it to Lovina, donations can be dropped off with Kerry (the owner) in *Piggy's Bar* on Poppies 2 in Kuta.

East Bali Poverty Project ℡0361/410071, ⓦwww.eastbalipovertyproject.org. Helps isolated mountain villages on the arid slopes of Gunung Agung and Gunung Abang in a number of ways, including education, nutrition, health and sustainable agriculture.

Gili Eco Trust c/o Big Bubble dive centre, Gili Trawangan ⓦwww.giliecotrust.com. Works to promote sustainable tourism on the island of Gili Trawangan. Projects include growing new coral reefs, recycling programmes, caring for cidomo horses and environmental education in schools. Visitors can participate in their monthly beach clean-up and more. See p.330.

Help the Children of Gili Meno ⓦwww .yacouba.org. If you visit Meno look out for postcards produced to support children from Gili Meno who attend the secondary school in Gili Trawangan. With uniform, food and boat transfers it costs €200 per child per year and without this support most of the island children never progress beyond primary school.

IDEP Foundation ⓦwww.idepfoundation .org. An Ubud-based NGO that promotes

sustainable-living programmes across Indonesia, including permaculture, micro-credit, fair trade and disaster response projects.

Kupu-Kupu Foundation ⓦwww .kupukupufoundation.org. Encourages sponsors and volunteers to help improve the lives of the 12,500 disabled children and adults in Bali. Sells inexpensive, high-quality handicrafts and jewellery made by disabled craftspeople at its shop in Ubud (see p.178).

Pondok Pekak Library and Learning Centre Jl Dewi Sita, Ubud ℡0361/976194, ⓔlibrarypondok@yahoo.com. A free library service in Ubud that offers all local children access to books and educational activities. Visitors can support the project by using the excellent adult-oriented library of English-language books (see p.182), by taking cultural classes here (see p.181) and by donating books and funds.

Sjaki-Tari-Us Foundation Off Jl Dewi Sita, Ubud ⓦwww.sjakitarius.nl. Works with disabled children and their families offering education, training and job opportunities.

Yayasan Senyum ⓦwww.senyumbali.org. Dedicated to helping fund operations for Balinese people with cranio-facial disabilities such as cleft palate. Visitors can assist by donating secondhand goods to their Ubud charity shop, the Smile Shop; see p.177.

Travel essentials

Addresses

Because the government has outlawed the use of English-language names, demanding that Indonesian names be used instead, a number of street names in resort areas such as Kuta (Bali) are known by two or more names (see box, p.77). Because of haphazard planning, frequent rebuilding and superstitions about unlucky numbers, street numbers are not always chronological – and may not be present at all. It's also quite common to use "X" where an adjacent property has been added, with the original building being, say, Jl Raya 200 and the new one becoming Jl Raya 200X.

Cookery and cultural classes

Short courses in Balinese cookery are available in Ubud (see p.181), Petitenget (see p.98), Tanjung Benoa (see p.113), Sanur (see p.131), Lovina (see p.259) and Munduk (see p.251), and at the *Alila* hotel in Candi Dasa (see p.216). Ubud is the most popular place to take workshops in art, dance, music, carving and other Balinese arts and crafts (see p.181 for details). You can learn batik painting in Kuta (see p.98).

Costs

Foreign tourists visiting Bali and Lombok, wherever they come from, invariably find that hotel rooms at all levels of comfort, goods and services are relatively inexpensive when compared with their home countries. However, the range of accommodation, restaurants and other opportunities means that it is just as easy to have a fabulously extravagant experience as a budget one.

Many tourist businesses, including hotels, dive operators, tour agents and car-rental outlets, quote for their goods and services in **US dollars** while others use **euros** (€); in the Guide, where dollars are mentioned they are always US dollars. Even where prices are displayed in US dollars or euros, though, you have the option of paying with cash, travellers' cheques, credit card or rupiah.

If you're happy to eat in local places, stay off the beer, use the public transport system and stay in the simplest accommodation, you could scrape by on a **daily budget** of £10/$17 per person if you share a room. For around £30/$50 a day per person if you share a room, you'll get quite a few extra comforts, like the use of a swimming pool, hot water and air-conditioning, three good meals and a few beers and you'll be able to afford tourist shuttle bus tickets to get around. Staying in luxury hotels and eating at the swankiest restaurants and chartering transport, you're likely to spend £75/$125 per day. The sky's the limit at this end of the market, with $1000-a-night accommodation, helicopter charters, dive or surf safaris, and fabulous gourmet meals all on offer.

Government-run museums and the most **famous temples** charge around Rp15,000 per person and **private art museums and galleries** Rp30,000–40,000. Tourist attractions, such as the Elephant Park at Taro (U$16) and Bali Treetop Adventure Park in Bedugul ($20) are even pricier. Youth and student **discounts** are rare but can be 50 percent where available. All visitors to any temple are expected to give a small donation (about Rp10,000).

Bargaining

Bargaining is one of the most obvious ways of keeping your costs down. Except in supermarkets, department stores, restaurants and bars, the first price given is rarely the real one, and most stallholders expect to engage in some financial banter before finalizing the sale; on average, buyers will start their counterbid at about 30 to 40 percent of the vendor's opening price and the bartering continues from there. Pretty much everything, from newspapers and cigarettes to woodcarvings and car rental is negotiable, and even accommodation rates can often be knocked down, from the humblest losmen through to the top-end places where potential guests ask about "low-season discounts".

Bargaining is an art, and requires humour and tact – it's easy to forget that you're quibbling over a few cents or pennies, and that such an amount means a lot more to an Indonesian than to you.

Crime and personal safety

While incidents of crime are relatively rare on Bali and Lombok, the importance of tourism to the economy, and the damage that adverse publicity could do, means that the true situation may be kept conveniently obscured. Certainly, the majority of visitors have trouble-free trips, but there have been instances of theft and assault on tourists.

It makes sense to take a few **precautions**. Carry vital documents and money in a concealed moneybelt: bum-bags are too easy to cut off in a crowd. Make sure your luggage is lockable (there are gadgets to lock backpacks) and be aware that things can quickly be taken from the back pockets of a rucksack while you're wearing it without you knowing. Beware of pickpockets on crowded buses or bemos and in markets; they usually operate in pairs: one will distract you while another gets what they can either from your pockets or your backpack.

Check the **security** of a room before accepting it, make sure doors and windows can be locked, and don't forget access via the bathroom. Female travellers should make sure there are no peepholes through into neighbouring rooms. Some guesthouses and hotels have safe-deposit boxes, which neatly solves the problem of what to do with your valuables while you go swimming. A surprising number of tourists do leave their valuables unattended on the beach and are amazed to find them gone when they return.

Keep a separate **photocopy** of your passport and airline ticket, or scan them in and store them online, so you can prove who you are and where you are going if you need to get replacements, and a separate list of travellers' cheque numbers along with the emergency phone number.

It's never sensible to carry **large amounts of cash**, and on Bali it's not necessary. However, on Lombok you may need to carry more than you would like because of the scarcity of moneychangers outside the resort areas. It's wise to keep a few dollars hidden somewhere away from your main stash of cash so that if you get your money stolen you can still get to the police, contact a consulate and pay for phone calls while you sort everything out. There are a number of potential rip-offs when you're changing money; see the box on p.63.

Something else to watch out for on Bali is being approached on the street by somebody wanting to ask a few questions about your holiday. These seemingly innocuous questionnaires provide information for **time-share companies**, who have a reputation for hassling visitors once they've divulged their details. Another ruse is for the "researchers" to offer you a prize as a reward for participating – usually a free dinner or tour – which invariably involves a trip to the time-share company's office. Advice on this is to never sign anything unless you've thought about it extremely carefully, examined all the small print – and then thought about it some more.

It's also worth being alert to the possibility of **spiked drinks** and to be aware that **gambling** is illegal in Indonesia and problems can arise from foreigners getting involved in this.

It is foolish to have anything to do with **drugs** in Indonesia. The penalties are very tough, even for simple possession, and you won't get any sympathy from consular officials. The horrendous fate that awaits foreigners arrested for drug use is described in *Hotel K: The Shocking Inside Story of Bali's Most Notorious Jail* (see p.396).

If you're arrested, or end up on the wrong side of the law for whatever reason, you should ring the **consular officer** at your embassy immediately (see p.59 for a list).

If you're driving, the chance of entanglement with the police increases; see p.33 for more.

Women travellers

Bali and Lombok do not present great difficulties for **women travellers**, either travelling alone or with friends of either sex; basic issues of personal security and safety are essentially the same as they would be at home. Women should take similar responsibility for their own safety, especially in bars and large parties.

However, an image of Western women as promiscuous and on holiday in search of sex is well established on both islands, although attitudes on Bali are a little more open-minded than most places on Lombok.

Observe how local women **dress** both on the streets and on the beach. While topless sunbathing is popular among tourists – and it's unlikely that local people will say anything directly – it's worth being aware how far outside the local dress code such behaviour is. Whatever you do on the beach, you should cover up when you head inshore, and visits to temples or festivals carry their own obligations regarding dress (see p.48).

There's a large population of **young men** on both Bali and Lombok known variously as Kuta Cowboys, mosquitoes (they flit from person to person) or gigolos, whose aim is to secure a Western girlfriend for the night, week, month or however long it lasts. Older women are increasingly targeted for attention. The boys vary considerably in subtlety and while the transaction is not overtly financial, the woman will be expected to pay for everything. You'll see these couples all over the islands, and if a Western woman and a local man are seen together, this is the first assumption made about their relationship. Local reaction is variable, from hostility in the more traditional villages through acceptance to amusement. Sex outside marriage is taboo in the Muslim religion, and young girls on Lombok are expected to conform to a strict moral code. On Bali things are changing and while sex outside marriage is not actually approved of, it is accepted that it happens –

In an emergency, call the police (☏110), ambulance (☏118) or fire service (☏113).

although marriage is still expected once the girl becomes pregnant.

Women involved in relationships abroad, either with local men or other travellers, should be aware of **sexual health issues**; see p.41.

Reporting a crime or emergency

If you have anything **lost** or **stolen** you must get a **police report** for insurance purposes, so head for the nearest police station (these are marked on the maps in the Guide). In areas without local police, such as the Gili Islands off the coast of Lombok, ask for the local village headman, *kepala desa* or *kepala kampung* in smaller villages, whose job it is to sort out the problem and take you to the nearest police. The police will usually find somebody who can speak some English, but it's a good idea to take along someone who can speak both Indonesian and English, if you can. Allow plenty of time for any bureaucratic involvement with the police. If you're unfortunate enough to be the victim of violent crime, contact your consulate at once (see consulate addresses on p.59).

Departure taxes

International: Rp150,000 from Bali, Rp100,000 from Lombok. Domestic: Rp40,000 from Bali and Rp25,000 from Lombok.

Electricity

Usually 220–240 volts AC, but outlying areas may still use 110 volts. Most outlets take plugs with two rounded pins.

Entry requirements

At the time of writing, only citizens of twelve (mostly Southeast Asian) countries are eligible for **visa-free visits** to Indonesia. Citizens of 64 other countries, including Britain, Ireland, most European states, Australia, New Zealand, Canada, the US, South Africa and

India, are able to buy thirty-day **visas on arrival** (VOA). These cover **stays of up to thirty days** and can be bought on arrival if entering and exiting Indonesia via one of the country's 44 **designated gateway ports**. In Bali, the visa-issuing gateways are Ngurah Rai Airport, Benoa Harbour and Padang Bai port; in Lombok, it's just Selaparang Airport. (Garuda has begun implementing a scheme to issue VOAs on board its flights; currently this is only available on direct Tokyo–Bali flights but more are planned.) The fee of $25 is payable in almost any currency; your passport must be valid for at least six months and you must be able to show proof of onward travel (a return or onward ticket) within thirty days. The thirty-day visa on arrival is **extendable** (see below).

Note that if you try to board a plane to Indonesia without having **a return ticket dated within thirty days** the airline will not let you check in, even if you're planning to extend your thirty-day visa when there. Your options are either to buy a sixty-day visa in advance (see below), or to buy a fully refundable or very cheap one-way ticket out of Bali, either online or, if you're already at check-in, at an airline desk. Budget airlines like Jetstar (Ⓦwww.jetstar.com) sell their Bali–Singapore flight for as little as $40.

If you're not on the list of 64 countries, if you're entering via a non-designated gateway, or if you want to **stay for up to sixty days**, you should buy a **visa in advance** from an Indonesian embassy or consulate. Forms and detailed lists of requirements can be downloaded from most Indonesian embassy websites (Ⓦwww .kemlu.go.id). Fees for single-entry sixty-day visas are £35/$45/Aus$60; for multiple entry £100/$100/Aus$165. In addition, you will need two passport photos and proof of onward travel (a return or onward ticket), and your passport must be valid for at least six months, or one year if applying for a multiple-entry visa. Many but not all visa-issuing embassies also require a recent bank statement showing a minimum balance (the UK specifies £1000) and a recent letter from your employer, educational establishment, bank manager, accountant or solicitor certifying your obligation to return home/leave Indonesia by the designated date.

It is possible to **extend thirty-day and sixty-day visas** by thirty days once you're in Indonesia. **Immigration offices** (*kantor imigrasi*) in Bali – Denpasar (see p.122), Kuta (see p.99) and Singaraja (Lovina; see p.259) – and in Mataram on Lombok (see p.312) will all do this for you, though the speed of service varies; you need to apply at least a week before your existing visa expires. The price should be $25, with an extra $15–20 levied locally if you want your paperwork fast-tracked. At the time of writing the fastest standard processing time is at Mataram (24hr, or less than 3hr for the fast-track option); Kuta and Singaraja offices take a week. You will need to fill out various easy forms, submit two passport photos and pay to have relevant passport pages photocopied.

Penalties for **overstaying your visa** are severe. On departure, you'll be fined $20 for each day you've overstayed up to a limit of sixty days. If you've exceeded the sixty-day barrier you're liable for a five-year prison sentence or a fine of Rp25,000,000.

Indonesian embassies and consulates abroad

For comprehensive listings of **Indonesian embassies and consulates** around the world, see the "Mission" page of the website of the Indonesian Ministry of Foreign Affairs at ⓦ www.kemlu.go.id.

Foreign embassies and consulates

Most countries maintain an **embassy** in the Indonesian capital, Jakarta, and some also have **consulates** in Bali; there are none on Lombok. Your first point of contact should always be the Bali consulate.

Australia Consulate in Bali: Jl Letda Tantular 32, Renon, Denpasar ☎ 0361/241118, ⓦ www .bali.indonesia.embassy.gov.au. Embassy: Jakarta ☎ 021/2550 5555, ⓦ www.austembjak.or.id.
Canada Contact the Australian consulate in Denpasar first. Embassy: Jakarta ☎ 021/2550 7800, ⓦ www.dfaitmaeci.gc.ca/jakarta.
Ireland Contact the UK consul in Sanur first.
Malaysia Embassy: Jakarta ☎ 021/522 4947, ⓦ www.kln.gov.my/web/idn_jakarta/home.
New Zealand Contact the Australian consulate in Denpasar first. Embassy: Jakarta ☎ 021/2995 5800, ⓦ www.nzembassy.com/indonesia.

Singapore Embassy: Jakarta ☎ 021/2995 0400, ⓦ www.mfa.gov.sg/jkt.
South Africa Embassy: Jakarta ☎ 021/574 0660, ⓦ www.southafricanembassy-jakarta.or.id.
UK Consulate in Bali: Jl Tirta Nadi 2 no. 20, Sanur ☎ 0361/270601. Embassy: Jakarta ☎ 021/2356 5200, ⓦ ukinindonesia.fco.gov.uk.
US Consulate in Bali: Jl Hayam Wuruk 188, Renon, Denpasar ☎ 0361/233605, ⓔ amcobali @indosat.net.id. Embassy: Jakarta ☎ 021/3435 9000, ⓦ jakarta.usembassy.gov.

Customs regulations

Indonesia's **customs regulations** allow foreign nationals to import one litre of alcohol, two hundred cigarettes or fifty cigars or 100g of tobacco, and a reasonable amount of perfume. Cars, laptops and video cameras are supposed to be declared on entry and re-exported on departure. Import restrictions cover the usual banned items, including narcotics, weapons and pornographic material, and foreigners are also forbidden to bring in any printed matter written in Chinese characters, Chinese medicines, and amounts of Rp5,000,000 or more in Indonesian currency. Indonesia is a signatory to the Convention on International Trade in Endangered Species (CITES), and so forbids import or export of products that are banned under this treaty, which include anything made from turtle flesh or turtle shells (including tortoiseshell jewellery and ornaments), as well as anything made from ivory. Indonesian law also prohibits the export of antiquities and cultural relics, unless sanctioned by the customs department.

Gay and lesbian travellers

As members of a society that places so much emphasis on marriage and parenthood, the Balinese are generally intolerant of homosexuality within their own culture, to the point where gay Balinese men will often introduce themselves to prospective lovers as hailing from Java, so as not to cause embarrassment to their own people. It's not uncommon for men to lead a gay lifestyle for ten or fifteen years before succumbing to extreme social pressure around the age of thirty, getting married and becoming fathers.

Lesbians are even less visible, but subject to similar expectations.

On the positive side, it's much more common in Bali and Lombok to show a modest amount of physical affection to friends of the same sex than to friends or lovers of the opposite sex, which means that Indonesian and foreign **gay couples** generally encounter less hassle about being seen together in public than they might in the West. Indonesian law is relatively liberal: the legal **age of consent** for both gay and heterosexual sex is 16.

Despite the indigenous aversion to gay culture, Bali's tourist industry has helped establish the island as one of the two main gay centres of Indonesia (the other being Jakarta). Young gay men from islands as far afield as Borneo gravitate to Bali in search of a foreign partner, and most end up in the Kuta area, where sophisticated Seminyak has become the focus of the island's small but enduring **scene**. Here, Jalan Camplung Tanduk has a burgeoning number of boutique gay bars and more out-there clubs (with drag shows, theme nights and the like). A mixed gay crowd of Indonesians and foreigners congregates in certain other Kuta venues, where they're welcomed without a problem. There are also established **cruising** areas in north Petitenget at the far northern end of Kuta beach, and on Alun-alun Puputan in Denpasar. Everything is a lot quieter and less overt on **Lombok**, where Senggigi clubs offer the best chance of access to the local gay scene.

A lot of gay visitors and expatriates do have **affairs** with Indonesian men, and these liaisons tend to fall somewhere between holiday romances and paid sex. Few Indonesians would classify themselves as rent boys – they wouldn't sleep with someone they didn't like and most don't have sex for money – but they usually expect to be financially cared for by the richer man (food, drinks and entertainment expenses, for example), and some do make their living this way.

The Utopia website (@www.utopia-asia .com) is an excellent **resource** for gay travellers in Bali and the rest of Indonesia. The Bali-based tour agencies Bali Friendly (@www.balifriendlyhotels.com) and Bali Gay (@www.baligay.net) recommend gay-owned and GLBT-friendly hotels, spas and package tours, while the umbrella organization for gays and lesbians in Bali and Lombok is Gaya Dewata (T0361/7808250, @gaya dewata@yahoo.com).

Insurance

It is vital to arrange **travel insurance** before travelling to Bali or Lombok, covering for medical expenses due to illness or injury, the loss of baggage and travel documents plus cancellation or curtailment of your journey. Most exclude so-called dangerous sports unless an extra premium is paid: in Bali and Lombok, this can mean scuba diving, kayaking and whitewater rafting.

Before buying a **policy**, check what cover you may already have. Your home-insurance policy may cover your possessions against loss or theft even when overseas; in addition, many credit cards include some form of travel cover and some private medical schemes, especially in Canada and US, may include cover when abroad. However, in many cases the coverage from these sources is pretty meagre and you'll

---

Rough Guides travel insurance

Rough Guides has teamed up with WorldNomads.com to offer great travel insurance deals. Policies are available to residents of over 150 countries, with cover for a wide range of adventure sports, 24hr emergency assistance, high levels of medical and evacuation cover and a stream of travel safety information. Roughguides.com users can take advantage of their policies online 24/7, from anywhere in the world – even if you're already travelling. And since plans often change when you're on the road, you can extend your policy and even claim online. Roughguides.com users who buy travel insurance with WorldNomads.com can also leave a positive footprint and donate to a community development project. For more information go to @www.roughguides.com/shop.

need to extend your cover or buy a new policy.

Specialist travel insurance companies usually offer the most comprehensive and competitive policies, or consider the travel insurance deal we offer (see box, p.60). Many policies can be chopped and changed to exclude coverage you don't need. With regard to medical coverage, ascertain whether benefits will be paid as treatment proceeds or only after your return home, and be sure to carry the 24-hour medical emergency number and the policy number with you at all times. Always make a note of the policy details and leave them with someone at home in case you lose the original. When securing baggage cover, make sure that the per-article limit – typically under £500/$900 – will cover your most valuable possession.

It can be more economical for couples and families travelling together to arrange joint insurance. Older travellers or anyone with health problems is advised to start researching insurance well in advance of their trip.

If you need to make a claim, you should keep receipts for medicines and treatment, and, if possible, contact the insurance company before making any major payment (for example, on additional convalescence expenses). In the event you have anything stolen, you must obtain an official report from the police.

Internet

There are scores of **Internet** centres in the main resorts on Bali and Lombok, most of which charge about Rp300 per minute, though big hotels usually charge very inflated rates. Access is patchy in the smallest and most remote towns. **Wi-fi** hotspots are becoming more common in restaurants and hotels and are highlighted in the Guide. See p.66 for advice on buying pre-paid local sim cards for **3G phones**, the cheapest way of getting mobile internet on your phone in Bali and Lombok.

Language lessons

Indonesian language lessons are available in Denpasar (see p.122), Kuta (see p.99), Ubud (see p.181) and Munduk (see p.251).

Laundry

Most hotels and losmen have a laundry service, and tourist centres have plenty of services outside the hotels as well.

Left luggage

Most losmen and hotels will store luggage. Bali's Ngurah Rai Airport has a left-luggage facility (see p.78) and the shuttle-bus operator Perama will store luggage for its customers.

Living and working in Bali and Lombok

Bali has a large and lively expat community, with significant numbers of foreigners choosing to make their homes in and around Ubud, Seminyak, Canggu and Sanur in particular; on Lombok, Senggigi and Gili Trawangan are the main centres. Visa regulations are complicated (see ⓦwww .kemlu.go.id) but some expats manage to work as English-language teachers in Kuta and Ubud, or as dive instructors in south Bali resorts or on the Gili Islands. Others export Indonesian fabric, clothes, jewellery, artefacts and furniture. The Living in Indonesia website (ⓦwww.expat.or.id) is a good resource on expat life, and the fortnightly free newspaper the *Bali Advertiser* (ⓦwww.baliadvertiser.biz) carries a "situations vacant" column.

Mail

Every town and tourist centre on Bali and Lombok has a **General Post Office** (GPO; *kantor pos*) where you can buy stamps (*perangko*) and aerogrammes (*surat udara*), and can post letters (*surat*) and parcels (*paket*). Most *kantor pos* keep official government office **hours** (Mon–Thurs 8am–2pm, Fri 8–11am, Sat 8am–1pm; closed on festival days and public holidays); exceptions are detailed in the Guide. In larger towns and resorts, you can also buy stamps and send letters and parcels from **postal agents**, who charge official rates but often open longer hours than the *kantor pos*. Post boxes aren't widespread, so it's best to post letters at GPOs or postal agents. Postage is expensive, with the current rates for **airmail postcards/letters** under 200g as follows: Australia and New Zealand Rp8000/8000, Europe Rp8000/10,000, US and Canada Rp8000/11,000. Airmail post takes about a week.

If the *kantor pos* doesn't offer a **parcel-packing service**, there will be a stall next door for getting your stuff parcelled up; don't bother packing it yourself as the contents need to be inspected first. Postal rates for parcels are also high: a parcel weighing less than 500g costs R100,000 to be airmailed to Europe or Rp75,000 to Australia; a 6–10kg parcel sent by sea costs Rp336,000 to Australia and Rp594,000 to the UK and could take up to three months. *Kantor pos* won't handle any parcels over 10kg or more than a metre long, but most shops can arrange **shipping** (from about $140 per cubic metre); reputable drivers will also often help organize shipping and can be a good source of advice, or try Pal Cargo (☎0361/466999, ⓦwww.palcargo.com).

Maps

For **Bali**, the best **maps** are Periplus Travel Maps (1:250,000; on sale worldwide). Periplus also produces the impressive *Bali Street Atlas*, which is exhaustively indexed and good for drivers. Maps of **Lombok** are less easy to come by and are best bought abroad or in Bali rather than on Lombok itself. Go for the Periplus Travel Maps sheet covering Lombok and Sumbawa (1:200,000).

The media

Most Balinese **newspaper** readers buy the daily *Bali Post* (ⓦwww.balipost.co.id), while non-Indonesian speakers read either its slimline counterpart, *Bali Post International* (ⓦinternationalbalipost.com) or the weekly *The Bali Times*, published every Friday but produced daily online (ⓦwww.thebalitimes .com). For Indonesian and international coverage there's the English-language daily *The Jakarta Post* (ⓦwww.thejakartapost .com) and, for more incisive journalism, the weekly **news magazine** *Tempo* (ⓦwww .tempointeractive.com), published in both Indonesian and English versions, but not widely distributed on Bali or Lombok. The online quarterly *Inside Indonesia* (ⓦinside indonesia.org) runs hard-hitting articles on

social and political change. Major **inter-national newspapers** are available in Bali's main tourist centres and digital-print services mean that some outlets can even sell them on the same day.

The government-operated **TV station** Televisi Republik Indonesia (TVRI) is dominated by soaps; Bali TV broadcasts in both Balinese and Indonesian. Most hotels also have satellite TV, which includes CNN, HBO and sometimes BBC World and ABC.

Paradise FM (100.9 FM; ⓦwww.balibaku .com; daily 8am–8pm) is a Bali-based English-language **radio** station aimed at tourists, broadcasting regular news bulletins, music and chat. Hard Rock FM Bali (87.8 FM; ⓦwww.hardrockfm.com) is another music station with English-speaking DJs, and Radio Republik Indonesia (RRI) broadcasts music, chat and news programmes 24 hours a day on 93.5 FM, with occasional English-language bulletins.

Money

The Indonesian **currency** is the **rupiah** (abbreviated to "Rp"). Notes commonly in circulation are Rp1000 (blue), Rp2000 (grey), Rp5000 (green and brown), Rp10,000 (pink or purple), Rp20,000 (green), Rp50,000 (blue) and Rp100,000 (pink). They are all clearly inscribed with English numbers and letters. Be warned that most people won't accept ripped or badly worn banknotes, so you shouldn't either. You'll commonly come across Rp100 (silver-coloured plastic), Rp500 (larger, round, bronze) and Rp1000 (large, round, bronze with silver rim) coins. Don't be surprised if cashiers in supermarkets give you sweets instead of small-denomination coins as change.

At the time of writing the **exchange rate** was $1 to Rp 8600, €1 to Rp12,400 and £1 to Rp14,100. For the current rate check out the useful "Travellers Currency Cheat Sheets" at ⓦwww.oanda.com.

Cash and travellers' cheques

Before you leave home, exchange facilities should be able to get some **cash** rupiah for you. However, rates are poor and you don't really need it; there are exchange counters at Bali's Ngurah Rai Airport and Lombok's Selaparang Airport which all open for arriving

Money-changing scams

Some unscrupulous exchange counters try to rip customers off, and there are several well-known **money-changing scams** practised in the bigger resorts, in particular in Kuta and Sanur on Bali.

Some common rip-offs

- Confusing you with the number of **zeros**. With nearly Rp20,000 to every pound it's easy for staff to give you Rp100,000 instead of Rp1,000,000.
- Giving you your money in Rp10,000 **denominations**, so that you lose track.
- Tampering with the **calculator**, so that it shows a low sum even if you use it yourself.
- **Folding notes** over to make it look as if you're getting twice as much as you are.
- Turning the lights out or otherwise **distracting** you while the pile of money is on the counter.
- **Stealing** some notes as they "check" it for the last time.
- Once you've rumbled them and complained, telling you that the discrepancy in the figures is due to "**commission**".

Some advice

- **Avoid** anywhere that offers a ridiculously good rate. Stick to banks or to exchange desks recommended by other travellers.
- Work out the total amount you're expecting beforehand, and write it down.
- Always ask whether there is commission.
- Before signing your cheque, ask for notes in **reasonable denominations** (Rp10,000 is unreasonable, Rp50,000 is acceptable), and ask to see them first.
- **Count your money** carefully, and never hand it back to the exchange staff, as this is when they whip away some notes without you noticing. You should be the last person to count the money.
- So long as you haven't already **signed** a travellers' cheque, you can walk away at any point. If you have signed the cheque, stay calm, don't get distracted, and count everything slowly and methodically.

passengers and ATMs at Ngurah Rai (but see p.64). Some cash in **US dollars** is useful to take with you, but take crisp new notes and avoid $100 bills, which can be hard to exchange; pre-1996 ones are not accepted at all.

Many people carry at least some of their money as **travellers' cheques**, which are widely accepted at banks and exchange counters across Bali and in the tourist centres of Lombok (Senggigi, the Gili Islands and Mataram). Outside these areas on Lombok, facilities are rarer (see Guide chapters for details), so be sure to carry enough cash. The best cheques are those issued by the most familiar names, particularly American Express in US dollars or pounds sterling, though numerous other currencies are accepted in the largest resorts. Keep the **receipt** (or proof of purchase) when you buy your travellers' cheques, as you may need to show it. Be aware that if you lose your passport your travellers' cheques will be useless as you can't encash them, so a backup access to funds (a credit or debit card) in case of emergency is useful.

In tourist centres, **exchange counters** are the most convenient places to cash

Lost or stolen credit cards/travellers' cheques

American Express ☏001-803-44-0176
MasterCard ☏001-803-1-887-0623
Visa Cards ☏001-803-44-1600

your cheques. They open daily from around 10am to 10pm and rates compare favourably with those offered by the banks. However, be wary of money-changing scams (see box, p.63), particularly in Kuta, Bali.

Normal **banking hours** are Monday–Thursday 8am–2pm, Friday 8am–noon and, in some branches, Saturday 8–11.30am, but these do vary. However, in many banks the foreign-exchange counter only opens for a limited period. Banks in smaller towns don't have foreign-exchange facilities.

Plastic

Major **credit cards**, most commonly Visa and MasterCard, are accepted by most mid- to top-end hotels and tourist businesses. However, outlets often add to your bill the entire fee that is charged to them (currently four percent), bumping costs up.

In Bali's and Lombok's biggest tourist centres you'll find **ATMs** that accept international cards, both Visa and MasterCard as well as Visa **debit cards**. If you can't find one, track down the local Hardy's supermarket – there's always at least one ATM attached. See the relevant sections of resort and city accounts for ATM locations; for an up-to-the-minute list, check ⓦwww .mastercard.com and www.visa.com. Note that currently some tourist centres, notably Amed, Padang Bai, Candi Dasa, Sidemen, Tirtagangga and Pemuteran on Bali, and Senaru/Rinjani and Kuta on Lombok have no international Visa ATM. Make sure you know what the charges are for using your cards to withdraw cash overseas. Be aware that your home bank may well block your card when you initially try to use it abroad, even if you've warned them of your trip, and it may take a couple of phone calls to sort this out – take the relevant telephone number with you.

Be careful when using your card – unlike machines at home, some of the Bali and Lombok machines only return your card *after* they've dispensed your cash, making it easier to forget your card. Visa TravelMoney (ⓦwww.visa.com) is a **pre-paid card** that works like a debit card in ATMs, hotels and other businesses and allows you to top it up as and when you wish.

Wiring money

If you get into financial trouble, getting money wired to you from home is fast but expensive. Money should be available for collection in local currency, from the company's local agent within twenty minutes of being sent via Western Union (ⓦwww .westernunion.com) or Moneygram (ⓦwww .moneygram.com); both charge on a sliding scale, so sending larger amounts of cash is better value. Money can be sent via the agents, telephone or, in some cases, the websites (see above). Check the websites for locations and opening hours. Getting money wired from a home bank to a local bank on Bali or Lombok can be tortuous and is best avoided.

Opening hours and public holidays

Opening hours are not straightforward in Bali and Lombok, with government offices, post offices, businesses and shops setting their own timetables.

Generally speaking, **businesses** such as **airline offices** open at least Monday–Friday 8am–4pm, Saturday 8am–1pm, with many open longer, but have variable arrangements at lunchtime. Normal **banking hours** are Monday–Thursday 8am–2pm, Friday 8am–noon and, in some branches, Saturday 8–11.30am, but these do vary and foreign-exchange-counter opening hours are often shorter. Main **post offices** operate roughly similar hours, with considerable variations from office to office for details see p.61. Postal agents in tourist areas tend to keep later hours. In tourist areas, **shops** open from around 10am until 8pm or later, but local shops in towns and villages open and shut much earlier with the exception of supermarkets in shopping centres, which generally open at least 10am–10pm. Local **markets** vary; some start soon after dawn with business completed by 10am, others open all day and only close up towards the end of the afternoon.

Government offices are widely reported as open Monday–Friday 8am–4pm; in fact there is much variability in different areas and departments – most close early on Friday and you'll generally be most successful if

Ramadan begins July 20, 2012; July 9, 2013; June 28, 2014.
Idul Fitri Aug 19, 2012; Aug 8, 2013; July 28, 2014.
Note that Islamic festivals depend on local sightings of the moon; actual dates may
vary by a day or two.

you turn up between 9am and 11.30am. Official government hours shorten during Ramadan; the best advice is to ring offices at that time to check before you make a long journey.

National public holidays

In addition to **national public holidays** celebrated throughout Indonesia (see box below) there are frequent local **religious festivals** occurring throughout the Muslim, Hindu and Chinese communities. Each of Bali's twenty thousand temples also has an anniversary celebration once every *wuku* year, or 210 days, local communities host elaborate **marriage** and **cremation** celebrations, and both islands have their own particular secular holidays.

All major **Muslim festivals** are national holidays; see box below. These, based on a lunar calendar, move backwards against the Western calendar, falling earlier each year. The ninth Muslim month is **Ramadan**, a month of fasting during daylight hours. It is much more apparent on Muslim Lombok than on Hindu Bali. Followers of the Wetu Telu branch of Islam on Lombok (see p.340) observe their own three-day festival of

Puasa rather than the full month. Many Muslim restaurants, although not tourist establishments, shut down during the day so it can be hard to get a meal in central and eastern parts of Lombok where you should not eat, drink or smoke in public at this time. However, in all other areas of Lombok you'll find Ramadan much less apparent. **Idul Fitri**, also called Hari Raya or Lebaran, the first day of the tenth month of the Muslim calendar, marks the end of Ramadan and is a national holiday. In fact, many businesses across Indonesia shut for a week and many hotels on Bali and Lombok get booked out with visitors from across the archipelago.

Phones

The cheapest way to make **international calls** (*panggilan internasional*) is generally via **Skype** at one of the many internet centres in the main tourist resorts; some internet centres charge standard internet rates for this service (around Rp300/min) but those with limited bandwidth capacity may charge considerably more. Some **local mobile phone networks** also offer very cheap rates for international calls, as low as Rp1000/min to Australia for example; see

National public holidays

January 1 New Year's Day (Tahun Baru).
January/Febuary Chinese New Year.
February/March Maulid Nabi Muhammad, birth of the Prophet.
March/April Balinese New Year (Nyepi).
March/April Good Friday and Easter Sunday.
April/May Waisak Day, anniversary of the birth, death and enlightenment of Buddha.
May/June Ascension of Jesus Christ (Isa Almasih).
May/June Al Miraj, Ascension Day.
July/August Idul Fitri, celebration of the end of Ramadan.
August 17 Independence Day (Hari Proklamasi Kemerdekaan).
November Muharram, Muslim New Year.
November/ December Idul Adha, the Muslim day of sacrifice.
December 25 Christmas Day.

Useful numbers and codes

International operator ☏101, 107
International directory enquiries ☏102
Domestic operator ☏100
Local directory enquiries ☏108
Long-distance directory enquiries ☏106

Phoning home

To phone home from a local mobile or a land line you need to preface your home country code with an **international access code**. Confusingly, Indonesia has many of these, depending on your phone provider and on current discounted deals. If you are using a local sim card or a **discount card** you need to ask the vendor which is the best international access code. If you're phoning from a **wartel** or **hotel**, ask the front desk which service they recommend. The two main operators of land lines and mobile networks are Telkom and Indosat. **Telkom**'s prime international access code is ☏007 (advertised as their "premium quality" service); the access code for their "budget service" (cheaper but possibly with a fuzzier connection) is ☏01017. The Indosat equivalents are ☏001 (premium), ☏008 (economy) and ☏01016 (VoIP).

To **call an international number**: dial the relevant international access code (as outlined above) + IDD country code (eg 44 for the UK, or 1 for the US) + area code (minus its initial zero if applicable) + local number.

Calling Bali and Lombok from abroad

Dial your international access code + 62 for Indonesia + area code minus its initial zero + local number.

below for advice on how to buy a local sim card and be sure to ask the vendor what the best access code is for the cheapest international calls.

If you don't have internet access or a local sim, your best bet is to use one of the privately run "telephone shops" or **wartel,** which are found all over Bali and Lombok; most open long hours, typically 7am–10pm. Some wartels are able to offer very cheap international calls, using pre-paid cards and VoIP (Voice over Internet Protocol) deals. Others, particularly those in outlying areas, charge according to rates set by **Telkom**, the government telecommunications service, plus a little extra. Telkom prices vary according to the time of day at the destination and are set out in full at ⓦwww.telkom .co.id; sample "standard" rates include: to Australia and the US Rp6640/min, to the UK Rp7520/min. The other main operator of international services is **Indosat** (ⓦwww .indosat.com), which charges identical rates.

A **local call** (*panggilan lokal*) is a call to any destination that shares the same area code and should cost in the region of Rp100/min, depending on distance and

time of day; calls to all other domestic destinations with a different area code are classed as **long-distance calls** (*panggilan inter-lokal*) and will cost more. Bali is divided into several **code zones**, and Lombok has two codes. Calls to **mobile phones** – whose numbers begin ☏08 – are more expensive. Some businesses have to rely on **satellite phones** (code ☏086812), which are costlier still.

Mobile phones

Most **UK**, **Australian** and **New Zealand** mobiles use GSM technology, which works fine in Indonesia, but contact your phone provider before leaving home to get international "roaming" switched on. If you have a **US** or **Canadian** triband phone it will probably need to be "unlocked" in order to work in Indonesia; check with your provider.

Buying a **local sim card** can be a useful alternative, especially as international calls from Indonesian mobiles can work out cheaper than via land lines. Buying a local **3G** sim card will make mobile internet a great deal cheaper than using roaming on your home mobile, though the availability of wi-fi in main resorts (see p.61) might mean that's unnecessary for your purposes. Mobiles are huge in Bali and Lombok and there are phone shops all over, even in villages. Staff may have to unblock your phone first and will also advise on the best sim card for your needs, bearing in mind local and international coverage. They should also fill you in on promotions and access codes for discounted calls; travellers' forums are also a good source of advice (see below). You should be able to get a basic sim card for Rp25,000, with a small amount of credit thrown in; 3G cards cost a little more. Some "lucky" or "easy-to-remember" sim numbers cost more so it's always worth asking if there's a cheaper number for sale. Top-up cards are sold at mobile-phone stalls everywhere. Sending a local SMS costs about Rp100, overseas SMS about Rp600; a 15MB data block for your 3G phone will cost about Rp5,000 but check online forums for advice on current deals.

Time

Bali and Lombok are on **Central Indonesian Time** (GMT+8, North American EST+13, Australian EST+2). There's no daylight saving.

Tourist information

Indonesia has no **overseas tourist offices** but in Australia is represented by Aviareps Oceania, Level 5, 68 Alfred St, Milsons Point, NSW 2061 ℡02 9959 4277, Ⓦwww.visit-indonesia.com.au.

District capitals across Bali and Lombok all maintain their own **government tourist office** (Mon–Thurs 8am–3pm, Fri 8am–noon; those in the main tourist centres keep longer hours) but they're generally concerned more with strategy and marketing than with travellers' queries. Lombok's provincial tourist office in Mataram (see p.310) is a notably helpful exception.

Government travel advice

Most Western governments maintain websites with travel information detailing some of the potential hazards and what to do in emergencies.

Australian Department of Foreign Affairs
Ⓦwww.dfat.gov.au
British Foreign & Commonwealth Office
Ⓦwww.fco.gov.uk
Canadian Department of Foreign Affairs
Ⓦwww.international.gc.ca
Irish Department of Foreign Affairs
Ⓦwww.foreignaffairs.gov.ie
New Zealand Ministry of Foreign Affairs
Ⓦwww.mfat.govt.nz
South African Department of Foreign Affairs
Ⓦwww.dfa.gov.za
US State Department Ⓦwww.state.gov

Listings magazines and tourist publications

Plenty of **free tourist magazines** supply information on Bali's and Lombok's sights, activities and events; they're generally available online as well as in hotels and restaurants in the main tourist centres.

Agung Ⓦwww.agungbali.com. Small-format periodical all about eastern Bali from Padang Bai to Amed.

Bali Plus Ⓦwww.baliplus.com. Compact monthly that covers tourist attractions, and lists and reviews restaurants, clubs, shops and spas.

the beat Ⓦwww.beatmag.com. Bali's premier nightlife listings magazine covers gigs, parties and clubs plus a few bars and restaurants. Fortnightly.

The Bud Ⓦwww.thebudmag.com. Quarterly glossy magazine focusing on Ubud and the surrounding area.

The Lombok Guide Ⓦwww.thelombokguide.com. Fortnightly newspaper that runs interesting features and general info on all aspects of visiting Lombok and the Gili Islands.

What's Up? Bali Ⓦwww.whatsupbali.com. Weekly foldout featuring day-by-day listings of club and live-music events; dance performances and major festivals; plus restaurant and shopping recommendations.

The Yak Ⓦwww.theyakmag.com. Lifestyle quarterly magazine for the Seminyak expat community and visitor.

Websites and forums

Online forums are great for up-to-the-minute information on everything from favourite hotels to shipping prices, DVD shops to sim-card deals.

Bali Discovery Ⓦwww.balidiscovery.com. Weekly tourism-related news from Bali's plus hotel and tour booking.

Bali Paradise Online Ⓦwww.bali-paradise.com. Features and links on everything from traditional architecture to car rental and the weather forecast. Also has a busy travellers' forum.

Bali Travel Forum Ⓦ www.balitravelforum.com. Active forum with lots of expert posters.

Lombok Lovers Forum Ⓦ lomboklovers .aforumfree.com. Lively and useful Lombok forum.

Travellers with disabilities

Indonesia makes few provisions for its disabled citizens, which clearly affects **travellers with disabilities**, although the situation is definitely improving year on year. At the physical level, kerbs are usually high (without slopes) and pavements/sidewalks uneven, with all sorts of obstacles; access to most public places involves steps (very few have ramps); public transport is inaccessible to wheelchair users (although Perama tourist buses will take them); and the few pedestrian crossings on major roads have no audible signal. On the positive side, many hotels comprise bungalows in extensive grounds and/or have spacious bathrooms, while the more aware are increasingly making an effort to provide the necessary facilities. These hotels are highlighted in the Guide and the Bali Paradise site opposite carries a round-up of big hotels that have accessible facilities.

For all of these reasons, it may be worth considering an **organized tour** or holiday – the contacts listed below will help you start researching trips to Bali and Lombok. Note

that a medical certificate of your fitness to travel, provided by your doctor, can be extremely useful; some airlines or insurance companies may insist on it.

Be sure to carry your complete supply of **medications** with you whenever you travel (including on buses and planes), in case of loss or theft. It's also a good idea to carry a doctor's letter about your drugs prescriptions with you at all times, particularly when passing through customs at Ngurah Rai or Selaparang airports, as this will ensure you don't get hauled up for narcotics transgressions. Assume that if anything happens to equipment, such as a wheelchair, spares will be hard to find, and a small repair kit may well come in very handy.

Contacts for travellers with disabilities

Bali Access Travel Jl Danau Tamblingan 31 ☎ 0361/851 9902, Ⓦ www.baliaccesstravel .com. Specialists in wheelchair-accessible travel in Bali, Lombok and Java including equipment rental, accessible vehicles, all-inclusive tours and home care services.

Ⓦ **www.bali-paradise.com** Follow the Special Needs Traveler link for detailed local information, suggestions and tips.

Ⓦ **www.bootsnall.com/guides** They produce an excellent guide to travelling with disabilities.

Ⓦ **www.emerginghorizons.com** Magazine with a huge range of worldwide travel information and inspiration for wheelchair users and slow walkers.

Ⓦ **thorntree.lonelyplanet.com** The "Travellers with Disabilities" forum is useful.

Guide

Guide

South Bali

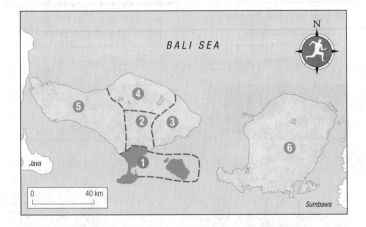

CHAPTER 1 # Highlights

* **Seminyak** Some of the finest dining, most luxurious hotels and most sophisticated shopping on Bali. See p.86

* **Kuta nightlife** Scores of easy-going bars, trendy clubs and packed dancefloors make Kuta *the* place to party. See p.95

* **Jimbaran beach barbecues** Delicious fresh fish is grilled over coconut husks and served at candlelit tables on the sand. See p.102

* **Surf beaches** Awesome breaks at Uluwatu, Dreamland, Bingin and Padang Padang surrounded by towering limestone cliffs. See p.104

* **Denpasar** Balinese city life in all its noisy, frantic glory. See p.113

* **Sanur** This green and relatively peaceful resort makes an appealing alternative to Kuta. See p.123

* **Nusa Lembongan** Laidback seaweed-farming island with great diving nearby. See p.134

* **Nusa Penida** Home to the Bali starling and an important temple, this spectacularly rugged island is well off the tourist trail. See p.139

▲ Surfboards, Kuta beach

South Bali

The triangle of mainly flat land that makes up **the south** is among the most densely populated in Bali. This is where you'll find the island's major **tourist resorts**: at Kuta and Jimbaran in the west, and Sanur, Nusa Dua and Tanjung Benoa in the east. The area is a surfers' paradise, pounded by some of the most famous and challenging breaks in the world. The vast majority of visitors head straight for brash, commercial **Kuta–Legian–Seminyak**, which sprawls down the southwest coast just 3km north of Bali's airport and is as famous for its shopping and nightlife – the most happening on the island by far – as its surf.

Bali's administrative capital, **Denpasar**, is also here, and while most tourists treat the city as little more than a transit point for cross-island journeys, it holds the island's best museum and makes an interesting contrast to the more westernized beach enclaves.

Across on the southeast coast, beach life is quieter and greener at **Sanur** and more luxurious and manicured at **Nusa Dua** and **Tanjung Benoa**, where watersports are the draw. Offshore lie three islands: handsome but little-visited **Nusa Penida**; tiny **Nusa Ceningan**; and resolutely relaxed **Nusa Lembongan**, with its exceptional diving and easy access from Sanur. South of Kuta, the **Bukit peninsula** offers peaceful, upmarket beachfront hotels at **Jimbaran** and fabulous **surf** and lively beach bases beneath the cliffs at and around **Uluwatu**, also the site of an important clifftop temple.

Kuta–Legian–Seminyak

The biggest, brashest resort in Bali, the **KUTA–LEGIAN–SEMINYAK** conurbation continues to expand from its epicentre on the southwest coast, 10km southwest of Denpasar. Packed with thousands of hotels, restaurants, bars, clubs, shops, spas and tour agencies, the 8km-long strip plays host to hundreds of thousands of visitors a year, many of them regular visitors here to party, shop or surf. It's a hectic place: noisy, full of touts, jammed with traffic and a scene of constant building work. Yet the hustle is mostly good-humoured and there are as yet no strip bars or high-rises (nothing over the height of a tall coconut tree, in fact).

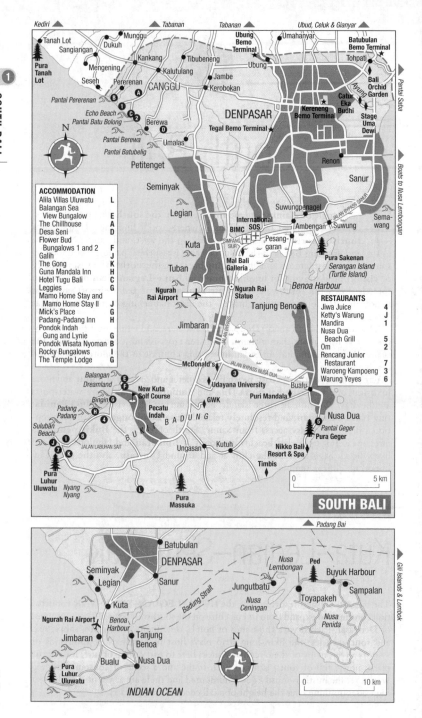

SOUTH BALI

Kediri ▲   ▲ Tabanan   Tabanan ▲   Ubud, Celuk & Gianyar ▲

Tanah Lot
Sangiangan
Pura Tanah Lot
Dukuh
Munggu
Mengening
Seseh
Pererenan
Pantai Pererenan
Echo Beach
Pantai Batu Bolong
Berewa
Pantai Berewa
Pantai Batubelig
Umalas
Petitenget
Seminyak
Legian
Kuta
Tuban
Kankang
Kalutulang
Tibuneneng
CANGGU
Jambe
Kerobokan
Ubung
Umahanyar
Ubung Bemo Terminal
Batubulan Bemo Terminal
Tohpati
Bali Orchid Garden
Catur Eka Budhi
Stage Uma Dewi
Kereneng Bemo Terminal
DENPASAR
Tegal Bemo Terminal
Renon
Sanur
Suwungpenagel
Semawang
Ambengan
Suwung
International SOS
BIMC
SIMPANG SIUR
Pesang-garan
Mal Bali Galleria
Ngurah Rai Airport
Ngurah Rai Statue
Tanjung Benoa
Jimbaran
Pura Sakenan
Serangan Island (Turtle Island)
Benoa Harbour
Bualu
Puri Mandala
Nusa Dua
Pantai Geger
Pura Geger
Nikko Bali Resort & Spa
Timbis
Kutuh
Ungasan
Pura Massuka
Nyang Nyang
Pura Luhur Uluwatu
JALAN LABUHAN SAIT
Suluban Beach
Padang Padang
Bingin
Balangan
Dreamland
New Kuta Golf Course
Pecatu Indah
BUKIT
BADUNG
GWK
Udayana University
McDonald's
JALAN BYPASS NUSA DUA
JALAN BYPASS

Pantai Saba ▶
Boats to Nusa Lembongan ▶

ACCOMMODATION

Alila Villas Uluwatu	L
Balangan Sea View Bungalow	E A
The Chillhouse	A D
Desa Seni	D
Flower Bud Bungalows 1 and 2	F
Galih	J
The Gong	K
Guna Mandala Inn	H
Hotel Tugu Bali	C
Leggies	G
Mamo Home Stay and Mamo Home Stay II	J
Mick's Place	G
Padang-Padang Inn	H
Pondok Indah Gung and Lynie	G
Pondok Wisata Nyoman	B
Rocky Bungalows	I
The Temple Lodge	G

RESTAURANTS

Jiwa Juice	4
Ketty's Warung	J
Mandira	1
Nusa Dua Beach Grill	5
Om	2
Rencang Junior Restaurant	7
Waroeng Kampoeng	3
Warung Yeyes	6

0   5 km

Padang Bai ▲

Batubulan
DENPASAR
Seminyak
Legian
Sanur
Kuta
Ngurah Rai Airport
Benoa Harbour
Jimbaran
Tanjung Benoa
Bualu
Nusa Dua
Pura Luhur Uluwatu
Badung Strait
Nusa Lembongan
Jungutbatu
Nusa Ceningan
Ped
Toyapakeh
Buyuk Harbour
Sampalan
Nusa Penida
INDIAN OCEAN

Gili Islands & Lombok ▶

0   10 km

For many travellers, it's not only the crowds and the assault on the senses that are off-putting, it's that the place seems so un-Balinese: *McDonald's*, Rip Curl and *Hard Rock* are all here and almost every bartender, waiter and losmen employee can employ some slang-ridden English or Japanese banter. But the resort is, in truth, distinctly Balinese: villagers still live and work here, making religious offerings, attending *banjar* meetings and holding temple festivals. Every morning and afternoon, the women place **offerings** in doorways, which you'll see on the street as you walk along. All three former villages have their own **temples**, but none is outstanding and nearly all lock their gates to tourists except at festival times, when visitors are welcome to attend as long as they're suitably attired (see p.48).

Some history

For centuries, Kuta was considered by the Balinese to be an infertile stretch of coast haunted by malevolent spirits and a dumping ground for lepers and criminals. In the seventeenth and eighteenth centuries it operated as a **slave port** when the Balinese rajas sold hundreds of thousands of people to their counterparts in Java and beyond. By the mid-nineteenth century, however, life had become more prosperous – thanks in part to the energetic Danish business trader **Mads Lange**, who set up home here in 1839. Lange's political influence was also significant and thanks to his diplomatic skills, south Bali avoided falling under the first phase of Dutch control when the north succumbed in 1849. Eventually the Dutch took control in 1906 following the mass ritual suicide in Denpasar of hundreds of members of the Badung court (see p.363).

In 1936 the Americans **Bob and Louise Koke** spotted Kuta's tourist potential and built a small hotel; they named it the *Kuta Beach Hotel* (now succeeded by the *Inna Kuta Beach*) and, until the Japanese invasion of 1942, the place flourished. World War II and its aftermath stemmed the tourist flow until the 1960s, when young travellers established Kuta as a highlight on the **hippie trail**. Homestays were eventually joined by smarter international outfits, and Kuta–Legian–Seminyak has since evolved into the most prosperous region of the island, drawing workers from across Bali as well as the rest of Indonesia.

The flood of fortune-seekers from other parts of Indonesia raised the ugly spectre of racism and religious tension, but no one could have anticipated the **October 12 bomb** attack in 2002, in which Muslim extremists from Java detonated two bombs at Kuta's most popular nightspots, *Paddy's Pub* and the *Sari Club*. Three years later, on October 1, 2005, bombs at Kuta Square and in Jimbaran killed twenty. The **Monument of Human Tragedy**, dedicated to the 202 people from 22 countries known to have been killed in the 2002 attack, now occupies the "Ground Zero" site of the original *Paddy's* on Jalan Legian. *Paddy's* has been rebuilt just down the road. For more on the bombings, see Contexts, p.367.

Arrival, information and local transport

Kuta, Legian and Seminyak all started out as separate villages but it's now impossible to recognize the demarcation lines. We've used the most common perception of the neighbourhood borders: **Kuta** stretches north from the Matahari department store in Kuta Square to Jalan Melasti; **Legian** runs from Jalan Melasti as far north as Jalan Arjuna; and **Seminyak** extends from Jalan Arjuna to the *Oberoi* hotel, where **Petitenget** begins. Petitenget feeds into Kerobokan and then north up to the string of **Canggu** area beaches, not strictly within the Kuta boundaries but close enough to share facilities. Kuta's increasingly built-up southern fringes, extending south from Matahari to the airport, are defined as **south Kuta/Tuban**.

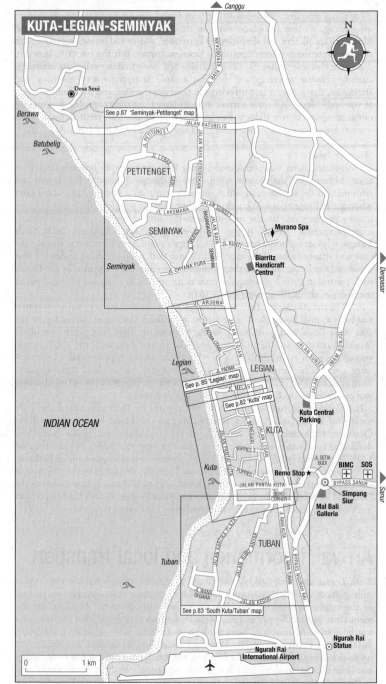

KUTA-LEGIAN-SEMINYAK

▲ *Canggu*

N

Berawa

Batubelig

● Desa Seni

JL RAYA KEROBOKAN

JALAN BATUBELIG

See p.87 'Seminyak-Petitenget' map

JL PETITENGET

JL LEBAK SARI

PETITENGET

JALAN RAYA KEROBOKAN

SEMINYAK

JL LAKSMANA

JALAN SUNSET

BASANGKASA

RAYA

SEMINYAK

Seminyak

JL DHYANA PURA

JL KUNTI

◆ Murano Spa

■ Biarritz Handicraft Centre

Seminyak

JL ARJUNA

JALAN SUNSET

JALAN IMAM BONJOL

▶ *Denpasar*

JL PADMA UTARA

JALAN LEGIAN

Legian

JL PADMA

LEGIAN

See p. 85 'Legian' map

JL MELASTI

See p.82 'Kuta' map

JALAN

INDIAN OCEAN

BENESARI

JALAN LEGIAN

KUTA

JALAN PANTAI KUTA

POPPIES

Kuta Central Parking

Kuta

POPPIES

JL SETIA BUDI

BIMC ✚ SOS ✚

JALAN PANTAI KUTA

Bemo Stop ★

BEMO CORNER

BYPASS SANUR

▶ *Sanur*

Simpang Siur

■ Mal Bali Galleria

JALAN KARTIKA PLAZA

JALAN KUBU ANYAR

JL RAYA KUTA

JL BYPASS NGURAH RAI

JL RAYA TUBAN

TUBAN

Tuban

JL WANA SEGARA

JALAN KEDIRI

See p.83 'South Kuta/Tuban' map

Ngurah Rai Statue ⊙

✈ Ngurah Rai International Airport

0   1 km

▼ *Jimbaran & Nusa Dua*

Alternative road names

Many roads in Kuta, Legian and Seminyak were initially named after the first or biggest hotel or restaurant built there. Though the roads have been given official names (often several of them in succession over the years), many local residents, taxi drivers and maps stick to older versions, and street signs are rarely consistent. The following are the most confusing examples. The **official name** is given in bold.

Jalan Kayu Aya (Petitenget) Previously called Jalan Laksmana and Jalan Oberoi – and now increasingly referred to as "Eat Street" because of the host of restaurants along its length.

Jalan Camplung Tanduk (Seminyak) Also known as Jalan Dhyana Pura and Jalan Abimanyu, and sometimes as Jalan Gado-Gado, after the restaurant at the western end.

Jalan Arjuna (Legian) Commonly referred to as Jalan Double Six after the famous nightclub located on the beach.

Jalan Yudistira (Legian) Until very recently this was Jalan Padma.

Jalan Pantai Arjuna (Legian) Also known as Jalan Blue Ocean Beach, after one of its hotels.

Jalan Werk Udara (Legian) Formerly called Jalan Bagus Taruna, and sometimes known as Jalan Rum Jungle, after a restaurant.

Jalan Bakung Sari (south Kuta/Tuban) Previously known as Jalan Singo Sari.

The resort's main road, which begins as **Jalan Legian** and becomes Jalan Raya Seminyak, runs north–south through all three main districts, a total distance of 5km. The bulk of resort facilities are packed into the 600m-wide strip between Jalan Legian in the east and the coast to the west, an area crisscrossed by tiny *gang* (alleyways) and larger one-way roads.

The other main landmark is **Bemo Corner**, a minuscule roundabout at the southern end of Kuta that stands at the Jalan Legian–Jalan Pantai Kuta intersection. The name is misleading as the Denpasar bemos don't actually leave from here, but it's a useful point of reference.

Arrival

If you're arriving in Bali by air, you'll land at **Ngurah Rai Airport**, just beyond the southern outskirts of Kuta. The main options for getting to Kuta–Legian–Seminyak from the airport are by taxi or bemo – for details see the box on p.78.

From elsewhere in the south, the few public bemos that still exist have limited routes through the Kuta area. Coming **from Denpasar**'s Tegal terminal, the dark-blue **Tegal–Kuta–Legian bemo** goes via Bemo Corner and runs clockwise via Jalan Pantai Kuta, Jalan Melasti and north up Jalan Legian as far as Jalan Yudistira (Jalan Padma), then does a U-turn to head back south down Jalan Legian to Bemo Corner again. For destinations a long way north of here, you're better off getting a taxi.

The dark-blue **Tegal–Kuta–Tuban (airport)–Bualu** route is fine if you're staying in the southern part of Kuta as drivers generally drop passengers on the eastern edge of Jalan Bakung Sari – a five-minute walk from Bemo Corner – before they turn south along Jalan Raya Kuta. Coming by bemo **from Jimbaran**, you'll probably be dropped off at the same place.

A **new public bus** service, the Trans-Sarbagita, has been planned for years and may have started operation by the time you read this. The first three routes are:

Puputan Square in Renon, Denpasar–GWK–Udayana University Campus near Jimbaran; Batubulan–Kuta Central Parking; Kuta Central Parking–Nusa Dua. They will all be potentially useful for visitors but at the time of writing the buses had yet to be delivered and prices were not fixed.

If arriving in Kuta by **shuttle bus**, you could be dropped almost anywhere, depending on your operator. Perama drivers drop passengers at their office on Jalan Legian, about 100m north of Bemo Corner, but may stop at spots en route if asked.

Ngurah Rai Airport

All Bali's international and domestic flights come into **Ngurah Rai Airport** 3km south of Kuta. For arrival and departure **enquiries** see ⊛www.baliairport.com or call ☎0361/751011 ext 5273 or ☎0361/751020 ext 5123.

Arrival

Queues can be lengthy at **immigration** (see Basics, p.58, for visa information). Inside the baggage claims hall, you'll find **ATMs** and **currency exchange** booths, while just outside the Arrivals building there are a number of **hotel reservations desks** (room rates starting at Rp200,000), along with **car rental** outlets for Traffica (☎0361/804 8899, ⊛www.traffica.co.id) and Trac Astra (☎0361/703333 ext 3211, ⊛www.trac.astra.co.id). The 24-hour **left-luggage** offices (Rp20,000–25,000/day/item) are located outside, behind the *McDonald's* between International Arrivals and Departures and to the right of Domestic Arrivals. The **domestic terminal** is in the adjacent building, where you'll find the counters of nearly all the domestic airlines serving Bali.

For **onward transport**, most mid-priced and upmarket hotels can arrange pick-up at the airport. Otherwise, the easiest but most expensive mode of transport anywhere on the island is **pre-paid taxi**, for which you'll find counters beyond the customs exit doors outside the International Arrivals area, and just outside the Arrivals doors in the domestic terminal; pay at the counter before getting into the taxi. **Fares** are fixed: currently Rp35,000–45,000 to Tuban/south Kuta; Rp50,000 to central Kuta (Poppies 1 and 2); Rp55,000 to Legian (as far as Jalan Arjuna); Rp60,000 to Seminyak. Further afield, you'll pay Rp60,000–75,000 to Jimbaran; Rp85,000–90,000 to Denpasar; Rp95,000 to Sanur or Nusa Dua; Rp195,000 to Ubud; or Rp335,000 to Candi Dasa.

If these prices are too steep you're better off avoiding the transport **touts** who gather round both the International and Domestic Arrivals areas and pick up a **metered taxi** on the road immediately outside the airport gates (turn right outside International and walk about 500m – they're not licensed to pick up inside the compound). Using the meter their rates for rides into Kuta–Legian–Seminyak will work out around thirty percent lower than the pre-paid taxi equivalents – the light-blue Blue Bird taxis are the most reliable.

Cheaper still are the dark-blue **public bemos** that often wait for customers on Jalan Airport Ngurah Rai across the road from the airport gates and whose route (daylight hours only) then takes in Jalan Raya Tuban on the way up to Kuta. Keep in mind that their schedules are random and may run no more than hourly, and that it's difficult to stash large backpacks in crowded bemos. The northbound bemos (heading left up Jalan Raya Tuban) go via Kuta's Bemo Corner, Jalan Pantai Kuta, Jalan Melasti and Jalan Legian (see p.77 for details), before continuing to Denpasar's Tegal terminal. You should pay around Rp5000 to Kuta, Legian or Denpasar, or twice that if you've got sizeable luggage.

If you want to go straight from the airport to **Ubud**, **Candi Dasa** or **Lovina**, the cheapest way (only feasible during daylight hours) is to take a bemo, first to Tegal terminal in Denpasar and then on from there; see the plan on p.116 for route outlines.

Information

There's an official **tourist office** behind the lifeguard post on the beach off Jalan Pantai Kuta (Mon–Thurs 10am–2pm, Fri 10am–noon; ℡0361/755660) and another at Jl Raya Kuta 2 (Mon–Thurs 9am–3.30pm, Fri 9am–1pm; ℡0361/766180). However, you'll get a lot more tourist information and details about forthcoming events from the bevy of **tourist newspapers and magazines** available at hotels and restaurants, including the fortnightly *Kuta Weekly*; see Basics, p.67, for details.

These journeys will involve two changes. More conveniently but a little more expensive, is to take a bemo or pre-paid taxi from the airport to Kuta's Bemo Corner, then walk 100m north up Jalan Legian to Perama's shuttle-bus office, where you can book yourself on to the next tourist shuttle bus, most of which run three or four times a day (see p.80).

Departure

For a small fee, any tour agent in Bali will **reconfirm** your air ticket for you if necessary. Most hotels in Kuta, Sanur, Nusa Dua and Jimbaran will provide **transport to the airport** for about Rp100,000–150,000. **Metered taxis** should be a little cheaper and **shuttle buses** are cheaper still: about Rp25,000 from Sanur, Rp50,000 from Ubud, Rp60,000 from Candi Dasa and Rp125,000 from Lovina. During daylight hours, you could also take the rather unreliable Tegal (Denpasar)–Kuta–Tuban **bemo** from Denpasar, Kuta or Jimbaran, which will drop you just beyond the airport gates for about Rp5000.

Airport **departure tax** is Rp150,000 for international departures and Rp30,000 for domestic flights.

Airline offices in Bali

Most **airline offices** are open Mon–Fri 8.30am–5pm and some also open Sat 8.30am–1pm; some close for an hour's lunch at noon or 12.30pm. Except where stated, all the following offices are at Ngurah Rai Airport. Websites are given here for domestic airlines only; websites for international carriers are given in Basics, p.29.

Air Asia airport plus Jl Legian Kaja 455, 3rd floor and Carrefour Supermarket, Jl Sunset ℡021/5050 5088; **Batavia Air** airport ℡0361/751011 ext 5336 and Jl Sunset ℡0361/767633, @www.batavia-air.co.id; **Cathay Pacific** ℡0361/753942, reservation from land line ℡0804/188 8888, from mobile ℡021/515 1747; **China Airlines** ℡0361/757298; **Eva Air** ℡0361/759773; **Garuda** ℡0804/180 7807 or ℡021/2351 9999 if calling from a mobile (both 24hr), airport Domestic ℡0361/751176, International ℡0361/768258, @www.garuda-indonesia.com, city check-ins in Sanur (see p.131), south Kuta/Tuban (see p.99), Nusa Dua (see p.113) and Denpasar (see p.122); **Hong Kong Airlines** Global Holidays, Jl Gurita 38 Kav 10, Sesetan, Denpasar ℡0361/725680; **Jetstar** 24hr contact ℡001/8036 1691; **Korean Air** ℡0361/768377; **Lion Air** ℡0361/765183, @www.lionair.co.id; **Malaysia Airlines** ℡0361/766925; **Mandala** Jl Diponegoro 98, Komp Kertawijaya Blok D/23, Denpasar, 24hr ℡0804/123 4567 or ℡021/5699 7000 from a mobile, @www.mandalaair.com; **Merpati** Jl Gatot Subroto 26, Denpasar ℡361/420999, @www.merpati.co.id; **Qantas** *Inna Grand Bali Beach Hotel*, Sanur ℡0361/288331; **Qatar Airways** airport ℡0361/760274, Discovery Shopping Mall, Tuban ℡0361/752222 ext 2; **Singapore Airlines/Silk Air** ℡0361/768388; **Sriwijaya Air** ℡0804/177 7777 or ℡021/2927 9777 from a mobile, Jl Sunset 1010, Blok D ℡0361/217 1099, @www.sriwijayaair-online.com; **Thai Airways** *Inna Grand Bali Beach Hotel*, Sanur ℡0361/281141; **Trans Nusa** Jl Sunset 100C, ℡0361/847 7395, @www.transnusa.co.id.

Moving on from Kuta

Bemos

To get from Kuta to most other destinations in Bali by **bemo** will almost always entail going via Denpasar, where you'll probably have to make at least one cross-city connection.

Dark-blue bemos to **Denpasar**'s Tegal terminal (Rp5000; 25min) run throughout the day, though the service can be sporadic and you may have to wait up to an hour; the easiest place to catch them is at the Jalan Pantai Kuta/Jalan Raya Kuta intersection, about 15m east of Bemo Corner, where they wait to collect passengers, although you can also get on anywhere on their loop around Kuta (see p.77 for details). From Tegal, other bemos run to **Sanur** and to Denpasar's other bemo terminals for onward connections; full details are on p.117 and on the map on p.118. Note that to get to Batubulan terminal (departure point for **Ubud**), the white Damri bus service from Nusa Dua may be quicker than taking a bemo to Tegal and another to Batubulan; you can pick it up at the Kuta fuel station on the intersection of Jalan Imam Bonjol and Jalan Setia Budi, about ten minutes' walk northeast of Bemo Corner. Dark-blue bemos from Tegal to Bualu and **Nusa Dua's** Bali Collection also pass this intersection, and will pick you up on Jalan Setia Budi if you signal. Some Tegal–Bualu bemos serve **Jimbaran** on the way, and there's also a dark-blue Tegal–Jimbaran bemo.

Shuttle buses and taxis

If you're going anywhere beyond Denpasar, the quickest public-transport option from Kuta is to take one of the tourist **shuttle buses** that run to the main tourist destinations on Bali, as well as some on Lombok and the Gili Islands. Every agency in Kuta–Legian–Seminyak offers "shuttle bus services": some are little more than one man and his van, others are more professional. Prices are always competitive; most travellers choose according to convenience of timetable and

Local transport

As more and more Balinese buy motorbikes, public **bemos** are in decline and it can be as much as an hour between services. All Kuta bemos are dark-blue and they all originate at Denpasar's Tegal terminal. For details of the routes, see p.77; local trips cost Rp5000.

Taxis and touts

Hundreds of **metered taxis** circulate throughout the resort, all with a "Taxi" sign on the roof. The most reliable are the light-blue Blue Bird Bali Taksi (T0361/701111). All charge an initial Rp5000 and then Rp4000 per kilometre, day or night; always check that the meter is turned on. A ride from, say, Jalan Arjuna in Legian down to the *Hard Rock Hotel* will cost around Rp20,000. You can often save time and money by walking a short distance to pick up a taxi heading in the correct direction in Kuta's long-winded one-way system.

Another option is the informal taxi service offered by the "Transport! Transport!" **touts** who hang around on every corner. For brief journeys the bargaining is often more hassle than it's worth, but they can be worthwhile for longer trips.

Cars, bikes and motorbikes

Every major road in the resort is packed with tour agents offering **car and motor-cycle rental** and many also offer bicycles: see Basics, p.33, for price guidelines and advice. Where it is legal to **park** beside the road, attendants generally charge Rp2000 to wave you in and out and keep an eye on your vehicle.

pick-up points. Drop-offs are usually at the operator's office at the destination rather than specific hotels.

Bali's biggest and best-known shuttle-bus operator is **Perama**, whose unobtrusive head office is located 100m north of Bemo Corner at Jl Legian 39 (daily 6am–10pm; ℡0361/751875, ⓦwww.peramatour.com). This is the departure point for all Perama buses, although you can pay an extra Rp10,000 to be picked up from your hotel as long as you leave on the early morning bus. At some destinations they take you to your hotel, while at others this costs extra. You can buy tickets on the phone; shuttle-bus tickets sold by other agencies are almost certainly not for the Perama service, whatever you're told. Typical fares include Rp50,000 to Ubud, Rp125,000 to Lovina and Rp350,000 to the Gili Islands (including boat transfer). See "Travel details", p.142, for a full list of destinations and frequencies.

If there are several of you, **taxis** can be good value for transport to other areas of south Bali: a ride to Denpasar will cost around Rp60,000, and to Nusa Dua or Sanur about Rp90,000.

Transport to other islands
Many Kuta travel agents sell **boat tickets** to Lombok, Nusa Lembongan and other Indonesian islands; Perama (described above) also offer integrated shuttle-bus and boat transport, while Island Promotions (see p.100) specializes in the Gili Islands. Details of the local Pelni office (for long-distance ferries to other parts of Indonesia) are on p.100.

All Kuta travel agents sell **domestic air tickets**. Typical one-way fares are Rp200,000 to Mataram on Lombok, Rp510,000 to Jakarta and Rp550,000 to Kupang, but special deals are frequently available if you search online. Full airport information is on p.78.

Most car-rental outlets can also provide a **driver** for the day, which is a good way of organizing a private tour. A recommended freelance English-speaking guide and driver is Wayan Artana (℡0812/396 1296, ⓔiartana@hotmail.com).

Accommodation

Of south Bali's main beach resorts, Kuta–Legian–Seminyak has by far the greatest amount and range of **accommodation**.

The inexpensive losmen are mainly concentrated in **Kuta** and **Legian** along with a decent share of good-value mid-range places. **Tuban**, **Seminyak** and **Petitenget** are dominated by more expensive – and often very stylish – accommodation, a lot of it right on the beach. The scene is much quieter in the **Canggu** area, whose beaches, at Batubelig, Berewa, Batu Bolong and Pererenan, are served by just a handful of hotels.

Kuta and Tuban

The vibe in **Kuta** is young and fun, bordering on the trashy. Hugely popular with backpackers and surfers, this is the most frantic part of the resort, and also the cheapest. The narrow lanes known as Poppies 1 and 2 and the maze of alleyways around and between them are the main accommodation hubs. The beach gets crowded, but it's a long, inviting stretch of fine sand.

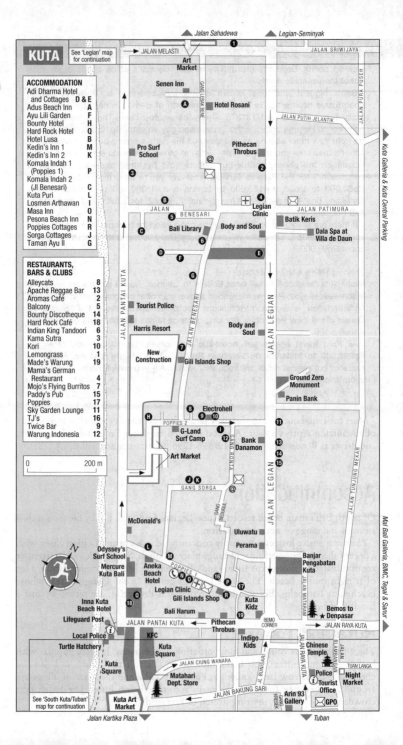

KUTA

See 'Legian' map for continuation

ACCOMMODATION
Adi Dharma Hotel and Cottages	D & E
Adus Beach Inn	A
Ayu Lili Garden	F
Bounty Hotel	H
Hard Rock Hotel	Q
Hotel Lusa	B
Kedin's Inn 1	M
Kedin's Inn 2	K
Komala Indah 1 (Poppies 1)	P
Komala Indah 2 (Jl Benesari)	C
Kuta Puri	L
Losmen Arthawan	I
Masa Inn	O
Pesona Beach Inn	N
Poppies Cottages	R
Sorga Cottages	J
Taman Ayu II	G

RESTAURANTS, BARS & CLUBS
Alleycats	8
Apache Reggae Bar	13
Aromas Café	2
Balcony	5
Bounty Discotheque	14
Hard Rock Café	18
Indian King Tandoori	6
Kama Sutra	3
Kori	10
Lemongrass	1
Made's Warung	19
Mama's German Restaurant	4
Mojo's Flying Burritos	7
Paddy's Pub	15
Poppies	17
Sky Garden Lounge	11
TJ's	16
Twice Bar	9
Warung Indonesia	12

0   200 m

Just beyond Kuta Square's Matahari department store, Kuta beach officially becomes **Tuban**, or **South Kuta**, and things quieten down a bit. This area is often the choice of families, as many hotels enjoy direct access to the beach. There are plenty of restaurants and shops along the main drag, Jalan Kartika Plaza, as well as the colossal Discovery Shopping Mall. No bemos run this way but the beachfront promenade runs from the lifeguard post near the corner of Jalan Pantai Kuta to the fence of the airport and it's about a thirty-minute walk from Kuta Square down to the *Holiday Inn Resort*.

Adi Dharma Hotel and Cottages Access from both Jl Legian 155 and Jl Benesari: hotel ☏0361/754280, cottages ☏0361/751527, both ⓦwww.adidharmahotel.com. A pleasant, central package-tourist-oriented operation with 37 contemporary-styled a/c "cottage" rooms in blocks of four just off Jl Legian, and 86 hotel rooms in a separate building off Jl Benesari. There are pools, a spa and a games room. ❼

Adus Beach Inn Off Gang Lebak Bene ☏0361/755419. There's more than one *Adus* in this area. To find this cheapie follow the signs to *Senen Inn* down the alleyway and *Adus* is on the left. Walking south along Gang Lebak Bene if you get to *Hotel Rosani* you've come too far. Simple rooms with cold-water bathrooms are dotted round the large family compound down a quiet residential lane. Fan ❶, a/c ❷

Ayu Lili Garden Jl Benesari ☏0361/750557. Good-quality rooms around a pool set in a quiet spot well back from the bustle of Jl Benesari. All rooms have hot water and a safe deposit box.

There's also one larger family house with kitchen. Fan ❷, a/c ❸, family house ❹

Bounty Hotel Poppies 2 ☏0361/753030, ⓦwww .bountyhotel.com. Long-established favourite of partying young Australians, this place is also for the "young at heart", as the publicity proclaims – and certainly for a fun vibe the *Bounty* is hard to beat. The 166 well-maintained terraced rooms all have a/c, hot water and cable TV and are set around two different pools – one open 24hr, and a quieter one that closes at 11pm. ❼

🏃 **Hard Rock Hotel** Jl Pantai Kuta ☏0361/761869, ⓦwww.hardrockhotels .net. With sleek, contemporary rooms and rock memorabilia all over the place, the atmosphere is lively and upbeat and works as well for couples as it does for families. Occupying a prime location across from the beach in the heart of Kuta, it boasts the largest free-form swimming pool in Bali, which includes an island in the middle. There's also a spa, a kids' club and *Hard Rock*'s own radio station. ❽

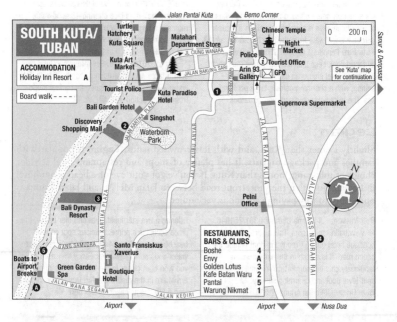

Holiday Inn Resort Jl Wana Segara 33 ☎0361/755577, ⓦwww.bali.holidayinn .com. Fabulously located right on the beach at Tuban, and offering activities, plus a gym and spa, this stylish resort caters brilliantly to families (eg with Rascals Kidz Club and Zone 12–18 for teenagers) as well as couples. It makes a good first or last stop on the island; the Departure Lounge ($30) offers excellent facilities between checking out and heading off to the airport. ❼

Hotel Lusa Jl Benesari ☎0361/753714, ⓦwww .hotellusakuta.com. Large, well-run, well-maintained place on Jl Benesari, just a short walk from the beach. There are rooms for every budget and the garden and pool are inviting. Fan ❷, a/c ❹

Kedin's Inn 1 Poppies 1 ☎0361/756771. This backpackers' favourite offers more than thirty large losmen rooms, built in two storeys around a garden compound and swimming pool. Fan/ac ❷, a/c and hot water ❸

Kedin's Inn 2 Gang Sorga, off Poppies 1 ☎0361/763554. Neat, well-maintained fan cottages in a cute garden with a pretty pool. The location is quiet but the beach and action are close by. ❸

Komala Indah 1 (Poppies 1) Poppies 1, no. 20 ☎0361/751422. Handily located terraced bungalows set around a courtyard garden. Rooms have fans and are clean and cheap. ❶

Komala Indah 2 (Jl Benesari) Jl Benesari ☎0361/754258. *Komala Indah*s seem to have cloned on Jl Benesari. This one is a few metres down a small lane that runs south off Jl Benesari. It's a friendly setup offering decent rooms with fan or a/c (these have hot water as well) in a pleasant garden a short walk from the beach. Fan ❶, a/c ❸

Kuta Puri Poppies 1 ☎0361/751903, ⓦwww .kutapuri.com. Less than a minute from the beach, this small hotel enjoys an unusually spacious setting, with a charming garden, large pool and spa. The terraced rooms and more luxurious bungalows (❼) are well-furnished in Balinese style. All have a/c and hot water and some have outdoor garden bathrooms. Booking is advisable. ❺

Losmen Arthawan Poppies 2 ☎0361/752931. The fan rooms with cold-water bathrooms tucked into a tiny central compound don't have any frills but all have an outside sitting area. For the budget-minded who want to be in the heart of the action, this is a winner. ❶

Masa Inn Poppies 1, no. 27 ☎0361/758507, ⓦwww.masainn.com. Central, well-priced, comfortable hotel, with two good pools and a sociable garden. Rooms in the two- and three-storey blocks come with a/c, hot water, cable TV and safety box. More expensive ones are at ground level and just a few steps from the pool. ❹

Pesona Beach Inn Poppies 1, no. 31 ☎0361/765778, ⓔpesonabeachinn@yahoo.com. Plain but comfortable a/c, hot-water rooms in two- and three-storey blocks set in a garden with a cute little pool that's right on Poppies 1 but away from the main fray. ❸

Poppies Cottages Poppies 1 ☎0361/751059, ⓦwww.poppiesbali.com. Twenty traditional-style a/c cottages set in a tranquil tropical garden with a bougainvillea-shaded swimming pool. Rooms are not up-to-the-minute chic but are charmingly furnished in local fabrics and all have shady terraces and garden bathrooms, plus all mod cons. Extremely popular so reserve ahead. ❼

Sorga Cottages Gang Sorga, off Poppies 1 ☎0361/751897, ⓦwww.hotelsorga.com. Comfortable and well-run place offering 48 good-value rooms in a three-storey block set around a smallish pool and restaurant. Fan ❸, a/c ❹

Taman Ayu II Jl Benesari ☎0361/754376. Seventeen spotless, comfortable, well-maintained rooms, all with hot water, tucked away in a quiet spot a few steps from all the action. Fan ❶, a/c ❸

Legian

Slightly calmer than Kuta, and with less-crowded sands, **Legian** is popular with families and package tourists. It has plenty of shops and restaurants, and a wider choice of mid-range hotels than Kuta. If you've got your eye on a beachfront hotel in Legian, note that the shorefront road between Jalan Melasti and Jalan Arjuna is open only to toll-paying cars and is very quiet.

Bali Niksoma Jl Padma Utara ☎0361/751946, ⓦwww.baliniksoma.com. This award-winning boutique hotel (just 57 rooms) is right behind the beach road. It is stylish in the extreme with fabulously chic but comfortable rooms, a stunning split-level pool and charming service. ❽

Blue Ocean Jl Pantai Arjuna ☎0361/730289. Offering a five-star location at one-star prices, this place occupies a prime, spacious spot on the beachfront road. The 24 rooms all have fans, hot water and cooking facilities. Fancy they aren't, but you won't get closer to the beach at this price anywhere in the resort. The Rip Curl School of Surf (see p.89) has its headquarters here. ❸

Hotel Kumala Jl Werk Udara ☎0361/732186, ⓦ www.hotelkumala.com. With two pools, extensive grounds and a good location just 250m from the beach and 50m from Jl Arjuna, this small, welcoming hotel is excellent value. Rooms in all categories are large and well furnished, and all have a/c, hot water and good bathrooms. Sometimes known as the *Grand Kumala* to distinguish it from the nearby *Kumala Pantai*. Booking essential. ④

Hotel Kumala Pantai Jl Werk Udara ☎0361/755500, ⓦ www.kumalapantai.com. Hugely popular, well-priced hotel with smart, comfortable a/c rooms, each with a balcony, bathtub and cable TV in a series of three-storey buildings set in grounds that run down to the seafront road. Has a good-sized pool. Reservations are essential. ⑥

The Island Gang IX off Jl Legian ☎0361/762722, ⓦ www.theislandhotelbali .com. Stunning little place tucked away in peaceful surroundings offering twelve luxury dorm spaces that are spotlessly clean and comfie (Rp250,000/ bed) and nine private rooms around a neat little pool. The atmosphere is chilled and friendly and the roof terrace to die for. Yoga classes and massage also available. Perfectly located a short

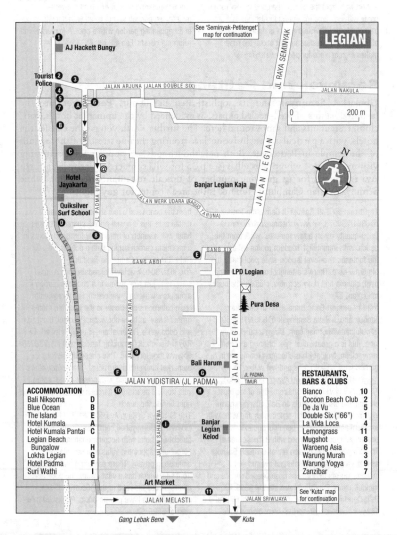

LEGIAN

ACCOMMODATION

Bali Niksoma	D
Blue Ocean	B
The Island	E
Hotel Kumala	A
Hotel Kumala Pantai	C
Legian Beach Bungalow	H
Lokha Legian	G
Hotel Padma	F
Suri Wathi	I

RESTAURANTS, BARS & CLUBS

Bianco	10
Cocoon Beach Club	2
De Ja Vu	5
Double Six ("66")	1
La Vida Loca	4
Lemongrass	11
Mugshot	8
Waroeng Asia	6
Warung Murah	3
Warung Yogya	9
Zanzibar	7

See 'Seminyak-Petitenget' map for continuation

See 'Kuta' map for continuation

AJ Hackett Bungy

Tourist Police

JALAN ARJUNA (JALAN DOUBLE SIX)

JL RAYA SEMINYAK

JALAN NAKULA

0   200 m

Hotel Jayakarta

Quiksilver Surf School

JL WERK UDARA

JL PADMA UTARA

JALAN PANTAI ARJUNA (BLUE OCEAN BEACH)

JALAN WERK UDARA (BAGUS TARUNA)

Banjar Legian Kaja

JALAN LEGIAN

GANG XIX

GANG ABDI

LPD Legian

Pura Desa

JALAN PADMA UTARA

Bali Harum

JALAN YUDISTIRA (JL PADMA)

JL PADMA TIMUR

JALAN SAHADEWA

Banjar Legian Kelod

Art Market

JALAN MELASTI

JALAN SRIWIJAYA

Gang Lebak Bene   Kuta

distance from the beach and from nightlife/shopping. Reservations essential. **⑤**

Legian Beach Bungalow Jl Yudistira ☎0361/751087, ✉legianbeachbunglow@yahoo.co.id. A small, inviting place with friendly staff and 25 simple but pleasantly furnished rooms set in a spacious garden close to the shops but not far from the beach. Very well priced considering its location and swimming pool. Fan **①**, a/c **②**, a/c and hot water **③**

Lokha Legian Jl Yudistira ☎0361/767601, ⓦwww.thelokhalegian.com. Good-value mid-range option, well placed for shops, restaurants and bars, and just a short walk from the beach. The good-quality rooms come with Bali-chic-minimalist furnishings that are also comfortable, while the pool is right in the heart of things and the restaurant just above the road makes a great place for people-watching. **⑦**

Padma Resort Jl Yudistira 1 ☎0361/752111, ⓦwww.padmaresortbali.com. Top-notch upper-bracket resort hotel set in extensive and glorious tropical gardens adorned with dramatic Balinese statuary running down to the beachfront road. Choose between accommodation in one of the hotel wings and larger deluxe "chalets"; some are wheelchair-accessible. There are five restaurants and three bars, two great pools (some rooms have direct access to the lagoon one), a Mandara spa and a complimentary kids' club. **⑧**

Suri Wathi Jl Sahadewa 12 ☎0361/753162, ⓦwww.suriwathi-group.com. Popular hotel with 46 small but well-maintained bungalow rooms, all with hot water, set in an appealing garden with a pool. A favourite with returning guests. Fan **③**, a/c **④**

Seminyak and Petitenget

Upmarket **Seminyak** and its sophisticated neighbour, **Petitenget**, are the favoured haunts of well-heeled expats, as evidenced by the upmarket hotels, bars, clubs, restaurants and shops found here. The further north you go the classier the hotels, with a particularly exclusive enclave fronting the fine stretch of shore south of the temple in Petitenget. Both neighbourhoods are popular with returning visitors, many of whom rent villas (see p.35 for villa contacts). Nearby Jalan Kayu Aya is famous for its growing number of upscale restaurants (see p.93), while Seminyak's Jalan Camplung Tanduk is the area's centre for **gay** nightlife.

The Breezes Bali Resort Jl Camplung Tanduk 66 ☎0361/730573, ⓦwww.thebreezesbali.com. Good-quality resort a few minutes' walk from the beach, with minimalist, modern rooms set around the fantastic two-level lagoon-style pool that's the big draw here. There's a tennis court, on-site spa, gym, cinema and daily activites, plus shuttle buses to Legian. **⑦**

Inada Losmen Gang Bima 9, off Jl Camplung Tanduk and Jl Raya Seminyak ☎0361/732269, ✉putuinada@hotmail.com. Down a quiet, leafy lane, this is a great-value spot offering a dozen large, clean, typically basic losmen rooms set in a garden yard, all with fans and hot water. **①**

The Oberoi Jl Kayu Aya ☎0361/730361, ⓦwww.oberoihotels.com. One of the most elegant and discreet hotels on Bali, offering charmingly appointed, traditional-style rooms and villas with excellent amenities set in beautiful and extensive beachfront grounds adorned with Balinese statuary. The designs and decoration are all uniquely Balinese, as is the atmosphere. Numerous awards and celebrity guests testify to its unsurpassed service and tranquil luxury. Published rates start at $355. **⑨**

Puri Cendana Jl Camplung Tanduk ☎0361/730869, ⓦwww.puricendanaresortbali.com. A short walk from the beach and a few steps from bars and restaurants, this a well-priced, characterful little hotel with a variety of attractively furnished rooms in a charming garden setting with a pool as well. **⑥**

Raja Gardens Jl Camplung Tanduk ☎0361/730494, ✉jdw@eksadata.com. A small setup with just nine rooms in a spacious garden just a minute's walk from the beach. Fan rooms with open bathrooms are closer to the pool, a/c rooms further away; all have hot water. Peaceful, family run and good value. Reservations strongly advised. **①**

Royal Beach Jl Camplung Tanduk ☎0361/730730, ⓦwww.mgallery.com. This cheerfully stylish, upmarket chain hotel, previously the *Sofitel*, offers rooms and villas (some with private pools) set in vast tropical beachfront gardens with two pools, one right beside the beach. **⑧**

The Samaya Jl Kayu Aya ☎0361/731149, ⓦwww.thesamayabali.com. Stunningly stylish beachfront hotel with accommodation in walled, gorgeously appointed villas that provide the ultimate in privacy. There are some on the beachfront site, which has a vast swimming pool, and others across the road in the "Courtyard" site, where all villas have private pools. Published rates start at $525. **⑨**

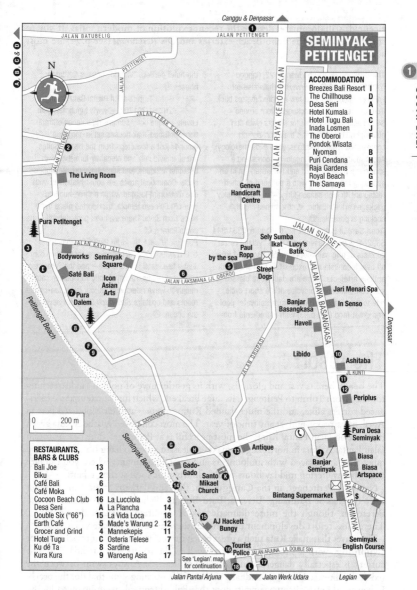

Canggu & Denpasar ▲

JALAN BATUBELIG

JALAN PETITENGET

A, B, C & D

N

SEMINYAK-PETITENGET

JALAN PETITENGET

JALAN LEBAK SARI

JALAN RAYA KEROBOKAN

ACCOMMODATION

Breezes Bali Resort	I
The Chillhouse	D
Desa Seni	A
Hotel Kumala	L
Hotel Tugu Bali	C
Inada Losmen	J
The Oberoi	F
Pondok Wisata Nyoman	B
Puri Cendana	H
Raja Gardens	K
Royal Beach	G
The Samaya	E

The Living Room

Geneva Handicraft Centre

JALAN SUNSET

Pura Petitenget

JALAN KAYU JATI

Sely Sumba Ikat   Lucy's Batik

Bodyworks   Seminyak Square

by the sea   Paul Ropp

Saté Bali   Icon Asian Arts

JALAN LAKSMANA (JL OBEROI)

Street Dogs

JALAN RAYA BASANGKASA

Pura Dalem

Jari Menari Spa

In Senso

Banjar Basangkasa

Haveli

Petitenget Beach

JALAN DRUPADI

Libido

Ashitaba

JL KUNTI

Periplus

JALAN SARINANDE

Pura Desa Seminyak

Seminyak Beach

0   200 m

Antique

Biasa

RESTAURANTS, BARS & CLUBS

Bali Joe	13
Biku	2
Café Bali	6
Café Moka	10
Cocoon Beach Club	16
Desa Seni	A
Double Six ("66")	15
Earth Café	5
Grocer and Grind	4
Hotel Tugu	C
Ku dé Ta	8
Kura Kura	9

La Lucciola	3
La Plancha	14
La Vida Loca	18
Made's Warung 2	12
Mannekepis	11
Osteria Telese	7
Sardine	1
Waroeng Asia	17

Gado-Gado

Santo Mikael Church

Banjar Seminyak

Biasa Artspace

Bintang Supermarket

JALAN RAYA SEMINYAK

JL VILLA LALU

$

AJ Hackett Bungy

Seminyak English Course

Tourist Police   JALAN ARJUNA (JL DOUBLE SIX)

Denpasar ▶

See 'Legian' map for continuation

Jalan Pantai Arjuna ▼   ▼ Jalan Werk Udara   Legian ▼

Canggu beaches: Batubelig, Berewa, Batu Bolong and Pererenan

North of Petitenget, the coastline unfurls via a succession of wild surfing beaches at **Batubelig**, **Berewa**, **Batu Bolong** and **Pererenan** (see map, p.74) – all of which can be dangerous for swimming. This area is loosely referred to as **Canggu** rather than Kuta, and while there are a couple of exceptional places to stay, restaurants or services are a bit further away. Inland, village streets and ricefields still dominate, despite the recent explosion of modern villas. If you're staying out here, the Echo Beach eateries and *Om Restaurant* (see p.94) are most accessible.

The Chillhouse Jl Kubu Manyar 22, Canggu ☎0813/5337 6872, ⓦwww.thechillhouse.com. Friendly, laidback spot a few hundred metres back from the sea. Various packages (from around $425/person/week) cater for surfers (with surf guiding and coaching) and their non-surfing companions (with massages, yoga and reflexology). Accommodation is in bungalows, rooms and a spacious loft (all with a/c and hot water) set in an appealing little garden, with a pool and attached restaurant. In high season (June–Aug) only weekly packages are available; at other times nightly booking is possible. ❹

Desa Seni Jl Subak Sari 13, Canggu ☎0361/844 6392, ⓦwww.desaseni.com. This "village resort" consists of original wooden houses sourced from all over Indonesia and exquisitely furnished with antique artefacts. There are daily yoga classes, a spa, complimentary bicycles (it's a short cycle ride to the beach at Batubelig), a saltwater pool and great food (see p.93) with ingredients from the hotel garden. "Village" houses ❽, larger houses ❾

Hotel Tugu Bali Jl Pantai Batu Bolong ☎0361/731701, ⓦwww.tuguhotels.com. Lovely, unique hotel comprising a series of traditional polished-teak houses set in gorgeous grounds just a few steps from the beach. Suites are all individually and elegantly furnished with beautiful antiques, and some have private plunge-pools. Communal areas are equally fabulous, with one restaurant located within a three-hundred-year-old Chinese temple, transported piece by piece from Java. There's a hotel pool, delightful spa and a library. ❾

Pondok Wisata Nyoman Pantai Pererenan ☎0812/390 6900, ⓔpondoknyoman@yahoo.com. Just a few steps from the sea – and the Pererenan surf break – this friendly, family-run losmen caters mainly to wave riders with its four large, fan-cooled rooms and upstairs *Surfwatch Café* with views of the ocean. ❸

The resort

The **beach** here is vast and glorious, with its gentle curve of golden sand stretching for 8km from Tuban to Petitenget, its huge breakers, which lure amateur and experienced surfers alike, and the much-lauded Kuta sunsets – at their blood-red best in April, but streaky-pink at any time of year. The most congested swathe is Kuta beach itself, along Jalan Pantai Kuta; the most peaceful is at Petitenget. The beach around Jalan Pantai Arjuna in north Legian makes a pleasant place to hang out, fronted by a quiet road and graced with sunloungers and several restaurants where you can laze away the sweltering midday hours while admiring the local surfing talent.

North of Petitenget, in the **Canggu** area, the sand darkens around the rougher little beaches at Batubelig, Berewa, Batu Bolong, Echo Beach (Batu Mejan) and Pererenan, though the more dramatic coastal panoramas here make up for it. There's less resort development up here but there are more private villas.

The waves that make Kuta such a great beach for surfers can make it treacherous for **swimming**, with a strong undertow as well as the rollers to contend with. The current is especially dangerous at the Canggu beaches. Always swim between the red-and-yellow striped flags, and take notice of the warning signs that dot the beach. If you need extra discouragement, note that Bali's lifeguards were involved in 187 rescues in 2010, but there were seven fatalities. **Lifeguards** are stationed in special towers all along Bali's southwest coast from Uluwatu on the Bukit to Seseh near Pererenan; the central lifeguard post is on the beach at the corner of Jalan Pantai Kuta.

Despite the crowds, Olive Ridley **turtles** return to Kuta's shores every year between June and October to lay their eggs late at night. To protect these much sought-after eggs from poachers and help the hatchlings survive, a hatchery has been established by the ProFauna organization and the Satgas community police beside the latter's office on the beach near the corner of Jalan Pantai Kuta. The

Learn to surf

Surfing **lessons** ("If you're not standing on your board by the end of your first lesson, the next one's free") are offered throughout the resort from about Rp150,000 per hour, but it pays to take a bit of care choosing your instructor; personal recommendation is always good and bear in mind that established **surf schools** are accredited and have insurance and qualified instructors. In the established schools prices average $35 for a half-day introduction in a group, or $95 for three full days. The schools below are on the maps on p.82 and p.85.

Odyssey's Surf School At the *Mercure Kuta Bali* on Jl Pantai Kuta ℡0361/742 0763, Ⓦwww.odysseysurfschool.com.

Pro Surf School Jl Pantai Kuta, just north of *Kama Sutra* club ℡0361/744 1466, Ⓦwww.prosurfschool.com. Uses Australian G-Boards for beginners. Accommodation is available on site with brilliant views of the surf across the road.

Quiksilver Jl Pantai Legian Kaja, next to *Jayakarta Hotel* ℡0361/731078, Ⓦwww.quiksilversurfschoolbali.com.

Rip Curl School of Surf *Blue Ocean* hotel, Jl Pantai Arjuna, Legian ℡0361/750459, Ⓦwww.ripcurlschoolofsurf.com. Also offers wakeboarding, kitesurfing, windsurfing and standup paddleboard lessons as well as equipment rental.

hatchlings are then released into the sea, usually in public ceremonies. For more on turtles in Bali, see p.108.

Surfing

Surfing is huge in Kuta and Poppies 2, Poppies 1 and Jalan Benesari in particular are crammed with board rental and repair shops, surf wear outlets and surfer-oriented bars. Surfing was supposedly introduced to Bali by American hotel-owner Bob Koke in 1936; these days, local and international surf championships are regular events. The best **time of year** for surfing off Kuta is during the dry season (April–Oct); at other times surfers head east to Sanur and Nusa Dua.

As Kuta is a sandy beach with no coral or rocks to wipe out on, it's the best place in Bali to learn to surf. Slightly more advanced breaks can be found further south in Tuban, accessed by boats from the lot at the west end of Jalan Wana Segara. North of Seminyak, in the Canggu area, there are reef breaks at Batu Bolong, Echo Beach and Pererenan. For general surfing info, see p.45; for surfari tours see p.91.

Diving and watersports

Most south Bali **dive** centres are based not in Kuta but in Sanur (see p.128 for a list) and as there's no diving directly off Kuta's shores they all include free transport to dive sites. A notable local outfit is AquaMarine Diving, at Jl Petitenget 2A (℡0361/738020, Ⓦwww.aquamarinediving.com).

Watersports also happen elsewhere, in Tanjung Benoa (described on p.111); any Kuta tour agent can make the arrangements.

Water parks and pools

Kuta's **Waterbom Park** on Jalan Kartika Plaza, Tuban (daily 9am–6pm; adults $26, ages 2–12 $16; 2-day passes to be used within a week $42/$26; Ⓦwww.waterbom.com) is a hugely popular aquatic adventure park, with water slides, a 150m-long macaroni tube, a lazy river with inner tubes and Climax, which features a 60m near vertical drop before blasting you into looping the loop. More self-consciously hip is the dazzlingly modern dining, drinking and lounging venue at *Cocoon Beach Club*, Jl Double Six, 66 (☎0361/731266, ⓦwww.cocoon-beach .com) that tempts punters in from 8am (until 3am) with its large pool and quality food and drink. On a much smaller scale, non-guests can use the charming little bougainvillea-shaded swimming pool at *Poppies Cottages* on Poppies 1 for Rp25,000; alternatively, if you eat at the *Aneka Beach Hotel* at the beach end of Poppies 1 you can use their pool for free.

Adrenaline kicks

Should you be so inclined, you can **bungee jump** off a 45m-high swimming-pool tower just back from the ocean on Jalan Arjuna, care of AJ Hackett Bungy (daily noon–8pm, Fri & Sat nights 2–6am; $99; ⓦwww.ajhackett.com); you can even jump on a BMX bike or motorcycle if that's your thing. The 2am jumps on weekends are predictably popular with tripped-out clubbers. Alternatively head skywards instead, via the **Bali Slingshot**, which catapults you 52m into the air in just over one second ("Kiss your a★★★ goodbye" as the publicity advises); it

Active days out

If you fancy something a bit more active than sunbathing, the following **activities** can be booked through travel agents, though it's worth checking prices online as discounts may be available. The bigger operators are Bali Adventure Tours (☎0361/721480, ⓦwww.baliadventuretours.com), See Bali Adventures (☎0361/794 9693, ⓦwww.seebaliadventures.com) and Sobek (☎0361/768050, ⓦwww.balisobek .com). These big operators all do free picks-up from hotels in Kuta, Sanur, Nusa Dua and Ubud, though it's worth enquiring with the others about free transport, too.

Camel safaris Camel rides on the beach near the *Nikko Bali Resort and Spa* in Nusa Dua from $20 for 30min, with Bali Camel Safaris (☎0361/776755, ⓦwww .balicamelsafaris.com).

Elephant trekking At the Elephant Safari Park in Taro (see p.187) with Bali Adventure Tours. From $86, including the 30min elephant ride.

Horseriding The Umalas Equestrian Resort in Kerobokan (☎0361/731402, ⓦwww .balionhorse.com) offers lessons and rides along the beach and through village areas (30min ricefield ride $25; 2hr beach ride $72). A similar outfit is Island Horse (☎0361/731407, ⓦwww.baliislandhorse.com), located in the Yeh Gangga area of west Bali (2hr at $56).

Kitesurfing Bali Kite Surf (☎0811/393919, ⓦwww.balikitesurf.com) and Bali Kitesurfing (☎0361/7899 013, ⓦwww.bali-kitesurfing.org) both offer lessons for beginners and advanced pupils, plus tours of the island to the best kitesurfing locations (from Rp900,000 for 2hr).

Mountain biking Guided downhill bike rides starting from the rim of the volcano in the Batur region are offered by See Bali Adventures, Bali Adventure Tours and Sobek (from $69; half-day).

Paragliding Exo-Fly (☎081/139 3919, ⓦwww.exofly.com) offers courses from two days upwards at Timbis on the Bukit.

Quad-biking, ATV and **buggy driving** Available through See Bali Adventures ($79–85). The trips are about 1hr30min–2hr, driving on tracks through the countryside.

Trekking Bali Adventure Tours offers guided treks (around 2hr 30min; from $64) in the Taro area, including through the Elephant Safari Park there.

Whitewater rafting and **kayaking** Raft the Class II–III rapids of the Ayung River (from $76/half day) with Sobek or Bali Adventure Tours; the latter also offers guided kayaking trips.

Surfaris

Numerous agents in Kuta sell "**surfari**" surfing tours to the mega-waves off East Java (including the awesome **G-Land surf break**; mainly March–Oct but ask about out-of-season options) plus breaks off the coasts of West Java, Lombok, Sumbawa and West Timor. **Prices** start from $275 for a four-day package at G-Land; **operators** covering G-Land include G-Land Bobby's Surf Camp, Jl Pantai Kuta 8B (☏0361/755588, ⓦwww.grajagan.com) and G-Land Surf Camp, Okie House, Poppies 2 (☏0361/750320, ⓦwww.g-landsurfcamp.com). Surf Desert Storm, Jl Poppies 2, (☏0812/365 8239, ⓦwww.surfdesertstorm.com) offers G-Land, Lakey Peak in Sumbawa, Desert Point and a seven-night Lembongan, Lombok, Sumbawa safari (minimum 12 people; $865) or you can charter a liveaboard surf boat to pretty much any break in the region through them. Surf Travel Online on Jalan Benesari (☏0361/737056, ⓦwww.surftravelonline.com) also runs trips to breaks all over. Surfaris can be organized for all levels of **ability** but you must come clean about your experience, or lack of it, with the operators. See Basics, p.45, for more on surfing safety.

operates opposite the *Bali Garden Hotel* at Jl Kartika Plaza 8X in Tuban (daily 11am until late; Rp250,000; ⓦwww.balislingshot.net).

Eating

There are hundreds, perhaps even thousands, of **places to eat** in Kuta–Legian–Seminyak, from tiny neighbourhood warung to design-obsessed "dining experiences". In general, the most sophisticated – and expensive – restaurants are in Seminyak and Petitenget, while there's often little to differentiate the tourist restaurants that line the roads and alleyways of Kuta and Legian (we've tried to select some of the standouts, below). Unless otherwise stated, all places listed below are **open** daily from breakfast-time through to at least 10pm.

Kuta's main **night market** (*pasar senggol*) on Jalan Blambangan, at the southern edge of Kuta, is sleepy and small but, with mains from Rp10,000, it's worth a walk if pennies are precious.

Kuta

Alleycats Off Poppies 2; look for the *Balita Inn* at the end of the alleyway. The home-from-home for hungry Brits, this courtyard café prides itself on dishing out authentic full English breakfasts (Rp45,000), monster mixed grills (Rp125,000) and kormas and Punjabi curries (pick your fire rating up to level 15).

Aromas Café Jl Legian. Delicious vegetarian food served in an open-sided garden dining room set away from the street. The menu includes Mexican, Italian, Indian and Indonesian dishes (Rp40,000–55,000), mostly made with organic ingredients. Also does an enticing range of desserts and lots of juices.

Balcony Jl Benesari. Occupying a breezy spot up above the bustle of the street, this surfer-themed place has a big Indonesian and international menu, specializing in tasty grills (mains from Rp40,000).

A huge drinks menu (the frozen margaritas are a steal at Rp20,000) and Illy coffee complete the offerings.

Indian King Tandoori Jl Benesari 40 ☏0361/919 8254. Tiny little Indian place offering cheap and tasty eats – the food is well cooked and nicely presented. Dosas start at Rp12,000 and there's a huge menu of vegetarian, meat and fish dishes (mains from about Rp30,000). Thalis are also available as is delivery in the Kuta area. There's another branch on Jl Camplung Tanduk in Seminyak.

Kori Poppies 2 ☏0361/758605 ⓦwww .korirestaurant.co.id. Peaceful, sophisticated setting just a few steps from the mania of Poppies 2. The wide-ranging menu takes in Indonesian, Thai and international dishes, including bangers and mash and items you grill yourself on sizzling hot stones (mains from about Rp70,000). The desserts are fabulous and there's an extensive drinks list. Not great for vegetarians, but otherwise definitely worth the price tag, particularly before 7pm when there's a ten percent discount.

Made's Warung Jl Pantai Kuta ⓦwww .madeswarung.com. This long-standing Kuta institution has been serving up great meals to travellers for decades, including Balinese and Indonesian fare (Rp25,000–150,000). The portions are large, the quality excellent and it's a splendid spot for people-watching. There's an offshoot on Jl Raya Seminyak in a rather more elegant setting.

Mama's German Restaurant Jl Legian ⓦwww .bali-mamas.com. Buzzy 24hr streetside spot with jolly service offering a vast menu of Indonesian and international meals, specializing, unsurprisingly, in German meals such as a sausage platter (Rp62,900), beef goulash (Rp69,900) and meat loaf (Rp57,500). Well-priced beer as well.

Mojo's Flying Burritos Jl Benesari ⓣ0361/764930 ⓦwww.mojosflyingburritos.com. This cheap and cheerful Californian-Mexican place offers great-quality nachos, enchiladas, quesadillas and tacos, plus the house speciality: build-your-own burritos (about Rp30,000). Margaritas (Rp45,000 and up) and mojitos (Rp35,000) are reasonable and free delivery is available. Branches in Seminyak (Jl Petitenget, Gang Prana), Petitenget (Jl Petitenget) and Ubud (Jl Raya Ubud).

Poppies Poppies 1 ⓣ0361/751059. This tranquil haven set away from the hustle beneath bougainvillea-draped pergolas is a Kuta institution, established in 1973 and so famous the road is named after it. There's a huge Indonesian (from Rp40,000 to the *rijsttafel* at Rp210,000 for two) and international menu (Rp50,000 and up) of well-cooked and well-presented food. There's also a breakfast menu from 8am. Worth reserving a table for dinner.

TJ's Poppies 1. Popular, long-running Californian/Mexican restaurant with comfie seating and tables set around a pond. The menu covers the full gamut of tortillas, fajitas and enchiladas (Rp50,000–60,000) and includes a great range of desserts plus, as you'd expect, margaritas shaken or frozen (from Rp65,000) and tequila shots (from Rp40,000).

Warung Indonesia Gang Ronta. Welcoming surfer-friendly warung where you can fill up on your own assortment of veg and non-veg *nasi campur* (Rp25,000 will fill up most folks) or order Indonesian staples (starting at Rp10,000) from the good-sized menu. Open noon to midnight.

South Kuta/Tuban

Envy *Holiday Inn Resort*, Jl Wana Segara 33. Fabulously located beachside bar/restaurant

serving lunch and then afternoon tea (3pm–5pm; available with martinis instead of tea if you prefer) before morphing into a great sunset bar with innovative cocktails (make your own mind up about the Breakfast Cocktail with gin and marmalade) and finally a restaurant offering offering pizza, pasta and grills (main courses from Rp100,000).

Golden Lotus *Bali Dynasty Resort*, Jl Kartika Plaza. Upmarket Chinese restaurant that's a hit with local Chinese and Indonesian families. Go for the all-you-can-eat Sunday buffet of sixty different types of dim sum (10am–2.30pm; Rp85,000, ages 5–12 Rp42,500). On other days, dim sum is served at the same times but ordered by the plate, and dinner is 6–10pm.

Kafe Batan Waru Jl Kartika Plaza. South Kuta branch of the Ubud stalwart, this streetside café directly opposite Waterbom Park serves specialities from across Indonesia (mostly Rp45,000–75,000), including spicy chicken from Lombok (*ayam Taliwang*), prawns in a Sumatran green chilli sauce (*udang lado hijau*) and Buginese red snapper fishermen's stew (*ikan woku belanga*). Also does international salads and sandwiches.

Pantai South Kuta. The menu features the usual Indonesian and international staples including plenty of seafood (mains Rp30,000 upwards) but it's the location, right on the beach (about a 10min walk south of Discovery Shopping Mall along the boardwalk) that's the real draw – you can enjoy the peace and watch the lights of Kuta and Legian twinkling from afar.

Warung Nikmat Just off Jl Kubu Anyar, next to the main entrance of *Hotel Baking Sari*, 50m west of the southern end of Gang Kresek. Ultra-popular lunchtime choice of everyone from workers to surfers where you assemble your own *nasi campur* from around fifty different East-Java-style dishes – beans with chilli, curried eggs, chicken curry, *urap*, tempeh and much more. The price depends on your selection but Rp25,000 should satisfy even the biggest appetite. Usually open until 2.30pm or so.

Legian

Bianco Jl Yudistira. White decor, high ceilings and whirling fans confirm the colonial theme here. The enormous menu offers half Italian and half Indonesian cuisine, with well-cooked, artfully presented mains from Rp45,000 (up to an Indonesian *rijsttafel* at Rp315,000 for two). The drinks list is equally vast and two-for-one offers and live music add to the allure.

Lemongrass Jl Melasti. Fantastic Thai restaurant serving all the Thai classics and then some from a huge menu including plenty of seafood and many vegetarian options. It isn't cheap (Rp50,000–60,000 for a main course) but portions are huge.

Mugshot Jl Padma Utara. Fabulous coffee – probably the best in the resort – supplemented by excellent snacks and light meals, as well as computers and wi-fi access.

Waroeng Asia Jl Arjuna 23. There's some superb Thai food to be had in Bali and this shady little café is no exception. Tourists and expats alike are drawn here for its speciality, palate-tingling, well-priced dishes (most mains around Rp35,000), including delicious curries, salads and spring rolls. Get there early to get a table.

Warung Murah Jl Camplung Tanduk. Popular with thrifty diners, especially at lunch times: select your own *nasi campur* medley from curries, tempeh, fritters and vegetable dishes (from about Rp20,000), or choose from the small menu featuring the usual Indo-Chinese suspects (from Rp18,000). They also have another place on Jl Kayu Aya.

Warung Yogya Jl Padma Utara 79. Another busy, unpretentious and cheap Indonesian eatery, where *nasi campur* (veg or non-veg) and a small menu of other Indonesian favourites costs around Rp16,000.

Zanzibar Jl Pantai Arjuna. One of a string of good, busy bar/restaurants set beside the car-free beachside road, boasting an upper deck that catches the breeze and good food from a wide-ranging menu including Italian food and grills. The pizzas from the wood-fired oven are a treat. Mains are mostly Rp40,000–70,000.

Seminyak and Petitenget

Biku Jl Raya Petitenget 888 ☎0361/857 0888. All-day breakfasts, all-day Afternoon Tea (including freshly baked scones and cream), cakes, great lunches and dinners, taking in curries, Indonesian food, burgers, meat pies and a great deal more, mean there's something for everyone at any time of the day. Located in an old Joglo with a wonderful atmosphere, an attached bookshop and tealeaf and tarot readings on Friday, Saturday and Sunday afternoons. Reservations advisable.

Café Bali Jl Kayu Aya ☎0361/736484. Incredibly popular place in "Eat Street" with an almost unbelievably eclectic menu; quesadillas nestle next to sushi rolls, dim sum, pasta, grills and Indian curry. This means all tastes are catered for in this atmospheric, high-ceilinged building with distressed white paint, whirling fans and a great buzz.

Café Moka Jl Raya Seminyak. Fabulous French bakery offering bread, pastries, cakes, quiche,

sandwiches, salads and more substantial meals. The a/c can be a life-saver, as can the coffee.

Desa Seni Jl Kayu Putih 13, Pantai Berewa, Canggu. Organic restaurant attached to this small boutique hotel (see p.88), with many of the vegetables grown in the hotel garden. The dishes (mostly about Rp65,000) are delicious: scrumptious salads, pastas and fish all make great use of local produce and the setting is wonderfully chilled.

Earth Café Jl Kayu Aya 99. Tasty vegetarian fare, predominantly organic, including *nasi campur*-style platters (Rp52,000 upwards), daily grain specials, "Bali boost" smoothies, interesting salads and lots more.

Grocer and Grind Jl Kayu Jati 3X ☎0361/730418. Pricey but excellent bistro/deli serving great coffee, cakes, pastries, soups, salads and sandwiches (Rp30,000 and up) as well as larger meals, including pasta, noodles, pies, grills and sausage and mash (Rp45,000–90,000). Local delivery available.

Hotel Tugu Jl Pantai Batu Bolong ☎0361/731701, ⓦwww.tuguhotels.com. The hotel offers a choice of wonderful dining spaces, including the *Bale Sutra*, which houses a three-hundred-year-old temple, the *Bale Puputan*, featuring memorabilia from the Dutch colonial era, and *Waroeng Tugu*, a simple, traditional kitchen. Relatively inexpensive à la carte options are available as well as a huge range of set menus, up to the amazing, multi-coursed Royal Tugudom, a meal in the style of the ceremonial dining of the Majapahit kingdom (Rp950,000/person).

Ku dé Ta Jl Laksmana ☎0361/736969, ⓦwww.kudeta.com. One of the most talked-about restaurants in south Bali, boasting a setting – a dramatic beachfront piazza embraced by a cloister that frames a stunning sea view – as breathtaking as the prices on its modern-European dinner menu (Rp290,000 for baby lobster risotto). A long, lazy breakfast, brunch or lunch on the loungers overlooking the beach is far more affordable (set breakfast Rp120,000 8am–noon or to 1pm on Sunday, lunch main courses Rp110,000–120,000) or come and enjoy the club vibe from 11pm to 2am.

Kura Kura *The Oberoi* hotel, Jl Kayu Aya ☎0361/730361, ⓦwww.oberoihotels.com. It doesn't get much more romantic than this: an open-sided pavilion in the glorious hotel grounds, with the sound of waves crashing on the shore. Service is sublime, with Indonesian, Indian (the home of *Oberoi* is India) and Modern European food to match. It would be possible to break the bank with main courses (mostly from Rp200,000–300,000) but the daily three-course Plats du Jour (Rp250,000 for lunch, Rp320,000 for dinner) offer great dining as well as stunning value.

La Lucciola Jl Petitenget, accessed by footpath from the Pura Petitenget car park, or from the beach ☎0361/730838. Built on the edge of the shore, this two-storey pavilion is a popular spot for sunset cocktails and romantic dinners under the glow of flaming torches. The Mediterranean-inspired menu (mains Rp125,000–255,000) takes second place to the setting, but includes prawn and snapper pie, grilled Black Angus steak and seafood stew. Lunch is less pricey but lacks the drama of the dining experience. Reservations advisable, especially for a sea-view table.

La Plancha Accessed by a footpath from Jl Camplung Tanduk or past the AJ Hackett Bungy. Great Spanish place on the beach with a chilled vibe serving a small menu of tapas favourites (Rp20,000), which you can also order as main courses, taking in salads, Spanish omelette, chicken and seafood. Come early to bag the cushions on the beach. Usually 7am–11pm but look out for parties until 3am.

Mandira Echo Beach. One of a row of eateries overlooking the sands at Echo Beach in Canggu, Mandira offers a typical tourist menu of international and Indonesian dishes (mains Rp20,000–50,000); the food is fine but, as with all these places, it's the beachside location that's the real star.

Om Jl Pantai Batu Bolong ☎0361/9640 4121. A few steps towards the beach from Hotel Tugu in Canggu, Om sports an ambitious organic menu that covers the whole world, with quesadillas nestling alongside sushi, fettuccine, rendang and pad thai (mains Rp50,000–70,000). Dishes are also available in small portions, so you can share a few. The high-ceilinged bale is welcoming and airy.

Osteria Telese Jl Pantai Kayu Aya. Osteria Telese stands out from its high-concept, high-price neighbours as a plain and simple Italian restaurant serving excellent food. The menu features a vast array of appetizing, well-cooked antipasti, pizza, pasta, meat and fish, with mains around Rp55,000–80,000 – which would barely get you a side order of French fries and a juice at some places nearby.

Sardine Jl Petitenget ☎0361/738202, ⓦwww.sardinebali.com. An imaginatively designed bamboo bale overlooking a private ricefield sets the scene for fabulous food and service at this fine-dining spot. Fish is the speciality here, and while the menu changes daily, depending on the catch of the day, everything is intricately and beautifully cooked and presented.

Nightlife and entertainment

Kuta–Legian–Seminyak has the liveliest and most diverse **nightlife** on the island, with scores of clubs and bars, many featuring live bands. Most places stay open until at least 1am, with several clubs continuing to churn out the sounds until 6am; there are always plenty of metered taxis around to get you home.

Women are unlikely to get serious hassle, though they'll be seriously chatted up by the resident gaggle of **gigolos** who haunt the dancefloors and bars. **Drugs** are also part of the Kuta scene and are widely available, but be aware that police setups are quite common and even the possession of small quantities for personal consumption can land you with a ten-year jail sentence.

Cultural entertainment doesn't get much of a look-in around Kuta, but there's one regular local **dance show** (and travel agents can arrange trips to shows further afield) and there's a **cinema** on the edge of the resort.

Bars, clubs and live music

Kuta's nightlife is extremely loud and laddish. It's the home of the jam jar (lethal, pint-sized cocktails of multiple spirits and mixers) and countless happy hours and the province of drunken tourists; if you want to join in, start at Paddy's Pub and follow the crowds. Up in **Legian**, **Seminyak** and **Petitenget** the scene is more sophisticated, with an ever-changing choice of trendy little lounge bars, some of them very chic, plus several **gay bars** on Jalan Camplung Tanduk (Bali Joe bar is the epicentre, next to the restaurant Antique on that road). If you want to connect with **local music**, consider a short trip out to Antida (ⓦserambi-arts-antida.com) at Jalan Waribang, off Jalan Bypass Ngurah Rai, on the eastern edge of **Denpasar**. It's a terrific, semi-outdoor hangout and a cool new venue for local acts, complete with a recording studio, stage and beer garden out the back.

In addition, all the clubs listed below stage frequent **live music** and special events, detailed in the free fortnightly **magazine** *the beat*, available throughout the resort. Check flyers, too, for big-name appearances. The following places typically **open** at around 6pm, closing at 1am or later.

Kuta and Tuban

Apache Reggae Bar Jl Legian 146. Kuta's primary reggae spot is dark and loud, with a sunken dance-floor and dread-heads grooving to the Rasta beats played live and by resident DJs. Open till 2am.

Boshe Jl Bypass Ngurah Rai 89X, Tuban. If you're into indie bands and prefer indoor clubs, chances are you'll like the *Boshe*: it has a great sound system and a "Local Session" every Tuesday night, featuring interesting local outfits.

Bounty Discotheque Behind *Paddy's* on Jl Legian, just south of Poppies 2 intersection. Infamous hub of bare-chested excess, housed in and around a novelty replica of Captain Bligh's eighteenth-century galleon. DJs play hip-hop and mainstream dance music, bands (mostly rock and punk) do their stuff at one of the live-music stages, and themed parties are a regular feature. Jam jars are of course the signature drink.

Hard Rock Café Jl Pantai Kuta. This place has a good reputation for its live music (including from Balinese bands) and stage shows, which attract big crowds. The food is good too; the headliners are, of course, the excellent burgers (from Rp159,000), with salads, steaks and grills also on the menu. Most shows start at 11pm; closes 2am (weekends 3am).

Kama Sutra Jl Pantai Kuta. Large, plush Indian-styled club and live-music venue that attracts capacity crowds with big-name bands from Jakarta and beyond.

Paddy's Pub Jl Legian 66, just south of Poppies 2 intersection. Part of the *Bounty* complex and just as popular, this huge, open-sided place gets crammed. Punters need little encouragement to enter the frequent drinking competitions and foam parties. Regular live music and reasonably priced beer.

Twice Bar Poppies 2. Perfect destination if you're into hardcore underground stuff – a great place to connect with alternative local music.

Sky Garden Lounge Jl Legian 61, across from the Poppies 2 intersection. Loud and jumping multi-storey venue with various rooms pumping different sounds and terraces with views across the resort.

Legian, Seminyak and Petitenget

Breeze *Samaya* hotel, Jl Kayu Aya, Petitenget. Sit at the bar or tables that line the shorefront boardwalk and enjoy the unparalleled sea view, swaying paper lanterns and illuminated palm trees, and hopefully you won't mind paying the top-dollar prices at this swanky hotel bar.

De Ja Vu Jl Pantai Arjuna 7X, Legian. Loud and jumping, sleek and slender beach-view lounge-bar where in-house DJs spin progressive house, electro and chill-out sounds to big crowds. Gets going about 11pm. Open 4pm to late.

Double Six ("66") Jl Pantai Arjuna. Large Legian institution that's massive for the hardcore dance music, huge sound-system, packed dancefloor and visiting big-name DJs (check flyers for info).

Hu'u Jl Laksmana, Petitenget. There's style and atmosphere aplenty at this hip drink 'n' dine experience. Sofas invite you to lounge or you can do the romance thing at the candlelit tables set around and behind the gem-like swimming pool. The DJ starts at 11pm and the pace ratchets up, aided by the bar's famous lychee Martinis. Daily 11am–1am, Sat & Sun until 2am.

La Vida Loca Jl Pantai Arjuna. Latin beats in this small spot just behind the beach.

Mannekepis Jl Raya Seminyak 2 ⓦ www.mannekepis-bistro.com. Describing itself as a jazz and blues bistro, this place has live music Thurs–Sat and a great international menu (plenty of Belgian specials) as well as snacks to accompany drinks. Dark wood and a friendly vibe all add to the attraction. 10am–1am.

Traditional dance and cinemas

The traditional Balinese **dance** – the Legong – is performed at Puri Seminyak (see map, p.87) for tourists every Tuesday evening (2hr; Rp80,000 at the door). It's an atmospheric setting and the only scheduled dance show in the resort area. However, many tourists find that the Kecak or Barong dances (see p.377 for more about these) are a bit more engaging than the stately Legong, especially for children, but for these you'll have to travel further afield on a tour or spend a couple of nights in Ubud (see p.152). Alternatively, look out for hotels offering Balinese dances to accompany dinner.

Kuta's Galeria 21 Cineplex **cinema** is inside the Mal Bali Galleria shopping complex at the Simpang Siur roundabout on Jalan Bypass Ngurah Rai, near the road to Sanur (☎0361/767022). Most mainstream films are shown in their original language with subtitles; the fortnightly freebie *Bali Advertiser* publishes the programme.

Shopping

Kuta–Legian–Seminyak has the best and most diverse **shopping** in Bali, especially for clothes, kids' wear, surfing gear, homewares and souvenirs. For a shopping expedition start at Bemo Corner and head up Jalan Legian, whose 6km of shops begin at the southern end with an emphasis on cheap, mass-market stuff, gaining in style and price as you reach Seminyak. Take side excursions into Jalan Arjuna (for cheap sarongs and clothes) and Jalan Camplung Tanduk, and end up in Jalan Kayu Aya, the Bond Street of Bali, where designers rule.

For basic necessities, cosmetics, groceries and kids' items, head for the **Matahari department store** in Kuta Square, the **Bintang Supermarket** on Jalan Legian, **Carrefour Supermarket** on the Sunset Road, or the colossal seafront **Discovery Shopping Mall** in south Kuta/Tuban, a good one-stop shopping destination with its scores of international and local brand-name clothing stores, plus several cafés for sustenance. All these places are open daily, at least 10am–10pm.

Many popular Balinese stores have morphed into **chains**, with several branches in the south and sometimes in Ubud. Note that addresses do change, so if there's somewhere you especially want to visit, it's worth checking the website (if there is one) in advance.

Art, books, DVDs and music

The resort is awash with **art** shops, mostly featuring agreeable but mass-produced canvases with little originality. There are secondhand **bookshops** along Poppies 1, Poppies 2 and Jalan Benesari, and Bali Library (see map, p.82) is excellent. Finally, there's no shortage of shops selling recently released pirate **CDs** and **DVDs** for Rp10,000.

Biasa Artspace Jl Raya Seminyak 34 ⊛www .biasaart.com. Light, airy commercial gallery in the heart of Seminyak specializing in modern Indonesian art; most of the work will be way above the average budget but this is always an interesting space.

Ganesha At *Biku* restaurant, Jl Raya Petitenget 888. This small outpost of the great Ubud bookshop (see p.178) has an excellent range of fiction and non-fiction, especially strong on Balinese subjects and mind, body and soul material.

Kenzo Jl Legian 457A, just south of the Jl Arjuna junction. Rather better canvases with more variety than is available in the usual mass-produced art places.

The Light Box J Kayu Aya 1. Original art from French photographer Laurence Laborie who presents his work in the front of a light box, creating a unique item. Limited editions from Rp1.6 million up to original works at Rp8million–10million.

Periplus *Made's Warung* Seminyak, Seminyak Square, Carrefour, Bali Galeria Mall, Discovery Shopping Mall ⊛www.periplus.co.id. This outstanding chain of English-language bookshops has branches throughout the resort and features novels and plenty of books about Bali and Indonesia among an eclectic non-fiction range.

Clothes and jewellery

Bali's **clothing** industry is based here in Kuta–Legian–Seminyak and the shops stock some great designs. The most stylish and exclusive boutiques are on northern Jalan Legian and Jalan Raya Seminyak. **Surfwear shops** also abound, with dozens of outlets throughout the resort, including Jungle Surf, Mambo, Quiksilver, Rip Curl, Hurley and Surfer Girl; you'll trip over them on Jalan Legian, in Kuta Square and in the Discovery Shopping Mall.

Biasa Jl Raya Seminyak 36, Jl Raya Seminyak 34 ⓦwww.biasabali.com. Also in Ubud. Specializes in light, elegant cotton and silk clothing for men and women.

Body and Soul Kuta Square and Jl Legian 162, Kuta, plus a factory outlet at Jl Raya Seminyak 16C ⓦwww.bodyandsoulclothing.com. Up-to-the-minute young and trendy fashions from this Oz-based company with stores all over Indonesia.

by the sea Jl Raya Seminyak 32, Jl Basangkasa 30, Jl Kayu Aya 20C, Jl Legian 186, Discovery Mall ⓦwww.bytheseatropical.com. Relaxed, casual and wearable fashions by Brazilian designer Renato Vianna for men, women and children.

Electrohell Poppies 2. Small shop selling street designs from a vast range of small independent Indonesian and Balinese designers.

Indigo Kids Jl Legian, Jl Legian, Jl Melasti, Jl Seminyak, Discovery Mall ⓦwww.indigokidsglobal .com. Bright, cotton childrens' clothes that are Aussie-designed and Indonesian-made – they do girls' stuff best.

Kuta Kidz Jl Pantai Kuta (Bemo Corner) and Jl Bakung Sari. Bright fabrics and cute designs for boys and girls under 12.

Paul Ropp Jl Patih Jelantik Blok Promenade 1 no. 8, Jl Raya Seminyak 39, Jl Kayu Aya 68, Seminyak ⓦwww.paulropp.com. Expensive, eye-catching, boho-chic fashions hand-tailored from stunning silk and cotton fabrics – subtle they aren't, fabulous they certainly are, even if not to all tastes.

Pithecan Throbus Jl Pantai Kuta, Jl Legian 368, Legian. Batik-print sarongs and clothes featuring modern reinventions of antique patterns plus unusual, classy handicrafts.

Street Dogs Jl Kayu Aya 60X ⓦwww.balibrass .com. Bold, brash jewellery that is totally different from much of the more delicate jewellery on offer throughout the resort. They have another outlet, Libido, at Jl Basangkasa 5.

Uluwatu Jl Pantai Kuta, Poppies 2, Jl Laksmana and several branches on Jl Legian ⓦwww .uluwatu.co.id. White, handmade Balinese lace and cotton clothes.

Handicrafts, souvenirs and homewares

The shops and stalls that line Poppies 1 and the Kuta end of Jalan Legian are the place to start looking for **artefacts**, **antiques** and other **souvenirs** from all over Indonesia. As with fashions, you'll find the most interesting and better-made items in Legian and Seminyak. For one-stop good-value shopping, the huge **oleh oleh shops** (warehouse-sized handicraft and souvenir supermarkets) detailed below are unbeatable.

Ashitaba Jl Raya Legian 353 and Jl Raya Seminyak 6. Intricate *ata*-grass basketware from Tenganan, fashioned into everything from mats to bowls.

Bali Harum Jl Pantai Kuta 28A and Jl Legian 419. Prettily packaged aromatherapy, toiletries, soaps, oils and incense.

Batik Keris Discovery Shopping Mall. Large range of batik clothes, housewares and souvenirs.

Biarritz Handicraft Centre Jl Sunset ⓦwww .biarritzhandicraft.com. Vast oleh oleh store with excellent (fixed) prices. Closed Sun.

Geneva Handicraft Centre Jl Kerobokan 100. ⓦwww.genevahandicraft.com. Multistorey oleh

oleh shop with the goods piled high and sold cheap.

Haveli Jl Raya Basangkasa 15 & 38 ⓦwww .haveli.com. Upmarket homewares, including hand-woven cotton drapes, tablecloths and cushions plus some clothing, all in fabulously luxurious fabrics and designs.

Icon Asian Arts Jl Kayu Aya 17 ⓦwww .iconasianarts.com. Works from all over Asia that are a definite cut above the usual tourist offerings; top quality and top prices but there's no harm in browsing.

Sarongs and traditional textiles

The cheapest places to buy everyday rayon and cotton **sarongs** are the street stalls and art markets of Kuta and Jalan Arjuna.

Lucy's Batik Jl Raya Basangkasa 88, Seminyak ⓦ www.lucysbatik.com. Breathtakingly beautiful collection of Javanese batik sarongs and scarves, from stamped cotton wraps up to exquisite hand-drawn silk versions (some woven with pineapple leaf fibre) that cost millions and may take four months to make.

Sely Sumba Ikat Jl Raya Basangkasa, Seminyak. Distinctive, mass-produced "primitive style" *ikat* wall hangings, scarves, bags and jackets from Sumba, Java and Flores.

Spas and beauty treatments

Every road in the resort appears to be lined with cheap and cheerful **day spas** offering massages, pedicures and manicures to every passing tourist from dawn until well after dark – or you can head down to the sea for a beachside kneading from one of Kuta's conical-hatted massage women (Rp50,000 for 60min). For something more luxurious, many of Kuta's high-end hotels have their own spas (the Mandara Spa at the *Padma Resort,* ⓣ0361/752111, ⓦ www.mandaraspa.com, see p.86 is a standout) that are open to non-residents; alternatively, the places below are good bets.

Bodyworks Jl Kayu Jati 2, Petitenget ⓣ0361/733317. Housed in earthy, Moroccan-style rooms set around a courtyard, this long-running and well-regarded treatment centre offers an extensive menu of massages (from Rp220,000) including Balinese, Javanese (*mandi lulur*), Thai, shiatsu, hot stone and aromatherapy. Hair treatments, manicures, facials and waxing are also available.

Dala Spa *Villa de Daun*, Jl Raya Legian ⓣ0361/756276, ⓦ www.villadedaun.com. Award-winning spa offering fabulous treatments in plush, luxurious surroundings just a short walk from Jalan Legian. Balinese massage costs from $54 or there's the Russian Caviar and Pearl Facial ($108) or packages from $95.

Jari Menari Jl Raya Basangkasa 47, Seminyak ⓣ0361/736740, ⓦ www.jarimenari.com. One of the most popular massage centres, not least because its masseurs are all male as, apparently, "they can maintain pressure more consistently from the beginning to the end of the treatment". Offers various programmes and massage styles (from Rp300,000 for 75min) and runs massage courses (see p.99). Also in Nusa Dua (see p.113). Reservations advisable.

Murano Spa Jl Dewi Saraswati (also known as Jl Kunti II), Seminyak ⓣ0361/738140, ⓦwww .muranospa.com. Well-regarded, excellent-value spa but tucked away a bit so take advantage of the free pick-up service. Massages (from Rp80,000), reflexology and packages (from Rp225,000 for 3hr) are available.

Courses and classes

If you tire of the sea, sun, sand and other resort entertainments it is possible to find some more **cultural and spiritual pastimes** tucked away amid the hedonism of the Kuta-Legian-Seminyak area – although if this is your reason for coming to Bali you'll be better off heading to Ubud, where far more of these pursuits are on offer.

Balinese cookery *Saté Bali* restaurant, Jl Kayu Aya 22A, Petitenget ⓣ0361/736734, ⓔ satebali @yahoo.com. Stand-alone 3hr classes, led by the former chef of Jimbaran's *InterContinental Resort* (9.30am–1.30pm; Rp375,000 including lunch).

Batik-painting Arin 93 Gallery, Gang Kresek 5, off Jl Bakung Sari, south Kuta ⓣ0361/765087. Taught by painter and batik artist Heru at his home; three-day workshops cost Rp600,000 including materials.

Dance Tango classes for all levels at Tango Bali Club, Jl Sari Dewi, Sunset Village @www .tangobali.com. All schools of dance for kids and adults are catered for at Dance Asia, Jl Sunset 48B, Seminyak ☎0361/8475891, @www .balidanceasia.com.

Indonesian language Seminyak Language School, Gang Villa Lalu, off Jl Raya Seminyak ☎0361/733342, @www.learnindonesianinbali .com. Short courses for tourists, family courses and longer 40hr courses are all available.

Massage Jari Menari, Jl Raya Basangkasa, Seminyak (☎0361/736740, @www.jarimenari .com) is a well-known massage centre offering day courses (Tues 9am–3.30pm; $170), also available in Nusa Dua (see p.113). Jamu Spa School, Jl Bypass Ngurah Rai 99X

(☎0361/704581, @www.jamuspaschool.com) offers courses from $275 for five days aimed at training professional massage therapists.

Yoga and meditation Up to five sessions per day (taking in Kundalini, Anusara, Vinyasa Flow, Dynamic Hatha and Yoga for Surfers) are available at the *Desa Seni* hotel, Jl Subak Sari 13, Canggu (☎0361/844 6392, @www.desaseni.com), as well as longer retreats and immersions. In addition, *The Island* hotel, Gang IX, off Jl Legian (☎0361/762722, @www.theislandhotelbali.com) offers three classes per day of Hatha and Surf Yoga; *Bikram Bali* (☎0361/769100, @www .bikrambali.com) has classes at Kuta Galleria; and *Jiwa Yoga and Dance* (☎0361/8413689, @www .jiwayogaanddance.com) offers daily classes in Petitenget.

Listings

Airline offices Garuda has a sales office and city check-in (24hr–4hr before departure) inside the *Kuta Paradiso* hotel, South Kuta (☎0361/761414 ext 7807, Mon–Fri 8am–4.30pm, Sat & Sun 9am–3pm; national call centre ☎0804/180 7807 or 021/2351 9999 from a mobile). For other international and domestic airline offices, see p.78.

Banks and exchange There are ATMs every few hundred metres throughout the resort. Be careful at exchange counters: there are several well-known scams (see p.63 for details). One chain of recommended moneychangers is PT Central Kuta, which has several branches on Jl Legian plus one on Jl Melasti, Legian. Another reputable moneychanger, PT Dirgahayu Valuta Prima (look out for the brilliant green sign) is on Jl Raya Kuta near Bemo Corner in Kuta. In Seminyak go to Maspintjinra at Jl Raya Seminyak 16A. If you do get caught in a money-changing scam, contact the community police (see below).

Dentist Bali Dental Clinic 911, 2nd Floor, Mal Bali Galleria, Simpang Siur roundabout, Jl Bypass Ngurah Rai ☎0361/766254, @www.bali911 dentalclinic.com. In addition, International SOS (see below) has a dentist.

Embassies and consulates See p.59.

Hospitals and clinics The nearest hospitals are in Denpasar; see p.122. In the Kuta area, most expats go to one of two reputable, private 24hr hospitals on the outskirts of Kuta, both of which have English-speaking staff, A&E facilities, ambulance and medivac services: Bali International Medical Centre (BIMC) at Jl Bypass Ngurah Rai 100X, near

the Simpang Siur roundabout on the road to Sanur ☎0361/761263, @www.bimcbali.com; and International SOS, just a few hundred metres further east at Jl Bypass Ngurah Rai 505X ☎0361/710505, @www.sos-bali.com. Consultations cost from $63. Smaller, cheaper places in the heart of the resort include Legian Clinic on Jl Benesari, Kuta ☎0361/758503 and Poppies 1 ☎0361/757326, which offer 24hr services. Consultations from Rp500,000. Nearly all the large, upmarket hotels have an in-house doctor.

Immigration office Jl Ngurah Rai, Tuban ☎0361/751038.

Left luggage All hotels and losmen will store your luggage if you reserve a room for your return; some charge a nominal fee. There's also left luggage at the airport (see p.78) and, for Perama customers, at the Perama office, Jl Legian 39, Kuta (daily 6am–10pm; Rp20,000 a week or part thereof; ☎0361/751875).

Pharmacies Inside the shopping malls and department stores; on every major shopping street; next to Legian Clinics on Jl Benesari and Poppies 1.

Police Community police, Satgas Pantai Desa Adat Kuta, are English-speaking and in 24hr attendance at their office on the beach in front of *Inna Kuta Beach Hotel* (☎0361/762871). Tourist police are further north on Jl Pantai Kuta (see map, p.82). The government police station is at Jl Raya Kuta 141, south Kuta ☎0361/751598.

Post offices Kuta's GPO is signposted and on Jl Selamat, between Jl Raya Kuta and Jl Blambangan in Tuban (Mon–Sat 8am–4pm); services include parcel packing and poste restante. There are many small postal agents elsewhere in the resort; see maps for other locations.

Travel agents Domestic and international airline tickets are available from the following agents, some of which also sell express boat tickets: Perama, Jl Legian 39, Kuta ☎0361/751875, ⓦwww.peramatour.com; KCB Tours, Jl Raya Kuta 127 (the main road to Denpasar, on the eastern outskirts) ☎0361/751517, ⓦwww.kcbtours.com; Mas Tour and Travel, Jl Gunung Salak 233,

Kerobokan ☎0361/732600, ⓦwww.mas-travel .com. Gili Islands transport and accommodation booking is available at Island Promotions, The Gili Islands Shop, Poppies 1 no. 12 (☎0361/753241) and Jl Benesari (☎0361/766220, ⓦwww .gili-paradise.com). Pelni boat tickets are sold at the Pelni office, about 500m south of Supernova Supermarket at Jl Raya Tuban 299 (9am–2pm; ☎0361/763963).

The Bukit peninsula

Some 4km south of Kuta, Bali's **Bukit peninsula** narrows into a sliver of land at Jimbaran before bulging out again into a limestone plateau that dangles off the south of the island. Officially called **Bukit Badung** (*bukit* means "hill" in Bahasa Indonesia), the plateau has more in common with infertile Nusa Penida across the water than with the lush paddies elsewhere in Bali. Farming is almost impossible here, but it's the dramatic, craggy coastline that fuels the local economy: surfers flock to the Bukit's famously challenging breaks, particularly those at Uluwatu and Padang Padang, while everyone else simply enjoys the glorious clifftop views from the burgeoning number of expat villas and coastal hotels.

This account follows an anticlockwise route around the peninsula, beginning at the fishing town of **Jimbaran**, which lies just a couple of kilometres south of the airport and has a fine beach and several luxury hotels. Continuing southwest, the road passes a number of inviting **surf beaches** before reaching **Uluwatu**, site of world-class breaks as well as one of Bali's major clifftop temples, perched on the island's far southwestern tip. Across on the southeast coast sits **Nusa Dua**, a purpose-built resort offering deluxe facilities but lacking in character, and adjacent **Tanjung Benoa**, a centre for watersports.

Public **transport** in the Bukit is sporadic at best, so it's a good idea to rent your own wheels. Motorbikes are often more practical than jeeps for negotiating the potholed tracks down to the surfing beaches.

Jimbaran

With its crescent of golden sand fronted by upmarket hotels, **JIMBARAN** makes a quieter, more authentic alternative to purpose-built Nusa Dua, and is just a few kilometres' drive from the temptations of Kuta. Easy access to the airport makes it a handy first or last night.

Jimbaran's *raison d'être* is **fish**, and every morning at dawn the town's fishermen return with hundreds of kilos for sale at the covered fish market in Kedonganan, at the northern end of Jimbaran beach. The market stays open all day if you want to go sightseeing, and every evening the day's catch is served up at the dozens of beach warung that specialize in **barbecued seafood**.

Other than lazing in the sun during the day (with a bit of plane-spotting for extra kicks) and munching fish at night, there's little to do in Jimbaran itself, though you can rent boogie boards on the beach and the Airport Rights **surf break**, halfway down the Jimbaran side of the airport runway, is within easy reach via chartered *prahu*. If **shopping** is more your thing, check out the extraordinary clothes on sale at the Paul Ropp shop, Jl Uuwatu 80, and the sophisticated designs of the ceramic specialist **Jenggala Keramik** (℡0361/703311, Ⓦwww.jenggala-bali.com; 9am–6pm), whose premises on Jalan Uluwatu II house their flagship store and factory, as well as a café, exhibition area and workshop space for pot-painting classes.

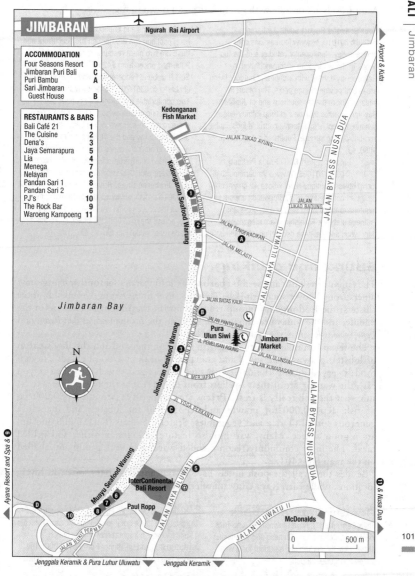

JIMBARAN

Ngurah Rai Airport

ACCOMMODATION
Four Seasons Resort — D
Jimbaran Puri Bali — C
Puri Bambu — A
Sari Jimbaran
 Guest House — B

RESTAURANTS & BARS
Bali Café 21 — 1
The Cuisine — 2
Dena's — 3
Jaya Semarapura — 5
Lia — 4
Menega — 7
Nelayan — C
Pandan Sari 1 — 8
Pandan Sari 2 — 6
PJ's — 10
The Rock Bar — 9
Waroeng Kampoeng — 11

Kedonganan Fish Market

Jimbaran Bay

JALAN TUKAD AYUNG
JALAN PANTAI KEDONGANAN
Kedonganan Seafood Warung
JALAN PENGRACIKAN
JALAN MELASTI
JALAN BATAS KAUH
JALAN PANTAI SARI
Pura Ulun Siwi
JL PEMELISAN AGUNG
Jimbaran Market
JALAN ULUNSIWI
JALAN KUMARASARI
JL MERJAPATI
Jimbaran Seafood Warung
JL YOGA PERKANTI
InterContinental Bali Resort
Muayu Seafood Warung
Paul Ropp
JALAN BUKIT PERMAI
McDonalds
JALAN RAYA ULUWATU
JALAN ULUWATU II
JALAN TUKAD BADUNG
JALAN RAYA ULUWATU
JALAN BYPASS NUSA DUA

Airport & Kuta
Ayana Resort and Spa & 9
D & Nusa Dua
11 & Nusa Dua

N

0 — 500 m

Jenggala Keramik & Pura Luhur Uluwatu — Jenggala Keramik

Arrival and information

There's a sporadic **bemo** service from Denpasar's Tegal terminal to Jimbaran, which runs via Kuta's eastern fringes and then on to Nusa Dua, or you can get a **taxi** from Kuta for about Rp50,000. No tourist shuttle buses serve Jimbaran. Metered taxis circulate around Jimbaran day and night.

There are **ATMs**, moneychangers and **internet** places on Jalan Raya Uluwatu.

Accommodation

Most **hotels** are upscale with grounds that run down to the beach.

Four Seasons Resort South Jimbaran ☎0361/701010, ⓦwww.fourseasons.com /jimbaranbay. Consistently voted one of the top hotels in the world, with accommodation in Balinese-style villas with indoor and outdoor living areas and private plunge pools. The resort is situated above the far southern end of Jimbaran Bay and facilities include a clifftop infinity-edge swimming pool, a spa, tennis courts, a kids' club and babysitting service. Published rates start at $680. ❾

🏃 **Jimbaran Puri Bali** Jl Yoga Perkanti ☎0361/701605, ⓦwww.jimbaranpuribali .com. Stylish boutique hotel whose 42 charmingly designed cottage and villa compounds are set in fabulous grounds filled with ponds, pools and Balinese statuary. Furnishings are elegant, with dark wood and Balinese decoration, complemented

by all mod cons and impeccable service. The large hotel pool and spa are right on the beachfront and there are two great restaurants to choose from. Published prices from $425. ❾

Puri Bambu Jl Pengeracikan, Kedongangan, north Jimbaran ☎0361/701468, ⓦwww.puribambu.com. This comfortable and deservedly popular place keeps its prices reasonable because there's no shorefront access. However, the beach is about a 3min walk away and the 48 large a/c rooms are positioned around a series of charming plant- and statue-filled courtyards, one of which also holds a good-sized pool. Upper-storey rooms are brighter. ❼

Sari Jimbaran Guest House Jl Pantai Jimbaran 2 ☎0361/704135, ⓦwww.bali-aquaholics.com. Small fan or a/c rooms around a good-sized pool just across the road from the beach make this place great value. Fan ❸, a/c ❹

Eating and drinking

The famous fresh fish and seafood **barbecues** at Jimbaran's **seafood warung** draw diners from all over southern Bali. There are over fifty warung, grouped in three clusters: the **Kedongangan** group is in the north; the **Jimbaran** ones are in the middle; and the **Muaya** restaurants are between the *Intercontinental Bali Resort* and *Four Seasons Resort* in the south.

The setup is similar in each one, with tables on the sand and **the day's catch** of lobster, prawns, fish, squid and crab grilled in the warung behind. Though food is served during the day (with sunloungers and towels provided if you eat), the warung are at their liveliest from sunset; eat at the busier places to be sure that the fish really is fresh. **Prices** are competitive (around Rp60,000/kg of fish, Rp160,000 for prawns and Rp350,000 for lobster) and include a generous spread of rice and vegetables. Seafood baskets (Rp150,000 and up) are a good choice. Many warung also feature Indonesian dishes and grilled meat. The most commonly recommended warung in each group are labelled on the map on p.101.

Besides these, all the posh hotels have **restaurants** and **bars**, often in lovely locations, while Jalan Raya Uluwatu offers local warung.

Restaurants and bars

Jaya Semapura Jl Raya Uluwatu 33. A no-frills local favourite that does Chinese and Indonesian dishes (mostly chicken and seafood) for a well-priced Rp15,000–22,000.

Nelayan At *Jimbaran Puri Bali*. This beachfront restaurant has a great location plus classy, intricate and innovative international cuisine (lunch Rp130,000 and up, dinner from Rp180,000). The real feast is the Lobster Menu (Rp495,000) which features lobster as a tartare, in lasagne and then sautéed.

PJ's Southern beachfront, also accessible via Jl Bukit Permai, south Jimbaran ☎0361/701010. This *Four Seasons* restaurant has a Bali-wide reputation for exquisite, and pricey, Mediterranean food (Rp200,000 and up) including wood-fired pizzas. It occupies a fine position beside the sand and twice a week runs the spectacular candlelight gourmet Beds on the Beach dinner (Tues & Sat; Rp1,500,000/person).

The Rock Bar At *The Ayana Resort and Spa* ⓦwww.ayanaresort.com At the base of the Bukit cliffs this glam bar reaps hosts of awards. Its location is incredible but with queues to get down,

queues to get in and then more queues to get back up, plus a vast army of camera-toting tourists, it's less like a bar than an attraction – you can even buy the T-shirt to prove you've been there. Wait until later in the evening for the music to get going and the vibe to heat up. Open 5–11pm (to 1am Fri & Sat).

Waroeng Kampoeng Jl Bypass Ngurah Rai 123. Located a kilometre east of the junction with Kampus Udayana (marked by a *McDonald's* and a *KFC*), this very popular local eatery offers a vast menu of Indonesian, Chinese and seafood dishes, including plenty of veggie options and sizzling food served on hot plates. No main courses over Rp25,000.

SOUTH BALI | Around the Bukit

Spa treatments

The Thermes Marins Spa at *The Ayana Resort and Spa* (☎0361/702222, ⓦwww .ayanaresort.com) has garnered numerous awards; its Spa on the Rocks treatment room set amid the rocks at the base of the Bukit cliffs is the subject of many a photograph. You'll pay dearly, though: treatments in this iconic location start at about Rp1.2million. Rather more affordable is the lovely beachside spa at *Jimbaran Puri Bali*, where massages start at about Rp600,000.

Around the Bukit

Just south of Jimbaran, the road climbs up onto the limestone plateau, where the typical **Bukit landscape** of cracked earth and the long brown pods of the ubiquitous kapok trees are brightened only by the occasional bougainvillea, bringing dramatic flashes of pink or purple. The thin, dusty soil supports cassava tubers, used to make tapioca flour, and grass-like sorghum, whose seeds are also pounded into flour. Farming is tough so, not surprisingly, many locals have cashed in on the area's new status as prime real estate. Property development has taken off, and in addition to the widening range of accommodation at the beaches that were until recently the preserve of surfers, the Bukit is now home to an ever-growing number of expats' dream homes, villas for rent and **super-luxury resorts** that are built to make the most of the marvellous scenery.

One of the most stunning of these is *Alila Villas Uluwatu* (☎0361/848 2166, ⓦwww.alilahotels.com; ⊙), perched on the clifftop (500 steps down to the beach) at the southern end of the Bukit. The villas have every imaginable luxury and the public areas are staggeringly stylish, but with published prices starting at $1070, staying here will be beyond the reach of many budgets. You may, however, want to splash out on a meal in the resort's well-regarded restaurants – *Warung* offers Indonesian dishes (mains Rp100,000–325,000) and *Cire* does Western food (3 courses from Rp450,000). Alternatively a drink in the *Sunset Cabanna*, suspended out from the edge of the cliff over hundreds of metres of nothing, is definitely worth a detour towards the end of the afternoon.

Garuda Wisnu Kencana (GWK)

Accessed from the main Jimbaran–Uluwatu road, the monumental **Garuda Wisnu Kencana** cultural park, or **GWK** (pronounced "Gay Way Kah"; daily

8am–10pm; Rp50,000), is a massive and incomplete project that's still being carved out of the hillside but welcomes tourists nonetheless. The focal point is a towering statue of the Hindu god Vishnu astride his sacred vehicle, the half-man, half-bird Garuda, which will measure 146m when completed. Critics have deplored the commercial rather than religious motivation of the venture and accused GWK's supporters of trying to turn Bali into a Hindu theme park (see p.392 for more on the "touristification" of Balinese culture). Visitors can climb the partially constructed statue and enjoy the commanding views of south Bali's coastlines from the restaurant. Big concerts and other performances are also staged here.

Surfing beaches

The Bukit's greatest assets are the **surfing beaches** along its breathtakingly craggy shorelines that get relentlessly pounded by the most thrillingly difficult breaks in Bali. Where once only hardcore surfers would endure the potholed tracks to get to them, a far bigger mix of visitors is now following suit as the roads are improved and new hotels are hollowed out of the clifftops. To date, the atmosphere in these secluded little enclaves – at **Balangan**, **Bingin**, **Padang Padang** and **Suluban** – is still pleasingly sand- and wave-oriented, although the construction at **Dreamland** means that it's definitely less magical than it used to be. Although the beaches are stunning, the **swimming** can be dangerous because of rips and reefs. The **breaks** are at their best from April to October.

Balangan and Dreamland

The quietest and most northerly of the surfing beaches is the long, white-sand **Balangan**, fringed by a shallow reef that makes swimming tricky but powers a speedy left-hand break at high tide. A handful of warung serving food and drink occupy the southern end of the beach, near the main break. You can **stay** up on the clifftop plateau here: *Flower Bud Bungalows 1* and *2* are great options (T0816/472 2310, Wflowerbudbalangan.com), providing accommodation in appealing *lumbung*-style bungalows with fans, attached cold-water bathrooms and deep verandas set in lovely gardens. *Flower Bud 1* (❹) has just six double and twin rooms, while *Flower Bud 2* (❺) has larger two- and three-bed rooms and a pool. At nearby *Balangan Sea View Bungalow* (T0812/367 9212, Wbalanganseaview bungalow.com; Rooms ❹–❺, *lumbung* ❻), accommodation is either in a room above the restaurant and pool, or in a *lumbung*-style bungalow with two bedrooms. Road access to Balangan is either via Dreamland, described below or directly (via 6km of twisting lanes) from the main Jimbaran–Uluwatu road.

West around Balangan's rocky southern point is the famous **Dreamland** beach, whose great surf and gloriously white sands have now been "improved" by the addition of concrete walkways and restaurants with sunloungers to rent, and the accompanying services of massage and manicures on offer – just the spot if you want to pretend you're in Kuta but with a towering cliff behind you. Surfers, on the other hand, come for the fast left and right peak and the chance of grabbing some unusually long rides. Much of the land around Dreamland is now part of the controversial **Pecatu Indah Resort**, with access to the beach via the resort's ostentatious entrance and eighteen-hole **New Kuta Golf Course** (T0361/848 1333, Wwww.newkutagolf.com), guarded by enormous statues of Garuda and Hanoman beside the main Uluwatu road. Follow the wide boulevards through the landscaped grounds for about 4km until signed down a short track to the Dreamland parking area; for Balangan follow the signed road running north before you reach the Dreamland parking.

Bingin

Fast developing into the liveliest of the Bukit surf beaches, **Bingin** enjoys the same great coastal scenery as its neighbours and equally rewarding **breaks** – short left-hand tubes close to shore and the long and peeling left-handers of "Impossibles" further out – but wins out with a superior choice of accommodation. The beach is soft and sandy but as with all these wave-lashed little gems, currents can be treacherous and there are large expanses of shallow reef just offshore. Access to the beach is via two different sets of very steep steps.

To reach Bingin, take the **coastal road**, Jalan Labuhan Sait, which is signed west off the main Uluwatu road, and then follow signs to Bingin, via a 2km side road to the parking area. *The Temple Lodge* **restaurant** is in a fabulous clifftop location and is open to non-residents (book before 4.30pm for the set dinner, at Rp160,000). *Jiwa Juice* restaurant (10am–6pm) on Jalan Labuhan Sait, about 200m inland from the Bingin turn-off, serves breakfasts, salads and sandwiches made from fresh bread, and offers **internet** access.

Accommodation

The cheapest **places to stay** in Bingin are the warung that almost literally tumble down the cliff face, many of them built hard against the rock, while more comfortable options can be found on the clifftop.

Leggies A few metres back from the northerly cliff edge ⓣ 0815/5890 8900. Excellent little place with eighteen fan-cooled rooms set around a large garden with plenty of space to relax and a small swimming pool. ❸

Mick's Place On the clifftop above the northerly steps ⓣ 0812/391 3337, ⓔ micksplacebali@yahoo.com.au. Occupying a stunning position right on the cliff edge, with just six elegant, contemporary-styled circular huts and a tiny infinity pool. You can get married here, too – and stay in the honeymoon suite with private pool ($300). ❼

Pondok Indah Gung and Lynie A few metres back from the northerly cliff edge ⓣ 0361/847 0933. Welcoming place offering ochre-painted rooms set round a garden, some of them in charming coconut-wood-and-thatch bungalows, others in two-storey buildings, all with fan and cold-water bathrooms. ❹

The Temple Lodge On the clifftop near the southerly steps ⓣ 0813/3921 9179, ⓦ www.thetemplelodge.com. Enjoying an unrivalled cliff-edge location, this creatively designed jewel has been constructed around existing rocks and trees from an inspired mix of limestone coral, reclaimed wood and Indonesian antiques. Its six bungalows all have great individual style, and there's a pool, yoga classes and Ayurvedic-influenced cuisine. Smallest suite ❻, larger suites ❼, with private lap pool ❽

Padang Padang

Back on Jalan Labuhan Sait, **Padang Padang**'s string of lodgings begins almost immediately, lining the roadside between the Bingin turn-off and the bridge that marks the steps down to the famous Padang Padang **break**. This is considered one of the classiest and most exciting surf spots in Indonesia, not least because of a twist in the final section. *Warung Yeyes* (1pm–midnight), between the turning to Bingin and Padang Padang, does great **pizza** among an international and Indonesian menu (mains from Rp28,000) and is the hangout of choice in the evening. The *Padang-Padang Inn*, about 400m west along Jalan Labuhan Sait from the Bingin turn-off and about the same from the Padang Padang bridge, offers plenty of **accommodation**, from simple bamboo rooms to more luxurious choices with hot water and air-conditioning (ⓣ 0361/847 0682, ⓦ www.padangpadanginn.com; fan ❶, a/c ❹). Near the bridge, the modern, purpose-built *Guna Mandala Inn* (ⓣ 0361/847 0673; ❷–❸) offers twenty good rooms with fans and cold-water bathrooms in two-storey blocks, plus a restaurant. **Motorbike rental** and **internet** facilities are available in the accommodation. The Padang Padang Open Stage features daily Kecak and Fire **dances** every evening at 6pm (Rp50,000).

Suluban

Suluban is another mesmerizing spot, complete with turquoise water and crashing white surf. But it's the famous **Uluwatu surf breaks** (named after the nearby temple) that are the headliners here: five separate left-handers, all of them consistent and surfable at anything from two to fifteen feet. Access to the breaks is down the steep steps beside the ultra-posh *Blue Point Bay Villas and Spa*. If you'd rather admire them from afar, over a good **meal**, head for *Ketty's Warung* (7.30am–10pm; mains Rp30,000–50,000) on the top of the cliffs, just by the steps, which delivers panoramic ocean views. Alternatively, *Rencang Junior Restaurant*, a couple of hundred metres towards Uluwatu, on the main road, has decent food, surfing movies and **internet access**.

Accommodation

If proximity to the ocean is the priority, choose one of the **places to stay** that line the track, about 200m long, from the parking barrier down to *Ketty's Warung* and *Blue Point Bay Villas and Spa*, at the top of the path down to the beach. However, there are also good options a bit further afield.

Galih About 100m beyond Blue Point parking barrier, 200m from the path down to the beach ☎0856/391 1211. Accommodation is in clean, new, good-quality tiled rooms set around a large garden, all with attached cold-water bathrooms. Fan ④, a/c ⑤

The Gong Jl Labuhan Sait ☎0361/769976, ✉thegongacc@yahoo.com. This chilled and friendly place run by ex-surfer Nyoman and family has fan-cooled terraced losmen rooms plus a large a/c room (⑦) that sleeps six, ranged around a small garden area with a pool. Building is underway to add more rooms. ③

Mamo Home Stay and **Mamo Home Stay II** On the road between the Blue Point parking barrier and the path down to the beach ☎0361/769882. Accommodation is in small fan (*Mamo*) or sparkling new a/c rooms (*Mamo II*) set in small compounds. All have attached cold-water bathrooms. *Mamo II* is nearer to the beach. Fan ③, a/c ⑤

Rocky Bungalows Jl Labuhan Sait ☎0361/769845. Comfortable fan and a/c rooms affording long-range sea views from their verandas, set in a large garden with a great little pool. Expansion is underway to add more rooms. Fan ④, a/c ⑤

Pura Luhur Uluwatu

One of Bali's holiest and most important temples, **Pura Luhur Uluwatu** (dawn to dusk; Rp3000 including sarong and sash rental) is superbly sited on the edge of a sheer rocky promontory jutting out over the Indian Ocean, 70m above the foaming surf, at the far southwestern tip of Bali – 18km south of Kuta and 16km west of Nusa Dua. Views over the serrated coastline to the left and right are stunning, and it's a favourite spot at sunset, especially with tour buses. The temple structure itself, though, lacks magnificence, being relatively small and for the most part unadorned.

Accounts of Uluwatu's early **history** are vague, but the Javanese Hindu priest Empu Kuturan almost certainly constructed a *meru* (multi-tiered thatched shrine) here in the tenth century. Pura Luhur Uluwatu is now sanctified as one of Bali's sacred **directional temples**, or *kayangan jagat* – state temples having influence over all the people of Bali, not just the local villagers or ancestors. It is the guardian of the southwest, is dedicated to the spirits of the sea and its festivals are open to all; during the holy week-long period of Galungan, Balinese from all over the island come here to pay their respects.

The temple complex

Climbing the frangipani-lined stairway to the temple's **outer courtyard**, you'll meet Uluwatu's resident troupe of macaques, who routinely steal earrings, sunglasses and cameras. Images of the elephant god Ganesh flank the temple entrance. Only worshippers are allowed inside but the temple extends to the cliff edge and the famous three-thatched *meru* is visible from along the cliff. A tiny courtyard in the temple contains a locked shrine housing an ancient statue, thought by some to be Nirartha, the influential fifteenth-century priest from Java, who possibly achieved his own spiritual liberation, or *moksa*, on this very spot.

You'll get some of the best **views** of Pura Luhur Uluwatu's dramatic position from the tracks that wind along the cliff edge to the left and right of the temple for a few hundred metres, affording fine, silhouetted vistas of the three-tiered *meru* perched atop the massive, sheer wall of limestone.

Practicalities

There is no public **transport** to Uluwatu, so if you don't have your own wheels the easiest option is to join a **tour** with a south-Bali operator (around Rp250,000) that visits the temple at sunset. These are timed to take in the nightly performances of the **Kecak** and **Fire Dance** at Uluwatu, which you can attend independently (6–7pm; Rp70,000).

Nusa Dua and Tanjung Benoa

Bali's most carefully designed high-end beach resort luxuriates along a coastal stretch of reclaimed mangrove swamp some 14km southeast of Kuta. This is **NUSA DUA**, a pristine, gated enclave that was purpose-built to indulge upmarket tourists, while simultaneously protecting local communities from the impact of mass tourism (see p.392 for the full story). The five-star hotels here all boast expansive grounds set behind a white-sand beach, but other than the **Pasifika art museum** and the **Bali Collection shopping centre** (daily 10am–10pm) there's little else in Nusa Dua: no *banjar*, noodle stalls or markets (for a serious shopping excursion, head to Kuta–Legian–Seminyak).

There are more signs of real life along the narrow sand bar that extends north from Nusa Dua. **TANJUNG BENOA**, as this finger-like projection is known, is dominated along its east-coast strip by more swanky hotels, tourist restaurants, shops and watersports facilities. But west of its Jalan Pratama thoroughfare, and at the top of the peninsula, village life rumbles on in areas that can be well worth exploring, if only to remind you that you are still in Bali. Tanjung Benoa's **beach** is more activity-based than the pristine stretches of Nusa Dua, but no less appealing for that: it can be great fun watching the latest brave souls strap themselves in to be hauled skywards, screeching all the way. In addition, Tanjung Benoa has the dubious distinction of being the centre of Bali's turtle trade (see box, p.108).

Just outside the gates of Nusa Dua the village of **BUALU** is where you'll find the densest concentration of *banjar*, temples, warung, family homes and commerce common to any small Balinese town, particularly along Jalan Srikandi – a worthwhile target if you want to explore beyond the manicured confines of Nusa Dua itself.

Don't confuse Tanjung Benoa with **Benoa Harbour** (Pelabuhan Benoa; described on p.131), which lies about a kilometre north across the water from Tanjung Benoa's northern tip. **Fast boats to Lombok**, Pelni boats to other parts of the Indonesian archipelago, sea planes and many excursion boats depart from Benoa Harbour, not Tanjung Benoa.

Tanjung Benoa and the turtle trade

According to the World Wildlife Fund, Indonesia is one of the world's most important countries for **marine turtles** and home to six out of the seven marine turtle species, all of which are endangered. The country provides nesting and foraging sites, as well as migration routes. The turtles are threatened by the destruction of their habitat and **nesting sites**, illegal trade and accidental capture in fishing boats. Female turtles will only lay their eggs on the beach where they themselves were born; on Bali these include beaches at **Kuta, Sanur, Nusa Dua, Tanjung Benoa, Jimbaran** and **Pemuteran**, nearly all of which have been affected by tourist development. The threats are many: turtles will not come ashore if there's too much light or noise; if vehicles compact the sand too tightly the females cannot dig their nests; hatchlings can easily get confused by bright lights and head for buildings and roads rather than the sea, when they hatch; and the predictability of the nesting sites makes the turtles highly vulnerable to hunters and egg poachers. Even where conditions are favourable, only one in a thousand eggs produces a turtle that survives thirty years to adulthood.

Bali has long been involved in the **turtle trade** and the fishing port of **Tanjung Benoa** has been at the heart of it, with turtles landed and slaughtered here for decades. The meat of the **green turtle**, which can weigh up to 180kg, has always been a popular delicacy on the island and has played an important part in certain religious rituals since time immemorial. The flippers are made into sate and the flesh ground down into the ceremonial *lawar* served at weddings, tooth-filing ceremonies and cremations.

It is estimated that between 1969 and 1994 **twenty thousand turtles** per year were landed in Tanjung Benoa for human consumption, plunging the population into severe decline (it has gone down by an estimated ninety percent in the last 130 years).

Arrival

For information on **airport arrivals** and transfers to Nusa Dua, see p.78. If you've splurged on a couple of nights of luxury out here you're unlikely to be hauling your bags on a bemo, and will probably arrive by metered **taxi** (about Rp80,000 from Kuta). For information on the **new bus service** from Kuta to Nusa Dua, see p.77.

Local transport

The resorts, restaurants and shops are strung over a distance of some 6km from the northern tip of Tanjung Benoa to southern Nusa Dua, so getting around can be a hot business. The shortest route between hotels is nearly always via the paved **beachfront walkway**, which begins in front of the *Ayodya Resort* at the far southern end of Nusa Dua and runs north to Tanjung Benoa's *Grand Mirage Resort*. It takes around two hours to amble from one end to the other and it's one of the nicest things to do in Nusa Dua, affording great views across to Gunung Agung in the east and Nusa Penida offshore. Alternatively you could capitalize on the flat terrain by **renting a bicycle** (around Rp20,000/hr from hotels or the outlet in the Bali Collection).

Another option is the free Bali Collection **shuttle bus**, which does a loop around all the big hotels and the shopping centre (approximately hourly, 10am–9pm), while **metered taxis** (an initial Rp5000, then Rp4000/km) circulate constantly. Some hotels also run their own free transport.

However, it's thought that things are now starting to improve. In 1999 Indonesia implemented a **turtle trade ban** amid international concerns about the diminishing turtle population and threats of a call for a tourist boycott of Bali. A breakthrough was made in 2005 when the Hindu Dharma Council of Indonesia decreed that substitutes such as drawings, cakes or other animals could be used for any endangered species, including green turtles, in religious rituals. The Council indicated that turtles can be used in rituals as long as they are unharmed and are released into the ocean afterwards in a gesture of symbolic sacrifice. In 2009 the government rejected a proposal by the Bali Governor of the time to set an annual quota of a thousand turtles for sacrificial ceremonies.

Where some two thousand or so green turtles were once landed at Tanjung Benoa every month, the current estimate is around two hundred, and it's clear that continued demand has driven the trade **underground**. It's a profitable business, with a single turtle fetching up to $550.

Campaign organizations and hatcheries

Travellers can help prevent the unnecessary slaughter of turtles by avoiding all products made from turtle flesh or tortoiseshell and by boycotting restaurants that serve turtle meat. For further information and to support **conservation efforts** look at Turtle Foundation (ⓦwww.turtle-foundation.org), ProFauna Indonesia in Denpasar (ⓣ0361/808 5800, ⓦwww.profauna.org) and the Jakarta branch of the World Wide Fund for Nature (ⓣ021/576 1065, ⓦwww.wwf.or.id).

Several concerned groups have established small **turtle hatcheries** on Bali and Lombok, including near the Satgas police post on Kuta beach (see p.88), at Reef Seen Aquatics in Pemuteran (see p.296), and on the Gili islands.

Car rental, with or without driver, can also be arranged through Nusa Dua hotels (from $35/day) or from Tanjung Benoa rental outlets on Jalan Pratama. All the big hotels in Nusa Dua offer organized **tours** to major sights in Bali and beyond.

Accommodation

In Nusa Dua and Tanjung Benoa four- and five-star **accommodation** is the norm. Rates booked via hotel websites or through agents start at around $125, excluding tax and a possible high-season supplement, which makes them very good value. The best have beachfront locations and great facilities.

Nusa Dua

The Laguna ⓣ0361/771327, ⓦwww.luxury collection.com/bali. A luxury hotel whose rooms are set around a series of lagoon-like swimming pools, complete with little sandy beaches, islands and waterfalls. The most expensive rooms have direct lagoon access and all have huge plasma TVs, DVD players and broadband access. There are several restaurants, a fitness centre, tennis courts, spa and beachfront gazebos. ⓭

The Westin Resort ⓣ0361/771906, ⓦwww .starwoodhotels.com. The massive lobby with soaring roof, attached shopping arcade and numerous ponds and pools sets the tone here. This is a typical *Westin*, with blocks of contemporary-styled rooms centred round the trademark, ultra-luxurious "heavenly" bed, plus a spa, gym and kids' club. Some rooms have been modified for wheelchair users. There are freshwater, saltwater and kids' pools. The Royal Beach Club is the luxury option with super-lux rooms, private lounge and other goodies. ⓭

Tanjung Benoa

Conrad Bali Jl Pratama 168 ⓣ0361/778788, ⓦwww.ConradHotels.com/Bali. Dramatically

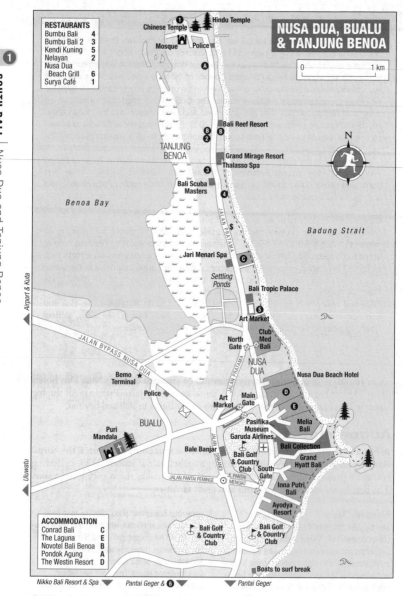

RESTAURANTS
Bumbu Bali	4
Bumbu Bali 2	3
Kendi Kuning	5
Nelayan	2
Nusa Dua Beach Grill	6
Surya Café	1

Chinese Temple
Hindu Temple
Mosque Police

NUSA DUA, BUALU & TANJUNG BENOA

0   1 km

Bali Reef Resort

TANJUNG BENOA

Grand Mirage Resort
Thalasso Spa

Bali Scuba Masters

Benoa Bay

Badung Strait

Jari Menari Spa

Settling Ponds

Bali Tropic Palace

Art Market

Club Med Bali

North Gate

NUSA DUA

Nusa Dua Beach Hotel

Bemo Terminal

Police

Art Market

Main Gate

BUALU

Puri Mandala

Pasifika Museum
Garuda Airlines

Melia Bali

Bali Collection

Bale Banjar

Bali Golf & Country Club

South Gate

Grand Hyatt Bali

Inna Putri Bali

Ayodya Resort

ACCOMMODATION
Conrad Bali	C
The Laguna	E
Novotel Bali Benoa	B
Pondok Agung	A
The Westin Resort	D

Bali Golf & Country Club

Bali Golf & Country Club

Boats to surf break

Nikko Bali Resort & Spa ▼   *Pantai Geger &* ⑥ ▼   ▼ *Pantai Geger*

modern architecture, strong, uncluttered lines, pale cream stone and dark wood give this deluxe chain hotel enormous style. A 33m-long lagoon pool dominates the resort, which has numerous restaurants, a spa, kids' club, daily yoga and a tennis programme among many other offerings. Service always gets great reviews and some rooms are

wheelchair-accessible. The beachfront wedding chapel is remarkable. ⑧

Novotel Bali Benoa Jl Pratama
☎0361/772239, ⑥www.novotelbali.com. Chic, charming and contemporary, this comfortable low-rise hotel spreads over both sides of the road. The cheaper rooms (non-beachside) all have a

balcony or small garden and are furnished with cream drapes and coconut-wood furniture and flooring, and there's a lovely, quiet pool here. Beachside options include good-value tropical terrace bungalows with larger gardens and fabulous bathrooms, and there's a larger pool over here. The beautifully planted grounds run down to an inviting stretch of beach. **❼**

🏃 **Pondok Agung** Jl Pratama 99 ☏ 0361/771143, ✉ pondok.agung @hotmail.com. Exceptionally welcoming and classy homestay, offering just nine stylish and comfortably furnished rooms, all with good, contemporary-look bathrooms and hot water and some with terraces, in cottages overlooking the prettily designed gardens. Great value. Fan **❸**, a/c **❹**

The resorts

Nusa Dua beach is long, white and sandy, though at low tide the reef is exposed and you're better off beachcombing than swimming. Halfway down the shoreline, the land blossoms out into two little clumps, or "islands" (Nusa Dua means "Two Islands"), with a temple standing on each one. If you want to venture beyond the beach, you could pay a visit to **Pasifika: Museum Pacific Asia** (daily 10am–6pm; Rp70,000), just north across the access road from the Bali Collection, which houses a wide-ranging and reasonably interesting display of art and artefacts from Asia and the Pacific, including Balinese paintings (although anyone with an interest in Balinese art would find it far more stimulating to visit Ubud).

Getting back to the beach, the far north of **Tanjung Benoa beach** is dominated by watersports facilities, though shore-life becomes more appealing further south, from the *Bali Reef Resort* downwards. Inland Tanjung Benoa has a few points of interest. At the northern tip, there's an impressive coral-carved **Hindu temple**, a gaudy red-painted **Chinese temple** and the restrained contours of a mosque within a few hundred metres of each other. Follow any of the lanes running west from the middle stretch of Jalan Pratama to find typical Balinese warung, fruit and veg stalls and family compounds.

For a different beach experience, head south towards the *Nikko Bali Resort & Spa*, and follow signs for **Pantai Geger** (about a 1km drive from the golf course or fifteen minutes' walk along the beach from *Ayodya Resort*). The broad, white-sand beach is quiet, with sunloungers for rent, although much of the southern end, below the clifftop temple, Pura Geger (which is also accessible via a more southerly road), is given over to seaweed farming (for more on which, see p.136). If you want to linger over a meal, the recommended *Nusa Dua Beach Grill* (see p.112) is here. If you don't have your own transport, and don't want to walk, you can take a metered taxi from the resort to Pantai Geger; an informal taxi service from Pantai Geger can take you back.

Sports and other activities

Tanjung Benoa is south Bali's **watersports** playground, with parasailing, water-skiing, jet-skiing, kayaking, wakeboarding and the rest all offered by at least a dozen similar shorefront watersports centres. Prices are the same at all of them ($20–35/15min session). The **snorkelling** trips are less interesting: all boats make for White Tower, a few minutes offshore, where the fish gather to gorge on the bread they're fed throughout the day. There are several PADI **Dive Centres** in the area; Bali Scuba Masters is at Jl Pratama 85 (☏ 0361/777156, Ⓦ www .baliscubamasters.com) and Waterworld (Ⓦ www.baliwaterworld.com) has counters at *The Laguna* and *The Westin Resort*. There is more choice in Sanur for divers; see the box on p.128 for details.

The main Nusa Dua **surf break** is a right-hander about 1km offshore (accessible by boat from a signposted point south of the *Ayodya Resort* and the golf course), while further north, a brief paddle beyond the *Club Med Bali*, "Sri Lanka" is a short, speedy right-hander.

The world-class, eighteen-hole, championship **Bali Golf and Country Club** (℡0361/771791, ⓦwww.baligolfandcountryclub.com) dominates the southern end of Nusa Dua and is open to all.

For **birdwatchers** an early morning at the settling ponds around the mangrove swamp to the north and west of Nusa Dua's North Gate can yield several species of kingfisher, as well as lots of water birds including white-vented Javan mynahs, Sunda teals and white-browed crakes.

Rounding out the activities, **Bali Camel Safaris** (℡0361/776755, ⓦwww .balicamelsafaris.com; from $20 for 30min) operate on the beach near the *Nikko Bali Resort and Spa*, near Pantai Geger.

Eating and drinking

You'll find the cheapest and most authentic Balinese **food** at the warung along the back lanes of **Tanjung Benoa** and on Jalan Srikandi in Bualu village. Besides these, Tanjung Benoa has a few notable tourist restaurants among its many unremarkable identikit options, while in **Nusa Dua**, the Bali Collection shopping complex houses a dozen restaurants but little atmosphere. The beachside *Cascade Bar* at the *Laguna Resort* is a prime spot for evening **drinks**, with a Happy Hour that stretches from 6pm to 8pm.

Bumbu Bali and Bumbu Bali 2 Jl Pratama, Tanjung Benoa. *Bumbu Bali 1* ℡0361/774502, *Bumbu Bali 2* ℡0361/772299. Founded and managed by renowned expat chef and food writer Heinz von Holzen, this is the most famous restaurant in the area. It serves classy Balinese cuisine in pleasant surroundings, with an open-plan kitchen. The menu includes enormous *rijsttafel* (vegetarian and meat options, from Rp185,000). Balinese cooking lessons are offered here (see p.113). Reservations suggested.

Eight Degrees South *Conrad Bali*, Jl Pratama 168, Tanjung Benoa ℡0361/778788, ⓦwww.Conrad Hotels.com/Bali. In a fabulous beachside location, with views in the day and a romantic atmosphere at night, this is a Mediterranean and seafood-accented restaurant. The lunchtime salads (from Rp105,000) and the pizzas (Rp135,000) are excellent value on a menu that can get rather pricey.

Kendi Kuning Just north of *Bali Club Med* ⓦwww .kendikuning.com. In a shady beachside location, this inviting spot serves up drinks and snacks plus Indonesian and international food. With mains from Rp24,000 and three-course set menus from Rp60,000, this is some of the best-value beachside food in the resort.

Nelayan Jl Pratama 101, Tanjung Benoa ℡0361/776868. Deservedly popular mid-priced place that is set far enough back from the road to avoid traffic noise. Offers a good selection of international and Indonesian dishes, including Balinese curries – vegetable, prawn, chicken and beef – and a range of fresh fish and seafood dishes (Rp45,000–120,000). Free local transport.

Nusa Dua Beach Grill Pantai Geger ℡0361/743 4779. Breezy café just behind the beach at Pantai Geger. Listen to the waves while savouring the seafood combination (Rp96,000) or any number of fish dishes and salads, and refuelling with a spirulina-laced power smoothie. Easiest road access is via the rough track to Pura Geger temple just south of *The Balé* villas.

Surya Café Jl Segara, Tanjung Benoa. Right at the top of the peninsula seafood is served Jimbaran style: you buy it by weight and if ordering a kilo or more you'll get potato wedges, rice, veggies and sauces thrown in. At Rp200,000 a kilo for fish, Rp175,000 for prawns, it isn't especially cheap, but the food is well cooked and it's fun to sit and watch the life on the water.

Spa treatments

All the top hotels have **spas** offering a full menu of traditional Balinese, Thai, Swedish and aromatherapy **massages**, as well as the popular Javanese *mandi lulur* (see p.47); reservations are advisable. The Mandara Spa at the *Nikko Bali Resort and Spa*, south of Nusa Dua (℡0361/773337, ⓦwww.mandaraspa.com) is part of the respected chain of East–West spas; the Thalasso Spa at the *Grand Mirage Resort*

(☎0361/773883, ⊛www.thalassobali.com) specializes in therapies using heated sea water and seaweed; and The Nusa Dua Spa at the *Nusa Dua Beach Hotel and Spa* has massage rooms in open *bale* by the beach. The well-regarded *Jari Menari*, which uses only male therapists, has an outlet in Nusa Dua at Jl Pratama 88X (☎0361/778084; from Rp300,000), just opposite the *Conrad Bali*, and also runs **massage classes**.

Listings

Airline offices Garuda has a sales office and city check-in (4–24hr in advance) in the Bali Collection complex, just inside Lobby A, by the west entrance (Mon–Fri 10am–9pm, Sat & Sun 1pm–9pm; ☎0361/770747, 24hr national call centre ☎0804/180 7807 or 021/2351 9999 if calling from a mobile). For other international and domestic airline offices, see p.78.

Banks and exchange There are several ATMs and moneychangers on Jl Pratama in Tanjung Benoa, and big hotels in both resorts do exchange. See p.63 for advice on moneychangers' scams.

Cooking lessons Balinese cooking lessons from $70 offered at *Bumbu Bali* restaurant in Tanjung Benoa (Mon, Wed & Fri; ☎0361/771256, ⊛www .balifoods.com).

Hospitals and clinics All Nusa Dua hotels provide 24hr medical service. See also p.99 for expat-oriented clinics near Kuta and p.122 for Denpasar hospitals.

Internet access At all hotels and on Jl Pratama in Tanjung Benoa.

Denpasar

Despite the roaring motorbikes and round-the-clock traffic congestion, Bali's capital, **DENPASAR**, remains a pleasant city at heart, centred on a grassy square, with just a few major shopping streets crisscrossing the core. Department stores and malls are mushrooming, but the older neighbourhoods, especially those in the north of the city, are still dominated by family compounds grouped into traditional *banjar* (village association) districts. There is also a marked influence of the sizeable immigrant communities, notably Javanese Muslims, Sasaks from Lombok

Moving on from Denpasar

Denpasar's four main bemo terminals serve destinations across the island; see the plan on p.116 for an overview. **Tegal** bemo terminal covers routes south of Denpasar, including Kuta (Rp7000), Legian (Rp7000), Tuban/Airport (Rp7000), Jimbaran (Rp15,000), Nusa Dua (Rp15,000) and Sanur (Rp6000), though frequencies on all these routes vary due to an ongoing drop in demand. **Kereneng** terminal covers Sanur (Rp5000), and these services are also quite erratic. **Batubulan** terminal (described on p.148) runs regular services to the Ubud area; to east Bali; parts of north Bali; and Nusa Dua, via Sanur (dropping passengers on the outskirts at the *Sanur Paradise Plaza* hotel) and the eastern outskirts of Kuta (see p.80). **Ubung** terminal (see p.274) runs frequent transport to north and west Bali, as well as to Padang Bai (for Lombok) and Java.

There are smaller bemo terminals on **Jalan Gunung Agung**, for transport to Canggu and Kerobokan (Rp5000); near the **Sanglah** hospital, for Benoa Harbour and Suwung; at **Wangaya** for Sangeh and Pelaga; and at **Suci** for Pulau Serangan.

For information on the new Trans-Sarbagita **bus services** see p.77, and for **airport** departure details, see p.78.

and Chinese-Indonesians, who together constitute a **large minority** of the city's population of more than 700,000.

Most tourists whiz into Denpasar as part of a day-trip from one of the southern resorts, lingering just long enough to tour the **Bali Museum** and browse the traditional **markets**. Very few stay overnight, although there's a reasonable choice of lodgings. In fact, the relative dearth of tourists – and accompanying facilities – is an attraction in itself, offering a rare chance to experience unadulterated urban

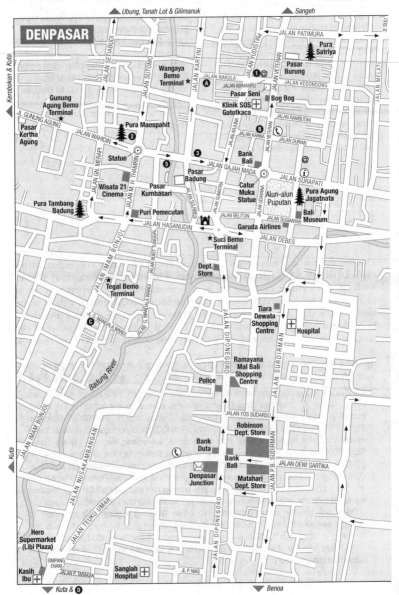

DENPASAR

▲ Ubung, Tanah Lot & Gilimanuk   ▲ Sangeh

Kerobokan & Kuta

JALAN PATIMURA
JL. SULI
JALAN SETIABUDI
Pura Satriya
JALAN YUDISTIRA
JALAN SUTOMO
JALAN KARTINI
JALAN NAKULA
Wangaya Bemo Terminal ★
JALAN ABIMANYU
JALAN VETERAN
JALAN KEDONDONG
Pasar Burung
A
Pasar Seni
Bog Bog
Gunung Agung Bemo Terminal ★
Klinik SOS Gatotkaca
JL. GUNUNG AGUNG
JALAN WAHIDIN
JALAN RAMBUTAN
Pasar Kertha Agung
Pura Maospahit
JALAN ARJUNA
JALAN VETERAN
JALAN KARNA
JALAN DURIAN
B
Statue
JALAN GN. MERAPI
JALAN H. THAMRIN
Bank Bali
JALAN GAJAH MADA
JALAN SURAPATI
@
Pasar Badung
JALAN SUMATRA
Catur Muka Statue
Wisata 21 Cinema
Pasar Kumbasari
JALAN SULAWESI
JALAN UDAYANA
Alun-alun Puputan
Pura Agung Jagatnata
Pura Tambang Badung
JALAN GN. AGUNG
Puri Pemecutan
JALAN BELITON
JALAN SUGIANYAR
Bali Museum
JALAN HASANUDIN
Garuda Airlines
★ Suci Bemo Terminal
JALAN DEBES
JALAN IMAM BONJOL
JALAN BAKTI TUNGGAL
Dept. Store
Tegal Bemo Terminal ★
JL. G. MANDALA WANG
JL. G. MANDALA WANG
C
Tiara Dewata Shopping Centre
Hospital
Pura Tambang
Badung River
JALAN DIPONEGORO
JALAN SURDIRMAN
Ramayana Mal Bali Shopping Centre
Police
JALAN IMAM BONJOL
JALAN NUSAKAMBANGAN
JALAN YOS SUDARSO
Robinson Dept. Store
Kuta
Bank Duta
Bank Bali
JALAN P.B. SUDIRMAN
JALAN DEWI SARTIKA
Denpasar Junction
Matahari Dept. Store
JALAN TEUKU UMAR
JALAN DIPONEGORO
Hero Supermarket (Libi Plaza)
SIMPANG ENAM
JALAN P. TARAKAN
Kasih Ibu
Sanglah Hospital
JL. P. NIAS

▼ Kuta & D   ▼ Benoa

Bali, not to mention cheaper food and shopping; the city also makes a feasible base for trips by public transport to attractions such as Tanah Lot, Mengwi, Sangeh and Batubulan.

Some history

Until the early twentieth century, control of the city – then known as **Badung**, like the regency it governed – was divided among several rajas, most notably those

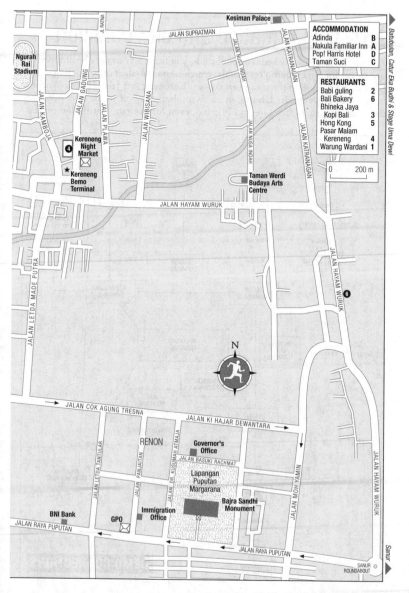

Kesiman Palace

JALAN SUPRATMAN

JALAN NUSA INDAH

JL. RATNA

JALAN KATRANGAN

ACCOMMODATION
Adinda B
Nakula Familiar Inn A
Pop! Harris Hotel D
Taman Suci C

RESTAURANTS
Babi guling 2
Bali Bakery 6
Bhineka Jaya Kopi Bali 3
Hong Kong 5
Pasar Malam Kereneng 4
Warung Wardani 1

0   200 m

Ngurah Rai Stadium

JALAN KAMBOJA

JALAN GADUNG

JALAN PLAWA

JALAN WIBISANA

JALAN NUSA INDAH

JALAN KATRANGAN

JALAN HAYAM WURUK

Kereneng Night Market

★ **Kereneng Bemo Terminal**

Taman Werdi Budaya Arts Centre

JALAN HAYAM WURUK

JALAN LETDA MADE PUTRA

JALAN HAYAM WURUK

N

JALAN COK AGUNG TRESNA

JALAN KI HAJAR DEWANTARA

RENON

JALAN LETDA TANTULAR

JALAN PANJAITAN

JALAN DR. KUSUMA ATMAJA

Governor's Office

JALAN BASUKI RACHMAT

Lapangan Puputan Margarana

Bajra Sandhi Monument

JALAN MOH YAMIN

JALAN HAYAM WURUK

BNI Bank

GPO

Immigration Office

JALAN RAYA PUPUTAN

JALAN RAYA PUPUTAN

SANUR ROUNDABOUT

Sanur

at the courts of Pemecutan (southwest Denpasar) and Kesiman (east Denpasar). Supremacy was wrested from them, however, by the insatiably expansionist Dutch. After Bali won independence from the Dutch in 1949, the island's administrative **capital** was moved to Badung from the north-coast town of Singaraja and the city was renamed Denpasar. Almost fifty years later Denpasar's status was upgraded again when, in 1992, it became a self-governing municipality, no longer under the auspices of Badung district.

Arrival, information and city transport

Arriving in Denpasar by bemo or public bus, you'll almost certainly be dropped at one of the four main **bemo terminals**, which lie on the edges of town: **Tegal**, on Jalan Imam Bonjol, in the southwest corner; **Kereneng**, off Jalan Hayam Wuruk, in east central Denpasar; **Ubung**, in its own suburb way off to the northwest on the main road to Tabanan (see p.274); and, even further out, **Batubulan** on the

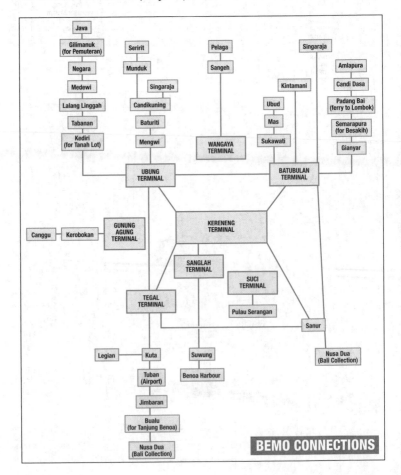

Cross-city bemo routes

As outlined below, some routes alter slightly in reverse because of the one-way system.

Yellow

Kereneng – Jl Plawa – Jl Supratman – Jl Gianyar – corner of Jl Waribang (for Barong dance) – Kesiman – Tohpati – **Batubulan**.
On the return route bemos travel down Jl Kamboja instead of Jl Plawa just before reaching Kereneng.

Grey-blue

Ubung – Jl Cokroaminoto – Jl Gatot Subroto – Jl Gianyar – corner of Jl Waribang (for Barong dance) – Tohpati – **Batubulan**.

Dark green

Kereneng – Jl Hayam Wuruk – corner of Jl Nusa Indah (for Taman Werdi Budaya Arts Centre) – Sanur roundabout (for Renon) – Jl Raya Sanur – **Sanur**.

Turquoise

Kereneng – Jl Surapati (for tourist office and Bali Museum) – Jl Veteran (alight at the corner of Jl Abimanyu for *Nakula Familiar Inn*) – Jl Cokroaminoto – **Ubung**.

Yellow or turquoise

Tegal – Jl Gn Merapi – Jl Setiabudi – Ubung – Jl Cokroaminoto – Jl Subroto – Jl Yani – Jl Nakula (for *Nakula Familiar Inn*) – Jl Veteran – Jl Patimura – Jl Melati – **Kereneng** – Jl Hayam Wuruk – Jl Surapati – Jl Kapten Agung – Jl Sudirman – Tiara Dewata Shopping Centre – Jl Yos Sudarso – Jl Diponegoro (for Ramayana Mal Bali shopping centre) – Jl Hasanudin – Jl Bukit Tunggal – **Tegal**.

Beige

Kereneng – Jl Raya Puputan (for GPO) – Jl Dewi Sartika (for Matahari and Robinson department stores) – Jl Teuku Umar – junction with Jl Imam Bonjol – **Tegal**.
The return route runs along Jl Cok Agung Tresna instead of Jl Raya Puputan.

Dark blue

Tegal – Jl Imam Bonjol – Jl Teuku Umar – junction with Jl Diponegoro (for Matahari and Robinson department stores) – Jl Yos Sudarso (for Ramayana Mal Bali shopping centre) – Jl Sudirman – Jl Cok Agung Tresna – junction with Jl Panjaitan (alight for the 500m walk to GPO) – Jl Hajar Dewantara – Jl Moh Yamin – Sanur roundabout – **Sanur**.

The return route goes all the way along Jl Raya Puputan after the roundabout, passing the GPO, then straight along Jl Teuku Umar and north up Jl Imam Bonjol to Tegal.

northeast fringes (see p.148). The plan opposite shows which terminal covers which routes. Getting from one bemo terminal to another is fairly easy, but can be time-consuming, as you have to wait for your bemo to fill up at each transit point.

For details on getting to Denpasar directly from **Ngurah Rai Airport**, see the box on p.142.

Information

Denpasar's **tourist office** is conveniently located near the Bali Museum on the northern perimeter of Alun-alun Puputan, at Jl Surapati 7 (Mon–Thurs 7.30am–3.30pm, Fri 8am–1pm; ☏0361/234569). Specific questions can be answered here, particularly about city transport and upcoming festivals, and they've a decent city map, but don't expect much more.

City transport

As in many other areas of Bali, public transport in Denpasar is in decline because of the huge rise in motorbike ownership. Although **public bemos** continue to shuttle between the city's bemo terminals, they now run infrequently, only departing when enough passengers show up, which could mean waiting for anything between five minutes and an hour. Nonetheless, we've detailed the most convenient routes in the text and there's a summary of the most useful routes on p.117. Nearly all Denpasar bemos are colour coded. Wave to hail one and state your exact destination before getting in. Tourists pay Rp5000 for a cross-city ride or Rp10,000 to Batubulan. For impartial advice on bemo routes and prices, ask at the controller's office rather than in the bemos themselves. If you can't find a bemo, metered **taxis** circulate around the city (an initial Rp5000, then Rp4000/km) or you can ring for one; Blue Bird Bali Taksi (☎0361/701111) are the most reliable.

Accommodation

Accommodation in Denpasar is geared more towards the Indonesian business traveller than the tourist trade, but there's one particularly inviting budget hotel and several other decent options.

Adinda Hotel Jl Karna 8 ☎0361/240435. Decent-value mid-range a/c hotel without much character but in a handy location just a few minutes from the museum and main sights. The 27 rooms are in three storeys around a central atrium restaurant and are clean. Deluxe rooms are much larger than standard and have balconies. Standard ❸, Deluxe ❹

Nakula Familiar Inn Jl Nakula 4 ☎0361/226446, ⓦwww.nakulafamiliarinn .com. Modern, well-maintained rooms, each with a balcony and the choice of fan or a/c in this welcoming family-style losmen. It's less than a 10min walk from the museum and about a 15min walk from Tegal bemo terminal. From Kereneng terminal, take an Ubung-bound bemo to the Jl

Abimanyu/Jl Veteran junction, from where it's a short walk to the hotel. Fan ❶, a/c ❷
Pop! Harris Hotel Jl Teuku Umar 74 ☎021/5296 0490, ⓦwww.popharris.com. Aimed mostly at business travellers, this is a functional, modern hotel on the Legian side of town, convenient for the business and shopping areas of Denpasar but a bit further from the historic sites. ❹
Taman Suci Jl Imam Bonjol 45 ☎0361/485254, ⓦwww.tamansuci.com. Modern, decently furnished mid-range hotel, just 50m south of Tegal bemo terminal. Good value and well equipped with hot water, a/c and TV in every room, plus the choice of main-street or rooftop view, but not terribly convenient for Denpasar's big sights. ❺

The City

Denpasar's central landmark is **Alun-alun Puputan**, the verdant square that marks the heart of the downtown area. The traffic island here is topped with a huge stone **statue of Catur Muka**, the four-faced, eight-armed Hindu guardian of the cardinal points, indicating the exact location of the city centre. The main road that runs west from the statue is **Jalan Gajah Mada**, lined with shop-houses and restaurants and, just beside the Badung River, a huge covered market, **Pasar Badung**. The most visited attractions dominate the eastern fringes of Alun-alun Puputan itself – the rewarding **Bali Museum** and the state temple, **Pura Agung Jagatnata**.

Denpasar's eastern districts are less enticing, but the art gallery at the **Taman Werdi Budaya Arts Centre** is worth a look, while the suburb of **Renon** is home to consulates and government offices. Modern Denpasar is epitomized on **Jalan Teuku Umar**, a long, neon-lit strip crammed with restaurants, malls and scores of mobile-phone outlets.

Alun-alun Puputan

Grassy **Alun-alun Puputan**, or Taman Puputan (Puputan Square), commemorates the fateful events of September 20, 1906, when the Raja of Badung marched out of his palace gates, followed by hundreds of his subjects, and faced the invading Dutch. Dressed entirely in holy white, with each man, woman and child clasping a golden *kris* (dagger), the people of Badung had psyched themselves up for a **puputan**, or ritual fight to the death (see p.363 for an eyewitness account of what happened). The final death toll was reported to be somewhere between six hundred and two thousand. The palace itself, just across Jalan Surapati on the north edge of the modern square, was razed and has since been rebuilt as the official residence of Bali's governor. The huge bronze statue depicting figures bearing sharpened bamboo staves and *kris* on the northern edge of the park is a memorial to the citizens who died in the *puputan*; it's an image that you'll see across the island.

The square hosts a commemorative **fair**, with food stalls and *wayang kulit* shows, every year on September 20.

The Bali Museum

Overlooking the eastern edge of Alun-alun Puputan on Jalan Mayor Wisnu, the **Bali Museum** (Museum Negeri Propinsi Bali; Sat–Thurs 8am–4pm, Fri 8.30am–12.30pm; closed public hols; Rp5000, children Rp2500, cameras Rp1000; on the turquoise Kereneng–Ubung bemo route) is Denpasar's top attraction and provides an excellent introduction to the island's culture, past and present. The museum compound itself is divided into traditional courtyards complete with *candi bentar* (split gates), *kulkul* (bell) tower, shrines and flower gardens.

The two-storey **Gedung Timur**, located at the back of the entrance courtyard, features archeological finds downstairs, including a massive **stone sarcophagus** that was hewn from soft volcanic rock around the second century BC, while the upstairs gallery is given over to an unexceptional display of traditional **paintings and woodcarvings**.

Through the traditional gateway that leads left off the entrance courtyard, the compact **Gedung Buleleng** holds fine examples of Balinese **textiles**, including the rare Kain *geringsing*, a complicated material that involves a lengthy and intricate dyeing and weaving technique practised only by the villagers of Tenganan (see p.194, for more).

Built to resemble the long, low structure of an eighteenth-century Karangasem-style palace, the **Gedung Karangasem** introduces the **spiritual and ceremonial life** of the Balinese – the cornerstone of the average islander's day-to-day existence – and is the most interesting section of the museum as it details the main religious ceremonies of Balinese Hinduism. The Balinese **calendars** on the right-hand wall are immensely complex and still widely used to determine all sorts of events from temple festivals to the starting day for the construction of a new house. For an explanation of the workings of the Balinese calendar, see p.43.

The theme of the **Gedung Tabanan**, a replica of a Tabanan regency palace, is **music and dance**, and its exhibits include masks, costumes and puppets. Most impressive are the Barong costumes, including the shaggy-haired **Barong Ket**, symbolizing the forces of good. Probably the most popular character, it looks like a cross between a lion, a pantomime horse and a Chinese dragon.

Pura Agung Jagatnata

Just over the north wall of the Bali Museum stands the modern state temple of **Pura Agung Jagatnata**, set in a garden of pomegranate, hibiscus and frangipani trees. Founded in 1953, it is dedicated to the supreme god, Sanghyang Widi Wasa, who is here worshipped in his role as "Lord of the World", or Jagatnata.

Carvings of lotus flowers and frogs adorn the tiny stone bridge that spans the moat around the temple's central gallery (access at festival times only) and scenes from the Hindu epics the *Ramayana* and *Mahabharata* decorate the gallery's outer wall. The temple's focal point is the looming five-tiered **padmasana** tower in the inner courtyard, balanced on a huge cosmic turtle. Built from blocks of white coral, the tower is carved with demons' heads and the bottom level displays the face and hands of Bhoma, the son of the earth, whose job is to repel evil spirits from the temple. The lotus throne at its summit is left empty for Sanghyang Widi

---

Markets and malls of Denpasar

Perhaps the best reason to visit Denpasar is to see the city's old-fashioned Balinese **markets**. The biggest and best is the chaotic **Pasar Badung**, located downtown in a traditional three-storey covered stone-and-brick *pasar* beside the Badung River, set slightly back off Jalan Gajah Mada. Trading takes place 24 hours a day, with buyers and sellers pouring in from all over the island. You'll find fresh fruit, veg and spices on the lower floors while those upstairs sell pretty much everything else imaginable, from buckets to boots and shoes to shovels.

Just west across the narrow Badung River from Pasar Badung, the four-storey traditional art market, **Pasar Kumbasari**, overflows with clothes, souvenirs, textiles, woodcarvings, paintings and sarongs – all the stuff that's on sale in the lanes of Kuta but without the crowds of tourists. With some well-honed bargaining skills you'll be able to pick up some bargains here.

Just to the east of Pasar Badung, Jalan Sulawesi, the narrow thoroughfare running from Jalan Hasanudin in the south to Jalan Gajah Mada in the north, is devoted to **fabric** of all descriptions, including batik, *songket* brocades and sari silks. Not far from here, the city's **gold quarter**, centred on the stretch of Jalan Hasanudin that runs west from Jalan Diponegoro to the river, has lots of jewellery outlets, but be aware that most of the designs cater to local tastes rather than tourist ones and it will pay to do some homework on the price of gold before embarking on the obligatory bargaining. Further north, **Pasar Burung**, the bird market, is a small but picturesque market full of **song birds** and the delicate cages that owners keep them in.

Tourists find the traditional markets picturesque and fun but for the Balinese they're for mundane day-to-day purchases; for their leisure time most Balinese head to the growing number of **shopping malls** that dot Denpasar. The newest is Denpasar Junction at the junction of Jalan Teuku Umar and Jalan Diponegoro, which has the most glam designer shops. Also popular are the Ramayana Mal Bali shopping centre, Jl Diponegoro 103 (Kereneng–Tegal and Tegal–Sanur bemos), the Matahari department store at Jl Dewi Sartika 4 (Tegal–Sanur bemo) and the Tiara Dewata shopping centre at Jl Sutoyo 55 (Kereneng–Tegal bemo); all carry high-street **fashions** and a few handicrafts. The malls generally **open** daily from 9.30am to 9pm, but many small shops in Denpasar close on Sundays.

Wasa to fill when descending to earth at festival times – the god is represented in a gold relief embossed on the back. In the southeast corner of the outer compound stands the **kulkul** tower, its split wooden bell still used to summon locals to festivals, meetings and temple-cleaning duties.

Twice a month, on the occasion of the full moon and new (or dark) moon, **festivals** are held here and *wayang kulit* shows are sometimes performed, from around 9pm to 11pm; ask at the nearby tourist office for details.

Taman Werdi Budaya Arts Centre

In the eastern part of town, on Jalan Nusa Indah, fifteen minutes' walk from the Kereneng bemo terminal, or direct on a Sanur-bound bemo, the **Taman Werdi Budaya Arts Centre** (daily 8am–3pm) was designed by one of Indonesia's most renowned architects, Ida Bagus Tugur. It consists of a number of performance spaces and is the location of the annual **Arts Festival** (usually between mid-June and mid-July; see ⓦwww.baliartsfestival.com for details), which is definitely worth seeking out for the huge programme of special exhibitions, competitions and shows.

The centre also houses a small **museum** (same hours; free), which aims to cover the history of Balinese arts – if you don't have time to visit the far superior Neka Art Museum in Ubud, it will at least give you a taste. It offers an overview of Balinese **painting**, including the classical *wayang* style, followed by works from the Ubud, Batuan and Young Artists styles (see p.168 for an explanation of these) up to more contemporary works. Other arts and crafts, including woodcarvings, masks, dance costumes, shadow puppets and jewellery are also on show.

Renon and Bajra Sandhi

Denpasar's administrative district, **Renon**, is on the southeastern edge of the city and served by Sanur-bound bemos. In among its wide tree-lined boulevards and imposing government offices stands the huge grey lava-stone **Bajra Sandhi** ("Balinese People's Struggle") monument (Mon–Fri 9am–4.30pm, Sat & Sun 9.30am–5pm; Rp2000; entrance just off Jalan Raya Puputan), at the heart of the **Lapangan Puputan Margarana** park. Designed by Taman Budaya's architect, Ida Bagus Tugur, to resemble a priest's bell, the monument's structure also symbolizes the date of Indonesia's Declaration of Independence – August 17, 1945 – with its eight entrances, seventeen corners and height that measures 45m. The upper floor contains a series of 33 dioramas illustrating edited episodes from Balinese history. Climb the spiral stairs to get a panoramic view across Denpasar's rooftops.

Eating

There are only a few tourist-oriented **restaurants** in Denpasar, so this is a good chance to sample Bali's cheap, authentic neighbourhood eateries. Note that smaller restaurants generally shut by 9pm.

Babi Guling Jl Sutomo. The roast suckling pig (*babi guling*) at this simple warung is considered the best in the city, and it's cheap too, at Rp17,000 a plate. There's no sign, but look for the open *bale* with low tables just north of Pura

Maospahit, opposite Bale Banjar Gerenceng. Closes around 6pm.

Bali Bakery Jl Hayam Wuruk 181. The Denpasar outpost of the well-known expat and tourist bakery in Kuta and Seminyak is the spot to head for if you're craving Western soups, salads, pastas, grills and a fabulous array of cakes and pastries. It isn't cheap, with most main courses around Rp40,000–70,000, but the a/c is a welcome respite from the city heat and they also do great breakfasts. Daily 8am–10pm.

Bhineka Jaya Kopi Bali Jl Gajah Mada 80 ⓦ www.kopibali.com. At this downtown outlet for Indonesia's Butterfly Globe Brand coffee you can sit down and sample a cup of premium, creamy Bali Gold and then choose which grade of beans to take away – from Bali, Sumatra or Kalimantan. *Kopi luwak* is also available (Rp100,000/cup). Mon–Sat 9am–4pm.

Hong Kong Jl Gajah Mada 99. Moderately priced a/c Chinese restaurant offering a huge, reasonably priced menu (mains Rp25,000–45,0000) including seafood and some vegetarian choices. Popular with middle-class Indonesian families, portions are big and the food well cooked.

Pasar Malam Kereneng Just off Jl Hayam Wuruk, adjacent to Kereneng bemo terminal. Over fifty vendors convene at this night market from dusk to dawn every night, dishing out super-cheap soups, noodle and rice dishes, *babi guling*, fresh fruit juices and cold beers for consumption at the trestle tables set around the marketplace.

Warung Wardani Jl Yudistira 2. The locals' favourite for good, filling plates of *nasi campur*, *nasi soto ayam*, *soto babad* (meat soup) and *gado-gado*, most of them costing just Rp25,000. Closes at 4pm.

Listings

Airline offices Garuda has a city check-in (4–24hr in advance) on the southeast corner of Alun-alun Puputan at Jl Sugianyar 5 (Mon–Fri 8am–4.30pm, Sat & Sun 9am–3pm; ☎0361/225320, national call centre ☎0804/180 7807 or 021/2351 9999 from a mobile). For other international and domestic airline offices, see p.79.

Cinema Cinema Wisata is at Jl Thamrin 29 ☎0361/423023, and there's a cinema at Denpasar Junction shopping mall.

Dance Tourist performances (about 2hr; Rp70,000) of the Barong (daily 9am) at the Catur Eka Budhi on Jl Waribang, in Denpasar's eastern Kesiman district, and the Kecak (daily 6pm) at the Stage Uma Dewi, also on Jl Waribang, about 300m south of the Barong dance stage. Batubulan-bound bemos from Ubung and Kereneng pass the corner of Jl Waribang, from where it's a short signposted walk.

Embassies and consulates See p.59.

Hospitals, clinics and dentists Sanglah Public Hospital (Rumah Sakit Umum Propinsi Sanglah, or RSUP Sanglah) at Jl Kesehatan Selatan 1, Sanglah (five lines ☎0361/227911–227915; Kereneng–Tegal bemo and Tegal–Sanur bemo) is the main provincial public hospital, with an emergency ward and some English-speaking staff. It also has Bali's only divers' recompression chamber (☎0361/257361 or mobile 0812/465 5281). Bali Med Hospital is a private hospital at Jl Mahendradatta 57X (☎0361/484747, ⓦ www.balimedhospital.co.uk). Most expats use BIMC or International SOS, both near Kuta (see p.99). International SOS also has a dentist, or see p.99.

Immigration Office Corner of Jl Panjaitan and Jl Raya Puputan, Renon (Mon–Thurs 8am–4pm, Fri 8–11am; ☎0361/227828).

Internet There's an internet place on Jl Kaliasem, the small road that heads north off Jl Surapati, alongside the tourist office (see map, p.114).

Language lessons Courses in Indonesian language at Indonesia Australia Language Foundation (IALF), Jl Raya Sesetan 190 ☎0361/225243, ⓦ www.ialf.edu.

Music and dance lessons Lessons and workshops in gamelan and Balinese dance at Mekar Bhuana Conservatory, Jl Gandapura III No.501X, Kesiman Kerthalangu ☎0361/464201, ⓦ www.balimusicanddance.com.

Pharmacies Several along Jl Gajah Mada and inside all the major shopping centres.

Phone There are Telkom offices at Jl Teuku Umar 6 and on Jl Durian, and wartels (phone offices) all over the city.

Police There are police stations on Jl Patimura and Jl Diponegoro; the main police station is in the far west of the city on Jl Gunung Sanghiang (☎0361/424346).

Post office Denpasar's poste restante (Mon–Sat 8am–6pm) is at the GPO, located on Jl Raya Puputan in Renon. The Sanur–Tegal and Kereneng–Tegal bemos pass the front door; otherwise, take the Tegal–Sanur bemo, get out at the Jl Cok Agung Tresna/Jl Panjaitan junction and walk 500m south.

Travel agent International and domestic airline tickets can be bought from Jatatur, Jl Surapati 47, ☎0361/261488, ⓦ www.jatatur.com. Get Pelni boat tickets from Jl Diponegoro 165 ☎0361/234680.

Sanur and around

With a 5km-long sandy beach, plenty of attractive accommodation in all price brackets and a distinct village atmosphere, **SANUR** makes an appealing, more peaceful alternative to Kuta, and is not as manufactured as Nusa Dua. Because it lacks the clubs and all-night party venues of Kuta, it can seem a bit tame to younger travellers (hence its nickname, "Snore"), but it has plenty of restaurants and makes a great place to bring the kids. It is also south Bali's main centre for diving, and works well as a base for exploring the island: Kuta is just 15km to the southwest, Ubud a mere forty minutes' drive north and Nusa Lembongan a short boat ride away.

Sanur was chosen as the site of Bali's first major beach hotel in the 1960s. This was the **Grand Bali Beach**, a high-rise that remains a blot on the Sanur seafront (currently part of the *Inna* hotel group). Though fashionable at the time, its architecture did not, thankfully, go down well locally and the Bali-wide edict against building anything higher than a coconut tree has held good ever since.

These days, Sanur is famous as the source of some of Bali's most powerful **black magic** and home of the most feared sorcerers and respected healers, or *balian*. It's not uncommon to hear stories of police enquiries that use the black-magic practitioners of Sanur to help track down criminals.

Arrival and local transport

Sanur is comprised of several districts. **North Sanur** incorporates Jalan Hang Tuah, which has just a few small hotels, and the area around the nearby *Inna Grand Bali Beach* hotel. South of Jalan Segara Ayu as far as Jalan Pantai Karang is **Sindhu**, location of many guesthouses, hotels, shops and restaurants. Less congested **Batujimbar** runs from Jalan Pantai Karang as far as the *Bali Hyatt*, while **Semawang** is the southern coastal strip from the *Bali Hyatt* to *Hotel Sanur Beach* and beyond, site of an increasing number of tourist-oriented shops, hotels and businesses. The more residential inland area covering Jalan Danau Poso and Jalan Bypass is **Blanjong**.

Pick up a copy of the free **booklet** *Sanur Community*, available in many tourist businesses and issued every two months, for details of what's happening locally.

Arrival

A **taxi** ride from central Kuta should cost about Rp60,000; otherwise, the fastest and most direct transport from most other tourist centres is by tourist **shuttle bus**. The drop-off point for the biggest operator, Perama, is Warung Pojok minimarket, Jl Hang Tuah 31 in north Sanur, from where you can continue by bemo or taxi.

It's also possible to reach Sanur by public **bemo** via Denpasar; dark-green bemos from Denpasar's **Kereneng terminal** (see p.113) run to the Jalan Bypass/Jalan Hang Tuah junction in north Sanur (15min), then Jalan Danau Beratan and Jalan Danau Buyan, before continuing down Jalan Danau Tamblingan to *The Trophy* pub in Semawang. Dark-blue bemos from Denpasar's **Tegal terminal** (see p.113) run direct to Sanur via Jalan Teuku Umar and Renon (30min) and then follow the same route as the Kereneng ones. **From Kuta**, you'll need to change bemos at Tegal in Denpasar or, from Kuta's eastern outskirts, take the white

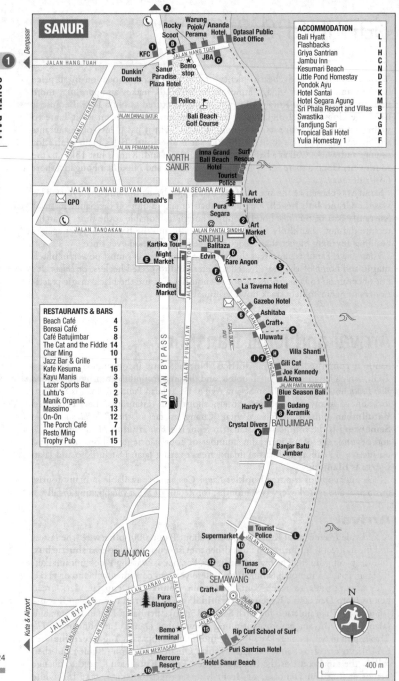

SANUR

SOUTH BALI

ACCOMMODATION

Bali Hyatt	L
Flashbacks	I
Griya Santrian	H
Jambu Inn	C
Kesumari Beach	N
Little Pond Homestay	D
Pondok Ayu	E
Hotel Santai	K
Hotel Segara Agung	M
Sri Phala Resort and Villas	B
Swastika	J
Tandjung Sari	G
Tropical Bali Hotel	A
Yulia Homestay 1	F

RESTAURANTS & BARS

Beach Café	4
Bonsai Café	5
Café Batujimbar	8
The Cat and the Fiddle	14
Char Ming	10
Jazz Bar & Grille	1
Kafe Kesuma	16
Kayu Manis	3
Lazer Sports Bar	6
Luhtu's	2
Manik Organik	9
Massimo	13
On-On	12
The Porch Café	7
Resto Ming	11
Trophy Pub	15

Denpasar

Kuta & Airport

N

0   400 m

Damri **bus**, which travels between Batubulan and **Nusa Dua**, and alight at the *Sanur Paradise Plaza* hotel on Jalan Bypass in north Sanur; you can also use this service if coming **from Ubud**, changing on to the Damri bus at Denpasar's **Batubulan** terminus (see p.148).

Local transport

Sanur stretches 5km from north to south, so the green and blue public **bemos** to and from Denpasar's two terminals (see "Arrival", above) can be useful for buzzing up and down the main streets; the tourist price is about Rp5000 for any local ride. Otherwise, flag down one of the numerous **metered taxis**: light-blue Blue Bird Bali Taksi (℡0361/701111) have the best reputation; all metered taxis charge an initial Rp5000, then Rp4000 per km, day and night. If you're planning a long trip, consider negotiating a fee with one of the roadside **transport touts**.

The transport touts also **rent cars** and **motorbikes**, as do many hotels and tour agencies. JBA is one of the few Sanur agencies to sell car insurance, and will also supply a **car with driver**; it's located at Jl Hang Tuah 54 in north Sanur (℡0361/286501, ⒲www.jbabali.com). See Basics, p.33, for vehicle rental advice and price guidelines, and for first-hand recommendations of Sanur drivers check the archives of the online travellers' forums listed on p.67.

Sanur is a good place for **bicycles**, which are available for rent (Rp20,000–35,000) along the beachfront promenade.

Most tourist businesses in Sanur offer **sightseeing tours** around Bali and to neighbouring islands. See "Listings", p.131, for some recommended travel agents.

Accommodation

There's **accommodation** to suit every pocket in Sanur, from low-budget homestays to gleaming five-star establishments. In general the quality is good and with more space and better facilities you get more for your rupiah or dollar here

---

Moving on from Sanur

Most hotels and losmen will arrange transport to the **airport** for around Rp100,000, or you can hail a metered taxi for slightly less.

The most painless way of moving on to most tourist destinations is by **tourist shuttle bus**, tickets for which are sold by tour agents. The largest, most reliable operator is Perama and their main agent and pick-up point is Warung Pojok minimarket, Jl Hang Tuah 31 in north Sanur (℡0361/285592, ⒲www.peramatour .com); you can pay an extra Rp10,000 for a hotel pick-up. Sample fares include Rp25,000 to Kuta/the airport, Rp60,000 to Padang Bai and Rp125,000 to Lovina. See "Travel details", p.142, for destinations and frequencies.

Moving on by **bemo** to anywhere on Bali entails going via the Denpasar terminals at Kereneng or Tegal. The latter is the departure point for services to the Kuta area, Jimbaran and Nusa Dua. For other destinations you have to make a cross-city bemo connection to the Ubung terminal for **the west and the north** (see p.274), or the Batubulan terminal for **Ubud and the east** (see p.148); the alternative for Ubud connections is to pick up the white Damri **bus** service, which runs direct to the Batubulan terminal (hourly until about 3pm), collecting passengers from near the *Sanur Paradise Plaza* hotel on Jalan Bypass in north Sanur.

Sanur is the main departure point for **boats to Nusa Lembongan**; see p.134 for full details.

than in Kuta–Legian–Seminyak. Obviously, access to the beach is a priority for many but there are also some brilliant gems where the longer distance from the shorefront is more than worthwhile.

Bali Hyatt Jl Danau Tamblingan, Semawang ☏0361/281234, ⓦwww.bali.resort.hyatt.com. The 36 acres of award-winning tropical gardens are the highlight of this long-established, upmarket hotel. Rooms are in a trio of ocean-facing or garden-view blocks and facilities include two swimming pools, a well-regarded spa, several restaurants and grounds that extend to the beach. Free shuttles to the *Grand Hyatt* hotel in Nusa Dua. **❾**

Flashbacks Jl Danau Tamblingan 110, Batujimbar ☏0361/281682, ⓦwww.flashbacks-chb.com. Great little place with just nine rooms and bungalows, all with hot water, some with fan, some with a/c and one with a kitchen. There are plenty of sitting areas in the small compound, set in a lush, atmospheric garden with a pool. Fan **❸**, a/c **❺**, with kitchen **❻**

Griya Santrian Jl Danau Tamblingan 47, Sindhu ☏0361/288181, ⓦwww.santrian.com. Popular mid-sized place with 98 spacious rooms in a garden compound that runs down to the beach. The newly renovated "deluxe" rooms are worth the extra money. There is also an art gallery which hosts interesting exhibitions, and three pools (one shoreside). **❼**

Hotel Santai Jl Danau Tamblingan 168, Batujimbar ☏0361/287314, ⓦwww.crystal-divers.com. Just behind the Crystal Divers shop, this is a good-value choice with a lively atmosphere offering large, good-quality rooms. All have hot water and are in two-storey blocks set around the pool in a pleasant courtyard. **❹**

Hotel Segara Agung Jl Duyung 43, Semawang ☏0361/288446, ⓦwww.segaraagung.com. Occupying a quiet spot down a residential *gang* just a couple of minutes' walk from the beach, this place offers twenty bungalows set in a spacious garden with a pool. The cheapest have fans and cold water; the pricier ones are far more comfortable. Fan **❹**, a/c **❻**

Jambu Inn Jl Hang Tuah 54, north Sanur ☏0361/286501, ⓦwww.jambuinn.com. Tiny, quiet place with twelve bungalows set round a cute garden with pool and there's also a bigger one (**❹**) with a living area and a spacious veranda. Convenient for boats to/from Nusa Lembongan. **❸**

Kesumasari Beach Jl Kesumasari 6, Semawang ☏0361/287824. Just 10m from the beach, this is the cheapest accommodation so close to the ocean in Sanur. The eleven rooms are decent, standard losmen style, all with hot water and some with traditional painted and carved wooden doors. Fan **❸**, a/c **❹**

Little Pond Homestay Jl Danau Tamblingan 19, Sindhu ☏0361/289902, ⓦwww.ellor-abali.com. With a small pool, free wi-fi and a choice of fan or a/c and hot water, this tiny setup is strikingly good value. The dozen terraced rooms are comfortably appointed and although there's no restaurant or other hotel facilities it's a few steps to the main road and a short walk to the beach. Fan **❶**, a/c **❸**

Pondok Ayu Gang Pudak, Jl Selanta ☏0361/284102, ⓦwww.pondok.com.au. Tucked away in a peaceful residential area on the west side of Jl Bypass, this hidden gem has just four rooms and a villa ranged around a lovely pool in charming gardens. Rooms are extremely well furnished, comfortable, spotless and superbly maintained, and service is great. Meals are available if you can't drag yourself away, and the beach is a short walk away (transport available). It's very popular and gets booked up months ahead so reservations are vital. **❻**

Sri Phala Resort and Villas Jl Hang Tuah III no. 5, north Sanur ☏0361/286479, ⓦwww.sriphala.com. Accessed from either Jl Bypass or Jl Hang Tuah, the accommodation is set far enough back, in a great garden, not to be bothered by the road noise. The large, well-cared-for and nicely decorated rooms come with tea-making facilities, lots of storage space and an outside sitting area. The gardens are lush and the pool lovely. **❺**

Swastika Jl Danau Tamblingan 128, Batujimbar ☏0361/288693, ⓦwww.swastika-bungalows.com. Deservedly popular mid-range place, whose 78 comfortable rooms (many with beautifully painted carved wooden doors and window shutters) are set round a delightful garden with two pools. The fan-cooled rooms have garden bathrooms, and all rooms have hot water and verandas. Named after the ancient Buddhist symbol, not the Nazi emblem. **❻**

Tandjung Sari Jl Danau Tamblingan 41, Sindhu ☏0361/288441, ⓦwww.tandjungsarihotel.com. Sanur's original boutique hotel was founded in 1962 and remains small and intimate, with 28 elegant, beautifully appointed traditional-style cottage compounds, each with a courtyard garden, shaded gazebo and garden shower. Many rooms feature antique Chinese floor tiles and all have refined Javanese batik furnishings. There's a large pool, and the garden runs down to the shore. Service is excellent. **❽**

Tropical Bali Hotel Jl Padang Galak, Gang Penyu Dewata 3/2 ☏ 0361/282524, ⓦ www.tropicalbali hotel.com. Situated in a completely rural setting about 5km north of Sanur, about a 5min walk from the (black sand) Pantai Galak beach, this little gem has just ten rooms, all immaculate, with a/c, hot water and great sitting areas looking out on the verdant garden and pool. There's transport to Sanur, or staff can make meals. Booking is vital. ❹

Yulia Homestay 1 Jl Danau Tamblingan 38, Sindhu ☏ 0361/288089. This long-established family-run place offers twenty appealing, comfortable, fan-cooled or a/c bungalows, some of which have hot water and all of which are clean, well-maintained and set in a lush garden, well back from the road. All have small sitting areas outside. Rates increase according to amenities (a/c and hot water) provided. ❶–❸

The resort

The entire length of Sanur's 5km **shoreline** is fronted by a partially shaded, paved esplanade, so it's easy to wander (or cycle) down the coast in search of the perfect spot. There are busy patches of beach around the *Inna Grand Bali Beach* in the north and, further south, in Sindhu, between the Sindhu Art Market and the *Tandjung Sari Hotel*, but other spots are much quieter. The **views** are great from almost any point along this coast: on a clear day, Gunung Agung's imposing profile dominates panoramas to the northeast, while out to sea you can see the cliffs of Nusa Penida.

A huge expanse of Sanur's shore is exposed at low tide and the reef lies only about 1km offshore at high tide; the **currents** beyond it are dangerously strong. This makes it almost impossible to swim here at low tide (though it's okay for paddling kids), but at other times swimming is fine and watersports are popular.

Watersports and golf

Sanur is a popular base for **divers** (for details of local dive operators, see box on p.128), but its own **dive sites**, along the east-facing edge of the shorefront reef, are only really of interest for refresher diving. The coral is not that spectacular, and visibility is only around 6–10m, with dives ranging from 2–12m, though the area does teem with reef fish.

Several outlets along the beachfront offer **snorkelling** trips ($30/person/hr, including gear) and three-hour fishing excursions ($95/person). They also rent out **watersports** equipment, including kayaks ($10/hr), windsurfers ($35/half-day) and jet skis ($30 for 15min), and can arrange parasailing, wakeboarding and water-skiing. Contact Segara Ayu Watersports on Segara Beach or Matahari watersports at a number of spots near *Mercure Resort* and *Sanur Beach Hotel*. From September to March, when the northwest winds blow offshore, there are several decent **surf breaks** off Sanur, including directly in front of the *Inna Grand Bali Beach*, in front of *Tandjung Sari* hotel, and about 1.5km offshore from the *Bali Hyatt*. You can rent surfboards and boogie boards ($6–10/hr) along the beachfront.

Sanur also has its own nine-hole **golf course**, the Bali Beach Golf Course, in front of the *Inna Grand Bali Beach* (☏ 0361/287733, ⓦ www.balibeachgolfcourse.com).

Bali Orchid Garden

The Balinese have a passion for tropical gardens and many buy their plants from the nurseries that line the roads between Sanur and Denpasar. The **Bali Orchid Garden** (daily 8am–6pm; Rp50,000; ⓦ www.baliorchidgardens.com) has turned itself into a paying attraction and encourages tourists who probably aren't thinking of taking a shrub home to come and browse the beautiful blooms

Dive centres in south Bali

Many of the outfits that sell **dive** excursions from shops in Kuta and Nusa Dua have their headquarters in **Sanur**. South Bali's dive sites are good for learners and those needing a refresher, but experienced divers usually prefer the dives off the east and north coasts of Bali, either arranging them from the south, or basing themselves nearer those places. For **general advice** on diving in Bali and Lombok, see p.45.

There is one **divers' recompression chamber** on Bali, located at Sanglah Public Hospital, Jl Kesehatan Selatan 1 in Denpasar (T0361/257361 or mobile 0812/465 5281).

Long-established PADI-certified dive centres in south Bali include:

AquaMarine Diving Jl Petitenget 2A T0361/738020, Wwww.aquamarinediving .com. UK-run PADI five-star resort.

Atlantis International Jl Bypass Ngurah Rai 350, Sanur T0361/284312, Wwww .balidiveaction.com. PADI five-star IDC Centre. Operates courses in English, French, Spanish, German and Indonesian.

Bali Scuba Jl Danau Poso 40, Blanjong, Sanur T0361/288610, Wwww.baliscuba .com. PADI five-star IDC centre that's known for its technical diving.

Blue Season Bali Jl Tamblingan 69XX, Batujimbar T0361/270852, Wwww .baliocean.com. PADI CDC centre. UK/Japanese-run.

Crystal Divers Jl Danau Tamblingan 168, Batujimbar T0361/286737, Wwww .crystal-divers.com. PADI CDC centre. Also runs tailored dive safaris all over Bali. UK-Danish-run.

anyway. The grounds are pleasingly landscaped and alongside the huge variety of orchids are other lovelies, including heliconias, bromeliads and tree ferns. You can also order gift boxes of cut flowers for taking overseas. The garden is 3km north of Sanur on Jalan Bypass, just beyond the junction with the coast road to Pantai Saba and Kusamba.

Eating

Sanur has dozens of tourist-oriented **restaurants** with a few that stand out from the pack. The beachfront cafés are great to catch the daytime breeze and have the added romance of candlelight at night. Of the swanky hotels, the *Trattoria Café* at the *Griya Santrian* manages beachside dining with the most style. The most authentic Indonesian food and cheapest eats are beyond the main drag, for example in the **night market** that sets up inside the Sindhu Market at Jalan Danau Tamblingan/Jalan Danau Toba and in the *gang* alongside Hardy's supermarket. Most places open daily, from breakfast time to nighttime.

Beach Café Beachfront walkway south off Jl Pantai Sindhu, Sindhu. The most sophisticated yet chilled of the beachfront cafés in this part of the beach has sea-view couches indoors as well as tables on the sand. Breakfasts are good – taking in eggs Benedict, frittatas and full English (from Rp39,000) – as are the dinner options, including "taster platters" that feature a selection of dishes (from Rp82,000), plus a kids' menu. Look out for

special events such as the Full Moon Festival with entertainment and special menus.
Bonsai Café Beachfront walkway just north of *La Taverna* hotel, accessed off Jl Danau Tamblingan, Sindhu. Breezy shorefront restaurant that serves typical tourist fare, including Mexican fajitas, seafood, steaks and pizzas. The owner's impressive nursery of bonsai is out back, beside the path from the main road.

Café Batujimbar Jl Danau Tamblingan 75A, Batujimbar. The menu (Rp40,000–225,000) at this relaxed Sanur institution includes roast vegetable salads, home-made mushroom-stuffed ravioli and crispy fried duck with mango and feta cheese, as well as mango pie, home-baked cakes and Bali-brewed Storm Beer. Live music nightly from 8pm. An attached deli sells bread, cheese and home comforts such as canned soup and cereal.

Char Ming Jl Danau Tamblingan 97, Semawang ☎0361/288029, ⊛www.charming-bali.com. Glorious restaurant housed in an elegant high-ceilinged open *bale* with wooden carvings and statues. Service is formal and the menu a mixture of French (frogs' legs, cassoulet) and Indonesian dishes (*rendang*, Balinese prawns) ranging from Rp65,000–195,000 for a main course, supplemented by an extensive wine list. If this is to your taste consider Char Ming's older sister, *Le Resto Ming*, at no. 105, slightly pricier and more sophisticated.

Kafe Kesuma Semawang Beach. A good southern finish if you're riding or walking the beachfront walkway, as the views and beach deteriorate into industrial non-chic further south. This shady beach-front café offers seafood, grills, international and Indonesian meals, all at good-value prices (Rp35,000 tops).

Kayu Manis Jl Tandakan 6, Sindhu. ☎0361/289410 Open 6.30–10pm. Head and shoulders above all other Sanur restaurants for ambition, taste and presentation. This is intricate and superb cooking from a small menu, in a tiny garden restaurant with less than a dozen tables and prices no higher than you'll pay at the beach.

Most dishes are Western with an Asian twist, with a strong presence of fish and seafood: think pan-fried snapper wrapped with bacon and a balsamic cream sauce, or a seafood skewer on a bed of risotto with chilli and tomato sauce. Reserve as far ahead as possible.

Luhtu's Sindhu Beach. Little spot on the beach serving, they claim, "the best coffee in Bali" – it is Illy and extremely good, so they may just be right. Add to this the small menu of fish and chips, grilled tuna, spring rolls, sandwiches and tasty cakes and this is a great spot to while away a few hours. Shuts at 6pm.

Manik Organik Jl Danau Tamblingan 85, Batujimbar ⊛www.manikorganikbali.com. Plenty of healthy eating options taking in soups, salads and shakes plus fruit and vegetable juices (including wheatgrass shots). Refills for water bottles available.

Massimo Jl Danau Tamblingan 228, Semawang. The vast array of home-made ice creams (Rp20,000) on offer at the *gelato* stand at the front of this genuinely south-Italian restaurant is enticing, but just an indication of the great food and vast menu within, covering all the Italian staples of pizza, pasta, meat and fish (Rp40,000). Widely regarded as producing the best Italian food in Sanur.

The Porch Café Jl Danau Tamblingan 110, in front of *Flashbacks*, Batujimbar. This small gem of a place packs a big culinary punch with a good range of breakfasts, bangers and mash, home-made pies and tapas plus Devonshire Tea, including scones. Eat out on the porch or in the a/c interior; works well at any time of the day or evening.

Nightlife and entertainment

Reggae **bands** and cover groups entertain drinkers and diners most nights at one or other of the beachside restaurants between *La Taverna* and Jalan Pantai Sindhu, but for **clubbing** action you'll need to head for Kuta. If you're carousing in Sanur after 10pm you might find it difficult to find a taxi, so ask bar staff to phone for a cab (☎0361/701111).

Bars and live music

The Cat and the Fiddle Jl Cemara 36, opposite *Hotel Sanur Beach*, Semawang ⊛www.catfiddle.com. There's live Irish music at least three nights a week at this Ireland-focused bar-restaurant. Plus Guinness, Jameson and Bushmills, of coursee, as well as steak and Guinness pie, Limerick salad and a Blarney Schnitzel. Open 7am to late (last food orders 11pm).

Jazz Bar & Grille Komplek Pertokoan Sanur Raya 15, next to *KFC* at the Jl Bypass/Jl Hang Tuah crossroads, north Sanur. In the bar jazz, blues and pop bands play live sets nightly from about 9.30pm; the atmosphere is mellow and it attracts a mix of locals, expats and tourists. The upstairs restaurant serves quality international food (Rp40,000–80,000). Daily 10am–2am.

Lazer Sports Bar Opposite *Gazebo Hotel* at Jl Danau Tamblingan 68, Sindhu. Big place dominated by big-screen-TV sports coverage and with pool tables and live music from local MOR bands to fill in the gaps.

On-On Jl Danau Poso 53, Blanjong. Expat hangout offering billiard tables in addition to drinks, food and TV.

Trophy Pub Jl Cemara, opposite *The Cat and Fiddle* in Semawang. Buzzy yet relaxed drinking spot with decent food as well.

Shopping

Compared to Kuta, Legian and Seminyak there are far fewer **shops** to browse in Sanur, though the souvenir stalls along the boardwalk sell much the same range. Boutiques and trendy giftware and homewares outlets feature in moderation but most lack the panache of the better Seminyak versions. Periplus **bookstore** has a branch in Hardy's Grosir supermarket.

A.Krea Jl Danau Tamblingan, Batujimbar. Great little shop with arts, crafts, textiles and souvenirs that are well chosen and out of the ordinary, including unusual recycled rice-sack bags and limited-edition photographs by A. A. Caya Wisanta.

Art markets Sanur's *pasar seni* (art market) stalls selling cheap cotton clothes, beachwear, sarongs, woodcarvings and other souvenirs are mainly clustered along the beachfront south from Jl Pantai Sindhu to the *Bali Hyatt* hotel.

Ashitaba Jl Danau Tamblingan 39, Batujimbar. Part of a small chain of good-quality Balinese basket-ware shops selling placemats, containers, handbags and more, all made from *ata* grass in Tenganan.

Balitaza Jl Danau Tamblingan 1, Sindhu. Small place with an excellent range of luscious toiletries and appetizing foods, all attractively packaged. For equally enticing toiletries, Bali Organic is across the road at no. 8.

Craft+ Jl Danau Tamblingan 39, Batujimbar and Jl Danau Poso 108, Semawang. Imaginative and well-presented handicrafts and textiles from small, easily transportable items to larger stuff that is best to admire but leave behind.

Edvin Jl Danau Tamblingan 17, Sindhu. Most of the hefty sculptures in this antiques emporium – gathered from across the archipelago – will

inevitably remain in Bali but there are some small, easily packable items that will make great souvenirs back home.

Gudang Keramik Jl Danau Tamblingan, Batujimbar. Ceramics shop that's an outlet for seconds produced by the high-quality Jenggala Keramik ceramics emporium in Jimbaran (see p.101). Slight imperfections get you a thirty percent discount.

Hardy's Grosir Jl Danau Tamblingan 193, Batujimbar. The entire top floor of Sanur's main supermarket is devoted to local handicrafts, with a large, if uninvitingly displayed, range of reasonably priced, fixed-rate souvenirs, from baskets to woodcarvings. Among other things, the ground-floor supermarket sells groceries, pharmacy items, sandals and motorbike helmets.

Pisces Jl Danau Tamblingan 105, Semawang. Describing itself as a "black and white clothing boutique", this friendly little place does what it says on the tin, selling light, easywear, tropical clothes that are highly covetable.

Rare Angon Jl Danau Tamblingan 17, Sindhu. Modern art gallery (one of the few in Sanur) featuring mostly but not exclusively paintings from local artists.

Uluwatu Jl Danau Tamblingan, Sindhu ⓦ www .uluwatu.co.id. Balinese chain selling white, handmade lace and cotton clothes.

Spa treatments

Many of Sanur's more expensive hotels have luxurious **spas** offering a range of treatments, including aromatherapy, reflexology and traditional Balinese massages, and the Javanese *mandi lulur* exfoliation scrub (see p.47), as well as facials and hair treatments. The most famous is the traditional village-style spa complex at the *Bali Hyatt* (☏0361/281234), where the ninety-minute Lulur costs $85. Alternatively, there's always the massage-and-manicure ladies who hang out on the beach, charging Rp50,000 for a half-hour massage.

Listings

Airline offices Garuda has a sales office and check-in (4–24hr in advance) inside the *Sanur Beach Hotel*, Semawang (Mon–Fri 8am–4.30pm, Sat & Sun 9am–3pm; ☎0361/288011 ext 1789, national call centre ☎0804/180 7807 or 021/2351 9999 from a mobile). For other international and domestic airline offices, see p.79.

Banks and currency exchange There are ATMs and exchange counters all over Sanur; see p.63 for advice on how to avoid exchange scams. Recommended exchange counters are PT Central Kuta inside Circle K, PT Maspintjinra, Jl Danau Tamblingan 18 and PT Made Putroe Bakri Valuata, Jl Tamblingan 50. If you're heading to Nusa Lembongan, note that there is currently no ATM on the island; the most convenient mainland ATMs en route are at the *Dunkin' Donuts* on the corner of Jl Hang Tuah (see map, p.124) and at the Permata Bank, where you can withdraw Rp3,000,000 in one transaction.

Cookery classes Learn to make Balinese dishes at Villa Shanti, Jl Tamblingan 47 (☎0361/288060; Rp300,000/person).

Embassies and consulates See p.59.

Hospitals and clinics All the major hotels provide 24hr medical service; if yours doesn't, try Dr Ari Sudhewa & Associates (☎0812/395 4567), a mobile English- and German-speaking doctor who serves the area. There are international clinics on the edge of Kuta (see p.99); the nearest hospitals are all in Denpasar (see p.122).

Pharmacies Several on Jl Danau Tamblingan, including Guardian Pharmacy next to Hardy's Grosir in Batujimbar.

Photographic tours Joe Kennedy, based at Jl Danau Tamblingan 51D (☎0361/282339, ⓦwww.josephkennedy.co.uk), customizes full-day tours to suit individual interests and abilities, taking in about three separate locations. Tours cost Rp2million for one person, Rp3million for two.

Police There's a 24hr Tourist Police post on Jl Danau Tamblingan, just south of the *Bali Hyatt* hotel. The police station (☎0361/288597) is on Jl Bypass in north Sanur, just south of the *Sanur Paradise Plaza* hotel.

Post office Sanur's main post office is on Jl Danau Buyan, Sindhu.

Travel agents International and domestic flights, plus organized tours, can be booked through: JBA, Jl Hang Tuah 54, north Sanur ☎0361/286501, ⓦwww.jbabali.com; Kartika Tour, Jl Danau Tamblingan 16, Sindhu ☎0361/782 5466, ⓦwww.balikartikatours.com; and Tunas Tour, Jl Danau Tamblingan 119, Semawang ☎0361/288581, ⓦwww.bali-tunas-tour.com. See p.134 for details of transport to Nusa Lembongan. Sanur is also the location for Bali Access Travel, Jl Danau Tamblingan 31 (☎0361/851 9902, ⓦwww.baliaccesstravel.com), specialists in wheelchair-accessible travel in Bali, Lombok and Java.

Benoa Harbour (Pelabuhan Benoa)

BENOA HARBOUR (Pelabuhan Benoa) is located off the end of a long causeway 5km southwest of southern Sanur, and is the arrival and departure point for many sailing trips and tourist **boat services**, including fast boats to the Gili Islands (see p.325) and luxury trips to Nusa Lembongan (see p.134), as well as for all Pelni ships from elsewhere in Indonesia, plus cruise liners.

The easiest way to reach Benoa Harbour is by **metered taxi**; it's a short ride of about Rp50,000 from Kuta. Sporadic public **bemos** also run between here and a stopping point near Denpasar's Sanglah hospital.

Tickets for long-distance **Pelni** boats to other islands must be bought in advance (booking opens three days before departure), either through travel agents or at the Pelni offices in Benoa Harbour (Mon–Fri 8am–4pm, Sat 8am–12.30pm; ☎0361/821377) or Kuta (see p.100). **Tickets** for tourist boats to Nusa Lembongan, fast boats to Lombok and sailing trips can be booked through any tour agent and include transfers to the harbour.

Nusa Lembongan, Nusa Ceningan and Nusa Penida

Due east of Sanur, the small islands of **Nusa Lembongan**, **Nusa Ceningan** and **Nusa Penida** rise alluringly out of the Badung Strait and make a refreshing escape from the hustle of south Bali. Encircled by breathtakingly clear water and plenty of healthy reef, they offer outstanding **diving** and challenging **surfing**, and several dramatic white-sand bays, though many of the **beaches** are

Diving, snorkelling and surfing around Nusa Lembongan

Protected as a marine conservation area, the reefs around Nusa Lembongan and Nusa Penida attract **divers** from all over south and east Bali, not least for the chance to swim with the one-tonne legendary local giant, the **mola mola** (oceanic sunfish), from July to October (see p.9). Many of the reefs are rewarding for **snorkelling** too, and **surfing** here is famously challenging.

Diving

Of the fourteen main dive sites, the two most famous are both **off Nusa Penida** and can get very crowded in peak season: **Manta Point** is renowned for manta rays, while **Crystal Bay** is known for its eponymously clear waters that boast up to 40m visibility, and for its *mola mola*. *Mola mola* and manta rays also frequent the **Toyapakeh** reef, with its huge coral boulders and pillars. Other local highlights include drift dives, turtles, octopus and white-tipped reef sharks.

The sea around Penida and Lembongan can be cold and is known for its treacherous **currents**, so it's important to dive with experts (see p.46 for advice on choosing a dive centre); some sites are for experienced divers only. Basing yourself on Lembongan not only cuts down on travel time and costs but also means you can get to the big sites before or after the crowds from mainland Bali. Reputable **dive centres** on Nusa Lembongan include World Diving Lembongan (℡0812/390 0686, ⓦwww.world-diving.com), based at *Pondok Baruna* bungalows in Jungutbatu, and Big Fish Diving at *Secret Garden* bungalows, also in Jungutbatu (℡0813/5313 6661, ⓦwww.bigfishdiving.com). One-day, two-dive packages average $79.

Snorkelling

Prime snorkelling spots off Nusa Penida include **Crystal Bay** (see p.142), the **Penida Wall** and **Malibu Point**; off Nusa Lembongan, and sometimes accessible from the shore if the tide is right, are **Mangrove Corner** (see p.137) and **Mushroom Bay**. Boats can be booked direct on the beach, or via your accommodation: it's about Rp150,000 per hour for four people including equipment around Nusa Lembongan, or Rp350,000 for a two-hour excursion to Crystal Bay. World Diving runs dedicated half-day snorkel trips for $25–35.

Surfing

The best surfing is from June to September and the main – mostly advanced – breaks are **Playgrounds**, **Lacerations** and **Shipwrecks**, all off Jungutbatu; there's also Mushroom Bay, and Ceningan Point in the channel between Lembongan and Nusa Ceningan. Dreamweaver (℡0813/3835 5228, ⓦwww.dreamweaver-surf.com) runs surf safaris incorporating Nusa Lembongan, Lombok and Sumbawa.

dominated by seaweed farming, which is the major occupation. **Nusa Lembongan** has nearly all the tourist facilities and is the obvious place to stay. It's very relaxed, with accommodation slotted in between village homes and yards filled with seaweed laid out to dry, and there's lots of potential for enjoyable trips on foot and by bicycle or motorbike. Tiny **Nusa Ceningan** is linked to southeast Lembongan by a bridge, but has few sights. **Nusa Penida** is larger and more rugged than Lembongan, but far less developed, making it ripe for a few days' adventurous exploration.

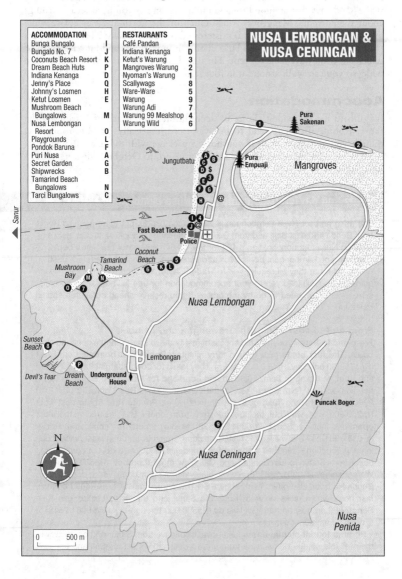

ACCOMMODATION	
Bunga Bungalo	I
Bungalo No. 7	J
Coconuts Beach Resort	K
Dream Beach Huts	P
Indiana Kenanga	D
Jenny's Place	Q
Johnny's Losmen	H
Ketut Losmen	E
Mushroom Beach Bungalows	M
Nusa Lembongan Resort	O
Playgrounds	L
Pondok Baruna	F
Puri Nusa	A
Secret Garden	G
Shipwrecks	B
Tamarind Beach Bungalows	N
Tarci Bungalows	C

RESTAURANTS	
Café Pandan	P
Indiana Kenanga	D
Ketut's Warung	3
Mangroves Warung	2
Nyoman's Warung	1
Scallywags	8
Ware-Ware	5
Warung	9
Warung Adi	7
Warung 99 Mealshop	4
Warung Wild	6

NUSA LEMBONGAN & NUSA CENINGAN

Pura Sakenan

Jungutbatu

Pura Empuaji

Mangroves

Sanur

Fast Boat Tickets

Police

Coconut Beach

Tamarind Beach

Mushroom Bay

Mushroom Beach

Nusa Lembongan

Sunset Beach

Lembongan

Devil's Tear

Dream Beach

Underground House

Puncak Bogor

Nusa Ceningan

N

Nusa Penida

0   500 m

Nusa Lembongan

Despite its growing popularity, **NUSA LEMBONGAN** retains its laidback, village vibe, its small population of just seven thousand concentrated in Jungutbatu in the north and Lembongan in the south. Most visitors stay in **Jungutbatu**, which has plenty of accommodation, while day-trippers flock to **Mushroom Bay**, which is slightly better for swimming. Seaweed farming dominates a lot of the shore, and much of the aquamarine waters too, but there are some pretty white-sand bays that are good for swimming as long as you heed local warnings about the currents. Mangroves fringe much of the north and east coast, while inland the copious intact forest is crisscrossed by sandy tracks. There are no cars (just a few pick-ups) and locals buzz about on motorbikes and bicycles, both of which are widely available for rent. The island is just 4km long and less than 3km wide, so you can **walk** around it in four hours.

Accommodation

Jungutbatu has the widest choice of **accommodation**, much of it fronting the shore. Rooms elsewhere tend to be overpriced, especially on Mushroom Bay, though you get better deals if you book a package with the day-tripping boats listed below. The island gets packed out from April to October, when it's vital to reserve ahead.

Boats and day-cruises to and from Nusa Lembongan

The main port for Nusa Lembongan is **Sanur** (see p.123), but there are also **boats** from Benoa and east Bali, and from Gili Trawangan and Lombok. Note that there's no **ATM** on Nusa Lembongan; see p.124 for the ATMs handiest for the Sanur boats.

Arriving on Lembongan, boats dock at different points along the beach depending on the tide, but they all require you to **wade** ashore. You'll be met by local "beach guides", who will lead you to your accommodation for free (all hotels pay commission), unless you need to go by motorbike. If you reserve ahead hotel staff should meet you.

From and to south Bali, Gili Trawangan and Lombok
From and to Sanur you have the choice of fast boats, a tourist shuttle boat and slow boats. The **fast boats** take around forty minutes. **Public fast boats** are cheapest (Rp175,000 one way, Rp250,000 return). They leave for Jungutbatu at 9am, 12.30pm and 4pm, returning at 8am, 10.30am and 3pm; and for Mushroom Bay at 2.30pm, heading back at 1pm. Buy tickets at the Optasal "Public Boat" office (℡0361/918 9900) on Jalan Hang Tuah near the *Ananda Hotel*. **Private fast boats** cost from Rp250,000 one way but include transfers from south Bali resorts; established operators include Scoot (℡0361/285522, ⊛www.scootcruise.com) and Rocky (℡0361/801 2324, ⊛www.rockyfastcruise.com), which both run at least twice a day in each direction – see their websites for schedules. Scoot also does a combination ticket from Sanur to Lembongan and **Gili Trawangan/Lombok** (Rp600,000); Blue Water Express (℡0361/723479, ⊛www.bluewater-express.com), which departs from Benoa Harbour, also offers Lembongan–Gili Trawangan transfers, as does Perama's fast boat, which picks up from Kuta and Sanur and travels to Lembongan then **Senggigi** (Lombok) and the Gili Islands (Rp500,000 through-ticket; ℡0361/751875, ⊛www.peramatour.com).

Perama tourist shuttle boats (as above) also leave from Sanur and connect with their reliable shuttle bus service from and to destinations across Bali and Lombok

---

Jungutbatu

Bunga Bungalo ☎0817/551826, ⓦwww
.bunga-bungalo.com. Just seven rooms crammed
into a tiny seafront compound at this lively and
popular place. Fan ❷, a/c ❸

Bungalo No. 7 ☎0366/24497, ⓦwww
.bungalo-no7.com. Good-value rooms beside the
beach, some with a/c, hot water and sea view, all
with verandas. The Bali Dive Academy dive centre
is here. Fan ❶, a/c ❹

Coconuts Beach Resort ☎0361/728088,
ⓦwww.coconutbeachresorts.com. Upmarket,
thatched circular bungalows (with fan or a/c) are
ranged up the hillside between Jungutbatu Beach
and tiny Coconut Beach, their huge windows giving
fine panoramas. There are two pools, but it's a stiff
climb from the public areas to the rooms. ❼

🏃 **Indiana Kenanga** ☎0366/24471, ⓦwww
.indiana-kenanga-villas.com. A design-
conscious boutique resort right on the beach, with
cosy, modern decor and original Balinese art.
Standard suites are in private compounds and have
DVDs and wi-fi; family villas sleep seven and come
with a pool and kitchen; there's also one cheaper
room. Has a pool, spa and gastronomic restaurant
(see p.138). Room ❻, suites ❼, villas ❾

Johnny's Losmen The cheapest beds on the
island, in a small plot just back from the beach.
Rooms are basic but tolerable, with fans and cold-
water bathrooms. ❶

Ketut Losmen ☎0813/3784 6555, ⓦwww
.ketutlosmen.net. A dozen well-built, attractive
rooms, a cut above the rest in attention to detail,
set in pretty gardens, and with a small seaside
pool. Some have a/c and hot water. Fan ❸, a/c ❺

Playgrounds ☎0817/474 8427, ⓦwww
.playgroundslembongan.com. The six rooms are set
up on the hillside off the southern end of the bay
and enjoy outstanding sea views (fan rooms are
upstairs and have prime panoramas). Interiors are
comfortable (cold water only) and there's a pool.
Two good-value family villas have their own plunge
pool and kitchenette. Rooms ❻, villas ❼

🏃 **Pondok Baruna** ☎0812/390 0686,
ⓦwww.world-diving.com. Plush, very clean,
a/c "garden" rooms are set round the pool just

(see "Travel Details" on p.142). They run to Jungutbatu (daily at 10.30am, return at
8.30am; 90min; Rp100,000); book one day in advance.

Public slow boats from Sanur are cheap but slow (about 2hr), and can be unnerv-
ingly crowded. Boats to Jungutbatu and Mushroom Bay leave at 8am (Rp60,000) and
there's another boat to Jungutbatu at 10.30am (Rp80,000). Buy tickets from the
Optasal "Public Boat" office, as for the public fast boats, above. The boats **return
from Jungutbatu** at 8am and Mushroom Bay at 7am.

From and to east Bali

You can **charter** a boat for up to six people from **Padang Bai** or **Candi Dasa** to Nusa
Lembongan for about Rp700,000, but choose wisely as waves can be huge.
Returning from Jungutbatu, it's often possible to cadge a lift with the empty
"Vegetable Boat" **to Kusamba** (10am from near the public boat office in Jungutbatu;
40min; Rp50,000); a chartered bemo on to Padang Bai costs about Rp25,000. The
boat takes a maximum of ten people and is not for the faint-hearted: it carries no life
jackets and you'll probably get wet.

Day-cruises

Lots of people just visit Lembongan for the day, on one of the many large-scale
organized **cruises** from south Bali, which all include transfers from your hotel. Some
boats are more luxurious than others but all offer snorkelling, watersports and lunch,
often at one of the huge pontoons moored offshore; most include a village or
mangrove tour of Lembongan as well. Prices start at $70, with discounted accom-
modation packages also available, and can be booked anywhere on Bali. Try the
following **operators**: Bali Hai (ⓦwww.balihaicruises.com); Bounty (ⓦwww
.balibountycruises.com); Island Explorer (ⓦwww.bali-cruise.com); or Sail Sensations
(ⓦwww.bali-sailsensations.com).

inland from the beach; cheaper, old-style fan rooms sit right on the shore and enjoy direct sea views, a bargain for the price. World Diving Lembongan is based here. Book well ahead as it's very popular. Fan ❶, a/c ❹

Puri Nusa ℡0366/24482, ℮purinusa@hotmail .com. A variety of losmen rooms and bungalows, all furnished to a good standard and spread around a big, tidy garden that runs down to the sea. A couple have sea views. Fan ❶, a/c ❹

🏃 **Secret Garden** ℡0813/3809 8815, ⓦwww.secretgardenbungalows.com. Run by an exceptionally welcoming British couple, this is a peaceful and great-value hideaway of nine large bungalows nicely spaced around a beautiful garden, 100m from the beach. Hammocks and movie nights contribute to the relaxed vibe, there's daily yoga and a pool is planned. Big Fish Diving is here. Fan ❶, a/c ❸

Shipwrecks ℡0813/3803 2900, ⓦwww .nusalembongan.com.au. Attractive, tranquil Australian-run retreat of just three large tropical-style villas set around a tranquil garden full of frangipani trees, 100m off the beach. There's a/c and garden bathrooms, wi-fi in the lobby and a pool on the cards. No kids, no smoking and a minimum two-night stay. ❻

Tarci Bungalows ℡0812/390 6300, ℮agustarci@yhoo.co.id. Popular seafront place

with a pool and eleven rooms and bungalows to suit different budgets; many can sleep three. A/c, TV, hot water and bathtubs at the top end. Fan ❶–❸, a/c ❸–❺

The rest of the island

Dream Beach Huts Dream Beach ℡0812/398 3772, ⓦwww.dreambeachlembongan.com. In peaceful isolation above the fantastic white-sand Dream Beach, the rooms and *lumbung*-style thatch-and-wood huts here have bamboo beds, fans and cold-water garden bathrooms. There's a shore-view pool and restaurant. Heed warning signs when swimming in the sea here as the waves can be big and there's an undertow. ❺

Mushroom Beach Bungalows Mushroom Bay ℡0366/24515, ⓦwww.mushroom-lembongan .com. These good-quality rooms are among the cheapest on the beach, in a panoramic location on the headland at the eastern end of Mushroom Bay, just a 2min walk from the island's prettiest beach (see opposite). Has a small pool. Fan ❺, a/c ❻

Nusa Lembongan Resort Mushroom Bay ℡0361/725864, ⓦwww.nusalembonganresort .com. The most luxurious resort on the island has a lovely infinity pool, a pretty garden and a sense of space that is lacking in many of Lembongan's other top-end options. Accommodation is in twelve spacious thatched cottages. ❽

Around the island

It's easy and pleasant to **walk** along the west coast to the best beaches, none of which is more than ninety minutes from Jungutbatu, or make use of the free transport offered by the more isolated restaurants (see p.138). If cycling around the island, set off in a clockwise direction to avoid a killer climb out of Jungutbatu to the south. The road is tarmac most of the way, although very broken in places. **Bikes** and **motorbikes** are best rented through staff at your accommodation and they can also arrange motorbike transport.

Seaweed farming

Seaweed is a source of two lucrative substances: **agar**, a vegetable gel used in cooking, and **carrageenan**, used in cosmetics and foodstuffs. But it's fussy stuff: it can only be cultivated in areas protected from strong currents but needs a flow of water through it. The temperature must not get too high, the salinity needs to be constant and, at low tide, the seaweed must remain covered by water. To **"farm"** seaweed, a bamboo frame is made to support lengths of twine. Farmers tie small pieces of seaweed – both **green** *cotoni* and **red** *spinosum* varieties (*cotoni* produces better-quality carrageenan and fetches at least twice the price) – to the twine, harvesting the long offshoots after 45 days. The seaweed is then dried and compressed into bales; 8kg of wet seaweed reduces to 1kg when dry. Seaweed farming is hard, physical work and the financial rewards are unpredictable: like all raw materials that sell on a world market, seaweed is subject to price fluctuations and market forces way beyond the farmer's control.

Jungutbatu

Strung out along the northwest coast, the village of **JUNGUTBATU** is the main tourist centre and has accommodation and restaurants all along the beachfront. The **beach** is no great shakes for swimming but it's very scenic: the mesmerizingly clear water is filled with wooden outriggers and rectangular seaweed-growing plots, and is perfect for horizon-gazing – Bali's Gunung Agung is easily visible from the southern end.

There are several places to **change money** (at poor rates) but no ATMs; Money-changer Gede, next to *Ketut's Warung*, cashes travellers' cheques and does Visa and MasterCard cash advances (eight percent commission, passport required). The village has several **internet** cafés but no post office, and there's a health centre (*klinik*). For **massages**, try the recommended Sub, at the southern end of the village; Ketut, at *Ketut's Warung*, does **reflexology healing**. The various **ticket offices** for the public boats and the private fast boats are towards the southern end of the beach; Perama is north of *Pondok Baruna*.

The west coast and Mushroom Bay

The best way to get to Mushroom Bay from Jungutbatu is via the **west-coast path**, a gloriously scenic route that can be walked in 45 minutes from *Pondok Baruna*. From the far southern end of Jungutbatu beach take the steps up to the path that runs past *Ware-Ware* restaurant and continues along the coast via *Playgrounds* hotel. A few minutes beyond *Coconuts Beach Resort*, tiny **Coconut Beach** is used by surfers heading for the breaks at Playgrounds and Lacerations. *Warung Wild* sits here alongside the drying seaweed and outriggers and sells drinks and snacks. Back on the path above the bay, continue southwest via exceptional views of the surf breaks, the turquoise water and Gunung Agung on the horizon, plus a burgeoning number of private villas, to rocky and unexceptional **Tamarind Beach**. At the far western end of Tamarind you need to head almost due west through scrub to pick up the path again, indistinct in places, at the top of the rise behind *Tamarind Beach Bungalows*. Within three minutes (150m) you should see a blue arrow marked on the path: follow this down a steep path to the shore to find **Lembongan's prettiest beach**. This beautiful white-sand (nameless) bay is backed by screw palms and usually all but empty of people. It's just north over a narrow promontory from Mushroom Bay and is more easily located when coming from Mushroom Bay, passing through the restaurant at *Mushroom Beach Bungalows* and continuing for a couple of minutes to the blue arrow. The sandy arc of **Mushroom Bay** itself is small, lined with overpriced accommodation, and always crowded with boats and day-trippers. If you ask locally you should be able to find the path to Sunset Beach and its recommended restaurant (see p.138) from Mushroom Bay, but easiest access is by road via Lembongan village (see below).

The north and east coasts

At the **northern tip of the island**, a flat 3km – easily covered by bicycle – from central Jungutbatu, there's good snorkelling, several warung and the chance to explore the extensive mangrove forest that fringes the northeast coast. To get there, follow the road that runs north through Jungutbatu and continue past the unremarkable sea temple, **Pura Sakenan**. At the end of the road, 1km beyond the temple, *Mangroves Warung* is one of several cafés where you can organize a half-hour **mangrove boat trip** through the eerie forest (Rp100,000 for up to four people). Boats are punted by bamboo poles so there's no engine noise to disturb the lizards, crabs and birds that inhabit the muddy forest floor; the trip is best at low tide when the roots are exposed (see p.291). Just in front of the warung there's reef that's good for **snorkelling**; you can rent equipment here and ask about currents.

Depending on the tide you can either swim to the reef, or take a boat to the reefs here or further afield, around Nusa Penida (see p.132).

A fork in the road 200m west of Pura Sakenan takes you along **the east coast**, via **Pura Empuaji** (700m southwest) and its two monumental *ficus* trees; this is the most venerated temple on the island (take a sarong and sash if you want to visit). The road wends its way between mangrove forest and cactus scrub, and the occasional house, and after another 5.5km reaches the turn-off for the yellow bridge across to Nusa Ceningan (see opposite). From here it's another 2km up to Lembongan village, then another 3km back to Jungutbatu.

Lembongan village and the southwest coast

LEMBONGAN, at the top of a steep hill 3km southwest of central Jungutbatu, is the largest village on the island and the location of the **Underground House** (open on request; donation), dug by a local man, Made Byasa, between 1961 and 1976, inspired by part of the *Mahabharata* (see p.378). It consists of several dank rooms, a well and ventilation shafts, and isn't for the claustrophobic.

Follow the main road west through the village to reach a T-junction and signs for Mushroom Bay, 750m down a side road. A left turn here leads 1km to **Dream Beach**, a beautiful little white-sand bay with clear, turquoise water and some dangerous currents: read the warning signs before you go for a dip. There's accommodation and a restaurant here, and it's just a few minutes' walk to dramatic little **Sunset Beach**, the site of *Scallywags* restaurant and pool (see below), but too risky for a swim.

Eating

In addition to the **restaurants** listed, food is served at most places to stay, and there are several very cheap local warung in Jungutbatu village.

Jungutbatu

Indiana Kenanga King-sized daybeds on the shorefront make this the perfect spot to enjoy Lembongan's fabulous sunsets – but such luxury doesn't come cheap: cocktails cost a whopping Rp90,000 (try the Marseille Lembongan, made with vodka, Pernod and fresh strawberries) and main dishes are Rp130,000–250,000. The chef is French and the short, classy gastronomic menu features coquilles St-Jacques and French choux patisserie.

Ketut's Warung 50m inland, signed just south of *Indiana Kenanga*. Homely warung that serves great Thai food, including recommended chicken with cashew nuts, plus pad thai and red and green curries for around Rp35,000.

Nyoman's Warung In a pretty spot overlooking seaweed farms about a 10min walk north up the road from *Puri Nusa*, Nyoman is known for her delicious fish – try her signature grilled jacket fish (*tabasan*; from Rp40,000), a local speciality.

Ware-Ware On a waterside deck with excellent views over seaweed farms and the mainland, this is a good choice at sunset. The fresh seafood is recommended, especially the tuna and *mahi-mahi* fillets (around Rp55,000).

Warung 99 Mealshop Good, inexpensive village-centre warung serving Indonesian and Chinese dishes, including *kolobak* (spicy meat and veg), *nasi campur* and *fu yung hai*, mostly for Rp20,000.

The rest of the island

Café Pandan At *Dream Beach Bungalows* on Dream Beach ☏0812/398 3772. Offers free transport, use of the hotel pool for Rp50,000, and a wide-ranging menu (most mains Rp45,000) encompassing Indonesian, Balinese and Thai curries, *pepes udang* (steamed prawns), baby tuna in spicy sauce and lots of cocktails.

Scallywags Sunset Beach, a 5min walk from Dream Beach ☏0828/9700 5656, Ⓦwww.scallywagsresort.com. Serving some of the most imaginative food on the island, this is an enjoyably sophisticated yet relaxed place to eat. During the day you have use of the sunloungers and pool as long as you spend Rp100,000; in the evening there's freshly barbecued barramundi, lobster and tuna steaks (mains from Rp55,000). Other highlights include four different breads, brandy pork pies, berry crumble, wheatgrass shots and imported wines. SMS or phone for free transport.

Warung Adi Mushroom Bay. The cheapest place to eat in this part of the island offers a small Indonesian and travellers' menu, with *nasi campur* for Rp20,000.

Nusa Ceningan

At the point where the channel between Nusa Lembongan and **NUSA CENINGAN** is narrowest, matching temples face each other across the crystal-clear water and a **bridge** links the islands. You can cycle or ride a motorbike across for a look at this totally rural island, just 4km long by 1km wide, but it's quite a challenge: the road is very rough in places, there are no signs, and gradients are steep. Forested and hilly, the island depends on seaweed farming and lacks swimmable beaches, though there is a famous **surf break**, Ceningan Point. You get great views of the break, plus Lembongan and Bali's southeast coast, from the top of the precipitous **Puncak Bogor** hill (unsigned).

Tourist facilities on Ceningan are few: apart from the overnight homestays that can be organized by the village ecotourism network, JED (☎0361/737447, Ⓦwww.jed.or.id), the only **place to stay** is *Jenny's Place* (☎0812/3627 7650, Ⓔ Paeittreim@yahoo.com), which occupies a magnificently dramatic spot in front of the Ceningan Point surf break. The wooden bungalows have awesome views of Lembongan and Bali from the upstairs bedrooms, plus kitchenettes and modern bathrooms downstairs. There's free use of a motorbike and breakfast is provided, but other **meals** have to be ordered in – your only other alternatives are the couple of warung in the village, about 500m southwest of the bridge.

Nusa Penida

Dominated by a harsh, dry, limestone plateau, with towering sea cliffs in the south, the ruggedly handsome island of **NUSA PENIDA** feels remote and quite different from mainland Bali. It was once used as a penal colony, a sort of Siberia for transgressive Balinese, and is famous as the home of the legendary demon I Macaling, whose beautiful temple, **Pura Dalem Penataran Ped**, is an important pilgrimage site for Hindus from all over Bali. Islanders have their own dialect and many live off seaweed farming and fishing; it's too dry for rice.

Despite offering first-class **diving** (see p.132), some of the most dramatic scenery in Bali, and the chance to see the elusive and endangered **Bali starling**, Nusa Penida has few tourist facilities and gets almost no foreign visitors. The obvious way to see it is on a day-trip from nearby Nusa Lembongan, but there is accommodation in the island's main towns of **Toyapakeh** and **Sampalan**, as well as near the temple in Ped.

Arrival and island transport

Most tourists arrive by chartered boat **from Nusa Lembongan**, pulling in at the village of Toyapakeh, which is separated from Nusa Ceningan by a channel less than 1km wide but over 100m deep in places. Boats depart from *Mangroves Warung* north of Jungutbatu (30min; Rp50,000/person if four people, or Rp300,000 return for the whole boat). There's also a public boat from Jungutbatu to Toyapakeh at 5.30am, which returns at 9.30am (45min). Coming direct **from Bali**, there's a daily public slow boat **from Sanur** to Toyapakeh (8am, returns 7.30am; 2hr 30min; Rp60,000); and **from Padang Bai** to Buyuk Harbour there are fast boats (up to 4 daily, 7am–noon; 45min; Rp25,000) and a RoRo vehicle ferry (leaves 2pm, returns 11.30am; 1hr; Rp18,000). Alternatively you can join a **day-cruise** from Bali with Quicksilver (Ⓦwww.quicksilver-bali.com; $80), which includes watersports off their huge pontoon at Toyapakeh.

Public **bemos** run between Toyapakeh and Sampalan, via Ped, between about 6am and 9am, but the best way to get around Nusa Penida is by **motorbike**.

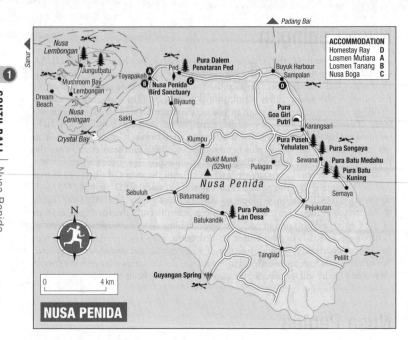

Motorbike drivers/guides wait at Toyapakeh harbour to meet arrivals from Lembongan, or you could call ahead to contact local English teacher and guide Gede Indra (℡0878/6084 8978, ✉indrajuana_putra@yahoo.com). Rp250,000 is a reasonable price for a full day of riding and guiding. You can also rent your own bike here for about Rp100,000 per day, though be warned that the island is a maze of remote lanes and signposts are few.

Around the island

Nusa Penida is roughly 22km long by 16km wide but because of the steep inclines and numerous back roads a full circuit is best spread over two days. If you've only got one, aim for a route that takes in **Pura Dalem Penataran Ped**, **Pura Goa Giri**, a **view** of the south-coast cliffs, and **Crystal Bay**.

Toyapakeh

Boats from Nusa Lembongan dock at **TOYAPAKEH**, whose attractive white-sand beach is mostly taken up by *jukung*, with the monstrous Quicksilver diving pontoon disfiguring the approach. There's nothing particular to see, just a small daily market and a tiny mosque, but there are a couple of places to **stay**. Right by where the boats dock, *Losmen Tanang* (℡0817/976 0575; ❶) has two ultra basic rooms. For something a bit more appealing, walk about 200m north along the beach (left, with your back to the sea) to find *Losmen Mutiara* (℡0819/1620 1753; ❶), which has eleven perfectly acceptable terraced en-suite fan rooms round a garden. (Incidentally, although *Mutiara* is associated with the Czech dive company MM Divers, you're advised to choose one of the established Lembongan dive companies listed on p.132 instead.)

Ped

The village of **PED**, 4km east of Toyapakeh, is famous for its hugely important temple, **Pura Dalem Penataran Ped**, which every day attracts van-loads of worshippers from across Bali, bearing copious offerings. The temple complex is always dressed to receive them, its dazzlingly smooth white limestone walls and fantastic carvings draped in ceremonial cloths of black-and-white *poleng* and gold-brocade *songket*. The temple is regarded as *angker*, a place of evil spirits; it is the home of the dreaded **I Macaling**, also known as **Ratu Gede** and **Jero Gde**, who brings disease, floods and ill fortune to the mainland and requires regular appeasement. There are actually four temples within the compound, one of which is dedicated to I Macaling; another has a dramatic sculpture of the half-fish, half-elephant deity of the sea, Gajah Mina.

In recent years, Ped has also become famous for offering the unique chance to see the rare **Bali starling** (*jalak putih Bali*), or Rothschild's myna (*Leucopsar rothschildi*), in the wild. Thanks to an innovative, community-focused programme run by the Friends of the National Parks Foundation (Ⓦwww.fnpf.org), this endangered, fluffy white bird – Bali's only remaining endemic creature, and the provincial symbol – is now flourishing on Nusa Penida, with a hundred of them micro-chipped and free to roam the island in safety. The easiest place to spot them is at the **Nusa Penida Bird Sanctuary** (daily, dawn to dusk; donation appreciated), on the western edge of Ped, a few hundred metres west of the temple, where they congregate for food; staff will lead you round the small site. The sanctuary also protects the even rarer lesser sulphur-crested cockatoo.

Nusa Boga (Ⓣ0828/367 4049; ●), diagonally across the road from the temple, makes a handy **lunch** stop while you're here, and offers four clean, tiled **rooms** around a garden, should you want to stay.

Sampalan and Pura Goa Giri Putri

SAMPALAN, 4km from Ped on the northeast coast, is the largest town on the island and has a couple of banks (but no foreign-card ATMs), plus a **market** (daily 6–10am) spread out behind the coast, with the bemo terminal in the middle. The nicest **place to stay** on Nusa Penida is across the road from the market: *Homestay Ray* (Ⓣ0366/23597; ●) has nine very clean fan rooms set around a courtyard designed in traditional style with intricately carved pillars and Kamasan paintings on the veranda. For good *nasi goreng* with a fabulous sea view, walk through the market to the sea then turn left to find the tiny **restaurant** *Warung Sri Ganesha*.

It's a spectacular ride south from Sampalan, along a road that hugs the coast and offers fine views of the photogenic patchwork of seaweed-farming plots as well as vistas of Lombok ahead. About 10km south, in the village of **Karangsari**, a steep flight of steps leads up to the limestone bat-cave temple of **Pura Goa Giri Putri** (Rp15,000). Squeeze through the narrow gap in the rock to enter a vast 300m-long cavern housing several small shrines, countless bats and a meditation cave; at the far end you emerge into daylight having walked right through the hill. Balinese people consider this a very powerful spiritual site.

The south coast and Crystal Bay

Turning inland at Sewana (or Suana), you climb dramatically to the central plateau and eventually reach the village of **Batukandik**. The amazing **south coast** of the island is accessible from here, its spectacular limestone cliffs rising sheer out of the ocean. A side road leads 7km south to the edge of the cliffs and a precipitous 200m descent to the **Guyangan freshwater spring** at their base. This is typical of the whole southern coast of the island; there are several spots where equally hairy descents to the sea are possible. Beyond Batukandik, turn left at Batumadeg to **Sebuluh**, where the road ends 200m beyond the village green and numerous paths run through the village to the cliffs. There are two **temples** here, one on a promontory linked to the mainland by an exposed ridge, and the other at the bottom of a path that winds down the cliff to a freshwater spring.

Returning to Batumadeg, the road skirts close to the summit of **Bukit Mundi**, at 529m the highest point on the island and crowned with dysfunctional wind turbines, then descends from the plateau, dropping through the village of Klumpu and on to **Sakti**. From here it's 3km southwest down a very steep hill to **Crystal Bay**, a pretty, greyish-sand beach with outstandingly clear water, good snorkelling and an offshore rock with a hole that's a popular dive site (see p.132). If you come in the afternoon, though, you'll likely have the water to yourself. There's a tiny stall selling drinks and snacks but no snorkel rental. From Crystal Bay it's 9km back to Toyapakeh.

Travel details

Bemos and public buses

It's almost impossible to give the frequency with which bemos and public buses run: see Basics, p.30, for details. Journey times given are the minimum you can expect. Only the direct bemo and bus routes are listed; for longer journeys you'll have to go via one of Denpasar's four main bemo terminals (full details on p.113).

Denpasar (Batubulan terminal) See p.188.
Denpasar (Kereneng terminal) to: Sanur (15–25min).
Denpasar (Tegal terminal) to: Jimbaran (40min); Kuta (25min); Ngurah Rai Airport (35min); Nusa Dua (Bali Collection; 35min); Sanur (25min).
Denpasar (Ubung terminal) See p.300.
Denpasar (Wangaya terminal) to: Sangeh Monkey Forest (45min).
Jimbaran to: Denpasar (Tegal terminal; 40min); Kuta (15min); Ngurah Rai Airport (10min).
Kuta to: Denpasar (Tegal terminal; 25min); Jimbaran (15min); Ngurah Rai Airport (10min); Nusa Dua (Bali Collection; 20min).
Ngurah Rai Airport to: Denpasar (Tegal terminal; 35min); Jimbaran (10min); Kuta (10min); Nusa Dua (Bali Collection; 20min).
Nusa Dua (Bali Collection) to: Denpasar (Batubulan terminal; 1hr); Denpasar (Tegal terminal; 35min); Kuta (20min); Ngurah Rai Airport (20min).
Sanur to: Denpasar (Kereneng terminal; 15–25min); Denpasar (Tegal terminal; 25min).

Perama shuttle buses

Kuta to: Bedugul (daily; 2hr 30min–3hr); Candi Dasa (3 daily; 3hr); Gili Islands (daily; 9hr 30min); Kintamani (daily; 2hr 30min); Lovina (daily; 4hr); Nusa Lembongan (daily; 2hr 30min); Padang Bai (3 daily; 2hr 30min); Sanur (4 daily; 30min); Senggigi (Lombok; 2 daily; 9hr); Ubud (4 daily; 1hr–1hr 30min).

Sanur to: Bedugul (daily; 2hr–2hr 30min); Candi Dasa (3 daily; 2hr–2hr 30min); Gili Islands (daily; 9hr); Kintamani (daily; 2hr 15min); Kuta/Ngurah Rai Airport (5 daily; 30min–1hr); Lovina (daily; 2hr 30min–3hr); Padang Bai (3 daily; 1hr 30min–2hr); Senggigi (Lombok; 2 daily; 8hr 30min); Ubud (4 daily; 30min–1hr).

Boats

Nusa Lembongan (Jungutbatu) to: Gili Trawangan (3 daily; 1hr–3hr 15min); Kusamba (daily; 40min); Nusa Penida (Toyapakeh; daily; 45min); Sanur (at least 10 daily; 40min–2hr); Senggigi (Lombok; daily; 1hr 45min); Teluk Kodek (Lombok; daily; 2hr).
Nusa Lembongan (Mushroom Bay) to: Sanur (1–3 daily; 40min–2hr).
Nusa Penida (Buyuk Harbour) to: Padang Bai (at least 2 daily; 45min–1hr).
Nusa Penida (Toyapakeh) to: Nusa Lembongan (Jungutbatu; daily; 45min); Sanur (daily; 2hr 30min).
Sanur to: Nusa Lembongan (Jungutbatu; at least 10 daily; 40min–2hr); Nusa Lembongan (Mushroom Bay; 1–3 daily; 40min–2hr).

Domestic flights

All flights depart at least once a day unless otherwise stated.
Denpasar (Ngurah Rai Airport) to: Bima (Sumbawa; 1hr 15min); Ende (Flores; 2hr); Jakarta (Java; 1hr 40min); Kupang (West Timor; 1hr 40min); Labuanbajo (Flores; 2hr 20min); Makassar (Sulawesi; 1hr 10min); Mataram (Lombok; 30min); Maumere (Flores; 2hr 20min); Ruteng (Flores; 3 weekly; 45min); Sumbawa Besar (Sumbawa; 1hr); Surabaya (Java; 45min); Tambolaka (Sumba; 5 weekly; 1hr 15min); Waingapu (Sumba; 3 weekly; 1hr 10min); Yogyakarta (Java; 1hr 10min).

Ubud and around

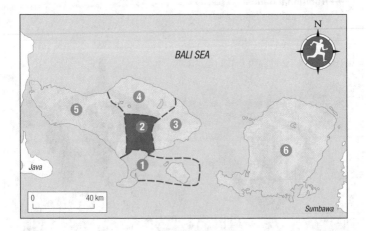

CHAPTER 2 # Highlights

✳ **Bali Bird Park** A vast and beautifully landscaped aviary, with elusive Bali starlings in residence. See p.148

✳ **A walk through the rice paddies** Classic vistas of emerald terraces and coconut groves, framed by distant volcanoes. See p.165

✳ **Neka Art Museum, Ubud** The finest collection of Balinese paintings on the island. See p.166

✳ **Traditional dance performances** Gods and demons flirt and fight by torchlight. See p.177

✳ **Alternative therapies** Take up yoga, visit a local healer, have a massage. See p.179

✳ **Cultural classes** Return home with a new skill in batik painting, silversmithing or Balinese cookery. See p.181

✳ **Gunung Kawi** Impressive eleventh-century rock-cut "tombs" in the valley of the sacred Pakrisan River. See p.187

▲ Yoga overlooking the Ubud paddyfields

Ubud and around

T he inland town of **Ubud** and its surrounding area form Bali's cultural heartland, home to a huge number of temples, museums and art galleries, where Balinese dance shows are staged nightly, a wealth of craft studios provide absorbing shopping, and traditional ceremonies and rituals are observed daily. Once away from the main thoroughfares, Ubud's lovely location is apparent, set amid lush, terraced paddies offering plenty of scope for hikes and bicycle rides, many of them with fine views up to the central mountains. The route to Ubud **north of Denpasar** connects a string of craft-producing towns where you can watch artisans at work and browse their wares. You'll need to venture out to the villages around Ubud, however, for a sense of old-fashioned Bali – to the classic settlements of **Penestanan** and **Peliatan**, for example, or to **Pejeng**, which still boasts relics from the Bronze Age.

Ubud lies within the boundaries of **Gianyar district**, formerly an ancient kingdom. (Gianyar itself, 10km east of Ubud, lies on the main route into east Bali and is described in Chapter 3, as are all the villages east of the T-junction at Sakah.) Roads around Ubud tend to run north–south down river valleys, making it difficult in places to travel east–west; this chapter reflects that restriction.

North of Denpasar

The stretch of road running 13km **north of Denpasar** to Ubud links a string of arts- and crafts-producing towns, all with long histories of artistic activity: Mas, for example, is famed for **woodcarvings**, Celuk for **silverwork**, and Batubulan for **stone sculptures**. In addition, there are several other pleasantly rural and peaceful routes northwards that take in some of the area's main attractions, such as the **Bali Bird Park** and **Bali Reptile Park** outside Batubulan, **The Green School** at Sibang Kaja and the **Putrawan Museum of Art** north of Penatih.

Batubulan and around

Barely distinguishable from the northeastern suburbs of Denpasar, **BATUBULAN** is the capital's terminal for public transport heading east and northeast, the home of famous Barong **dance troupes**, and respected across the island for its **stone-carvers**. There's also a **bird park** and a **reptile park** here. The town is strung out

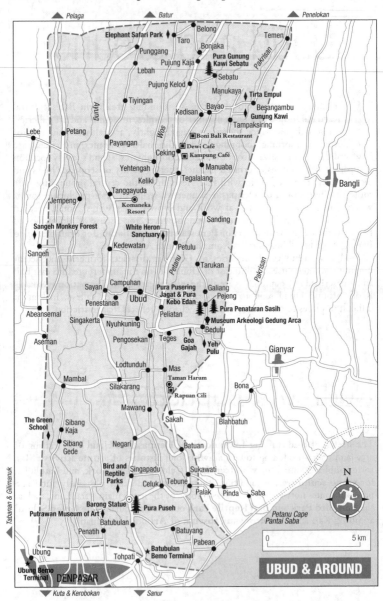

UBUD & AROUND

Carved in stone: for gods, rajas and tourists

The traditional function of **stonecarved statues and reliefs** was to entice and entertain the gods and to ward off undesirable spirits and evil forces. The **temples** in south Bali generally do this in a restrained way, being built mainly from red brick with just a few flourishes of carved volcanic tuff or *paras* (though Batubulan's Pura Puseh is an exception), but the northern temples, which are often built entirely from the easy-to-carve *paras*, are a riot of vivacious curlicues. Outstanding northern examples include the Pura Dalem in Jagaraga, Pura Beji and the Pura Dalem in Sangsit and, most famously, Pura Meduwe Karang at Kubutambahan. In the east, Bangli's Pura Kehen is not to be missed.

Rajas and high-ranking nobles also commissioned fantastic carvings for their **palaces** (*puri*). Few outlasted the early twentieth-century battles with the Dutch, but one notable survivor is the Puri Saren Agung in Ubud, the work of Bali's most skilful stonecarver, **I Gusti Nyoman Lempad** (see p.164). These days, **hotels** are the modern *puri*, and many of the older, grander ones were built in the Bali-baroque *puri-pura* style, with plenty of exuberant stone-carved embellishments. **Gateways** normally feature the most elaborate carvings, in keeping with their function as both a practical and symbolic demarcation between the outer and the inner world, whether they're leading to the inner temple courtyard or giving access to palace compounds or hotels.

Sculptures of *raksasa* giants often guard temple and hotel gates, and most other freestanding stonecarvings destined for homes and gardens in Bali and abroad still take their inspiration from traditional subjects, including Hindu deities and mythological characters and creatures. The vast majority are made in the workshops of **Batubulan**, which is the best place to buy small or large sculptures.

over 3km along the main road, bound by the bemo/bus station in the south and the huge **Barong statue** at the Singapadu/Celuk junction in the north.

Roadsides throughout Batubulan are crowded with ranks of **stone statues** in front of dozens of workshops and galleries. Most of these shops deal in a range of images and stone types (see the colour section, *The Crafts of Bali and Lombok*, for a guide). Some sell carvings imported from Java, where much of the stone now originates, and most also deal in cheaper, mass-produced artworks that are moulded (rather than carved) from lava-stone "concrete"; see Basics, p.51, for details.

Pura Puseh

As you'd expect in a town so renowned for stonecarving, the main temple, **Pura Puseh**, is exuberantly decorated. Its unusual design features a five-tiered gateway tower inspired by Indian religious architecture, as well as a number of Buddha images not normally associated with Bali's Hindu temples. The rest of the iconography, however, is characteristically and flamboyantly Balinese: a grimacing Bhoma head overlooks the main gateway and, to his right, the god Wisnu poses astride a bull; to the right of him, Siwa stands ankle-deep in skulls and wears a string of them around his neck. Pura Puseh is 250m east off the main road, from a signed junction about 250m south of the Barong statue.

Traditional dance shows

The spectacular **Barong dance**, in which the lion-like Barong Ket is pitted against the widow-witch Rangda, is performed for tourists at various venues around Batubulan (daily 9.30–10.30am; Rp80,000) including the stage next to Pura Puseh and the Denjulan Barong and Kris stage, 300m south down the main

Denpasar road from the Pura Puseh junction. Both stages are served by Ubud–Batubulan bemos. Additionally, in the evenings, there's a double bill of the **Kecak** and the **Fire Dance** (daily 6.30–7.30pm; Rp80,000; Ⓦwww.sahadewabali.com) at the Barong Sahadewa stage on Jalan SMKI, signed off the main road about 500m south of the Pura Puseh junction. If you're looking for good, cheap food after the show, head to Batubulan's bemo terminal, which is transformed into a **night market** after sundown.

Bali Bird Park and Bali Reptile Park

Both the Bali Bird Park and the neighbouring Bali Reptile Park (not to be confused with the inferior reptile park in Mengwi) are great fun. The parks are about 3.5km northwest of Batubulan bemo terminal. All bemos or buses between Batubulan and Ubud or Gianyar can drop you at the Singapadu/Celuk intersection from where it's about 400m west.

Home to some 250 species of mostly Indonesian birds, the **Bali Bird Park** (Taman Burung; daily 9am–5.30pm; joint ticket with Reptile Park $25.85, children $12.92; Ⓦwww.bali-bird-park.com) is beautifully landscaped around enormous aviaries. Highlights include birds of paradise, bright scarlet egrets, the rhino hornbill and iridescent blue Javanese kingfishers. And you shouldn't miss the severely endangered Bali starling, Bali's only endemic bird (see p.141 for more).

The highlights at the **Bali Reptile Park** (same hours and ticket) include the green tree pit viper, which is very common in Bali, and very dangerous, and the astonishing 8m-long reticulated python, thought to be the largest python in captivity in the world. There's also a Komodo dragon and visitors are invited to cuddle up to one of the park's scaly green iguanas.

Putrawan Museum of Art

East of the main road to Ubud, about 2km from Batubulan as the crow flies (though more than 4km by road), the **Putrawan Museum of Art**, also known as **PUMA** (Mon–Sat 9am–5pm, Sun noon–5pm; $3; Ⓦwww.museumpuma.com) is a remarkable, largely ignored, collection of sculpture from across Indonesia including works from Flores, Nias, Kalimantan and Sumba, supplemented by jewellery and other artefacts. The *ana deo*, ancestral figures from Flores, and *tau tau*, effigies of the dead, from Sulawesi are especially compelling. Given that tourist shops are awash with reproductions of these, this is a fabulous chance to see the real thing. The museum is situated in the grounds of the *Alam Puri Resort*, about 3km north of Denpasar on the small road through the village of Penatih. If you haven't got your own transport, a taxi from Denpasar is the easiest way to get here.

Singapadu and the back roads to Ubud

The main road from Denpasar divides at Batubulan's Barong statue roundabout, the principal artery and bemo routes veering right (east) to Celuk (see p.150), and the left-hand (north) prong narrowing into a scenic **back road**, which cuts through a series of traditional villages as far as Sayan, a few kilometres west of Ubud, before continuing to Payangan and eventually to Kintamani.

Just over 1km north of the T-junction, you'll pass through the charming village of **SINGAPADU**, a classic central-Bali settlement of house and temple compounds behind low walls. Some of Bali's most expert **mask-carvers** come from this village (see box below), but as most work only on commissions from temples and dance troupes, there's no obvious commercial face to this local industry.

Some 13km north of Singapadu the road runs through the village of **Sayan**, located in the spectacular Ayung river valley, site of several top-flight hotels (see Ubud accommodation, p.159). Ubud is just 3km east from Sayan, via Penestanan and Campuhan.

The Green School

On a parallel road north from Denpasar at Sibang Kaja, **The Green School** (tours 3pm Mon & Wed, book in advance; Rp100,000 suggested donation; ℡0361/469875, ⓦwww.greenschool.org) makes a fascinating excursion. Opened in 2008 by John and Cynthia Hardy, owners of a successful jewellery business and Bali residents for more than thirty years, the aim is to educate pupils (aged 3–17) in emotional, spiritual and environmental issues alongside the more traditional subjects. Interesting from an **educational** point of view, the school is also fabulous architecturally as it consists entirely of open-sided **bamboo structures**; the main bridge and multistorey Heart of School are quite simply works of art. It is accessible by motorcycles or bicycle (via Silakarang and Mambal Market), about 13km from Ubud. Sibang Kaja is about 8km north of Ubung terminal in Denpasar, and bemos from there to Mambal Market pass through the village, though it's another couple of kilometres to the school from the main road. A taxi from Denpasar is also an option.

Masks

Carved wooden **masks** play a crucial role in traditional Balinese dance-dramas. Many are treated as sacred objects, wrapped in holy cloth and stored in the temple when not being used, and given offerings before every public appearance. There's even an annual festival day for all masks and puppets, called Tumpek Wayang, at which actors and mask-makers honour their masks with offerings. The main centres of mask-making on Bali are **Singapadu** and **Mas**. Such is the power generated by certain masks that some mask-makers enter a trance while working.

Traditional masks fall into three categories: human, animal and supernatural. Most **human** masks are made for performances of the *Topeng*, literally "Masked Drama" (see p.381), while **animal** masks are generally inspired by characters from the Hindu epic the *Ramayana*. Most sacred of all are the fantastical **Barong** and **Rangda** masks, worn in many dramas by the **mythical creatures** representing the forces of good and evil.

The main road to Ubud

All the towns described below lie on the main **bemo route** between Denpasar's Batubulan terminal and Ubud. With private transport they are easily visited on a day-trip from Ubud or from the southern resorts; access from Sanur is particularly easy, with Batubulan less than 10km from its northern outskirts.

Celuk

Immediately east of Batubulan is **CELUK**. Known as the "silver village", it is a major centre for **jewellery** production, and the silversmiths welcome both retail and wholesale customers – though designs are often less innovative than in Kuta's shops. Many of the outlets have workshops or factories where visitors can watch the silversmiths at work. The smaller, lower-key Celuk outlets are along Jalan Jagaraga (a back road to Singapadu), which runs north from the western end of the main road, Jalan Raya; among dozens of possibilities, you could try family-run Ketut Sunaka at no. 28. In the centre of the village on Jalan Raya it's impossible to miss the monolithic frontage of Angel to Angel, decorated with cavorting white figures (daily 8am–6pm; ☎0361/295999, ⓦwww.angeltoangel.net). The inside of the showroom, and the jewellery on sale there, are equally eye-catching. Batubulan–Ubud **bemos** pass through Celuk, but the shops and workshops are spread out over a 3km stretch.

Sukawati

The lively market town of **SUKAWATI**, 4km east of Celuk, is a major arts-and-crafts shopping destination. It's convenient for public transport as Ubud–Batubulan **bemos** stop in front of the town's **art market** (*pasar seni*), which trades every day from dawn till dusk inside a traditional two-storey building on the main road, Jalan Raya Sukawati. Here you'll find a tantalizing array of artefacts, paintings, fabrics, clothing and basketware, piled high on stalls that are crammed together. The scrum, and parking, are so bad that a second market, **Pasar Seni Guwang**, operates about a kilometre to the south offering the same range of stuff but in slightly less frenetic surroundings.

Sukawati is also famous for its *wayang kulit*, or **shadow-puppetry**, a traditional form of entertainment that's still popular across the island. The puppets (*wayang*) are made out of animal hide, perforated to let the light shine through in intricate patterns, and designed to traditional profiles that are instantly recognizable to a Balinese audience. To visit the workshops inside the homes of the makers look out for signs on Jalan Padma (the road that runs east off Jalan Raya, one block south of the *pasar seni*) and Jalan Yudisthira, which runs parallel to Jalan Raya a few hundred metres to the east.

There are several cheap **warung** on Jalan Raya Sukawati, including the tiny *Warung Vegetarian Karuna Vittala*, about 1km north of the Pasar Seni on the east side of the road.

Batuan

Northern Sukawati merges into southern **BATUAN**, another ribbon-like roadside development, which was the original home of the **Batuan style of painting** (see box, p.168, for more about this style) and is now a commercial centre for all styles of Balinese painting.

Batuan is dominated by large **galleries** lining the main road, while smaller studios are tucked away in the traditional neighbourhoods to the west; look out for "painter" signboards above their gateways. On the west side of the main road, the **I Wayan Bendi Gallery**, named after the most famous exponent of the Batuan style of painting, displays some of the great man's work, while the sprawling **Dewa Putu Toris**, another large commercial enterprise, is also worth a visit; it's located 250m west off the southern end of the main road, in the *banjar* of Tengah – turn west at the *raksasa* (demon-giant) statue and follow the signs. Just before the gallery you'll pass Batuan's main temple, **Pura Desa–Pura Puseh** (dawn to dusk; donation), graced with appropriately elaborate gold-painted woodwork.

At the northern limit of Batuan, a plump stone statue of a well-fed baby Brahma (officially known as Brahma Rare and unofficially as the **Fat Baby statue**) marks the Sakah turn-off to Blahbatuh and points east (see p.196), while the main road continues north.

Mas

Long established as a major **woodcarving** centre as well as for traditional *topeng* and *wayang wong* masks, **MAS** is a rewarding place both to browse and to buy. However, be warned that it stretches 5km from end to end and its reputation means that prices are high.

The best place to start is the gallery and home of one of Bali's most famous woodcarving families, the **Njana Tilem Gallery** (daily 9am–5pm; ℡0361/975099, Ⓦwww.tilem.com), approximately halfway along the Mas–Ubud road, about 2km north of the baby Brahma statue. It displays the work of **Ida Bagus Nyana** (also spelt Njana) and his son, **Ida Bagus Tilem**; see the box below for more about the artists, whose descendants still run the workshop, shop and gallery displaying some of their finest originals. The quality and craftsmanship here is breathtaking. Once you've seen the best, you're ready to browse the street, but be aware you'll need to bargain hard.

The **Setia Darma House of Masks and Puppets** (Ⓦwww.setiadarma.org) on Jalan Br Tegan Bingin, to the east of the village on the way to Tengkulak, houses a

---

The woodcarvers of Mas

Woodcarving, like all the arts in Bali, was traditionally used only to decorate temples and palaces, but the early twentieth century saw a growing interest in **secular subjects** and a rise in creativity. Artists began to court the burgeoning tourist market with carvings of nudes, lifelike animals and witty portraits, and a whole new genre evolved in just a few years.

By the mid-1930s, however, creativity and standards were slipping, so a group of influential artists and collectors established the **Pita Maha** foundation to encourage Bali's best carvers to be more experimental. One of these carvers was **Ida Bagus Nyana**, from the village of Mas, who from the 1930s to the 1960s produced works in a range of innovative styles, including abstract elongated human figures, erotic compositions of entwined limbs, and smooth, rounded portraits of voluptuously fat men and women. His son, **Ida Bagus Tilem**, was particularly famous for his highly expressive pieces fashioned from contorted roots and twisted branches. Works by both artists are on show at the Njana Tilem Gallery in Mas (see above). The Jati artist **I Nyoman Cokot** developed a "free-form" style that turned monstrous branches into weird, otherworldly creatures, while his son, **Ketut Nongos**, lets his supernatural beings emerge from the contours of weatherworn logs and gnarled trunks.

The legacy of these trailblazers can be seen in almost every souvenir shop in Bali, many of which sell goods that suffer from the same lowering of artistic standards that those artists sought to combat. Few **contemporary woodcarvers** have attained the same status as the stars of the Pita Maha.

huge collection of more than 1200 masks and 4700 puppets from around the world, with plenty from Bali and Indonesia, including a fine array of *topeng* masks and *wayang kulit* puppets. There's not enough space for the whole collection to be displayed but a good selection is on show in the glorious antique houses from Java that comprise the museum. The only feasible way to get here is with your own transport; it's about a 5km cycle ride from the bottom of Jalan Monkey Forest in Ubud.

Mas itself is served by all Ubud–Batubulan **bemos**, which zip through the village and will stop anywhere on request. *Taman Harum Cottages*, at the southern end of Mas, is a charming place to **stay** and is reviewed on p.160. Non-guests are welcome to eat at its **restaurant**, or you could try *Rapuan Cili* (daily 8am–6pm), which overlooks local ricefields; to find it, continue beyond *Taman Harum* for 500m, then follow the signs 300m east down a side road.

Museum Rudana, Teges

The chief reason to visit the village of **TEGES**, sandwiched between Mas to the south and Peliatan to the north, is to see the contemporary Balinese paintings at the **Museum Rudana** (Mon–Sat 9am–5pm, Sun noon–5pm; Rp20,000; Ⓦwww .museumrudana.com). The exhibitions here change, and do not always focus exclusively on modern art, but the museum's core collection includes plenty of works by the big hitters of the contemporary scene. They include **Nyoman Gunarsa** (see p.202), **Made Budhiana** and **Made Wianta**, all of whom are associated with the influential Sanggar Dewata Indonesia style (see the box on p.168 for more on this). Museum Rudana is 800m north of the Nyana Tilem Gallery in Mas and about 1.5km south of the junction with Jalan Peliatan; from central Ubud, it's a ten-minute ride on the Batubulan bemo, or an hour's walk.

Ubud

Ever since the German artist Walter Spies arrived here in 1928, **UBUD** has been a magnet for any tourist with the slightest curiosity about Balinese arts and traditions. It is now a fully fledged resort, visited by nearly every holidaymaker on the island, even if only as part of a day-trip.

Although it's fashionable to characterize Ubud as the "real" Bali, especially in contrast with Kuta, it bears little resemblance to a typical Balinese town. Organic cafés, riverside bungalows and craft shops crowd its centre, chic expat homes and international hotels occupy some of the most panoramic locations, and side streets are dotted with spas and alternative treatment centres. It even hosts an annual literary **festival**, the Ubud Writers and Readers Festival (Ⓦwww.ubudwriters festival.com), every October, and the Bali Spirit Festival of world music, dance and yoga every March (Ⓦwww.balispiritfestival.com). There is major development along the central thoroughfare, Jalan Wanara Wana, known to everyone by its unofficial name of **Jalan Monkey Forest** – a kilometre-long street of hotels, restaurants, tour agencies and souvenir shops – and the core village has expanded to take in the neighbouring hamlets of **Campuhan**, **Penestanan**, **Sanggingan**, **Nyuhkuning**, **Padang Tegal**, **Pengosekan** and **Peliatan**. That said, traditional practices are still fundamental to daily life in Ubud and the atmosphere is an appealing blend of ethnic integrity and tourist-friendly comforts. The local people really do still paint, carve, dance and make music, and hardly a day goes by without some kind of religious festival in the area. Appropriately, Ubud is now a recognized centre of **spiritual tourism**, a place where visitors can experience indigenous healing practices as well as any number of imported therapies.

The surrounding countryside and traditional hamlets give ample opportunity for exploration on foot or by bike, and **shopping** is a major pastime too, with Balinese carvers and painters selling their wares alongside expat fashion designers and artists. Ubud's **restaurants** and **accommodation** also set the town apart: imaginative menus are the norm here (with vegetarians well catered for), and hotels and homestays tend to be small and charming. Linger for a few days, preferably in family-run accommodation, and you'll get an intriguing glimpse of the daily rhythms of traditional Bali. In fact, Ubud is a convenient base or stopover on any trip: the volcanic peak of Gunung Batur is just 40km north; local tour operators offer sunrise treks up Gunung Agung; and it takes less than two hours on a tourist shuttle bus or bemo to reach the east-coast beach of Candi Dasa.

Some history

Ubud's emphasis on the arts really evolved at the beginning of the twentieth century: before that time its energy had been concentrated on fighting other Balinese kingdoms and then the Dutch. In 1900 the Ubud court was obliged to join its neighbour, the Gianyar royal family, in asking for the protection of the Netherlands Indies government against other land-hungry rajas. As a Dutch protectorate with no more wars to fight, the Sukawati family and the people of Ubud were free to follow artistic and musical pursuits. **Cokorda Gede Agung Sukawati** (1910–78) cultivated the arts, and actively encouraged foreign artists to live in his district. The most significant of these was the artist and musician **Walter Spies**, who established himself in the hamlet of Campuhan in 1928. Over the next nine years, Spies introduced new ideas to Ubud's already vibrant **artistic community**. A crowd of other Western intellectuals followed in his wake, including the Dutch artist Rudolph Bonnet and the American musician Colin McPhee, who between them injected a new vigour into the region's arts and crafts, which have thrived ever since.

Arrival and information

Perama runs several daily **shuttle-bus** services to Ubud from all the major tourist centres on Bali and Lombok. Their Ubud terminus is inconveniently located at the southern end of Jalan Hanoman in Padang Tegal, about 750m from the southern end of Jalan Monkey Forest, and 2.5km from the central market. There's no local bemo or taxi service from here; you can either pay an extra Rp10,000 for the Perama drop-off service or you can take your chances with touts offering free transport to whichever accommodation they are promoting. Other shuttle-bus operators are more likely to make more central drops (some even offer a door-to-door service), but check this before booking.

All public **bemos** terminate in front of Ubud's central market. If coming from Batubulan (Denpasar) you can alight in **Peliatan** en route; if heading for **Campuhan**, **Sanggingan** or **Penestanan**, you can connect on to a west-bound service at the market (see "Moving on", p.156). For **Nyuhkuning**, you'll either have to walk from the market (about 30min) or negotiate a ride with a transport tout.

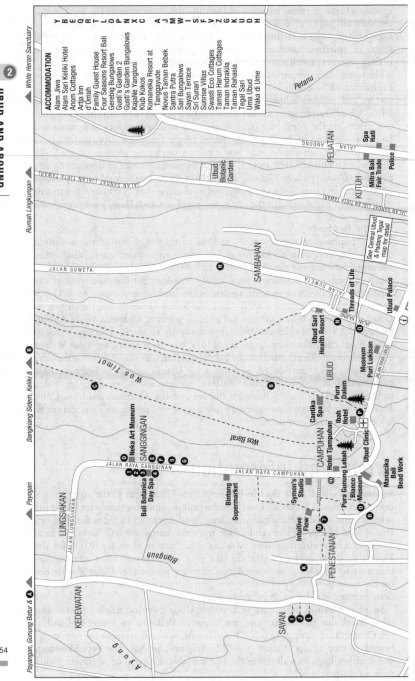

ACCOMMODATION

Alam Jiwa	Y
Alam Sari Keliki Hotel	B
Anom Cottages	E
Arjia Inn	Q
d'Omah	R
Family Guest House	T
Four Seasons Resort Bali	L
Gerebig Bungalows	O
Gusti's Garden 2	P
Gusti's Garden Bungalows	N
KajaNe Yangloni	X
Klub Kokos	C
Komaneka Resort at Tanggayude	A
Novus Taman Bebek	J
Santra Putra	M
Sari Bungalows	W
Sayan Terrace	I
Sri Sunari	S
Sunrise Villas	F
Swasti Eco Cottages	V
Taman Harum Cottages	Z
Taman Indrakila	G
Taman Rahasia	K
Tegal Sari	U
Uma Ubud	D
Waka di Ume	H

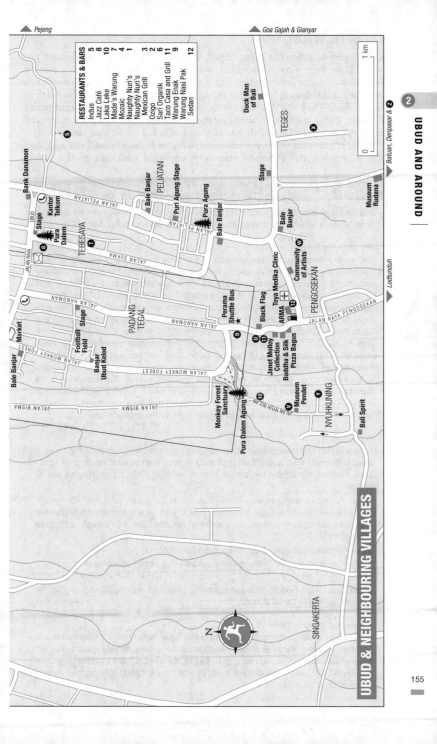

UBUD & NEIGHBOURING VILLAGES

RESTAURANTS & BARS

Indus	5
Jazz Café	8
Laka Leke	10
Made's Warung	7
Mozaic	4
Naughty Nuri's	1
Naughty Nuri's Mexican Grill	3
Ozigo	2
Sari Organik	6
Taco Casa and Grill	11
Warung Enak	9
Warung Nasi Pak Sedan	12

Information

Ubud's **tourist office** (daily 8am–8pm; ☎0361/973285) is centrally located just west of the Jalan Raya Ubud/Jalan Monkey Forest intersection. Staff provide schedules of dance performances and festivals, sell tickets for dance shows, run inexpensive day-trips to local sights and sell shuttle-bus tickets for Perama and their competitors. They also dish out copies of the excellent free **Ubud Community booklet**. Other useful publications are the free *Ubud Life* (every three months) and the glossy quarterly *The Bud* (free in selected hotels and restaurants; also on sale).

If you're planning to do any serious walking or cycling around the area, buy the worthwhile *Bali Pathfinder* **map** from any local bookstore or the widely

---

Moving on from Ubud

Numerous **shuttle buses** run out of Ubud every day to destinations all over Bali, and there's also a cheaper but more time-consuming network of public **bemos**.

By shuttle bus

Bali's ubiquitous **shuttle-bus** operator, Perama, is the longest-running and most reliable transport provider out of Ubud and serves all major tourist destinations, including the airport. **Perama**'s head office is inconveniently located in Padang Tegal at the far southern end of Jalan Hanoman (daily 7am–10pm; ☎0361/973316, ⓦwww .peramatour.com), but the buses do pick-ups from central Ubud's main thorough-fares for an extra Rp10,000 and tickets are also available from the tourist office and some travel agencies. Sample fares include Rp50,000 to Kuta, Rp100,000 to Lovina and Rp350,000 to the Gili Islands (including Perama boat transfer). See "Travel details", p.188, for a full list of Perama destinations and frequencies. Other shuttle-bus services come and go, but may offer more convenient schedules: the tourist office keeps an up-to-date list of operators and sells tickets. The alternative is the transfer service offered by transport touts and some losmen and hotels. For Pemuteran, Gilimanuk and other parts of **northwest Bali**, take a shuttle bus to Lovina and then change on to a westbound bemo for the last coastal stretch.

By bemo

Only a limited number of direct **bemo** services run from Ubud, normally departing at least half-hourly from about 6am until around 2pm, then at least hourly until about 5pm. They all leave from the central market on Jalan Raya Ubud. **Routes** are as follows:

Ubud–Peliatan–Mas–Sukawati–Celuk–**Batubulan**/Denpasar (chocolate-brown or light-blue bemos). Change in Batubulan (see p.148) for services across **Denpasar** and convoluted connections to **southern resorts**, the **southwest** and **Java** (see p.116).

Ubud–Tegalalang–Pujung–**Kintamani** (brown bemos).

Ubud–Campuhan–Neka Museum–Kedewatan–Payangan–**Kintamani** (brown or bright-blue bemos).

Ubud–Goa Gajah–Bedulu–**Gianyar** (turquoise or orange bemos). Change in Gianyar for connections to **Candi Dasa**.

Boat and airline tickets

Many Ubud travel agents sell Perama **bus and boat tickets** for the Gili Islands and Lombok, as well as international and domestic **airline tickets** (see p.182 for recommendations). The easiest way to **get to the airport** from Ubud is by shuttle bus (Rp50,000/person); transport touts charge about Rp200,000 per car. Airport information is on p.78.

available *Bali Street Atlas* (Periplus). Another good investment, though less widely available, is the slim volume, *Bali Bird Walks*, written by the local expat ornithologist Victor Mason.

Local transport and tours

The most enjoyable way of seeing Ubud and its immediate environs is **on foot** via the tracks through the rice paddies and the narrow *gang* that weave through the more traditional *banjar*.

Bicycles are an excellent way to get around, too, if you avoid the busier roads; they can be rented from outlets along Jalan Raya Ubud, Jalan Monkey Forest and Jalan Hanoman (from Rp20,000/day). There are countless possibilities for interesting **bike rides** in the area.

There are no metered **taxis** in Ubud, so you have to bargain with the **transport touts** who hang around on every corner; typically, you can expect to pay around Rp25,000 between the market and Nyuhkuning or Sanggingan in a car, half this on a motorbike. Most outlying hotels provide free transport in and out of central Ubud.

It's also possible to use the public **bemos** for certain short hops (generally charged at Rp5000): to get to the Neka Art Museum, flag down any bemo heading west; for Pengosekan or Peliatan take any bemo heading for Batubulan; and for Petulu use the orange bemos to Pujung or the brown bemos to Tegalalang and Kintamani.

Guided walks, treks and other activities

Ubud is especially good for **guided walks** and cycling tours but there are also plenty of other **activities** on offer.

Bicycle tours Downhill rides from Gunung Batur, via villages, temples and traditional homes, costing around Rp350,000–450,000. Bali Bike Baik Tours ☎0361/978052, Ⓦwww.balibike.com; Bali Eco Cycling ☎0361/975557, Ⓦwww.baliecocycling.com; Banyan Tree Bike Tours ☎0813/3879 8516, Ⓦwww.banyantreebiketours.com; Happy Bike Cycling Tour ☎0819/9926 0262, Ⓦwww.happybiketour.com; Jegeg Bali Cycling Tours ☎0812/3677 9429, Ⓦwww.jegegbalicycling.com.

Bird walks Bird-spotting walks in the Campuhan area, organized by expat author Victor Mason. Bali Bird Walks ☎0812/391 3801, Ⓦwww.balibirdwalk.com; Tues, Fri, Sat & Sun 9am; $33, including lunch and the use of shared binoculars.

Cultural and ecological walks Guided walks with an emphasis on learning about traditions and local life from Rp200,000. Bali Nature Walks ☎0817/973 5914, Ⓦwww.balinaturewalks.com; Bali Off Course ☎0361/369 9003, Ⓦwww.balioffcourse.com; Keep Walking Tours ☎0361/973361, Ⓦwww.balispirit.com/tours/bali_tour_keep_walking.html.

Elephant treks At the Elephant Safari Park in Taro, 13km north of Ubud; see p.187.

Sunrise mountain treks Gunung Batur (from $45) and Gunung Agung (from $99). Bali Sunrise Trekking and Tours ☎0818/552669, Ⓦwww.balisunrisetours.com; Keep Walking Tours (see above) and Jegeg Bali (see above).

Traditional medicine walks Traditional herbalists Ni Wayan Lilir and I Made Westi show how to identify native medicinal plants in the Ubud countryside ($18). Herb Walk ☎0812/381 6024, Ⓦwww.baliherbalwalk.com.

Whitewater rafting and kayaking On the Ayung River just west of Ubud, the 2hr courses cover about 8km and cross Class 2 and 3 rapids. See box on p.90 for contacts.

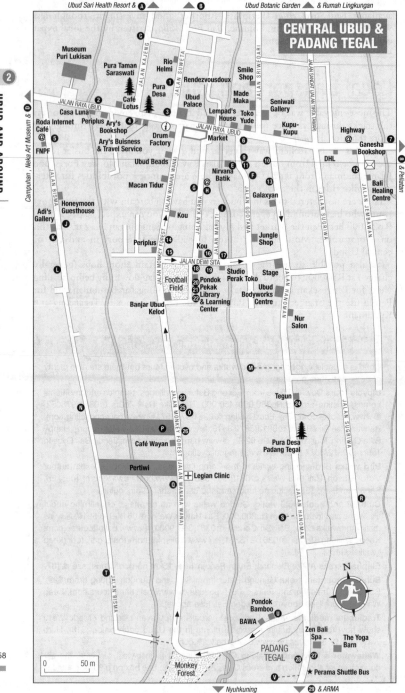

CENTRAL UBUD &
PADANG TEGAL

Ubud Sari Health Resort & Ⓐ   Ⓑ   Ubud Botanic Garden ▲ & Rumah Lingkungan

Museum
Puri Lukisan
Pura Taman
Saraswati
Rio
Helmi ①
Rendezvousdoux
Smile
Shop
Made
Maka
Seniwati
Gallery

Ⓒ
JALAN KAJENG
JALAN SUWETA
JALAN SRIWEDARI
JALAN SANDAT (JALAN TIRTA TAWAR)

Pura
Desa
Ubud
Palace
Lempad's
House
Toko
Yude
Kupu-
Kupu

JALAN RAYA UBUD ②
Café
Lotus
③

Casa Luna
Roda Internet
Café @
Periplus ⑤
Ary's
Bookshop
Ary's Buisness
& Travel Service
④
ⓘ
JALAN RAYA UBUD

Market
Ⓓ Camphuan, Neka Art Museum &

FNPF

Ubud Beads

Macan Tidur

Adi's
Gallery
Ⓚ
Honeymoon
Guesthouse
Ⓙ

JALAN BISMA

Periplus ⑭
⑮

Banjar Ubud
Kelod

JALAN DEWI SITA
Football
Field
⑱
⑲
⑳
㉑
㉒
Pondok
Pekak
Library
& Learning
Center
Studio
Perak Toko
Stage
Ubud
Bodyworks
Centre

Highway @ ⑦
Ganesha
Bookshop
⑥
⑨ ⑪
Nirvana
Batik
@ Ⓕ
Ⓗ Ⓖ
Galaxyan ⑬
⑩
DHL
Ⓔ
Bali
Healing
Centre
⑫
& Peliatan ⑧

Kou
JALAN WANARA WANA
JALAN KARNA
JALAN MARUTI
JALAN GOOTAMA
Ⓘ
Kou
⑯ ⑰
Jungle
Shop

JALAN MONKEY FOREST

Nur
Salon
JALAN HANOMAN
JALAN SUGRIWA
JALAN JEMBAWAN

Ⓜ

Ⓝ
JALAN MONKEY FOREST (JALAN WANARA WANA)
㉓
㉕ Ⓞ
Ⓟ ㉖
Café Wayan

Pertiwi

+ Legian Clinic
Ⓠ

Tegun
㉔
Pura Desa
Padang Tegal

JALAN SUGRIWA
JALAN HANOMAN
Ⓡ
Ⓢ

JALAN BISMA
Ⓣ

Pondok
Bamboo
BAWA
Ⓤ
Zen Bali
Spa
㉘ ㉗
The Yoga
Barn
★ Perama Shuttle Bus
Ⓥ ㉙ & ARMA

PADANG
TEGAL

Monkey
Forest

N

▼ Nyuhkuning

0   50 m

ACCOMMODATION		RESTAURANTS & BARS	
Artja Inn	C	Ary's Warung	4
Donald	F	Bali Buddha	12
Gandra House	G	Bamboo Bar	15
Gusti's Garden 2	D	Bar Luna	9
Gusti's Garden		Batan Waru	17
Bungalows	A	Black Beach	
Jati Homestay	M	Restaurant	13
KajaNe Mua	P	Bollero	16
Komaneka Resort		Café des Artistes	5
at Bisma	N	Café Havana	19
Komaneka Resort		Clear	10
at Monkey Forest	O	Cinta	23
Komaneka Resort		DeliCat	21
at Rasa Sayang	Q	Ibu Oka	3
Nick's Hidden		Ibu Rai	14
Cottages	L	Jazz Café	8
Nick's Homestay	S	Kafé	24
Nick's Pension	J	Laughing Buddha Bar	26
Nirvana Pension		Mojos Flying Burritos	7
and Gallery	E	Nomad	6
Putri Ayu	T	Rai Pasti, Warung	
Sania's House	H	and Tailor	25
Sayong House	I	Ryoshi	2
Sehati Guesthouse	U	Shisha XL Lounge	20
Teba House	R	Siam Sally	27
Tegal Sari	V	Sjaki's Warung	22
Uma Sari Cottages	K	Taco Casa and Grill	29
Waka di Ume	B	teraZo	1
		Tutmak	18
		Warung Enak	28
		Warung Lokal	11

Most transport touts and tour agencies along Jalan Monkey Forest offer **car and motorbike rental**; see Basics, p.33, for price guidelines and advice. A reputable and efficient car-rental place is Ary's Business and Travel Service (℡0361/973130, ℮arys_tour @yahoo.com), near Ary's Bookshop on Jalan Raya Ubud. Note that if you're driving northwards, ie uphill, to Kintamani or to the north coast, it's worth getting something more powerful than the cheapest Jimny.

Tours

Although the Ubud tourist office and all travel agencies offer programmes of standard **tours** (generally Rp125,000–200,000/person; two people minimum), it's usually more rewarding to hire your own **driver** and design your own itinerary. A day-trip to Kintamani, for example, could cost you just Rp450,000 all in, for up to four people. Recommended freelance drivers include Nyoman Suastika (℡0813/3870 1962, ⓦwww .nyoman-suastika.tripod.com), or you can arrange one through almost any car-rental outlet.

Most tour agencies advertise inclusive trips to local **festivals** and **cremations** (for more on which, see p.372) although you can simply check the details at the tourist office and attend independently. Note that whether you go to a temple ceremony with a group or on your own, formal dress (sashes and sarongs) is required.

Accommodation

Ubud offers a good choice of **accommodation**, particularly in **family homestays** in traditional compounds. There are plenty of more upscale options too, many of them incredibly luxurious, and plenty with rice-paddy or river views. All accommodation listed below is marked on a **map** – either the Central Ubud and Padang Tegal map (opposite) or the Ubud and neighbouring villages map (p.154).

Central Ubud and Padang Tegal

The kilometre-long **Jalan Monkey Forest** is the most central and commercial part of town, while the smaller roads, such as Jalan Karna, Jalan Maruti, Jalan Gootama, Jalan Kajeng and Jalan Bisma, for example, retain a more peaceful atmosphere but may be further from the tourist facilities.

The *banjar*, or neighbourhood, of **Padang Tegal**, which is centred on Jalan Hanoman, is marginally quieter than Jalan Monkey Forest but has plenty of shops and restaurants. Depending on the location, you may be quite a hike from the marketplace.

Artja Inn Jl Kajeng 9 ☎0361/974425. Set away from the road behind a family compound in a cute garden, this classic losmen offers six fan-cooled bamboo-walled cottages. Cold water ①, hot water ②

Donald Jl Gootama 9 ☎0361/977156. Tiny but well-run homestay offering four sprucely maintained fan-cooled bungalows in a secluded garden compound. Cold water ②, hot water ③

Gandra House Jl Karna 8 ☎0361/976529. Ten typical losmen-style rooms inside the quiet but central family compound. All rooms have fans, cold-water bathrooms and verandas. ②

🏃 **Gusti's Garden 2** Jl Abangan, about 150m walk north from Jl Raya Ubud ☎0361/971474, ✉gustigarden@hotmail.com. Overlooking the paddies on the western fringes of central Ubud, these nicely designed, clean, comfortable rooms are popular so reservations are advisable. Also has a grotto-like swimming pool. ④

Gusti's Garden Bungalows Jl Kajeng 27 ☎0361/973311, ✉gusti_garden@yahoo.com. Sixteen pleasant rooms, all fan-cooled with hot water, set around a swimming pool in a peaceful location. ③

Jati Homestay Jl Hanoman, Padang Tegal ☎0361/977701, ⓦwww.jatihs.com. Set well away from the road, the ten fan rooms – with bamboo furniture and hot-water bathrooms – enjoy rice-paddy views. Run by a family of painters, there's an art gallery on site and art lessons are available. Charges per person so singles are good value. ④

🏃 **KajaNe Mua** Jl Monkey Forest ☎0361/972877, ⓦwww.kajane.com. Popular resort with villa compounds offering one to four rooms, all with private pool in addition to the inviting main pool. The chic modern Balinese or antique-themed interiors come with good facilities and excellent service, and there are plenty of activities on offer. Smaller, quieter outposts are located in the countryside south of Ubud (KajaNe Yangloni) and in Tulamben on the north coast. ⑧

Komaneka Resort at Monkey Forest Jl Monkey Forest ☎0361/976090, ⓦwww.komaneka.com. Perennially popular boutique hotel offering large, fabulously stylish a/c bungalows. Some have private pools, and there's a beautiful hotel pool and spa. Service is excellent. Two other wonderful locations are offered in and near Ubud, with another in the pipeline – check the website for details. ⑨

Nick's Pension Jl Bisma ☎0361/975636, ⓦwww.nickshotels-ubud.com. Ranged down the valley side with a lovely pool, all the rooms have hot water and verandas. The small site doesn't

feel too densely packed. *Nick's Hidden Cottages* are less central and a smaller setup (☎0361/970760; fan ④, a/c ⑤) while *Nick's Homestay* (☎0361/975526; ③), off Jl Hanoman, is cheaper with fan rooms in the family compound – guests there can use the pools in the other two locations. Fan ④, a/c ⑤

Nirvana Pension Jl Gootama 10 ☎0361/975415, ⓦwww.nirvanaku.com. Six comfortably furnished and artistically decorated rooms, all with fan and hot water, in the traditional house compound of painter and batik teacher Nyoman Suradnya (see p.181). ④

Putri Ayu Jl Bisma, access on foot also via the *Pertiwi* compound ☎0361/972590, ⓦwww.putriayucottages.com. Quiet, friendly place with easy access to central Ubud, offering nine enormous a/c rooms in two buildings. There are floor-to-ceiling windows, huge verandas and excellent breakfasts. ④

🏃 **Sania's House** Jl Karna 7 ☎0361/975535. This hugely popular backpackers' place has more than twenty good-quality, well-maintained fan or a/c rooms (some in multistorey buildings) close to the market. There's even a small pool. The drawback is that with so much accommodation in the small compound it can feel somewhat cosy. Cold water ③, hot water ④

Sayong House Jl Maruti ☎0361/973305, ✉sayong_ubud@yahoo.com. Ten simply furnished rooms, all with hot water, set around a garden at the end of a quiet lane. There's a swimming pool across the lane. Fan ③, a/c ④

Sehati Guesthouse Jl Monkey Forest ☎0361/976341, ⓦwww.sehati-guesthouse.com. Smashing little place in a quiet location near the Monkey Forest. The clean rooms have hot water and a/c, as well as good verandas or terraces. ④

Teba House Jl Sugriwa 59 ☎0361/971179, ⓦubudtebahouse.com. Neat, budget place in a quiet but convenient location; rooms, all with hot water and good verandas, are set in a small garden. Fan ②, a/c ③

🏃 **Tegal Sari** Jl Hanoman, Padang Tegal ☎0361/973318, ⓦwww.tegalsari-ubud.com. Exceptionally appealing set of 24 tastefully furnished rooms, all with fan, a/c and hot water, in two-storey buildings overlooking the paddyfields. There's thoughtful service, massage facilities and a pool and cookery classes, free local transport, day-treks and village visits are all offered. Convenient for the Perama office. Hugely oversubscribed, so book as far in advance as possible. ④

Uma Sari Cottages Jl Bisma ☎0361/972964, ⓦwww.umasari.com. Comfortable rooms with fan or a/c (all have hot water) in two-storey buildings in a quiet but convenient spot. All have terraces or verandas overlooking the ricefields and there's a small pool. Fan ❹, a/c ❺

🏃 **Waka di Ume** About 1.8km north along Jl Suweta from Ubud market, in the hamlet of Sambahan ☎0361/973178, ⓦwww.wakadiumeubud.com. Delightful accommodation

designed in the distinctive *Waka* natural-chic style. Each room has a picture-perfect rice-paddy view and the hotel has a beautiful pool, a spa and a restaurant with stunning views as far as the Bukit. Cooking classes are available, and service is excellent. Regular shuttles into central Ubud. ❼

Tebesaya, Peliatan, Nyuhkuning and Mas

Tebesaya is a residential area around fifteen minutes' walk east from Ubud market. Further east again, the neighbourhood of **Peliatan** harbours a couple of excellent and quiet places to stay. **Nyuhkuning** is a peaceful village just ten minutes' walk from the bottom of Jalan Monkey Forest through the Monkey Forest – somewhat eerie in the evening. There's also a charming hotel in the woodcarving village of **Mas**, 6km south of Peliatan.

🏃 **Alam Jiwa** Nyuhkuning ☎0361/977463, ⓦwww.alamindahbali.com. Spacious accommodation gorgeously located by a small river, affording dramatic views of ricefields and Gunung Agung. Service is friendly and there's a pool and free transport into Ubud. This is one of a small local chain of delightful hotels in Ubud and Gili Trawangan. ❻

🏃 **Family Guest House** Jl Sukma 39, Tebesaya ☎0361/974054, ⓔfamilyhouse@telkom.net. Friendly place offering eight well-maintained, fan-cooled bungalows in the family compound, all of them with stylish furniture and most with hot water and large verandas. The top-end options are huge and especially good value. ❹

Sari Bungalows Off the southern end of Jl Peliatan, Banjar Kalah, Peliatan ☎0361/975541, ⓔironkic @hotmail.com. The twelve simple bungalows (some with hot water) are among the cheapest in Ubud; all have small verandas. Great value. ❶

Sri Sunari Jl Gunung Sari, Peliatan ☎0361/970542, ⓦwww.sunari-bali-inn.com. Just

four large, tastefully furnished fan-cooled rooms and a saltwater pool In the middle of paddyfields about 2km from Ubud market. Bicycle rental is available. ❺

Swasti Eco Cottages Nyuhkuning ☎0361/974079, ⓦwww.baliswasti.com. Thoughtfully tended hideaway with spacious accommodation in rooms and bungalows. There's a pool and spa, as well as an organic vegetable garden, which supplies the restaurant (offering French, Thai, Indian and Indonesian dishes). A family house is also available. Rooms ❻, house ❼

Taman Harum Cottages In the compound of Tantra Gallery, Jl Raya, southern Mas ☎0361/975567, ⓦwww.tamanharumcottages .com. The two-storey villas and suites are the best choice here, affording fine ricefield views from upstairs. All rooms have a/c and hot water and there's a pool, restaurant, free transport to Ubud (20 min) and cultural classes can be arranged. Rooms ❺, villas and suites ❻–❼

Campuhan, Sanggingan, Bangkiang Sidem and Keliki

West of central Ubud, **Campuhan** and **Sanggingan** hotels are reached via Jalan Raya Ubud, the busy main road, which is not a particularly pleasant walk, but public bemos run this way and some hotels offer free transfers. Rural **Bangkiang Sidem**, on the other hand, is accessible via a delightful path from the edge of Campuhan (about a 30min walk). If you're staying in the remote but charming village of **Keliki**, you'll probably need transport.

Alam Sari Keliki Hotel Keliki ☎0361/981420, ⓦwww.alamsari.com. The inviting a/c bungalows overlook ricefields and coconut groves about 10km north of Ubud. There are also two-bedroom family units and a three-bedroom villa, along with a restaurant, spa and swimming pool. A kids' programme and art and culture classes are also

available. The hotel has bikes you can borrow and runs a free shuttle to Ubud. ❻

Anom Cottages Sanggingan ☎0361/977234, ⓦwww.anomcottages.com. This small setup has just six rooms (all have hot water, one has a/c) in a small garden with a pool. Accommodation is appealing without being swanky and prices for this location (dominated by far more expensive options), are excellent. Fan ❹, a/c ❺

Klub Kokos Bangkiang Sidem ☎0361/978270, ⓦwww.klubkokos.com. Comfortable accommodation in a variety of sizes, complete with a huge pool, a restaurant, on-site art gallery, library and kids' games room. Located a lovely 25min (1500m) walk from the Campuhan bridge, partway along the Campuhan ridge walk (see p.171), and also accessible by road. Rooms ❻, family unit ❼

Sunrise Villas Jl Raya Sanggingan, Sanggingan/Campuhan ⓦwww.baliretreatcenter .net. Fourteen lovely, spacious rooms, all with hot water, some with a/c, perched on the valley side with breezy verandas plus glorious views of the Campuhan ridge (cheaper rooms have garden views). There's a pool and meditation/yoga are specialities but not obligatory. Weekly packages available. Garden view ❻, valley view ❼

Taman Indrakila Jl Raya Sanggingan, Sanggingan/Campuhan ☎0361/975017, ⓦwww .tamanindrakila.net. Offering a five-star view at two-star prices, this is a low-key operation with seven cottage rooms ranged along the hillside, all affording spectacular panoramas over the Campuhan ridge. Rooms are in traditional style with carved doors, netted beds and plain decor. Also has a pool. Fan ❹, a/c ❺

Uma Ubud Jl Raya Sanggingan ☎0361/972448, ⓦwww.uma.como.bz. Fabulous resort of 29 white-walled compounds containing luxurious accommodation set along the side of the Wos river. Part of the super-luxury *COMO* group (whose other Bali property is the nearby, world-famous *Como Shambala*), there's an emphasis on wellbeing, with complimentary daily yoga classes and morning walks. ❾

Penestanan

Occupying a ridge and river valley between Campuhan and Sayan, **Penestanan** is a picturesque hamlet whose ridgetop is increasingly occupied by villas, many of which can be rented (see p.35 for leads). There are also some good mid-range accommodation options up here and in the village below (places in the village below are referred to as *kelod* or *kaja* in the following listings). Ridgetop access is by foot or motorbike, while village accommodation has the advantage of road access.

Gerebig Bungalows Penestanan Kelod ☎0813/3701 9757, ⓦwww.gerebig.com. Appealing rooms and bungalows, all with fan and hot water and some with kitchen facilities, set a short distance from the road amid local ricefields. The swimming pool is a bit further out in the fields. Two-bedroom houses are also available. ❺

d'Omah Penestanan Kelod ☎0361/976622, ⓦwww.domahbali.com. Small, deservedly popular hotel offering twenty rooms, suites and a villa all with a/c and hot water, set in a lush garden with two pools, a spa and restaurant. Rooms/suites ❻, villa ❼

Santra Putra Ridgetop ☎0361/977810, ⓦwww .wayankarja.com. Eleven fan rooms with hot water and great verandas or balconies overlooking the garden. Accessible on foot via the Campuhan steps or by motorcycle from the Penestanan side. ❹

Taman Rahasia Penestanan Kaja ☎0361/979395, ⓦwww.balisecretgarden.com. A classy little boutique hideaway in the heart of the village. The seven large a/c rooms are pleasingly furnished with tasteful artworks and local fabrics and have deep verandas or balconies. There's a restaurant, small pool, a spa, and a charming garden. Also has a cooking school for in-house guests (see p.181). Not recommended for children. ❼

Sayan and Kedewatan

Overlooking the spectacular Ayung river valley about 3km west of central Ubud, **Sayan** and **Kedewatan** are famous for their luxurious resorts, all of which capitalize on the dramatic panoramas.

Four Seasons Resort Bali at Sayan Sayan/Kedewatan ☎0361/977577, ⓦwww.fourseasons .com/sayan. Considered to be one of the world's top hotels, this resort is built on several levels in the Ayung river valley. The suites and villas are beautifully appointed and fabulously comfortable

and villas also have private pools. Service is impeccable and the two-tier pool and other communal areas are stunning. Rates from $460. ❾

🏃 **Novus Taman Bebek** Sayan ☎0361/975385, ⓦwww.novushotels .com. Seven villas and four suites built in airy colonial style with verandas, sliding screens and carved doors. Lush foliage obscures some of the Ayung River terrace views but the atmospheric garden is a winner. There's a pool and spa, transport to Ubud (10min) and meals can be provided. ⑧

Sayan Terrace Sayan ☎0361/974384, ⓦwww .sayanterraceresort.com. These enormous rooms and villas with fan and a/c, all with huge windows and verandas, make the most of the fine Ayung River views. There's an inviting pool and a restaurant and transport to central Ubud. Rooms ❼, villa ⑧

Central Ubud

Covering the area between Jalan Raya Ubud in the north and the Monkey Forest in the south, and between the Campuhan bridge in the west and the GPO in the east, **Central Ubud**'s chief draws are its restaurants and shops. However, it does hold a few notable sights, including Ubud's oldest art museum, **Puri Lukisan**, the **Seniwati Gallery of Art by Women** and the **Threads of Life** textile gallery.

Museum Puri Lukisan

The **Museum Puri Lukisan** on Jalan Raya Ubud (daily 9am–5pm; Rp40,000; ⓦwww.museumpurilukisan.com) is best visited as an adjunct to the far superior Neka Art Museum, 2km west in Sanggingan (see p.166). Set in well-maintained gardens, Puri Lukisan ("Palace of Paintings") was founded in 1956 by the Ubud *punggawa* Cokorda Gede Agung Sukawati and the Dutch artist Rudolf Bonnet.

It's worth noting that significant redevelopment is underway so the arrangement of galleries may change in the near future. The **First Pavilion**, Pitamaha Gallery, located at the top of the garden, is largely given over to prewar Balinese paintings, mostly black-and-white **Batuan-style** and early **Ubud-style** pictures depicting local scenes (see p.168 for more on all these styles). There's also a good selection of distinctive drawings by I Gusti Nyoman Lempad (see p.164). Several fine **woodcarvings** from the 1930s to the 1950s are also here, including the surreal earth-goddess *Dewi Pertiwi* by Ida Bagus Nyana (see p.151 for more about this artist), the sinuous *Dewi Sri* by I Ketut Djedeng and I Cokot's much-emulated *Garuda Eating Snake*.

In the **Second Pavilion**, to the left on the way up the garden, the Ida Bagus Made (1915–1999) Gallery showcases the artist's work alongside other postwar Balinese work, including those in the naive expressionist **Young Artists** style that originated in nearby Penestanan in the 1960s. Also in this pavilion you'll find paintings in the **Ubud style**, including *Balinese Market* by Anak Agung Gede Sobrat, as well as works in the so-called **modern traditional** style, such as I Made Sukada's *Battle Between Boma and Krishna*.

In the **Third Pavilion**, to the right on the way up the garden, the Wayang Gallery houses the collection of **wayang-style** paintings as well as temporary exhibitions.

Pura Taman Saraswati

Commissioned in the 1950s by Cokorda Gede Agung Sukawati, the member of the Ubud royal family who focused his energies on developing the arts (see p.153), **Pura Taman Saraswati** is the work of the prolific royal architect and stonecarver I Gusti Nyoman Lempad, who set the temple complex within a delightful lotus-pond garden. It's dedicated to Saraswati, the goddess of learning, science and literature. A **restaurant**, *Café Lotus*, now capitalizes on the garden view. Access to the temple is via a lane next to the restaurant. Walk

Lempad

Many of Ubud's most important buildings are associated with the venerable sculptor, architect and artist **I Gusti Nyoman Lempad** (c.1862–1978), among them Puri Lukisan, Pura Taman Saraswati and Ubud Palace. Lempad came to Ubud with his family at the age of 13, where he found favour in the court of the Sukawatis, for whom he worked for most of his life. A versatile **artist** who designed temples, carved stone reliefs, built cremation towers and produced ink drawings, Lempad was an influential figure and an important member of the Pita Maha arts association, which he co-founded with his friends Cokorda Gede Agung Sukawati and Rudolf Bonnet. A **traditionalist** in certain matters, Lempad would only work on propitious days and is said to have waited for an auspicious day on which to die; by that time he was thought to be approximately 116 years old. The best places to see his drawings are the Neka Art Museum and Museum Puri Lukisan.

Lempad lived on Ubud's Jalan Raya for almost a century in a **house** that still belongs to his family, and which is open to the public as a showroom for artists working under the "Puri Lempad" by-line (daily 8am–6pm; free).

between the lotus ponds to the red-brick *kori agung* (temple entrance). The straight route into the temple courtyard is blocked by an unusual **aling-aling** (the wall device built into nearly every temple to disorient evil spirits), which is in fact the back of a rotund statue of a *raksasa* (demon guardian). Inside the **courtyard** the main lotus-throne **shrine** is covered with a riot of *paras* carvings, with the requisite cosmic turtle and *naga* forming the base, while the tower is a swirling mass of curlicues and floral motifs.

Seniwati Gallery of Art by Women

Balinese women feature prominently in the paintings that fill the Neka Art Museum and the Museum Puri Lukisan, but there is barely a handful of works by women artists in either collection. To redress this imbalance, British-born artist Mary Northmore-Aziz established the **Seniwati Gallery of Art by Women** at Jalan Sriwedari 2B (Tues–Sun 9am–5pm; free; Ⓦ www .seniwatigallery.com), which represents more than seventy female artists from Bali, Java, Kalimantan and overseas who are resident in Bali. There are regular children's art classes and there's a small shop selling cards as well as their famous *Women Artists of Bali* calendar.

The small but charming permanent collection covers the range of mainstream Balinese art styles. Notable artists include **Ni Made Suciarmi**, whose childhood was spent helping with the 1930s renovations on the Kerta Gosa painted ceilings in Semarapura, and who continues to work in the *wayang* style; Batuan-born **Ni Wayan Warti**, who excels in the traditional style of her village, producing dark and detailed scenes; and the well-known painter **I Gusti Agung Galuh**, who works chiefly in the popular Ubud style. **Gusti Ayu Kadek Murniasih**, better known as **Murni** (1966–2006), was known for her witty and uninhibited style, which made her one of Bali's most famous modern artists.

Threads of Life Indonesian Textile Arts Center

The small **Threads of Life Indonesian Textile Arts Center and Gallery** (daily 10am–7pm; free; Ⓦ www.threadsoflife.com) at Jl Kajeng 24 is devoted to exquisite hand-woven textiles from across the islands of Indonesia, including Bali,

Sumba, Timor, Java and Sulawesi. Though they were all produced using natural dyes and ancient methods, the textiles are modern works, commissioned by the Threads of Life foundation in an attempt to keep Indonesia's historic textile art alive. This is a complex and highly skilled art, and severely endangered, not least because a single weaving can take two years to complete. The gallery displays superb weavings alongside plenty of information on their origins, the weavers, the processes involved and the meaning of the most important motifs. The centre also sells beautiful, if pricey, **textiles** and runs regular **classes** on traditional textile appreciation (see p.181).

A rice-paddy walk through Ubud Kaja

Running east of, and almost parallel to, the Campuhan ridge walk (see p.171) is the possibility of an almost circular **rice-paddy walk** that begins and ends in the northern part of Ubud known as **Ubud Kaja** (*kaja* literally means "upstream, towards the mountains"). The walk takes about two and a half hours round-trip and is flat, though there's not much shade. About 800m into the walk the *Sari Organik* café makes a lovely place for a break (see p.176) and you can refill water bottles here too.

The walk begins from the western end of **Jalan Raya Ubud**, just before the overhead aqueduct, where a track leads up to the *Abangan Bungalows* on the north side of the road. Head up the slope and, at the top, follow the track, which bends to the left before straightening out, passing *Gusti's Garden 2* bungalows and heading north to *Sari Organik*, passing Cantika Spa on the way. From here the route is straightforward, following the track, which is paved in places, for about 3km as it slices through gently **terraced ricefields** fringed with coconut palms; you should see scores of beautifully coloured dragonflies, and plenty of **birdlife**, including, possibly, iridescent blue Javanese kingfishers. There are a number of art shops/studios where you can get a drink en route.

After about an hour and a quarter, the track ends at a sealed road. For the most straightforward version of the walk, turn around here and retrace your steps.

Alternatively, if you want a bit of an adventure, turn right onto the road, which rises, curves and then falls to cross the river. The **southbound track** starts almost immediately after the bridge and runs east of the river. After five minutes of following the track through the village, it forks; take the right fork, keeping the water channel on your right. Another five minutes later a dirt path heads up into the paddyfields to your left; take this path. At this point the southbound track becomes totally indistinct and for the next thirty minutes you should try to follow the narrow paths along the top of the ricefield dykes, sticking roughly to a southerly direction and keeping the river in view on your right. You'll inevitably wind in and out on the paths through the paddies rather than being able to head straight-as-an-arrow south. Don't forget to look back at the amazing **views of Gunung Agung** (cloud cover permitting): with the mountain in the background and the conical-hatted farmers working in the glittering ricefields, these views are perfect real-life versions of the Walter Spies-style paintings you see in the museums and galleries of Ubud. After thirty minutes or so you'll see a rough path about five or six metres below you to the right on the riverbank. Scramble down some rough-cut muddy steps to reach the path. This will lead you back to Ubud through some light forest and then paddyfields.

Twenty-five minutes after the scramble down you'll reach the **outskirts of Ubud**. When the path forks take the left fork steeply down to a stone bridge. The road bends right, passes a school and becomes Jalan Kajeng, a little road paved with graffitied-covered stones that runs down to Jalan Raya Ubud in ten minutes or so. The stones are inscribed with the names, messages and doodlings of everyone who helped finance the paving of the lane.

Campuhan, Sanggingan and Penestanan

Sited at the confluence of the rivers Wos Barat and Wos Timor, the hamlet of **CAMPUHAN** (pronounced *cham-poo-han*) extends west from Ubud as far as the *Hotel Tjampuhan*, and is famous as the home of several of Bali's most charismatic expatriate painters, including the late **Antonio Blanco**, whose house and gallery have been turned into a museum; the late **Walter Spies**, whose villa remains inside the *Hotel Tjampuhan*; and **Symon**, who still paints at his studio-gallery across the road from the hotel.

North up the hill, Campuhan turns into **Sanggingan** (though few people bother to distinguish it from its neighbour), and it's here that you'll find Bali's best art gallery, the **Neka Art Museum**. If you don't fancy walking or cycling along the busy main road, you can take any west-bound **bemo** from the market in Ubud.

Heading up the steps in Campuhan (see map, p.154) takes you up onto the **Penestanan ridge**, a picturesque route across to the still traditional hamlet of Penestanan down in the next valley. In the 1960s **Penestanan** became famous for its so-called **Young Artists**, who forged a naive style of painting that's since been named after them. Some are still painting, but Penestanan's current niche is **beadmaking**, and the village has several shops selling intricately decorated items.

The Neka Art Museum

Boasting the most comprehensive collection of Balinese paintings on the island, the **Neka Art Museum** (daily 9am–5pm; Rp40,000; ⓦwww.museumneka.com) is housed in a series of pavilions alongside the main Campuhan/Sanggingan road, about 2.5km from central Ubud. English-language labels are posted alongside the paintings, with Balinese, expatriate and visiting artists all represented. The museum shop sells a couple of recommended **books** about the collection, notably *Neka Art Museum: The Heart of Art in Bali* by Suteja Neka and Garrett Kam, which is essentially a catalogue of the highlights of the collection and *Perceptions of*

Walter Spies in Campuhan

The son of a German diplomat, **Walter Spies** (1895–1942) left Europe for Java in 1923, and relocated to Bali four years later. He set up home in Campuhan and devoted himself to the study and practice of Balinese art and music. He sponsored two local gamelan orchestras and was the first Westerner to attempt to record **Balinese music**. Together with the American composer Colin McPhee, he set about transposing gamelan music for Western instruments, and with another associate, Katharane Mershon, encouraged Bedulu dancer I Wayan Limbak to create the enduringly popular dance-drama known as the **Kecak**.

Spies was an avid collector of Balinese **art**, and became one of the founding members of the Pita Maha arts association in 1936. He is said to have inspired, if not taught, a number of talented young Ubud artists, among them the painter Anak Agung Gede Sobrat, and the woodcarver I Tegelan. Characteristic of Spies's own Balinese works are dense landscapes of waterlogged paddies, peopled with conical-hatted farmers – a distinctive style that is still much imitated. There's currently only one Walter Spies painting on show in Bali; it's at the Agung Rai Museum of Art in Pengosekan.

In 1937 Spies retired to the village of Iseh in the east, turning his Campuhan home into a **guesthouse**, the first of its kind in the Ubud area. He died in 1942, drowning when the ship deporting him as a German national in World War II was bombed in the Indian Ocean. The guesthouse became *Hotel Tjampuhan*.

Paradise: Images of Bali in the Arts by Garrett Kam. For more on the **styles of art** on display, see the box on p.168.

First Pavilion: Balinese Painting Hall

The first pavilion surveys the three major schools of **Balinese painting** from the seventeenth century to the present day. The collection opens with examples of the **Kamasan style**, including work from contemporary Kamasan artists such as Ida Bagus Rai in *Rajapala Steals Sulasih's Clothes* and *The Pandawa Brothers In Disguise*, in which classical elements are fused with a more modern sensuality. These are followed by works representing the **Ubud style**, including *The Bumblebee Dance* by **Anak Agung Gede Sobrat**. Finally come the dark and densely packed **Batuan style** canvases, including the dramatic *Busy Bali* by **I Wayan Bendi**, which delineates the effect of tourism on the island, and **I Made Budi**'s 1987 work, *President Suharto and His Wife Visit Bali*.

Second Pavilion: Arie Smit Pavilion

The top floor of the second pavilion is devoted to the hugely influential Dutch expatriate artist **Arie Smit**. His work is instantly recognizable by the bold, expressionist tone; many of the paintings, including *A Tropical Garden By the Sea*, have a breathtakingly beautiful Cézanne-like quality.

The ground-floor hall is given over to **contemporary Balinese art**, which includes expressionist, figurative and abstract works – a clear indication of the vibrancy of modern art on the island. The styles range widely from the huge abstract canvases of I Made Sumadiyasa to the unsettling wooden sculptures of I Made Supena.

Third Pavilion: Photography Archive Center

The third pavilion houses an archive of black-and-white **photographs** from Bali in the 1930s and 1940s, taken by the American **Robert Koke**. He and his wife Louise founded the first hotel in Kuta in 1936. His photographic record includes village scenes, temple festivals and cremations, but its highlights are the pictures of the dance performances and the portraits of the Kebyar dancer Mario and of the Kecak choreographer I Wayan Limbak. The photos are labelled with extracts from Louise Koke's book *Our Hotel in Bali* (reviewed on p.396).

Fourth Pavilion: Lempad Pavilion

The late **I Gusti Nyoman Lempad** (see box, p.164) is the subject of the fourth pavilion, which holds the largest collection of his pictures in Bali. Among his best-known works is a series on **Men and Pan Brayut**, the well-known folk story about a poor couple and their eighteen children (see box, p.201 for more on this).

Fifth Pavilion: Contemporary Indonesian Art Hall

The fifth pavilion focuses on works by formally trained Indonesian artists, whose style is often labelled "Academic". Outstanding examples include large oils by Javanese-born **Anton Hwang** (Anton Kustia Widjaja), who moved to Ubud in 1969, and **Abdul Aziz**'s much-reproduced diptych entitled *Mutual Attraction*.

Sixth Pavilion: East-West Art Annex

The upstairs galleries feature the paintings of **foreign artists in Bali**, including the Dutch painter **Rudolf Bonnet**'s sensual portraits, including *Temptation of Arjuna*. The bright Gauguin-esque oils of Swiss-born **Theo Meier** draw on the lurid light and tropical emotions of Bali, in contrast to the Dutchman **Willem Gerard Hofker**'s minutely observed crayon studies of temples, such as *Temple at Campuhan*,

Art historians group **Balinese painting** into six broad **schools**: *wayang* (also known as classical or Kamasan), Ubud, Pengosekan, Batuan, Young Artists, and Modern or Academic.

Wayang or Kamasan style

The earliest Balinese painters drew their inspiration from the *wayang kulit* shadow plays, using two-dimensional figures to depict episodes from the same religious and historical epics that were played out on the stage. Variously known as the **wayang style**, the **classical style** or the **Kamasan style** (after the east Bali village where the most famous *wayang*-style artists came from), this is the most traditional genre of Balinese art, and the one that's been the least influenced by Western techniques and subjects. The oldest surviving examples are the eighteenth-century temple banners, calendars and astrological charts housed in the **Nyoman Gunarsa Museum** near Semarapura (see p.202). To see Kamasan art in situ you need to visit the old palace in Semarapura, where the ceilings of the **Kerta Gosa** and Bale Kambung pavilions retain their *wayang*-style painted ceilings; these were done by artists from Kamasan in the early nineteenth century but have been retouched several times (see p.200).

All *wayang*-style pictures are packed full of people painted in **three-quarter profile**, with caricature-like features and puppet-like poses. There is no perspective, and stylized symbols indicate the location; pictures are often divided into scenes by borders of mountains, flames or walls. Traditional *wayang* artists limit their palette to red, blue, yellow, black and white.

As with the *wayang* puppets, the **characters** in the paintings are instantly recognizable by their facial features and hairstyles and by their clothes, stance and size. Convention requires, for example, that "refined" characters (heroes, heroines and others of noble birth) look slightly supercilious, and that their bodies be svelte and elegant. "Coarse" characters, on the other hand, such as clowns, servants and demonic creatures, have bulbous eyes, prominent teeth and chunky bodies.

The *wayang* style is still popular with modern artists and continues to be centred on the village of **Kamasan**, which has many studios open to the public.

Ubud style

By the 1930s Balinese painters were starting to experiment with more **naturalistic techniques**, including perspective and the use of light and shadow, and to reproduce what they saw at the market, at the temple and in the ricefields. The village of Ubud was at the heart of this experimentation so the style has been dubbed **Ubud style**. Expatriate artists **Walter Spies** and **Rudolph Bonnet**, both resident in the Ubud area in the 1930s, are said to have had a big influence; they also helped set up the **Pita Maha arts foundation**, whose mission was to promote innovation and individual expression.

Though the Ubud style is more naturalistic than *wayang* art, the pictures are still unrealistically crammed with busyness and **activity**, every corner filled with detail. Every palm leaf and blade of grass is painstakingly delineated, every sarong pattern described, but people are rarely given much individuality, their faces usually set in a rather stylized expression.

Most of the best-known Ubud-style artists are represented in the major Ubud art museums, among them the highly rated **Anak Agung Gede Sobrat**.

Pengosekan style

During the 1960s, a group of young painters working in the Ubud style and living in the village of Pengosekan on the outskirts of Ubud came up with a new approach, subsequently known as the **Pengosekan style**. From the Ubud-style pictures, the Pengosekan school isolated just a few components, specifically the **birds,** butterflies, insects and flowering plants, and magnified them to fill a whole canvas. The best Pengosekan paintings look delicate and lifelike, generally depicted in soothing pastels, and reminiscent of classical Japanese flower and bird pictures – some fine examples can be seen in the Community of Artists showroom run by the descendants of the original Pengosekan artists, in their village, as well as in the Seniwati Gallery in Ubud.

Batuan style

In contrast to the slightly romanticized visions of events being painted by the Ubud-style artists in the 1930s, a group of painters in nearby Batuan were taking a more quizzical approach. Like the *wayang* artists, **Batuan-style** painters filled their works with scores of people, but on a much more frantic scale. A single Batuan-style picture might contain a dozen apparently unrelated scenes – a temple dance, a rice harvest, a fishing expedition, an exorcism and a couple of tourists taking snapshots – all depicted in fine detail that strikes a balance between the naturalistic and the stylized. By clever juxtaposition, the best Batuan artists, such as the Neka Art Museum exhibitors **I Wayan Bendi**, **I Made Budi** and **Ni Wayan Warti**, can turn their pictures into amusing and astute comments on Balinese society. Works by their precursors, the original Batuan artists, **Ida Bagus Made Togog** and **Ida Bagus Made Wija**, focused more on the darker side of village life, on the supernatural beings that hang around the temples and forests, and on the overwhelming sense of men and women as tiny elements in a forceful natural world.

Young Artists style

A second flush of artistic innovation hit the Ubud area in the 1960s, when a group of teenage boys from **Penestanan** started producing unusually expressionistic works, painting everyday scenes in vibrant, non-realistic colours. Encouraged by Dutch artist and Penestanan resident **Arie Smit**, who gave them materials and helped organize exhibitions, they soon became known as the **Young Artists**, a tag now used to describe work by anyone in that same style. The style is indisputably childlike, even naive: the detailed, mosaic-like compositions of scenes from daily life are crudely drawn with minimal attention to perspective, outlined in black like a child's colouring book, and often washed over in weird shades of pink, purple and blue.

All the major museums have works by some of the original Young Artists from the 1960s, the most famous of whom include **I Ketut Tagen**, **I Wayan Pugur**, **I Nyoman Londo**, **I Nyoman Mundik** and **I Nyoman Mujung**. The Neka Art Museum in Ubud devotes a whole gallery to Arie Smit's own work (see p.167).

Academic and Bali modernism

Bali's modern artists, both indigenous and expatriate, are sometimes labelled as **Academic**, meaning that they've studied and been influenced by Western modernism but have settled in Bali and paint Balinese subjects. Many of the best-known are graduates from the Yogyakarta Academy of Fine Arts in Java, and some are or have been part of the **Sanggar Dewata Indonesia** art movement, whose style – loosely defined as Balinese Hindu abstract expressionism – has been the dominant form of modern Balinese painting since the 1970s. Although the style has been somewhat devalued by the countless poor-quality abstracts sold in souvenir shops across Bali, works by the most famous Academics – including **Affandi**, **Anton H** and **Abdul Aziz**, all from Java, the Sumatran-born **Rusli**, and from Bali, **Made Wianta**, **Nyoman Gunarsa**, **Nyoman Erawan** and **Made Budiana** – are on show at the Ubud museums and the Nyoman Gunarsa Museum near Semarapura. Of these important modern artists, Made Wianta is probably the best known internationally; he represented Indonesia in the Venice 2003 Biennale, with a video installation on the Kuta bombings.

Ubud. Also on show are some erotically charged portraits by the Catalan-born **Antonio Blanco**, whose studio-gallery is nearby; the Australian **Donald Friend**'s charmingly fanciful Chagall-esque evocations of his Sanur home, including *Batujimbar Village*; and the Dutchman **Han Snel**'s striking *Girls Carrying Offerings*.

Not all the impressions of Bali come from outside Asia: the dynamic *Gabor-Pendet Dance* is by **J. Elizalde Navarro** from the Philippines, while the striking works *Fight to the Finish*, *The Gambler* and *Barong and Rangda Dance* are by the Javanese expressionist **Affandi**.

Symon's Studio

With its eye-catching outdoor displays, the studio-gallery of American-born artist **Symon** (daily until about 9pm; free; ⓦwww.symonstudios.com), across the road from the *Hotel Tjampuhan*, is hard to ignore. The multi-levelled building is a gallery packed with Symon's paintings, sculptures and other creations, as well as a working atelier for the artist and his assistants. Symon has lived in Bali since 1978 and is best known for his vividly coloured portraits of sensual young Balinese men. He also works on the northeast coast of Bali. An insightful book about Symon's work, *Property of the Artist* by Philip Cornwel-Smith, is available at the Ubud studio, as well as at some local bookshops.

Blanco Museum

Just down the main road into Ubud from Symon's Studio, beside the Penestanan turn-off, the former home of the flamboyant Catalan artist **Antonio Blanco** – complete with gilded pillars and sweeping Spanish balustrades – is open to the public as the enjoyably camp **Blanco Renaissance Museum** (daily 9am–5pm; Rp50,000; ⓣ0361/975502, ⓦwww.blancomuseum.com; phone ahead for free transport).

Dubbed "the Bali Dali", Blanco (1911–99) specialized in **erotic paintings** and drawings, particularly portraits of Balinese women in varying states of abandon. As with countless other Western male artists before and since, Blanco fell for a local girl, Ni Ronji, soon after arriving in Ubud in 1952, singling her out as his top model and later marrying her. Blanco's collection also includes multimedia pieces, plus lots of idiosyncratic picture frames created from unorthodox materials. The museum garden contains a small aviary housing two pairs of rare **Bali starlings** (see p.141).

Penestanan

Just west of the Campuhan bridge, but invisible from the main road, the traditional hamlet of **PENESTANAN** is accessible from the side road that turns off beside the Blanco Museum, but the most atmospheric approach is via the steep flight of steps a few hundred metres further north along Jalan Raya Campuhan, just south of Symon's Studio. The steps climb the hillside to a narrow west-bound track, which passes several arterial north–south paths leading to panoramic **views** (many of which have been appropriated by new villas), then drops down through ricefields into the next valley, across a river and through a small wooded area, before coming to a crossroads with Penestanan's main street. Go straight across (west) if you're heading for Sayan (600m away), right for *Taman Rahasia* hotel (200m, see p.162), or left for the circular walk back through the village to the Blanco Museum in Campuhan (1.5km). For sustenance en route, *Made's Warung*, *Lala and Lili's* and the *Yellow Flower Café* are relaxed places on the ridgetop, all offering cheap **food** (*Yellow Flower Café* also

The Campuhan ridge walk

Campuhan means "the place where two rivers meet" and the confluence of the Wos Barat and the Wos Timor is marked by **Pura Gunung Lebah** (also known as Pura Campuhan). The track that extends north along the grassy spine behind Pura Gunung Lebah forms part of a pleasant two-hour circular **walk** around the outskirts of Campuhan and Sanggingan. Alternatively, if you continue the complete length of the ridge, you'll eventually reach **Keliki** (7km) and **Taro** (13km) before joining the Sayan road to **Kintamani** (32km). All routes are feasible on a **mountain bike**, but be prepared for some significant undulations and a few steps.

If you're starting **from central Ubud**, walk (or take a bemo) west from Ubud market almost as far as the Campuhan bridge, turning north off the main road about 100m before the bridge, into the entrance of the *Ibah* hotel, where an immediate left fork takes you down some steps to the Pura Gunung Lebah. The track heads right around the temple walls and climbs up onto the ridge, where it undulates for a stretch before levelling out along the flattened **ridgetop** between the two river valleys. The perspective from this section is breathtaking: to the left lie the steep banks of the Wos Barat valley; to the right, the eastern panorama across the Wos Timor valley is of savannah, coconut groves, the rocky river gorge and Gunung Agung in the distance. You'll walk through a seemingly endless carpet of **alang-alang grass** swaying in the breeze – a valuable resource used for thatching houses and shrines.

About twenty minutes from Pura Gunung Lebah, the track passes through the first ridgetop settlement, site of the *Klub Kokos* hotel (see p.162) and, beyond, about 1500m of sculpted ricefields before reaching the traditional hamlet of **Bangkiang Sidem**. *Karsa Kafe* is a good stop for refreshments along here. Just beyond the village temple, you arrive at a larger sealed road; turn left on the road for the round trip back to Campuhan road, or continue straight on for Keliki.

Once you've turned left, the road cuts through a swathe of ricefields, drops down steeply towards the Wos Barat and then climbs up through the hamlets of **Payogan** and **Lungsiakan** before reaching **Jalan Raya Sanggingan**. From here you can either flag down any bemo heading east for the ten-minute ride into Ubud, or continue walking for twenty minutes east down to the Neka Art Museum, or twenty minutes west to Kedewatan and the main Kintamani road.

has a Sunday organic buffet at 6.30pm; Rp60,000/person). Down in the village *Bayu's Kitchen* makes an equally appealing refuelling stop. For **accommodation** in this area, see p.162.

Penestanan's main claim to fame is as the original home of the **Young Artists** (see box, p.168 for more about this style of painting). You can still find scores of painters in Penestanan and some **galleries** showcasing various styles. The people of Penestanan are also the most skilful **bead**-workers on the island, adorning an amazing array of items with hundreds of painstakingly strung beads. Their work is on sale in shops in Penestanan and across Bali; visit Manacika Bali Bead Work in the village.

The Monkey Forest and Nyuhkuning

Ubud's best-known tourist attraction is its **Monkey Forest Sanctuary** (daily 8.30am–6pm; Rp20,000, children R10,000; Ⓦ www.monkeyforestubud.com), which occupies the land between the southern end of Jalan Monkey Forest and the northern edge of the woodcarvers' hamlet of **Nyuhkuning**. The focus of numerous day-tours because of its resident troupe of over three hundred malevolent but photogenic long-tailed **macaques**, the forest itself is small and disappointing, traversed by a concrete pathway and with little exceptional flora to look at. The only way to visit is on foot: the entrance is fifteen minutes' walk south from Ubud's central market, and a stroll around the forest and its temple combines well with a walk around neighbouring Nyuhkuning.

Five minutes into the forest, you'll come to **Pura Dalem Agung Padang Tegal**, the temple of the dead for the *banjar* of Padang Tegal (you can borrow the requisite sarong and sash at the temple entrance, for which a small donation is requested). You'll find half a dozen stonecarved images of the witch-widow **Rangda** (see p.197) flanking the main stairway – hard to miss with her hideous fanged face, unkempt hair, metre-long tongue and pendulous breasts. Two of the Rangda statues are depicted in the process of devouring children – a favourite occupation of hers.

You can stop for **refreshments** just south of the temple at the *Laka Leke* café, beside the road into Nyuhkuning; the café also stages free dance performances for diners on Balinese buffet evenings (Mon, Wed, Fri & Sat 8pm; Rp150,000/ person). There are other small restaurants further along the road.

Nyuhkuning

Continuing south from the Pura Dalem Agung Padang Tegal, the road enters the **woodcarvers' village** of **NYUHKUNING**, a pleasingly quiet place for a wander and the site of several charming, small hotels (see p.161). The road is dotted with shops selling the carvers' handiwork but the atmosphere is more low-key and workshop-oriented than in the more famous woodcarving centre of Mas – and prices are better too. Many of the carvers will give woodcarving lessons to interested tourists. Works by the famous Nyuhkuning carver, the late I Wayan Pendet, are exhibited in the tiny **Museum Pendet** (daily 10am–5pm; free). Just beyond the museum, beside the football field, the road branches. Heading straight on, along the peaceful **main street**, you'll pass walled family compounds for the 600m to the main road. A left turn here leads into the next village of Pengosekan (1km to the east; see below). If you turn right towards the *Bali Spirit* hotel, a right turn north again leads back up to the football field at the top of the village, from where you can head back to the Monkey Forest and central Ubud. The *Laka Leke* café (see above) or the smaller warung in the village are all possible lunch stops.

Pengosekan

At the southern end of Jalan Hanoman, the road enters **PENGOSEKAN**, known locally as the centre of the Pengosekan Community of Artists, a cooperative founded in 1969 to help villagers share resources, exhibition costs and sales. The cooperative was so successful that most of the original members have since established their own galleries, but the spirit of the collective lives on in the **Pengosekan Community of Artists showroom** (daily 9am–6pm). As with other local communities of artists, the Pengosekan painters developed a distinct style (see box, p.168 for details). Their art also features increasingly on carved picture frames, boxes and small pieces of furniture. It's about a thirty-minute walk here from central Ubud, or catch any Ubud–Batubulan bemo.

Agung Rai Museum of Art (ARMA)

Pengosekan's main attraction is the impressive **Agung Rai Museum of Art**, or **ARMA** (daily 9am–6pm; Rp40,000; ☎0361/976659, ⓦwww.armamuseum .com). Founded by Ubud art dealer Anak Agung Rai, its collection nearly matches that of the Neka Art Museum; there's also an excellent public-access **library** and research centre here, and an open-air dance stage. Access is either via Jalan Hanoman or through the main gateway on the Pengosekan–Peliatan road. See box on p.168 for information about all the Balinese schools of painting.

From the main entrance, pass through the temporary exhibition hall and across the garden to the large **Bale Daja** pavilion. The downstairs area celebrates the life and work of Walter Spies (see box, p.166) and includes life-size reproductions of his work along with some typical Ubud-style paintings such as I Ketut Sepi's *Cremation Ceremony* and Anak Agung Gede Sobrat's *Baris Dance*. Its upstairs gallery gives a brief survey of the development of Balinese art, though the labels aren't that helpful. Historically speaking, you should begin with the **wayang-style** canvases that are hung high up on the walls overlooking the central well, which are in typical seventeenth-century style, though experts think that they date from much later. Ida Bagus Belawa's *Cock Fighting* is thought to have been painted in the 1930s and is a good example of a modern subject done in traditional two-dimensional style.

Also on this floor, the **Batuan-style** art focuses on real life too; the works are instantly recognizable by their extraordinary detail. *The Island of Bali* by the popular I Wayan Bendi is a fine example: crammed with archetypal Balinese scenes, it's also laced with satire, notably in the figures of long-nosed tourists poking their camera lenses into village events. If you look closely you'll find a surfer in the picture too. Look out also for the pen-and-ink cartoons of I Gusti Nyoman Lempad, an important Ubud character (see p.164).

Across the garden, the **Bale Dauh** is dedicated to works by expatriate artists and the content reads like a directory of Bali's most famous expats, with works by Rudolf Bonnet, Miguel Covarrubias, Donald Friend, Theo Meier, Antonio Blanco and Arie Smit. The gallery also includes works by expat Asian artists Chang Fee Ming (Malaysia) and Damas Mangku (Java). The highlight is *Calonarang* (1930) by **Spies** himself, a dark portrait of a demonic apparition; this is the only Spies painting currently on show in Bali. The other major work is the *Portrait of a Javanese Nobleman and His Wife* (1837) by the Javanese artist **Raden Saleh**, considered to be the father of Indonesian painting. The rest of the floor is given over to modern Indonesian painting, including works by **Ruang Affandi** and some strikingly powerful abstracts by I Made Sumadiyasa.

Ubud Botanic Garden

Lush, tranquil **Ubud Botanic Garden** (daily 8am–6pm; Rp50,000; Ⓦwww .botanicgardenbali.com) occupies a steep-sided river valley in the *banjar* of Kutuh Kaja, 1.7km north of Jalan Raya Ubud. The garden features plants from all over Indonesia, including heliconias, orchids and bromeliads, and there's also an Islamic Garden and a maze. It works well as a green retreat, with its thoughtfully designed open-air meditation court and strategically sited seating. The garden is accessed via Jalan Tirta Tawar and takes about half an hour to reach on foot, passing through villages and ricefields.

Petulu and the heron sanctuary

Every evening at around 6pm, hundreds of thousands of herons fly in from miles around to roost in the village of **PETULU**, immediately northeast of Ubud – quite a spectacle. To find this **white heron sanctuary**, follow Jalan Andong north from the T-junction at the eastern edge of Ubud for about 1.5km, then take the left-hand (signed) fork for a further 1.5km. Lots of public bemos ply Jalan Andong, but you'll have to walk the section from the fork. A visit here in the evening is a good way to round off a daytime visit to the botanic garden (see p.173).

Birdwatchers might be able to distinguish the four species of wading birds that frequent the heronry – the **Javan pond heron**, the **plumed egret**, the **little egret** and the **cattle egret** – but for everyone else the sheer volume of birds is spectacle enough.

It isn't clear why the birds have chosen to make their home in Petulu, though locally it's claimed that the birds are **reincarnations** of the tens of thousands of men and women who died in the civil war that raged through Bali in 1966. Many of the victims were buried near here, and the birds are said to have started coming here only after an elaborate ceremony was held in the village in memory of the dead.

Eating

Ubud is packed full of **places to eat** and there are more vegetarian and organic options than anywhere else on the island. Most restaurants shut at about 10pm. Where phone numbers are given for restaurants outside central Ubud it's worth calling to ask about free transport. If it's a picnic you're after, the **organic food markets** opposite *Pizza Bagus* restaurant (Sat 9.30am–2pm) or at the ARMA restaurant (Wed 9.30am–2pm), both in Padang Tegal, offer the goods.

Central Ubud and Padang Tegal

Bali Buddha Jl Jembawan 1 Ⓦwww.balibuddha .com. The original Ubud organic café offers a vast menu of healthy drinks, sandwiches made with traditional or rye, spelt and red rice breads, raw-food meals, salads, soups and main courses (up to Rp55,000). There's a shop downstairs, plus a noticeboard for yoga and language classes and houses for rent. They also have a café in Kerobokan and a shop on the Bukit.

Bollero Jl Dewi Sita Ⓦwww.bollerobali .com. An airy restaurant with friendly service dishing up exceedingly well-cooked and well-presented Balinese, Asian and international dishes (mains Rp32,000–62,000) in relaxed surroundings. The desserts are extremely tempting, and there are cocktails and a small wine list.

Café des Artistes Jl Bisma 9X Ⓦwww.cafe desartistesbali.com. Sophisticated place with changing exhibitions by local artists and a tasty menu that features half a dozen steak dishes (from

---

Save the water bottle, save the world...

... by **reusing** your plastic water bottle. Discarded plastic bottles don't decompose and are expensive and wasteful to manufacture. The Bali Cantik Tanpa Plastik (**Plastic Free Bali**) Campaign is working to get rid of *all* plastic, including bags (see their Facebook page). In the meantime, to help minimize the rubbish problem, you can **refill** your plastic water bottle with the filtered water supplied at certain clued-up outlets in Ubud for less than what it would cost to buy a replacement. These include:

Jl Bisma: *Roda Internet Café*.

Jl Dewi Sita: *Tutmak* restaurant; Pondok Pekak Library and Learning Centre; and *Sjaki's Warung*.

Jl Hanoman: *Kafe* restaurant at no. 44B.

Jl Jembawan: *Bali Buddha* café.

Jl Kajeng: *Rumah Roda* losmen at no. 24.

Rice-paddy walk: *Sari Organik* café.

Rp74,000), home-made pastas, escargots (Rp45,000) and moules (Rp48,000) plus a good-value monthly special (Rp125,000 for 3 courses). Also offers over forty imported wines and Hoegaarden beer.

Clear Jl Hanoman ⓦ www.clear-café-ubud.com. This relative newcomer to the healthy-eating restaurant scene in Ubud offers an excellent range of organic raw, vegan, vegetarian and seafood dishes, drawing culinary inspiration from across the globe. The design is eye-catching and with mains from Rp30,000 it won't break the bank.

DeliCat Off Jl Dewi Sita. This is the place for a glass of wine and accompanying Camembert, Danish Blue, salami or smoked salmon (sandwiches from Rp30,000), or meatballs and mash (Rp40,000) – and there's a whole page on the menu for sausages (Rp45,000).

Ibu Oka Jl Suweta. This open-sided warung attracts queues of diners for its *babi guling* (roast suckling pig), which is cooked fresh every day (Rp30,000 with rice and *sambal*). It's open from 11am until the food runs out (about 5.30pm).

Ibu Rai Jl Monkey Forest ⓦ www.iburai.com. Hugely popular long-time tourist favourite that serves up Indonesian, Asian and international dishes in bustling surroundings and at reasonable prices (mains Rp42,000–75,000). *Bollero* is their quieter offshoot around the corner.

Kafe Jl Hanoman. Extremely popular with expats and visitors, the vast and enticing "organically inspired" menu includes salads (especially fine), soups, stews, stir fries, noodles and sandwiches supplemented by healthy juices. Mains range upwards from Rp29,000. *Little Kafe* is a small branch at the Yoga Barn (see p.180) and offers more raw food and Ayurvedic dishes.

Mojo's Flying Burritos Jl Raya Ubud ⓣ 0361/920 9422. Great-quality Californian-Mexican nachos, enchiladas, quesadillas and tacos. The speciality is the build-your-own burritos (about Rp30,000 depending on what you have). Margaritas and mojitos are reasonably priced, and free delivery is available.

Nomad Jl Raya Ubud 35 ⓦ nomad-bali.com. Serving local, Asian fusion and international dishes with style, *Nomad* offers a small but inviting menu ranging through Malaysian *laksa*, Thai prawn salad and Japanese *gyozas* (mains at Rp35,0000– 95,000). There are plenty of cocktails, too, including dessert cocktails such as Butterscotch Seduction and Death by Chocolate.

Rai Pasti, Warung and Tailor Jl Monkey Forest. Walk past the shirts to the restaurant tables for views of a local paddyfield and of the swanky *Three Monkey's* restaurant nearby. They dish up cheap and cheerful Indonesian and international meals (mains from Rp27,000) in pleasant surroundings.

Ryoshi Jl Raya Ubud ⓣ 0361/972192. Besides offering a decent selection of sushi, this branch of the Bali-wide chain of Japanese restaurants has a great menu of appetizers plus a huge variety of main courses taking in noodles, rice dishes, teriyaki and grilled skewers. Delivery available.

Siam Sally Jl Hanoman, Padang Tegal ⓦ www .siamsally.com. Above-average Thai cuisine in a relaxed setting featuring all the usual mainstays, including soups, curries, noodles and holy basil dishes (mains Rp58,000 upwards) with plenty of veggie and vegan options. Service is friendly and there's also weekly live music. Owned by the team that runs *teraZo* (pan Asian and international), *Batan Waru* (Indonesian) and *Cinta* (grills), other Ubud restaurants that are consistently popular.

Sjaki's Warung Off Jl Dewi Sita. In a lovely, quiet location overlooking the football field, this warung serves up cheap, good-quality mainstays (*nasi goreng* is Rp25,000). It also acts as a training and fund-raising business for the Sjaki-Tari-Us Founda-tion, which works with the mentally disabled and their families. There's a small shop attached.

Taco Casa and Grill Jl Pengosekan. Smashing little spot, popular with expats and tourists alike, serving excellent food that covers all the usual Mexican bases (burritos, tacos, quesadillas, fajitas and enchiladas) with big, good-value portions (Rp20,000–45,000). There's a small cocktail list including margaritas (Rp34,000–39,000).

Tutmak Jl Dewi Sita ⓦ www.tutmak.com. While this chilled spot is great for just about everything covered by its international and Indonesian menu, it's best for its exceptionally good coffee, cakes and pastries (the cinnamon rolls are sublime). It also does fine breakfasts – "The Works" costs Rp47,500.

Warung Enak Jl Pengosekan ⓣ 0361/972911, ⓦ www.warungenakbali.com. The menu ranges across the whole of Indonesia in this atmospheric, high-ceilinged *bale*. The *rijsttafel*, at Rp175,000/ person, is the way to hit all the highlights, and for the adventurous there's snail sate on offer. For the less intrepid, well-cooked soups, sates, curries, noodles and rice dishes are the mainstays (mains from about Rp45,000).

Warung Lokal Jl Gootama 7. This typical Balinese warung selling *cap cay, nasi campur, nasi goreng* and the like at good prices (main meals mostly Rp15,000–20,000) attracts a clientele of savvy foreigners and locals.

Campuhan, Sanggin-gan, Penestanan and Pengosekan

Indus Jl Raya Sanggingan ⓦ www.casalunabali .com. Affording great daytime views across to the

Campuhan ridge, this place is run by the same team behind *Bar Luna* and *Casa Luna* in central Ubud. The menu is a mix of Balinese, Asian and Western cuisine (main courses from Rp55,000); breakfasts are especially delectable. Free transport from *Casa Luna* (see map, p.158) and live Latino music every Monday and Friday from 7.30pm.

Made's Warung Penestanan ridge. One of several excellent options along the Penestanan ridge, serving well-priced travellers' favourites, including cheap juices (Rp7500), good *nasi campur* (Rp22,000) and (with 24hr notice) Balinese smoked duck (Rp195,000 for two).

Mozaic Jl Raya Sanggingan ☏0361/975768, ⓦwww.mozaic-bali.com. This multi-award-winning restaurant, regarded as one of the best in Asia, showcases the talents of French-American chef Chris Salans. The French- and Asian-inspired menu changes daily: splash out on the Discovery (Rp650,000) or Chef's Tasting menu (Rp850,000) for the full experience, or go for less pricey à la carte options. Reservations essential.

🏃 **Naughty Nuri's** Jl Raya Sanggingan. Long-running warung where the barbecued spare ribs (Rp75,000) are the highlight, drawing in diners from far and wide. This is the original and best *Naughty Nuri's*, directly opposite the Neka Museum. About 200m down the road, *Naughty Nuri's Mexican Grill* is a tarted-up version with a huge Mexican menu in addition to the ribs.

🏃 **Sari Organik** (aka *Bodag Maliah*) Off Jl Abangan, about 800m walk north from the aqueduct on western Jl Raya Ubud: follow signs from *Abangan Bungalows*. About 20min into the Ubud Kaja ricefield walk described on p.165, this ultra-chilled café has gorgeous views and delicious home-grown organic produce. The food (Rp30,000–48,000) is almost entirely home-made and includes great veggie kebabs, chicken and salads. Fireflies add extra sparkle in the evening. Daily 8am–8pm.

Warung Nasi Pak Sedan Jl Raya Pengosekan. Probably the cheapest meal in town; *nasi campur ayam* (the house speciality) costs Rp10,000. Open 7.30am–5pm.

Nightlife and entertainment

Ubud is no hotbed of hedonistic **nightlife**. Most tourists go to an early-evening Balinese **dance performance** before catching last orders at a restaurant at around 9pm. Alternative entertainment is limited to the **live music** staged at some of the town's **bars** and restaurants.

There's no cinema in Ubud but *Black Beach* Italian restaurant (ⓦwww .blackbeachubud.blog.com) on Jalan Hanoman shows Italian **films** with English subtitles on Wednesdays and English films on Thursdays on its rooftop terrace. The Yoga Barn at the southern end of Jalan Hanoman in Padang Tegal hosts an eclectic programme of Monday Night Movies every other Monday from 7.30pm (Rp20,000 or 85,000 including dinner from 6pm; ⓦwww.theyogabarn.com).

Bars and live-music venues

The **bar** scene can be very quiet in Ubud, so choose a **live-music night** to be sure of a decent crowd. Where phone numbers are given, free transport within the Ubud area is usually available.

Ary's Warung Jl Raya Ubud. This chic streetside lounge bar is ideal for people-watching while you sip on pricey martinis and champagne cocktails. All the usual spirits and beers and a large wine cellar are available. Daily 10.30am–10pm.

Bamboo Bar Jl Dewi Sita. Regular live music and a loud and lively vibe make this one of the best central places for a late-night session. The food is reasonable too. Daily until late.

🏃 **Café Havana** Jl Dewi Sita ⓦwww .cafehavanabali.com. This is where Ubud comes to shake its booty during live Latin music

(Thurs eve & Sun afternoon) and salsa class sessions (Wed & Sat 5–6pm; Rp100,000/person). At other times this great spot just dishes up tasty Cuban and Caribbean dishes washed down with a vast array of cocktails featuring Havana Club rum.

Jazz Café Jl Sukma 2, Peliatan ☏0361/976594, ⓦwww.jazzcafebali.com. Ubud's long-running jazz bar and restaurant stages quality live jazz – the best in Ubud. Tues–Sun 7.30–10.30pm.

Laughing Buddha Bar Jl Monkey Forest ⓦwww .laughingbuddhabar.net. Small, relaxed bar in the heart of Jl Monkey Forest; there's a big drinks menu plus plenty of nibbles and tapas to share alongside some larger meals. Sunset Happy Hour stretches from 4pm to 8pm and there's regular live music. Daily 8am–midnight.

Ozigo Jl Raya Sanggingan ☎0361/974728. The closest thing Ubud has to a Kuta-style club: DJs, theme nights and live music nightly from 10pm.

Shisha XL Lounge Jl Monkey Forest 129X ⓦ www.xlshishalounge.com. This comfortable, chilled-out place overlooking the football field stays open late and features DJs and live music plus a menu that takes in escargots, Dutch *bitterballen* (croquettes), burgers and kebabs. The drinks menu includes sangria and ice-cold beer and the shishas are Rp75,000. Daily noon–3am.

Dance and drama

The Ubud region is an important centre of **Balinese dance** and **gamelan** and boasts dozens of performance groups. Between them they stage up to nine different dance shows every night in the area; the tourist office publishes the schedule (which is also available at ⓦ www.ubud.com) and arranges **free transport** to outlying venues. **Ticket prices** are fixed and cost Rp70,000–80,000 from the tourist office, touts and at the door. Performances generally start between 7pm and 8pm, and it's free seating, so arrive early for the best spot.

The **Kecak** (Monkey Dance) and the **Barong** (Lion Dance) are the most accessible and visually interesting, while the **Legong** is more refined and understated. Unusual shows worth seeking out include the unique **all-female** Kecak Srikandhi. For more on Balinese dance, see p.377.

If you have only one evening to catch a show, consider seeing whatever is playing at **Puri Saren Agung** (**Ubud Palace**), opposite the market in the centre of Ubud. The setting is atmospheric, with the courtyard gateway and staircase furnishing a memorable backdrop. The Kecak that's staged twice a month on the nights of the full and dark moon at the **ARMA** in Pengosekan (see p.172), the Cak Rina, is also worth a special effort to catch, as it's an unusually fiery and humorous version.

Shopping

Shopping for arts and crafts is a major pastime in Ubud: there are outlets in all its neighbourhoods, but if you're short on time the **market** in central Ubud is a good one-stop venue and overflows with stalls selling pretty much anything you could want. For a shopping excursion around the central area, Jalan Monkey Forest, Jalan Hanoman and Jalan Dewi Sita are the best roads. You might also want to explore the specialist "craft villages" on the Denpasar–Ubud road (see pp.150–152). The 24-hour **minimarts** that dot the Ubud streetscape and Bintang Supermarket (daily; 8am–10pm), on Jalan Raya Campuhan, stock all major essentials, from suntan lotion to beer. Most Ubud shops **open** daily, often until 9pm; many can organize shipping if required. Unless otherwise stated, all of the places below are in central Ubud.

Too much luggage?

Need to make room in your luggage for new purchases? Donate unwanted clothes, books, bric-a-brac and anything else "so long as it's not alive" to the Yayasan Senyum **charity shop**, The Smile Shop, on Jalan Sriwedari (ⓦ www.senyumbali.org). Profits help fund operations for Balinese people with cranio-facial disabilities such as cleft palate. You can, of course, also buy cheap secondhand stuff at the shop too. The Jungle Shop on Jalan Gootama works in a similar way, supporting the work of the Sumatran Orangutan Society (ⓦ www.orangutans-sos.org).

Arts and crafts

Adi's Gallery and Sweet Komang's Gallery Café Jl Bisma 12. Modern art gallery with a changing display of works for sale and an attached café with seats inside and out. With *nasi goreng* at Rp17,000, you don't have to be an art-lover to appreciate this place.

Duck Man of Bali Jl Raya Goa Gajah, about 1.5km east along the road to Goa Gajah. Known for its phenomenal gallery of wooden ducks in all sizes and styles, carved by "the duck man", Ngurah Umum, and his assistants.

Nekat Just off the path to *Sari Organik* restaurant (see p.176). This gallery in the middle of the paddies displays the striking and deceptively simple pop-naive paintings by the idiosyncratic Pandi.

Rio Helmi Jl Suweta 5 ⊛ www.riohelmi.com. Small gallery of the respected expat photographer. With limited edition prints from $125 to more than $1000, it's the mass-market prints (Rp50,000) and the chance to see some great photographs on display that are the main attraction here.

Sjaki's Warung Off Jl Dewi Sita. A small shop attached to the warung selling a range of items made by the young learning disabled that the project helps; jewellery, art and small gifts are all on offer.

Books

Ary's Bookshop Jl Raya Ubud. Extensive stock of books and maps on Bali and Indonesia.

Ganesha Bookshop Jl Raya Ubud, corner of Jl Jembawan ⊛ www.ganeshabooksbali.com. The best bookshop in Bali, with a huge stock of new books on all things Balinese as well as numerous secondhand books.

Periplus North end of Jl Monkey Forest, Jl Raya Ubud and inside Bintang Supermarket on Jl Raya Campuhan, Campuhan. Well-stocked Bali-wide chain.

Pondok Pekak Library and Learning Centre Jl Dewi Sita. Plenty of well-priced secondhand books available for sale, rent and part-exchange.

Rendezvousdoux Jl Raya Ubud 14. Secondhand bookshop and café with decent food and comfy chairs so you can try before you buy.

Clothing, jewellery and accessories

Bali Harum Jl Raya Ubud. Stocks a wide range of Balinese toiletries in cute packaging.

Black Flag Jl Hanoman, Padang Tegal. Small shop offering a variety of up-to-the-minute stylish street clothes by a range of small Balinese independent fashion designers including Furious, Dynamite and Nothing.

Galaxyan Jl Hanoman ⊛ www.galaxyanjewels .com. Unusual and glorious (and gloriously

expensive) range of jewellery made from silver, copper and gold wire, some of it crocheted into shape. A great antidote to much of the overly delicate jewellery on offer in Bali.

Janet Molloy Collection: Goddess on the Go Jl Raya Pengosekan, Padang Tegal. Features eco-friendly, travel-friendly, stylish clothes made from beech tree fibres. The colour range is great and there are bags and jewellery as well.

Kado Jl Dewi Sita ⊛ www.saraswatipapers.com. Small outlet for Saraswati papers, handmade in Bali from recycled papers and including fresh flowers. The results are superb cards, notebooks, photograph albums, picture frames and wrapping papers that are all excellent gifts.

Kou Jl Dewi Sita and Jl Money Forest. Sells a small but fabulous range of home-made jam (mango, pineapple and guava, passion fruit and tangerine), Kusamba sea salt and handmade soaps.

Paul Ropp Jl Raya Sayan, Sayan. Extraordinary clothing (see p.97).

Pithecan Throbus Jl Monkey Forest. Top-quality silks and cottons printed with updated batik designs, which are then made into a range of clothing and charming gift items.

Studio Perak Jl Raya Ubud, Jl Hanoman and Jl Dewi Sita ⊛ 0361/973371, ⊛ www.studioperak .com. Stylish silver jewellery to suit all tastes from the folks who run the silversmithing courses (see p.181). It's also possible to purchase jewellery here produced by inmates at Kerobokan jail in an initiative established with the help of Studio Perak.

Ubud Bead Shop Jl Monkey Forest. Fun bead shop with an enormous selection and all the bits and pieces you need to make your own necklaces, bracelets and so on.

Crafts, textiles and souvenirs

Buddhas and Silk Jl Raya Pengosekan, Padang Tegal. Classy handicrafts from across Indonesia including plenty of textiles, pictures and ceramics. Worth taking a walk out here from central Ubud.

Kafe Jl Hanoman 44B. Tiny area in the restaurant for handicrafts, books, food and toiletries. The bags from recycled materials by the XSProject Group are the greatest fun.

Kupu-Kupu Jl Raya Ubud. Small outlet for inexpensive works produced by disabled woodcarvers, kite-makers, painters, bead workers and weavers, under the auspices of the Kupu-Kupu foundation (see Basics, p.55). Staffed by the artists.

Macan Tidur Jl Monkey Forest ⊛ www .macantidur.com. Stunning selection of arts, crafts, textiles and antiques from across Indonesia. Prices are at the top of the range but so is quality.

Made Maka Jl Sriwedari, opposite the Seniwati gallery. The little stone carvings of garden guardians are really so ugly they're cute – and just about transportable in your luggage if you buy nothing else.

Mitra Bali Fair Trade Jl Andong. You can show your support for local craftspeople at the little shop in Andong, where a changing range of crafts is on offer.

Tegun Jl Hanoman 44. Indonesian artefacts big and small from across the archipelago, including textiles, statues, puppets, jewellery, and wooden bowls and gifts.

Toko Yude Jl Raya Ubud. Stunning array of sarongs from Java including hand-painted cotton classics from Yogya and silk beauties.

Musical instruments

The Drum Factory Two shops on Jl Monkey Forest. The largest hand-drum manufacturer in Indonesia offers more than two hundred percussion instruments of all shapes and sizes. Some will even fit in the luggage.

Pondok Bamboo Far southern end of Jl Monkey Forest, Padang Tegal. Sells a full range of Balinese instruments made from bamboo, including *genggong* and the bamboo gamelan. The musician owner teaches music and is also a *dalang* shadow-puppet master; he performs here every Mon (*Ramayana*) & Thurs (*Mahabharata*) at 8pm (Rp75,000).

Spa treatments, yoga and alternative therapies

Arty, spiritual-minded Ubud is Bali's centre for **holistic practices** and **alternative therapies**, and also offers plenty of traditional **spa and beauty treatments** (for more on these, see p.47). For more information on holistic activities and therapies in Ubud and the rest of Bali, visit the website of the **Bali Spirit** network (ⓦ www .balispirit.com), which also runs Ubud's annual Bali Spirit Festival of world music, dance and yoga every March (ⓦ www.balispiritfestival.com). This aspect of Ubud has magnified greatly since the movie *Eat, Pray, Love* was released in 2010, following up on the book of the same name: see below for details of Ni Wayan Nuriasih, who featured in the book. The healer and artist Ketut Liyer, also a major character, lives in Pengosekan. Anyone in the village will direct you to him; however, he is very elderly and was not in good health when this book went to press. Unless otherwise stated, all of the places below are in central Ubud.

Bali Botanica Day Spa Jl Raya Sanggingan, Sanggingan ☎ 0361/976739, ⓦ www.balbotanica .com. Cute little day spa overlooking a small flower garden and river where the signature treatments are Ayurvedic (2hr 30min; Rp495,000) and herbal massage. Massages start from Rp150,000 (1hr 15min) and packages are available.

Balinese Traditional Healing Centre Jl Jembawan 5, but in future may also work from Rumah Lingkungan, Banjar Jungjungan, about 1.5km north of Ubud Botanic Garden ☎ 0361/8843042, ⓔ balihealer@hotmail.com. Fourth-generation Balinese healer Ni Wayan Nuriasih uses a combination of local herbal medicine plus Chinese and Ayurvedic practices, massage and *jamu* to treat her clients. Her popularity has soared since the publication of Elizabeth Gilbert's bestselling spiritual memoir, *Eat, Pray, Love* (reviewed on p.396), in which Wayan plays a major role. Tourists generally receive a traditional health spa treatment designed to address medical issues and rejuvenate the skin

(2–3hr; Rp850,000) which includes a "Body reading" diagnosis, a "Body balancing" massage, plus *jamu* to take away.

Cantika Jl Sok Wayah ☎ 0361/7944425, ⓦ www .indoline.net/santika. Location is all with this little place on the ricefield walk described on p.165, en route to *Sari Organik*. An hour's massage is Rp100,000 and facials, hair treatments, manicures and pedicures are also available using their own products.

Honeymoon Guesthouse Jl Bisma ☎ 0361/973282, ⓦ www.casalunabali.com. Offers beginners' and intermediate sessions that are a blend of hatha and vinyasa yoga. Mon–Wed, Fri & Sat 8–9.30am.

Intuitive Flow Ridgetop, Penestanan ⓦ www .intuitiveflow.com ☎ 0361/977824. Specializing in Yoga Pranala but also featuring other yoga schools, meditation and healing therapies, there are regular classes at the centre on the Penestanan ridgetop with brilliant views from the studio windows.

Jamu: herbal tonics for health and beauty

Ubud has long been famous for its **herbal medicine** – *ubad* means "medicine" in Balinese – known both for the medicinal plants that flourish around the Campuhan river gullies and for the local healers who know how to use them.

The pills, pastes and potions distilled from medicinal herbs are collectively known as **jamu** and are widely used throughout Bali (and the rest of Indonesia), both in the treatment of serious ailments and for general wellbeing. Healers usually **make their own** *jamu* from herbs they may have picked or even grown themselves and will have a standard range of special, secret, mixtures to prescribe to their patients as pills or for use in infusions; often they'll custom-make *jamu* for particular conditions as well. Commonly used mainstream plants include turmeric, ginger, galangal and garlic, but there are countless others. See p.179 for details of a couple of Ubud **healers** who also treat tourists and p.157 for information on guided herb-walks. Some *jamu*-makers don't offer healing sessions but simply hawk their home-brews around the market in old glass bottles. Several Ubud spas and cafés also serve ready-made *jamu* drinks to tourists, including *Bali Buddha*, reviewed on p.174.

Commercially produced *jamu* is also a huge industry and tends to focus more, but not exclusively, on the wellbeing side of things. Sex and beauty enhancers for men and women are predictably big sellers, as are diet and breast-enlargement elixirs, but there are also plenty of products for cleansing the blood, easing joint pain and muscle ache, improving circulation and dealing with skin conditions. The reputable brands use entirely natural ingredients, often to recipes that are familiar to those who make their own and, like home-made *jamu*, should have no side effects at all (though it's always best to seek local advice first). Pharmacies sometimes sell these commercial powders and pills but there are also dedicated *jamu* shops, like the one towards the eastern end of Ubud's Jalan Raya. Commercial *jamu* is distinc-tively packaged, often carrying a helpful graphic, like a pulsating knee joint (arthritis) or a smiling, muscular male (better sex), and the most vital information is usually also given in English.

Nur Salon Jl Hanoman 28 ☏0361/975352, ✉nursalonubud@yahoo.com. Ubud's first massage and beauty salon has been in operation since the 1970s and enjoys a very good reputation; the *mandi lulur* treatments are especially famous (from Rp175,000 for 1hr 30min) and the seaweed massages (Rp180,000) are also popular. The special packages are good value. The salon occupies a traditional Balinese compound and treatment rooms are designed in keeping. Uses male masseurs for male customers.

Spa Hati Jl Andong 14, Peliatan ☏0361/977578. Small, unpretentious spa offering a small programme of two- and four-hand massages and *lulur* treatments (from Rp165,000) and use of a jacuzzi and cute little swimming pool. Profits help fund the work of Bali Hati Foundation community projects (for more on which see Basics, p.54).

Ubud Bodyworks Centre Jl Hanoman 25 ☏0361/975720, ⓦwww.ubudbodyworkscentre .com. Well-respected centre for massage and spiritual healing where you can book an appointment with master healer Ketut Arsana ($50 for 30min) or with one of his staff (from Rp160,000/hr). Also offers traditional baths and massages, beauty treatments, acupressure, energy balancing, herbal healing and reflexology, and yoga sessions, and sells essential oils.

Ubud Sari Health Resort Jl Kajeng 35 ☏0361/974393, ⓦwww.ubudsari.com. The most serious of Ubud's health and beauty centres, with an on-site swimming pool and health restaurant. Treatments (from $15) include massage, reflex-ology, reiki, sports massage and yoga. You can also stay at the resort's tranquil bungalows (ⓖ) or book an all-inclusive healing week from $625 for six days.

Uma Ubud Sanggingan ☏0361/972448. Sunday-morning yoga class followed by a top-quality Uma Ubud breakfast. Rp295,000.

The Yoga Barn Southern Jl Hanoman, Padang Tegal ☏0361/970992, ⓦwww.theyogabarn.com. The Yoga Barn runs a big programme of yoga classes in various disciplines along with pilates, dance and meditation. It also offers yoga retreats (3–9 days at $400–1800) and yoga teacher-training.

Courses and workshops

With so many creative types in residence, Ubud is a great place to get learning: there are tourist-oriented **courses** in everything from batik to yoga. In addition to the more formal venues listed below, it's always worth asking advice from the more traditional homestays, whose managers are often dancers, musicians or painters. For yoga courses, see p.179. Unless otherwise stated, all of the places below are in central Ubud.

Arts, crafts, music, dance and traditional culture

ARMA Cultural Workshops Jl Raya Pengosekan, Pengosekan ☏0361/976659, ⓦwww .armamuseum.com. Museum-endorsed classes (mostly 2hr; $25–50) in Balinese painting, woodcarving, batik, gamelan, dance and theatre, silver, basket weaving, traditional architecture, Hinduism, astrology and making offerings.

Café Havana Jl Dewi Sita ⓦwww.cafehavanabali .com. Regular salsa classes (Wed and Sat 5–6pm; Rp100,000/person).

Jati Homestay Jl Hanoman, Padang Tegal ☏0361/977701, ⓦwww.jatihs.com. Painting (Rp100,000/hr) and dancing (Rp75,000/hr) lessons arranged on an individual basis.

Lingsir Paperie Jl Dewi Sita ☏0361/977984. Papermaking classes (Mon–Thurs & Sat 10am–noon, Rp175,000).

Museum Puri Lukisan Cultural Workshops Jl Raya Ubud ☏0361/971159, ⓦwww.mpl-ubud .com. Serious, reputable classes at Ubud's oldest art museum covering batik, woodcarving, beadwork, classical painting, basketry, kite-making, mask-painting, shadow-puppet-making, gamelan and Balinese dance.

Nirvana Batik Course Jl Gootama 10 ☏0361/975415, ⓦnirvanaku.com. Renowned batik artist I Nyoman Suradnya runs one- to five-day courses in batik painting (Rp485,000/day, including materials). His family also runs the *Nirvana Pension* guesthouse (see p.160).

Nyuhkuning woodcarving shops Nyuhkuning. There are plenty of willing teachers in this village of woodcarvers; just ask at any of the shops.

Pondok Pekak Library and Learning Centre Jl Dewi Sita ☏0361/976194, ⓔlibrarypondok @yahoo.com. "Art of Bali" beginners' classes in dance, gamelan, painting, woodcarving, making offerings and jewellery (Rp75,000–200,000). Book at least one day in advance.

Sari Api Jl Suweta, ☏0361/977917, ⓔsariapi @indo.net.id. Courses in ceramic-making from the Canadian ceramicist Susan Kohlik.

Sehati Guesthouse Off the southern end of Jl Monkey Forest, Padang Tegal ☏0361/976341, ⓦwww.sehati-guesthouse.com. Learn the elements of Balinese dance from a graduate of Denpasar's prestigious school of performing arts (Rp100,000/hr).

Studio Perak Jl Raya Ubud, Jl Hanoman and Jl Dewi Sita ☏0361/973371, ⓦwww.studioperak .com. Courses in silversmithing: in half a day you can produce your own ring or pendant (Rp250,000 inclusive of 5g of silver).

Threads of Life Indonesian Textile Art Center Jl Kajeng 24 ☏0361/972187, ⓦwww.threadsof life.com. Scheduled weekly lectures (Tues & Weds) on Indonesian textile appreciation (Rp150,000 for one or two people, Rp50,000/person for three or more). Contact them for details.

Cookery and language

Café Wayan Jl Monkey Forest ☏0361/975447, ⓦwww.alamindahbali.com. There are seven choices of lessons (2hr; Rp350,000) featuring various menus, given at the *Laka Leke* restaurant in Nyuhkuning village.

Casa Luna restaurant Jl Raya Ubud ☏0361/973282, ⓦwww.casalunabali.com. Famous, long-running half-day Balinese cooking workshops (from Rp300,000) run by *Fragrant Rice* author Janet de Neefe.

Paon Cooking Class Laplapan village ☏0813/3793 9095, ⓦwww.paon-bali.com. Well-regarded classes (from Rp350,000) that get rave reviews. Free pick-up in the Ubud area.

Pondok Pekak Library and Learning Centre Jl Dewi Sita ☏0361/976194, ⓔlibrarypondok @yahoo.com. Intensive Indonesian language courses (24hr, usually over 4 weeks; Rp900,000) and individual lessons (Rp120,000/1hr 30min), plus Balinese lessons (Rp150,000/1hr 30min).

Secret Garden Cooking School Taman Rahasia hotel, Penestanan Kaja ☏0361/979395, ⓦwww .balisecretgarden.com. One- and two-day courses in Balinese cooking offered to guests staying at the hotel. Cooking school and accommodation packages from $290.

Tegal Sari hotel Jl Hanoman, Padang Tegal ☏0361/973318, ⓦwww.tegalsari-ubud.com. Half-day courses in Balinese and Indonesian cuisine (Rp350,000 including lunch).

Warung Enak Jl Pengosekan, Padang Tegal
℡0361/972911, ⊛www.warungenakbali.com.
These classes come with a different set menu on

each day (Mon, Wed & Sat 7am–1pm; Rp450,000).
Vegetarian menu available on request.

Listings

Banks and exchange There are ATMs and money-changers throughout central Ubud (see p.63 for details of common scams). PT Central Kuta is a recommended exchange counter in the Circle K supermarket opposite Museum Puri Lukisan.

Embassies and consulates See p.59.

Hospitals, clinics and dentists Toya Medika Clinic is at Jl Raya Pengosekan (℡0361/978078). Ubud Clinic, which also has a dental service, is at Jl Raya Campuhan 36 (℡0361/974911, ⊛www.ubud-clinic.com); it's open 24hr, is staffed by English-speakers and will respond to emergency call-outs. For anything serious, the nearest hospitals are in Denpasar (p.122).

House rental Check the noticeboards at *Bali Buddha* café, Jl Jembawan, Bintang Supermarket, Jl Raya Sanggingan and *Kafe*, Jl Hanoman 44B.

Internet access Efficient internet centres include Highway, Jl Raya Ubud (open 24hr; ⊛www.highway bali.com) and *Roda Internet Café*, Jl Bisma 3.

Libraries The Pondok Pekak Library and Learning Centre off Jl Dewi Sita (daily 9am–9pm) has lots of books about Bali, English-language novels, a comfortable upstairs reading room and a children's library. The Agung Rai Museum of Art (ARMA) has the island's best library of books about Bali, including famous esoteric works and language books.

Phones Wartel Telkom is at the eastern end of Jl Raya Ubud (daily 8am–9pm) and also has credit-card phones outside. Most internet centres offer international phone services and also have Skype.

Police The main police station is on the eastern

edge of town, on Jl Andong. There's a more central police booth at the Jl Raya Ubud /Jl Monkey Forest crossroads.

Post office The main office, at Jl Jembawan 1 (Mon–Sat 8am–5pm, Sun & hols 9am–4pm), has poste restante and a parcel-packing service at the back. There are postal agents throughout Ubud where you can buy stamps and send mail and parcels.

Safety boxes For rent at Rp15,000/day at Ary's Bookshop, Jl Raya Ubud (daily 8.30am–9pm).

Travel agents Ary's Business and Travel Service, Jl Raya Ubud (℡0361/973130, ℮arys_tour @yahoo.com) provides general travel agency services including car and motorbike rental. Perama, Jl Hanoman, Padang Tegal (℡0361/973316, ⊛www.peramatour.com) sells shuttle-bus tickets and offers a range of other travel services. Friends of the National Parks Foundation (FNPF), Jl Bisma 3 (℡0361/977978, ⊛www.fnpf .org) is the place to go for information about the Bali starling project in Nusa Penida and advice on arranging a visit to the island (see p.139).

Volunteering The Ubud area hosts a number of charitable foundations that can use a helping hand for varying lengths of time, although needs vary (see Charities and volunteer projects, p.54 for more details). Sjaki-Tari-Us Foundation (⊛www.sjakitarius.nl) at Sjaki's Warung and BAWA, Jl Monkey Forest 100X (⊛www.bawabali. com) both welcome volunteers; contact them in advance.

East of Ubud

Slicing through the region immediately **east of Ubud**, the sacred rivers Petanu and Pakrisan flow down from the Batur crater rim in parallel, framing a narrow strip of land imbued with great spiritual and historical importance. This 15km-long sliver has been settled since the Balinese Bronze Age, around 300 BC, and now boasts the biggest concentration of antiquities on Bali. From the stone sarcophagi and Bronze Age gong of **Pejeng** to the eleventh-century rock-hewn hermitage at **Goa Gajah** and fourteenth-century **Yeh Pulu reliefs**, these relics all lie within 7km of Ubud.

Access by **bemo** is easy from Ubud – take any Gianyar-bound service – and similarly straightforward by bike or motorbike. This area also combines well with Tirta Empul and Gunung Kawi, 11km further north, and direct bemos connect the two.

Goa Gajah

Thought to have been a hermitage for eleventh-century Hindu priests, **Goa Gajah** (Elephant Cave; daily 8am–5pm; Rp15,000, children Rp7500, including sarong rental) is a major tourist attraction, owing more to its proximity to the main Ubud–Gianyar road than to any remarkable atmosphere. Besides the cave itself, there's a traditional bathing pool here, as well as a number of ancient stone relics.

Descending the steps from the back of the car park, you get a good view of the elegant rectangular **bathing pool**. Such pools were usually built at holy sites, either at the source of a holy spring as at Tirta Empul or, like this one, near a sacred spot, so that devotees could cleanse themselves before making offerings or prayers. Although the water still flows, the pool is now maintained for ornamental purposes only.

The carvings that trumpet the entranceway to the hillside cave are impressive, if difficult to distinguish. The **doorway** is a huge gaping mouth, framed by the upper jaw of a monstrous rock-carved head that's thought to represent either the earth god Bhoma, or the widow-witch Rangda, or a hybrid of the two. It would have served both as a repeller of evil spirits and as a suggestion that on entering you were being swallowed up into a holier world. Early visitors interpreted it as an elephant's head, which is how the cave got its modern name.

Passing into the monster's mouth, you enter the dimly lit T-shaped **cave**, hewn by hand to serve as meditation cells or possibly living quarters, for the priests or ascetics. Legend describes how the mythical giant Kebo Iwa gouged out the cells and the carvings here with his powerful fingernails in just one night.

Outside the cave, in a small pavilion to the left of the gateway, is a weather-worn statue of a woman surrounded by a horde of kids. This is the folk heroine **Men Brayut**, who has come to epitomize a mother's struggle against poverty (see box, p.201). Men Brayut is known as the goddess Hariti in Buddhist literature, and this statue, along with a number of other relics found nearby, have led archeologists to believe that the site may have a **Buddhist** as well as a Hindu history.

Practicalities

To get to Goa Gajah, either walk, cycle or drive the 3km east from Ubud's Jalan Peliatan, or take an Ubud–Gianyar **bemo**, which will drop you at the entrance. The car park borders the main Ubud–Gianyar road. You can also walk between Yeh Pulu (see below) and Goa Gajah through the ricefields, but you'll need to hire one of the guides who hang around both at Yeh Pulu and Goa Gajah.

Yeh Pulu

In contrast with the overcrowded and rather overrated carvings at Goa Gajah, the rock-cut panels amid the ricefields at **Yeh Pulu** (daily 7am–6pm; Rp15,000, children Rp7500 including sarong rental) are delightfully engaging, and the site is often empty.

Chipped away from a cliff face, the 25m-long series of Yeh Pulu **carvings** are said to date back to the fourteenth or fifteenth century. They are thought by some historians to depict a five-part story and while the meaning of this story has been lost, it's still possible to make out some recurring characters and to speculate on the connections between them; local people, however, simply describe the carvings as showing daily activities from times past.

The small **spring** after which the site is named (*yeh* means "holy spring", *pulu* "stone vessel") rises close by the statue of Ganesh that is carved into the final niche and is sacred – hence the need for all visitors to wear temple dress. The Balinese believe that all water is a gift from the spirits so whenever the spring fails, special ceremonies are required to restore a harmonious flow.

Practicalities

The prettiest approach to Yeh Pulu is **on foot** through the rice terraces behind Goa Gajah, but you'll need a guide – they wait for customers at both sites and charge Rp200,000 for one or two people. Guides can also take you on the two-hour return ricefield **walk** from Yeh Pulu to the rice temple Dukuh Kedongan, with the chance of a dip in the Petanu River (Rp250,000 for one or two people); or there are longer variations (3–5hr), which continue either to the village of Segana or to the Durga Kutri temple, Pura Bukit Dharma Durga Kutri, in the village of Kutri (see p.196) or a trek of similar length to the village of **Tengkulak** via the Campuhan river. All of these cost about Rp400,000 for one or two people.

If you're using the Ubud–Gianyar **bemo**, get off at the Yeh Pulu signs just east of Goa Gajah or west of the Bedulu crossroads, then walk the kilometre south through the hamlet of Batulumbang to Yeh Pulu. If driving, follow the same signs through Batulumbang until the road peters out, a few hundred metres above the stonecarvings. *Made's Warung* is well located at the end of this road and serves a simple menu of **snacks** and rice dishes.

Pejeng

Inhabited since the Bronze Age, and considered a holy site ever since, the village of **PEJENG** and its immediate environs harbour a wealth of religious antiquities, from carvings and rock-cut *candi* to bronze artefacts and massive stone statues. Some of these have been left in their original location, alongside riverbeds or buried in the paddyfields, while others have been housed in local temples. Several have also been carted off to museums, here and in Denpasar, Jakarta and Amsterdam. The remains have rather an esoteric appeal, and the area gets relatively few visitors.

Pejeng's three main **temples** all lie within a few hundred metres of each other on the Bedulu–Tampaksiring road, and are clearly signposted. Coming from Ubud, take a Gianyar-bound **bemo** to the Bedulu crossroads and then either wait for a Tampak-siring-bound bemo, or walk the kilometre to the temples. The alternative route from Ubud – by bike or motorbike – is the fairly scenic but severely undulating 5km-long **back road** that heads east from the Jalan Raya Ubud/Jalan Peliatan junction at the eastern edge of Ubud, passes the *Maya Ubud* hotel, and then zigzags through paddies and small villages before finally emerging at the market on the main road, just 25m north of Pura Penataran Sasih (turn right for the temple). Entry to each temple is by **donation**; the obligatory sarong and sash can be borrowed at each one.

For **food** in Pejeng, the car park opposite Pura Penataran Sasih is lined with simple warung.

Pura Penataran Sasih

Balinese people believe **Pura Penataran Sasih** to be a particularly sacred temple, because this is the home of the so-called Moon of Pejeng – hence the English epithet **Moon Temple**.

The crafts of Bali and Lombok

Bali and Lombok are among the world's best destinations for traditional crafts, as famous for their flamboyant stone-carved temples as their sumptuous gold brocades. Woodcarvings, sculptures and handwoven fabric are some of the most tempting buys, particularly in the Ubud area and in the villages of East Bali, while Lombok produces beautiful pots. There is surprising diversity, too, with age-old forms still popular but increasingly updated with a sleek, contemporary twist.

Carved stone statue ▲

Stonecarving

Stonecarvings are Bali's most public art form, gracing the facades and interiors of homes, hotels and temples. Because many are chiselled from quick-to-erode volcanic tuff, they need to be renewed often, so the craft thrives. Religious and secular buildings tend to feature similar iconography, with deities and demons appearing alongside playful scenes of daily life. North Bali **temples** in Jagaraga, Sangsit and, most famously, Kubutambahan (see p.266) are sculpted with scenes of everything from love-making to beer-drinking parties. Bali's most famous stonecarving centre is **Batubulan**, where roadside stalls sell statues of mythical figures, Buddha heads and pagoda lanterns as well as modern, indoor abstracts carved from slinky white Javanese limestone.

Stonemasons shop near Ubud ▼

Carving wood ▼

Art markets and how to bargain

Some of the most enjoyable places to shop for lower-grade crafts are the traditional *pasar seni*, or **art markets**. Visitors will find everything from sarongs and ceremonial fabric to woodcarvings and T-shirts for sale. Every sizeable town has a *pasar seni*, but some of the best are in Denpasar, Ubud and Sukawati. These markets are also great places to hone your **bargaining** skills (for more advice, see p.56). It's standard practice all over Indonesia to haggle for your purchase and in general, assume that the vendor's opening price is well over the odds. Begin with a counter offer that's at least thirty percent less and negotiate from there – and always remain good-humoured. In swankier shops asking about the availability of a discount can sometimes get a reduction.

Woodcarving

The oldest Balinese **woodcarvings** are those that decorate the doors and pillars of **temples** and **palaces**, often in the shape of mythological beings that protect the building from evil influence. Denpasar's Bali Museum has some good examples (see p.119), and many losmen and hotels boast beautiful traditional-style wooden **doors**. Reproduction antique-style doors and furniture are sold in Batubulan, Mas and Seminyak. **Mas** is a centre for the best and most expensive woodcarving outlets, but more affordable carvings are produced in **Nyuhkuning** and **Ubud**. Villages along the Tegalalang-Pujung road churn out non-traditional artefacts like brightly painted mobiles.

Traditional textiles

Nearly a century after Western fashions started filtering into Indonesia, **cloth** still has a **ritual purpose** on Bali and Lombok where it is worn, given or hung at important rites-of-passage ceremonies such as tooth-filing and first hair-cutting. **Pacung** in north Bali is a renowned centre for sacred striped *bebali* cloth. Bali's indigenous textile industry has always focused on the **ikat** technique, in which the yarn is tie-dyed into the finished design before weaving begins, particularly the weft-*ikat* or *endek* of **Gianyar** and the highly complex double *ikat* or *gringsing* of **Tenganan**. It's possible to see weavers at work in both those places, as well as in **Sidemen**, **Seraya** and **Singaraja**. To see brocaded weft-*ikat* or *songket* being woven, visit **Sukarara** on Lombok, which produces exuberantly coloured versions that are popular for weddings. Javanese-style **batik** is currently more fashionable

▲ Craft stalls on the Tegalalang–Pujung road

▼ Batik sarongs for sale

You'll find additional background information on crafts traditions inside the Guide chapters. For more on woodcarving, see p.151; for more on stonecarving, see p.147. For advice on where and how to shop, see p.52.

Batik detail ▲

Lombok pots ▼

Potter in the village of Penujak, Lombok ▼

for sarongs and shirts; the shops on Denpasar's Jalan Sulawesi stock hundreds of batik designs (see p.120). For exquisite examples of locally woven cloth, go to the Bali Museum in Denpasar (see p.119) and the Threads of Life Textile Arts Center in Ubud (see p.164).

Basketware

The historic Balinese village of **Tenganan** is celebrated for its distinctive, very finely woven basketware made from *ata* grass. They come in every imaginable shape and size, from the tiniest boxes to ones that are big enough for you and your laundry. **Pengosekan** is known for its palm-leaf baskets in eye-catchingly bold designs. On Lombok, the village of **Loyok** specializes in bamboo baskets.

Lombok pots

Traditional **pottery** has become big business in Lombok and also finds its way to Bali's shops. It's centred in the villages of **Banyumulek** and **Penujak**, where the techniques for producing the distinctive water vessels, as well as the more modern bowls, vases and lamp bases, are passed down from mother to daughter. They work the local grey clay by hand using a round stone and a wooden paddle. After firing, the potters apply slip (liquid clay) and polish the surface to a deep shine. Modern designs incorporate etching, inlays and paintings.

The moon in question is a **large bronze gong**, shaped almost like an hourglass, suspended high in its tower at the back of the temple compound. It probably dates from the Balinese Bronze Age, from sometime during the third century BC, and – at almost 2m long – is thought to be the largest such kettledrum ever cast. Legend tells how the gong once served as the wheel of a chariot that transported the moon through the skies, at which time the wheel shone just as brightly as the moon itself. The Balinese treat the Moon of Pejeng as sacred and make offerings to it whenever they need to move it.

The **temple** itself was once the most important in the area, and whatever the origins of the gong, it would have been used for the same purposes as the modern *kulkul* – to summon the people of Pejeng to ceremonies, to announce war, and also to invite rain to fall.

Pura Pusering Jagat

About 100m south down the main road from Pura Penataran Sasih, **Pura Pusering Jagat**, the "Temple of the Navel of the World", is famous for its elaborately carved metre-high **stone jar**, used for storing holy water. Carved in the fourteenth century from a single block of sandstone, the jar's reliefs are thought to depict a scene from the Hindu myth "The Churning of the Sea of Milk", in which the gods and the demons compete for the chance to extract, distil and drink the elixir of immortal life.

Housed in a nearby pavilion is another significant icon, the metre-high phallic *linggam* and its female receptacle, the *yoni* – this is an important shrine visited by many newlywed and infertile couples.

Pura Kebo Edan

Pura Kebo Edan, some 200m south of Pura Pusering Jagat, is also considered lucky for childless couples. The attraction here is the massive, lifelike phallus of the huge stone man, nicknamed the **Pejeng Giant**, who is nearly 4m tall and is depicted dancing on a prone female figure thought to represent the earth. He is said to possess six penises in all; aside from the one swinging out for all to see, one is supposed to have dropped to the ground during his dancing, and four more are said to be hidden inside him, awaiting the correct point of the dance before emerging. His principal penis is pierced from front to back with a huge bolt-like pin, probably a realistic reference to an age-old Southeast Asian practice designed to increase women's sexual pleasure. The giant's identity is debatable; he is possibly Bhima, one of the chief characters from the *Mahabharata* or the Hindu god Siwa, who harnessed enormous cosmic power whenever he danced.

Museum Arkeologi Gedung Arca

Pejeng's government-run **Museum Arkeologi Gedung Arca**, 500m south of Pura Penataran Sasih (Sat–Thurs 8am–3pm, Fri 8am–12.30pm; free, but a donation to your guide is expected) houses an eclectic assortment of artefacts found in the area, ranging from Paleolithic chopping tools to bronze bracelets and Chinese plates, though labels are limited and many pieces have been moved to the Bali Museum in Denpasar (see p.119).

The most interesting exhibits are the huge **sarcophagi**. These massive coffins, up to 3m long and fashioned from two fitted sections of hollowed-out stone, probably date back to about 300 BC. They were designed to hold adult skeletons (those placed in the smallest vessels would have been flexed at knees, hips and shoulders), and only the more important members of a community would have merited such an elaborate burial. Bronze jewellery, coins and weapons were found in some of the sarcophagi.

North of Ubud

All three major roads **north of Ubud** lead eventually to Gunung Batur and its huge crater (covered in Chapter 4). Whether you go via **Payangan** to the west, **Tegalalang** directly to the north, or **Tampaksiring** to the east, the villages and paddyfields along each route make for a pleasant drive. Distances are comparable, about 40km to Batur whichever way you go, but the most significant tourist sights are located along the most easterly route, around the Tampaksiring area.

The most frequent and reliable **bemo** service running north from Ubud is on the **central route** via Tegalalang and Pujung; there are frequent bemos along the first section of the **westerly route**, as far as Payangan, but only some of them continue as far as Kintamani. For the **easterly route** via Tampaksiring, you'll need to change bemos at the Bedulu crossroads, just over 5km from he market in Ubud by road.

Although there's little of specific interest on the **westerly route**, which takes you via Campuhan and Payangan, this is the quietest, least congested and prettiest of the three, and the best if you have **private transport**. The villages on the way are picturesque and in Payangan you pass the village's famously huge roadside banyan tree. The road eventually brings you to Pura Ulun Danu Batur (see p.241) on the Batur–Kintamani road, about 5km west of Penelokan.

Tegalalang, Ceking and Sebatu

The **central route** up to Gunung Batur begins at the eastern edge of Ubud, from the point where Jalan Raya Ubud intersects with Jalan Peliatan (if you're heading up here on a bicycle, you might prefer the more peaceful route that starts on central Ubud's Jalan Suweta).

Seven kilometres north of Ubud, the village of **TEGALALANG** and its environs produce a wide range of **handicrafts** and **home accessories**, and the entire length of the 12km-long Ubud–Tegalalang–Pujung road is lined with shops displaying their wares, which include painted wooden mobiles, animals and figurines; wrought iron lamp stands, tables and artefacts; glass mosaic and wooden frames for pictures and mirrors; and much else besides. On a clear morning the **views** become increasingly spectacular as you pass through Tegalalang, with Bali's greatest mountains looming majestically ahead – Gunung Batur to the north, and Gunung Agung to the east – and rice terraces providing the classic foreground.

In **CEKING**, the village just north of Tegalalang, there's no shortage of well-stocked souvenir shops, and several **restaurants** make the most of the vistas, including the *Kampung Café*, overlooking the valley and, a few hundred metres further north, the homely *Dewi Café*.

If you continue north along the main road for another 18km, you'll reach the Gunung Batur crater rim. Alternatively, a right turn at *Dewi Café* takes you along the scenic back road – where the quieter and more isolated *Boni Bali Restaurant* (Ⓦwww .bonibalirestaurant.com) can be found a few hundred metres after the turn – to the village of **SEBATU**, 6km beyond, site of the uncrowded **Pura Gunung Kawi Sebatu** water-temple complex (daily 8am–5pm; Rp15,000, including sarong rental). Not to be confused with the quite different and more-visited Gunung Kawi in nearby Tampaksiring, the Sebatu temple is built on the site of holy springs, whose water is channelled into seven walled **bathing pools** – four for public bathing and three, at the spring itself, for special cleansing rituals. Many of the temple's wooden shrines and *bale* are carved with exquisite, brightly painted floral motifs.

Taro and the Elephant Safari Park

Turning left off the main Kintamani road a couple of kilometres beyond Pujung Kelod, a signposted little road leads you 6km west to the village of **TARO** and its Elephant Safari Park. While the imported pachyderms are a relatively recent claim to fame for Taro, it has long been renowned among the Balinese for its small herd of sacred white **Brahmin cows**.

The **Elephant Safari Park** (daily 8am–6pm; $16, children $8, family discounts available; Ⓦwww.baliadventuretours.com) occupies a landscaped area of fields and forest to the south-east of the village and is home to more than two dozen elephants brought over from Sumatra, where they had been trained to work in the logging industry but were then abandoned when the industry declined. The park admission fee allows you to feed the animals, admire their painting skills and watch them having their baths. There's also an elephant museum and luxurious on-site accommodation at the *Elephant Safari Park Lodge* (Ⓦwww.elephantsafariparklode.com; ⑨). The chief attraction, however, is the half-hour leisurely, swaying elephant **safari ride** offering an elephant's eye view of the countryside ($45, children $32; purchasers get fifty per cent off admission). Most people visit the park as part of a **tour**, which includes transport, a meal and the safari ride ($86/$58 or nighttime safari $99/$69); book at any travel agent or directly with the park. There's a restaurant inside the park.

Tampaksiring

The most **easterly route** from Ubud to the mountains takes you along the Bedulu–Penelokan road, passing through Pejeng before reaching **TAMPAK-SIRING**, 11km further on, a fairly nondescript town that's the access point for nearby **Gunung Kawi** and **Tirta Empul**. Gianyar–Bedulu–Tampaksiring **bemos** terminate near the market in the centre of the long settlement. There's no public bemo service between Tampaksiring and Penelokan, about 20km north, but you should be able to charter one. Gunung Kawi is an easy walk north of the market in Tampaksiring and you should be able to charter a bemo in the market to Tirta Empul. There are several simple warung in the market area for refreshments.

Gunung Kawi

Hewn from the rocky walls of the lush, enclosed valley of the sacred Pakrisan River, the eleventh-century royal "tombs" at **Gunung Kawi** (daily 8am–5.30pm; Rp15,000, children Rp7500 plus donation for sarong rental) occupy a lovely spot and are a lot quieter than most other archeological sites, not least because you have to descend 315 steps to reach them. Access is signed via Jalan Bayubrata, which heads east off the main road a few hundred metres north of Tampaksiring's market.

The *candi* are huge reliefs, chiselled from the riverside cliff face to resemble temple facades. Originally the surface would have been decorated with plaster carvings, but now all that's left are the outlines of a single false door on each one. The most likely **theory** about these "tombs", or *candi*, is that they were erected as memorials to the eleventh-century king Anak Wungsu and his queens. The four Queens' Tombs are thought to be for Anak Wungsu's minor consorts, while the five Royal Tombs across the river probably honour the king and his four favourite wives. The slightly higher *candi* at the far left end is believed to be Anak Wungsu's. As there are no signs of bones or ashes in the *candi*, it appears that they weren't actual tombs, yet over the false door of each were found inscriptions (most of them unreadable) thought to be names or titles.

The complex also contains an extensive **cloister**, which probably accommodated the tombs' caretakers. On the way back to the steps you can branch off left through the fields to reach the so-called **Tenth Tomb**, a five-minute walk away. Believed to have been erected in memory of an important member of the royal household, this *candi* stands on its own, framed only by rock-cut cloisters.

The staircase is lined with souvenir stalls and drinks stops and *Kafé Kawi* at the top is a good spot to recover after the ascent.

Tirta Empul

Balinese from every corner of the island make pilgrimages to **Tirta Empul** (daily 7am–6pm; Rp15,000, children Rp7500), signposted off the main Tampaksiring–Kintamani road, about 500m north of the turn-off to Gunung Kawi. They come to spiritually cleanse themselves and cure their physical ailments by bathing in the **holy springs**. Legend describes how the springs were first tapped by the god Indra during his battle with the evil Mayadanawa, an early ruler of the Pejeng kingdom. Mayadanawa had poisoned the nearby river and made Indra's retainers sick, so Indra pierced the earth to release a spring of pure and sacred water – the elixir of immortality – that would revive his flagging troops. The new spring was named Tirta Empul, and has been considered the holiest in Bali ever since the tenth century, if not longer. A **temple** was built around the springs and the complex is now an extremely popular destination, both for Balinese and foreign tourists.

The **bathing pools** are sunk into the ground of the temple's outer courtyard, fed by the water from the springs in the inner sanctuary. Men, women and priests have segregated sections in which to immerse themselves, though most just splash their faces. However, for pregnant women and anyone who's just recovered from a long illness, Tirta Empul is one of three places in which they must bathe for a special ritual called *melukat*. This ceremony requires immersion in the waters of each of Bali's three holiest springs: the "holy waters of the mountain" at Tirta Bungkah, the "holy springs of the plain" here at Tirta Empul and the "holy springs of the sea" at Tirta Selukat at Pura Dalem Pingit.

Travel details

Bemos and public buses

It's almost impossible to give the frequency with which bemos and public buses run: see Basics, p.30, for details. Journey times given below are the minimum you can expect. Only the direct bemo and bus routes are listed; for longer journeys, you'll have to go via Denpasar's Batubulan terminal or Gianyar (see p.195).

Batubulan (Denpasar) to: Amlapura (2hr 30min); Bangli (2hr 30min); Candi Dasa (2hr); Celuk (10min); Gianyar (1hr); Kintamani (1hr 30min); Klungkung (1hr 30min); Mas (35min); Nusa Dua (1hr); Padang Bai (for Lombok; 1hr 40min); Peliatan (45min); Semarapura (1hr 20min); Singaraja (Penarukan terminal; 3hr); Sukawati (20min); Tegalalang (1hr 15min); Ubud (50min).

Ubud to: Campuhan/Sanggingan (5–10min); Celuk (40min); Denpasar (Batubulan terminal; 50min); Gianyar (20min); Goa Gajah (10min); Kedewatan (10min); Kintamani (1hr); Mas (15min); Peliatan (5min); Pujung (25min); Sukawati (30min).

Perama shuttle buses

Ubud to: Bedugul (daily; 1hr 30min); Candi Dasa (3 daily; 1hr 30min–2hr); Gili Islands (daily; 8hr); Kintamani (daily; 45min); Kuta/Ngurah Rai Airport (5 daily; 1hr–1hr 30min); Lovina (daily; 1hr 30min–2hr); Nusa Lembongan (daily; 2hr 30min); Padang Bai (3 daily; 1hr–1hr 30min); Sanur (5 daily; 30min–1hr); Senggigi (Lombok; 2 daily; 7hr 30min–11hr 30min).

East Bali

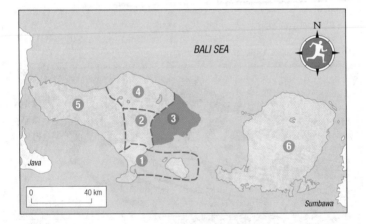

N

BALI SEA

④

⑤

②

③

Java

① ⑥

0   40 km

Sumbawa

CHAPTER 3 # Highlights

✳ **Nyoman Gunarsa Museum**
An exquisite (if dusty)
collection of historic cloth
paintings from Kamasan.
See p.202

✳ **Gunung Agung** Bali's highest
and most important mountain
looms majestically over every
district of the east – everyone
can enjoy the sight, and the
seriously fit can climb it.
See p.202

✳ **Sidemen** There's great
accommodation and classic
rice-terrace scenery in this
small upland village.
See p.208

✳ **Candi Dasa** This relaxed
resort makes an ideal base for
exploring the east. See p.213

✳ **Tirtagangga** Enjoy glorious
mountain and rice-paddy
views, an attractive water
palace and gentle treks
through typical Balinese
countryside. See p.223

✳ **Amed** A dramatic coastline
with prime diving and
snorkelling just offshore.
See p.226

▲ Rice terraces near Tirtagangga

East Bali

The **east of Bali** is dominated both physically and spiritually by the majestic, picture-perfect volcanic cone of **Gunung Agung**. The Balinese orientate their villages and homes towards this mountain, literally "Great Mountain", and after a few days in the region you'll probably fall under its spell too. Immediately beneath its awesome bulk unfurls a landscape of dense forests, narrow river valleys and sweeping rice terraces, making for a scenic drive, or hike, whichever direction you travel in. The far east, by contrast, especially around the coastal centres of **Amed** and **Tulamben**, lies within the rain shadow and is much drier and less productive, and correspondingly poorer. Most of east Bali comes under the administrative district of **Karangasem**, where villagers still follow a traditional way of life, mostly living off the land or from the sea. There are tourist centres but on a far smaller scale than in the south or around Ubud, and the lack of crowds, absence of commercial pressures and refreshingly unadulterated green vistas are a large part of the east's appeal. And with Bali being so small, you can easily base yourself in this part of the island without missing any of the highlights.

The main tourist hubs are along the coast, particularly at **Candi Dasa**, a low-key resort that compensates for its less than perfect beaches with good facilities and handy transport connections. Nearby, funky little **Padang Bai** is the port for boats to the Gili Islands and Lombok, and also makes a decent diving base in its own right. The biggest-hitting **dive centres**, though, are in the northeast, at **Amed**, which has lots of accommodation and plenty of reef close to shore, and nearby **Tulamben**, site of a famous shoreside wreck.

Inland, Gunung Agung and its Mother Temple, **Besakih**, are major attractions. Climbing this most magnificent of volcanoes is a significant challenge, but a rewarding one. The temple, however, can disappoint, as much for its persistent touts as for its sometimes misty outlook.

You might find some of the region's other temples more satisfying, especially the venerable Pura Kehen in **Bangli**, with its splendid sculptures. The east also has a rich artistic heritage associated with its ancient courts: **Semarapura** and the nearby painters' village of **Kamasan** keep the traditional art of classical *wayang* painting alive, while there's a chance to enjoy palace architecture at the Puri Agung in **Amlapura**. The district capital of **Gianyar** is justly famous for its beautiful *endek* weaving, and there's even more exquisite textile art, in the form of the rare double *ikat*, produced at **Tenganan**, a traditional Bali Aga village that's home to descendants of the early inhabitants of Bali. For classic rice-terrace vistas and village walks, it's hard to beat a stay in **Tirtagangga** or **Sidemen**, both offering attractive accommodation in tranquil settings.

The small-format glossy magazine *Agung* (W www.agungbali.com) is a good source of **information** about the east and is widely distributed throughout the

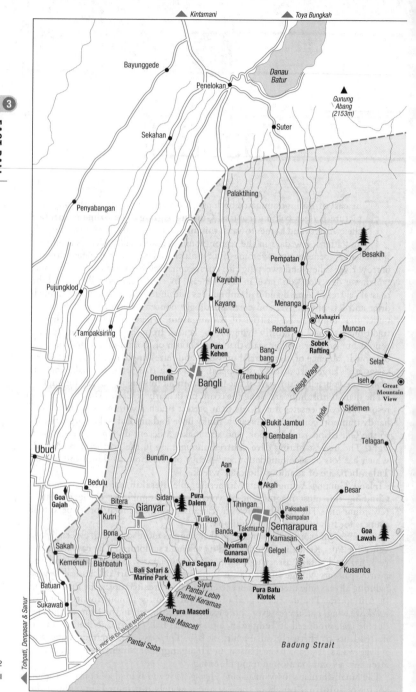

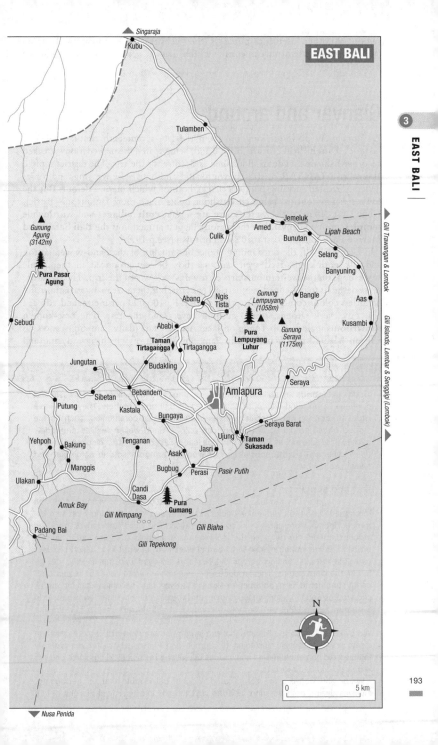

EAST BALI

Singaraja

Kubu

Tulamben

Gunung
Agung
(3142m)

Pura Pasar
Agung

Jemeluk

Amed   Lipah Beach

Culik   Bunutan

Selang

Banyuning

Sebudi

Abang   Ngis   Gunung   Bangle   Aas
          Tista   Lempuyang
                         (1058m)
Ababi   Kusambi

Taman   Tirtagangga   Pura   Gunung
Tirtagangga   Lempuyang   Seraya
                               Luhur   (1175m)

Jungutan   Budakling

Putung   Sibetan   Bebandem   Seraya

Kastala   Amlapura

Yehpoh   Bakung   Bungaya

Tenganan   Ujung   Taman
                       Asak   Sukasada
Manggis   Jasri
                       Seraya Barat
Ulakan   Bugbug   Perasi   Pasir Putih

          Candi
          Dasa   Pura
Padang Bai   Gili Mimpang   Gumang

Amuk Bay

Gili Tepekong   Gili Biaha

N

0   5 km

Nusa Penida

region. Another useful resource is the website for Karangasem Tourism (www.karangasemtourism.com), which has a very handy calendar of upcoming festivals.

Gianyar and around

An immensely powerful kingdom from the late seventeenth century, Gianyar became a **Dutch Protectorate** in 1900 and, being spared the depredations wreaked on other Balinese kingdoms, flourished as a centre for the arts. The district capital, also called **GIANYAR**, is still known for its handsome *endek* weaving, and for its delicious roasted suckling pig (*babi guling*), both of which merit a detour. But the town sees few tourists, being far outshone by its much more famous sub-district, Ubud, just 10km to the west. There are several **craft villages** and worthwhile **temples** around Gianyar, but the region's biggest attraction is the **Bali Safari and Marine Park**, off the coast road south of town (see p.197).

In Gianyar itself, the outstanding choice and quality of the hand-woven cotton and silk **endek** (tie-dyed weft *ikat*; see box below) produced in the textile workshops on the western outskirts of town is well worth the trip. The signature *endek* design is fuzzy-edged geometrical patterns, but there are many variations and countless colour combinations; prices start at Rp100,000 per metre, and you can also buy *endek* sarongs, shirts, cushion covers and the rest. The best-known **showrooms** include Cap Togog on Jalan Astina Utara (daily 8am–5pm) and Cap Cili on Jalan Ciung Wenara (daily 9am–5pm), both of which have dyeing and

---

Traditional textiles

Traditional **fabrics** are still fashionable for clothes and furnishings in Indonesia and continue to be hand-woven in some areas of Bali and Lombok. They also have **ritual functions**, with specific weaves used in certain ceremonies, such as the striped *bebali* produced in Pacung (see p.267). Hand-woven textiles are widely available for sale across Bali and Lombok (see p.52) and are often displayed to their best advantage on the special carved **wooden hangers** sold in some *ikat* and souvenir shops.

Ikat and songket

Easily recognized by the fuzzy-edged motifs it produces, **ikat** weaving is common throughout Indonesia, woven on backstrap, foot-pedal or, increasingly, on semiautomatic looms, from either silk, cotton or rayon. The word *ikat* derives from the Indonesian verb "to tie", and the technique is essentially a sophisticated tie-dye process. Bali is quite unusual in favouring **weft-ikat**, or **endek**, in which the weft yarn (the threads running across the fabric) is tie-dyed into the finished design before the warp begins. This produces the distinctive blurred edge to the predominantly geometric and abstract designs. **Gianyar** has several excellent *endek* showrooms and workshops (see above), and there's a highly regarded producer in **Sidemen** (see p.209); on Lombok, the weavers of **Sukarara** (see p.349) are the ones to seek out.

Warp-ikat (in which the threads that run lengthwise are tie-dyed) is more common elsewhere in Indonesia, including on Sumba and Flores, whose textiles typically feature bold humanoid motifs and images of real and mythological creatures and are widely sold in Bali's resorts.

Warp- and weft-*ikat* are complicated enough, but **double ikat**, or **geringsing**, involves dyeing both the warp and the weft threads into their final designs before

weaving workshops on site (open to the public 9am–4pm except hols); also on Jalan Ciung Wenara is Bakti (daily 8am–5pm, no workshop).

Practicalities

Gianyar has useful **bemo** services from and to Ubud and Denpasar's Batubulan terminal, both of which terminate near *Babi Guling Gianyar*, on the corner of Jalan Ngurah Rai and Jalan Jata. Most of the other services, including those to Candi Dasa and Batur (see "Travel details", p.234) pick up and drop off outside Hardy's Supermarket on Jalan Ngurah Rai.

The Gianyar government **tourist office** is at Jl Ngurah Rai 9 (Mon–Thurs 7.30am–3pm, Fri 6.30am–2pm; ℡0361/943401). There's currency **exchange** opposite the Ubud bemo stop and an international **ATM** outside Hardy's. Nearby, off Jalan Berata, the main **market** takes place every three days (best before noon), although there are always some stalls here.

With Ubud so close, there's no reason **to stay** overnight, but should you wish to, you'll find clean fan and air-conditioned rooms in a small compound at the perfectly acceptable *Pondok Wisata Gianyar* (℡0361/942165; ❸), across from Hardy's, just off Jalan Ngurah Rai at Jalan Anom Sandat 10X.

To sample Gianyar's famous *babi guling*, which is roasted **suckling pig** stuffed with chillies, rice and spices and served with *lawar* (chopped meat, vegetables and coconut mixed with pig's blood), try *Depot Melati*, Jl Ngurah Rai 37, or *Babi Guling Gianyar* on Jalan Jata; expect to pay about Rp15,000. They serve from early morning until they sell out; get there by noon to be sure of a feast, or try the night markets after 5pm.

they're woven together; a double-*ikat* sarong can take five years to complete. There are just three areas in the world where this method is practised – India, Japan and **Tenganan** in eastern Bali. Not surprisingly, *geringsing* is exceedingly expensive to buy, and has acquired an important ritual significance. At first glance, *geringsing* can look similar to the warp-*ikat* of Flores, because both use the same dye combinations, but the Tenganan motifs have a highly charged spiritual meaning, and their geometric and floral designs are instantly recognizable to the people of Bali.

The art of embroidered *ikat*, or supplementary-weft weaving, is known as **songket**. This uses metallic gold and silver yarn to add tapestry-like motifs of birds, butterflies and flowers onto very fine silk (or, increasingly, rayon or artificial silk). *Songket* sarongs are worn on ceremonial occasions, and dancers wear *songket* sashes. **Sukarara** in Lombok is the best place to see *songket* being woven.

Batik and perada

Despite being more common than *ikat* for everyday and formal wear on Bali and Lombok, nearly all **batik** fabric is imported from Java. The batik process involves drawing patterns on the fabric in dye-resistant wax, then dyeing and re-waxing as necessary to create complex multi coloured designs that look the same on both sides. Screen-printed batik is generally inferior as the dyes don't penetrate to the reverse side.

A special type of batik called **perada** is used for ceremonial outfits and ornaments. This is the gold-painted cloth that you'll see fashioned into temple umbrellas, adorning some sacred statues, and worn in the Legong and other traditional dances. The background colour is nearly always bright green or yellow, sometimes purple, and onto this is painted or stamped a symbolic design (usually birds or flowers) in either gold-leaf paint or, more commonly today, a bronze- or gold-coloured pigment.

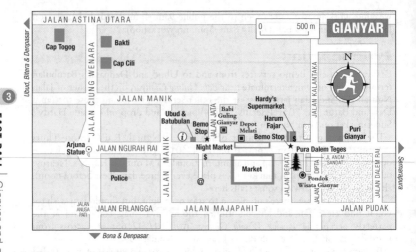

Bona & Denpasar

Around Gianyar

KUTRI, 4km west of Gianyar, is the site of an interesting temple, **Pura Bukit Dharma Durga Kutri**. Head up the staircase from the temple's inner courtyard to the top of the hill, where you'll find the statue of the many-armed goddess **Durga** slaughtering a bull and brandishing a conch shell, flames, bow and arrow, javelin and shield. Many people believe that the carving actually depicts **Mahendratta**, the alter ego of the legendary widow-witch Rangda (see box opposite), and that this is her burial place. An unusual way of visiting Kutri is to walk there from the Yeh Pulu rock carvings east of Ubud (3–5hr), for which you'll need a guide (see p.183). Coming from Gianyar, the easiest way to get here is on a bemo bound for Denpasar's Batubulan terminal.

At the village of **Blahbatuh**, 5km south of Kutri, the main road is lined with **bamboo-furniture** workshops. Nearby, **Bona** and **Belaga** villages also make bamboo furniture, as well as **baskets** and other artefacts woven from rattan, palm and *alang-alang* grass. At **Kemenuh**, 7km southwest of Gianyar, the speciality is **woodcarving**, and there are workshops all along the road to Goa Gajah, 5km north.

The widow-witch Rangda makes an especially gruesome appearance at the **Pura Dalem** (unlocked on request; Rp50,000) in **SIDAN**. This temple of the dead, dating from the seventeenth century, drips with grisly carvings and statues of the terrible Rangda squashing babies, along with depictions of the punishments that await evil-doers in the afterlife – which include having your head sawn off and being boiled in a vat. The temple is 2km east of Gianyar then 1km north up the main Gianyar–Bangli road and served by bemos between the two towns; as the entry fee is offputtingly high, you may simply want to admire the external carvings, which are also impressive.

The coast south of Gianyar

The coast **south of Gianyar** is fringed with long, black-sand beaches and offers some fine views of Gunung Agung. It's mainly surfing territory, though, notably at **Pantai Keramas**, as the current is too treacherous for swimming and the shoreline has suffered drastic erosion.

The first of several important **temples** along this stretch of coast is ornate **Pura Masceti**, the directional temple, or *kayangan jagat* (see p.371), for the south; it's by the beach, about 7km south of Gianyar, 14km east of Sanur.

But the big draw for tourists is **Bali Safari and Marine Park** (Mon–Fri 9am–5pm, Sat, Sun & hols from 8.30am; $35 or $50 with transport from Kuta/Sanur; ☎0361/950000, ⓦwww.balisafarimarinepark.com), which attracts several thousand visitors a day to its landscaped grounds housing animals from Indonesia, India and Africa (white tigers, Komodo dragons and Sumatra tigers among them). There's also a water park, the "Bali Agung" theatrical extravaganza, and animal rides and shows. If you don't have a problem with wild animals being kept in captivity then this is a pretty good example, and most visitors spend the entire day here. You can also **stay** in the park at *Mara River Safari Lodge* (☎0361/747 5000, ⓦwww.marariver safarilodge.com; ❼), whose balconies overlook an enclosure frequented by white rhinos, Chapman zebras and oryx; there are night safaris and a pool. The park is about 1.5km east of Pura Masceti, 7km southeast of Gianyar and 15km east of Sanur, just off the coastal highway, Jalan Bypass Prof Dr Ida Bagus Mantra.

Black-sand **Pantai Lebih**, 1km east of the Safari Park, is crowded with fishing boats and famous for its dozen or so very popular warung serving **fresh seafood** (most open daily until 10pm). Menu highlights include the local speciality *sate languan* (fish grilled with green coconut, spices and brown sugar), *ikan bakar* (charcoal-grilled fish in banana leaf) and *ikan pepes* (fish steamed in banana leaves); they're great value, with set meals from Rp15,000. Across the highway from the sea, Lebih's **Pura Segara** (Sea Temple) is associated with magical forces, and holds an annual ceremony to placate the demon I Macaling, who is believed to bring disease and ill fortune from Nusa Penida across the Badung Strait (p.141).

Pura Batu Klotok, on the beach at **Pantai Batu Klotok**, 7km east of Lebih, is one of four highly revered state temples in Klungkung district. The sacred statues from the Mother Temple, Besakih, are brought here during the annual cleansing ritual of *malasti*. From here it's 9km on to Kusamba and then 20km to Candi Dasa (see p.213).

Rangda, Queen of the Witches

Sporting a mane of unkempt hair, tusk-like teeth, a tongue that hangs to her knees, and enormous, pendulous breasts, **Rangda**, Queen of the Witches, is a terrifying spectacle wherever you encounter her. And she is everywhere: on stage in religious dance-dramas, as a larger-than-life statue at temples, in paintings and on textiles. To the Balinese, she represents evil, death and destruction.

It's possible that Rangda is based on a real woman, **Mahendratta**, a Javanese princess who married the Balinese prince Udayana and bore him a son, Erlangga, in 1001 AD. According to legend, Udayana later banished Mahendratta for practising witchcraft. When Udayana died, Mahendratta, now a *rangda* (widow), used her powers to call a plague upon her son's kingdom. Erlangga duly dispatched a troop of soldiers to kill her, but they failed, despite stabbing her in the heart. In desperation, Erlangga asked for assistance from the holy man Empu Bharadah, who used Rangda's book of magic to both restore her victims to life, and destroy the witch by turning her own magic on herself. Both Mahendratta and Empu Bharadah are thought to be associated with Bali's Mother Temple, Besakih (see p.202).

The Rangda story is widely enacted across Bali, most commonly during the **Barong** and **Calonarang** dramas (see p.379). She always speaks in the ancient Kawi language, spiced with plenty of grunts and cackles. Even in performances of the story the figure of Rangda is believed to have remarkable powers, and prayers precede each show to protect the actors from the evil forces they are invoking.

BANGLI

N

Penelokan

Pura Kehen

JALAN SRIWIJAYA

Sasana
Budaya
Arts Centre

Pura
Penyimpenan

JALAN ERLANGGA

Rendang

Police

Indomaret

JALAN NUSANTARA

Demulih & Tampaksiring

Trimurti
Statue

JALAN KUSUMAYUDHA

Bangli
Inn

JALAN MAJAPAHIT

Hospital

Night
Market

Bemo
Terminal

Market

JL RAMBUTAN

JALAN MERDEKA

JALAN NGURAH RAI

Football
Field

Pura Dalem
Pengungekan

0   500 m

Bunutin, Sidan & Gianyar

Bangli

Situated between Gianyar and the volcanoes of Batur, the district capital of **BANGLI** is a cool and spacious market town whose extravagantly carved temples are well worth making the effort to visit. Its most famous sight is the ancient **Pura Kehen** (daily 6am–6.30pm; Rp3500), a gem among Bali's temples and thought to have been founded in 1206. Rising in **terraces** 1.5km north of the centre, its mossy stairway is lined with statues of human and mythical creatures, led by a pair of elephants at the base, and crowned by a leering Bhoma above regal red-and-gold carved doors. In the **outer courtyard** a massive banyan tree hides a *kulkul* tower among its branches, and a small compound, guarded by *naga* under a frangipani tree, houses a stone that reportedly glowed with fire when the site of the temple was decided. The **inner courtyard** contains an eleven-roofed *meru*, dedicated to Siwa, and other shrines dedicated to mountain gods.

Across the road, the lavishly restored **Pura Penyimpenan** (Temple for Keeping Things) contains three ancient bronze inscriptions (*prasasti*) dating from the ninth century, which suggests Pura Kehen could be much older than some believe.

It's a pleasant walk to the temple of the dead, **Pura Dalem Pengungekan**, at the opposite end of town, where exuberant carvings cover the outside walls. Depicting the fate of souls in hell and heaven as witnessed by Bhima, one of the Pandawa brothers (see box, p.378), these show a riot of knives, pleading victims, flames and decapitated bodies. There are also appearances by the widow-witch Rangda, and stories of Siwa, Ganesh, Uma and Rakshasha.

Practicalities

Bangli is served by **bemos** from Gianyar and is also on the Denpasar (Batubulan)–Singaraja (Penarukan) route. The best place to stay is the *Bangli Inn*, Jl Rambutan 1 (☎0366/91518; ❷), which has clean rooms with attached cold-water bathrooms built around a small courtyard. During the day, the bus/bemo terminal has several **food** stalls and after dark it transforms into a small **night market**. There's an international **ATM** at the BNI bank on Jalan Nusantara.

Semarapura (Klungkung) and around

Famous as a centre of classical Balinese art, Klungkung's district capital, **SEMAR-APURA** (also frequently referred to as **KLUNGKUNG**), makes an enjoyable day out, especially from Padang Bai, which is just half an hour away by bemo. The highlight is the rare painted ceiling of the **Kerta Gosa** pavilion inside the Taman Gili palace gardens. The lively market is also a fun browse and there's more classical art on the outskirts: in the village of **Kamasan**, home to modern-day artists working in the *wayang* style, and at the **Nyoman Gunarsa Museum**, which houses Bali's best collection of historic Kamasan art.

Some history

Semarapura became a centre of the arts towards the end of the seventeenth century, when Bali's Majapahit rulers relocated here from their **court** at Gelgel, 4km to the south (Gelgel was believed to have fallen under a curse). The political power of the Majapahits was by then on the wane, with breakaway kingdoms such as Gianyar rising to prominence, but their sophisticated artistic and literary culture endured, its greatest legacy being the classical paintings that adorn the Kerta Gosa in Semarapura's palace grounds. The court remained at Semarapura until the early twentieth century and was one of the last two strongholds against the Dutch invasion. Rather than submit to the colonial power, on April 28, 1908, Semarapura's *dewa agung* (king) led two hundred members of his family and court in the traditional **puputan** (ritual suicide), marching into the line of fire. A monument opposite the Taman Gili commemorates this.

Arrival, information and accommodation

Semarapura is served by **bemos** from Padang Bai, Gianyar, Sidemen and Denpasar. Some Padang Bai bemos conveniently terminate on (and pick up from) Jalan Nakula, just outside the market, but the main **bus and bemo terminal**, Terminal Kelod (also known as Terminal Galiron), is about 1km south of the town centre. If you're heading up to Besakih via Semarapura, you can pick up a bemo going to Rendang or Menanga (see p.205) on Jalan Gunung Rinjani just north of the main

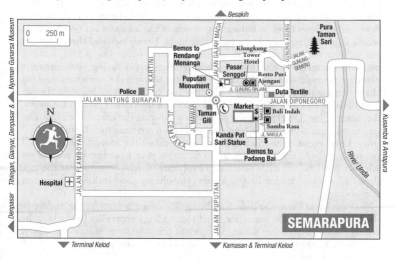

crossroads in the centre of town. The crossroads are marked by the **Kanda Pat Sari statue**, which guards the four cardinal directions, and both Taman Gili and the market are just a few steps from it. There are a couple of international **ATMs** on the two arms of Jalan Nakula, just outside the market entrance.

Most tourists visit for just a few hours, but there's pleasant **accommodation** at *Klungkung Tower Hotel*, Jl Gunung Rinjani 18 (T0366/25637, Etowerhotel07 @yahoo.co.id; ❸–❹), which has nicely decorated, air-conditioned rooms with hot-water bathrooms and street-view verandas. Climb to the top of the tower for a panoramic view of the city.

The Town

Though the big attraction in town is the Taman Gili, Semarapura also has an important **market**, Pasar Umum Semarapura (daily from dawn until about 1pm), which is well worth a browse. The market is at its largest and busiest every three days, but even on normal days it's a fun place to shop, especially good for *songket* fabric and offering baskets, as well as the usual sarongs, kids' toys and fruit and veg. The shops on nearby Jalan Diponegoro are also well known for **fabric**: Duta Textile at no. 71 stocks exceptional silk and cotton sarongs and shimmering *kebaya* material.

Taman Gili and the Kerta Gosa

Built around 1710, and largely destroyed by the fighting in 1908, **Taman Gili**, or "Island Gardens" (daily 7.30am–5pm; Rp12,000), is all that remains of the original **Semarapura palace**. It's an attractive complex of lily ponds, pavilions and graceful statues, and its indisputable highlight is the superb painted ceiling of the **Kerta Gosa**. This is Bali's only example of *wayang*-style classical art still in situ (see p.168 for more on classical Balinese art) and was painted by artists from nearby Kamasan (see opposite), probably in the early nineteenth century. Despite its historical importance, the pavilion is open to the elements and located next to the city's busiest junction so the pictures are not in prime condition, though they have undergone several major restorations over the years.

The Kerta Gosa is sometimes described as a criminal court, which adds poignancy to the pictures of gruesome punishments on the ceiling, but it's more likely to have been a debating chamber. It has nine levels of paintings. **Level one**, nearest the floor, shows scenes from an Indonesian version of the *Thousand and One Nights*, in which a girl, Tantri, weaves tales night after night. **Levels two and three** illustrate the "Bhima Swarga" story (part of the *Mahabharata* epic; see p.378), and the punishments meted out to souls in the afterlife, such as having your intestines extracted through your anus for farting in public. Bhima is the aristocratic-looking chap with moustache, tidy hair, a big club and a long nail on his right thumb. **Level four** shows the "Sang Garuda", the story of the Garuda's search for *amerta*, the water of life. **Level five** is the *palalindon*, predicting the effects of earthquakes on life and agriculture, while **levels six and seven** continue the "Bhima Swarga" story. **Level eight** is the "Swarga Roh", which details the rewards the godly will receive in heaven; unfortunately, it's so far above your head that it's hard to see whether good behaviour is worth it. **Level nine**, the *lokapala*, right at the top, shows a lotus surrounded by four doves symbolizing good luck, enlightenment and salvation.

Near the Kerta Gosa, the **Bale Kambung** (Floating Pavilion), in the middle of the lotus pond, was the venue for royal tooth-filing ceremonies (see p.389). Its ceiling is slightly less finely drawn; six levels of paintings cover Balinese astrology, the tales of Pan Brayut (see box opposite) and, closest to the top, the adventures of Satusoma, a Buddhist saint.

The tale of Men and Pan Brayut

Blessed – or lumbered – with eighteen children, **Men and Pan Brayut** ("Mother and Father Brayut") may be desperately poor, but their scrapes are typical of any Balinese family. So goes the popular Balinese folktale that has inspired countless artists, including the mural painters of Semarapura's Bale Kambang hall, the Ubud artist I Gusti Nyoman Lempad (see p.164) and the stonecarvers of Pura Dalem Jagaraga, near Singaraja (see p.265). The fullest account of the couple's story is related in an epic **poem** called *Gaguritan Brayut*, housed in Singaraja's Gedong Kirtya library.

According to one version of the **story**, the reason that Men Brayut has so many children is her uncontrollable appetite. When hungry, she gets irritable and rows with her husband, Pan Brayut. After fighting, the couple always make up in the time-honoured fashion – hence the constantly expanding clan. Another version puts the size of the family down to Pan Brayut's insatiable desire for his wife, which he acts upon regardless of place or circumstance.

Men Brayut is both full-time mother and part-time weaver, so her husband does most of the domestic chores; these scenes from daily life – cleaning the yard, cooking ceremonial dishes – feature in many paintings. Eventually, after all their hard parenting, Men and Pan Brayut renounce the material world and enter a retreat (still common practice, especially among elderly Balinese men), leaving their home and its contents to be divided among the children.

Although illustrations of the Brayut story always emphasize its **Hindu** elements, with lots of scenes showing offerings and temple ceremonies, Men Brayut is also associated with **Buddhist** lore. In this mythology she is said to have evolved from an evil ogress named Hariti who spent her time devouring children until she converted to Buddhism and became not only a protector of children, but also a fertility goddess. Statues of Men Brayut in her Hariti manifestation can be found at Goa Gajah, near Ubud, and at the temple in Candi Dasa.

The **Museum Daerah Semarapura** at the back of the Taman Gili grounds contains a motley collection including *kris* (daggers), textiles and Barong costumes, but labels are scant.

Eating

For **food**, head for Jalan Nakula, where *Bali Indah* at no. 1 and *Sumba Rasa* at no. 5 have small English menus; or there's *Restaurant Puri Ajengan* at the *Klungkung Tower Hotel*. The hot-food stalls of the lively Pasar Senggol **night market** occupy the western end of Jalan Gunung Rinjani after dark.

Around Semarapura

If your interest in classical Balinese art has been piqued by the Kerta Gosa ceiling, consider making a visit both to the artists' studios in nearby **Kamasan** itself, and to the unrivalled collection of historic Kamasan art at the **Nyoman Gunarsa Museum**.

Kamasan

As the home of the original nineteenth-century Kerta Gosa artists, and the source of subsequent generations of restorers and commercial artists, the village of **KAMASAN**, just outside Semarapura, has given its name to the classical school of art with which it is so closely associated. Numerous artists have open studios in their homes in the village, particularly in the neighbourhood of Banjar Sanging, the turning to which is 500m south and east of Semarapura's Kelod bemo terminal, from where it's another 500m or so. Among the most famous local names here are **I Nyoman Mandra** and **Ni Made Suciarmi**, the latter being one of Kamasan's very few women artists (she is also represented at the Seniwati Women's Art Gallery in Ubud; see p.184). Most of the work on sale is either inexpensive small cloth pictures or reproductions of traditional calendars, depicting mythological stories in muted classical colours.

Nyoman Gunarsa Museum

Try not to be discouraged by the dilapidated carbuncle of a building, the birds nesting inside it, or the high ticket price: the **Nyoman Gunarsa Museum** (Mon–Sat 9am–4pm; Rp50,000) is well worth a lengthy browse. The big attraction is the large and rather special collection of Kamasan **cloth paintings**, some of which probably date back to the eighteenth century. Highlights include several ten-metre-long *ider ider* – ceremonial banners depicting mythological tales that were traditionally hung under the eaves of a palace or temple building. Labels are informative and the art is supplemented by antique doors, carved gamelan ornaments and examples of *wayang kulit* puppets that echo the origins of the classical style. The top floor is dedicated to paintings by the museum founder, **Nyoman Gunarsa**, one of Bali's foremost modern artists, who still works from his studio on the premises; his distinctive style is high-energy abstract oil and watercolour interpretations of traditional Bali themes, especially dancers.

The museum is 5km west of Semarapura, just beyond the village of Takmung on the Gianyar road; any Amlapura–Gianyar **bemo** will drop you outside.

Gunung Agung, Besakih and around

Visible throughout eastern Bali and even from Nusa Lembongan and west Lombok across the sea, the classic volcanic cone of **Gunung Agung** is a majestic presence from any angle. It is the spiritual centre of the island: Balinese people believe the spirits of their ancestors dwell here, and several important temples, including **Besakih**, the Mother Temple, and **Pura Pasar Agung**, are sited on its slopes. Villages and house compounds are oriented towards the mountain, and many people sleep with their heads towards it. At 3142m, Gunung Agung is also Bali's highest peak and the focus of challenging **climbs** to its summit; there are reputable trekking guides in the villages of Muncan and Selat, on the **Amlapura–Rendang road**.

Besakih

The major draw in the east of Bali is undoubtedly the vast **Besakih** temple complex (daily 8am–5pm; Rp15,000), the most venerated on the island. On a clear day it can be a magnificent sight, the multi-tiered shrines of the twenty-plus temples busy with worshippers in traditional dress bearing elaborate offerings and the whole complex framed against the stark grandeur of the sacred volcano. But Besakih also has a reputation as a place of unpleasant hassle, and its jumble of buildings, unremarkable in many ways, are closed to non-Hindus, who must stay outside the low walls; even the towering hulk of Gunung Agung is often invisible behind enveloping cloud. You might well end up wondering why you bothered.

Some history

It's likely that Besakih was a religious site long before the start of recorded history. Pura Batu Madeg (Temple of the Standing Stone), in the north of the complex, suggests megalithic connections through its ancient terraced structure

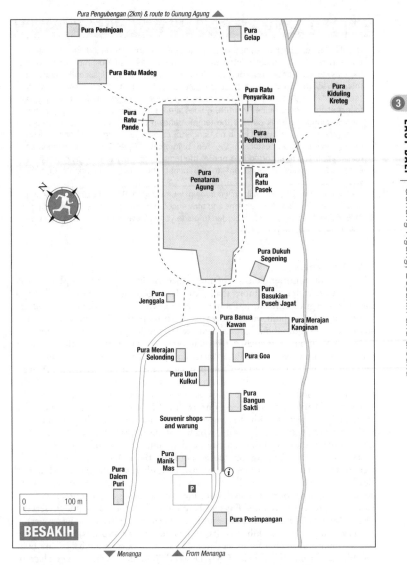

Pura Pengubengan (2km) & route to Gunung Agung ▲

Pura Peninjoan

Pura Gelap

Pura Batu Madeg

Pura Kiduling Kreteg

Pura Ratu Penyarikan

Pura Ratu Pande

Pura Pedharman

Pura Penataran Agung

Pura Ratu Pasek

Pura Dukuh Segening

Pura Jenggala

Pura Basukian Puseh Jagat

Pura Banua Kawan

Pura Merajan Kanginan

Pura Merajan Selonding

Pura Goa

Pura Ulun Kulkul

Pura Bangun Sakti

Souvenir shops and warung

Pura Manik Mas

Pura Dalem Puri

P

ⓘ

0   100 m

BESAKIH

Pura Pesimpangan

▼ Menanga   ▲ From Menanga

based around a central stone. However, Besakih's founder is generally believed to be **Sri Markandeya**, a priest who came from eastern Java at the end of the eighth century. An important ceremony occurred in 1007, widely thought to be the cremation rites of **Queen Mahendratta**, origin of the Rangda legend (see box, p.197). Already an important temple by the time of the **Majapahit** conquest of Bali in 1343, Besakih then became the **state temple** of the powerful Gelgel and Semarapura courts. An **earthquake** damaged the buildings in 1917 and **renovations** were needed after the 1963 eruption of Gunung Agung (see box, p.206). As a result, the temples are a mix of old and new, and restoration work is always ongoing.

203

Guides at Besakih

Besakih has established an appalling reputation over the last decade as a place of nonstop hassle. The problem stemmed from the hundreds of local men who styled themselves as **guides**, **guardians** or **keepers** of the temple, insistently attached themselves to tourists and then demanded large sums in payment for their "services". The official advice is to engage only properly badged guides; they can be found at the tourist office. In truth, guides are hardly needed: stick to the paths running along the walls outside the temples shown on the map on p.203, wear a sarong and sash, and you'll be in no danger of causing any religious offence. If you do employ a guide, establish the **fee** beforehand: Rp40,000 is a reasonable minimum. If you're escorted into one of the temples to receive a blessing you'll be expected to make a "donation" to the priest, the amount negotiable through your guide.

If you're including Besakih in your own tour using a Balinese driver, they will probably warn you of the problems and may encourage you to visit a different temple. At Besakih itself drivers are forbidden to guide you or translate for you and won't be able to negotiate on your behalf.

The temples

The **Besakih complex** consists of more than twenty separate **temples**, spread over a site stretching for more than 3km. It's a good idea to begin with **Pura Penataran Agung** (the Great Temple of State), which is both the largest and the most dramatic. It's built on **six terraces**, with more than fifty *bale*, shrines and stone thrones inside; about half are dedicated to specific gods, while the others are for ceremonial purposes such as receiving offerings, or accommodating the gods during festivals. A path skirts Pura Penataran Agung's perimeter wall, from which you can see most of the terraces (the best views are from the west side). A giant stairway, lined by seven levels of **carved figures**, leads to the first courtyard; the figures to the left are from the *Mahabharata* and the ones to the right from the *Ramayana*. As worshippers process through the first courtyard they symbolically sever their connection with the everyday world, before proceeding through the *kori agung* into the second courtyard, which contains the *padmatiga*, the three-seated lotus throne dedicated to Brahma, Siwa and Wisnu, where all pilgrims pray.

Beyond Pura Penataran Agung, the *meru* of **Pura Batu Madeg**, rising among the trees to the north, are enticing, while **Pura Pengubengan**, the most far-flung of Besakih's temples, is a good 2km through the forest. As you wander around the complex, look out for representations of the manifestations of the supreme God, in particular differently coloured **flags and banners**: black for Wisnu (the Preserver), red for Brahma (the Creator) and a multicoloured array for Siwa (the Destroyer).

Every temple in Besakih has its timetable of **ceremonies**; see ⓦwww .karangasemtourism.com for exact dates. The most important annual ceremony is the Bhatar Turun Kabeh (The Gods Descend Together), which takes place in March or April and lasts a month, with the high point on the full moon of the tenth lunar month. At this time, the gods of all the shrines are believed to come and dwell in Besakih, drawing worshippers from all over the island. Besakih's biggest ceremony is Eka Dasa Rudra (see box, p.206), held every hundred years. The Panca Wali Krama occurs every ten years and involves a 42km-long, three-day procession from the coast to the temple.

Practicalities

Arrive early morning or late afternoon to avoid the worst of the crowds. Without your own transport, the easiest way of getting to Besakih is to take an **organized**

tour, but check how much time you'll have there; anything less than an hour isn't worth it.

If you're using **public transport**, bemos from Semarapura go as far as Menanga, from where you should be able to hire an ojek to the temple. Bemos also run from Amlapura (via Selat and Muncan) to Rendang, with some continuing to Menanga. Most bemos run in the morning, but dry up in the afternoon. There are no public bemos north of Menanga to Penelokan, or between Rendang and Bangli.

The Besakih **tourist office** (daily 7am–6pm), on the right, just beyond the car park, is staffed by the local organization of guides who will pressure you to make a donation and engage their services (both are unnecessary but difficult to resist; see box opposite). The rule about wearing a **sarong and sash** appears to be inconsistently applied but you'll definitely need them if you're in skimpy clothing; you can rent them (from Rp20,000) but it's easier to bring your own.

Accommodation near Besakih is limited. *Lembah Arca* hotel (T0366/530 0552; ❷–❸), on the road from Menanga, about 2km before the temple complex, has basic cold-water rooms. A much more luxurious option is *Mahagiri*, in Rendang, about 9km from Besakih, which also does good **food** (see p.207). Alternatively, there's cheap food at *Depot Mawar* in Menanga, on the left as you turn off to Besakih, and a few warung on the walk up to Besakih from the car park.

Climbing Gunung Agung

Two main **routes** lead up Gunung Agung, both long and hard. One starts from Besakih and the other from further east, at the mountain's other main temple, Pura Pasar Agung. Whichever route you take, you'll need to set out in the middle of the night to be at the top for the **sunrise** (6–7am); clouds often obscure the view by late morning. It's essential to take a **guide** and you'll also need strong footwear, warm clothes for the summit, a good torch (ideally a head lamp to leave both hands free for climbing) and water and snacks; for the descent, a stick is handy.

Climbing is not permitted at certain **times of the year** because of religious ceremonies at Besakih or Pura Pasar Agung. The dry season (April to mid-Oct) is the best time to climb; wind and rain can render the ascent too dangerous or may mean aborting an attempt, so take advice from a reputable English-speaking guide. There have been fatalities due to a combination of slippery conditions and poor footwear.

The routes

From Pura Pasar Agung (see p.207), at an altitude of 1600m, it's at least a three-hour climb with an ascent of almost 2000m, so you'll need to set out by 3am from the temple, depending on how fit you are. The track initially passes through forest, ascending onto bare, steep rock. It doesn't go to the actual summit, but ends at a point on the rim that is about 100m lower. From here, the summit masks views of part of the island and, between April and September, the sunrise on the horizon, but you'll be able to see Lombok's Gunung Rinjani, the south of Bali and Gunung Batukaru and look down into the 500m crater.

From Besakih (950m; see p.202), the climb is longer (5–7hr) and much more challenging; you'll need to leave between 10pm and midnight. This path leads to the **summit** of Agung, with views in all directions. The initial climb is through forest, but the path gets very steep, very quickly, even before it gets out onto the bare rock, and you'll soon need your hands to haul yourself upwards. The descent is particularly taxing from this side and feels very precarious when you're already exhausted; allow at least five hours to get down.

A less-used route, **from Dukuh Bujangga Sakti**, inland from Kubu on the northeast coast, is offered by M&G Trekking (see p.217). Starting out at an altitude of 300m, the climb is greater but not as steep as the other routes. You begin in the afternoon, camp on the mountain at 1750m and complete the three hours to the summit pre-dawn. The north of Bali is drier so is less often shrouded in cloud. You can walk round the rim to the absolute summit if you climb from this side and can see the sunrise on the horizon all year round.

Trekking guides

As this is a serious climb you need to have confidence in your **guide** and be able to communicate well with them. For these reasons it's strongly advised to climb with an established trekking guide such as those listed here; the freelance guides who hang round Pura Pasar Agung and Besakih tend to have very limited English and may not be as safety-conscious.

It's possible to arrange your trek through accommodation and tour agents nearly anywhere in Bali, but there are obvious advantages to basing yourself as close as possible to the mountain. In the village of **Selat**, a half-hour drive from Pura Pasar Agung, **Gung Bawa** (T0812/387 8168, Wwww.gb-trekking.blogspot.com) is a highly experienced and dependable guide and speaks excellent English. He charges Rp350,000 per person (minimum two people) from Pura Pasar Agung and Rp500,000 from Besakih and can supply a head torch, jacket and even shoes if necessary. He also offers an overnight option that leaves Selat at midday and camps

1963

The year **1963** is recalled as a time when the gods were displeased with Bali and took their revenge. Ancient texts prescribe that an immense ceremony, **Eka Dasa Rudra** – the greatest ritual in Balinese Hinduism – should be held every hundred years for spiritual purification and future good fortune. Before 1963, it had only been held a couple of times since the sixteenth century. In the early 1960s, religious leaders believed that the trials of World War II and the ensuing fight for independence were indicators that the ritual was once again needed, and these beliefs were confirmed by a **plague of rats** that overran the entire island in 1962.

The climax of the festival was set for March 8, 1963, but on February 18, **Gunung Agung**, which had been dormant for centuries, started rumbling; fire glowed within the crater and ash began to coat the area. Initially, this was interpreted as a good omen sent by the gods to purify Besakih, but soon doubts crept in. Some argued that the wrong date had been chosen for the event and wanted to call it off. However, by this time it was too late: President Sukarno was due to attend, together with a group of international travel representatives.

By March 8, black smoke, rocks and ash were billowing from the mountain, but the ceremony went ahead, albeit in a decidedly tense atmosphere. Eventually, on March 17, Agung **erupted** with such force that the top 100m of the mountain was ripped apart. The whole of eastern Bali was threatened by poisonous gas and molten lava, villages were engulfed, and between a thousand and two thousand people are thought to have died, while the homes of another hundred thousand were destroyed. Roads were wiped out, some towns were isolated for weeks, and the ash ruined crops, causing serious food shortages and great hardship. Some villagers fled as far afield as Lombok.

Despite the force of the eruption and the position of Besakih high on the mountain, a relatively small amount of damage occurred to the temples, and the **closing rites** of Eka Dasa Rudra took place on April 20. Subsequently, many Balinese felt that the mountain's eruption at the time of the ceremony was an omen of the civil strife that engulfed Bali in 1965 (see p.366).

In 1979, the year specified by the ancient texts, Eka Dasa Rudra was held again, this time passing off without incident.

at 2560m ($120). Selat has a couple of places to stay, both of which can also organize treks up Gunung Agung (see below).

In **Muncan**, 5km west of Selat, English teacher I Ketut Uriada (☏0812/364 6426) has climbed Agung several hundred times and still sometimes accompanies tourists, or sets them up with his assistant. Small groups who book ahead can spend the previous evening at his house; he charges $35 per group of up to three people from Pura Pasar Agung, or $70 from Besakih.

Slightly further away but with a wide choice of scenic accommodation and many guide services is the village of **Sidemen**, 18km from Pura Pasar Agung (see p.208). **Tirtagangga** is also a convenient base, with comfortable accommodation and other attractions nearby (see p.223). In the big resorts, there's M&G Trekking in **Candi Dasa** (see p.217); Bali Sunrise 2001 in **Ubud** (see p.157); and Perama (bookable through their offices in most tourist centres or at ⓦwww .peramatour.com).

The Rendang–Amlapura road

From **Rendang**, 14km north of Semarapura on the main route to Kintamani, a picturesque **road** heads 32km east **to Amlapura**, running beneath Gunung Agung via ricefields, forest and deep river valleys. The scenery is good but the going is slow, the potholed road crowded with trucks bringing charcoal-coloured sand down from the mountain. **Bemos** connect Rendang with Amlapura, and also serve Menanga to the north, for Besakih (see p.205). If you've got wheels, it's well worth making the short detour off the Amlapura road, signed 1km east of Rendang, for **food** or an overnight **stay** at *Mahagiri* (☏0812/381 4775, ⓦwww .mahagiri.com; ❻), which looks straight across a stunning valley filled with rice terraces to Gunung Agung. It has a dozen attractive fan-cooled bungalows with hot-water bathrooms and a pool. Many tours stop here en route to Besakih for the expensive but classy buffet lunch (Rp80,000).

Muncan and Pura Pasar Agung

Continuing east, you cross the River Telaga Waja, whose serpentine 14km-long descent is used by **whitewater rafting** companies such as Sobek (ⓦwww.99bali .com), and pass through **MUNCAN**, a possible base for climbing Gunung Agung (see p.205). A further 5km brings you to the western edge of Selat and the turn-off to the important **Pura Pasar Agung**, directional temple for the northeast, and, at 1600m above sea level, one of the two main starting points for Gunung Agung ascents. The road to the temple is an ear-poppingly steep climb of 10km through bamboo stands and acacia forests, in countryside scored by deep lava-carved gorges. The temple itself, however, is probably not worth a special journey, though on a clear morning you do get fine views.

Selat and Alas Tunggal

With Pura Pasar Agung so close, **SELAT** is an obvious base for **treks up Gunung Agung** (see p.205). It's served by public **bemos** from Gianyar, Amlapura and Denpasar's Batubulan terminal (mornings only). The recommended **guide** Gung Bawa is based here, around the corner from the police station at the west end of town (see opposite). Nearby, 200m west of the post office, 1km west of the Sidemen road junction, the genial Yandi offers basic **accommodation** at *Pondok Wisata Puri Agung Inn* (☏0852/3025 3672; ❷) and also organizes ascents of Gunung Agung (from Rp500,000 for one or two people, excluding transport). There's accommodation of a different order at *Great Mountain View* (☏0858/5701 3416, ⓦwww .greatmountainbali.com; ❹) in **ALAS TUNGGAL**, 3km south and east of Selat (5km north of Sidemen). The upscale bungalows here enjoy full-frontal views of

Gunung Agung across a gorgeous swathe of ricefields. As well as treks up Agung (Rp600,000 for two), there are cooking classes and opportunities for yoga and meetings with traditional healers.

It's just 8km south from Selat to Sidemen (see below), but continuing towards Amlapura instead you soon pass *Warung Makan Wayan* (daily 10am–7.30pm) on Selat's eastern edge, which serves excellent, cheap, Indonesian **food** and is presided over by the larger-than-life Wayan, who trained at the five-star *Amankila* hotel in Candi Dasa. From here it's 20km to Amlapura (see p.221), or about the same to Tirtagangga (see p.223).

Sidemen and around

The upland village of **SIDEMEN** sits within a quintessential Balinese setting of tiered rice terraces, coconut groves and the coursing Unda river, beneath the looming profile of Gunung Agung. It makes a glorious base for a few days, with a burgeoning number of scenic places to stay, opportunities for gentle ricefield treks, and easy access to Pura Pasar Agung for the challenging sunrise climb up Gunung Agung. It's also perfectly feasible to explore Besakih from here, and even Batur, which is just 48km, or a ninety-minute drive, to the northwest. Even if you don't intend to stay, you can appreciate some of the area's scenery from the road that begins at Selat (8km north of Sidemen; see p.207) and drops down to Paksabali, 16km southwest of Sidemen on the main Semarapura–Kusamba road. **Bemos** travel this route from Semarapura.

Artists Walter Spies (see p.166) and Theo Meier both lived in this area in the 1930s and 1940s, in **Iseh**, 3km to the north, and Anna Mathews wrote her evocative *Night of Purnama* about her life in the village before and during the **1963 eruption** of Gunung Agung. Although the Sidemen area was carpeted in ash by the eruption (see p.206) it did not suffer the same devastation as the northern slopes and the soil has since benefited from the extra fertilizer, as the endless *sawah* show.

Accommodation

The **accommodation** area is west off the main road, in **Dusun Tabola**. The access road forks 400m west of the main road; the following listings give directions from the fork. Many of the places to stay are small-scale "villas", often with just half a dozen rooms, constructed in prime spots scattered across the ricefields. As it's reasonably cool here at night almost none have air-conditioning; few have restaurants, either, but many have kitchenettes. Bring earplugs to muffle the cacophony of the nightly frog chorus.

Jana's Home Stay 100m along the left-hand fork ☎0813/3806 2202. There's only one room here, but it's spacious and very nicely done and has an attractive bathroom. You get views across the rooftop to the distant hills but not of the ricefields. ❸

Khrisna Home Stay 120m along the left-hand fork ☎0815/5832 1543, ✉pinpinaryadi@yahoo .com. Just a couple of clean, well-furnished rooms (one of them en suite) in the compact family compound of Sidemen's English-speaking nurse and his wife. ❷, en suite ❸

Kubu Tani 800m along the left-hand fork ☎0819/1633 2880 or 0366/530 0519, ⓦwww.kubutani.com. One of several places run by the Lihat Sawah family, this comprises four exceptionally attractive two-storey villas. Built in wood and thatch to a sophisticated Bali-modern/antique design, they are huge and beautifully appointed. Verandas give onto a profuse garden and have great ricefield and Agung views. Can sleep four. ❺

Pondok Wisata Lihat Sawah 100m along the right-hand fork ☎0819/1633 2880 or 0366/530 0519, ⓦwww.lihatsawah.com. Run by the local English teacher and his family, this is the liveliest place to stay, with a dozen rooms, from simple cold-water options to very comfortable deluxe bungalows with hot water and pretty views; there's also a very nice family villa. There are lots of activities, an on-site restaurant and lovely staff, and a small pool is planned. Prices are for dinner, bed and breakfast. Rooms ❸, bungalows ❹, villa ❺

Villa Sawah Indah 1100m along the left-hand fork ☎0819/1633 2880 or 0366/530 0519. Overlooking a fine amphitheatre of rice terraces, the five large and stylishly decorated villa-style rooms here have picture windows, colour-washed bathrooms and prettily tiled floors. Has connecting rooms and a kitchenette and dining area. ❹

Around the village

The main activity in these parts is **ricefield appreciation**, either from the comfort of your veranda or on a walk through the fields to nearby villages and temples. Guesthouses can supply a basic sketch map or you can take a guide for your first outing (Rp50,000/group/hr). Alternatively, head up to the main road and you can buy beautiful *endek* and *songket* (gold- and silver-thread) **weaving** and watch it being made on foot looms at the Pelangi workshop (daily 8am–5pm) on the main road at the southern end of the village. The tiny shop opposite produces traditional **lontar-palm** paintings.

Lihat Sawah runs **cooking courses** and arranges whitewater rafting on the Telaga Waja (see p.207), and Jana, at *Jana* restaurant (☎0813/3806 2202), leads **treks up Gunung Agung** (Rp700,000 for one or two people) and rents motorbikes (Rp60,000). There's no car rental, but a recommended local **driver** and guide is Ketut Lagun (☎0812/362 2076, ✉ketut_lagun@yahoo.com).

There is a postal agent and **currency exchange** (Mon–Sat 10am–4pm) on the main road, 25m south of the accommodation turn-off, but the nearest international ATM is in Semarapura.

Eating

The main **restaurants** are *Warung Lihat Sawah*, near *Kubu Tani*, 800m along the left-hand fork, which serves the same good menu of Thai, Indonesian and European food as its sister restaurant at *Pondok Wisata Lihat Sawah* guesthouse (mains Rp35,000–45,000); and *Jana*, beside the fork, which does cheap and tasty Indo classics including *nasi campur*, plus some Thai and European food as well.

Padang Bai and around

PADANG BAI, the tiny port village for boats to the Gili Islands and Lombok, has developed into a small, laidback travellers' centre and is also known for its **diving**. Its beaches are tiny, but its youthful vibe, funky cafés, cheap accommodation and live-music bars may keep you lingering longer than you intended. There's a daily market and shops stocking basic necessities, but for anything major you'll need to head to Candi Dasa (20min away by bemo) or Semarapura (30min). The main local sight is the temple at **Goa Lawah**, on the way to Semarapura.

Arrival

Perama runs **shuttle buses** to Padang Bai from all the main tourist centres (see "Travel details", p.234). **Bemos** and **minibuses** from Amlapura, Candi Dasa, Semarapura and Denpasar's Batubulan terminal terminate at the port entrance about 300m from the main hotel area. Fixed-price taxis from **Ngurah Rai**

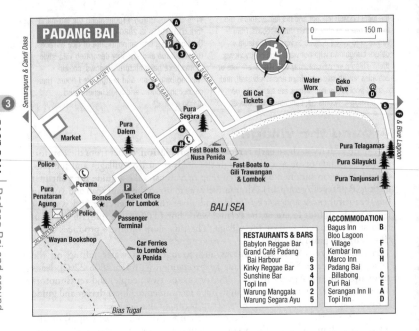

Airport cost Rp315,000 (2hr). For information on **boats** to the Gili Islands, Lombok and Nusa Penida, see the box opposite.

Accommodation

Except for *Bloo Lagoon*, none of the accommodation is more than ten minutes' walk from the ferry port or jetty, or more than 200m from the sea. This also means that nowhere is out of earshot of the ferry announcements and horn blasts, which resound through the village 24/7.

Bagus Inn ☏0813/3896 7025. A proper family-compound homestay with just five fan rooms, including two with private terraces, hot water and rooftop views towards the harbour. **②**, rooftop rooms **④**

Bloo Lagoon Village ☏0363/41211, ⊛www .bloolagoon.com. This village-like compound of 25 privately owned, eco-conscious villas sits on top of a hill, a 5min walk from the main centre and 2min from Blue Lagoon beach. The two- and three-bedroom villas are all slightly different but all have big decks and coastal views, plus kitchenettes. There's a pool and restaurant, and wi-fi. **⑦**

Kembar Inn ☏0363/41364. Popular, traveller-oriented guesthouse with nice staff, decent rooms on several floors and a generous buffet breakfast. There are common sitting areas but no private balconies (and few external windows) except on the top floor, which has a huge terrace plus a/c and hot water. Fan **②**, a/c **③**

Marco Inn ☏0813/3919 8241, ⓔbalihomefromhome@hotmail.com. A tiny place with welcoming staff and eight cheerfully painted cold-water rooms set round a courtyard off the harbourfront road in the village. Rooms have more furniture than you'd expect for the price and upstairs ones have nice rooftop sea views. Very cheap. **①**

Padang Bai Billabong ☏0363/41399. One of the few cheap places with a decent garden, this has four simple two-storey *lumbung* bungalows with very basic downstairs bathrooms, and eight plain bungalows nearer the road. **①**

Puri Rai ☏0363/41385, ⊛www.puriraihotels .com. Good-value, mid-range hotel with an amazing three pools for its 34 large, comfortable and nicely furnished rooms. Upstairs rooms are brighter and those at the back are the quietest. Fan **④**, a/c **⑤**

Serangan Inn II ☏0818/0550 2124, ⓔputuadi56@yahoo.com. You get spotless,

Arranging onward transport from Padang Bai is easy, with frequent boats to the Gili Islands and Lombok and any number of tour agencies keen to sell you tickets.

Boats to the Gili Islands and Lombok

See p.306 for Lombok arrival info and for other routes to Lombok.

Car ferry to Lembar An hourly service that operates 24hr and takes four hours. Tickets are Rp36,000 per person; motorbikes Rp101,000 (including two people); cars from Rp659,000 (including passengers). See p.33 for information on taking rental vehicles between the islands.

Perama tourist boat to the Gili Islands and Senggigi Boats serve all three Gili Islands (about 4hr; Rp300,000) before continuing to Senggigi (5hr; Rp300,000). Operates daily at 1.30pm, except for two days' maintenance each month (see Ⓦwww.peramatour.com). Perama also do a car ferry-and-bus combo to Senggigi (9.30am; 6hr; Rp100,000).

Fast boats to Gili Trawangan and Teluk Kodek At least five different operators offer services to Gili Trawangan (1hr 30min–2hr; Rp350,000–660,000) and Teluk Kodek, south of Bangsal on mainland Lombok (1hr 30min; same price), most leaving Padang Bai between 8.30am and 9.30am, with additional departures in high season. Tickets – which do not include onward shuttles to Gili Meno or Gili Air – are sold by shops and freelance agents throughout Padang Bai and the price varies a lot, according to demand and your bargaining skills. Full-price tickets include transfers from south Bali. The most expensive service is the *Gili Cat* (Ⓣ0361/271680, Ⓦwww.gilicat.com, or book at *Made Restaurant*); others include *Ocean Star* (Ⓣ0818/0572 0243, Ⓦwww.gilifastboat.com) and *Sea Marlin* (Ⓣ0361/977247, Ⓦbaliseamarlinexpress.com).

Boats to Nusa Penida

Fast boats to Buyuk Harbour Boats depart from just west of the jetty (up to 4 daily, 7am–noon; 45min; Rp25,000), and a large RoRo vehicle ferry to Buyuk departs from the port at 2pm (1hr; Rp18,000).

Shuttle buses and bemos

Perama shuttle buses Services depart from the Perama office near the port (daily 7am–5pm; Ⓣ0363/41419, Ⓦwww.peramatour.com) to major destinations in Bali and Lombok, including Ubud, Kuta and Sanur (see "Travel details", p.234). There are plenty of other shuttle services advertised throughout the resort.

Bemos and public minibuses Departures are from the port entrance (mostly in the morning) and run to Amlapura via Candi Dasa (Rp10,000), and Semarapura (Rp10,000); minibuses serve Batubulan.

---

high-quality rooms (and some hot water) at this three-storey place at the top of the village, plus good views across the village to the sea. Note, however, that it's across the road from the loud live-music bars *Babylon* and *Kinky* so look elsewhere if you want an early night. Fan ❷, a/c ❹
Topi Inn Ⓣ0363/41424, Ⓦwww.topiinn.com. Very

traveller-friendly guesthouse and restaurant (see p.212) with five simple rooms (some en suite) plus a common area that doubles as an open-plan dorm (Rp50,000/person) with mattresses and mosquito nets (security boxes are available). Runs tours and transport, and has internet and wi-fi. Reserve rooms ahead by email as it's very popular. ❶

The beaches

The **village beach**, between *Made's Restaurant* and *Topi Inn*, is normally crowded with *jukung* (traditional wooden outrigger boats), though you can swim here and it's often busy with local families on Sundays.

There are half a dozen rewarding dive sites around **Padang Bai** and **Blue Lagoon**, whose hard and soft corals attract eels, wrasses, turtles, flatheads, lion fish and sharks; Spanish dancers, too, are frequently spotted on night dives. At nearby **Jepun** there's a decent artificial reef and the wreck of a 15m fishing boat, which is great for stingrays and reef fish. It's ideal for novice divers and macro photography, and good for **snorkelling**, too. The reefs of Candi Dasa and, further afield, Nusa Lembongan and Nusa Penida, are also within reach.

All **dive centres** in Padang Bai stick to a price agreement, with two local dives costing $55 excluding equipment. Long-established outfits include the UK/Australian-run Geko Dive (℡0363/41516, ⊛www.gekodive.com) and the German Water Worx (℡0363/41220, ⊛www.waterworxbali.com). See p.46 for general advice on selecting a dive operator.

Most tourists head instead for the tiny whiteish-sand bays immediately over the headlands to the east and west, both within walking distance. They get crowded and aren't always pristine but they're better than nothing. **Bias Tugal** (also known as **Pantai Kecil**) is a fifteen-minute walk to the west of the port; go past the post office on Jalan Penataran Agung and then left up a rubbly track, which is quite steep in parts. The beach here has a few tiny warung, and is overlooked by the skeleton of a long-abandoned hotel project.

Alternatively, a five-minute walk along the left fork just east of *Topi Inn* will bring you to the pretty but miniature cove of **Blue Lagoon**, not much more than 100m long. You can snorkel here at high tide but beware the serious undertow and high coral. The two restaurants rent snorkel gear as well as sunloungers (Rp10,000) and you're sure to find a couple of massage ladies and sarong-sellers in attendance.

Eating, drinking and nightlife

Fresh seafood is the speciality in Padang Bai's **restaurants**, especially *mahi-mahi*, barracuda, snapper and prawns. Several tiny **live-music bars** open onto the car park inland from the jetty, with tables spilling out onto the street and a battle of the sound systems nightly from around 9pm.

Babylon Reggae Bar Tiny, perennially busy late-night drinking and music venue with local musos playing the Javanese hit *Welcome to my Paradise*, *La Bamba* and the rest. Next door is *Kinky* reggae bar, and the two meld into one big party come late evening.

Grand Café Padang Bai Harbour Classy and popular harbour-view place with comfy rattan chairs, free wi-fi, lots of cocktails, a dozen "bio" health juices, and cappuccinos. The food is good and includes pizzas, *sate campur*, grilled fish with garlic sauce, kebabs and steaks. Mains from Rp35,000.

Sunshine Bar Tiny bar with only four tables, serving cocktails and staging regular live music, just like at nearby *Babylon*.

Topi Inn Has a menu several centimetres thick, with great bread, cakes, cappuccinos and a ton of imaginative vegetarian dishes – including Mediterranean and Greek salads – as well as the usual Western and Indonesian standards (mains from Rp43,000). Sells dried fruit and other takeaway snacks, does water refill and has wi-fi (for a fee) and internet.

Warung Manggala A cut above many, complete with candles, tablecloths and powerful ceiling fans, and serving good food – chicken Kiev, tzatziki, seafood kebabs (from Rp38,000) – plus free bar snacks with your Bintang.

Warung Segara Ayu At the top of some steps on the way to Blue Lagoon (cut through for a short cut), this breezy, homely warung has harbour views, does cheap fruit juices (Rp6000) and makes excellent, inexpensive *nasi goreng* (Rp19,000).

Listings

Banks and exchange There are exchange counters in the village and on the seafront. BRI bank has an ATM that accepts Cirrus and Master-Card but not Visa; the nearest Visa ATM is in Semarapura.

Bookshop Secondhand books for sale and exchange at Wayan Bookshop, Jl Penataran Agung, across from the access road to Bias Tugal Beach (Mon–Sat 9am–6pm).

Courses You can do courses in batik, *ikat*, basket-weaving, Balinese dance, sculpture, cooking, *wayang kulit* and more at *Topi Inn* (☎0363/41424, ☜www.topiinn.com), from Rp75,000.

Doctor Highly regarded, English-speaking Dr Nisa can be contacted via Water Worx Dive Centre (☎0811/380645). The nearest hospitals are at Semarapura (see p.119) or Denpasar (see p.122).

Goa Lawah

As Bali's directional temple for the southeast, **Goa Lawah** (Bat Cave; daily 7am–7.30pm; Rp6000 plus Rp3000 sarong rental), by the coast, 7km west of Padang Bai, is always busy with worshippers who travel here in community groups to perform rites associated with significant life events. Discreetly watching the spectacle of the various **ceremonies**, both in the temple compound and at the shrine on the beach across the road, is part of the appeal of a visit here. The other highlight is the **cave** at the base of the cliff, which heaves with fruit bats. It is supposedly the start of a tunnel that stretches 30km inland to Pura Goa in Besakih and is said to contain the cosmic *naga* Basuki. If you engage a local guide to show you round, establish the fee beforehand; Rp30,000 is reasonable.

The warung along the road just west of Goa Lawah are famous for their **fresh fish** dishes. One of the most highly rated is the simple *Warung Lesehan Merta Sari* (daily 8am to about 7pm), on Jalan Kresna in the village of **Desa Pesinggahan**; to find it, turn off the main road 1.5km west of Goa Lawah and continue straight for 1.2km. For a bargain Rp15,000 you get a delicious set meal of fish soup, fish sate, steamed fish and rice and veg.

Any **bemo** between Padang Bai and Semarapura will drop you at the Goa Lawah temple; to get to *Warung Lesehan Merta Sari* ask to be dropped at the junction, then walk.

Candi Dasa and around

East Bali's main tourist hub, **CANDI DASA** is a relaxed resort with plenty of comfortable accommodation in all price brackets, some good restaurants, rewarding **diving** and lots of opportunities for day-trips and treks. All of which makes it an enjoyable and convenient base for the quieter, less commercial corners of east, central and north Bali. Its one significant drawback is its disappointing **beach**, now all but eroded out of existence and fronted by a phalanx of groynes and a sea wall. You can still swim in the sea here, and some hotels do have little patches of sand out front, but for anything approaching a beautiful beach you have to head 9km east to the lovely **Pasir Putih**. Given the lack of a beach scene, and the minimal nightlife, Candi Dasa attracts a slightly older crowd and is increasingly popular with expat villa owners.

Just 3km north of Candi is the famous traditional Bali Aga village and weaving centre of **Tenganan**, while to the east there's the locally important hilltop temple of **Pura Gumang**. Candi Dasa is also well placed for excursions to Besakih and Tirtagangga, and further afield to Amed; it's also easy to arrange treks from here up Gunung Agung and Gunung Batur.

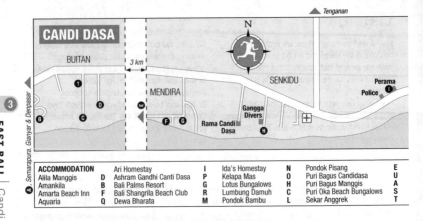

ACCOMMODATION		Ari Homestay	I	Ida's Homestay	N	Pondok Pisang	E
Alila Manggis	D	Ashram Gandhi Canti Dasa	P	Kelapa Mas	O	Puri Bagus Candidasa	U
Amankila	B	Bali Palms Resort	G	Lotus Bungalows	H	Puri Bagus Manggis	A
Amarta Beach Inn	F	Bali Shangrila Beach Club	J	Lumbung Damuh	C	Puri Oka Beach Bungalows	S
Aquaria	Q	Dewa Bharata	M	Pondok Bambu	L	Sekar Anggrek	T

Arrival, information and transport

Candi Dasa is a two-hour drive from Ngurah Rai Airport; airport **taxis** charge Rp335,000, or Candi hotels will pick you up for Rp350,000. The resort is well served by **shuttle buses** from main tourist destinations, including those operated by Perama (see p.234 for schedules and p.32 for sample prices). **Buses** and minibuses from Denpasar's Batubulan terminal pass through Candi Dasa en route to Amlapura, as do orange **bemos** between Padang Bai and Amlapura. As hotel development in the Candi Dasa area extends for about 8km along the main Denpasar–Amlapura road, these bemos are also handy for travelling in and out of central Candi and can be flagged down anywhere en route; some outlying hotels also offer free **local transport**.

There's no official tourist **information** office in Candi Dasa, but the east Bali magazine *Agung* (Ⓦ www.agungbali.com), available for free at local hotels and restaurants, is a good read and carries ads for restaurants and tour agents.

Accommodation

Accommodation in **central Candi Dasa** is clustered along the main road and the beachfront immediately to the east and west of the lagoon. Just east of here is the quieter enclave around **Jalan Puri Bagus**. Further west, there's a decent beach at **Mendira**, beyond which the villages of **Buitan** and **Manggis** have some nice places to stay.

Central Candi Dasa

Central Candi Dasa is handy for restaurants and shops, but avoid rooms that are within earshot of the busy main road. Many central hotels have attractive shore-front restaurants or seating areas that are well away from traffic noise; they're all built above a sea wall so access to the water is by steps down.

Ari Homestay ☏ 0817/970 7339, Ⓔ garyv18 @hotmail.com. A classic little Aussie-run budget guesthouse with a cheap, no-frills dorm (Rp55,000/ bed), well-priced en-suites, huge cooked break-fasts, guests' appreciation graffitied on the walls and a tiny hot-dog café. The cheaper rooms are close to the road, all have fans and some have hot water. Cold water ❶, hot water ❷

Ashram Gandhi Canti Dasa ☏ 0363/41108, Ⓦ www.ashramgandhi.com. This Gandhian ashram occupies a gorgeous location between the lagoon and the ocean and rents a few simple but attractive bungalows. Guests take part in the daily puja, yoga and meditation as much or as little as they wish, but may not smoke or drink on site. Volunteer placements are also possible. Rates are

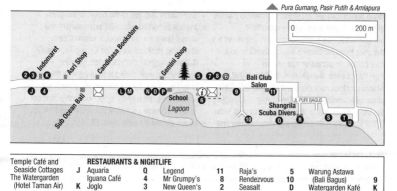

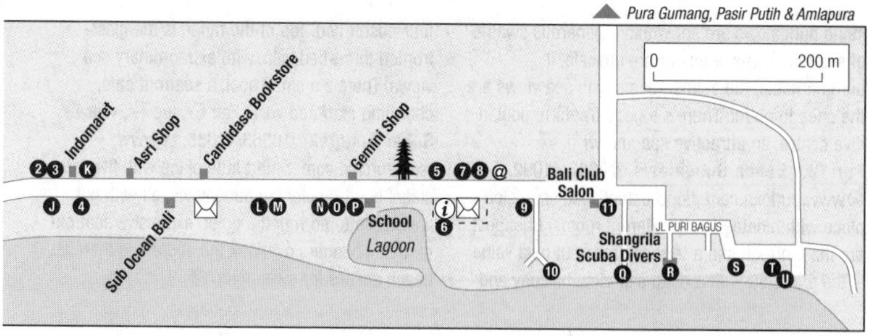
Pura Gumang, Pasir Putih & Amlapura
0
200 m
Indomaret
Asri Shop
Candidasa Bookstore
Gemini Shop
Sub Ocean Bali
Bali Club Salon
School
Lagoon
JL PURI BAGUS
Shangrila Scuba Divers
2 3 K
J 4
L M
N O P
5 7 8 @
6
9
11
10
Q
R
S
T
U

		RESTAURANTS & NIGHTLIFE							
Temple Café and Seaside Cottages	J	Aquaria	Q	Legend	11	Raja's	5	Warung Astawa (Bali Bagus)	9
The Watergarden (Hotel Taman Air)	K	Iguana Café	4	Mr Grumpy's	8	Rendezvous	10	Watergarden Kafé	K
		Joglo	3	New Queen's	2	Seasalt	D		
		Le 48	6	Nyoman's Café	1	Vincent's	7		

for two and include three vegetarian meals a day. Booking is essential. ④

Dewa Bharata ⓣ0363/41090. Eighteen good-value, old-style Balinese bungalows positioned in facing rows within a profuse garden that ensures privacy. All have hot water, some have a/c and sea views, and there's a pretty pool and seafront restaurant. Fan ③, a/c ④

Ida's Homestay ⓣ0363 41096, ⓔjsidas1@aol.com. Still within its original coconut grove, this is a little enclave of rustic Bohemia. The five good-sized wooden bungalows are designed for the climate and have almost no glass, just mosquito nets, fans and cold-water garden bathrooms. There's a lovely shorefront deck and breakfast area plus a tiny patch of sandy beach – and wi-fi. ②

Kelapa Mas ⓣ0363/41369, ⓦwww.welcometokelapamas.com. Set in an award-winning garden of coconut palms, shrubs and lush lawns, this is a calm, popular spot. Bungalows are clean if spartan (a/c and hot water are available but the sea-view fan rooms have the best location), there's a small seafront bar and sunbathing area, plus wi-fi in the restaurant. Fan ③, a/c ④

Pondok Bambu ⓣ 0363/41534, ⓦwww.pondokbambu.com. A dozen comfortable, scrupulously clean, mid-range bungalows decked out, of course, with bamboo beds, tables and chairs; all have a/c, hot water and TV, and there's wi-fi too. The garden runs down to the shore and has a small pool and a good, idyllically located sea-view restaurant. ⑤

Temple Café and Seaside Cottages ⓣ0363/41629, ⓦwww.balibeachfront-cottages.com. An excellent choice, not least for its breezy seafront tables and sunloungers, above steps down to the stony shore. The fifteen nicely furnished bungalows come in a range of standards and prices, from fan and cold-water versions to those with a/c, sea view and very good hot-water bathrooms, but they are all good value. Wi-fi on site. Fan ②, a/c ④

The Watergarden (Hotel Taman Air) ⓣ0363/41540, ⓦwww.watergardenhotel.com. Just thirteen delightful bungalows in this most Balinese of garden settings, where lush planting screens each thatch-roofed cottage and every private veranda overlooks its own carp-filled lily pond. Bungalows are in several shallow tiers with uppermost ones getting the most light; all have a/c but there are no TVs. There's wi-fi around the pretty swimming pool, as well as a spa and a good restaurant (see p.218). ⑦

Jalan Puri Bagus

A quiet alternative to central Candi, and no more than ten minutes' walk from the main restaurants, **Jalan Puri Bagus** still has patches of banana and coconut plantation among its growing number of small hotels and expat villas.

Aquaria ⓣ0363/41127, ⓦwww.aquariabali.com. In a tiny, secluded, shorefront compound at the edge of a banana grove, this modern, mellow version of a losmen offers half a dozen contemporary-styled terraced rooms set around a striking little ionized pool. There are also a couple of sea-view villas, wi-fi throughout, and one of Candi's best restaurants on site. Fan ④, a/c ⑤, villas ⑦

Puri Bagus Candidasa ⓣ0363/41131, ⓦwww.candidasa.puribagus.net. There's a refreshing feeling of space here, as the 47 large, detached,

stone bungalows are set within a generous swathe of seafront lawns. Interiors are upscale, if unremarkable: the deluxe rooms with sea views are the ones to go for. There's a good freeform pool, a dive centre, an attractive spa and wi-fi. ⑦
Puri Oka Beach Bungalows ☎0363/41092, ⓦwww.purioka.com. Long-established shoreside place with nineteen very different rooms. Cheapest are the fan rooms in a terraced row, but best value is the a/c room with a deep sea-view balcony and

four-poster bed. Top of the range is the glass-fronted three-bed villa, with extraordinary sea views. There's a small pool, a seafront café, charming staff and wi-fi. Fan ❸, a/c ❻, villa ❽
Sekar Anggrek ☎0363/41086, ⓦwww .sekarorchid.com. Smart little place with five large, clean, good-quality fan bungalows, all with hot water, scattered round a quiet, expansive seafront garden. Loungers overlook the shore and there is beach access for swimming. ❸

Mendira

Accommodation in the village of **Mendira** fronts some of Candi's nicest beach but is several kilometres from the heart of the resort so you might want to rent a motorbike.

Amarta Beach Inn ☎0363/41230. This great-value place overlooks one of the best beaches along the Candi Dasa shoreline, with white sand, clear water and a pontoon for chilling on and snorkelling off. The ten fan bungalows are large and all have a sea view; the shoreside restaurant has a good reputation, especially for fish, and there are hammocks, plus internet if you bring your own laptop. ❷

Pondok Pisang ☎0363/41065, ⓦwww .pondokpisang.com. A remote but lovely haven at the end of a rough track through a banana grove, 2km from the main road. The six idiosyncratic, two-storey fan bungalows are furnished in boho-chic style, with plenty of sea-worn wood, and the garden fronts a (partially sandy-bottomed) shore, with beautiful decks jutting over the water. ❺

Buitan and Manggis

Staying at **Buitan** (sometimes also known as **Balina**) means you'll need transport to reach central Candi Dasa; further west again, 6km out of central Candi, **Manggis** village offers several very nice hotels, including one of Bali's most luxurious.

Alila Manggis Manggis ☎0363/41011, ⓦwww.alilahotels.com. Impressive, popular hotel situated in a shoreside coconut grove with rooms ranged around a gorgeous pool. Though the beach is stony, you can swim in the sea and there's a spa, cycling and trekking, imaginative cultural tours, kids' programmes and a variety of cooking courses. The excellent *Seasalt* restaurant is here (see p.218) and there are free shuttles to central Candi and Tenganan. ⑦
Amankila Manggis ☎0363/41333, ⓦwww .amanresorts.com. Jetset hideaway in its own private bay featuring super-deluxe hillside villas with awesome coastal views. For Rp400,000 a day, at the manager's discretion, non-residents can use the Beach Club facilities (which include a 45m pool), although you won't be allowed in the much-photographed three-tiered main pool up above. Villas from $800. ❾

Lumbung Damuh Buitan ☎0363/41553, ⓦwww.damuhbali.com. Ultra-chilled, traveller-friendly little hideaway of five creatively designed *lumbung* beside a tiny patch of shore. Bedrooms are upstairs, with sitting areas and hot-water bathrooms below. There is wi-fi, free use of boogie boards and canoes, and home-cooked bread for breakfast, but no restaurant. ❸
Puri Bagus Manggis Manggis ☎0363/41304, ⓦmanggis.puribagus.net. Prettily located in a village setting a couple of kilometres from the coast, this tiny boutique hotel has just seven elegant, if slightly dark, a/c rooms. Two have stunning views of ricefields and hills (others overlook a garden courtyard) and the pool is gorgeously sited in the fields across the road. There's free transport to the sister hotel by the sea (see p.215). ⑦

The resort

Candi Dasa is an ancient settlement, and its **temple**, opposite the lagoon, is believed to have been founded in the eleventh century. The statue of the fertility goddess Hariti in the lower section of the temple, surrounded by children, is a focus for pilgrims (the name Candi Dasa originally derives from "Cilidasa", meaning ten children).

Candi's fortunes as a tourist destination have risen and fallen with the state of its **beach**. Serious erosion is said to date back to the 1980s when the reef was destroyed to produce lime for the tourist building boom; more recently, shore-front building and poorly designed sea walls have likely exacerbated the problem. The government has made various attempts to restore the beach and import sand; large groynes now protrude into the sea and pockets of sand have accumulated behind some of them. The groynes make it impossible to stroll any distance along the shore, but that does deter hawkers and also makes each patch of coast feel private to individual hotels. The views are still lovely, encompassing craggy nearby outcrops as well as the impressive bulk of Nusa Penida on the horizon.

Trekking and cycling

There's good **trekking** in the Candi Dasa area. One of the most popular routes begins at **Kastala**, near Tirtagangga (see p.225), and takes you downhill to the Bali Aga village of **Tenganan** just outside Candi, an easy two- to three-hour walk with excellent rice-terrace views and the chance to visit a village or two en route. A longer version begins in **Tirtagangga** itself and continues via the blacksmiths' village of **Budakaling** (5–6hr). Mudi at M&G Trekking (☎0813/3815 3991, ⓦwww.mudigoestothemountain.com) charges Rp300,000 per person for the Kastala trek. He also organizes treks up Gunung Batur (Rp750,000/person); ascents of Gunung Agung (Rp750,000/person from Pasar Agung, Rp990,000 from Besakih, and Rp1,100,000 for the overnight route from Dukuh; for more details, see p.205); and a 55km **cycling tour** from Muncan via Tirtagangga to the coast at Amed (Rp750,000).

Diving and snorkelling around Candi Dasa

Just off the coast, the outcrops known as **Gili Tepekong**, **Gili Biaha** and **Gili Mimpang** offer excellent **diving**, although it's not suitable for beginners as the water can be cold and the currents strong. There are several walls, a pinnacle just off Mimpang, and dramatic scenery at boulder-lined Tepekong Canyon. The current is too strong for the growth of big coral, but the fish include barracuda, tuna, white-tipped reef shark, *mola-mola*, turtles and manta rays. **Prices** start at $75 for two local dives excluding equipment. Candi is also within day-tripping distance of the reefs at Padang Bai, the wrecks at Tulamben and Amed, and the challenging sites around Nusa Lembongan and Nusa Penida.

Well-regarded **dive centres** in Candi Dasa include British-run Shangrila Scuba Divers at Bali Shangrila Beach Club, Jl Puri Bagus, and with a counter at *Bali Palms Resort*, Mendira (☎0813/3733 5081, ⓦwww.shangrilascubadivers.com); and Gangga Divers, at *Lotus Bungalows*, Senkidu (☎0363/41796, ⓦwww.lotusbungalows.com /diving.html). See p.46 for general advice on choosing a dive centre.

Snorkelling

The local reef is gradually rejuvenating and there is now **snorkelling** just offshore, stretching for about a kilometre westwards from just in front of *Puri Bagus Candidasa*. The **currents** can be hazardous, though, so don't venture too far out and stay aware of your position at all times. Jepun, near Padang Bai (see p.212), is also rewarding. You can arrange snorkelling trips with local boat-owners: it's Rp250,000 for two hours for up to three people, including equipment, to the islands off Candi Dasa or to Pasir Putih (see p.219), or Rp350,000 to Jepun.

Eating and nightlife

There's a good range of **restaurants** in and around Candi Dasa, from cheap tourist-oriented warung to sophisticated hotel dining. Some offer free transport from hotels around the resort. **Nightlife** is low-key and things are usually pretty quiet by 10pm. The main entertainment is **live music**, staged at different restaurants through the week, from about 8pm: try *New Queen's*, where visiting musicians are often invited to jam with the in-house band; the sometimes rowdy *Legend* (☎0363/41636 for free local transport); or *Iguana Café*. *Raja's* shows videos and there are music videos, sports and films, wi-fi and fast internet at *Mr Grumpy's*.

Central Candi Dasa and Jalan Puri Bagus

🏃 **Aquaria** Jl Puri Bagus ☎0363/41127, ⓦwww.aquariabali.com. The tiny restaurant overlooking the hotel pool serves delicious, inventive food such as ginger-spiced prawns, organic chicken, rye-bread sandwiches and imported cheese. The fixed-price menu changes daily (Rp75,000 for two courses; browse the week's menu at the hotel entrance) and includes veggie options and a kids' menu.

Joglo There's classy, notably good Indonesian food at this small, gardenside restaurant. The beef *rendang* is especially recommended (Rp60,000).

Le 48 (Le Quarante Huit) ☎0363/41177, ⓦwww.le48bali.com. Though the retro red-chrome bowl chairs, Audrey Hepburn photos and waitresses clad in single black gloves seem rather pretentious for middle-of-the-road Candi, the food at this design-conscious hotel-restaurant is genuinely sophisticated. Highlights include the frozen carrot cappuccino, *mahi-mahi* ceviche and signature Bemo to Bangli cocktail ("hot"). Mains cost from Rp39,000 and though there is a wine list you can bring your own for Rp100,000 corkage. Free wi-fi.

Rendezvous *Asmara Bungalows* ☎0363/41929. This attractively sited seafront restaurant emphasizes quality ingredients – grass-fed beef, free-range chicken and home-made bread – and does decent-value seafood and vegetarian set meals (from Rp85,000) as well as Thai tom yam kung, pumpkin cake and health drinks. Phone for free local transport.

🏃 **Vincent's** ☎0363/41368, ⓦwww .vincentsbali.com. Central Candi's best has a relaxed, arty vibe – jazz on the sound system, Van Gogh repros on the walls and a separate lounge bar, dining room and garden restaurant. The food is great: fresh and scrumptious seafood and Greek salads, pan-fried potatoes with all main dishes, calamari Parmigiano and the signature chocolate mousse cake to round it all off. Mains cost Rp55,000–110,000 and imported wines start at Rp40,000 a glass. Arrive early for dinner or reserve ahead as it's very popular.

Warung Astawa (Bali Bagus) You get excellent value at this typical tourist warung, with set three-course meals of Indonesian standards, many of them fish-based, from Rp55,000.

Watergarden Kafé ☎0363/41540. Choose from over seventy Indonesian, international and seafood dishes, including good steaks, plus vegetarian, nut- and wheat-free options (mains Rp35,000–150,000). The attached hotel stages frequent culinary events, from suckling pig specials to German-style beer festivals, and there's free wi-fi and free local transport.

The outskirts

Nyoman's Café Buitan. One of a trio of cheap and cheerful places on the road to the beach, with a selection of Indonesian and Western favourites including local seafood (mains about Rp20,000).

Seasalt *Alila* hotel, Manggis ☎0363/41011, ⓦwww.alilahotels.com. The premier dining experience in eastern Bali features a delectable range of Asian, fusion and vegetarian dishes, with plenty of local specialities (mains from Rp90,000). Try a selection as tapas, as a *nasi campur* set, or in the signature *megibung* eight-dish feast, which includes spicy beef, chicken sate and snapper with ginger (Rp475,000 for two).

Listings

Banks and exchange There are moneychangers on the main street but no international ATMs. The nearest reliable international ATMs are a bemo ride away in Amlapura or Semarapura.

Car, motorbike and bicycle rental Cars and motorbikes are best rented through your accommo-dation. Sub Ocean Bali in central Candi has a few bicycles to rent, as do a couple of nearby shops.

Doctor English-speaking Dr Nisa (☎0811/380645) is based between Candi Dasa and Padang Bai and will do hotel visits. The nearest hospitals are in Amlapura, Semarapura and Denpasar.

Massage and spas Beach massages are available throughout the resort (Rp60,000/hr), or try Accessories, next to *Temple Café and Seaside Cottages* (Rp80,000). Bali Club Salon and Spa (daily noon–8pm; ☎0363 41166 for free transport) has "doktor fish" that supposedly nibble the rough skin off your feet (Rp30,000/10min). There are classy spas at the *Alila* hotel (☎0363/41011; from $50 for a stay-all-day three-treatment package) and the *Puri Bagus Candidasa* (daily 11am–9pm; from Rp300,000; ☎0361/41131 for free transport).
Shops New and secondhand books at Candi Bookstore; daily necessities at Indomaret minimarket, Asri Shop and Gemini Shop.

Tours and onward transport To put together your own day-trip, you'll be looking at Rp350,000–500,000/day for vehicle, driver and petrol; Ketut Lagun (☎0812/362 2076, ✉ketut_lagun @yahoo.com) is a highly recommended local driver and guide. A private transfer to the airport/ Kuta area costs about Rp350,000 or you can use one of the many shuttle buses, which charge Rp60,000. Perama (☎0363/41114, ✆www .peramatour.com) does hotel pick-ups and runs shuttle buses to major Bali and Lombok destinations (see "Travel details", p.234).

Pura Gumang

At the top of the pass about 3km northeast out of Candi, on the way to Pasir Putih, monkeys crowd around roadside stalls at the point where worshippers begin their hour-long walk up to hilltop **Pura Gumang**. This is one of the most important temples in the area and affords a fine panorama inland to Gunung Agung, down to the coast and even across to Gunung Rinjani on Lombok. Every two years, usually at full moon in October, four of the local villages – Bugbug, Bebandem, Jasri and Ngis – participate in a huge ceremony, complete with trance dances, that begins with a procession up to Pura Gumang. It attracts up to eight thousand people, especially new parents, who bring along hundreds of roast suckling pigs. To get to the temple, catch an Amlapura-bound **bemo** from central Candi and alight by the stalls. Concrete steps and then a steep path head seawards to the temple.

Pasir Putih

Everyone in Candi bemoans the loss of the beach, but there is, for the moment at least, a highly satisfying alternative, 9km northeast at the famously beautiful **Pasir Putih** (White Sand Bay). The less than straightforward access, via a steep and rutted track, is part of the appeal: the black-and-whitish-sand bay feels wild and remote, backed by palms and forest remnants, and sheltered by rocky headlands. The aquamarine water is perfect for swimming and the reef just offshore offers decent snorkelling. The beach is lined along part of its course with a dozen shacks providing meals and massage plus snorkel and sunlounger rental (Rp10,000/day); *Gusti's* is friendly and good value. All of this will change, however, if the rumoured development by a big Korean investor comes to fruition.

Access is from the village of **Perasi**, immediately east of **Bugbug** on the road to Amlapura, about 6km from Candi. There are two routes from here: the first (unsigned) is immediately opposite a temple; the second is a few hundred metres further east and has a tiny sign for White Sand Beach/Jalan Pasir Putih. Both lead 3km to the coast via a ticket office (Rp2500) and dauntingly rough track. An **ojek** will drive you there and back, and wait all day for you, for Rp60,000 from Candi, or it's Rp200,000 for a car plus driver.

Tenganan

When the Javanese Majapahit conquered Bali in 1343, imposing religious reforms and a caste system on the island, those that rejected the Javanization of Bali withdrew to their village enclaves to live a life based around ritual and ceremony.

The founding of Tenganan

In the days before the Majapahit invasion of Bali, **King Bedaulu** ruled the island. Legend has it that one day his favourite horse went missing, and so he offered a large reward for its return. When the horse was discovered – dead – near Tenganan, the king announced that he would give the local people the land within which the stench of the rotting animal could be smelled. One of the king's ministers was sent to adjudicate, and he and Tenganan's headman set out to decide the boundaries. The smell of the horse could be detected over a huge area. The lines were duly drawn and the minister departed. At this point, the devious village headman took out from under his clothes the piece of rotting horse meat with which he had fooled the minister. The limits of the village lands are still the ones set at that time, and cover more than ten square kilometres.

Nearly seven centuries later they are still a distinct group, known as the **Bali Aga** or Bali Mula, the "original Balinese", who adhere to a strict, archaic code in their social and religious lives. One of the most famous Bali Aga villages is **Tenganan Pegringsingan**, a wealthy settlement of 625 families set among forest and hills 3km north of Candi Dasa. It's a major day-trippers' destination, known not only for its traditional architecture but also as the only place in Indonesia that produces the celebrated **geringsing** cloth. It's also the finishing point of a popular and scenic trek that begins in either Kastala or Tirtagangga (see p.225). West across the river from Tenganan Pegringsingan, the twin Bali Aga settlement of **Tenganan Dauh Tukad** is smaller, with just 275 families, and much less famous, but also worth a visit.

The Bali Aga are followers of the Indra sect of Hinduism and trace their ancestral links to Orissa in India rather than to Java like most Balinese. Among other things, their exacting customary law determines on which of the three village streets they can live and who they may or may not marry. Most of the daily rites are inaccessible to the public, but there are many **festivals** where visitors are welcome; see Ⓦ www.karangasemtourism.com for exact dates. One of the most dramatic is the month-long Usaba Sambah, generally in May and June, which includes ceremonial duelling known as *perang padan* or *mekare-kare*, in which bare-chested men fight each other with thorny pandanus leaves.

To gain insight into daily life in the two Tenganan villages you'll need a **guide**: these are provided free of charge in Tenganan Dauh Tukad, or consider joining a tour organized through the village ecotourism network, JED (Ⓣ0361/737447, Ⓦ www.jed.or.id). The road to Tenganan Pegringsingan is a pleasant 3km **walk** uphill from the western end of Candi Dasa or you can take an **ojek** for about Rp10,000. Tenganan Dauh Tukad is also 3km from Candi, signed off the same road, part way up the hill. To walk between the two villages shouldn't take long but you'll need a guide; going by road it's about 4km.

Tenganan Pegringsingan

Laid out around three cobbled, vehicle-free avenues that run north–south, **TENGANAN PEGRINGSINGAN** (admission by donation) rises in a series of terraces, its family compounds hidden behind high walls of thatch, adobe and brick. Communal activities and meetings take place in thatched *bale* on the main street and there are plenty of handicraft stalls set out here too.

Tenganan's most famous craft is the unique and highly prized **geringsing** or double *ikat* (see p.194) that gives this village its name. Dyed in a limited natural palette of brown, deep red, indigo and tan, and designed with deeply symbolic motifs, *geringsing* is revered throughout Bali as sacred cloth, able to ward off evil and having an important role in tooth-filing and cremation ceremonies. One of the best-known outlets is the **Indigo Art Shop**, run by I Wayan Kondri, whose family is still involved in every stage of *geringsing* production. This starts with the making of the dye from locally grown indigo and tree bark; the dye then needs to be applied to both the warp and the weft threads in the "double-*ikat*" tying and dying process that makes *geringsing* so special. He will explain the meaning of the most common motifs and show you his collection of exquisite weaves, which start at $110 for a scarf.

Glossy, golden, tightly woven **basketwork** made from *ata* grass is another painstakingly crafted village product. The grass has to be split, woven, boiled, dried and then smoked, all of which means it can take a month to produce a single item. **Traditional calligraphy** is another attractive Tenganan craft. Pictures and symbols are incised on narrow lengths of *lontar* palm, which are then strung together to create a concertina-like book.

Tenganan Dauh Tukad

Nearby **TENGANAN DAUH TUKAD** (entry by donation) is much less visited. Part of its appeal is that every visitor is accompanied by a local guide, which is a great chance to learn about village life and customs; guides are free but a tip is appreciated. At first glance Tenganan Dauh Tukad looks less traditional than its neighbour, as it has many more modern additions, mainly because of rebuilding following a serious earthquake in 2004. But it's also greener and more peaceful, again with a series of broad terraced streets ascending the hillside. It's also less commercial, because the village forbids displaying wares in the street, so to see the weaving, basketware and other crafts you need to go inside the family homes. However, the quality and variety is better in the other village.

Amlapura and around

Formerly known as Karangasem, **AMLAPURA** was renamed after the 1963 eruption of Gunung Agung, when the outskirts of the town were flattened by the lava flow. (Balinese people sometimes change their names after serious illness in the belief that it will bring about a change of fortune.) It's the capital of Karangasem district, and has a significant history, but the modern town is quiet and unhurried, with just enough to keep you busy for an hour or two. It also makes a handy pit stop on the popular day-trip circuit from Amed via the scenic coastal route (see p.231), with alternative accommodation and food at **Seraya Barat**, 6km east around the coast.

The main sights in and around town are associated with the **Karangasem court**. Once so powerful that in the seventeenth century it established Balinese rule over several Lombok principalities, Karangasem was later severely weakened by feuding between its rival factions and by the mid-nineteenth century was itself ruled from Lombok. Following the Dutch conquest of Lombok in 1894, **Anak Agung Gede Jelantik**, a member of the Lombok ruling family, was appointed regent of Karangasem by the colonialists. He was succeeded in 1908 by his nephew, **Anak Agung Anglurah**, the last raja of Karangasem before Independence and famous as the architect of the water palaces at Tirtagangga and **Taman Sukasada** in Ujung. Their relatives continue to occupy the **Puri Agung Karangasem** palace in Amlapura and ties with Lombok are still strong: many Balinese in the west Lombok city of Cakranegara have family in Karangasem, and the sizeable Muslim community in Amlapura traces its ancestry back to the period when Karangasem was under Lombok rule.

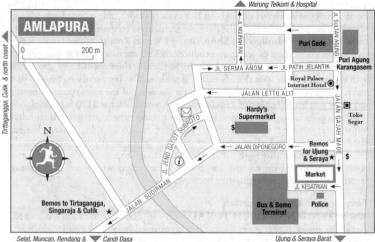

Built during the Dutch period at the end of the nineteenth century by the raja of Karangasem, Anak Agung Gede Jelantik, **Puri Agung Karangasem** (daily 8am–5pm; Rp10,000) is still home to descendants of the royal family and offers a rare chance to see a partially renovated palace home. Areas open to the public include the elegantly airy **Maskerdam** guest house, with its beautiful doors carved with three-dimensional reliefs of birds, animals and foliage. It was used for greeting VIP guests; inside there are a few pieces of period furniture and a gallery of historic photographs. Elsewhere in the compact but artfully tranquil gardens is the **Bale Kambang** (Floating Pavilion), encircled by a lotus pond, which is for meetings, dancing and dining. Wander round the compound, via the edges of the current-day family quarters, for views down over the rest of the town and across to Lombok – at one time under Karangasem rule; the peaks of Gunung Agung and Gunung Lempuyang frame the vista.

Practicalities

Amlapura has useful **bemo services** from and to Padang Bai via Candi Dasa (orange), Gianyar, and Rendang via Muncan and Selat (green), which all use the terminal in town. Bemos to Culik via Tirtagangga leave from the turn-off on the outskirts of town, as do dark-red minibuses to Singaraja. This turning is marked by a huge black-and-white pinnacle, a monument to the fight for independence, which is adorned with a Garuda. There are also buses and minibuses from the terminal to Singaraja, with some continuing to Gilimanuk. Bemos to Ujung and occasional services to Seraya (blue) leave from the southern end of Jalan Gajah Made, not far from the terminal. As elsewhere on Bali, bemos are most frequent in the early morning; in the afternoon you may end up chartering on some routes.

Most people stop off in Amlapura for a couple of hours on their way elsewhere. However, there is **accommodation** on Jalan Gajah Made at *Villa Amlapura* (aka *The Royal Palace Internet Hotel*; T 0857/3930 1697, E theroyalpalaceinternethotel @yahoo.com; ❸), which has rather dark, cold-water fan rooms in a small compound just south of Puri Agung Karangasem. For more upscale accommodation, and a sea view, consider heading east to Seraya Barat instead (see opposite). The neighbourhood **warung** *Toko Segar* on Jalan Gajah Made serves a few inexpensive Indonesian dishes.

There's an international (Visa) **ATM** at Hardy's shopping centre and **exchange** facilities at BRI on Jalan Gajah Made.

Taman Sukasada (Ujung Water Palace)

In a rural location 5km south of central Amlapura stands the largest of the three extravagant water palaces conceived by the last raja of Karangasem, Anak Agung Anglurah. **Taman Sukasada**, also known as the **Ujung Water Palace** (daily 7am–6pm; Rp10,000), dates from 1921 but was all but destroyed by the 1963 eruption of Gunung Agung. Renovations have attempted to recreate the stately tranquillity of its ponds, floating pavilions, ornamental bridges and pagodas, but the concrete relief carvings and statuary are not a patch on the more impressive originals at Taman Gili in Tirtagangga, nor the pretty elegance of Puri Agung Karangasem in Amlapura. Nonetheless it's a serene spot, served by **bemos** from Amlapura, and worth a visit if you're en route to Amed via the scenic coastal route (see p.231). There are a couple of warung on site.

Seraya Barat

If you're on a leisurely tour of east Bali, or simply want a place to stop between Amlapura and Amed, the wild, dramatic black-stone shore at **SERAYA BARAT**, 1km east of Ujung, 6km from central Amlapura or 24km from Amed, has a couple of options. The sea here is too dangerous for reliable swimming but the gorgeous white sands of Pasir Putih are a twenty-minute drive away (see p.219) and the views to Nusa Penida and Lombok are awesome.

There's good **food** and sea views at *Kebun Impian* guesthouse (☎0813/3872 1842, ⓦwww.holiday-rentals.co.uk/property65990; ❹), where diners can also use the swimming pool. A few hundred metres further east, the luxurious hideaway *Seraya Shores* (☎0813/3841 6572, ⓦwww.serayashores.com; ❻) comprises seven enormous, individually designed Bali-style **villas** in a great seafront garden, plus a beautiful shoreside pool; the restaurant isn't open to non-guests, however.

Tirtagangga and around

Famous for its whimsical mid-twentieth century water palace and its strikingly pretty landscape of plunging rice terraces and dramatic mountain peaks, **TIRTAGANGGA** is a popular day-trip destination but also makes an enjoyable stopover between Amed and Candi Dasa. There are countless possibilities for gentle ricefield treks and more strenuous full-day hikes, and it's significantly cooler than on the coast. Much of the accommodation enjoys fine panoramas, especially the quieter places in the neighbouring villages of **Temaga**, 1.5km to the south, and **Ababi**, 2.5km north, both of which are well off the main road; these villages feel remote but the accommodation is just ten to fifteen minutes' walk through the ricefields from central Tirtagangga. On a clear day you get fine views of Gunung Lempuyang to the east, on whose slopes stands **Pura Lempuyang Luhur**, a worthwhile local trip.

Arrival and information

Tirtagangga is served by **minibuses** and **buses** plying between Amlapura and Singaraja, and by Perama charters from Candi Dasa (Rp125,000/person, minimum two). The Perama agent in Tirtagangga is trekking guide Komang Gede Sutama,

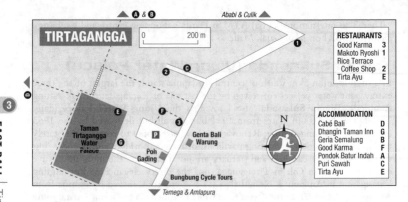

who is based at the Poh Gading **tourist information** shop. He can also arrange cheap private bemo charters on to Amed, Candi and Padang Bai (Rp80,000–130,000/bemo). There are **moneychangers** in the village but rates are better in Candi Dasa; the nearest international **ATM** is in Amlapura, 6km south.

Accommodation

Staying in central Tirtagangga puts you near a choice of warung but also within earshot of the busy road; staying further away means a greener and quieter outlook but a ten- or fifteen-minute walk into the centre.

Cabé Bali Temega, a 10min easy (flat) walk from Tirtagangga ℡0363/22045, ⊛www.cabebali.com. Encircled by ricefields with views to Agung and the Lombok Strait, the four large and supremely tasteful bungalows here have day beds from which to soak up the glorious surroundings, and a pool. The genial German–Indonesian hosts foster a relaxed atmosphere and the Indonesian food (served to guests only) is top-notch. Discounts for longer stays. ❻

Dhangin Taman Inn ℡0363/22059. Close to the Water Palace, with a sitting area and some pricier rooms overlooking the pools, this also has the cheapest beds in Tirtagangga. All rooms are simple, with cold-water bathrooms; a few are jazzed up with mirror-mosaic murals. ❶

Geria Semalung Ababi, a steep 15min walk down to Tirtagangga ℡0363/22116, ⊛www.geriasemalung.com. A forest hideaway of five attractively furnished hot-water bungalows on the crown of the hill, with fine views across to Gunung Lempuyang and down to the rice terraces below. ❸

Good Karma ℡0363/22445. Central spot set a decent distance back from the road, with four clean, tiled rooms in a small garden in the paddyfields. ❷

Pondok Batur Indah Ababi, a steep 10min walk down to Tirtagangga ℡0363/22342, ℅pondok baturindah@yahoo.com. Five large, clean, tiled rooms (one family-sized) with hot water in a small family compound with fine views to Lempuyang. Phone for a pick-up from Tirtagangga. ❷

Puri Sawah ℡0363/21847, ⊛www.purisawah.com. Set just off the main road, this British–Balinese-run place has a great restaurant, the *Rice Terrace Café*, and four nicely furnished rooms (one with hot water). Upstairs rooms are lightest and have the best views. ❸

Tirta Ayu ℡0363/22503, ⊛www.hotel tirtagangga.com. Occupying a compact corner of the Water Palace, where once the raja would stay, this has just five luxurious Bali-style villas and a swimming pool. Villas have sunken bathtubs, wi-fi and verandas but the views are mainly from the restaurant, which enjoys a prime outlook over the palace. ❼

Taman Tirtagangga Water Palace

Tirtagangga's only real sight, **Taman Tirtagangga Water Palace** (daily 7am–7pm; Rp10,000; ⊛www.tirtagangga.com) was built in 1946 by Anak Agung Anglurah, the last raja of Karangasem, and is the finest manifestation of his obsession with pools, moats and fountains. Constructed on the site of a holy spring just off the main road, it's actually a water **garden** rather than a palace, a confection of terraced ponds, pretty shrubs and water burbling from the mouths of sculpted water buffaloes and nymphs, the pools flashing orange with very well-fed carp. Two of the upper-level pools are even open to the public for **swimming** (Rp6000, kids Rp4000), though it's mostly local kids who use them.

Trekking and other activities

Surrounded by classic Balinese landscapes of terraced ricefields, rambutan, vanilla and banana plantations, tiny villages and distant volcanic peaks, Tirtagangga is an excellent base for gentle walks and challenging **treks**. Every guesthouse offers a range of programmes and there are also some specialist local **guides**, notably the reputable Komang Gede Sutama (contact him through his Poh Gading Tourist Information shop, ☎0813/3877 0893, or at *Good Karma* restaurant), who covers the most options. Choose from easy local hikes to longer versions that take you to Tenganan village above Candi Dasa (2–6hr depending on where you start the walk; see p.217): the **Kastala to Tenganan** section (2hr) is a real highlight. Prices average Rp35,000 per person per hour. More strenuous routes take you to Amed (Bunutan) via the mountaintop Pura Lempuyang (9hr; Rp850,000/guide, including luggage transfer if required), to Gunung Seraya, and up Gunung Agung (Rp1,200,000, but see p.205). Nyoman Budiarsa's shop at *Genta Bali Warung* on the main road (☎0363/22436) sells a **map** of local walks (Rp3000) and he also works as a **guide**.

Bungbung runs backroads **cycling** tours; contact them at their office in Tirtagangga (☎0812/3765 3467, ⓦsites.google.com/site/bungbungbikeadventure/; from Rp250,000) or at *Geria Semalung* guesthouse.

After all that activity, you may well need a **massage**: I Made Putu Tungtang from Ababi is highly recommended (☎0812/392 6321; Rp80,000/hr).

Eating

Most accommodation has a **restaurant** attached.

Good Karma Choose from a big tourist menu (mains Rp25,000 and up) that also includes Balinese specialities like *dendang be siap* (roast chicken, potatoes and spicy *bumbu* sauce).

Makoto Ryoshi Japanese café with tip-top views to the distant Lombok Strait. On the menu are *udon* and *soba* noodle dishes, including chilled *zaru soba*, plus chicken teriyaki; mains around Rp30,000.

Rice Terrace Coffee Shop *Puri Sawah* guesthouse. Excellent baguettes plus salads, baked potatoes, delicious cheesy crêpes, plenty of vegetarian choices, kids' sausage and chips and the best apple crumble around. Mains about Rp35,000.

Tirta Ayu The classy, innovative food at this upscale restaurant gets rave reviews, with the vast, pricey menu ranging from Vietnamese rice paper rolls to *tom yam*, duck in Hoisin sauce and pizza. The location within the Water Palace grounds is great, too, with views across the gardens and pools.

Pura Lempuyang Luhur

Visible to the northeast from Tirtagangga, less than 12km away, Gunung Lempuyang is a sacred peak and site of **Pura Lempuyang Luhur**, one of the *kayangan jagat* or directional temples of Bali, giving spiritual protection from the east. The temple gleams white on the mountain slopes and offers exceptional views. A daunting two-hour climb, up 1700 steps from the car park, will get you to the principal temple, which is believed to be the dwelling place of the god Genijaya, but the vistas, including of Gunung Agung perfectly framed in the *candi* *bentar*, makes it all worthwhile. The **courtyard** contains a stand of bamboo, and on festival days the priest makes a cut in the bamboo to release holy water. From the temple, a ninety-minute climb up another staircase brings you to the **summit** of **Gunung Lempuyang** (1058m), where there's another temple.

The temple car park is 8km from **Abang**, itself 3.5km north of Tirtagangga on the Culik road. Bemos only cover the 2km from Abang to **Ngis Tista**, (except during festivals when they go all the way to the temple), so it's best to organize your own transport. Festival days are the best time to visit (see ⓦwww .karangasemtourism.com for dates), when the temple swarms with worshippers carrying offerings all the way up the staircase.

The Amed coast

The entire fifteen-kilometre stretch of coast **from Culik to Aas** in the far east of Bali is known as **AMED**, although this is the name of just one village in an area of peaceful bays, clear waters and dramatically undulating topography. One of Bali's poorest regions, notorious for its dusty soil and subsistence economy based around fishing and salt production, Amed is also blessed with abundant reefs, many of them close to shore. As word spreads about the exceptional **snorkelling** and **diving** around here, tourist facilities are beginning to mushroom, with accommodation now available in every village bay. **Jemeluk**, with its dive centres and restaurants, is a good choice if you don't have your own transport; **Bunutan** has some very nice places to stay; and **Banyuning** is great for snorkelling. If you're not here for the snorkelling or diving, there are some day-tripping possibilities, but be warned that the **beaches** are not Bali's finest, being mostly black, stony and shadeless (though they do get paler and sandier east of **Lipah**), and generally busier with traditional wooden outriggers (*jukung*) than sunloungers. The scenery, however, is magnificent: as the coast road crests one headland after another, the scalloped bays and aquamarine waters sparkle beneath the folds of the stark volcanic hills behind.

Arrival

Access to Amed is via **Culik**, 9km northeast of Tirtagangga, 10km southeast of Tulamben. All public transport between Amlapura and Singaraja passes through Culik. From here, **bemos** sometimes run via Amed to Aas in the morning, but as you'll probably end up chartering one it may be easier to arrange through transport with a company such as **Perama** (ⓦwww.peramatour.com), who charge Rp125,000 per person (minimum two) to any Amed area hotel from Candi Dasa or Padang Bai, less from Tirtagangga.

Moving on from Amed

Tourist **transport** services are offered in almost every village, and through hotels, to all major destinations on Bali, including the airport. Fast boats run direct from Amed to **Gili Trawangan** and **Lombok** (1hr 15min–1hr 45min; Rp450,000–600,000 depending on demand) and leave at about 9am, daily in high season but sometimes less often in low season. Contact Amed Sea Express (ⓣ0878 6305 3149, ⓦwww .amedseaexpress.com) or Kuda Hitam (ⓣ0817/471 4503, ⓦwww.kudahitam.com). Big-engined fishing boats can also be chartered to the Gili Islands (Rp700,000/ two-passenger boat; 4hr); ask at your accommodation, but don't expect much comfort, or life jackets.

Diving and snorkelling at Amed

Amed's reefs are popular with divers from all over Bali and by late morning can be very crowded with day-trippers. Local dive operators tend to set off early in the day to get a head start on incomers, which is one of several good reasons to base yourself here.

Diving

The main diving area is at **Jemeluk**, where a massive sloping terrace of hard and soft coral leads to a wall dropping to a depth of over 40m. Gorgonian fans, basket sponges and table coral are especially good, there's plenty of fish (including schools of red-tooth trigger fish and sergeant majors), plus sharks, wrasses and parrotfish. Advanced divers rate **Gili Selang**, an islet off Bali's eastern tip, about 5km south of Aas, with its pristine reef, pelagics and exciting currents. There's the Japanese Wreck at **Banyuning** (see below) and a dramatic drift dive at **Bunutan**, with schools of barracuda and giant barrel sponges. **Tulamben** (see p.232) is a twenty-minute drive away and most dive centres offer safaris to sites further afield.

There are countless **dive centres** in the Amed area, but see our general advice on p.46 before choosing one. All the established places will collect you from your accommodation. Prices average $70/75 for two dives at Jemeluk/Banyuning/Bunutan (without/with boat), $70 at Tulamben and $80 at Gili Selang. Among the most reputable dive centres in the area are: **Jukung Dive** in Jemeluk/Congkang (T0363/23469, Wwww.jukungdivebali.com); **Puri Wirata Dive School** in Bunutan (T/0363/23523, Wwww.diveamed.com); and **Euro Dive** in Lipah (T0363/23605, Wwww.eurodivebali.com).

Snorkelling

Banyuning has the area's best snorkelling, at the **Japanese Wreck**, which lies in shallow water (6–12m) just 20m offshore; the small freighter is overgrown with soft corals and is frequented by pygmy seahorses, leaf scorpionfish and a number of nudibranchs. If you're staying elsewhere you can charter a boat to the wreck: from Jemeluk it's a forty-minute ride and costs Rp200,000 per two-person boat for the whole excursion. There's rewarding reef in **Jemeluk** too, especially in the exceptionally clear water around the headland beside *Villa Coral Café*, and also in a long stretch in front of *Café Amed* and *Ganesh Amed*. **Snorkel sets** can be rented everywhere.

Transport and tours

Transport along the Amed coast is scant. For transport within the Amed area you'll either need to rent your own **motorbike**, available in every village for about Rp50,000 per day, or get a lift on the back of one – there are ojek and transport touts all over. **Car rental**, with or without driver, is best arranged through your accommodation.

The most popular **tours** on dry land include the sightseeing loop via the spectacular coast road to Ujung (see p.231), with stops at Taman Sukasada Water Palace, Amlapura and Tirtagangga. The mountain and temple at Pura Lempuyang Luhur (see p.225) make another enjoyable outing, plus there are hikes inland up the slopes of Gunung Seraya. Prices range from Rp200,000 per person for a tour on the back of a motorbike to Rp500,000 per group for a car plus driver. Treks up Gunung Agung can also be arranged from Amed (about Rp1,000,000; see p.205).

Accommodation

Room rates throughout Amed are very season-sensitive and many places up their prices by forty percent in peak periods; we have therefore shown prices as **low-season/high-season**, where applicable. Such is the pressure on accommodation

THE AMED COAST

Jemeluk

Congkang

Amed

Jukung
Dive

Tukad Se

Eco-
Dive

Culik

ACCOMMODATION

Amed Café Hotel	C	Geria Giri Shanti	B	Puri Wirata	I
Anda Amed	J	Kembali Beach		Villa Coral Café	F
Baliku	P	Bungalows	A	Waeni's Sunset	
Blue Moon Villas	N	Le Jardin	L	View Bungalows	H
Eka Purnama	O	Life in Amed	M	Wawa Wewe II	K
Galang Kangin	E	Meditasi	Q		
Ganesh Amed	D	Prema Liong	G		

▼ Tirtagangga & Candi Dasa

in July and August that budget rooms can be impossible to find unless you've booked and paid way ahead. During this time villagers commonly accommodate backpackers in their homes up tracks off the main road, asking at least Rp150,000 per couple.

Jemeluk and Congkang

With a decent spread of accommodation, a useful supply of tourist facilities and excellent diving and snorkelling just offshore, **Jemeluk** (6km from Culik) makes a good Amed base. West of *Amed Café* is officially **Congkang**, though development is contiguous so the two are effectively indistinguishable.

Amed Café Hotel (Pondok Kebun Wayan)
☎0363/23473, ⊛www.amedcafe.com. One of the biggest outfits in Amed, with thirty rooms, plus a pool, dive centre, internet access and minimarket, this is a useful budget/mid-range option. Rooms in all categories are spacious and nicely furnished; the cheapest have fans and cold water and are right by the road. Fan ❸/❹, a/c ❹/❺
Galang Kangin ☎0363/23480, ⊛gkamed.blog69 .fc2.com, ℮bali_amed_gk@yahoo.com. Ten extremely clean, good-value rooms, some of them in two-storey blocks right on the beach, all with fine sea views (upstairs fan ones are best value), plus some bungalows in a garden across the road. A/c and hot water are available. Fan ❷/❹, a/c ❹/❺
Ganesh Amed ☎0859/3516 2475, ⊛www .ganeshamed.com. With a small shorefront pool, direct beach (and reef) access and some sea views, this is well priced for its location and facilities. The cheapest of the six rooms are cosy and close to the road; others are nearer the sea, in large, sparsely furnished bungalows with huge bathrooms. Fan ❸/❹, a/c ❹/❺

Geria Giri Shanti ☎0819/1665 4874,
⊛www.geriagirishanti.com. Friendly, well-run budget option with five good-sized, sparklingly clean and thoughtfully outfitted bungalows (good mosquito nets, nice fabrics, lots of hangers, long mirrors) just above the road. All have fans and hot water. ❷/❸
Kembali Beach Bungalows ☎0817/476 8313, ⊛www.kembalibeachbungalows.com. Café-au-lait-coloured shutters and simple but chic a/c interiors make these eight beachside bungalows an appealing choice; most enjoy sea views from their verandas. There are lounging *bale* and a small pool in the garden plus good snorkelling offshore. ❹/❺
Villa Coral Café ☎0813/3852 0243, ⊛www .balivillacoral.com. Tucked beneath the headland, this place feels more private than many and there's some of Amed's best snorkelling right out front. Two beachfront villas sleep up to five people and there are four rooms behind these, with partial or no sea views. All have a/c (rates are discounted if you want fan only). Rooms ❸/❹, villas ❺/❻

Bunutan

Bunutan (8km from Culik) has some of the nicest accommodation in the area, many enjoying great views. Places are quite spread out though, divided by a steep headland crowned with *Waeni's*, so you'll probably need transport.

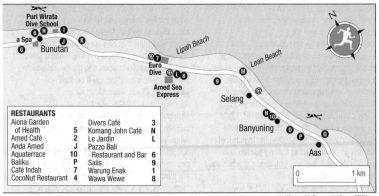

RESTAURANTS		
Aiona Garden of Health	5	
Amed Café	2	
Anda Amed	J	
Aquaterrace	10	
Baliku	P	
Café Indah	7	
CocoNut Restaurant	4	
Divers Café	3	
Komang John Café	N	
Le Jardin	L	
Pazzo Bali Restaurant and Bar	6	
Sails	9	
Warung Enak	1	
Wawa Wewe	8	

Kusambi, Seraya & Ujung ▼

Anda Amed ☎0363/23498, ⓦwww
.andaamedresort.com. There's plenty of style
at this modern, chic, well-thought-out British-run
boutique hotel. The ten generously sized bungalows
are widely spaced on the hillside to give maximum
privacy and the best ocean views. All have bathtubs
and a/c and some have kids' funky cubby-hole beds
too. There's a large pool and innovative restaurant.
Probably the only hotel in east Bali with pet ducks. ⓺

Prema Liong ☎0363/23486, ⓦwww.bali-amed
.com. Up a steep path high above the road, the
three tall-roofed, two-storey, thatched bamboo
cottages here have great lounging areas on deep
verandas and fine views across the shrub-filled
garden to the sea. All have attractive furnishings,
fans and cold-water bathrooms, plus an extra bed
in the roof space. ⓷/⓸

Puri Wirata ☎0363/23523, ⓦwww.diveamed
.com. One of Amed's larger hotels, this resort-like
outfit is associated with one of the top dive centres
and is a good choice if smaller places are booked
up. The seafront compound has two pools and

thirty good-quality rooms of varying luxury (fan or
a/c); most have some sort of sea view. ⓹

Waeni's Sunset View Bungalows
☎0363/23515, ⓦwww.baliwaenis.com. Unsurpassed views from all eight rooms at this gloriously
sited spot atop the headland between east and
west Bunutan. Views inland encompass Gunung
Agung, while the Lombok Strait glitters ahead.
Interiors are spacious and attractively done in
modern style (though the cheapest "standard"
room has a party wall that stops short of the top).
Go for the mid or top bracket. A/c and hot water
are available. Fan ⓸, a/c ⓸/⓹

Wawa Wewe II ☎0363/23522, ⓦwww
.bali-wawawewe.com. Book far in advance for this
good-value little set of beachfront bungalows,
whose family-friendly accommodation is especially
popular with French tourists. The ten simply
furnished Bali-style cottages nearly all have loft
spaces with kids' beds, a/c and partial or total sea
views. There's an infinity pool in the compact
shorefront compound. ⓸/⓺

Lipah, Lean, Selang, Banyuning and Aas

Lipah beach (10km from Culik) has reasonable snorkelling, though accommodation tends to be overpriced. Beyond lies a quartet of quiet village bays – **Lean**
(11km from Culik), **Selang** (12km), **Banyuning** (13km) and **Aas** (15km) – with
just a few places to stay on each. Banyuning is a good choice as it has the best
snorkelling in the Amed area.

Baliku Banyuning ☎0828/372 2601,
ⓦwww.amedbaliresort.com. Just four luxuriously appointed and indulgently spacious villa-style
bungalows – each with kitchenette, a/c, day bed and
bathtub – in a steep plot across the road from the
Japanese Wreck. The veranda views of the reef,
Lombok, and nearby hills are breathtaking. There's a
pool and well-regarded restaurant. ⓺

Blue Moon Villas Selang ☎0812/362 2597,
ⓦwww.bluemoonvilla.com. The killer choices here
are the three shorefront suites. From their fabulous
verandas, on the headland above the aquamarine
sea (steps drop down to the water), you can even
see the fish beneath you. Interiors are elegant and
pretty, with kids' cubby-hole beds. The nine
bungalows on the inland side of the road are

equally attractive, with partial sea views. Has three small pools, one exclusively for the suites. Bungalows ⑤, suites ⑥

Eka Purnama Banyuning ☏ 082/8372 2642, ⓦ www.eka-purnama.com. An excellent budget choice, especially for snorkellers, with four robust bamboo bungalows in a garden from whose verandas you can practically see the reef fish across the road. Bungalows have fans and cold-water bathroom; a/c rooms are planned. ③/④

Le Jardin Lipah ☏ 0363/23507, ⓔ limamarie @yahoo.fr. With its four good-value, thatch-roofed fan and a/c bungalows in a lovely garden, this place is the best deal on Lipah beach. It has a good restaurant too. Fan ③, a/c ④

Life in Amed Lean ☏ 0363/23152, ⓦ www .lifebali.com. Petite and pretty little beachside

gem, where the eight bungalows all have traditional carved doors, antique-style furniture and extra beds in the loft. There are also a couple of beachfront villas that can sleep bigger groups. Though the hotel compound is tiny it has a small pool and gives direct access to the beach, which offers decent snorkelling. Wi-fi on site. Bungalows ⑤/⑥, villas ⑦

Meditasi Aas ☏ 0828/372 2738, ⓦ http://meditasi.8m.com. Hatha yoga and laughing yoga are practised everyday at this relaxed little collection of large bamboo bungalows whose huge sliding screens reveal private sea views from their verandas. Interiors are simple, with fans, mosquito nets and garden bathrooms. It's a quiet village beach, with a sandy corner and some snorkelling. ④

The beaches

The whole area takes its name from **Amed**, the westernmost of the coastal villages, just 3km from the junction town of Culik; its traditional occupations of fishing and salt production are starting to give way to tourist development but there's nothing of special interest there yet. Much more of a tourist centre is **Jemeluk**, 6km from Culik, and the adjacent hamlet of **Congkang**, which between them have plenty of accommodation, restaurants and a good dive shop along the narrow, shrub-lined road. At low tide a swathe of beach is revealed here, and though there's almost no shade, *Café Amed* rents out sunloungers. There's good snorkelling in front of many of the hotels, and especially beneath the headland by *Villa Coral Café* bungalows. Continuing east over the headland brings you first to **Bunutan** and then to **Lipah**, both of which have plenty of accommodation. After that it's over headland after headland to the peaceful little villages and their bays at **Lean**, **Selang**, **Banyuning** and eventually **Aas** (15km from Culik). These eastern beaches get progressively less stony, and the sand gets yellower; Banyuning has the area's best **snorkelling**, at the Japanese Wreck just offshore (see box, p.227). The beach at Banyuning also has some shade, plus snorkel rental, a couple of cheap warung, and accommodation with restaurants at the north end, though it's not great for sunbathing.

Eating

Except where otherwise stated, all **restaurants** open for breakfast and continue serving until about 10pm.

Jemeluk

Amed Café Beachfront tables make this a pleasant place to refuel between snorkel forays, and it's nice at sunset too. There's squid curry and fish sate on the standard menu, and Balinese classics such as *sate lilit* (minced seafood sate) if you order three hours ahead. Mains Rp34,000–55,000.

Divers Café Relaxed and sociable spot, whose speciality, *ikan pepes bakar* (fish grilled in banana leaves), is recommended.

Warung Enak About 750m west of Jukung Dive in the hamlet of Tukad Se.

The home-style Indonesian cooking at this small restaurant is well worth the walk. Go for the deliciously spicy *gado-gado* or the melt-in-the-mouth chicken sate, or opt for a bit of everything in the recommended *nasi campur*. Portions are generous and everything's beautifully presented. Mains from Rp25,000.

Bunutan

Aiona Garden of Health This rather grandly titled "holistic health resort" takes itself very seriously but does indeed have the only Ayurvedic vegetarian restaurant for miles around. Its organic menu includes power protein soup, potato pie, wholegrain bread, hibiscus sorbet and chocolate cake, supplemented by aloe vera and kombucha drinks. Mains from Rp35,000. Open noon–3pm for lunch, and for dinner at 6pm if you reserve by 3pm.

Anda Amed Highlights from the creative menu here include tuna tempura, mushroom risotto and the perennially popular barbecued pineapple with chocolate-and-coconut dip. Mains around Rp50,000.

CocoNut Restaurant *Santai Hotel Bali*. The food at this traditionally styled, seafront hotel restaurant gets top marks for its nouvelle presentation. Barbecued fish and beef *rendang* are specialities (mains cost Rp50,000–110,000) and the desserts, including key-lime pie, are delicious.

Pazzo Bali Restaurant and Bar A busy, attractively decorated restaurant featuring live music on Friday nights, an extensive drinks list and a long menu of good Indonesian and Western fare (mains from Rp35,000). Free wi-fi.

Lipah, Lean, Selang and Banyuning

Aquaterrace Selang. Good Japanese food at this tiny B&B, including prawn tempura, sushi and okonomiyaki. Dishes from Rp30,000.

Baliku Banyuning ☏ 0828/372 2601, ⊛ www .balikudiveresort.com. Come to this hotel restaurant for lunch and you get free transport from the Amed area plus use of the pool, as well as premier snorkelling across the road. The menu is wide-ranging and includes tuna burgers, falafels, *mahi-mahi* with lime sauce and aubergine lasagne.

Café Indah Lipah. Located right on the beach, this place does the usual Indo and Euro standards, with discounts for customers of nearby Euro Dive.

Le Jardin Lipah. Offers a changing daily menu, tailored to its many French guests, plus cakes and delicious home-made yoghurt.

Komang John Café *Blue Moon Villas*, Selang. Serves a recommended Indo–European menu, from Balinese curry to mango crumble, plus imported wines. Mains Rp45,000–70,000.

Sails Lean/Lipah headland ☏ 0363/22006, ⊛ restaurantamedbali.com. Perfectly positioned on the headland and designed in contemporary minimalist style to make the most of the 180° sea views, this is Amed's destination restaurant. The food (from Rp55,000) has a Pacific–Asia accent – chilled tomato soup, Thai-style fishcakes, lamb rissoles, *mahi-mahi* fillet, and wine "made from Australian juices" – and there's free transport in the Amed area.

Wawa Wewe Lipah. Restaurant and bar that stages live music every Wednesday and Saturday.

Listings

Banks and exchange Amed has no ATMs: the closest is in Amlapura, some 30km away. There are moneychangers in all the main villages, offering poor rates; very few hotels accept credit cards.

Cooking lessons At *Amed Café* in Jemeluk.

Internet Most villages have at least one place with internet access.

Massage "a" Spa in Bunutan offers traditional *lulur* scrubs, massages and facials in an attractive setting

(☏ 0813/3823 8846, ⓔ a_spatrad@yahoo.com; daily 10am–7pm; from $18/hr; phone for free transport).

Shopping Amlapura is the nearest main shopping centre, but the Amed Café Minimarket in Jemeluk is well stocked with basic necessities and also sells swimming goggles and fresh fruit. *Ganesh Amed* hotel in Jemeluk sells secondhand books as well as silver jewellery and there's more jewellery at Crystal Mountain Jewellery in Lipah.

The coast road from Aas to Ujung

One of the highlights of the Amed area is **the coast road** that connects **Aas**, the southernmost village of the Amed strip, with **UJUNG**, 25km to the southwest. It's a gloriously scenic high-level route that works well as part of a **day-trip loop** – via Amlapura and Tirtagangga, with a possible side trip to Pura Luhur Lempuyang, then back via Culik. Many Amed hotels offer this as an excursion.

Continuing south and west around the coast from Aas, the scenery is breathtakingly dramatic, with hills sweeping up for hundreds of metres from the coast. The narrow, steeply undulating and sometimes broken road snakes through dry mountain land used in the wet season for growing peanuts, soya beans and corn and overlooked by the hulking profiles of Gunung Lempuyang and Gunung Seraya. It turns inland at **Kusambi**, about 4km from Aas and marked by a massive beacon; this is the most easterly point of Bali – on clear days Lombok is visible, 35km across the strait. Another 14km further, on the fringes of the small market-centre of **SERAYA**, the local **weavers' cooperative**, Kelompok Karya Sari Warna Alam, is well worth a stop. They grow their own cotton and dye it in the traditional way with indigo and bark harvested from the workshop garden; you can watch the spinners and weavers at work and then buy their beautiful scarves and sarongs, recognizable by their muted, natural tones. From here the road heads down to the coast, and 4km southwest to accommodation and food at **Seraya Barat** (see p.223), then to **Ujung Water Palace**, 1km further on (see p.223), and **Amlapura**, 5km beyond.

Tulamben

North of Amed, the parched landscape is cut with folds and channels, relics of the lava flow from the 1963 eruption of Gunung Agung, which rises dramatically inland. The main focus of tourist attention in these parts is the village of **TULAMBEN**, site of Bali's most popular dive, the **Liberty wreck**, which lies just 30m offshore. Up to a hundred divers a day come to explore this most accessible of wrecks and, with several hotels and dive shops nearby, it's perfectly feasible to

---

Diving at Tulamben

Tulamben's underwater treasure trove, the **Liberty wreck**, lies on a sandy slope just 30m offshore, making this one of the most accessible wrecks in Southeast Asia and a gift for novice divers. There are plenty of entrances and some sections are in shallow water, making it a good **snorkelling** site too. The wreck is encrusted with soft coral, gorgonians and hydrozoans plus a few hard corals, providing a wonderful habitat for around three hundred species of resident reef fish and another hundred species that visit from deeper water. Night dives are especially good. Built in 1915 in the US as a steamship, the 120m-long *Liberty* was carrying a cargo of rubber and rail parts when it was torpedoed on January 11, 1942, 15km southwest of Lombok. Attempts to tow the ship to port at Singaraja failed and it was beached at Tulamben, where it lay until 1963, when earth tremors accompanying the eruption of Gunung Agung shifted the *Liberty* into the water once more.

Although most people come to Tulamben for the wreck, there are plenty of other sites to explore – enough to fill a week or more. Many divers rate the **Tulamben Drop-off**, aka "The Wall", off the eastern end of the beach, at least as highly as the wreck itself. It comprises several fingers of volcanic rock that drop to 60m and are home to an enormous variety of fish, including unusual species such as comets, as well as black coral bushes. At **Batu Kelebit**, two huge boulders with coral-covered ridges are frequented by sharks, barracuda, jacks, manta rays, *mola-mola* and tuna. **Palung Palung** is suitable for beginners as well as experienced divers and has hard and soft coral and an enticing variety of marine life from depths of 3m to 40m. **Tulamben Coral Garden** and **Shark Point** are self-descriptive, with black-tip reef sharks the draw at the latter. The locally famous muck dive at **Secret Seraya** is good for boxer crab, harlequin shrimp, ghost pipe fish and tiger shrimp.

Dive centres
Tauch Terminal (℡0363/22911, ⊛www.tulamben.com), Tulamben Wreck Divers (℡0363/23400, ⊛www.tulambenwreckdivers.com) and Werner Lau at *Siddhartha Dive Resort and Spa* (℡0363/23034, ⊛www.wernerlau.com) are among the most established **dive centres** in the area. They charge around $66 for two local dives and offer dive-and-accommodation packages as well as trips further afield, to Amed, Pemuteran and Nusa Penida.

base yourself here for a few days. That way you can pick your dive times to avoid the crowds of day-trippers, who clog the wreck between 11.30am and 4pm. The beach is black and stony and the village itself has nothing else much to offer, so if you're looking for more of a resort atmosphere you might be better off choosing one of the hotels just outside central Tulamben, or considering Amed (13km east) or even Lovina, 75km west. For attractions between Tulamben and Lovina, see p.267.

Arrival

Tulamben is about 10km northwest of Culik and served by Singaraja–Amlapura public **buses** and minibuses, and by Perama shuttle buses from Candi Dasa; see "Travel details", p.234.

You can **change money** in central Tulamben but the closest **ATM** is in Amlapura. There's **internet access** at Tulamben Wreck Divers and *Tauch Terminal Resort*, which also has wi-fi.

Plenty of women on the beach offer **massages** (Rp60,000/hr), or there are luxurious **spa** treatments at *Tauch Terminal* and *Siddhartha Dive Resort and Spa*.

Accommodation

Most of the **accommodation** in **central Tulamben** is in a cluster between the sea and the Culik–Singaraja road. More upmarket places are scattered within a 5km radius east and west **along the coast** and will pick you up on request.

Bali Coral Bungalows Central Tulamben
☏0363/22909. Small, simple outfit with ten fan and a/c bungalows in a little compound near the sea (no views though). **3**

Batu Belah Sekar Karang Batu Belah, 5km east of central Tulamben
☏0817/975 5214, ⓦwww.eastbaliresort.com. A very inviting little Balinese–British-run oasis in a superbly peaceful and panoramic spot right on the shore. The five bright, high-standard bungalows are wheelchair-accessible and child-friendly and all have sea views, a/c, TV and hot water. There's a swimming pool and good restaurant (see p.234), plus boat trips for snorkelling and fishing. **6**

Liberty Dive Resort Central Tulamben
☏0813/3776 2206, ⓦwww.libertydiveresort.com. Nine large, good-quality rooms in a small two-storey block just 200m up the lane from the *Liberty* wreck. There's a/c, large balconies and hot water throughout, plus a small pool, wi-fi in public areas and energetic staff. **4**

Matahari Tulamben Resort Central Tulamben
☏0363/22916, ⓦwww.divetulamben.com. With some of the cheapest accommodation in Tulamben, this place is often busy, but don't expect many frills: the fifteen rooms (some with a/c and hot water) are crammed into a narrow seafront compound, none have views and most are pretty dark. There's a tiny pool, a dive centre and a restaurant. Fan **2**, a/c **4**

Puri Madha Central Tulamben ☏0363/22921. In an unbeatable location, set around an expansive shoreside garden right in front of the *Liberty* wreck. The priciest of the fifteen rooms are attractively furnished, with a/c and hot water as well as ocean views; the cheapest have fans and are very basic. Fan **1**, a/c **4**

Scuba Seraya Resort 3km east of central Tulamben ☏0819/1610 1060, ⓦwww.scubaseraya.com. Upscale dive resort with Bali-style maisonettes and villas in a spacious beachside garden, plus a pool and dive centre. One of Bali's best muck dives, Seraya, is just offshore. **7**

Siddhartha Dive Resort and Spa Kubu, 3km west of central Tulamben ☏0363/23034, ⓦwww .siddhartha-bali.com. Classy dive resort with a dramatic contemporary design, 32 elegant bungalows, generous beachfront grounds and a spa. The on-site Werner Lau dive centre (see p.232) gives you access to several house reefs, plus there's a spa and a huge pool. Good single-occupancy rates. ❼

Tauch Terminal Resort Central Tulamben ☏0363/22911, ⓦwww.tulamben.com. The most luxurious accommodation in central Tulamben has a lively buzz, a highly regarded dive centre and a good location in landscaped gardens fronting the coast. Most rooms enjoy sea views and all have a/c and modern art on the walls. There's a pool and a luxurious spa, too. ❼

Eating

There aren't really any standout **restaurants** in Tulamben, but *Tauch Terminal Resort* has an attractive seafront location and a varied menu that even runs to Häagen-Dazs ice cream. *Wayan Restaurant and Bar* on the main road does a big range of Indonesian and Western main courses, including fettuccine, prawn sate, fish tempura and beef stroganoff (Rp30,000–75,000). If you have your own transport, the restaurant at *Batu Belah Sekar Karang* hotel, 5km east, makes a scenic stop on any trip along the coast, where you can indulge in British fish and chips and meat pie (mains Rp38–110,000) besides the usual Balinese fare.

Travel details

Bemos and public buses

It's almost impossible to give the frequency with which bemos and public buses run: see Basics, p.30, for details. Journey times given are the minimum you can expect.

Amlapura to: Air Sanih (2hr); Candi Dasa (20min); Culik (45min); Denpasar (Batubulan terminal; 2hr); Gianyar (1hr 20min); Gilimanuk (4hr 30min); Lovina (3hr 30min); Padang Bai (45min); Seraya (40min); Singaraja (Penarukan terminal; 3hr); Tirtagangga (20min); Tulamben (1hr); Ujung (20min).
Bangli to: Denpasar (Batubulan terminal; 1hr 30min); Gianyar (20min); Singaraja (Penarukan terminal; 2hr 15min).
Candi Dasa to: Amlapura (20min); Denpasar (Batubulan terminal; 2hr); Gianyar (1hr); Padang Bai (20min).
Culik to: Aas (1hr 30min); Air Sanih (1hr 30min); Amed (20min); Amlapura (45min); Bunutan (45min); Jemeluk (30min); Lipah Beach (1hr); Selang (1hr 15min); Singaraja (Penarukan terminal; 2hr 30min); Tirtagangga (30min); Tulamben (1hr).
Gianyar to: Amlapura (1hr 20min); Bangli (20min); Batur (40min); Blahbatuh (30min); Candi Dasa (1hr); Denpasar (Batubulan terminal; 1hr); Semarapura (30min); Ubud (20min).
Padang Bai to: Amlapura (45min); Candi Dasa (20min); Gilimanuk (3–4hr); Semarapura (30min).
Semarapura to: Besakih (45min); Denpasar (Batubulan terminal; 1hr 20min); Gianyar (20min);

Padang Bai (30min); Rendang (30min); Sidemen (30min).
Sidemen to: Semarapura (30min).
Tirtagangga to: Air Sanih (2hr); Amlapura (20min); Culik (30min); Singaraja (2hr 30min); Tulamben (1hr).
Tulamben to: Air Sanih (1hr); Amlapura (1hr); Culik (30min); Singaraja (2hr); Tirtagangga (1hr).

Perama shuttle buses

Amed to: Candi Dasa (2 daily; 1hr 30min).
Candi Dasa to: Amed (2 daily; 1hr 30min); Bedugul (daily; 2hr 30min); Kuta/Ngurah Rai Airport (3 daily; 3hr); Lovina (daily; 3hr 30min); Padang Bai (3 daily; 30min); Sanur (3 daily; 2hr); Tirtagangga (2 daily; 1hr); Tulamben (2 daily; 2hr); Ubud (3 daily; 1hr 30min).
Padang Bai to: Candi Dasa (3 daily; 30min); Kuta/Ngurah Rai Airport (3 daily; 2hr 30min); Lovina (daily; 3hr); Sanur (3 daily; 1hr 30min); Ubud (3 daily; 2hr).
Tirtagangga to: Candi Dasa (2 daily; 45min).
Tulamben to: Candi Dasa (2 daily; 2hr).

Boats

Amed to: Gili Trawangan (up to 2 daily; 1hr 15min); Lombok (Teluk Kodek; up to 2 daily; 1hr 45min).
Padang Bai to: Gili Trawangan (at least 5 daily; 1hr 30min–4hr); Lembar, Lombok (hourly; 4hr); Nusa Penida (Buyuk Harbour; up to 5 daily; 45min–1hr); Senggigi, Lombok (daily; 5hr).

4

North Bali and the central volcanoes

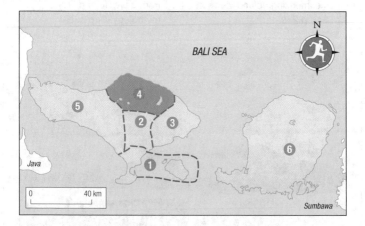

CHAPTER 4

Highlights

✳ **Gunung Batur** Bali's most climbed volcano rises within a spectacularly scenic caldera. See p.239

✳ **Bedugul** This highland region shelters a trio of sacred crater lakes, several important temples and a botanical garden with a treetop adventure park. See p.245

✳ **Munduk** Village tourism in the hills: good accommodation, enjoyable treks and mesmerizing upland views. See p.249

✳ **Lovina** Though the beaches are not Bali's finest, this laidback resort makes a good base for northern exploring. See p.252

✳ **Sekumpul Waterfall** Bali's best: seven cascades tumble dramatically into a verdant valley of clove plantations and rice terraces. See p.265

✳ **Pura Meduwe Karang** The liveliest example of north-Balinese temple carving, depicting vivid scenes from daily life and Hindu mythology. See p.266

▲ Danau Batur, with Gunung Batur rising behind

North Bali and the central volcanoes

Heading into **north Bali** from the crowded southern plains, you soon enter a cool and far less populated mountainous landscape. The centre of the island is occupied by the volcanic masses of the **Batur** and **Bedugul** areas, where dramatic peaks shelter crater lakes, and market gardens line the shores. Most visitors come to the Batur area to enjoy the exhilarating views from the crater rim or to trek up **Gunung Batur**, the most climbed peak in Bali, which still sends up occasional puffs of smoke. The Bedugul area, around **Danau Bratan**, offers more lakes and mountains, though on a smaller scale, and vast swathes of highland clove and coffee plantations, especially around the village of **Munduk**. Several important temples preside over the central lakes, notably **Pura Ulun Danu Bratan**, a popular destination for Balinese pilgrims and foreign day-trippers alike.

The mountains drop steeply to the **north coast**, occasionally softening into gentler hillsides and emerald-green rice terraces, the slopes and coastline dotted with villages. For hundreds and possibly thousands of years, the north of Bali was the part of the island most open to foreign influence, as Indian, Chinese and Arab traders plied their wares through the north coast, most recently via the port and former Balinese capital of **Singaraja**. This persisted into the early twentieth century with the start of the KPM steamship service from Java in 1924, making north Bali the tourist gateway to the island. It was only when Ngurah Rai Airport opened near Denpasar in 1969 that the tourist emphasis shifted firmly to the south. Today, Singaraja remains the biggest city in the north, capital of the administrative district of **Buleleng**, under whose jurisdiction the entire north coast falls. It holds relatively little of interest for twenty-first-century tourists, however, the vast majority of whom base themselves at the nearby beach resort of **Lovina** instead. From here, there's easy access to decent diving and snorkelling, as well as to a plethora of waterfalls and the idiosyncratic temples north Bali is known for.

The Singaraja–Gilimanuk road threads along the north coast, taking in Lovina and opening up connections to Java, and **public transport** also plies the three main southbound roads through the mountains to Denpasar – from Seririt via Pupuan, Singaraja via Bedugul, and Kubutambahan via Batur. This makes many of the sights in the north accessible by bus or bemo, although you'll need a vehicle to explore the scenic back roads.

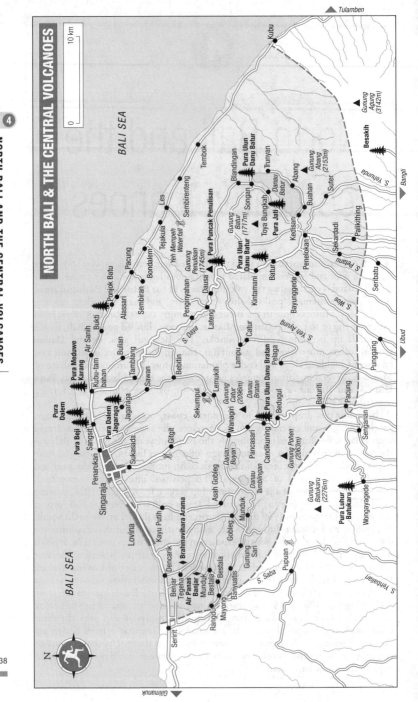

NORTH BALI & THE CENTRAL VOLCANOES

0   10 km

Tulamben

Gilimanuk

BALI SEA

BALI SEA

Kubu

Besakih

▲ *Gunung Agung (3142m)*

S. Yehunda

Bangli

▲ *Gunung Abang (2153m)*

Abang

Pura Ulun Danu Batur

Blandingan

Trunyan

Danau Batur

Suter

Buahan

Songan

Pura Jati

▲ *Gunung Batur (1717m)*

Toya Bungkah

Kedisan

Palikithing

Sekardadi

S. Petanu

Ubud

Tembok

Les

Sembirenteng

Pacung

Bondalem

Tejakula

Yeh Mempeh Waterfall

Pura Puncak Penulisan

▲ *Gunung Penulisan (1745m)*

Dausa

Penginyahan

Lateng

Pura Ulun Danu Batur

Batur

Kintamani

Penelokan

Bayunggede

S. Wos

Seribatu

Bunty Jung

Ponjok Batu

Bukti

Air Sanih

Alassari

Sembiran

Kubu-tambahan

Bulian

Tamblang

Sawan

Bebitin

Lemukih

Catur

Lampuh

Pelaga

Punggang

S. Daya

Pura Meduwe Karang

Pura Dalem

Pura Beji

Sangsit

Penarukan

Pura Dalem Jagaraga

Jagaraga

Gitgit

Sukasada

Sekumpul

Wanagiri

▲ *Gunung Catur (2096m)*

Danau Bratan

Pura Ulun Danu Bratan

Bedugul

Pancasari

Candikuning

▲ *Gunung Pohen (2063m)*

Baturiti

Pacung

Senganan

Yeh Jung

Singaraja

Lovina

Kayu Putih

Brahmavihara Arama

Asah Gobleg

Munduk

Gobleg

Danau Buyan

Danau Tamblingan

Gunung Sari

Pupuan

S. Saba

▲ *Gunung Batukaru (2276m)*

Pura Luhur Batukaru

Wongayagede

S. Yehballan

Seririt

Benjar

Tegeha

Air Panas Banjar

Dencarik

Munduk

Bestala

Bestala

Banyuatis

Rangdu

Mayong

N

S. Yehballan

Batur and Bedugul

The lakes within the volcanic craters of the **Batur** and **Bedugul** areas are the source of water for a vast area of agricultural land and, as the home of the goddess of the lake, Ida Batara Dewi Ulun Danu, are pivotal to Balinese Hinduism. The cool mountain air, trekking opportunities and good transport links have long made this region a favourite with local and foreign visitors.

Gunung Batur and Danau Batur

A spectacularly scenic area of dramatic volcanic peaks encircling a turquoise crater lake, the **Batur** area was formed thirty thousand years ago by the eruption of a gigantic volcano. The vast rim of the outer caldera spans 13.5km by 10km, with the still active **Gunung Batur** (Mount Batur; 1717m) at its heart. A major trans-Bali road runs along the west side of the crater rim, affording magnificent high-level views from the dozens of "panoramic restaurants" that line its course, and a side road gives access to the crater lake, **Danau Batur**, on its floor. Not surprisingly, this is one of Bali's most popular tourist destinations. Hundreds of day-trippers come for lunch in the village of **Penelokan** on the crater rim but you can also explore the villages along the lakeshore, stay the night and make the fairly straightforward sunrise trek up Gunung Batur itself, Bali's most climbed mountain. The Batur area is sometimes referred to as **Kintamani**, after one of the three main villages on **the crater rim**; there is accommodation up here, and a good trekking guide, but most overnighters stay down **by the lake**, usually at **Toya Bungkah**, where you can also start the mountain climb, and then recover in nearby hot springs. Lakeside **Kedisan** has hotels too, and is the departure point for boat trips to the Bali Aga cemetery at **Trunyan**. South of Kedisan, **Buahan** is the quietest spot of all, and **Songan**, at the northern end of the lake, is the start of walks up to the crater rim.

Sadly, the Batur area has developed a reputation for **hassles**. The persistent **hawkers** in Penelokan and aggressive hotel touts on motorbikes are hard to avoid, while the local association of trekking guides makes it almost impossible to climb the mountain unguided. The remarkable scenery, however, is worth the stress.

Eruptions at Gunung Batur

Gunung Batur has **erupted** more than twenty times since 1800. In 1917, a major eruption killed over a thousand people, but the lava stopped just outside the temple of Batur village, which was then situated in the crater beside the lake. Considering this a good omen, the population stayed put until August 3, 1926, when another eruption engulfed the village and residents were relocated onto the rim. The longest-lasting eruption started in September 1963, a few months after the massive explosion of Gunung Agung (see p.206), and continued for eight months. At Yehmampeh, on the road around the base of the mountain, you'll see lava flows from an eruption in March 1974. The newest crater, Batur IV, was formed during the eruption that began on August 7, 1994, and continues to erupt periodically. It's startling to see the volcano still smoking, but according to local belief it's better that Batur lets off a little steam regularly rather than saving it up for a major blow.

The crater rim

Spread out along the crater rim's road for 11km, the villages of **Penelokan, Batur** and **Kintamani** virtually merge. The big attraction is of course the view, at its most sensational from Penelokan, though the **museum** offers a decent introduction to the geology of the area and there are two very important **temples** up here too.

Arrival and information

The crater rim is included in many **day-trips** from the major resorts but Kintamani is also on **bus** and **bemo** routes from Ubud, and between Singaraja (Penarukan) and Denpasar (Batubulan) via Bangli. The road along the rim is one of the main routes between the north and south coasts, so public transport is frequent. Perama **tourist shuttle buses** run to the crater rim from Ubud, Kuta and Sanur, but not in the opposite direction. Once in the area, there are bemos along the rim, and lakeside hotels can arrange local and onward transport. Sobek (ⓦwww.balisobek.com; $79) runs downhill **cycling** trips from the Batur area with transport from tourist centres.

Entry to the Batur area is Rp10,000 per person, payable at booths on the access roads from Bangli and Ubud. There's an international **ATM** in the car park of the *Lakeview Hotel* in Penelokan but changing money elsewhere isn't easy.

Bear in mind that you're at quite a high altitude on the crater rim – Kintamani village is about 1350m above sea level – so the nights are **chilly** and you'll be glad of a sweater even in the day, especially when the mist descends.

Accommodation

Most people who **stay** in the Batur area base themselves down by the lake (see p.242) but there are a couple of alternatives on the rim. Commanding the finest

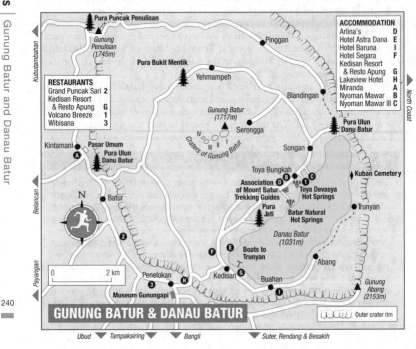

views is the *Lakeview Hotel* (℡ 0366/51394, ⓦ www.indo.com/hotels/lakeview; ❹), right on the edge of the rim in Penelokan. It's not the most refined of hotels, but every room has hot water, thick quilts and unsurpassed vistas over the crater and the lake; the "deluxe" rooms (❺) are the most modern. Hotel staff can arrange sunrise treks up Gunung Batur ($70/person). There are no views at all at *Miranda* (℡ 0366/52022; ❶), a budget homestay in Kintamani, whose en-suite rooms are basic (with squat toilets and *mandi*) but clean. The big draw is that the owner, Made Senter, is a respected **trekking guide** (see box, p.242). *Miranda* is 100m north of Kintamani market (Pasar Umum) and all public transport passes the door.

Penelokan and the Museum Gunungapi Batur

Literally meaning "Place to Look", **PENELOKAN** (1450m) enjoys the area's most majestic views, encompassing the full splendour of the stark volcanic landscape: Danau Batur lies far below, with Gunung Batur and Gunung Abang (2153m) towering on either side.

When you've had your fill of the view, head for the **Museum Gunungapi Batur** (Batur Volcano Museum; daily 9am–3pm; Rp10,000), located on the Bangli road, just south of the junction with the crater-rim road. It does a pretty good job of summarizing the history, mythology and geology of Batur, with scale models showing the changing face of the local topography, along with informative computer animations on volcano systems and an exhibit on the Pacific's "Ring of Fire". Upstairs, a viewing deck with binoculars gives you a close-up of the real thing, cloud-cover permitting.

Pura Ulun Danu Batur

The second most important temple on Bali after Besakih, **Pura Ulun Danu Batur** (Rp10,000 including sarong rental) honours **Ida Batara Dewi Ulun Danu** (Dewi Danu for short), the goddess of the crater lake, who is believed to control the water for the irrigation systems throughout Bali. Her hugely influential representative on earth is the temple's high priest, the Jero Gde, who is appointed on the death of his predecessor by a virgin priestess in a trance. He plays a vital role within Bali's sophisticated *subak* irrigation system and farmers come to confer with him about plans and conflicts, accepting his word as final.

The temple is one of the highly venerated *kayangan jagat*, or directional temples, protecting Bali from the north, and was relocated from the crater to its present position, 4km north of Penelokan, after the 1926 eruption (see box, p.239). The most significant of its countless shrines is the **eleven-roofed meru** in the inner courtyard, dedicated to both the goddess of the lake and the god of Gunung Agung. The drum in the *kulkul* tower is beaten 45 times each morning to honour the 45 deities worshipped in the temple.

Pura Puncak Penulisan

Built on the summit of Gunung Penulisan (1745m), about 5km north along the crater rim from Kintamani in the village of Sukawana, **Pura Puncak Penulisan** (admission by donation) is the highest temple on Bali and one of the most ancient, being referred to in ninth-century inscriptions. There are 333 steps to the top temple, **Pura Panarajon**, which is dedicated to Sanghyang Grinatha, a manifestation of Siwa and god of the mountains. Up here, *bale* shelter ancient lingga and statues from the eleventh to thirteenth centuries, including a wedding portrait believed to be of King Udayana and Queen Mahendratta, the source of the Rangda myth (see box, p.197).

Eating

The crater rim is packed with unprepossessing coach-tour **restaurants** offering expensive buffet lunches and panoramic views. One of the better options is *Grand Puncak Sari*, about 1km north of Penelokan, towards Batur, which also has an outdoor terrace (buffet Rp35,000, Balinese set lunch Rp80,000). Closer to Penelokan, on the opposite side of the road, *Wibisana* is good value (main courses about Rp15,000).

Around the lake

Filling the bottom of the ancient crater, 500m below its rim, are the emerald waters of **Danau Batur**, the largest lake in Bali (8km long and 3km wide) and one of the most glorious. Home of Dewi Danu, the goddess of the crater lake, Danau Batur is especially sacred to the Balinese and is believed to feed springs in other parts of the island. Several villages line the shore, notably **Kedisan**, **Buahan** and **Toya Bungkah**, which all have tourist accommodation, and **Songan**, site of an important temple and a footpath up the mountain. Vegetable plots fringe the shoreline, growing tomatoes, cabbages, onions and potatoes in the temperate, fertile soils; lake-fishing is the other main source of income, along with tourism.

The road to the lakeside drops down from the crater rim at Penelokan. Occasional public **bemos** from Penelokan go as far as Songan on the western side of the lake and Abang on the eastern side; the tourist fare to any of the lakeside accommodation is about Rp10,000, or several times that if you charter. Hotels can organize transfers from Penelokan and beyond. If you come with your own

---

Climbing Gunung Batur

Batur remains **active** and the authorities sometimes close the mountain. Check the current situation at ⓦwww.vsi.esdm.go.id – it's mostly in Indonesian but it is clear if any mountain is on alert. The **dry season** (April–Oct) is best for climbing.

There's a choice of **routes up Gunung Batur**. If you have your own wheels, the easiest option is to drive to **Serongga**, off the Yehmampeh road, west of Songan. From the car park, it's thirty minutes to an hour to the highest peak and largest of the caldera's inner craters, **Batur I**. Steam holes just below its rim confirm that this volcano is far from extinct, although the crater itself is grassed over.

The most common walking routes up to Batur I are from **Toya Bungkah** and **Pura Jati**. The path from Pura Jati is shadeless and largely across old lava fields. From Toya Bungkah, numerous paths head up through the forest (one starts just south of *Arlina's guesthouse*); after about an hour you'll come out onto the bare slope of the mountain, from where paths ascend steeply through slippery black volcanic sand to the tiny warung perched on the rim of Batur I. Allow two to three hours to get to the top from either start and about half that time to get back down; sunrise treks up this route depart at about 4am.

A **medium-length trek** involves climbing to Batur I, walking around its rim and then descending by another route. The **long-trek** option, sometimes called the **Exploration** (about 8hr in total) involves climbing up to Batur I, walking around to the western side, then descending to Batur II, Batur III and down to Toya Bungkah or Yehmampeh.

Guides and organized treks

Anyone who climbs Batur is under intense pressure to engage a guide from the **Association of Mount Batur Trekking Guides**, or PPPGB (ⓣ0366/52362), which has offices in Toya Bungkah and at Pura Jati. A guide is anyway essential for all sunrise treks (which require route-finding in the dark) and for the longer hikes and

vehicle, be warned that tourist **cars and motorbikes** are sometimes vandalized when parked at trailheads, so either leave yours at your accommodation while you trek, or take a driver to stay with it.

Kedisan and Buahan

At the bottom of the steep 3km road from Penelokan, the lakeside village of **KEDISAN** is the departure point for boats to Trunyan's cemetery (see p.244) and has a limited choice of places to stay. Turning right at the T-junction here brings you to the quietest and most attractive part of the lake, especially around and beyond the village of **BUAHAN**, 2km from Kedisan, where the eastern shore is lined with market gardens and fish-farming paraphernalia and offers some of the finest lake views of Gunung Batur. Dizzy at *Hotel Astra Dana* leads **treks** up the hill above Trunyan (Rp300,000/person) and he and all the other hotels also arrange Mount Batur climbs (see box below). *Hotel Baruna* can arrange **cycling** trips around the lake ($20).

Accommodation and eating

Much of the **accommodation** in Kedisan is extremely basic but there are a couple of appealing options. For **food** with a superlative view across the water to Batur's dimpled southeastern flank, it's hard to beat *Kedisan Resort & Resto Apung*, where you can choose to dine on a pontoon on the lake itself, or on the shoreside terrace; *ikan mujair* (freshwater fish) grilled to a crisp and smothered in garlic and chilli is a speciality. At *Hotel Baruna* in Buahan, the proprietor boasts of the very freshest fish dinners, from lake to plate in just thirty minutes.

less well-trodden paths; these routes are trickier and it's important to stay away from the most active parts of the volcano. If you are doing the climb in daylight either from Serongga or to Batur I from Toya Bungkah or Pura Jati, you don't really need a guide, but you will probably get intensely hassled and perhaps even intimidated into hiring one anyway.

Guide **prices** are clearly displayed in the Association's offices: Rp300,000 per guide for a four-hour sunrise trek for two people, Rp450,000 to the main crater, Batur I (5hr), and Rp600,000 for craters I, II, III and IV (6hr). You'll pay extra for breakfast on the mountain and transport to the trailhead, if required. Be absolutely clear which route you are doing and whether the price you have agreed is per person or for the group.

Many people find it's more straightforward to organize their trek through a **local hotel** or with a tour agent, though this is more expensive. Made Senter at *Miranda* homestay in Kintamani (☏0366/52022) is well regarded and leads sunrise climbs up Gunung Batur (Rp350,000/250,000/person, including transport, for groups of two/ four) and Gunung Abang (Rp500,000/person for two), and less strenuous four-hour treks on the crater rim (Rp400,000/person for four). *Arlina's* guesthouse in Toya Bungkah (☏0366/51165, ✉arlinas_ardana@yahoo.co.id) and *Hotel Astra Dana* in Kedisan (☏0813/3858 1983, ✉dizzy_made2@yahoo.com) charge Rp300,000 per person for the sunrise trek and *Baruna Cottages* in Buahan (☏0366/51378, ⊛www .barunacottages.com) does a sunrise trek via three craters plus accommodation for $50 per person.

It's also easy to arrange treks through **tour agencies** around Bali, with pick-ups from your hotel in Ubud, Candi Dasa or any south-Bali resort at around 2am and no need to stay over in Batur. Try Bali Sunrise Tours (☏0818/552669, ⊛www.balisunrisetours .com), Pineh Bali Tours (☏0813/3845 9739, ⊛www.pinehbalitours.com) or M&G Trekking (☏0813/3815 3991, ⊛www.mudigoestothemountain.com).

Hotel Astra Dana 500m west of the T-junction, Kedisan ☏ 0813/3858 1983, ✉ dizzy_made2 @yahoo.com. The dozen rooms here are ultra basic (the cheapest have cold-water bathrooms), but they're by the lake, surrounded by vegetable plots, with the best views in this village, including of Gunung Abang. ❶–❸

Hotel Baruna Just east of Buahan ☏ 0366/51378, ⓦ www.barunacottages.com. A cut above most other local accommodation, this place has several large, well-furnished rooms with panoramic windows and hot-water bathrooms, in a small compound just across the quiet, narrow road from the lake. Free transport from Ubud, plus trekking and cycling packages. ❹

Hotel Segara 300m west of the T-junction, Kedisan ☏ 0366/51136, ✉ hotelsegara@hotmail.com. A big outfit with 38 adequate losmen rooms set round a yard, plus some slightly posher options with hot water. Wi-fi available. Cold water ❷, hot water ❺

Kedisan Resort & Resto Apung 200m east of the jetty, Kedisan ☏ 0366/51627, ⓦ kedisan.com. In a great location by the shore, this is a good mid-range option with attractive, comfortably appointed *lumbung*-style thatch-and-wood bungalows set just back from the lake. ❹

Trunyan

Famous for leaving its dead to decompose in the open rather than cremating or burying them, the rather forbidding and notoriously unfriendly village of **TRUNYAN** is a less than edifying tourist destination and one that's best avoided. It's one of Bali's few remaining **Bali Aga** communities, inhabited by descendants of the "original Balinese" who rejected the Javanization of their island when the Majapahit invaded in 1343 and have maintained their distinctive customs ever since. Unfortunately you don't get much insight into Bali Aga life in Trunyan, but you do get a lot of hassle and requests for donations. All you're likely to see are a few artfully arranged bones in the tiny **cemetery** at Kuban (Rp10,000), plus the towering banyan tree that supposedly prevents the corpses from smelling. If you're interested in the Bali Aga, go to Tenganan village near Candi Dasa in east Bali instead (see p.219).

For those intent on visiting the Trunyan cemetery, access is by chartered **boat** from the jetty in Kedisan (20min; 8am–5pm; Rp385,000/boat for up to seven people).

Toya Bungkah and around

The village of **TOYA BUNGKAH**, 8km from Penelokan, is the lakeside's main accommodation centre and a starting point for climbs up Gunung Batur. The Association of Mount Batur Trekking Guides is also here (see box, p.242).

A couple of kilometres south of the village, **Batur Natural Hot Spring** (daily 7am–7pm; Rp80,000 including towel; ⓦ www.baturhotspring.com) is the perfect place to recover from your trek. An attractive public spa, it has three pools, one of them swimming-pool sized, filled with natural spring water that's up to 35°. You can eat here too. The much pricier hot springs in the middle of Toyah Bungkah are run by *Toya Devasya* (daily 8am–7pm; Rp150,000; ⓦ www.toyadevasya.com), whose ludicrously overpriced villas cost from $486 a night.

About 4km south of Toya Bungkah, **Pura Jati**, dedicated to the god Wisnu, has some fine carvings. One of the routes up the mountain starts near here.

Accommodation and eating

Accommodation in Toya Bungkah is pretty grotty and most people stay just one night. All the listed options have inexpensive **restaurants** on site, with *ikan mujair*, a local fish from the lake, the highlight on most menus. For a little bit more atmosphere, try *Volcano Breeze*, a garden-style restaurant on a quiet track down to the lake.

Arlina's ☏ 0366/51165, ✉ arlinas_ardana@yahoo .co.id. At the southern end of the village, with clean rooms (some with hot water) and small verandas set round a yard. Cold water ❷, hot water ❸

Nyoman Mawar (Under the Volcano) ☏ 0366/51166. Offering the cheapest rooms in the area, with especially good prices for singles, this is a friendly spot and fine for the price. ❶

Nyoman Mawar III (Under the Volcano III) ☎0813/3860 0081. A warm welcome and great views at this six-room place overlooking the owner's vegetable fields and the lake at the far end of the village. Rooms are simple but clean, with cold-water bathrooms. Canoes are available for rent. ❸

Songan and Yehmampeh

At the northwestern end of the lake, 4km beyond Toya Bungkah, the village of **SONGAN** is the location of **Pura Ulun Danu Batur**, believed to be one of the oldest temples in Bali and not to be confused with the bigger temple of the same name up on the crater rim. A ceremony is held here every ten years to honour the goddess of the lake, involving the ritual drowning of buffaloes, pigs, goats, chickens and geese, all adorned with gold ornaments. Not many bemos serve Songan and you may end up **walking** to or from Toya Bungkah, either along the road or via the lakeside track.

Directly behind the temple in Songan, a **footpath** winds up onto the rim of the outer crater and you can follow tracks to explore the tiny villages of traditional bamboo huts whose inhabitants farm the steep, dry hillsides. There are some fine views down to the north coast and back to Abang, Agung and even Rinjani on Lombok. With a good supply of food and water (it gets hotter the further down you go), the adventurous should be able to locate the paths down **to Bali's north coast** where you can pick up public transport west to Air Sanih or east to Tulamben.

From the junction in the middle of Songan, a **road** runs anticlockwise around the base of Gunung Batur, passing through the small village of **Yehmampeh** on its way to Penelokan, a scenic route of about 26km. It takes you past **Pura Bukit Mentik**, known as Lucky Temple because lava from the 1974 eruption surrounded it but caused no damage. The lava fields from that eruption now supply the grey-black building stone *paras* and sand that is ferried continuously from the area.

Routes to the north coast

It's 40km from Kintamani down through the foothills **to Kubutambahan** on the **north coast** (see p.266), from where Singaraja is 7km west and Air Sanih is 6km east. This road is one of Bali's main north–south routes, busy with trucks, cars and tourist buses, but it takes you through some pretty scenery, with mountains to the west and increasingly verdant valleys and forested ridges descending to the coast.

An attractive alternative route runs via the **back road to Bondalem**, a north-coast village that's 15km east of Air Sanih and 4km west of Tejakula (see p.267). The narrow, twisting, very steep and very scenic 16km road is signed off the main Kubutambahan road at **Lateng**, 13km from the market at Kintamani, and 500m after the end of the village of Dausa. The main road swings left on a sharp bend and there's a row of shops on the right at the start of your turning; this back road is known locally as the Tejakula road. It initially descends through vegetable gardens and stands of cloves, cocoa, coffee and avocado with great views of neighbouring ridges and west towards Gunung Batukaru. After about 10km the temperature rises significantly, and coconut plantations stretch all the way to the north coast.

The Bedugul region and Munduk

Domestic tourists come by the coachload to eat strawberries, enjoy the cool temperatures and admire the lakes and cloud-capped hills of the **Bedugul region**, an upland resort area (altitude 700m and above) that's also of great significance in Balinese Hinduism. The resort takes its name from the village of

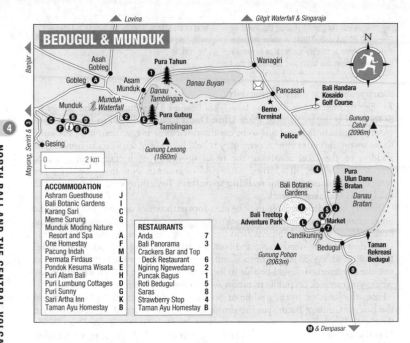

ACCOMMODATION

Ashram Guesthouse	J
Bali Botanic Gardens	I
Karang Sari	C
Meme Surung	G
Munduk Moding Nature Resort and Spa	A
One Homestay	F
Pacung Indah	M
Permata Firdaus	L
Pondok Kesuma Wisata	E
Puri Alam Bali	H
Puri Lumbung Cottages	D
Puri Sunny	G
Sari Artha Inn	K
Taman Ayu Homestay	B

RESTAURANTS

Anda	7
Bali Panorama	3
Crackers Bar and Top Deck Restaurant	6
Ngiring Ngewedang	2
Puncak Bagus	1
Roti Bedugul	5
Saras	8
Strawberry Stop	4
Taman Ayu Homestay	B

Bedugul, one of several small settlements up here, but is also often referred to simply as the Lake Bratan area. **Danau Bratan** itself is the largest and most visited of the three spiritually charged crater lakes around Bedugul and lies in the lee of towering Gunung Catur (2096m), the caldera's highest peak. It's presided over by the much photographed shoreside temple **Pura Ulun Danu Bratan**, an important pilgrimage site for the Balinese, but there's recreation here too, with canoes and motorboats for hire. Fruit and vegetables flourish in the temperate climate and frequent rainfall of Bedugul, Bali's market garden heartland, and so do the plants in the **Bali Botanic Gardens**, which offers rewarding birdwatching as well as the chance to swing through the trees at **Bali Treetop Adventure Park**.

There is accommodation both on and around the lake, in the adjacent village of **Candikuning**, and in the Botanic Gardens themselves, but many foreign visitors prefer to base themselves away from the resort atmosphere, in the village of **Munduk**, 20km northwest. A shining example of sustainable village tourism, with exhilarating panoramas, plenty of places to stay and a range of activities, Munduk also offers the opportunity to trek around the area's two smaller, far less commercial lakes: **Danau Buyan** and, particularly, **Danau Tamblingan**, with its venerable temples, forest hikes and wooden sampans.

Danau Bratan is 53km north of Denpasar and 30km south of Singaraja on the main **Denpasar–Mengwi–Singaraja road**; no direct route links it to Batur. Approaching from the south, the road rises through a series of small villages before reaching the crater rim at Candikuning, then descends and skirts the western shore of Danau Bratan before climbing again to the pass at Wanagiri, where it begins the steep drop to the northern plains and Singaraja, via the waterfalls at Gitgit (see p.264). There are **bemo** services along the main road, to and from Denpasar (Ubung; 1hr 30min) and Singaraja (Sukasada; 1hr 30min). Perama **shuttle buses** between Ubud and Lovina make a stop in Candikuning.

Trekking around Bedugul

The Bedugul area offers plenty of opportunities for **trekking**. You can hire guides through your accommodation, at *Puncak Bagus* restaurant between the two lakes (see p.249) and at the Danau Tamblingan ticket office, where printed price lists detail an enticing menu of options. Routes **from Tamblingan** are the most popular, especially the one-way trek over to Lake Buyan (4hr; Rp460,000), a short forest hike to Pura Dalem, returning by canoe on the lake (2–3hr; Rp280,000), and the strenuous trek to Jatiluwih (6–8hr; Rp1 million). **Prices** are for one guide and up to four people; for the longer treks you need to hire a driver to meet you at the finish.

Candikuning and Danau Bratan

The village of **CANDIKUNING**, situated above the southern shores of Danau Bratan, is the main base for the lake and the **Bali Botanic Gardens**. Accommodation and restaurants line the highway through the village, as well as the side road to the gardens.

Candikuning's daily **market**, between the gardens and the lakeside temple, is always busy with visitors stocking up on local strawberries, mandarins, orchids and roses; it sells sarongs and souvenirs too. In the far corner of the market, near *Crackers Bar and Grill* (see p.248), you'll find the AdoptA Co-op shop, set up by five widows of the 2002 Bali Bomb (see p.54); they sell T-shirts with humorous slogans. There are **moneychangers** in the market and in the car park at Pura Ulun Danu Bratan (rates are poor).

Perama **tourist shuttle buses** pass through Bedugul on their Ubud–Lovina route and will drop you at any of the hotels on the main road; their office and pick-up point (℡0368/21011, ⓦwww.peramatour.com) is at the *Sari Artha* losmen, just north of the market. Local bemos also beetle around the area.

Accommodation

Because of the cool climate up here (down to 10° at night), no accommodation offers fans or air-conditioning: it's thick quilts and hot water that you'll be more interested in.

Ashram Guesthouse Candikuning ℡0368/203 3222. Occupying a scenic spot rising in steep, floral terraces from the lakeshore, this is a large place (nothing like an ashram, however) with a range of options, from grimly basic rooms with shared cold-water bathrooms to comfortable bungalows with hot water, verandas and good views across Danau Bratan. It rents canoes and is a 10min walk from Pura Ulun Danu Bratan. Basic rooms ❶, bungalows ❸

Bali Botanic Gardens Within the Botanic Gardens ℡0368/22050, ⓦwww.balibotanic garden.org. There are three different sets of accommodation within the gardens, from a VIP hotel-style block to cottages and a small guest-house. Some rooms enjoy pretty views, the cheapest share bathrooms but all have hot water, free breakfast and complimentary entry to the Botanic Gardens. Book well ahead. Shared bathroom ❷, cottages ❺

Pacung Indah 9km south of Bedugul, on the main road just north of Pacung ℡0368/21020, ⓦwww.pacungbali.com. A comfortable option if you have your own transport, where the well-furnished bungalows all have hot water, satellite TV, wi-fi and great views across the deep valley from the communal terrace. The owners are Australian and Aussie breakfasts are included. ❸

Permata Firdaus Just outside the entrance to the Botanic Gardens ℡0368/21531. Six very clean, very cheap, good-value losmen rooms with hot water in a residential lane 400m from the gardens. ❶

Sari Artha Inn Just north of the market, Candikuning ℡0368/21011. Cheap and centrally located rooms and bungalows with or without hot water, all with verandas, set in a nice garden but with no lake views. Cold water ❶, hot water ❸

Bali Botanic Gardens and Bali Treetop Adventure Park

Conserving some two thousand species of tropical montane plants, from ferns and countless orchids to cacti, medicinal plants, multiple bamboos and an extensive collection of begonias, **Bali Botanic Gardens** (Kebun Raya Eka Karya Bali; daily 7am–6pm; Rp7000/person, parking Rp6000 for cars, Rp3000 for motorbikes; Ⓦ www.balibotanicgarden.org) is a cool and tranquil park that sits at an altitude of 1250–1450m. It's also rich in birdlife, with sightings that might include brown honeyeaters and grey-cheeked green pigeons among the 97 species recorded here. You can drive around the gardens (an additional Rp12,000/car; motorbikes prohibited) though it's probably more fun to take it slowly and just wander; bring a sweater as it's often cool (and wet) up here. The gardens get busy with picnickers at weekends, but during the week it's very quiet. You can also stay in the gardens (see p.247). Access to the Botanic Gardens is via a 700m side road from a well-signed junction just south of Candikuning market.

One great reason to visit is the chance to literally swing through a stand of the gardens' majestically tall *rasamala* (*Altinga excelsa*) trees at **Bali Treetop Adventure Park** (daily 9am–6pm; $20, child under 12 $13, family $50; Ⓦ www.balitreetop .com), in the southwest corner of the Botanic Gardens. Six very enjoyable circuits of ropeways, bridges, platforms and zip lines have been constructed here, up to 20m off the ground but designed to suit all levels, from 4-year-olds upwards. Safety gloves and harnesses are provided, along with guides. Packages are available from the southern resorts, including a visit to Pura Ulun Danu Bratan (adult $48, child $38, family $148). Avoid weekends if possible.

Danau Bratan

Situated at 1200m above sea level and thought to be 35m deep in places, the crater lake of **Danau Bratan** is surrounded by forested hills, with the bulk of Gunung Catur rising sheer behind. It becomes frenetic with watersports at weekends but the scenery more than compensates for the buzz of motorboats.

The lake and its goddess are worshipped in the beautifully sited temple of **Pura Ulun Danu Bratan** (daily 7am–5pm; Rp10,000), one of the most photographed and highly revered in Bali. Built in 1633 by the raja of Mengwi on a small promontory on the western shore of the lake, it's dedicated to Dewi Danu, source of water and hence fertility for the land and people of Bali. Shrines dot the shore and perch on islets in the lake, with the mountains rising dramatically behind. Closest to the bank, the eleven-roofed *meru* is dedicated to Wisnu and Dewi Danu. There's no public access to the shrines but, crowds and clouds permitting, they still look fabulous from the shoreline. For an even better view, hire a tiny wooden **sampan** (Rp55,000 for 30min for up to four people; Rp70,000 with a guide) from the nearby office and paddle round the other side of the temple-islands. You can also hire speedboats here (from Rp102,000 for 15min for up to four people).

Eating

Most **restaurants** in the area cater for the **lunchtime** trade. For cheap food, try the *kaki lima* (stalls) that line the road along the lakeside south of Pura Ulun Danu Bratan, or the warung in the temple car park.

Anda Across the road from the turning to the Botanic Gardens, Candikuning. One of the few places serving meals after 7pm, this place does inexpensive Indonesian and Chinese food (from Rp20,000).

Crackers Bar and Top Deck Restaurant In the back corner of Candikuning market. An unexpected find behind the market stalls, this expat-owned sports bar and restaurant serves sandwiches, burgers and fish and chips.

Roti Bedugul On the main road just north of the market, Candikuning. Recommended bakery and café that makes delicious bread and sells filled pitta wraps, sandwiches, burgers, apple pie and croissants. Daily 8am–4pm.

Saras 2km south of Bedugul. One of many similar restaurants lining the main road into Bedugul and catering to tour-bus diners, this one has fine views across to Gunung Agung, fresh strawberry juice and good *kampung* (free-range) grilled chicken. Mains from Rp27,000.

Strawberry Stop About 1500m north of the temple. The café at this small strawberry farm majors on desserts – strawberries with cream or ice cream, in milkshakes or in pancakes – but also does standard Indo-European mains like *nasi goreng*, fried noodles and jaffles.

Pancasari and Danau Buyan

The village of **PANCASARI**, 4.5km north of Candikuning, has a small bemo terminal (busiest in the morning), where you should alight if you're on your way to Munduk. This is also where you should turn off for **Danau Buyan**, whose southern shore is reached via a 3km road. It's driveable but would also make a pleasant walk, via allotments, fish farms and gardens planted with gladioli and dahlias. The lake is generally quiet and the ticket booth (Rp5000) in the car park at the end of the road may or may not be staffed. There are no restaurants or other facilities. Tracks head off into the forest that fringes the lake, including to Danau Tamblingan (see below), or you can simply sit lakeside and soak up the tranquil scene.

Danau Tamblingan

Danau Tamblingan (Rp5000) is the smallest and most atmospheric of Bedugul's three lakes, once contiguous with Danau Buyan to the east (before a massive landslide in 1818), now separated by a forested shoulder of land. **Trekking** between the two lakes is a popular activity (see p.247), best arranged through your accommodation or with the guides at the ticket office in the car park, from where it's ten minutes' walk down to the lakeside. You can also rent **wooden dugouts** to paddle around the lake (from Rp140,000). On the shore, **Pura Gubug** has eleven-, nine- and five-roofed *meru* and is dedicated to Dewi Danu, the goddess of the lake. Several other temples overlook the shoreline, including the ancient Pura Dalem Tamblingan on the east side. Villagers grow hydrangeas, marigolds and mandarins in the fertile, lake-watered soils, fish for carp, and rear cattle on the *tunjung* (lotus) that grows on the lake. The path around the western shore is a renowned **birdwatching** area, with sightings of babblers, woodpeckers, ground thrushes and malkohas all possible.

If you're not on foot, access to Danau Tamblingan is via the **road** that runs west from **Wanagiri**, 2km north of Pancasari, along the ridge above the northern shore of Danau Buyan. You get excellent views over both lakes from the **restaurant** tables at inexpensive *Puncak Bagus*, about 3km west of Wanagiri, where local treks can also be arranged. Another 2km west the road divides: take the left fork to reach the Danau Tamblingan car park after about 3km. There's **accommodation** about 100m before the car park, within easy reach of the lake, at *Pondok Kesuma Wisata* (☏0817/472 8826; ❸), with hot-water bungalows ranged around a garden.

Munduk and around

Overlooking slopes thick with clove trees and dotted with coffee plantations and rice terraces, the village of **MUNDUK** is an appealingly low-key centre of village tourism, with ample accommodation, refreshingly cool temperatures and commanding vistas. Cloud-gazing and **trekking** across the hills to nearby villages are the main pastimes (bring warm clothes and raingear), with cooking courses and cultural workshops also available. It's also a good base for exploring the rest of the Bedugul area, especially lakes Tamblingan and Buyan.

The **Dutch** administration also relished Munduk's scenery, fertile soils and cooler climate (it's 500–700m above sea level) and from about 1910 built a guest-house and various weekend homes here, some of which are still standing. There's little else to the village, save a small **market** towards the western end.

Arrival, information and local transport

Munduk is 8km west of Danau Tamblingan, 20km northwest of Candikuning and 20km southeast of Seririt. Access by public transport is possible but circuitous and is more reliable in the early morning. **Bemos** travel up to Munduk from Seririt, itself easily reached by bemo from Pemuteran or Lovina on the north coast. There are also one or two bemos from Denpasar's Ubung terminal (get there before 8am if possible); return bemos to Ubung and Singaraja leave Munduk very early, between 4am and 7am, though ask locally about an afternoon run. Coming from southern resorts or Ubud your best option is to take the Perama **shuttle bus** to Bedugul (Pancasari) and then a bemo to Munduk, which may need to be chartered (around Rp100,000).

The privately run **tourist information** office (Mon–Sat noon–9pm, shorter hours in low season; ☎0812/3633 6791, ⓦwww.lawangbali.com) in the centre of the village has **internet** access and can arrange accommodation and treks. It also keeps a price list of **charter transport** out of Munduk (which can be arranged everywhere): Rp170,000 per car to Bedugul, Rp190,000 to Lovina, Rp320,000 to Pemuteran or Rp340,000 to Ubud. **Motorbikes** are widely available for rent.

Accommodation

Because of the steep gradients in the area, some **hotels** are built below rather than above the road, and many offer fine views.

Karang Sari ☎0813/3845 5144, ⓔkarangsari _guesthouse@yahoo.com. With glass doors and verandas that overlook the pretty garden to the hills beyond, this is an appealing guesthouse at the west end of the village. The six rooms are spacious and nicely decorated and all have hot water. ❸
One Homestay Jl Selau ☎0852/3718 8980, ⓔone_homestay@yahoo.com. Four simple and exceptionally cheap rooms within the family compound behind the owner's shop and restaurant, off a quiet side road and below street level. Good views and some hot water. Cold water ❶, hot water ❷
Puri Alam Bali ☎0812/465 9815, ⓦwww .purialambali.com. The thirteen attractively furnished rooms here at the eastern end of the village all have hot water, good beds, comfortable verandas and expansive outlooks. The cheapest room is roadside; others are set more quietly below the road. From the restaurant you can see the

famous big tree at Gesing, several kilometres to the west. ❸–❹
Puri Lumbung Cottages ☎0362/701 2887, ⓦwww.purilumbung.com. Delightful, eco-conscious accommodation in a range of cottages set around ricefields and gardens, all with verandas that make the most of the mesmerizing panoramas across clove plantations to the hills and the Pemuteran coastline. There's a spa, too, and a big programme of village activities. Puri Lumbung also administers two mid-priced village homestays, *Puri Sunny* (❹) and *Meme Surung* (❹), where some of the plain rooms offer views; and a remote four-room cabin with no electricity, *Tamblang Nature Cabin* (❹), near Lake Tamblingan, a 30min trek from the road. ❻
Taman Ayu Homestay ☎0813/3755 6127. Welcoming little family homestay with three cheap and simple rooms below the road (two with views), and an excellent warung (see opposite). ❶

The village and around

There's really not a great deal to see in Munduk itself, though you could pass a pleasant half hour perusing the food and household goods at the village **market**, or looking for remnants of colonial **Dutch architecture** along the main street.

The main pastime is **trekking** in the surrounding countryside, something best organized using one of the local guides from the village cooperative; they charge

Cloves

It was the search for **cloves**, among other spices, that first drove Europeans to explore the Indonesian archipelago, and for hundreds of years they were one of the region's most lucrative exports. Native to certain islands of the Moluccas (the original "Spice Islands"), cloves are now grown mainly in Maluku, Sumatra, Sulawesi and Bali. You'll spot the tall trees in the hills around Bedugul, Tamblingan and Munduk and if you're there during harvest time, from August to October, you'll see death-defying pickers on rickety ladders and huge piles of drying cloves beside the road – buds that must be picked before the petals open, after which the amount of clove oil declines sharply.

Bali's cloves end up in Java for the manufacture of Indonesia's pungent **kretek cigarettes**. These consist of up to fifty percent cloves mixed with tobacco, and demand is so great that the former clove capital of the world now imports them from Madagascar and Zanzibar to supplement local production.

Rp40,000–70,000 per hour per guide, depending on whether you need an expert English-speaking guide or just someone to show you the way. The tourist information office has a rudimentary sketch map, though paths aren't always obvious (or present). Most treks are scenic rural hikes through clove and coffee plantations, via market gardens growing blue hydrangeas (used for offerings), vanilla and mandarins, and through ricefields and villages. The famously huge **banyan tree** at **Gesing** – 70m high, thought to be around 700 years old, and with a vast tangled root system that you can climb inside – is a popular destination (3hr from Munduk), as is **Munduk Waterfall** (about 1km east of Muduk), the most worthwhile of several falls in the area. Treks to and between lakes Tamblingan and Buyan are also well worth doing (see p.247), or you could try climbing Gunung Lesong (1860m).

Munduk is a good place to try your hand at Balinese **cooking**: courses cost from Rp50,000 and vary in complexity; ask at any of the village restaurants. *Puri Lumbung* also offers an exceptionally diverse range of **cultural workshops** (from $12 for up to two people), including in herbal medicine, Indonesian language, making offerings, Balinese music classes and spiritual discussions. They also host an open classical **dance class** for local kids three times a week and run a downhill **cycling** trip to the fishing village of Sangar Langit.

North Bali Safari Tour (T 0812/464 7847, @ nymnkok@yahoo.com) does **car tours** in style, in an open-topped bright red VW, to plantations and villages in the area, as well as to Bedugul's Botanic Gardens (Rp450,000/car for a full-day tour).

Eating

Every place to stay in Munduk has an attached **restaurant**, but don't expect *haute cuisine*. *Puri Lumbung* has the most extensive, and expensive, menu, while the warung at *Taman Ayu* serves exceptionally good *pisang rai* (steamed banana fritters with coconut and palm sugar) as well as *sate lilit siap* (chicken with coconut and lemongrass) and Balinese *lawar*. About 4km east of Munduk, you can soak up the fine high-level views at *Ngiring Ngewedang* while munching through their small menu of Indo-Chinese dishes and sandwiches (from Rp25,000); they roast and grind coffee and staff will explain the process.

To the north coast via Mayong or Asah Gobleg

Heading to the north coast along the main Seririt road from Munduk you'll pass through the ridge villages of Gunung Sari and Banyuatis before reaching **Mayong** and its prettily sited **restaurant** (see p.260) and then continuing down to Seririt.

An alternative and less travelled route to the north coast from the Munduk/Tamblingan area takes you down a minor route from the Wanagiri road above Lake Tamblingan. It descends slopes rich in banana, durian, papaya and jackfruit trees to Asah Gobleg and then drops through Selat before reaching the coast at **Anturan**, towards the eastern edge of Lovina. You'll need a decent road map to explore these byways. Hidden within a large plantation in the village of **ASAH GOBLEG**, 4km from the lake road, 10km from Munduk, and enjoying entrancing views across the misty hills, is *Munduk Moding Nature Resort and Spa* (☏0811/381 0123, ⓦwww.mundukmodingplantation.com; ➐). It's a remote and luxurious retreat, 1200m above sea level, where each **villa** is privately set overlooking endless plantation forest – growing a mix of coffee, dadap, mandarin and papaya trees, along with hydrangeas, pineapples, turmeric and lemongrass – and picture windows capture the magnificent prospect and the prolific birdlife. Suite rooms are also available. A breathtakingly located infinity swimming pool gilds the experience, and activities include treks to the lakes and the huge banyan tree at Gesing (see p.251), horseriding, village tours and cycle rides.

The north coast

The **north coast** of Bali is a rugged and, in places, dramatic landscape, the northern flanks of the mountains dropping steeply towards sweeping black-sand beaches. The land is parched towards the east, where lava flows from the last eruption of Gunung Agung are still visible. To the west, more fertile soil and more rain results in some finely sculpted rice terraces.

Most visitors head straight for the beach resort of **Lovina**, which, as the main tourist centre in north Bali, offers the full complement of facilities and makes a relaxing base for exploring the region. A few kilometres east, the city of **Singaraja** was until the mid-twentieth century the capital of Bali and the busiest port on the island. These days, however, it serves only as the capital of **Buleleng regency**, which incorporates the whole north coast. The city's most important relic is its Gedong Kirtya, the only library of *lontar*-palm books in the world. In the villages just beyond Singaraja's eastern perimeter are some exuberant **temple carvings**, as well as several large **waterfalls** in the hills to the south. East again, there is isolated accommodation along **the northeast coast** towards Tulamben.

Lovina and around

Stretching along 8km of grey-sand beach, **LOVINA** is north Bali's primary beach resort, encompassing the coastal villages of Pemaron, Tukad Mungga, Anturan, Banyualit, Kalibukbuk, Kaliasem and Temukus. **Kalibukbuk** is the tourist hub, bursting with accommodation and restaurants, but development here, and throughout Lovina, is on a far smaller scale than anywhere in south Bali. The potential of the area was spotted by the last raja of Buleleng, Anak Agung Panji Tisna, who built a hotel in Kaliasem in the 1960s and devised the name Lovina, said to be a contraction of "Love Indonesia". Today, Lovina is best known for its **dolphin-watching** and proximity to good **snorkelling** and **diving** sites, and for its easy access to waterfalls and temples. The disappointment, however, is the **beach**. A swathe of blackish sand that tends to scruffiness, with some natural shade but no sunloungers, and a proliferation of beached fishing boats and persistent hawkers, it's not Bali's most inviting. Much else about the resort is a plus, though, with hotels to suit all budgets, dramatic views inland across the surrounding fields and plantations to the hills beyond (and countless tour agents only too happy to help you explore them), good transport links and a relaxed atmosphere.

Among many enticing day-tripping destinations, the most popular are the **Buddhist monastery** and **hot springs** at Banjar, 10km west, and the temples and waterfalls east of Singaraja, within 30km of the resort. The crater lakes of Bedugul and the hillside village of Munduk are also just an hour and a half away.

Arrival, information and local transport

Lovina's easternmost district, Pemaron, is only 6km west of the city and transport hub of Singaraja, and access from most parts of Bali is straightforward. Perama **tourist shuttle buses** connect Lovina with tourist centres across Bali (see "Travel details", p.268); their office is in Anturan but for an additional Rp10,000 you can be dropped off elsewhere. From the east of Bali, you'll come via Singaraja: its Banyuasri terminal is a twenty-minute **bemo** ride away (Rp7000). From Denpasar, there are Ubung–Singaraja services via Pupuan, and minibuses to Seririt for local bemo connections. Inter-island **buses** from Java to Singaraja pass through Lovina as do Gilimanuk–Singaraja and Amlapura–Gilimanuk services, and all local buses and bemos from west Bali.

Lovina's **tourist office** (Mon–Sat 8am–8pm; ☏0362/41910 mornings only) is on Jalan Raya Kalibukbuk.

For **local transport** around Lovina, there are frequent **bemos** during daylight hours between Singaraja and Seririt, which all travel the length of Jalan Raya (Rp5000 for a local ride within the Lovina area), but after dark you'll need to negotiate with the transport touts.

Accommodation

The bulk of Lovina's **accommodation** is concentrated in Kalibukbuk, with the quieter options well away from the main road, Jalan Raya. Other neighbourhoods should be easily accessible by public transport during daylight hours. During peak season (June–Aug & Dec) everything gets quite busy, so booking ahead is a good idea.

Kalibukbuk

Centred around two side roads, Jalan Bina Ria and Jalan Mawar, **Kalibukbuk** is the heart of Lovina and chock-full of accommodation, restaurants and tourist facilities. A beachfront walkway links the ocean ends of the two roads.

Frangipani Beach Villas Jl Kartika ☏0819/3655 2532, ⓦwww.frangipanibeachvillabali.com. Upscale contemporary homestay where the five a/c rooms, designed in creamy limestone with clean modern lines and all with TV and rain showers, are set round a lawn and pool just back from the shore. The beach here is quiet, at least a 10min walk from the restaurants and shops of central Kalibukbuk, at the end of a long residential lane. ❼

Harris Homestay Off Jl Bin Ria ☏0362/41152. Sparklingly clean, exceptionally cheap German-run backpackers' accommodation. The five rooms in the tiny compound are all attractively furnished and very well maintained, with fans and cold-water bathrooms. ❶

Padang Lovina Off Jl Bina Ria ☏0362/41302, ⓔpadanglovina@yahoo.com. Good, clean, central

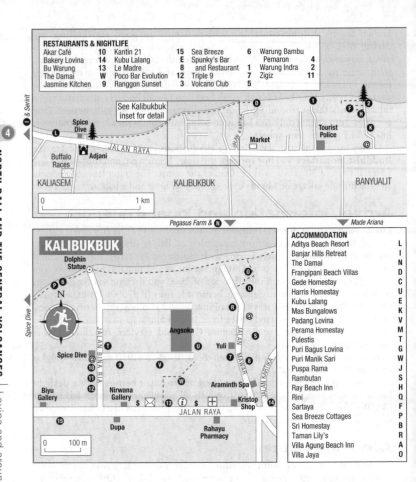

RESTAURANTS & NIGHTLIFE							
Akar Café	10	Kantin 21	15	Sea Breeze	6	Warung Bambu	
Bakery Lovina	14	Kubu Lalang	E	Spunky's Bar		Pemaron	4
Bu Warung	13	Le Madre	8	and Restaurant	1	Warung Indra	2
The Damai	W	Poco Bar Evolution	12	Triple 9	7	Zigiz	11
Jasmine Kitchen	9	Ranggon Sunset	3	Volcano Club	5		

KALIBUKBUK

ACCOMMODATION	
Aditya Beach Resort	L
Banjar Hills Retreat	I
The Damai	N
Frangipani Beach Villas	D
Gede Homestay	C
Harris Homestay	U
Kubu Lalang	E
Mas Bungalows	K
Padang Lovina	V
Perama Homestay	M
Pulestis	T
Puri Bagus Lovina	G
Puri Manik Sari	W
Puspa Rama	J
Rambutan	S
Ray Beach Inn	H
Rini	Q
Sartaya	F
Sea Breeze Cottages	P
Sri Homestay	B
Taman Lily's	R
Villa Agung Beach Inn	A
Villa Jaya	O

fan and a/c terraced accommodation in a two-storey block overlooking a small garden with a tiny pool. Fan ②, a/c ③

Pulestis Jl Bina Ria ☏0362/41035. Funky guesthouse with distinctive jazzy paintwork, 21 comfortable rooms with the option of hot water and a/c, plus a tiny pool with a fun waterfall feature. Fan ②, a/c ③

Puri Manik Sari Off Jl Bina Ria ☏0362/41089. Very cheap fan-cooled bungalows with hot water in a pretty garden. ①

Rambutan Jl Mawar ☏0362/41388, ⓦwww.rambutan.org. Exceptionally good facilities – two pools, wi-fi, a spa, fitness centre, kids' areas and music room – give this very nice UK–Balinese-run hotel the edge over most others in Lovina. It's in extensive grounds and has thoughtfully designed Bali-style cottages with great

bathrooms, plus some one- and two-room villas. Fan ③, a/c ⑤, villas ⑦

Rini Jl Mawar ☏0362/41386, ⓦwww.rinihotel .com. One of Lovina's larger hotels, whose thirty rooms and bungalows, ranged around a pleasant garden and pool, come in various styles and prices. The pricier a/c rooms are apartment-sized, with enormous, well-furnished verandas and equally generous bedroom space. The cheapest fan rooms are decent enough and everything's very clean. ②–④

Sea Breeze Cottages Beachfront ☏0362/41138. In a great beachside position behind the *Sea Breeze* café, this is a tiny outfit of just seven rooms, five of them attractive stilted wooden bungalows with pretty furnishings, a/c and hot water; the best are beside the small pool and have sea views. Fan ③, a/c ④

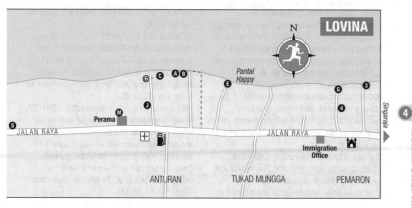

Taman Lily's Jl Mawar ☎0362/41307, ⓦwww.balilovinahotel-tamanlilys.com. Small Dutch–Balinese-run place with a row of six spotless and comfortably furnished bungalows in a lush garden. All have hot water and mini bars. Fan ❷, a/c ❹

Villa Jaya 100m off Jl Mawar ☎0362/700 1238, ⓦwww.villajaya.com. A quiet little place in a semi-rural spot 50m back from the beach. The six clean, tiled rooms have modern hot-water bathrooms and a choice of fan or a/c. There's a dinky pool and a restaurant. Fan ❷, a/c ❸

East of Kalibukbuk: Banyualit, Anturan and Pemaron

The **Banyualit** side road, Jalan Laviana, runs down to the sea 1.5km east of Kalibukbuk and is quiet and green, with banana palms still dotted between the various small warung and hotels. It's favoured by long-stay and older tourists from northern Europe.

There's more of a travellers' vibe in the small fishing village of **Anturan**, 1.5km east of Banyualit, though most accommodation here is not noticeably cheaper than in Kalibukbuk. It is quieter, however, and many places are on or very close to the village beach. There's snorkellable reef in front of Kubu Lalang, and the Perama office is nearby. Out on a limb at the far eastern end of Lovina is **Pemaron**, where ricefields are still in evidence.

Gede Homestay Anturan ☎0362/41526, ⓦwww.gedehomestay.com. Well-liked and cheap travellers' losmen with nine simple fan and a/c rooms in two compact rows just behind the beach. Fan ❶, a/c ❸

Kubu Lalang Anturan/Tukad Mungga ☎0362/42207, ⓦwww.kubulalang.com. Just beyond the eastern edge of Anturan village, close to a stretch of reef, this well-run place has just five thatched wood-and-rattan two-storey bungalows. Furnishings have arty touches, there are comfortable day beds on the verandas and a couple have ocean views. All have fans, some have hot water. Breakfasts include veggie and Indian versions, and there's a good restaurant attached (see p.258). Cold water ❸, hot water ❹

Mas Bungalows Jl Laviana, Banyualit ☎0362/41773, ⓦwww.masbungalows.com. Good-value little place considering it has a decent pool

and hot water throughout, but book ahead as it attracts long-stay guests, mostly from the Netherlands. Fan ❷, a/c ❸

Perama Homestay Anturan ☎0362/41161. Run by the local branch of Perama and located behind their shuttle bus office, this is both convenient and exceptionally cheap if you book at least two nights. Fan and a/c rooms are large and very clean and set round a garden just a short walk from the beach. ❶

Puri Bagus Lovina Pemaron ☎0362/21430, ⓦwww.lovina.puribagus.net. Upscale hotel that's part of the *Puri Bagus* chain (also in Candi Dasa and Ubud). The forty large, airy, elegantly simple Bali-style cottages occupy extensive seafront grounds quite a distance from most restaurants and facilities, at the far eastern end of Lovina. With a/c, wi-fi, a good pool and a charming spa it's good value, especially the standard rooms. ❼

255

Puspa Rama Anturan ℡0362/42070, ℮agungdayu@yahoo.com. You'll get the absolute cheapest rates here if you phone ahead and avoid coming with a transport tout. Rooms overlook a large garden a short walk from the beach; one has a/c and some have hot water. ❶–❷

Ray Beach Inn Jl Laviana, Banyualit ℡0362/41088, ℮lovina09@hotmail.com. A dozen cheerily decorated, tiled-floored rooms in a two-storey building looking out onto a small garden strip. A/c and hot water is available and there's a small spa. ❸

Sartaya Jl Laviana, Banyualit ℡0362/42240, ℮kembarsartaya@hotmail.com. Two rows of light, bright, good-quality, good-value, clean, tiled bungalows, some with hot water and a choice of fan or a/c, facing each other across a small garden. Fan ❷, a/c ❸

Sri Homestay Anturan ℡0362/42213, ℰwww .bluebali.co.uk. The big plus point here is that every one of the nine terraced rooms has a full-frontal view of the sea. Interiors are pleasant enough and come with fan or a/c; some have hot water. Fan ❷, a/c ❸

Villa Agung Beach Inn Anturan ℡0362/41527, ℰwww.agungvilla.com. A popular spot whose bright, modern fan and a/c rooms have good hot-water bathrooms and verandas, some with sea views. Family rooms have kids' bunks. There's a tiny pool but the real draw is the upstairs lounge and library offering great ocean views. Fan ❸, a/c ❹

West of Kalibukbuk and inland

Kaliasem doesn't have many restaurants but is an easy walk, along the beach or the highway, from central Kalibukbuk. **Inland** you're away from the commercial hustle at Banjar Tegeha, near the Buddhist temple; or there's the supremely luxurious retreat in the hills of Kayu Putih.

Aditya Beach Resort Kaliasem ℡0362/41059, ℰwww.adityalovina.com. Large, mid-range place whose 64 rooms front one of the nicer, less cluttered stretches of the beach, about a 10min walk west of Kalibukbuk. Top-end, deluxe bungalows are nicely furnished and have a/c and partial sea views; the budget rooms suffer a little from road noise but are fresh, and the upper-storey ones are pretty good. There's a pool, wi-fi and extensive gardens. Budget rooms ❹, deluxe bungalows ❻

Banjar Hills Retreat Jl Vihara, Banjar Tegeha ℡0815/5808 3880, ℰwww.balibanjarhills.com. Just 200m from the Buddhist monastery (see p.260), 10km from Kalibukbuk, this is a tiny place on its own on the edge of the village. Its four a/c bungalows are bright and modern and enjoy expansive views down to the coast. There's a small kidney-shaped pool and a restaurant. ❸

The Damai Kayu Putih ℡0362/41008, ℰwww.damai.com. Elegant luxury in a panoramic hillside location 4km inland from Kalibukbuk makes this the best in Lovina. Fourteen superbly appointed butler-serviced villas, some Bali-style with jacuzzis, others contemporary with up to three bedrooms and a private pool, are furnished with antiques and widely spaced around the expansive and charming organic gardens. There's a spa and scenically sited pool and a top-notch restaurant (see p.258). Free transport into Lovina. ❽

The resort

Joining one of Lovina's early-morning **dolphin trips** is almost obligatory – the dolphins themselves are honoured with an oversized statue at the beach end of Jalan Bina Ria – and most visitors also do some **snorkelling** or **diving**. If you're swimming off the beach in Lovina, be careful where you tread as there are lots of spiny sea urchins in places.

On dry land, **horseriding** and **waterfall treks** are a popular diversion – and see the details of cookery and art workshops given on p.259. It's also possible to visit the home and **art studio** of local painter Made Ariana, which is clearly signed 100m south off Jalan Raya Banyualit (℡0813/3845 9153, ℮made_ariana @hotmail.com). He specializes in abstract expressionist acrylics on huge canvases, mostly exploring philosophical and spiritual themes; he's exhibited in Holland and is happy to talk visitors through his work.

You can occasionally witness local **buffalo races** (*sapi gerumbungan*) in Kaliasem, one of the few places on Bali where this colourful tradition can still be seen.

> ## Dolphin trips
>
> Lovina is famous (or infamous) for dawn trips to see the **dolphins** that frolic off the coast: opinions are evenly split between those who think it's grossly overrated and those who consider it one of the best things on Bali.
>
> A flotilla of simple *prahu* hewn from a single tree trunk with a bamboo stabilizer on each side head out to sea at sunrise, providing lovely views of the coast and the central mountains. The ensuing scenario is comical, as one skipper spots a dolphin and chases after it, to be followed by the rest of the fleet, by which time, of course, the dolphin is often long gone. It's pretty much the luck of the draw: some days there is little to see while on others the dolphins cavort around and under the boats in a grand display. If you can see the funny side, it's a good trip, and very, very occasionally **whales** have been spotted.
>
> **Prices** are fixed, currently Rp60,000 per person for the two-hour excursion; book directly with the skippers on the beach or through your accommodation. There's a maximum of four passengers per boat.

They're usually staged on Independence Day (Aug 17), and in September (along with various other cultural performances) when the **Sail Indonesia** (Ⓦwww .sailindonesia.net) rally from Darwin to Singapore makes its stop at Lovina.

Diving and snorkelling
Situated between Pemuteran and Pulau Menjangan to the west and Tulamben and Amed to the east, Lovina is well placed for **diving**. The local reef, perhaps unfairly, has a reputation as being uninteresting for experienced divers, though there's an excellent range of fish, and artificial reef is encouraging coral growth; you'll need a boat to reach it though. Spice Dive (Ⓣ0362/41512, Ⓦwww .balispicedive.com), on the Kaliasem beachfront and on Jalan Bina Ria, is Lovina's longest-established **dive centre** and charges from Rp430,000 for local dives, or Rp615,000 to Menjangan, Tulamben or Amed. See p.46 for general advice on choosing dive companies. Local **snorkelling trips** can be arranged through any hotel, or directly with boat skippers on the beach (Rp60,000/ person for up to 2hr). Agents also organize snorkelling trips to the premier reefs at Pulau Menjangan (see p.293) for about Rp250,000 per person.

Trekking and horseriding
The most interesting **trek** in the area is the hike to Sekumpul Falls and nearby villages (see p.265), 30km east of Lovina. *Rambutan* hotel (Ⓣ0362/41388, Ⓦwww.rambutan.org) offers this as a full-day outing for Rp500,000 per person including lunch, as does Maha Nara (contact them through *Warung Bambu Pemaron* in Pemaron; Ⓣ0362/ 31455, Ⓦwww.mahanara.com; Rp430,000). Adjani (Ⓣ0812/3623 2019, Ⓦwww.adjanibali.com) leads half-day hikes in the hills around the traditional Bali Aga village of Sidetapa, including a visit to the Buddhist monastery and hot springs in Banjar (see p.260; Rp250,000/person).

Up in the hills around the village of Kayu Putih, 4km south of Kalibukbuk, Pegasus Farm (Ⓣ0858/5746 9576, Ⓦpegasus-organic-farm.blogspot.com) offers **horseriding** tailored for all ages, from short pony rides to two-hour rural treks (from Rp60,000), as well as free therapeutic riding for the disabled.

Eating
Kalibukbuk has by far the greatest choice of **places to eat** but several of the further-flung restaurants will pick you up for free if you phone ahead.

Kalibukbuk

Akar Café Jl Bina Ria. Green is the theme of the decor and the food at this cute little vegetarian café. There's cushion seating overlooking a rivulet at the back and an excellently varied menu that includes Middle Eastern mezze plates, veg and beetroot lasagne, quiches and five different salads, plus health juices, speciality teas and great ice creams. Most mains Rp40,000.

Bakery Lovina Jl Raya. Delicious white- and brown-bread sandwiches made with pâté, imported cheeses, chorizo and the like (from Rp30,000). Also croissants, cheesecakes and lots of other tempting cakes, as well as salads and a full range of lattes, iced coffees and ice creams.

Bu Warung Jl Raya. Probably the best-value food in Kalibukbuk, this tiny place serves a small menu of around a dozen well-cooked Indonesian and Western mains (Rp15,000), plus sandwiches, delicious avocado salads, pancakes and fried bananas.

Jasmine Kitchen Off Jl Bina Ria. Famously good Thai food in classy surroundings (mains mostly Rp40,000–54,000), including aromatic massaman curries, pad thai, tom yam soups and delectable desserts (Rp18,000). There's Hatten wine and Bintang on the menu or you can bring your own for Rp20,000 corkage.

Le Madre Jl Mawar. Little garden restaurant serving Italian food (the chef used to work at the upscale Italian *La Lucciola* restaurant in Seminyak) – carbonara, home-made bruschetta, pizzas, freshly baked focaccia – plus a few Indonesian dishes. Mains from Rp40,000.

Sea Breeze On the beach. Great for sunset drinks, and with a decent enough menu covering Western, Indonesian and seafood dishes (mains Rp30,000–55,000). The cakes and desserts are good, from daily specials that include crumble, brownies, lemon meringue pie and chocolate mousse. Acoustic music most nights just after sundown.

East of Kalibukbuk and inland

The Damai *The Damai* hotel, Kayu Putih ⓣ0362/41008, ⓦwww.damai.com. The most exquisite dining in northern Bali, where the imaginative, prize-winning fusion menu uses organic produce from the garden and changes daily. For an outstanding introduction go for the six-course taster dinner (Rp495,000), or there's three courses for Rp360,000, and Sunday brunch. Free transport from the Lovina area.

Kubu Lalang Anturan/Tukad Mungga ⓣ0362/42207, ⓦwww.kubulalang.com. A huge and imaginative menu – all cooked on the premises and entirely without MSG – that includes home-made bread, eleven different salads, stuffed crêpes, cauliflower curry and several other Indian dishes, plus seafood and plenty of veggie options. Mains Rp48,000–79,000. Free transport in the Lovina area.

Ranggon Sunset Jl Pura Penimbangan Barat, Pemaron ⓦwww.ranggonsunset.com. The Pemaron seafront, a short walk east along the beach from the *Puri Bagus Lovina* hotel, is popular with courting couples, who come to snack at the many stalls here. *Ranggon Sunset* is one of several more formal restaurants here, just back from the sea, and very popular with locals for its good-value set meals (from Rp17,500) and its seafood, including fish sate, tempura prawns and *gulai ikan* (Malaysian fish curry).

Spunky's Bar and Restaurant Beachfront, Banyualit. In an unbeatable shoreside location, serving the usual travellers' dishes.

Warung Bambu Pemaron Jl Puri Bagus Lovina, Pemaron ⓣ0362/31455, ⓦwarung-bambu.mahanara.com. In an attractive ricefield setting, the Balinese and Indonesian food here – sates, Balinese curries, tuna with aromatic sauce steamed in banana leaves – is all cooked from scratch (without MSG) and comes in generous portions; the rich and deliciously spiced *gado-gado* is especially recommended. Mains cost Rp27,000–40,000. There's Balinese dancing every Wed & Sun evening, paintings by Symon for sale (see p.170) and cooking classes (see opposite) and treks available (see p.260). Free transport in the Lovina area.

Warung Indra Jl Laviana, Banyualit. Neat, friendly little place with just four tables and a huge menu of Western and Indonesian standards; most mains are Rp30,000 and there are plenty of vegetarian choices.

Drinking and nightlife

Nightlife in Lovina is low key, with live music the main attraction, though there are also a few places that advertise "sexy dancers" and there's a locals' karaoke (hostess) scene too.

Kantin 21 Jl Raya, Kalibukbuk. Live-music bar, with an emphasis on reggae (rasta colours predominate), plus a good drinks list and cocktails by the jug. Daily 6pm–midnight.

Poco Bar Evolution Jl Bina Ria, Kalibukbuk. Popular spot with regular live music and drinks until at least midnight. Cocktails from Rp50,000.

Triple 9 Jl Mawar ⓦwww.triple9-lovina.com. Invitingly comfy sofas, free wi-fi, live sports TV and a reasonable happy hour (with free bar snacks) all make this an enjoyable place to spend an evening; food is also available. Daily 11am–midnight.

Volcano Club Jl Raya, Banyualit. Lovina's only club is housed in a strange concrete-cave of a building and is more of a hit with locals and domestic tourists. Mostly plays loud dance music, with occasional live bands. Sat from 6pm until about 2am; Rp25,000 including one free drink.

Zigiz Jl Bina Ria, Kalibukbuk. Tiny, lively bar with nightly live acoustic guitar from about 8pm, plus sports TV. Daily 4pm–midnight.

Spa treatments

As an alternative to the **massages** given by the ladies on the beach, there are plenty of hotels and day spas offering **treatments**. On Jalan Mawar in Kalibukbuk, Araminth Spa (☎0362/41901, ⓦwww.arunaspa.com) has an extensive menu, including *mandi lulur* scrubs (see p.47), vaginal steaming, and Ayurvedic massage (from Rp150,000); and *Rambutan* hotel (☎0362/41388, ⓦwww.rambutan.org) has cute therapy rooms and does a one-hour Bali massage for Rp130,000 as well as reflexology therapy given by a local healer. In Pemaron there's the fairly luxurious Jaya Spa at *Puri Bagus Lovina* (☎0362/21430, ⓦwww.lovina.puribagus .net; from Rp210,000).

Courses and workshops

Taking a **cookery class** for a couple of hours is a popular activity here. Most include hotel transport and a trip to the market, and you get to eat your efforts; all have a vegetarian option. Adjani (☎0812/3623 2019, ⓦwww.adjanibali.com; $25–30) runs classes in Kaliasem; *Warung Bambu Pemaron* restaurant (☎0362/31455, ⓦwww.mahanara.com; from Rp300,000) offers various classes including one all about sweets; Putu's Cooking (☎0813/3856 3705, ⓦwww.not-nasi-goreng.com; Rp200,000) takes place at the family home in Kalibukbuk.

Expat European artists Carola and Guy, based in Banyualit, run workshops in **painting** and **furniture restoration** (☎0813/3916 1879, ⓦwww.artventurebali .com; from Rp300,000).

Listings

ATMs On Jl Raya Kalibukbuk, between Jl Mawar and Jl Bina Ria.

Car, motorbike and bicycle rental Established car rental companies include Yuli Transport (☎0362/41184) on Jl Mawar; and Dupa, Jl Raya Kalibukbuk (☎0362/41397), which can also sell you proper rental car insurance (Rp100,000 for 10 days' cover). Motorbikes are available everywhere; for bicycles there are several outlets on Jl Mawar.

Doctor Dr Made Widiadnyana has a practice on Jl Raya Kalibukbuk (Mon–Sat 4–8pm; ☎0362/41314). The nearest hospital is in Singaraja (see p.264).

Immigration office Kantor Imigrasi, Jl Raya Pemaron, ☎0362/32174; visa extensions take a week (see p.59).

Police Jl Raya Banyualit, ☎0362/41010.

Shopping Nirwana Gallery, Jl Raya Kalibukbuk, sells a vast selection of fixed-price souvenirs and textiles.

Tours and onward transport Freelance driver Made Wijana (☎0813/3856 3027, ⓔmade_wijana @hotmail.com) is recommended for tours and transfers around the north; expect to pay around Rp450,000 for a full day. There are plenty of transport services to major destinations across Bali, Lombok and Java, including the efficient, Bali-wide Perama tourist shuttle buses, based in Anturan (daily 8am–10pm; ☎0362/41161, ⓦwww.peramatour .com; see "Travel Details"). Other operators run to Amed (Rp80,000/person), Kintamani (Rp80,000), Padang Bai (Rp110,000) and Pemuteran (Rp125,000), and most will sell you fast-boat tickets to Gili Trawangan (see p.211) as well as connecting transport to Padang Bai (about 4hr drive). Dupa, Jl Raya Kalibukbuk (☎0362/41397), sells airline tickets.

Yoga Regular classes at the Banana Plantation in Kaliasem; enquire at *Akar Café* on Jl Bina Ria (Rp50,000).

Around Lovina

The main sights around Lovina are the **Buddhist monastery** and **hot springs** at Banjar, about 10km west. With your own vehicle, the hills **inland from Seririt** make for a scenic drive. A kilometre beyond the western limits of Lovina, Jalan Singsing leads 1km south to the **Singsing (Daybreak) waterfalls**, an unexciting little cascade channelled via the rice terraces.

Brahmavihara Arama

Bali's largest Buddhist monastery, the **Brahmavihara Arama** (rarely closed; donation includes sarong rental; ℡0362/92954), is primarily a place of meditation, but it welcomes casual visitors and its shrines and prayer halls occupy a fine upland location with good views to the north coast. It combines well with a visit to the nearby hot springs at Banjar (a 3km walk away, via the market; see below) and is just 200m from the attractive accommodation at *Banjar Hills Retreat* (see p.256).

A Thai-style gold Buddha is the centrepiece of the main temple and there's also a Nepalese-style *stupa* (dome-shaped shrine) in the peaceful grounds. Most striking is the (scaled-down) grey lava-stone replica of East Java's Borobodur temple, set in serene frangipani gardens; it houses a mediation hall with limestone reliefs of the life of the Buddha.

The monastery is in the village of **Banjar Tegeha**, 10km southwest of Lovina. Catch any westbound bemo to **Dencarik**, where ojek wait to take you the last, steep 3km.

Air Panas Banjar

The traditional-style bathing pools and **hot springs** at **AIR PANAS BANJAR** (daily 8am–6pm; Rp5000) sit in exceptionally pretty surroundings, enclosed in a dell of palm trees and forest. They're hugely popular with locals and tourists alike, who come to soak in the silky soft, slightly sulphurous waters. There are lockers, changing rooms and spa treatments, and a small restaurant overlooking the pools. Dozens of stalls on the approach lane sell towels and swimwear. Come in the morning to avoid the crowds; weekends are especially busy.

The springs are 1.25km south of the central market in Banjar Tegeha, 3km from the Brahmavihara Arama Buddhist monastery on the other side of the village (see above). Coming from Kalibukbuk in Lovina, take the main road west for 8km, then follow signs south for 2.5km to reach the springs.

Inland via Seririt

With your own transport, you can take a scenic **inland drive** through the countryside south of Seririt, 12km west of Lovina, initially along the Denpasar road (Seririt itself is covered in Chapter 5). The road climbs through paddyfields and vineyards, splitting after 7km at **Rangdu**. The right-hand fork heads across the mountains via Pupuan to the south coast, while the left fork goes through Mayong, Banyuatis and Gunungsari to Munduk (see p.251) and on up to Danau Tamblingan and Danau Buyan. In **MAYONG**, the roadside restaurant *Bali Panorama* (9am–6.30pm, and for dinner on request; ℡0821/4704 9827, ✉mayong_bali@yahoo.com) makes a nice stop: it serves mostly organic Indonesian standards (from Rp25,000), accompanied by lovely paddyfield views, and staff can organize local treks if contacted in advance (from Rp75,000/person for a 2hr trek). Jero Made Karsini Murjasa, the proprietor, is a keen conversationalist and always willing to offer advice on spiritual matters.

Just beyond Mayong, take the small left turn for "Desa Bestala", which leads to the village of **Bestala**, where you should turn left by the statue of the independence fighter. The road then winds down into the valley, across the river and up the other side to the hamlet of **Munduk Bestala**, famous for its durians (Jan and Feb are the main season). Turn right at the T-junction in the village and if you've a decent map it's possible to navigate to **Pedawa** and **Sidetapa**, two traditional Bali Aga villages that still retain their narrow lanes and high-walled compounds. For guided walks in the Sidetapa area, contact Adjani in Lovina (see p.257).

Singaraja and around

The second-largest Balinese city after Denpasar, **SINGARAJA** has a population of over 100,000 and a spacious feel to it, with its broad avenues, imposing monuments and colonial bungalows set in attractive gardens. There are, however, few obvious reminders of its former days as the capital of Bali or its role as seat of the Dutch administration for the Lesser Sunda Islands (which included Bali and all the islands east to Timor); the harbour's status as Bali's primary port has also long been

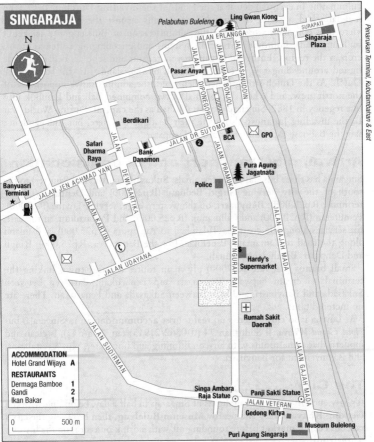

relinquished to Benoa in the south. But you can still see the shop-houses and narrow streets of the original trading area: Jalan Hasanuddin is known as Kampung Bugis and Jalan Imam Bonjol as Kampung Arab after the Muslim Bugis settlers from Sulawesi whose descendants still live in the area. And Singaraja is still the capital of the Buleleng district: images of **Singa Ambara Raja**, the winged lion symbol of Buleleng, appear all over the city – "Singa Raja" means "Lion King".

Accommodation isn't particularly enticing in Singaraja and there are only a couple of sights, notably the specialist **library** of books made from *lontar*-palm leaves, but you can spend a few interesting hours exploring here, best done as a day-trip from Lovina, a twenty-minute bemo ride to the west. All points eastwards are easily accessible, including the fabulous temples of **Pura Meduwe Karang** – best of the bunch – **Sangsit** and **Jagaraga**, plus the spectacular **Sekumpul Falls**.

Some history

When **Gusti Ngurah Panji Sakti** founded the kingdom of **Buleleng** in the seventeenth century, he built a new palace called Singaraja at the heart of his north-coast territory, then extended his dominion to Karangasem, Jembrana and parts of eastern Java. The regency's influence fluctuated over the next 150 years, culminating in eventual defeat at the hands of the **invading Dutch** in 1849, who had launched a series of extended campaigns against the north coast. The victorious colonialists took over the administration of Buleleng and set about building roads, improving irrigation systems and encouraging coffee as a cash crop in the region; European journalists, merchants and scholars began to settle in and around Singaraja, even as the south of the island was still battling the Dutch. As the Dutch strengthened their hold, the administrative importance of the north grew, and when the colonial power combined Bali and Lombok into one regency in 1882, Singaraja was established as the **capital**. During World War II, the invading **Japanese** also made their headquarters here, but Independence saw the Balinese capital move south to Denpasar.

Arrival, city transport and accommodation

Singaraja has three bus and bemo terminals: **Sukasada**, (also called Sangket) to the south of the city, serving Gitgit, Bedugul (Rp25,000) and Denpasar (Ubung terminal; Rp25,000); **Banyuasri**, on the western edge, serving Lovina (Rp7000), Pemuteran (Rp20,000) and Gilimanuk (Rp25,000); and **Penarukan**, in the east, for services along the coast via Tulamben to Amlapura (Rp25,000), and inland along the road to Kintamani, Penelokan (for the Batur area; Rp25,000), Bangli and Denpasar (Batubulan terminal).

Small **bemos** (flat rate Rp7000) ply main routes **around town** linking the terminals – cream between Banyuasri and Penarukan, dark-red between Sukasada and Banyuasri, and blue between Sukasada and Penarukan. There are no metered taxis.

As Lovina is so close, there's no real tourist **accommodation** in Singaraja, but *Hotel Grand Wijaya*, Jl Sudirman 74 (℡0362/21915; fan ❶, a/c ❸), is clean and modern, has some rooms with air-conditioning and hot water, plus a restaurant, and is convenient for Banyuasri.

The City

It's easy enough to see the highlights of Singaraja in half a day, beginning with the **Gedong Kirtya** library and nearby **Museum Buleleng**, then browsing the city's raucous central **market** before rounding off with a drink or a meal on the historic **waterfront**.

Gedong Kirtya

Singaraja's best-known attraction is the esoteric but surprisingly interesting **Gedong Kirtya**, Jl Veteran 20 (Mon–Thurs 8am–3.30pm, Fri 8am–2.30pm; donation expected), the only library of **lontar manuscripts** in the world. There are over six thousand of these texts, all inscribed on leaves from the *lontar* palm, bound between wooden boards measuring 35cm by 3cm, and covering Balinese religion, customs, philosophy, folklore, medicine, astrology and black magic. Due to the humidity on Bali, the palm-leaf books only last between fifty and a hundred years, so the library's decaying manuscripts are copied onto new *lontar* leaves, ensuring the survival of this ancient art. It's an inordinately lengthy process, which begins with the soaking and then boiling of the palm leaves, continues with many days of pressing, and culminates in the precise and painstaking work of engraving the text on to the leaf, then rubbing it with lamp black to make it visible. The library also conserves *prasasti*, inscribed **bronze plates** from the tenth century, which are among the oldest written records on Bali. It's a scholarly place, but visitors are welcome; a member of the library staff will show you round.

The library is located in the palace grounds of the Puri Agung Singaraja; blue Sukasada–Penarukan **bemos** pass the entrance.

Museum Buleleng and Puri Agung Singaraja

Not far from the Gedong Kirtya, and also within the palace compound of Puri Agung Singaraja, is the unglamorous but quite well-labelled **Museum Buleleng** (Mon–Thurs 8am–3.30pm, Fri 8am–2.30pm; donation welcome). It contains some pictures by the Dutch artist W.O.J. Nieuwenkamp (he of the famous bicycle stonecarving at Pura Meduwe Karang in nearby Kubutambahan; see p.266), and a lot of portraits of Buleleng heroes, including the kingdom's founding father, **Gusti Ngurah Panji Sakti** (see opposite). Of particular interest are the locally found ancient artefacts, including Stone-Age tools and Bronze-Age jewellery, as well as various eighth-century Buddhist items found in Kalibukbuk in Lovina, all testament to north Bali's trading history.

At the back of the compound, behind the museum, are the residential quarters of **Puri Agung Singaraja**, also known as Puri Gede Buleleng (daily 9am–5pm; entry by donation), the restored palace of the former royal family of Buleleng. Concise displays summarize the lives of previous rulers, in particular that of Anak Agung Panji Tisna (1908–78), the **last Raja of Buleleng**, a novelist, founder of Lovina and a Christian convert. His descendants still live in the palace.

The market and the waterfront

The commercial hub of traditional Singaraja is the thronging covered **market**, Pasar Anyar, off Jalan Diponegoro (daily 1am–11pm). It's at its busiest in the very early morning but at any time of day you can buy your live chickens and ducks here and stock up on temple offerings, sarongs and any number of handmade knives. Just outside, pavement hawkers peddle herbal potions along Jalan Diponegoro. If you're after quality textiles, however, head across to Berdikari **endek weaving workshop**, Jl Dewi Sartika 42 (showroom daily 7.30–3.30pm, workshop closed Sun), which produces fine silk and cotton *ikat* in vibrant colours and striking designs. The fabric is made on the premises and you can watch every stage of the process (see box, p.194), from the laborious tying of the weft to the hand-dyeing and weaving.

A few minutes' walk north of the market, **Pelabuhan Buleleng**, the **waterfront**, is a pleasant place to wander and, especially, to eat (see p.264); it's the site of the ancient harbour of Buleleng, though now it's hard to imagine that this was once the busiest port on Bali. Just around the corner, the Chinese temple **Ling**

Gwan Kiong (admission by donation) is a neat red-and-white confection of shrines, statues, plaques and bridges.

Eating

Gandi **restaurant**, at Jl Jen Achmad Yani 25 (set back off the road at the edge of the square and car park), is a good, central place to eat, with a cheap menu of Chinese, Indonesian and seafood dishes, including fried rice with crab, from Rp25,000. For better views and a wider choice head for the waterfront, to Pelabuhan Buleleng (cream-coloured Banyuasri–Penarukan bemos will drop you at the waterfront entrance, marked by an archway, on Jalan Erlangga). Here, four restaurants occupy a corner each of a jetty built over the water, offering sea breezes and fine coastal views: *Ikan Bakar* does seafood, *Dermaga Bamboe* does Indonesian standards, and there are burgers and pizzas too. Food carts also congregate on the seafront. As darkness falls, the **night market** in the Jalan Durian area near Pasar Anyar springs into life.

Listings

Banks and exchange International ATMs at BCA on Jl Dr Sutomo (exchange counter Mon–Fri 10am–2pm), Hardy's on Jl Ngurah Rai and Bank Danamon on Jl Dr Sutomo.

Bus tickets (long-distance) Menggala, Jl Jen Achmad Yani 76 (☎0362/24374), operates daily night buses to Surabaya (Rp130,000; 9hr), leaving at 7pm, arriving at Probolinggo and Pasuruan in East Java, access points for the Bromo region, in the middle of the night. Safari Dharma Raya, Jl Jen Achmad Yani 84 (☎0362/23460), leaves every afternoon at 3pm for Yogyakarta (12hr; Rp215,000) and Jakarta (26hr; Rp330,000).

Hospitals The best medical facility in Singaraja (and north Bali) is the private hospital Parama Sidhi, about 200m west of the Banyuasri terminal on the road to Lovina, Jl Jen Achmad Yani 171 (☎0368/29787). There's a public hospital, Rumah Sakit Daerah, on Jl Ngurah Rai (☎0362/41046).

Supermarket Hardy's on Jl Ngurah Rai (8am–10.30pm) is three floors of local shopping including a supermarket. There's another Hardy's and a Carrefour supermarket at the Singaraja Plaza complex on Jl Surapati.

South of Singaraja

South of the city, 10km along the road to Bedugul and spread over a 3km stretch, are three well-signposted **waterfalls** at **GITGIT** (daily 8am–5.30pm; Rp5000 at each). They get very busy, and are not a patch on Sekumpul Falls (see opposite), which can also be reached easily from Singaraja, but only if you have transport. The main **Gitgit Falls**, a 40m single drop, is the one nearest to Singaraja; 2km south is the **Multi-Tiered Falls** with pools for swimming in; and 1km further towards Bedugul are the underwhelming **Twin Falls**. Local belief suggests that couples coming to Gitgit will eventually separate – but it doesn't seem to deter the hordes of visitors. All **buses** between Singaraja (Sukasada terminal) and Denpasar via Bedugul pass Gitgit.

East of Singaraja

A trio of small and otherwise unremarkable villages east of Singaraja have some of the most engaging **temple carvings** on Bali and make an excellent day-trip from Lovina, ideally combined with a hike to Bali's most beautiful falls, **Sekumpul Waterfall**. The temple villages are served by **bemos** from Singaraja's Penarukan terminal (which is 3km east along Jalan Surapati from the Pelabuhan Buleleng waterfront), but for Sekumpul you'll need your own wheels. The temples are all open daily, from about 7am to 6pm.

Sangsit

The village of **SANGSIT**, 2km east of Singaraja's Penarukan terminal, is famous for two fine examples of exuberant north Balinese temple carving. The pink-sandstone **Pura Beji** (admission by donation, sarong rental included), 200m north off the main road, is dedicated to Dewi Sri, the rice goddess, and its every surface drips with carvings of animals, plants, masks, humans and monsters, both old and new.

The red roofs of **Pura Dalem Sangsit** are visible across the fields 400m northeast of Pura Beji. Its front wall vibrantly depicts the rewards that await the godly in heaven and, more luridly, the punishments lined up for the evil in hell: stone blocks on the head, women giving birth to strange creatures and sharp penises descending through the tops of skulls.

Jagaraga

About 500m east along the main road from Sangsit, then 4km south, **JAGARAGA** was the site of two immense battles between the Balinese and the Dutch. In 1848, the Balinese, led by local hero Gusti Ketut Jelantik, won with huge loss of life, their sixteen thousand troops fighting with lances and *kris* against three thousand well-armed Dutch. The two forces met here again in 1849, when the Dutch finally took control of the entire Buleleng regency (see p.262).

Scenes from daily life before and after the Dutch takeover are depicted in lively detail at **Pura Dalem Jagaraga** (Rp10,000), about 1km north of the village, whose graphic late nineteenth-century stonecarved temple reliefs are among the most photographed in Bali. The best carvings are on the outside front walls, though they're now quite eroded in places; an English-speaking guide is often on hand to interpret them. Those on the left of the main gateway show village life before the Dutch invasion – kite-flying, fishing, climbing coconut trees; next to them you see the Dutch arriving by car, boat, plane and bicycle, destroying the community. On the right-hand side is a much reproduced carving of two Dutch men driving a Model T Ford, being held up by bandits. Nearby, a statue of folk-character Pan Brayut shows him being crawled over by some of his scores of children (see box, p.201). On the inside of the right-hand wall the crocodile eating the man is taken to represent the Dutch conquering Bali.

Sekumpul Waterfall

Bali's most dazzling falls, **Sekumpul Waterfall** (dawn to dusk; Rp5000), tumble 70m in seven dramatic cascades down a remote and beautiful valley filled with clove, cacao and coffee trees and framed by coconut palms, rice terraces and the mountains beyond. The falls are between two villages: **Sekumpul**, 11km south of Jagaraga (21km from Singaraja or about 30km from Lovina), and **Lemukih**, 2km further south up the same road.

With your own transport, easiest access to the falls is via Sekumpul; they're signed 9km south of Jagaraga. A ten-minute walk from the Sekumpul ticket booth and café, just past *Kadek's* drinks and organic spices stall, and you have a fantastic view over the waterfalls. Then a steep and sometimes slippery flight of three hundred concrete steps leads you to the bottom of the chasm; water levels permitting, you can wade across the river and walk another ten minutes to reach a swimmable pool beneath the falls. Return the same way.

You can also arrange **guided treks** between Sekumpul and Lemukih, via the falls, taking in the various plantations and rice terraces as well as a swim. Lovina agents offer this (Rp300,000–500,000/person all inclusive; see p.257), or contact organic farmer and guide Kadek Ardita at his drinks stall on the path from Sekumpul (☏ 08523/704 4245); he charges Rp200,000 for up to three people for a three-hour trek (excluding entry and transfers, which he can also arrange).

Pura Meduwe Karang

The most arresting temple in the area is the lavishly carved **Pura Meduwe Karang** (admission by donation, sarong rental included) at **KUBUTAMBAHAN**, 7km east of Singaraja's Penarukan terminal (300m east of the Kintamani road junction) and served by frequent yellow bemos. Dedicated to Batara Meduwe Karang, the temple ensures divine protection for crops grown on dry land, such as coconuts, maize and groundnuts. It's built on a grand scale: the terraces at the front support 34 figures from the *Ramayana* (see p.380) including the giant Kumbakarna battling with hordes of monkeys from Sugriwa's army.

Inside, the walls are decorated with **carvings** of Balinese folk, including elderly people and mothers with babies. In the inner courtyard, and typical of northern temples, a large rectangular base links the three central shrines, called the *bebaturan*. It is here, on the outer left wall, that you'll find one of the most famous stone reliefs on Bali: a cyclist (possibly the Dutch artist W.O.J. Nieuwenkamp, who first visited Bali in 1904 and explored the island on a bicycle) wearing floral shorts, with a rat about to go under the back wheel, apparently being chased by a dog.

The northeast coast

Beyond Kubutambahan, the black-sand beaches along **the northeast coast** are quiet and local, mostly cleaner than around Lovina, if often stony. If you have your own transport and like the peaceful life, there are a number of hotels along here that could make an enjoyable base, especially in **Air Sanih**, and further east, en route to Tulamben, at **Tejakula**, **Sembirenteng** and **Tembok**. You're generally restricted to hotel food and tours if you don't have wheels but **bemos** from Singaraja's Penarukan terminal to Amlapura all pass this way.

Air Sanih

AIR SANIH, 13km east of Singaraja's Penarukan terminal, is a locals' beach resort with some not very inspiring cold **springs** (daily 6am–6pm; Rp4000). It's popular for its short-time accommodation catering to Balinese couples who need to get away from the village for a few hours, and while that doesn't make it seedy it does mean that many **places to stay** aren't that interested in having overnight foreign guests. There are, however, a couple of standout exceptions that are oriented towards foreign tourists and would make delightful bases. Down at sea level, set in lush tropical gardens right on the black-sand shore, 🅰 *Cilik's Beach Garden* (☏0812/360 1473, 🅦www.ciliksbeachgarden.com; ❻) is a gem, with two huge Bali-style bungalows, one villa and one *lumbung*-style cottage, each furnished with antiques and a library of books. Inland and across the road, 700m uphill, *Mimpi Bungalows* (☏0813/3857 9595, 🅦www.mimpibali.com; ❹), offers great panoramas of the coast, plenty of breeze and several relaxation areas around the pretty garden and pool. The two rooms and three bungalows (all with fans and hot water) are very clean and comfortable and the owner, a German nurse, can advise on interesting day-trips, meetings with a spiritual healer and the best local beach.

Pacung and around

About 12km east of Air Sanih, the road climbs a headland at **PONJOK BATU** with views along the coast. The impressive **temple** here was founded by the sixteenth-century Javanese priest Nirartha after he used his spiritual powers to bring a shipwrecked crew back to life and many Balinese drivers stop to pray and receive a blessing.

Less than 1km east of the temple, in the village of **PACUNG**, *Villa Boreh* (☎0858/5724 0068, Ⓦwww.bali-villa.org; Ⓞ) is a pretty spot on the black beach, whose six delightful, differently styled **villas** and two pools sit within a luscious garden. There's a reef for snorkelling and an attached spa. Also in Pacung, the award-winning cooperative **Surya Indigo Handweaving Centre** (daily from about 10am) is well worth a visit. It's famous for producing the striped *bebali* cloth used for ritual purposes in Bali (especially for babies' six-month ceremonies, and at the Galungan festival) and you can watch every stage of the process on the premises, from the dyeing of the silk and cotton threads with the natural colours produced from plants grown in the garden to the weaving on the traditional *cagcag* (backstrap) looms. The all but expired art of hand-weaving *bebali* was only revived here in 2000 but now the cooperative supplies sacred cloth to villagers and top hotels around Bali. Prices start at about Rp200,000 for cotton *bebali* (180cm by 60cm).

From Pacung, 100m west of Surya Indigo, it's 3km inland to **SEMBIRAN**, an ancient Bali Aga village (see p.220), but today little obviously distinguishes it from any other village in Bali. Another kilometre east brings you to **Bondalem**, from whose eastern fringes a signed, quiet **back road** leads 26km up to Kintamani (see p.245).

East to Tulamben

Secluded in a suitably tranquil shorefront garden in **TEJAKULA**, 4km east of Bondalem (with no direct car access), environmentally and socially conscious *Gaia-Oasis* (☎0812/385 3350, Ⓦwww.gaia-oasis.com; Ⓞ) is a collection of eighteen differently designed one- and two-bedroom **bungalows**, all with large verandas and kitchenette; they're rented out collectively by their owners. There's free yoga twice a day, with a monthly roster of changing yoga teachers, plus a pool and spa, and a programme of interesting village-culture tours.

About 2km beyond, at **LES**, a sign points inland to **Yeh Mempeh Waterfall** (entry by donation), questionably dubbed the highest waterfall in Bali (about 40m). It's 1.5km through the village to a parking area then a twenty-minute walk through the forest to the falls and a pool deep enough to swim in during the wet season (Oct–March). Even in the dry season it is picturesque as the water bounces down the rock face into an ice-cold pool at the bottom.

Right on the shore at the eastern perimeter of **SEMBIRENTENG**, about 7km east of Tejakula, *Alam Anda Dive and Spa Resort* (☎0812/465 6485, Ⓦwww.alamanda.de; bungalows Ⓞ, villas with private pool Ⓞ) is lively and popular and makes an appealing, good-value alternative **diving base** to Tulamben, which is a half-hour drive away; there are also two house reefs just offshore. The dive centre is part of the highly regarded Werner Lau stable (Ⓦwww.wernerlau.com). Accommodation is attractive, mostly in air-conditioned bungalows and a few private-pool villas, all set within extensive landscaped grounds with a large pool. The **restaurant** serves Western and Indonesian food supplemented by some German favourites and makes a good place to stop on a drive along the north coast.

Another 4km further east, in **TEMBOK**, the super-luxurious *Spa Village Tembok* (☎0362/32033, Ⓦwww.spavillage.com; Ⓞ) is an away-from-it-all retreat, featuring Bali-modern **rooms** and villas, a glorious pool, exceptional service, and a vast number of spa treatments from Bali and Malaysia (the home of the *Spa Village* concept). Prices start at $400 for full board including a daily spa treatment. However, it is pretty isolated – 22km east to Tulamben.

Travel details

Bemos and public buses

It's almost impossible to give the frequency with which bemos and public buses run: see Basics, p.30, for details. Journey times given are the minimum you can expect.

Air Sanih to: Amlapura (2hr); Culik (1hr 30min); Gilimanuk (3hr); Singaraja (Penarukan; 30min); Tirtagangga (2hr); Tulamben (1hr).

Bedugul to: Denpasar (Ubung; 1hr 30min); Singaraja (Sukasada; 1hr 30min).

Kintamani to: Bangli (1hr); Denpasar (Batubulan; 2hr); Singaraja (Penarukan; 1hr 30min); Ubud (40min).

Lovina to: Amlapura (3hr 30min); Gilimanuk (2hr 30min); Seririt (20min); Singaraja (Banyuasri; 20min).

Munduk to Denpasar (Ubung; 2hr); Seririt (45min).

Penelokan to: Bangli (45min); Buahan (30min); Denpasar (Batubulan; 1hr 30min); Gianyar (50min); Singaraja (Penarukan; 1hr 30min); Songan (45min); Toya Bungkah (30min).

Singaraja (Banyuasri terminal) to: Gilimanuk (2hr 30min); Lovina (20min); Seririt (40min).

Singaraja (Penarukan terminal) to: Amlapura (3hr); Culik (2hr 30min); Denpasar (Batubulan; 3hr); Gianyar (2hr 20min); Kubutambahan (20min); Penelokan (1hr 30min); Tirtagangga (2hr 30min); Tulamben (1hr).

Singaraja (Sukasada terminal) to: Bedugul (1hr 30min); Denpasar (Ubung; 3hr); Gitgit (30min).

Perama shuttle buses

Bedugul to: Kuta (daily; 2hr 30min–3hr); Lovina (daily; 1hr 30min); Sanur (daily; 2hr–2hr 30min); Ubud (daily; 1hr 30min).

Lovina to: Bedugul (daily; 1hr 30min); Candi Dasa (daily; 3hr–3hr 30min); Gili Islands, Lombok (daily; 8hr); Kuta/Ngurah Rai Airport (daily; 3hr); Padang Bai (daily; 2hr 45min); Senggigi, Lombok (daily; 10hr); Sanur (daily; 2hr 30min–3hr); Ubud (daily; 3hr 30min–4hr).

West Bali

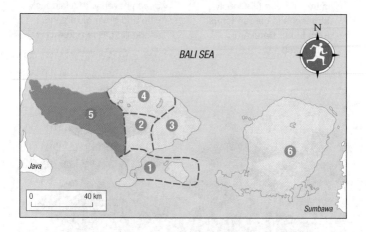

CHAPTER 5   # Highlights

❋ **Tanah Lot** Perched like a sea bird on a wave-lashed rock, this is Bali's most visited temple. See p.275

❋ **Yeh Gangga** A dramatic stretch of remote black-sand beach with just a couple of exceptional places to stay. See p.279

❋ **Gunung Batukaru** Bali's second-highest mountain is the site of a fabulously atmospheric garden temple, Pura Luhur Batukaru. See p.280

❋ **Jatiluwih road** Quintessentially Balinese scenery featuring swathes of luscious rice terraces lines this sinuous road. See p.280

❋ **Pulau Menjangan** Make the most of the crystal-clear waters and spectacular reefs off this tiny island. See p.291

❋ **Pemuteran** Small, relaxed beach haven with a laidback vibe and great diving and snorkelling. See p.294

▲ Pura Luhur Batukaru

West Bali

parsely populated, mountainous and in places extremely rugged, **west Bali** stretches from the northwestern outskirts of Denpasar across 128km to Gilimanuk at the island's westernmost tip. Connected in ancient times to Java by a tract of land (now submerged beneath the Bali Strait), the region has always had something of a Javanese character. When Java's Hindu Majapahit elite fled to Bali in the sixteenth century, the Javanese priest Nirartha started his influential preaching tour of Bali from the west – leaving the region with a trinity of stunning clifftop temples at **Tanah Lot**, **Rambut Siwi** and **Pulaki**. More recently, west Bali's Muslim population has increased so much that in the region to the west of Negara, mosques now seem to outnumber temples and a good percentage of the male population wears a small black *peci*.

Apart from making the obligatory visits to the big attractions just west of Denpasar – Pura Tanah Lot, Mengwi's **Pura Taman Ayun** and **Sangeh Monkey Forest** being the main draws – few tourists linger long in west Bali. Yet the southwest coast holds some fine black-sand beaches, and good surf at **Balian Beach** near **Lalang Linggah** and **Medewi**, while the cream of Bali's coral reefs lie off the northwest coast around **Pulau Menjangan**, near the little beach haven of **Pemuteran**. Bali's only national park, **Bali Barat National Park**, is also here. The island's second-highest peak, the sacred **Gunung Batukaru**, dominates many west Bali vistas and its southern slopes nourish the most fertile paddies in Bali, not least in the area around **Jatiluwih**, focus of a famously scenic drive. Bali's rice-growing culture is celebrated in a museum in nearby **Tabanan**. For areas that lie in Batukaru's rain shadow, however, the picture is quite different, with both the extreme west and some stretches of the northwest suffering from arid and infertile land.

Despite the lack of tourist centres in the west, there are several exceptional **hotels** both on the coast and in inland villages, most of them quiet and well off the usual tourist route. The southwest coast is served by **public transport** from Denpasar's Ubung terminal, and the northwest coast from Singaraja: both services terminate at **Gilimanuk**, from where car ferries shuttle across the Bali Strait to Java.

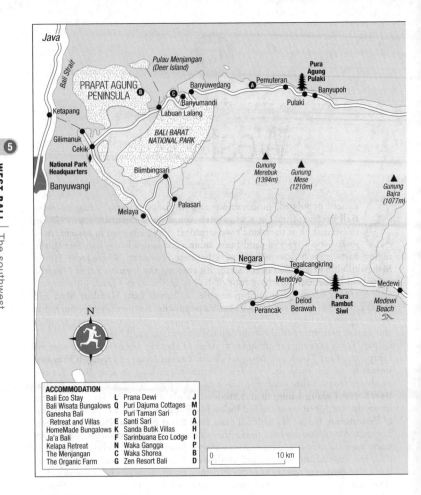

ACCOMMODATION

Bali Eco Stay	**L**	Prana Dewi	**J**
Bali Wisata Bungalows	**Q**	Puri Dajuma Cottages	**M**
Ganesha Bali		Puri Taman Sari	**O**
Retreat and Villas	**E**	Santi Sari	**E**
HomeMade Bungalows	**K**	Sanda Butik Villas	**H**
Ja'a Bali	**F**	Sarinbuana Eco Lodge	**I**
Kelapa Retreat	**N**	Waka Gangga	**P**
The Menjangan	**C**	Waka Shorea	**B**
The Organic Farm	**G**	Zen Resort Bali	**D**

0   10 km

The southwest

From the **Ubung** terminal in Denpasar's northwestern suburbs (see p.274), all westbound buses and bemos follow the busy main road through a string of unexciting little towns. After 15km, the road reaches the village of **Kapal**, one of the shrine-making centres of Bali: the pavements are lined with every conceivable permutation in stone, concrete and wood, some roofed with wiry black *ijuk* thatch made from sugar-palm fibres. The road branches just west of Kapal, the northbound fork being a major artery for Bedugul and Singaraja via the seventeenth-century temple complex at **Mengwi**, with a side road to the **Sangeh Monkey Forest**. Continuing west towards Gilimanuk, the road reaches a crossroads at Kediri, access point for the coastal temple of **Pura Tanah Lot**. Kediri lies on the outskirts of **Tabanan**, the district capital, from where you can get transport to **Yeh Gangga beach**.

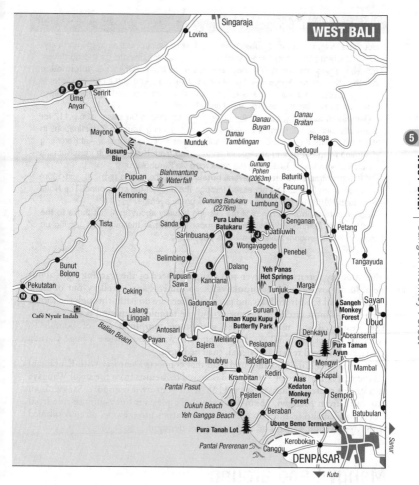

Sangeh Monkey Forest

Monkeys have a special status in Hindu religion, and a number of Balinese temples boast a resident monkey population, respected by devotees and fed and photographed by tourists. The **Monkey Forest** (Bukit Sari) in the village of **SANGEH**, 21km north of Denpasar, is the most atmospheric of these, its unruly inhabitants the self-appointed guardians of the slightly eerie **Pura Bukit Sari** (daylight hours; donation). According to local legend, the forest was created when Rama's general, the monkey king Hanuman, attempted to kill Rama's enemy Rawana by squashing him between two halves of the sacred Mount Meru. In the process, part of the mountain fell to earth at Sangeh, with hordes of Hanuman's simian retainers still clinging to the trees, creating Bukit Sari and its monkey dynasty. The temple was built some time during the seventeenth century, among sacred nutmeg trees that tower 40m high. It is best appreciated in late afternoon, after the tour buses have left, when both forest and temple take on a ghostly aspect missing from the island's

South Bali's terminus for all public transport to west Bali (as well as to the north and Java) is **Ubung bus and bemo station** on Jalan Cokroaminoto on the northwest fringes of Denpasar (see p.274). Bays are clearly marked and there's an **information booth** in the centre. Where there's a choice between a bemo and a bus, the latter is usually cheaper because it takes longer. For destinations served by Ubung and a guide to journey times, see "Travel details" on p.300.

Bemos run **to Ubung** from all the other bemo stations in Denpasar (see p.117 for trans-city routes), but there are no direct routes to Ubung from other destinations in the south, so for these you'll need to change at least once in Denpasar – at Kereneng if coming **from Sanur** and at Tegal when travelling **from Kuta**, though from Kuta it's much faster to take a **taxi** along the back road via Kerobokan.

If you get stranded there are several **hotels** behind the Ubung terminal, just 100m away on Jalan Pidada and accessed through the back of the compound. The *Hotel Niki Rusdi* (☎0361/416397; Fan ❶, a/c ❷) is pretty average.

Services **to Gilimanuk** run until the evening (usually about 9pm) but those **to the north coast** (Seririt and Singaraja) are most frequent in the mornings, drying up through the afternoon; travel as early as possible.

other monkey forests. Whenever you visit, take heed of the warning signs about the absurdly over-confident **monkeys**: keep cameras and jewellery out of sight and remove all food from bags and pockets. There are no paths through the forest, but a track almost circles its perimeter and the temple compound is easy to find. The weathered and moss-encrusted grey-stone **temple** is out of bounds to everyone except the monkeys, but beyond the walls you can see a huge Garuda statue, stonecarved reliefs and tiered, thatched *meru*.

Sangeh is on a minor northbound road that connects Denpasar with Kintamani via the junction village of Petang, and is served by **bemos** from the small Wangaya terminal in central Denpasar (see p.113). With your own transport, Sangeh is an easy drive from Mengwi, 15km southwest, or a pleasant forty-minute ride from Ubud. Sangeh also features on every **tour** operator's programme, often combined with Mengwi and Tanah Lot, and sometimes Bedugul.

Mengwi and around

The town of **MENGWI**, some 18km northwest of Denpasar, has a glittering history as the capital of a once powerful kingdom and is the site of an important temple, **Pura Taman Ayun**. From the early seventeenth century until the late nineteenth, the rajas of Mengwi held sway over an extensive area, comprising parts of present-day Badung, Tabanan and Gianyar districts. Their fortunes eventually waned, however, and in 1885 the kingdom of Mengwi was divided between Badung and Tabanan. Descendants of the royal family still live in the Mengwi area, and one of their palaces, **Puri Taman Sari** in nearby Umabian, is now a luxury homestay.

Pura Taman Ayun

The state temple of the former kingdom of Mengwi, **Pura Taman Ayun** (daily 8.30am–5.30pm; Rp3000, children Rp1500; sarong not required) is thought to have been built by Raja I Gusti Agung Anom in 1634. Designed as a series of terraced courtyards, the complex is surrounded by a moat to symbolize the mythological home of the gods, Mount Meru, floating in the cosmic ocean. The **inner courtyard** is encircled by its own little moat and is inaccessible to the public except at festival time, although the surrounding wall is low enough to give a reasonable view of the two-dozen multi-tiered **meru** within. The most important are the three that honour Bali's holiest mountains; their positions within the courtyard correspond to their location on Bali in relation to Mengwi. Thus, the eleven-roofed structure in the far northwest corner represents Gunung Batukaru; the nine-roofed *meru* halfway down the east side symbolizes Gunung Batur; and Batur's eleven-roofed neighbour honours Gunung Agung. The Batur *meru* has only nine tiers because the mountain is significantly lower than the other two.

Pura Taman Ayun is just east off the main Mengwi–Singaraja road and easily reached by **bemo** from Denpasar's Ubung terminal (30min). Coming from Gilimanuk or other points on the west coast, you'll need to change bemos at Tabanan's Pesiapan terminal.

Puri Taman Sari

One very good reason to visit this area is to stay at the *puri* (palace) of a branch of the Mengwi royal family. Located in the tiny village of **Umabian**, about 5km northwest of Pura Taman Ayun, *Puri Taman Sari* (☏0361/747 2420, ⓦpuritamansari.com; ⑤) has rooms, suites and villas with plenty of modern comforts in a traditional compound close to classic rice terraces. Cultural activities include making offerings, and gamelan and dance lessons are also available. The rural environs are a pleasure to explore on foot or by bicycle and Alas Kedaton Monkey Forest (see p.279) is also nearby. Access to *Puri Taman Sari* is via Denkayu on the Mengwi–Bedugul–Singaraja road.

Pura Tanah Lot and around

Dramatically marooned on a tiny, craggy rock, pounded by the ocean, sitting just off the southwest coast, **PURA TANAH LOT** is regarded as especially holy by the Balinese and among tourists holds a deserved reputation as one of Bali's top sights. Fringed by frothing white surf and glistening black sand, its elegant multi-tiered shrines have become the unofficial symbol of Bali, appearing on a vast range of tourist souvenirs. It's a huge tourist trap of course, particularly at sunset, and a busy tourist village encircles the temple approach, but get there early morning and it's still a striking sight.

Arrival and information

Though there are occasional **bemos** from Denpasar's Ubung terminal direct to Tanah Lot, you'll probably end up having to go via **Kediri**, 12km northeast of the temple complex on the main Denpasar–Tabanan road. All Ubung (Denpasar)–Gilimanuk buses and bemos pass through Kediri (30min), whose bemo station is at the crossroads where the road branches left for Tanah Lot, right for central Tabanan and straight on for Gilimanuk via the bypass. Kediri–Tanah Lot bemos (25min) run fairly regularly in daylight hours, more frequently in the morning.

With your own transport, the prettiest **route to Tanah Lot** is via Kerobokan and Beraban, passing through classic rice terraces and traditional villages. Alternatively, come via the *subak* rice museum in nearby Tabanan (see p.278), or make a slight detour to the ceramic-producing village of Pejaten (see p.277). When it's time to leave you can arrange charter transport at the transport posts around the parking area (for example, to Kuta it will be Rp150,000), or telephone for a metered taxi – enquire at the **information office** in the parking area (℡0361/880361, ⓦwww .tanahlot.net; 7am–7pm). You'll find an **ATM**, several **exchange** booths and a wartel in Tanah Lot's tourist village, in front of *Dewi Sinta Cottages* hotel.

Accommodation

Tanah Lot all but dies after the last tour bus pulls away at about 7.30pm, so there's little incentive to stay here overnight, though there are a few **hotels**. The most convenient is *Dewi Sinta Cottages*, located in the tourist village beside the temple approach (℡0361/812933, ⓦwww.dewisinta.com; ❸), which has air-conditioned bungalows in reasonable grounds with a swimming pool and spa. Better value and set well away from the commercial clutter, about 700m back along the access road from the temple car park, *Pondok Wisata Astiti Graha* (℡0361/812955; Fan ❶, a/c ❸) is surrounded by ricefields and offers clean if rudimentary en-suite rooms with hot water. On an entirely different scale, the super-swanky five-star *Pan Pacific Bali Nirwana Resort* (℡0361/815900, ⓦwww.panpacific.com; ❼) occupies extensive grounds, has four swimming pools (strong currents make swimming in the sea dangerous here) and a highly praised Greg Norman-designed eighteen-hole golf course (℡0361/815960, ⓦwww.nirwanabaligolf.com).

The temple

Pura Tanah Lot (daylight hours; Rp10,000) is said to have been founded by the Hindu priest **Nirartha**, who sailed to Bali from Java during the sixteenth century. Legends describe how he was drawn to the site by a light beaming from a holy spring, but his arrival was not welcomed by the local priest, who demanded that the rival holy man leave. In response, Nirartha meditated so hard that he pushed the rock he was sitting on out into the sea. This became the Tanah Lot "island". He dedicated his new retreat to the god of the sea and transformed his scarf into poisonous snakes to protect the place. Ever since, Pura Tanah Lot has been one of the holiest places on Bali.

Because of its sacred status, only devotees are allowed to climb the stairway carved out of the rock face and enter the compounds; everyone else is confined to the patch of grey sand around the base of the rock, which gets submerged at high tide. When the waters are low enough, you can take a sip of **holy water** (*air suci*) from the spring that rises beneath the temple rock (donation requested) or view the holy coral **snakes** that frequent nooks in the cliff face. Otherwise, your best option is to climb up to the mainland **clifftop** for the best viewing angle. During the daytime most people loiter at the cliffside restaurants immediately to the south of the temple rock, but if you follow the clifftop path northwest instead, you'll also be rewarded with a panoramic view of the Bukit plateau on Bali's southernmost tip. The coast path continues north past small weather-beaten shrines that watch over the wild grey sands below and eventually reaches Yeh Gangga, about two hours' walk away (see p.279). Every evening at sunset (6.15pm; Rp50,000) the temple complex hosts a performance of the **Kecak dance** in its wonderfully atmospheric setting.

Eating

The coastal path alongside the temple complex is packed with **restaurants** affording prime views and predictably inflated prices. A cheaper option is *Depot Dini* next to *Pondok Wisata Astiti Graha*, about 700m before the Tanah Lot car park, where *nasi goreng* costs just Rp17,000.

Pejaten

About 6km northeast of Tanah Lot and signposted west off the Kediri–Tanah Lot road, the village of **PEJATEN** is famous as the place where most Balinese roof tiles and roof-crown ornaments (*ketu*) are made. Of more interest to tourists is the distinctive Pejaten **ceramic ware** designed with distinctive frog, gecko and monkey embellishments and glazed in pastel greens, blues and beiges. Although Pejaten ceramics are sold in the big resorts, you should get better prices and a bigger choice in the village itself, particularly at Tanteri's Ceramic shop in Banjar Simpangan in the centre of the village (☎0361/831948, ⓦtantericeramic.com). There are kilns dotted all over the village, each of them fuelled by coconut husks, which lie in piles along the roadside – this is about as industrial as rural Bali gets.

Tabanan and around

Despite being the former capital of the ancient kingdom of Tabanan and the administrative centre of Bali's most fertile district, **TABANAN** is a medium-sized town with little to encourage a protracted stop. Its one outstanding feature is the **Subak Museum**, an ethnographic exhibition about rice farming in Bali. To the north of the town, the **Bali Butterfly Park** and **Alas Kedaton Monkey Forest** offer quiet diversions that are unlikely to be overrun with visitors, and the visitor programme in the village of **Tunjuk** provides an insight into everyday rural living.

Arrival, information and accommodation

All Ubung (Denpasar)–Gilimanuk buses and **bemos** bypass Tabanan town centre, dropping passengers at the **Pesiapan terminal**, a major transport hub on the northwest edge of town serving Denpasar and Gilimanuk. Bright-yellow city bemos shuttle from Pesiapan into the town centre, 1.5km east, where you'll find **banks**, **ATMs**, **internet** access and the **post office**, on Jalan Gajah Mada and its continuation, Jalan Pahlawan. Several regional bemo services run out of Pesiapan, including to Kediri (for Tanah Lot and Taman Ayun in Mengwi), plus Yeh Gangga. For **accommodation**, if you get stranded the *Kuskus Indah Hotel* (☎0361/815373; fan ❶, a/c ❸), has clean rooms just a few metres west of the Pesiapan bemo station at Jl Pulau Batam 32. For an

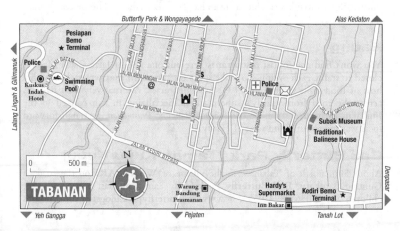

extended stay in the area, however, Yeh Gangga beach, 8km southwest (see p.279), and Lalang Linggah (Balian beach; see p.284), further west again, are much more enticing options.

The Town

Tabanan's two most interesting, though under-visited, sights are located on the eastern edge of town, within 100m of each other. The **Subak Museum** is signposted off the main Tabanan road in Banjar Senggulan, 1.5km east of Tabanan town centre and about the same distance west of the Kediri T-junction; the **Traditional Balinese House** is signed from the Subak Museum itself. Coming from Ubung, either alight at the Kediri junction and walk the 1.5km, or switch to a town-centre bemo at the Pesiapan terminal.

Subak Museum

Tabanan district has long been a major rice producer, and the **Subak Museum** or **Mandala Mathika Subak** (Mon–Thurs & Sat 8am–5pm, Fri 8am–1pm; Rp5000, children Rp3000) celebrates the role of the rice farmers' collectives (the *subak*) by describing traditional farming practices.

One of the most interesting displays explains the complex **irrigation system** used by every *subak* on the island – an unmechanized process that's been in operation since at least 600 AD. An underground tunnel connects the river water supply to the *subak* area, feeding hundreds of small channels that crisscross the land. A network of tiny wooden dams regulates the water flow along these channels: small wooden weirs block and divert the water, while lengths of castellated wood, called *tektek*, determine both the volume and the direction of the flow. Also worth looking out for are the **spiked wooden tweezers** for catching eels from the waterlogged paddies at night, and the **wooden nets** used to trap dragonflies, which are prized as delicacies by the Balinese.

Traditional Balinese House

Less than 100m from the Subak Museum, the **Traditional Balinese House** (same hours and ticket as Subak Museum) was purpose-built to illustrate the layout of a typical village home, comprising a series of thatched *bale* (pavilions) in a walled compound. Each *bale* has a specific function and its location is determined by the sacred Balinese direction *kaja* (towards the sacred Gunung Agung mountain) and its counterpoint *kelod* (away from the mountain, or towards the sea). For more information on Balinese architecture and a plan of a traditional house compound, see p.387.

Eating

You won't find any tourist **restaurants** here but one side of Jalan Gajah Mada is closed to traffic each evening to make space for the **night market**, packed with a host of food stalls serving up all the local delicacies. Alternatively *Ikan Bakar* is across the road from Hardy's supermarket, specializing in fish cooked in the Jimbaran barbecued style, or try *Warung Bandung Prasmanan*, a straightforward local warung about 700m west of Hardy's.

Bali Butterfly Park (Taman Kupu Kupu)

About 5km north of Tabanan, in the village of **WANASARI** on the road to Gunung Batukaru, **Bali Butterfly Park** (daily 8am–5pm, last entry 4pm; $6, children $3; ℡0361/894 0595, ⓦwww.balibutterflypark.blogspot.com) houses an impressive variety of butterflies from all over Indonesia (plus insects and spiders) in its small but pretty garden. The best time to visit is in the morning when the butterflies flit around most energetically. You'll need your own **transport** to get here, or you could try chartering a bemo from central Tabanan or Pesiapan terminal.

Tunjuk

The tiny, traditional village of **TUNJUK**, about 9km north of central Tabanan, hosts an interesting and pretty authentic "village life" programme organized through **Taman Sari Buwana** (reserve ahead on ☎0361/742 5929, ⓦwww.balivillagelife.com; $59 including transfers). It features visits to the local elementary school and a typical house compound that is home to fifteen different families (all related); there's also a rice-farming demonstration, a walk through the local area, cooking and lunch.

Alas Kedaton Monkey Forest

The monkeys at **Alas Kedaton Monkey Forest** (daily 8.30am–6pm; Rp10,000, children Rp5000), 3km north of the Kediri junction, are marginally less aggressive than many of their cousins elsewhere in Bali; if monkeys are your thing and/or the other monkey forests in Bali are too far away, this is a good place to get up close and personal in a simian way. Beware of getting landed with a (human) guide, whose main concern will be steering you to the souvenir stalls on the edge of the temple car park. Access to Alas Kedaton is via Kediri: either take a bemo from Denpasar's Ubung terminal to Kediri, then charter another one for the final 3km, or drive to Kediri, then follow signs for Marga.

Yeh Gangga beach

Heading west out of Tabanan, nearly every minor road that branches off south leads to the coast, a barely developed stretch of black sand notable for its strong currents and weird offshore rock formations. One of the most appealing sections is at **YEH GANGGA**, 10km southwest of Tabanan, whose two exceptionally attractive places to stay make this a good base from which to explore the area if you have your own transport. The currents make the sea too dangerous for swimming, but it's a dramatic scene, punctuated by huge rocks, and the **beach** stretches for miles in both directions. You can walk along the coast to Tanah Lot in around two hours, and the Pejaten ceramics village (see p.277) is within easy cycling distance.

The access road to Yeh Gangga is signposted off the main road about 4km west of the Kediri junction, or can be reached via back roads from Tanah Lot. At the end of the road you'll come to relaxed, unpretentious *Bali Wisata Bungalows* (☎0361/744 3561, ⓦwww.baliwisatabungalows.com; ❹), where a dozen spacious, fan-cooled and air-conditioned **bungalows**, some with hot water, are set in a shorefront garden, with nothing but the sea (with Java in the far distance) and the rice paddies in sight. There's a large saltwater swimming pool and massage service, plus plenty of information on local activities, car and motorbike rental, daily transport into Tabanan and a good **restaurant** – handy, too, if you're staying elsewhere in the area (though it's advisable to ring ahead).

About 1km northwest along the coast is *Waka Gangga* (☎0361/416256, ⓦwww.wakaexperience.com; bungalow ❽, villa with private pool ❾), one of the *Waka* group of small luxury hotels. Its ten exquisite, circular bungalows and two pool villas are scattered across terraced rice paddies and beautifully constructed from their trademark dark woods, rough-cut stone and natural fabrics; each has huge windows affording panoramic views of the ocean and ricefields. There's a swimming pool, restaurant and a spa.

North to Gunung Batukaru

Much of inland southwest Bali lies in the shadow of massive **Gunung Batukaru** (sometimes spelled Batukau; 2276m), the second-highest mountain on the island after Gunung Agung and one of the holiest. On the lower slopes of the holy mountain stands the beautiful **Pura Luhur Batukaru**, the focus of many pilgrimages.

Gunung Batukaru and its hinterland forms the **wettest** region of Bali, and the dense tropical rainforest that clothes the uppermost slopes has been designated a nature reserve, a particularly rewarding area for **birdwatching**. Lower down, on the gentler slopes that effectively stretch all the way to Tabanan, 21km southeast of Pura Luhur, the superior soil provides some of the most productive agricultural land on the island: the rice terraces around **Jatiluwih** are particularly scenic. Because of Batukaru's cool, damp microclimate, it's worth bringing warm clothes and rain gear up here, even if you're only making a brief visit to Pura Luhur Batukaru (817m above sea level) or are planning to stay in comfort in **Wongay-agede**, in eco-chic style in **Sarinbuana** or organically in **Munduk Lumbung**.

From Tabanan, with your own **transport**, you have a choice of two main **routes to Pura Luhur Batukaru**. The following account describes a circular tour to the temple and back, going up via Penatahan and Wongayagede and returning via Jatiluwih, Senganan and Penebel. Sarinbuana is accessed by a different road, described on p.283.

Most **tour** operators offer trips to Pura Luhur Batukaru, usually taking in the Jatiluwih rice terraces and either Pura Taman Ayun at Mengwi or Bedugul's Pura Ulun Danu; all prices include transfers from the main southern resorts. Adventure companies use the area for **mountain-biking**, **ATV** and **quad-bike** tours (see box, p.90).

Tabanan to Wongayagede (via Tengkudak)

Beyond Tabanan the main route to **Wongayagede** and Pura Luhur Batukaru passes the butterfly park in Wanasari (see p.278) and continues via archetypal Balinese scenes of shrub-lined villages and rice terraces before reaching a junction at **Buruan**. The right-hand fork will take you up to Gunung Batukaru via Penebel, Senganan and Jatiluwih, and is described in reverse on p.282.

In **TENGKUDAK**, at the northern edge of the village, about 500m before the road enters Wongayagede, the Catholic **church** (*gereja*) of St Martinus de Pons now draws its congregation from just five local Christian families, and is likely to be locked, but the facade is an interesting example of Balinese Christian architecture. Several Christian motifs have been carved onto an otherwise typical red-brick facade and the whole structure is crowned with a four-tiered Hindu-style *meru* tower.

Wongayagede

A night or two in **WONGAYAGEDE**, the village nearest to Pura Luhur Batukaru, is a rewarding experience. Remote and extremely scenic, it offers ample opportunity to explore the tranquil countryside and make the challenging trek up Gunung Batukaru.

The village is 2km south of the temple car park and the only **place to stay** here is the tranquil *Prana Dewi* (☎0361/736654, ⓦwww.balipranaresort.com; ❺), signposted west off the main road through the village (north of the side road to Jatiluwih). Occupying an idyllic spot within the ricefields and enjoying views of majestic Gunung Batukaru, *Prana Dewi*'s twelve stylish bungalows are thoughtfully designed with traditional features, picture windows and verandas, and are widely spaced amid the garden's streams and ponds; there are no fans or air-conditioning as it's cool up here at 636m. The **restaurant** is worth visiting in its own right: it serves lots of home-grown red rice, organic vegetables, salads and brown bread as well as curries and pasta (main courses Rp35,000–59,000). You can arrange **guides** for the

---

Climbing Gunung Batukaru

Because of the sacred status of Gunung Batukaru, most local villagers make the long trek up to the **summit** temple of this holy mountain once a year on the occasion of their own village temple ceremony. A few tourists also **climb** to the top, but it's quite an undertaking: a guide is essential and the best month is July, with the November–March rainy season being out of the question because of dangerously slippery trails, not to mention the high leech population. Gunung Batukaru is a long-extinct volcano and the dense **rainforest** that covers the slopes offers few clearings from which to admire the view, but a knowledgeable guide will point out some of the interesting plants, birds and butterflies, and perhaps even one of the resident rhesus monkeys. Constant shade and low-lying cloud make the atmosphere damp and the trails potentially hazardous whatever the season, so bring warm clothes, rainwear and decent shoes.

Of the several **routes** up Gunung Batukaru, the most accessible start from hotels in Sarinbuana (see p.283), Wongayagede (see above) and Sanda (see p.299). The Sarinbuana route is the easiest (about 4hr to the top) and Sanda the most taxing (about 6hr), though all three routes converge at a point known as Munduk Ngandang for the final two-and-a-half-hour slog to the **summit**. On a clear day the crater of Batukaru and the lakes of Bedugul plus Lombok and Java are visible. Camping near the top is an option, giving you the advantage of being up there for sunrise. For an easier hike, consider simply doing the route to Munduk Ngandang and back. The descent from the summit usually takes three to five hours.

Guides for Batukaru treks can be arranged through the hotels mentioned above, or with the guys who hang around Pura Luhur Batukaru. They all offer short hikes partway up the slopes to various of the mountain's shrines as well as return day-hikes to the summit; arrangements for overnight stays should be discussed direct. The temple guides **charge** per guide and do not supply water or food (note that beef is not permitted on the mountain): Rp250,000 per guide for jungle trekking (2–3hr) or Rp800,000 for the day-return to the summit with a maximum group size of eight. Booking a guide through your hotel usually costs more (from Rp600,000/person to the summit and back), but this includes transport to and from the start/finish, food and water and they may also supply more than one guide per group.

Gunung Batukaru trek here (see box, p.281), as well as for less taxing local walks. *Prana Dewi* also holds regular yoga and meditation **retreats** (from $380 for four nights/five days full-board).

Pura Luhur Batukaru

Usually silent except for its resident orchestra of cicadas and frogs, **Pura Luhur Batukaru** (Rp10,000 donation includes sarong and sash) is one of Bali's nine directional temples (*kayangan jagat*), the guardian of the west, and does full justice to its epithet the "Garden Temple". The grassy courtyards are planted with flowering hibiscus, Javanese ixora and cempaka shrubs, and the montane forest that carpets the slopes of Gunung Batukaru encroaches on the compound's perimeters. The monuments are encrusted with moss, and a web of paths fans out to solitary shrines set further into the forest. Batukaru's **bird** population includes bright green woodpecker-like barbets, scarlet minivets, olive-green grey-headed flycatchers and possibly even scarlet-headed flowerpeckers in the temple treetops.

Pura Luhur Batukaru is thought to have become a holy site in the eleventh century and was later consecrated by the rajas of the kingdom of Tabanan who made it into their state temple and dedicated shrines here to their ancestral gods. Many of the thatched *meru* now standing inside the **inner sanctuary** still represent a particular branch or ancestor of the Tabanan royal family. The most important shrine, though, is the unusual seven-tiered pagoda, which is dedicated to Mahadewa, the god of Gunung Batukaru. To the east of the main temple compound, a large square **pond** has been dug to represent and honour the gods of nearby Danau Tamblingan, which lies immediately to the north of Gunung Batukaru. Pura Luhur continues to play an important role in the lives of Balinese Hindus. Members of local *subak* groups draw holy water from the pond for use in agricultural ceremonies, and at the annual Galungan festivities truckloads of devotees travel long distances to pay their respects and make offerings.

In deference to Pura Luhur's extremely sacred status, there are strict **rules of admission** posted at the entrance. Aside from the usual prohibitions, such as menstruating women and those who have been recently bereaved, Batukaru also bars pregnant women and new mothers (who are considered ritually impure for 42 days after the birth), as well as "mad ladies/gentleman".

Wongayagede to Tabanan (via Jatiluwih)

The road to Jatiluwih branches east from Wongayagede about 2.5km south of Pura Luhur, and then winds through some of the most famous rice-paddy vistas on Bali, offering expansive panoramas over the gently sloping terraces and, afternoon cloud cover permitting, background shots of Gunung Batukaru as well. This whole area is known as **JATILUWIH**, after the hamlet of the same name, and has been designated a tourist site, which means every visitor has to pay a Rp10,000 toll (children Rp5000) to drive through. The road twists through ever more lush landscapes, dense with banana trees, *kopi bali* coffee plantations, fields of chilli peppers and tomato plants, ferns and *dadap* trees. Several **restaurants** make the most of the glorious vistas. Between May and October, Big Tree Farms, an organic farm near Jatiluwih (℡0361/461978, ⓦwww.bigtreebali.com) hosts six-course evening **Firefly Suppers**.

About 11km from Wongayagede, the road arrives at the **Senganan** road junction. The quickest route to the north and south coasts is the northeast (left) fork, a good 7.5km road that feeds into the main Denpasar–Bedugul–Singaraja artery at Pacung, 6km south of Bedugul and 25km north of Mengwi. For the slower, more scenic route to Buruan and Tabanan, take the southbound (right) fork that runs via the sizeable market town of **Penebel**.

At the Senganan junction it is also possible to follow the signs leading further north up the slopes of the mountain to the village of **Munduk Lumbung** and ⚒ *The Organic Farm* (☎0813/5337 6905, ⓦwww.theorganicfarmbali.com; all inclusive ❼), a small slice of rural paradise. **Accommodation** here is comfortable with electricity, thick mattresses and mosquito nets, but all water is carried in by the staff and it's a bit of a walk to the bungalows. While it's perfectly acceptable to sit and gawp at the stunning scenery all day, the real delight is to wander in the village with the owners, visit local houses, the hot springs, walk in the jungle, go on local cycle rides and learn about the organic farm. One of the owners, Wayan, is a great cook and the food is simply stunning. The farm does offer day programmes or, if you ring in advance, it is possible to stop by for **lunch**.

Sarinbuana and around

A few kilometres west of Wongayagede, the little village of **SARINBUANA**, tucked away in a remote spot on the southwestern slopes of Gunung Batukaru, is surrounded by some particularly inviting **accommodation**. The original is the delightful and award-winning *Sarinbuana Eco Lodge* (☎0361/743 5198, ⓦwww.baliecolodge.com; ❼ larger houses for four ❽), an exceptional place to stay run by committed environmentalists. Its five jungle-chic bungalows are dotted around a garden clearing in the rainforest, with rooms designed to make the most of the jungle surround-sound (provided by dozens of different birds among other creatures) and views across unadulterated forest. The *Lodge* is a genuinely community-conscious project: it grows its own organic fruit and veg, organizes **workshops** in Indonesian, Balinese calligraphy, massage, cookery and carving, and supports a local football team. Plenty of **activities** are offered, too, such as local guided walks to the summit of Gunung Batukaru (see p.281) and elsewhere, plus mountain-bike trips, including one all the way down to the coast. There are natural swimming pools and a waterfall in the grounds, and *Lodge* staff can also fix up cheaper **homestay** accommodation in the village (❹).

Sarinbuana Eco Lodge is located at 750m above sea level, on the edge of the *banjar* of **Biahan** in Sarinbuana village. Coming from south Bali or Ubud, access is via a road that begins 7km west of Tabanan, at kilometre-stone 30, and runs 15km north via the villages of Gadungan and Dalang; you can also get here via **Bajera** further west. Sarinbuana village itself is a couple of kilometres beyond the *Lodge*. Roads in the area are variable, so it's probably wise to ring the *Lodge* before setting off to find out which route is preferable at any time.

About a kilometre south of the *Lodge*, along the road through Gadungan and Dalang, *HomeMade Bungalows* (☎0815/5835 4611, ⓔabaduda@gmail.com; ❺) offers five simple but attractive bungalows made from recycled timbers with grass roofs and deep patios for relaxing.

Roughly 5km from the *Lodge* in **Kanciana** village, *Bali Eco Stay* (☎0813/3804 2326, ⓦwww.baliecostay.com; ❼) is also an organic venture with three fabulously large wooden bungalows with deep verandas and stunning views over the local organic ricefields. There's a local pool for swimming at a nearby waterfall and power is supplied by a small hydro-electric scheme. Cooking classes are available and the views from the restaurant at the top of the site are glorious.

The coast road to Medewi

Few tourists venture further west than Tanah Lot, but the stretch of coast beyond Tabanan holds some nice surprises at the black-sand beaches of **Balian** and **Medewi**. Just beyond Medewi, the spectacular cliff-side temple of **Pura Rambut Siwi** is almost as gloriously located as Tanah Lot but far less crowded with visitors.

The main road divides 16km west of Tabanan at the village of **Antosari**, splitting the thundering westbound Gilimanuk and Java traffic from the vehicles heading to Seririt and the north coast. The northbound road, served by Ubung (Denpasar)–Seririt buses and bemos, climbs through some impressive mountain scenery and is described on p.298.

To Lalang Linggah and Balian beach

Heading west through Antosari, the road to Gilimanuk drops down to the coast, affording fine sea views with southeast Java on the horizon, along with tantalizing inland panoramas of paddyfields. You can make more of these views by stopping off at *Soka Indah* hotel in **Soka**, where the road hits the coast (kilometre-stone 45). The tour-group-oriented *Gazebo* restaurant here has fine coastal views and you can follow the path from the car park down to the sea (Rp2000 for non-guests).

About 10km west of Antosari, the Gilimanuk road zips through **LALANG LINGGAH**, the village closest to **Balian beach**, a spiritually charged spot at the mouth of the Balian River. Its caves and headlands are frequented by priests and shamen, while surfers head here for the offshore breaks. The area is a pleasantly low-key place to hang out, for anybody, whether surfer or not, with some appealing accommodation – though take local advice on the vicious **current**, which makes almost the whole beach too dangerous for casual swimmers. Fields of rice run down to the grey-sand beach, spiked by occasional cashew trees and stands of clove, cinnamon and cocoa bushes. There are a few tracks to explore here and inland, up the course of the river, or just head west along the 30km-long beach.

All Ubung (Denpasar)–Gilimanuk **bemos** and buses pass through Lalang Linggah; they take about an hour and a quarter from Ubung or about half an hour from Medewi. Coming from the north coast you can take any Seririt–Ubung bemo as far as Antosari and then change onto the Ubung–Gilimanuk service. It's about 800m from the main road to the beach. All the accommodation can arrange onward **transport** to destinations throughout Bali (for example, Kuta Rp350,000). *Pondok Pitaya* **changes money** and there is **internet access** at the *Burger Gallery* at Suraberata Market, where the side road to Balian Beach leaves the main road.

Accommodation and eating

Balian Beach offers a growing choice of **accommodation**. Originally catering to surfers, this is now a laidback spot for anyone on any budget to while away a few days – as long as swimming in the sea is not a priority. None of it is more than five minutes' walk from the sea, with some set along the village road that runs down to the coast and the rest along the narrow shorefront road itself. A growing number of villas with rooms are also available to rent. All the following places are accessed via the road that runs south off the main Gilimanuk road, signed "Gajah Mina". For **food**, there are a few daytime warung on the beach, or try *Toki's Restaurant and Bar*

Volcanoes and ricefields

Situated in one of the most seismically active areas on the planet, Bali and Lombok are dominated by a series of majestic volcanoes. Their awesome peaks and deep crater lakes have great spiritual significance and their fertile volcanic soils nourish the abundant ricefields that fill the steeply terraced valleys. Even as a visitor you sense the power of these mountains as they loom over distant vistas, inspiring thoughts of summiteering or at the least inviting a gentle hike through the lush green paddyfields.

A temple ceremony at Besakih ▲

Gunung Rinjani and its crater lake, Segara Anak ▼

Gunung Agung

Gunung Agung's classic volcanic cone presides over every landscape in eastern Bali and on a fine day is even visible from Lombok across the Bali Strait. At 3142m it is the highest mountain on Bali and its most important. It is the spiritual centre of the island: many Balinese Hindus prefer to sleep with their heads towards Agung and it is always the corner of a ricefield closest to the mountain that gets planted first. The mother temple, **Besakih**, sits high on Agung's southwestern flanks and pilgrims trudge the mountain paths to make offerings to the spirits of ancestors believed to reside there. The fit and adventurous can engage a guide for the hard overnight slog to the summit for sunrise and views that take in much of the island. Agung is worthy of respect; it last erupted in 1963 (see p.206) with deadly and long-lasting results, and solidified lava flows are still visible today.

Gunung Rinjani

Rising to 3726m, **Gunung Rinjani** on Lombok is one of the highest peaks in Indonesia and the most challenging and rewarding trek on either island. It requires three tough days to reach the summit and get back, but shorter, equally rewarding hikes take in the crater rim and its magnificent views over the lake of **Segara Anak** and the still active volcanic cone of **Gunung Baru**. Alternatively you can simply admire the mountain from villages on its lower slopes, notably **Senaru** on the northern flank and **Tetebatu** on the southern. Considered sacred by both Hindus and Wetu Telu Muslims, the lake is also the focus of many pilgrimages, especially on full-moon nights and during Pekelem festival, usually in November.

Gunung Batur

The almost lunar landscape around **Gunung Batur** (1717m) in north Bali draws hundreds of tourists every day. The views are stunning. Batur's dramatic, and still active, volcanic cone rises beside the turquoise lake of **Danau Batur**, seen to finest advantage from the road that skirts the rim of the vast outer crater. Treks to the mountain top for sunrise take a bit of puff but most people can do it in only two or three hours and hikers are rewarded by fabulous views across near and distant peaks. After the descent, the hot springs beside the lake are ideal for easing tired muscles. The goddess of the crater lake is honoured at **Pura Ulun Danu Batur** on the crater rim; her bounty is seen as crucial to the continuing fertility of the island.

Lakes and temples

Pura Ulun Danu Bratan is the most photographed temple on Bali and with good reason. Built on a series of islands, its shrines appear to float on the surface of the lake against a backdrop of forested mountains. It's a striking spot but certainly not peaceful, as scores of pilgrims and busloads of tourists add to the traffic on the nearby main road; hire a pedal boat to find a more tranquil viewpoint.

The nearby lakes of **Tamblingan** and **Buyan** are less accessible, less frequented and arguably more atmospheric. Visit some of their small but venerable shoreside temples on a guided hike between the two lakes, via forests that are rich in birdlife. **Gunung Batukaru** is the furthest west of Bali's volcanic peaks, its upper slopes and summit thick with jungle, its primary temple, **Pura Luhur Batukaru**, full of dark, moss-encrusted statues and encroaching rainforest.

▲ Trekking on Gunung Batur

▼ Pura Ulun Danu Bratan

Ricefields

The quintessentially Indonesian landscape of valleys sculpted into terraces of startling green ricefields, or *sawah*, is common throughout the islands. The fertile volcanic soil, plentiful sunshine and regular downpours create ideal growing conditions that sustain at least two crops a year, and an ancient system of *subak* (irrigation cooperatives; see p.389) helps ensure that resources are shared.

Many restaurants and hotels occupy beautiful locations overlooking ricefields, and there are plenty of scenic drives too. Better still, go for a walk, either by yourself or on an organized **ricefield trek**, taking in traditional villages, fruit orchards, craft workshops and of course those all important paddyfields. Our favourite areas include Jatiluwih (see p.282), Sidemen (p.209), Munduk (p.250), Tirtagangga (p.225), Sekumpul (see p.265) and Tetebatu (p.346).

Rooms with a view

▶▶ **Alam Jiwa**, Ubud. Dramatic long-range views of Gunung Agung with classic ricefields in the foreground; all from your own balcony. See p.161

▶▶ **Kubu Tani**, Sidemen. Veranda vistas across the tropical garden to the ricefields and Gunung Agung. See p.208

▶▶ **Mahagiri**, Rendang. Extraordinary outlook across a valley of paddies to Agung. See p.207

▶▶ **Prana Dewi**, Wongayagede. A classic vista of ricefields and forest, framed by Gunung Batukaru. See p.281

▶▶ **The Organic Farm**, Munduk Lumbung. Glorious outlook across forest and jungle to the peaks around Gunung Batukaru. See p.283

▶▶ **Rinjani Mountain Garden**, near Senaru, Lombok. Panoramic views encompassing Rinjani and the surrounding fields. See p.344

at *Pondok Pitaya*, which has an unbeatable location overlooking the waves (and refills plastic water bottles). Alternatively, *Tom's Garden Café* at *Pondok Pisces* is cheaper and has a good range of Indonesian favourites with plenty of veggie options.

Ayu Homestay ☏0878/6328 1244. Just up from the beach, offering a range of fan rooms, some bigger than others and some with upstairs verandas and good views. Nothing fancy but good value. ❷–❸

Kubu Balian Beach ☏0815/5861 5061, ⓦwww .kububalian.com. If this falls within your price bracket or you're travelling as a family or in a larger group, this place is unbeatable. It's located up on the hill above the beach with just four huge, well-built and well-maintained "bungalows" (some have two storeys), with deep verandas, a pool, hot water and kitchens. Bungalows sleep two (❹), four (❻) and six (❼) people.

Made's Homestay ☏0812/396 3335. Just on the corner where the road turns left and starts down to the beach, this homestay offers three basic rooms (with fan and cold water) in a quiet

spot with good countryside views from the restaurant. ❸

Pondok Pisces Shorefront road and riverside ☏0361/780 1735, ⓦwww.pondokpiscesbali.com. This long-running little place offers a range of comfortable accommodation (all of it fan-cooled) in rooms, bungalows and villas in two different locations; near the road to the beach and in a garden location beside the Balian River. Swimming in the river is safe. The larger places are suitable for families. Rooms ❺, villas ❻–❼

Pondok Pitaya ☏0819/9984 9054, ⓦwww .baliansurf.com. Set at the end of the road just before the beach, this place has ten pretty basic rooms, some bigger than others, all with fan and cold water. The big draw here is the pool just above the beach and the brilliantly laidback restaurant area. ❹

Medewi beach

As it skirts the coastline, the 25km stretch of road between Lalang Linggah and Medewi beach crosses more than a dozen rivers, each one streaming down from the Batukaru mountain range, watering kilometre after kilometre of stunningly lush land en route. Rice paddies dominate the landscape, some even dropping to the shoreline, but this area is also a big producer of coconuts, vanilla pods, cloves, cocoa beans and coffee. If you're passing through, a pleasant and popular place for a **meal** with sea breezes is *Café Nyuir Indah* at kilometre-stone 60, which has a vast array of Indonesian, including vegetarian, food at reasonable prices (*nasi goreng* Rp10,000).

MEDEWI village sits on the main Tabanan–Gilimanuk road at kilometre-stone 72, served by frequent bemos and buses (about 2hr from Ubung), and is famous for its surf. Its black-sand **beach** is used primarily by local fishermen, but is fronted by a small enclave of sea-view bungalows catering mainly to **surfers**: the light current and fairly benign waves make this a popular spot for novices. You can also rent boats here, for snorkelling or fishing.

Accommodation and eating

The **accommodation** is located along the short lane (300m or so) leading from the main road to the coast and along the beach itself. All the places to stay have attached **restaurants**.

CSB Beach Inn About 600m east of central Medewi, via beach or road ☏0813/3866 7288. A quiet, well-kept losmen with eighteen large, clean, en-suite fan and a/c rooms offering views over the shorefront ricefields and the 300m track through them that leads down to the beach. Some rooms have hot water. Fan ❸, a/c ❹

Gede Medewi beachfront ☏0812/397 6668. Super-cheap accommodation in eight primitive but acceptable en-suite rooms (fan and cold water) in two-storey blocks behind the restaurant that's right on the shore. ❶

Hotel Pantai Medewi, aka **Medewi Beach Cottages** Medewi beachfront ☏0365/470 0080. The cheapest fan rooms here are poor value though their more expensive a/c cottages with hot water in outdoor bathrooms occupy seafront positions and are set in pleasant gardens with a swimming pool. Fan ❷, a/c ❻

Kelapa Retreat Pekutatan, 5km east of central Medewi ☏ 0361/805 3535, ⊛ www.balikelapa .com. This place is in a whole different league of style, opulence and cost from anything else in the area. The villas are startling white and minimalist, with straight lines and modern art; they range down to the pool, coast and restaurant and feature every imaginable luxury. ❽

Mai Malu The first accommodation on the road to the beach from the main road ☏ 0365/470 0068,

✉ elga.rumley@yahoo.com. Eight simple but clean and reasonably maintained rooms just behind the restaurant. All have fans and cold-water bathrooms attached. ❶

Puri Dajuma Cottages Pekutatan, 3km east of central Medewi by road, or a 30min walk along the shore ☏ 0365/43955, ⊛ www.dajuma .com. Well-located seafront hotel with suites in a new block and bungalows in the lush tropical garden, with pool, spa and *hammam*. All rooms are comfortable and attractive with a/c and hot water in garden bathrooms. There's a programme of cultural workshops and interesting trips around the region and as far as eastern Java. ❼

Pura Rambut Siwi

When the sixteenth-century Hindu priest Nirartha sailed across from Java, he paused at this spot 16km west of modern-day Medewi and pronounced it a holy site. On leaving, he donated a lock of his hair to the villagers, who duly erected a temple and named it **Pura Rambut Siwi**, "the temple for worshipping the hair" (donation Rp10,000 including sarong), which is now highly revered by the Balinese. It is easily reached on one of the Denpasar–Gilimanuk **bemos** or **buses**, which drop you at the head of the 750m access road to the temple.

Nirartha's hair is enshrined, along with some of his clothing, in a sandalwood box buried deep inside the central three-tiered *meru* in the inner courtyard, which is inaccessible to casual visitors but can be admired from alongside its south-facing **kori agung** (gateway). Built in tiers of red brick and ornamented with fierce stonecarvings of open-mouthed Bhoma, the gateway gives direct access to the cliff face and frames a stunning view of the Bali Strait. The figure that stands in the middle of the stairway, staring out to sea with his right arm raised, is said to be looking sorrowfully at Java (you can see Mount Bromo quite distinctly from here), bemoaning the ascendance of Islam over the Hindu kingdom of Majapahit. Gently stepped garden terraces of frangipani and stubby palm trees connect the outer gateway with the **shrine to Dewi Sri**, goddess of rice and of water, and hence of prosperity, that balances on the cliff edge. Descending the rock-cut steps to the charcoal-black-sand beach, you'll find a string of tiny cave temples tucked into the cliff face to the left of the stairway.

The far west

The coast road continues west from Medewi and Pura Rambut Siwi to the town of **Negara**, formerly the home of the Jembrana royal family and still the administrative capital of Jembrana district. It is graced with wide boulevards, a large number of mosques and a noticeably Islamic feel – though there's no particular reason to stop. Beyond Negara, the landscape of the **far west** changes dramatically, becoming noticeably drier and more rugged. The thickly forested, cloud-capped mountain slopes shelter very few villages and much of the land is protected by

Bali's Forestry Department, with the most important habitats conserved as **Bali Barat National Park**. Few tourists explore the park – the only one on the island – but it can be rewarding for birdwatchers and also harbours some of Bali's best coral reefs, around **Pulau Menjangan** (**Deer Island**).

If you're arriving from Java, the port town of **Gilimanuk** will be your first introduction to Bali. Other than Bali's most famous chilli-chicken restaurant there's little to detain you in the town itself, but the Menjangan reefs and Pemuteran beach are just a few kilometres away, and good transport connections enable you to head either straight to Pemuteran or Lovina on the north coast or to Denpasar with connections to Ubud or the southern resorts.

Gilimanuk

Situated on the westernmost tip of Bali, less than 3km from East Java, the small, ribbon-like town of **GILIMANUK** is used by visitors mainly as a transit point for journeys to and from Java. A 24-hour ferry service crosses the Bali Strait so few travellers linger, and there's nothing much to see here except the silhouettes of Java's great volcanoes across the water. The **Bali Strait** is a notoriously difficult stretch of water to negotiate: although Bali and East Java are so close, the water is just 60m deep, and the current treacherous. (Despite this, it is occasionally swum; the world record, set in May 2006, is currently 29 minutes and 30 seconds). During the ice ages, it's likely that a land bridge connected the two islands, which both rest on the continental plate known as the Sunda shelf, enabling humans and other animals to walk between the two – something which may become a reality once more, if the controversial plans to construct a modern-day Bali–Java bridge ever come to fruition.

Skeletons and pottery shards found around Gilimanuk show that this area was inhabited at least as far back as 3000 BC and some of the Neolithic remains are on show at one of the archeological sites near the bay, **Museum Manusia Purba** (Mon–Fri 8am–4pm; donation; ☎0365/61328).

The one significant attraction round here is the chance to "**muck dive**" the cold, shallow, silty waters of Gilimanuk's **Secret Bay**, just east of the port, where juvenile fish and rare marine species are prolific and especially rewarding for macro-photographers. Any dive operator in Pemuteran (see p.296) or the south (see p.128) can organize a trip.

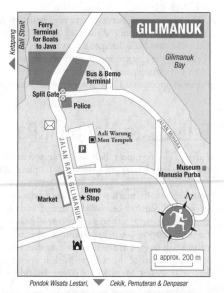

The other big draw is Gilimanuk's reputation for the finest **ayam betutu** (steamed chilli-chicken) on Bali (see below).

Practicalities

Gilimanuk's **bus** and **bemo terminal** is across from the ferry terminal and operates frequent

Pondok Wisata Lestari, ▼ *Cekik, Pemuteran & Denpasar*

Crossing to Java

Crossing the Bali Strait between Bali and Java is easy: there are no formalities, and onward transport facilities from both ports are frequent and efficient. If you're travelling quite a way into Java, to Probolinggo (for Mount Bromo), for example, or to Surabaya, Yogyakarta or Jakarta, the easiest option is to get an all-inclusive ticket from your starting point in Bali. The cheapest **long-distance buses** run out of Denpasar's Ubung bus and bemo terminal (see p.274), with pick-up points in Tabanan, Negara and sometimes Gilimanuk, but there are also more expensive **tourist shuttle buses** and **bus-and-train** combinations operating from tourist centres.

Ferries shuttle between Gilimanuk and Ketapang (East Java) and back again 24 hours a day (every 10min; 45min including loading and docking). **Tickets** are issued as you board: for foot passengers they cost Rp5700 (Rp4200 for children), for motorbikes Rp14,000–27,000 and cars Rp94,000 (including driver and passengers). Note that most car-rental agencies on Bali prohibit tourists from taking their vehicles to other islands (see p.33 for more).

Arriving in **Ketapang**, on Java, the Banyuwangi Baru train station is about 100m north of the ferry terminal and runs services to Surabaya, Probolinggo and Yogyakarta. The long-distance bus terminal is Sri Tanjung, 2km south of Ketapang and served by frequent bemos from the ferry terminal.

services to and from Denpasar's Ubung terminal, 128km away via Negara and the southwest coast; Singaraja, 88km away via Lovina; Padang Bai; and Amlapura. Services operate around the clock to Denpasar and Singaraja and from 4am to 4pm to Amlapura. Infuriatingly, at the time of writing, no **ATMs** in Gilimanuk were accepting foreign cards.

Accommodation in Gilimanuk is not tourist-oriented, as it's intended mainly for minimal overnight stops (which includes the brothel trade) or for long-stay contract workers. If you have to spend the night, try the twenty-room *Pondok Wisata Lestari* losmen and **restaurant** (T0365/61504; fan ❶, a/c and hot water ❸), about 2km southeast of the port along the road to Cekik, or 1.5km north of the Bali Barat National Park headquarters.

The most famous purveyor of **ayam betutu** is *Asli Warung Men Tempeh* (9am–6pm), whose simple warung at the back of the old bemo station is always crowded with fans. The late Men Tempeh's fiery recipe, now reproduced by her husband, entails slathering the chicken in a mouth-blasting mix of garlic, galangal, turmeric, ginger, chilli and shrimp paste and serving it with extra *sambal* (Rp33,000/half plate – plenty for most appetites). There are several copycat outlets in the area.

Bali Barat National Park

Parts of westernmost Bali are protected as **Bali Barat National Park** (**Taman Nasional Bali Barat**), whose 190 square kilometres of savannah, rainforest, monsoon forest, mangrove swamp and coral reef are home to a range of small animals, prolific marine life and approximately 160 species of bird – including a very small number of the elusive and endangered **Bali starling**, Bali's one true endemic creature, although if you really want to see it, a trip to Nusa Penida is a far better option (see p.139 for more information). This was also once the province of the Bali tiger, but the last one was shot here in the 1930s.

Just a fraction of the national park is open to the public and its biggest attraction by far is **Pulau Menjangan** (**Deer Island**), whose spectacular **coral reefs** draw snorkellers and divers from all over Bali. On dry land, encroachment and illegal tree-felling has degraded some of the forest and the handful of rarely-trekked **trails** are only worth it for the reasonably rewarding birdwatching, though you can also take a **boat trip** through the shoreline mangroves. If it's thrilling scenery you're after then trekking the slopes of the central volcanoes – Agung (see p.202), Batur (see p.239) or Batukaru (see p.280) – is decidedly more rewarding than the national park.

Arrival and information

The **national park headquarters** (Mon–Fri 8am–4pm) is conveniently located in the village of **CEKIK**, beside the Denpasar–Gilimanuk–Singaraja T-junction, 3km south of Gilimanuk; **getting here** is easy, as it's passed by all public transport between Ubung (Denpasar) and Gilimanuk, and between Singaraja and Gilimanuk (both routes are also useful for access to trail-heads). Anyone who enters Bali Barat National Park must be accompanied by a park **guide** and have a **permit**, which can both be arranged through the park headquarters or the branch offices at the campsite 100m north of the headquarters, at the Labuan Lalang jetty (see p.292), or at the crossing centre at Banyumandi.

Most of the **guides** are English-speaking and knowledgeable about the flora and fauna of Bali Barat; they don't necessarily need to be booked in advance and it does appear that charges are negotiable. The basic fee is Rp350,000 for a two-hour trek for up to two people (Rp450,000 for three to five people); more specialized treks will be more, for example, birdwatching for two to four hours (Rp500,000 for two people). If you don't have your own transport you'll also be expected to pay for any necessary bemo or boat charters. Having arranged a guide, the fee for most treks should include the Rp20,000 national park **permit**.

All the hotels in Pemuteran, 28km northeast of Cekik, organize **day-trips** to the park.

Accommodation and eating

Visitors are not permitted to **camp** in the park, but you can ask for permission to pitch your tent at Labuan Lalang's beach or, if student and other groups aren't in residence, at the Cekik national park headquarters, though that isn't necessarily a cheap option at Rp100,000 per person with only a toilet in the way of facilities. Otherwise, the closest decent **guesthouse** is *Pondok Wisata Lestari*, about 1.5km north of the park headquarters on the road into Gilimanuk; see p.288 for details. Alternatively, make for the appealing accommodation at Pemuteran (see p.294), 28km along the road towards Singaraja.

The upmarket **resorts** closer to or accessed from Labuan Lalang, rather than Cekik, offer guided walks and diving and snorkelling excursions. The fourteen elegantly simple wilderness bungalows plus two villas at *Waka Shorea* (T0362/94666, Wwww.wakaexperience.com; **7**) are just across the water from Pulau Menjangan on the shore of the Prapat Agung Peninsula, only accessible by hotel shuttle-boat from the Labuan Lalang jetty area. A couple of kilometres east of Labuan Lalang, at kilometre-marker 17, *The Menjangan* (T0362/94700, Wwww.themenjangan.com; **8**) offers top-class indulgent accommodation in the forest, at the beach or on the cliffs. There are plenty of activities on offer and the resort has its own riding stables. The highlight, however, is the **restaurant** in *The Tower*, a multi-storey wooden tower offering the best views of the whole area alongside your lunch, or a superbly romantic ambience after dark (sunset is the time to arrive to get the best of both worlds). It's open to non-residents; phone ahead for a reservation.

Other than at the resorts, there are no warung or food hawkers inside the national park, but carts set up outside the Cekik park headquarters every day. The nearest restaurant is at *Pondok Wisata Lestari*, 1.5km north up the road to Gilimanuk, or there are several warung at the Labuan Lalang jetty, 13km east of Cekik.

Exploring the mainland areas

The mainland sections of the park fall into two main areas: one north of the road between Cekik and Labuan Lalang, occupying the **Prapat Agung Peninsula**, and one south of the road, encompassing the neighbouring peaks of **Gunung Klatakan** and **Gunung Bakingan**.

Prapat Agung Peninsula and Teluk Terima

If your main interest is bird-spotting, opt for visiting the **Prapat Agung Peninsula**, whose monsoon forest harbours a large **bird population**, including flocks of the common yellow-vented bulbul and the loud-chirping black-naped oriole (1–2hr trek; Rp500,000 for two people). Other possible sightings include parakeets and fantails; the green jungle fowl; the pinky-brown spotted dove, which has a distinctive call; the black drongo, completely black save for its red eyes; and the tiny, bright-yellow-breasted olive-backed sunbird. This peninsula is also home to the last few Bali starlings that remain in the park. It is also possible to explore the peninsula by boat and walking or by **safari tour**, taking a vehicle along the beach for 15km each way (3–6hr; Rp800,000 for two people) or it is possible to get all the way round on a motorcycle. All of these options can be arranged at the park headquarters.

The two-hour walk around **Teluk Terima**, the bay west of the Labuan Lalang jetty and park office, passes through monsoon forest and coastal flats. It's a fruitful area for early-morning sightings of sea eagles, dollar birds and even the rufous-backed kingfisher, plus monkeys, deer and metre-long iguanas.

Gunung Klatakan–Gunung Bakingan trail

The **trail** between **Gunung Klatakan** and **Gunung Bakingan** (7hr; Rp825,000 for two people) is the most strenuous of the Bali Barat hikes. It starts at the Sumber Klampok ranger post and ascends the slopes of Gunung Klatakan and Gunung Bakingan, before returning to the main road a few kilometres east of Sumber Klampok. En route you pass through an area known as Watu Lesung, where grinding stones, possibly dating back to prehistoric times and now considered to be holy, were found. For the most part, the trail ascends through **tropical rainforest** thick with ferns, vines, spiky-stemmed rattan and viciously serrated pandanus palms, plus various epiphytic orchids. You're unlikely to spot much **wildlife** on this trail, but you'll probably hear the black monkeys swinging through the uppermost canopy, and you may stumble across a fearsome-looking wild boar – short-sighted and a bit stupid, boars tend to charge in a straight line regardless of where their prey happens to be, so just run away in zigzags if you encounter one. The most dramatic of the **birds** up here are the hornbills, while other commonly sighted birds include the multicoloured banded pitta, the bluey-grey dollarbird, the talking mynah, and the red-and-green jungle fowl. If you want to visit the area but don't fancy such a long hike, shorter treks are also possible; talk to the guides.

Gilimanuk Bay boat trip

An alternative to trekking in the area is to take a **boat trip** round mangrove-lined **Gilimanuk Bay**. Tiny *jukung* for two people cost Rp650,000 for two hours and should be arranged through the national park guides; you have to pay the permit fee on top. Note that the current off this shore is dangerously strong so it's not advisable to swim here, and sunbathing isn't that tempting either, as the beaches seem to end up with all the plastic bottles and other debris washed in across the Bali Strait.

Mangroves are best seen at low tide, when their exposed aerial roots form knotted archways above the muddy banks. Not only are these roots essential parts of the trees' breathing apparatus, but they also reclaim land for future mangroves by trapping debris into which the metre-long mangrove seedlings can fall. In this way, mangrove swamps also stabilize shifting mud and protect coastlines from erosion and the impact of tropical storms.

Boatmen should be able to get you close enough to the mangroves to spot resident **fiddler crabs** whose claws are said to be so strong they can open a can of beans. You might see **mudskippers** as well, specially adapted fish that can absorb atmospheric oxygen when out of the water, as long as they keep their outsides damp. **Crab-eating** or **long-tailed macaques** hang out along the shore, too, filling their outsized cheek pouches with fruit, mussels, small mammals and crabs (they're very good swimmers and divers).

On the exposed reef you'll see **sea cucumbers**, **sea horses**, and various species of **crab**, as well as heaps of seashells. You might also spot some dark-grey **Pacific reef egrets**.

Pulau Menjangan (Deer Island)

By far the most popular part of Bali Barat National Park is **Pulau Menjangan (Deer Island)**, a tiny uninhabited island 8km off the north coast, whose shoreline is encircled by some of the most spectacular **coral reefs** in Bali. Most visitors rate this as the best snorkelling spot on Bali, and divers place it high on their list too. Many divers and snorkellers come on organized **tours** from the south but it's cheaper and less tiring to base yourself at the nearby north-coast resorts of Pemuteran (see p.294) or Lovina (see p.252). For snorkellers it can work out even cheaper to head to Labuan Lalang or Banyumandi, the access ports for Menjangan, and club together with other tourists to hire a boat. As the island comes under the jurisdiction of the national park, hiring a **guide** is essential, but both the guide and boat transport can be arranged at the jetties in Banyumandi or Labuan Lalang without first checking in at the Cekik headquarters.

All snorkelling boats anchor off Menjangan's southeastern corner. If you take lunch, you can picnic on the beach there; there's no **food** or **water** on the island, nor any shade. Nor is there anything much to see, save for a small shrine and a freshwater spring, although a path encircles the flat, sandy-soiled island, which can be covered in about an hour.

The departure points for Pulau Menjangan are **Labuan Lalang**, just east of Teluk Terima, 13km from Cekik and 15km west of Pemuteran, or **Banyumandi**, 7km to the east of Labuhan Lalang. The only advantage of using Labuan Lalang is that it's right next to the main road, while Banyumandi is just over a kilometre from the main road. All Singaraja-bound **bemos** and **buses** from Gilimanuk (30min) or Cekik (20min), or any Gilimanuk-bound bemo or bus from Lovina (2hr) or Pemuteran (30min) ply the main road. If you're coming from the southwest coast, take any Ubung (Denpasar)–Gilimanuk bus or bemo to Cekik, then change onto the Singaraja-bound service. At each jetty there are **national park offices** (daily 7am–3pm), as well as **warung** where you can have a meal and buy food and water to take with you.

The **hiring of boats** to Pulau Menjangan from both spots is well organized through the national park offices. Boats can be hired at any time of day up to about 2pm (underwater visibility is best in the morning); they hold up to ten people and prices are fixed at Rp330,000 for a round trip of up to four hours, which includes thirty minutes' journey time each way. In addition to boat rental, you must pay Rp75,000 for a national park guide, who usually snorkels with you, plus Rp20,000 per person for the national park entry fee, Rp60,000 per person per hour national park snorkelling fee and Rp3000 insurance. The boat can be hired for as many extra hours as you like for Rp25,000 per hour (plus extra for the guide), and you can rent mask, fins and snorkel from the office for Rp40,000 a set. There are occasional reports of **thefts** from the boats while snorkellers are underwater, so leave valuables in your hotel and bring minimal money out with you, or keep it in a waterproof neck-pouch.

Life on the reef

Coral reefs are living organisms composed of a huge variety of marine life forms. The foundation of every reef is its ostensibly inanimate **stony coral** – hard constructions such as boulder, cabbage patch, mushroom and brain coral that feed on plankton, depend on direct sunlight for photosynthesis and extract calcium carbonate (limestone) from sea water. The polyps use this calcium carbonate to build new skeletons outside their bodies and this is how a reef is formed. It's an extraordinarily slow process, with colony growth averaging somewhere between 0.5cm and 2.8cm a year.

Fleshy, plant-like **soft coral**, such as dead man's fingers and elephant's ear, is also composed of polyps, but with flaccid internal skeletons built from protein rather than calcium. The lack of an external casing means the polyps' vivid colours are much more visible. **Horny coral**, or gorgonians, like sea whips and sea fans, are a cross between stony and soft coral. The marine animals, **sea anemones**, have the most obvious, and poisonous, tentacles of any marine creature, using them to trap fish and other large prey.

The algae and plankton that accumulate around coral colonies attract a catalogue of **reef fish**. Most are small, with exotically patterned skins for camouflage against the coral, and flattened bodies, broad tails and specially adapted fins for easy manoeuvring around the tiniest crannies. **Butterfly fish**, **moorish idols**, **clownfish**, **surgeonfish**, **trumpetfish** and **parrotfish** are among common reef dwellers.

The Menjangan reefs

The clear, shallow water between the mainland and Pulau Menjangan is protected from excessive winds and strong currents by the Prapat Agung Peninsula, and its **reefs** are mostly in good health, not least because patrols by national park officials and local dive operators has helped put a stop to the highly destructive practice of dynamite fishing. The reefs form a band 100m to 150m around the coastline, offering plenty of different **dive sites**, with drop-offs of 40m to 60m, first-class wall dives, and superb visibility ranging from 15m to 50m. As so many of the walls top out reasonably close to the surface, the snorkelling is also highly attractive. The larger pelagics aren't common visitors as the area is so protected from the colder currents from the open ocean but the area is a phenomenally rich trove of sea fans, barrel sponges, sea corals and all manner of soft and hard corals, and is a haven for masses of **reef fish**, nudibranchs and other reef dwellers. Popular sites include **Garden Eel Point** and **Pos II**, while for the more experienced the **Anker Wreck**, an old wooden *prahu*, sits at 45m off the western tip of the island.

Pura Jayaprana

For the best aerial view of Pulau Menjangan, stop off at **Pura Jayaprana** (donation), 12km east of Cekik and 1km west of Labuan Lalang. The temple itself is unimpressive, but its location at the top of a long flight of steps is superb, with panoramas that take in the island, its translucent waters and the shadows of the coral reefs beneath. Pura Jayaprana enshrines the grave of the eponymous local seventeenth-century folk hero who was murdered because the king wanted to marry the young man's wife. The wife, Layonsari, remained faithful to the memory of her dead husband and chose suicide over marriage to the king. The young couple's grave is in the shrine's inner courtyard.

Larger, less frequent visitors to the reefs of Bali and Lombok include the **moray eel**, **barracuda**, **sharks** and **manta rays**, whose extraordinary flatness, strange wing-like fins and massive size – up to 6m across and weighing some 1600kg – make it an astonishing presence. Weighing up to twice as much as rays, **mola mola** (also known as **oceanic sunfish**) measure some 3m top to bottom and about 2.5m end to end but you'll need to head across Bali to the south coast for a glimpse, though they are occasionally spotted off Nusa Lembongan. **Turtles** occasionally paddle around reef waters, too, but are fast becoming endangered in Bali (see p.108).

The reefs of Bali and Lombok also support countless species of **invertebrates**, including **sponges**, **nudibranchs** or **sea slugs** and the slug-like **sea cucumber**, which lies half-buried on the sea bed where it constantly ingests and excretes so much sand and mud that the combined force of those sea cucumbers in a three-square-kilometre area can together redistribute one million kilogrammes of sea-bed material a year.

Of the reef's numerous spiny echinoderms, the **sea urchins** have evil-looking black spines up to 35cm in length, though some varieties are covered in short, blunt spines or even flower-like pincers. The **crown-of-thorns starfish** is protected by venomous spines, which sheath the twenty or so "arms" that extend from its body and can measure up to 50cm in diameter. Disastrously for many reefs, the crown-of-thorns starfish feeds on coral, destroying as much as fifty square centimetres of stony coral in a 24-hour period.

The northwest coast

East of Cekik, the main Gilimanuk–Singaraja road emerges from Bali Barat National Park at Teluk Terima and runs along the narrow strip of the **northwest coast** between the sea and the mountains, passing Labuan Lalang and the Banyu-mandi turnings, access points for Pulau Menjangan (Deer Island; see p.291). Gradually the terrain becomes more interesting with dramatic mountain slopes dominating inland views as far as **Pemuteran**, a peaceful beach haven offering plenty of opportunities for snorkelling and diving. Continue east and you'll soon reach an even smaller hideaway at **Ume Anyar**, before the road divides: head east for Lovina and Singaraja (covered in Chapter 4) or south for the cool, refreshing hills around **Sanda** and **Belimbing**.

Pemuteran and around

The little fishing village of **PEMUTERAN**, 28km east of Cekik, is a pleasantly low-key area and a good place to base yourself for diving and snorkelling (both nearby and at Pulau Menjangan), especially as the small cluster of shoreside accommodation catering for every budget seems to make a conscious effort not to upset the village ambience. You can swim and snorkel in the safe, calm waters off the tree-shaded black-sand beach and make trips to the national park.

Arrival and information

All Gilimanuk–Singaraja **buses** and **bemos** pass through Pemuteran and will drop you in front of your chosen hotel; they take about thirty minutes from Labuan Lalang (or 1hr 20min from Lovina). If coming from Ubud or the south-coast

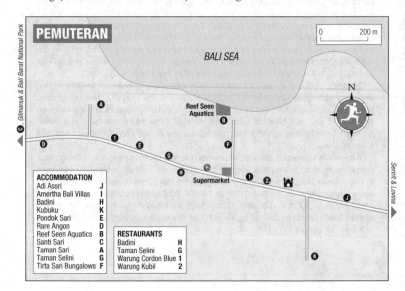

resorts, your fastest option is to take a **tourist shuttle bus** to Lovina and then hop on to a bus or bemo.

There are a couple of local shops on the main road and broadband **internet** at some hotels, as well as an internet café on the main road. The closest ATM is in Seririt (see p.298) but you can **change money** and travellers' cheques at *Rare Angon* homestay. The hospital in Seririt is the best option for minor ailments but for anything serious you'll have to go to one of the hospitals or clinics in Denpasar/Kuta (see p.122 & p.99).

Accommodation

All Pemuteran **accommodation** is accessed from the Gilimanuk–Singaraja road; the most attractive places occupy beachfront land. In high season, many places get booked up by divers, so it's best to reserve as far ahead as possible.

Adi Assri ☏0362/94838, ⓦwww.adiassri.com. Good-quality mid-range place with spacious grounds that go down to the beach. The attractive, comfortable bungalows feature plenty of natural wood. There are two restaurants, a spa and two pools. ⑤

Amertha Bali Villas ☏0362/94831, ⓦwww.amerthabalivillas.com. Fourteen glorious villas set in extensive, immaculate beachside grounds. Each villa has a number of self-contained suites which share a private pool. The spacious seafront garden also has its own large pool and restaurant. Suites ⑦

Badini ☏0813/5612 5711, ⓔoktadwina@yahoo .com. Basic but clean fan and cold-water rooms tucked behind the restaurant on the south side of the road. They're among the cheapest rooms in the resort and have nice little verandas. There's also a larger bungalow. ❸

Kubuku ☏0362/700 5225, ⓦwww.kubukubali .com. Just nine rooms in a large garden on the south side of the main road, so a bit of a walk to the beach. The two fan-cooled single rooms (❶) are a cheap option for individual travellers and all are clean and well-kept. Fan ❸, a/c ❹

Pondok Sari ☏0362/94738, ⓦwww.pondoksari .com. A lovely collection of large, stylishly designed a/c cottages all with attractive garden bathrooms spaced around a beautiful, mature tropical garden that runs down to the beach. Also has six deluxe options plus a villa, a pool and a spa. Minimum booking of six nights in the high season. Standard ❻, deluxe ❼, villa ❽

Rare Angon ☏0362/94747, ⓔrareangon@yahoo .co.id. Although it's across the main road, this tiny homestay is just 200m from the main beach area. Offers fan and a/c rooms in a small garden set back from the road. Fan ❹, a/c ❺

Reef Seen ☏0362/93001, ⓦwww.reefseenbali .com. Small row of good-quality bungalows with a/c and hot water set in the gardens of the beachside dive centre. Divers get priority with the accommodation but if they aren't full landlubbers can squeeze in. ❻

Santi Sari ☏0815/571 7629, ⓦwww.santisari hotel.com. Lovely, tranquil spot just 7km west of Pemuteran with ten gorgeous suites overlooking the coast (there's an adults-only policy). Rooms are vast, bathrooms stupendous and suites share private pools. The Mediterranean-accented gourmet restaurant offers plenty of fish and vegetarian options. The coastal and inland views are great and it doesn't come much more peaceful than this. ❽

Taman Sari ☏0362/93264, ⓦwww.balitamansari .com. A lovely place to stay, with an enormous range of accommodation from attractive bungalows, through suites to luxurious pool villas There's a pool, beachside restaurant and spa. Bungalows ❺, suites ❻, villas ❼

Taman Selini ☏0362/94746, ⓦwww.tamanselini .com. Small, elegant outfit with well-furnished bungalows, large garden bathrooms and day beds on the spacious verandas. The beachfront garden is lovely and there's a pretty pool and a Greek restaurant. ❼

Tirta Sari Bungalows ☏0878/6313 1567 ⓔwisnu_gupta@yahoo.com. Pretty little set of comfortable bungalows in a small garden, just back from the coast but also away from the main road. Fan ❹, a/c ❺

The beach and around

Development in Pemuteran centres on the curving palm-fringed **beach**, around a kilometre long from end to end, which is framed by the inland hills. Hotels discreetly line the beach, with their restaurants the most obvious signs of occupation, but it's all pretty quiet and low-key. The chief activities in Pemuteran – apart from lying on the black-sand **beach** – are **snorkelling** and **diving**. There are more than a dozen impressive reefs within very easy reach of Pemuteran's shore, to suit all interests and levels of ability, and marine life ranging in size from the occasional whale shark, turtle, giant clam or manta ray down to tiny nudibranchs and glass shrimp via corals, fans, sponges and fish such as, grouper, sweetlips, pipefish, surgeonfish, triggerfish, and wrasse. Most divers and snorkellers based in Pemuteran will take at least one trip to nearby **Pulau Menjangan** but there are also plenty of underwater reasons to linger in Pemuteran.

Diving and snorkelling aside, all the Pemuteran hotels organize **day-trips** to local sights as well as **hikes** through Bali Barat National Park. Reef Seen Aquatics offers sunrise and sunset **boat rides**, and also runs a **turtle-hatching** project at its dive centre (Rp25,000 donation, plus Rp100,000 to release a turtle). Green, Olive Ridley and hawksbill turtles all have nesting sites in the Pemuteran area, but all three species are fast becoming endangered (see box, p.108), and their eggs are particularly prized. To combat this, Reef Seen purchases eggs from fishermen for a little above market price and the turtles are hatched and reared before being released off the Pemuteran coast; seven thousand have been released in the last two years.

Pemuteran reefs

Local people and local dive operators have, in recent years, developed a real understanding of the **environmental value** of the reefs and considerable efforts have been made to repair earlier damage caused by the bad practices of local fishermen and unavoidable environmental factors. One initiative was the Karang Lestari Pemuteran project (ⓦ www.globalcoral.org), just off the Pemuteran shore, using the pioneering "**Biorock**" process, which encourages new growth by continuously passing a low electrical current through the stony coral, causing minerals to build up at about four times the normal speed (see box, p.330 for more on this process). The **Reef Gardeners** is an initiative to train local people as divers to maintain the Biorock structures, carry out work to maintain the health of the reefs and establish new sites.

Pemuteran dive centres

Pemuteran's **dive centres** all run diving and snorkelling trips to local reefs as well as to Pulau Menjangan; some also go to Gilimanuk's Secret Bay, to Puri Jati near Seririt, and to Tulamben on Bali's east coast. Several do night dives, nitrox diving and macro-photography trips. On the beach in front of the hotels, between *Sari Amertha* and *Taman Selini*, you'll find Reef Seen Aquatics (☎0362/93001, ⓦwww.reefseenbali .com); Werner Lau at both *Pondok Sari* and *Matahari Beach Resort* (*Pondok Sari* ☎0362/92337, *Matahari* ☎0362/92312, ⓦwww.wernerlau.com); Sea Rovers Dive at *Hotel Adi Assri* (☎0811/385 7118, ⓦwww.searovers.net) and Bali Diving Academy Pemuteran at *Taman Sari* (☎0361/270252, ⓦwww.scubali.com).

Two boat **dives** on the Pemuteran reefs averages Rp1.03million including all equipment; two dives around Pulau Menjangan costs about Rp1.25million inclusive of equipment and national park fees. **Dive courses** are available. **Snorkelling** trips cost Rp160,000 per person to the Pemuteran reefs (2hr plus equipment rental), or about Rp400,000 per person to Menjangan (6hr plus equipment rental and national park fees of Rp20,000 entrance plus Rp60,000 snorkelling fee), though small groups of snorkellers will probably find it cheaper if less convenient to arrange boats from Labuan Lalang or Banyumandi (see p.292). If you just want to do your own thing and snorkel off the beach, the village association booth on the beach between *Pondok Sari* and *Taman Sari* rents out equipment (Rp50,000 for three hours).

Of the naturally occurring sites, **Canyon Wreck**, featuring a 30m wooden Bugis schooner resting in a coral canyon, is among the more dramatic. Of the artificially created sites, the **Ships Graveyard**, where three fishing boats have been sunk to attract coral growth and fish life, is one area that features Biorock structures and is suitable for snorkellers as well as divers. **Temple Garden** consists of a 4m-high temple gateway and ten large statues, which have been submerged to provide a stunning underwater landscape as they are now beautifully covered in fans and attracting all sorts of marine life.

The **map** at Reef Seen Aquatics dive centre gives a good overview of all the sites.

Eating

All the hotels have **restaurants** serving freshly caught seafood, as well as the usual range of tourist and Indonesian standards, often in a beachside location. *Taman Selini's* menu of Greek dishes includes recommended mezze sets for Rp78,500, and their chocolate cake is fabulous (Rp32,900). *Warung Cordon Blue* on the main road has a vast, ambitious menu of Balinese, Asian and Western dishes in pretty blue and white surroundings (mains from Rp35,000) while the snack bar right beside the beach at *Reef Seen* offers sandwiches, drinks and cakes in the hours of daylight. Other good restaurant options include *Badini,* where the cocktails (Rp45,000) are a good bet and *Warung Kubil*, which has just four tables and a tiny menu (*nasi goreng* Rp15,000).

To Seririt and the road south

Seven kilometres east of Pemuteran, the stark **Pura Agung Pulaki** peers down from the top of a weatherworn cliff face, making for a good viewpoint. The temple's history dates back to the sixteenth-century Javanese priest Nirartha, but the buildings are modern and overrun by a band of grey macaques. Most bemo drivers stop here on their first trip of the day to make an offering at the temple's roadside shrine and get sprinkled with holy water dished out by the attendant priest.

With its cool sea breezes, relatively temperate climate and moderately fertile soil, the stretch of the northwest coast between Pulaki and Seririt, 30km to the east, is ideal for **vines** and Bali's main wine-producer, Hatten Wines, has a big vineyard in this area, where grapes are harvested year-round. The other significant industry around here is **pearl farming**. Should you be in the market for a $29,000 necklace, or simply a $49 pendant – or are just interested in the process – you might want to visit the Atlas North Bali Pearl visitor centre and gallery, 14km east of Pemuteran in the village of Penyabangan – it's 700m along a track from the main road. Tours are offered daily (10am–3pm; 45min; Rp50,000, children under 14 free; @www.atlassouthseapearl.com.au) and feature an introduction to the four-year growing process and advice on how to distinguish real from fake pearls and freshwater from seawater ones. If you just want to browse the shop or buy it's open 9.30am–5.30pm.

Ume Anyar and Puri Jati

Continuing east, about 1.5km short of Seririt you reach the village of **UME ANYAR**, where signs point you north off the main road to the accommodation. The local beach, sometimes known as **Puri Jati**, or PJ, is famous as a **muck-diving** destination (the practice of diving in sandy-bottomed bays in search of the elusive marine life that hides there). It's rich in juvenile fish and rare species and particularly good for macro-photography, so several dive operators around Bali run trips here.

The most established **place to stay**, *Zen Resort Bali* (T0362/93578, Wwww .zenresortbali.com; ●), 600m from the road and about 250m from the beach, commands fine views over surrounding vineyards and to the sea beyond, and makes a tranquil base, not least because of the extensive programme of thirty different Ayurvedic therapies offered here (there's a resident Ayurvedic doctor and a number of therapists). Its fourteen air-conditioned rooms are stylishly contemporary (the "sunset"-view ones are best and enjoy huge terraces and sunken patio baths) and there's also a beautiful infinity pool, daily yoga and meditation sessions plus an in-house diving centre. Closer to the beach, *Ganesha Bali Retreat and Villas* (T0821/4530 4627, Wganesha-bali.com; ●) offers eight great-quality villas with all amenities and a lovely spa, pool and restaurant, all of which are set back a little from the beach. Chinese and herbal medicine, as well as massage, are the specialities here and there are medicinal herbs growing in the grounds. For larger groups or families, the *Ja'a Bali* villa (T0061/416 974 611, Wwww.jaabali.com; $1500/week) is a beautifully appointed three-bedroom villa right on the coast nearby.

Seririt

The town of **SERIRIT** is chiefly of interest to travellers as a junction and for its banks and **ATMs** (there's a BNI bank and ATM on Jalan Gajah Mada near the market). The main north-coast road slices through the town centre, travelled by frequent dark-red Gilimanuk–Lovina–Singaraja bemos (Lovina is 13km to the east); this is also the departure point for the scenic back road to Munduk, Danau Bratan and Bedugul (see p.250). Most importantly, though, Seririt stands at the head of the most westerly route between the north and south coasts, described below, and served by frequent Seririt–Ubung (Denpasar) **bemos**.

To the south coast

The road from Seririt to the south coast commands some breathtakingly lovely views as it crosses through the mountains, rice-growing valleys and small hilltop villages of Bali's central spine. Seven kilometres south of Seririt the road branches southeast for Mayong and Danau Tamblingan, an area that's described on p.249. On the southbound road, the first great viewpoint comes 12km south of Seririt, after **Busung Biu**, where you can stop in a lay-by to admire the vista of rice terraces tumbling down into the valley, framed by the peaks of Gunung Batukaru to the southeast.

The road divides at the village of **Pupuan**, 22km south of Seririt, the site of a 100m-high waterfall called **Blahmantung**. Despite the height, the falls are less than spectacular, only really worth visiting in February or March when water levels are high from several months of rain. The 1.7km-long access road is steep and rutted, signed just beyond the southernmost limit of Pupuan; you can walk it in about half an hour.

Pupuan to Pekutatan (via Tista)

From Pupuan, the more westerly route takes you on a slow, twisting course west via the ridgetop settlements of **Kemoning** (where you can veer off south, via Ceking and Bangal, down a road that ends just west of Balian beach; see p.284) and **Tegalasaih**, and then south through clove plantations to **Tista**. Beyond Tista, the road parallels the Pulukan River and soon passes right through the middle of an enormous fig tree at **Bunut Bolong** (a famous local sight but not worth a special trip). About 10km south of the tree, the road comes to a T-junction at **Pekutatan** on the main Tabanan–Gilimanuk road, 2km east of Medewi beach (see p.285).

Pupuan to Antosari (via Sanda and Belimbing)

The easterly branch of the road from Pupuan drops down through glorious mountainscapes affording impressive views of Gunung Batukaru to the east. On the way, you'll pass dozens of **coffee plantations**, many of them protected by liberal plantings of spindly-looking *dadap* ("coral") trees, the dead leaves of which provide fertilizer for the coffee plants, while the roots anchor the soil and prevent erosion. **Cacao** is also a big crop round here, and **cloves** too, which you often see drying on mats beside the road.

In the village of **SANDA**, about 30km from Seririt, one former coffee plantation has been turned into a small, charmingly colonial-style **hotel** and **restaurant**, ⚑ *Sanda Butik Villas* (☏0828/372 0055, ⓦwww.sandavillas.com; ❼), whose stylish rooms have enormous enclosed verandas overlooking the neighbouring plantations. A small patch of the original coffee plantation has been incorporated into the gorgeous hotel garden and there's a saltwater pool here, too, though the 761m elevation on the slopes of Gunung Batukaru means the temperature in Sanda is always refreshingly cool. In the early mornings you get grand views of Batukaru, and it's possible to hire a guide here for the **trek** from the village to the summit and back (see p.281 for more on climbing Gunung Batukaru), as well as for other local trips.

Some 11km further south, in a pretty valley in the village of **BELIMBING** sits the *Kebun* **hotel** (☏0361/780 6068, ⓦwww.kebunvilla.com; ❻), whose accommodation is located down the valley sides (visitors must be able to cope with steps) with lovely valley views and a great little swimming pool at the bottom. Trekking and cycling can be arranged. Even if you don't stay you can soak up the glorious views from a seat in the breezy **café** up on the roadside, which has an excellent Indonesian and international menu (main courses Rp40,000–50,000). There are a few other places to eat locally; *Warung Made* on the roadside a short distance south of *Kebun* also makes the most of the views.

Just over 8km south of Belimbing, the road meets the Denpasar–Gilimanuk highway at **Antosari** (see p.284), 16km west of Tabanan.

Travel details

Bemos and public buses

It's almost impossible to give the frequency with which bemos and public buses run: see Basics, p.30, for details. Journey times given are the minimum you can expect. Only direct bemo and bus routes are listed; for longer journeys, you'll have to go via either Denpasar's Ubung terminal (see p.274), Gilimanuk (see p.287), or Singaraja's Banyuasri terminal (see p.262). The nearest shuttle bus service runs out of Lovina on the north coast (see p.253).

Gilimanuk to: Amlapura (4hr); Antosari (2hr 15min); Cekik (10min); Denpasar (Ubung terminal; 3hr 15min); Kediri (for Tanah Lot; 2hr 45min); Labuan Lalang (for Pulau Menjangan; 25min); Lalang Linggah (for Balian beach; 2hr 15min); Lovina (2hr 15min); Medewi (1hr 45min); Negara (1hr); Padang Bai (5hr); Pemuteran (1hr); Seririt (1hr 30min); Singaraja (Banyuasri terminal; 2hr 30min); Tabanan (2hr 30min).
Pemuteran to: Cekik (50min); Gilimanuk (1hr); Labuan Lalang (for Pulau Menjangan; 30min); Lovina (1hr 15min); Seririt (45min); Singaraja (Banyuasri terminal; 1hr 30min).

Ubung (Denpasar) to: Antosari (1hr); Bedugul (1hr 30min); Cekik (3hr); Gilimanuk (3hr 15min); Jakarta, Java (24hr); Kediri (for Tanah Lot; 30min); Lalang Linggah (for Balian beach; 1hr 15min); Medewi (1hr 30min); Mengwi (30min); Munduk (30min); Negara (2hr 15min); Pupuan (2hr); Sanda (1hr 30min); Seririt (2hr); Singaraja (Sukasada terminal; 3hr); Solo (Java; 15hr); Surabaya (Java; 10hr); Tabanan (35min); Yogyakarta (Java; 15hr).

Boats

Gilimanuk to: Ketapang (East Java; every 10min; 45min).

Lombok and the Gili Islands

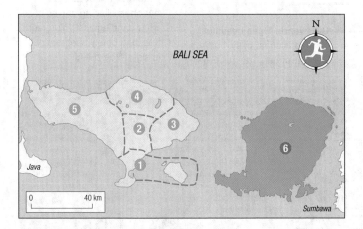

CHAPTER 6 # Highlights

✳ **Lombok pottery** From egg-cups to urns, Lombok's beautiful, distinctive pots make great souvenirs.
See p.312 & p.347

✳ **Sekotong and the Secret Islands** A dozen rarely visited islands offering excellent snorkelling, great diving and world-class surf.
See p.314

✳ **Senggigi** Choose your beach carefully and enjoy the best of Lombok's main resort.
See p.318

✳ **Gili Islands** Three beautiful car-free islands: busy, buzzy Gili Trawangan, tranquil Gili Meno and lively but local Gili Air. See p.324

✳ **Gunung Rinjani** The toughest mountain climb in either Lombok or Bali, but you can also just admire the view from the foothills. See p.340

✳ **Tetebatu** A chance to experience Sasak village life on Rinjani's southern slopes, with pretty views and enjoyable waterfall hikes.
See p.345

✳ **Kuta and the south-coast beaches** Blinding curves of white sand against wild green hills, and barely another soul in sight. See p.349

▲ Senggigi

Lombok and the Gili Islands

Located 35km due east of Bali, **Lombok** is inevitably compared with its more famous neighbour, although it differs in almost every way – physically it's drier, drought-prone and more rugged; culturally it is Islamic, with a far less developed artistic heritage; and even its flora and fauna are distinct, Lombok being on the Australasian side of the bio-geographical divide known as the Wallace Line (see box, p.308). Lombok also offers a very different experience for the visitor, with large tracts of unadulterated wilderness, plenty of empty beaches and a lot less traffic and commerce. Things are changing fast, but Lombok's essential character remains intact and accessible rather than buried beneath a veneer of tourist development.

The majority of Lombok's 3.1 million inhabitants are indigenous Muslim **Sasaks**. Their history is not well documented but they probably converted to Islam in the sixteenth century, with a minority following the animist-influenced Wetu Telu branch (see p.340). About ten percent of the population are of **Balinese** origin, practising Balinese Hinduism, introducing themselves as Balinese even though their families may have been on Lombok for several generations, and speaking both Balinese and Sasak. The history of the two islands has long been interlinked. The east Balinese kingdom of Karangasem invaded west Lombok in the seventeenth century and established a Balinese community that still thrives in modern-day Mataram. West Lombok's Balinese rulers extended their dominion over east Lombok, and were later also granted control of Karangasem by the invading Dutch. But the disempowered Sasaks of east Lombok fought back and in 1894 the Dutch seized the chance to take control, bringing the entire island of Lombok (and Karangasem) under colonial rule until Indonesian independence. In 1958 Lombok and neighbouring Sumbawa became jointly administered as the province of **Nusa Tenggara Barat**, or NTB (West Nusa Tenggara), with Mataram the provincial capital.

Measuring 80km by 70km, Lombok is slightly smaller than Bali. The mountainous **north** is dominated by the bulk of the sacred volcano **Gunung Rinjani**, at 3726m one of the highest peaks in Indonesia and a popular trekking destination. Most of the population lives in the **central plains**, in a broad, urbanized corridor that runs right across the island, from the capital, **Mataram**, in the west, to the port of **Labuhan Lombok** in the east. Lombok's largely agricultural **economy** is focused around this region, producing rice, cassava,

◄ Padang Bai, Benoa Harbour, Serangan Harbour, Nusa Lembongan & Amed

◄ Padang Bai (Bali)

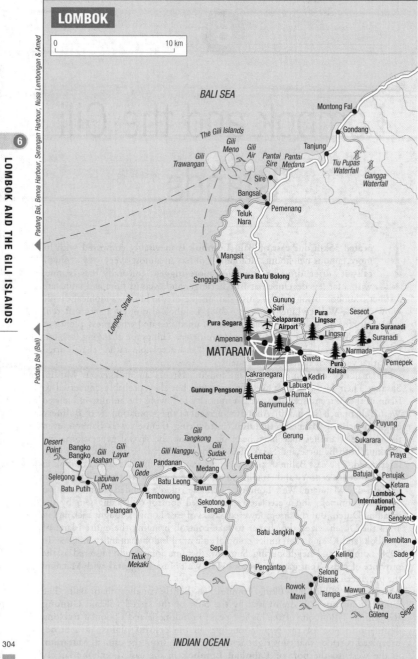

LOMBOK

0   10 km

BALI SEA

The Gili Islands

Gili Trawangan
Gili Meno
Gili Air

Montong Fal
Gondang
Tanjung

Pantai Sire
Pantai Medana

Tiu Pupas Waterfall
Gangga Waterfall

Sire
Bangsal
Pemenang

Teluk Nara

Mangsit

Senggigi
Pura Batu Bolong

Gunung Sari

Selaparang Airport
Pura Lingsar
Seseot

Pura Segara
Lingsar
Pura Suranadi

Ampenan
Suranadi

MATARAM
Sweta
Narmada

Lombok Strait

Cakranegara
Kediri
Pura Kalasa
Pemepek

Gunung Pengsong
Labuapi
Rumak

Banyumulek

Puyung

Gerung
Sukarara

Praya

Gili Tangkong
Gili Sudak

Gili Nanggu
Lembar
Batujai
Penujak

Desert Point
Bangko Bangko
Gili Layar
Gili Asahan
Pandanan
Medang
Ketara

Gili Gede
Batu Leong
Tawun
Lombok International Airport

Selegong
Labuhan Poh
Tembowong
Sekotong Tengah

Batu Putih
Sengkol

Pelangan
Batu Jangkih

Rembitan
Sade

Sepi
Keling

Teluk Mekaki
Blongas
Pengantap

Selong Blanak

Rowok
Mawi
Tampa
Mawun
Kuta

Are Goleng
Seger

INDIAN OCEAN

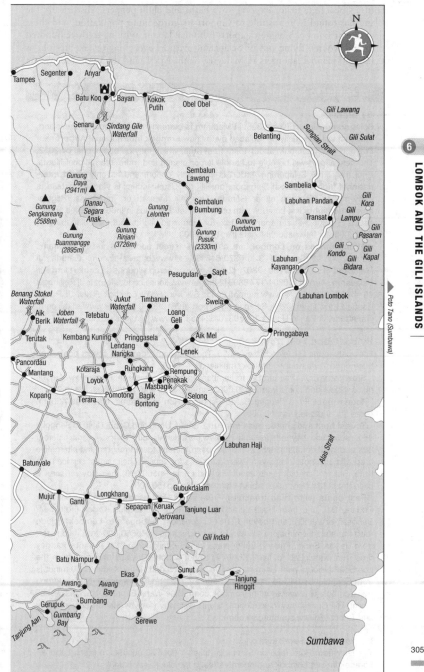

Tampes

Segenter • Anyar

Batu Koq • Bayan • Kokok Putih • Obel Obel

Senaru • *Sindang Gile Waterfall*

Belanting

Gili Lawang

Gili Sulat

Sungian Strait

Gunung Daya (2941m)

Danau Segara Anak

Gunung Lelonten

Sembalun Lawang

Sembalun Bumbung

Sambelia

Gunung Sengkareang (2588m)

Gunung Buanmangge (2895m)

Gunung Rinjani (3726m)

Gunung Pusuk (2330m)

Gunung Dundatrum

Labuhan Pandan

Transat

Gili Kora

Gili Lampu

Gili Pasaran

Labuhan Kayangan

Gili Kondo

Gili Kapal

Gili Bidara

Pesugulan • Sapit

Labuhan Lombok

Benang Stokel Waterfall

Aik Berik

Joben Waterfall

Tetebatu

Jukut Waterfall

Timbanuh

Loang Geli

Swela

Pringgabaya

Kembang Kuning • Pringgasela

Aik Mel

Terutak

Lendang Nangka

Lenek

Pancordau

Mantang

Kotaraja

Rungkang

Rempung

Loyok

Penakak

Kopang

Pomotong

Masbagik

Terara

Bagik Bontong

Selong

Labuhan Haji

Batunyale

Longkhang

Gubukdalam

Mujur • Ganti

Sepapan • Keruak • Tanjung Luar

Jerowaru

Gili Indah

Alas Strait

Batu Nampur

Ekas

Sunut

Tanjung Ringgit

Awang

Awang Bay

Gerupuk

Bumbang

Gumbang Bay

Serewe

Tanjung Aan

Sumbawa

cotton, tobacco (a major export), soya beans and chilli peppers. Historically the island has found it impossible to support its burgeoning population, and these days one of Lombok's biggest exports is human labour, with up to three hundred men and women flying out of Selaparang Airport every day to take up jobs as maids and manual labourers in Malaysia, Saudi Arabia and the UAE. Meanwhile

Travelling to Lombok

By plane
Selaparang Airport (see p.308) in Mataram is currently the only one on the island, though it will eventually be replaced by the new **Lombok International Airport** near Praya in south Lombok, about 15km from Kuta, which may be operational by 2012. The new airport will be able to handle larger planes and more international flights. Until that time, Selaparang Airport is your only option, and its only direct **international flights** are from Singapore on Silk Air. Usual access is **via Bali** instead, a thirty-minute flight on either Garuda, Lion Air, Merpati or TransNusa. Regular **domestic flights** link Lombok with other international hubs in Indonesia (see "Travel details", p.356). The **departure tax** for domestic flights out of Selaparang is Rp25,000; for international flights it's Rp100,000.

Airline offices on Lombok are as follows (street addresses are in Mataram): Batavia Air, Jl Sriwijaya 3 ☏0370/648998, ⓦwww.batavia-air.com; Garuda, Jl Majapahit 1 ☏0804/180 7807 (24hr), ⓦwww.garuda-indonesia.com; Lion Air, Selaparang Airport ☏0804/177 8899 (24hr), ⓦwww.lionair.co.id; Merpati, Jl Pejanggik 69 ☏0370/621111, ⓦwww.merpati.co.id; Silk Air, *Hotel Lombok Raya*, Jl Panca Usaha 11 ☏0370/628254, Selaparang Airport ☏0813/3990 3128, ⓦwww.silkair.com; TransNusa, Jl Panca Usaha 28 ☏0370/624555, ⓦwww.transnusa.co.id.

By boat (and bus) from Bali
For boats to the Gili Islands, see p.325. The following information covers boats, and bus connections, to the Lombok "mainland".

Slow ferry From Padang Bai to Lembar. An hourly service that operates 24 hour, takes 4 hour and costs from Rp36,000; can take cars and motorbikes. See p.211.

Tourist boat From Padang Bai to Senggigi. Run by Perama, leaves at 1.30pm, takes 5hr and costs Rp300,000.

Tourist boat and shuttle bus From Kuta, Sanur, Ubud and Candi Dasa to Senggigi or Lembar and beyond. Perama (ⓦwww.peramatour.com) offers several different bus-and-boat combinations, with pick-ups from main tourist resorts (and alternative drop-offs also possible); see relevant accounts for details. Their fastest service from Kuta, Bali to Senggigi takes about 3hr and costs Rp500,000; their slowest service uses the public ferry, takes about 8hr and costs Rp150,000.

Fast boats (with road transfers) From south Bali resorts via Benoa, Sanur or Padang Bai, and from Nusa Lembongan, to Teluk Nara/Teluk Kodek (both near Bangsal) or Lembar and beyond. Tickets for most fast boats to Lombok include road transfers from major Bali resorts; average price is Rp660,000 (less if you start from Benoa, Sanur, Padang Bai or Nusa Lembongan; see p.211) and total journey time from Kuta, Bali to Teluk Kodek is about 4 hour. Onward transport from the Lombok harbours near Bangsal is not usually included: Teluk Kodek is 30 minutes from Senggigi by private car (Rp175,000/car). Fast-boat operators include: Baruna Bali Lombok (ⓦwww.barunabalilombok.com); Blue Water Express (ⓦwww.bwsbali .com); Gili Cat (ⓦwww.gilicat.com); Island Getaway (ⓦwww.island-getaway.com); and Scoot (ⓦwww.scootcruise.com).

By boat from Sumbawa
The ferry from Poto Tano on Sumbawa takes 1 hour 30 minutes to reach Labuhan Lombok in east Lombok and operates round the clock (see p.348).

the provincial government is encouraging diversification on Lombok itself, with **tourism** one of several potential growth industries.

The main focus of Lombok tourism is its coast, most famously and successfully the trio of tiny islands known collectively as the **Gili Islands**: Gili Trawangan, Gili Meno and Gili Air. But Lombok offers many other shorelines that are equally stunning and far less crowded, especially around the **south coast**, which centres on the small surfers' resort of **Kuta**, and around **Sekotong** and **the southwest peninsula**, with its many enticingly tranquil white-sand islets. The most developed coastal resort is **Senggigi**, on the west coast, which makes the most convenient base for a Lombok stay, if not necessarily the most charming. Despite the many attractions, the **tourist presence** on Lombok is nowhere near as pervasive as on Bali. The island hosts only about 600,000 tourists a year, compared to the more than two million annual visitors that descend on Bali. As a result it's easy to find remote villages, unspoilt coastline and people still living traditional lives. However, **facilities** are often minimal and unsophisticated: you will find plenty of chic and luxurious accommodation on cosmopolitan Gili Trawangan, and in Senggigi, Pantai Sire and Pantai Medana, but elsewhere choices are fewer and simpler.

For local features and current **information**, consult the fortnightly *The Lombok Guide* (⊛www.thelombokguide.com) and browse the Lombok Lovers Forum (⊛lomboklovers.aforumfree.com), an invaluable place to post queries and scour the archives.

West Lombok

West Lombok – stretching from remote **Sekotong** and the southwest peninsula, through the port of **Lembar**, to the city of **Mataram**, then north to the established resort of **Senggigi** and its satellite beaches – has Lombok's biggest concentration of tourist facilities. With Selaparang Airport, and a major port and bus station in this area, most visitors pass through at some point.

Mataram and around

MATARAM is Lombok's principal city and the capital of Nusa Tenggara Barat province, or NTB (which comprises Lombok and the neighbouring island of Sumbawa). A sprawl of half-a-dozen districts, the city stretches about 8km west to east and is just 5km south of the tourist resort of Senggigi. Sights are thin on the ground and accommodation unappealing, so most visitors come for just a few hours, chiefly to browse the **markets** and the **Mataram Mall**, Lombok's most modern and best-stocked shopping emporium, and perhaps to visit the **museum** and sample some authentic Sasak food. Selaparang Airport is also in Mataram, but is to be replaced by the new airport at Praya in central Lombok (see opposite).

The administrative centre is **Mataram** itself, a district of broad, tree-lined avenues and imposing government buildings, including the immigration office, but not much else of interest. Immediately to the east, **Cakranegara**, or Cakra (pronounced *chakra*), is the commercial heart of the city and centres around the

The Wallace Line

Bali and Lombok are separated by the 35km-wide Lombok Strait, which is over 1300m deep in places. An imaginary boundary, the **Wallace Line**, runs through it, marking a division between the distribution of Asian and Australasian wildlife.

The boundary is named in honour of the nineteenth-century British naturalist **Sir Alfred Russell Wallace**. He suggested that during the ice ages, when the levels of the world's oceans dropped, animals were able to range overland from mainland Asia all the way down through Sumatra and Java to Bali, but were halted by the deep waters of the Lombok Strait. Similarly, animals from the south could roam only as far as Lombok on the other side of the strait.

Some evidence supports his theory. Bali and the islands to the west have creatures mostly common to **mainland Asia** (rabbits, monkeys, tigers), while the wildlife on Lombok and the islands to the east is more characteristic of **Australia and New Guinea** (parrots, marsupials, platypus and lizards).

However, research has since shown that many animal species are common to both Bali and Lombok; for example, you're likely to see crab-eating macaques and silver leaf monkeys both in Bali Barat National Park and on the slopes of Gunung Rinjani. Today naturalists refer not to Wallace's Line but to a zone of transition from the Asian type of animal life to the Australasian; in honour of Sir Alfred, this is known as "**Wallacea**".

buzzing **Mataram Mall**. It was the capital of Lombok in the eighteenth century, during the height of Balinese ascendancy on the island, and is still the most Balinese area of the island. Two of the city's main sights – **Puri Mayura** and **Pura Meru** – date from the Balinese period. In the far west of the city, closest to Senggigi, the old port town of **Ampenan** flourishes around the mouth of the Kali Jangkok. This is the most traditional and atmospheric part of the city, with narrow streets and a maze of shop-houses once inhabited by Chinese and Arab traders, plus the chaotic **Kebon Roek market**. The regional museum and tourist information office are both here.

Within easy reach of Mataram are several worthwhile attractions, including the **potteries of Banyumulek**, the formal gardens at **Taman Narmada** and the Hindu–Muslim temple of **Pura Lingsar**.

Arrival, information and city transport

Mataram is Lombok's busiest transport hub and has the most useful tourist information office on the island.

Arriving by air

Until the new Lombok International Airport opens in Praya (see p.306), all flights will continue to use tiny **Selaparang Airport** (℡0370/622987) in the north of the city. There's currency exchange, an ATM, hotel and tour desks at domestic arrivals (100m from international arrivals), as well as a **taxi** counter with fixed-price fares: Mataram Rp29,000; central Senggigi Rp57,500; Bangsal Rp115,000; Lembar Rp115,000; Kuta 225,000; and Senaru Rp360,000. For lower prices walk out of the airport gates and hail a metered taxi on the road. See the map opposite and p.338 for public transport details from the airport to Bangsal (for the Gili Islands).

Arriving by bus or bemo

If you're arriving by bus or bemo from anywhere except Senggigi, you'll come into **Mandalika bus terminal**, Lombok's main transport hub. It's in the suburb of

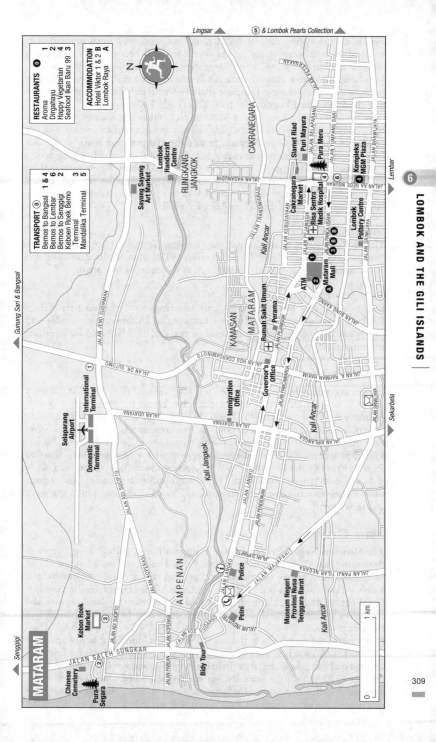

MATARAM

Chinese Cemetery

Pura Segara

JALAN SALEH SUNGKAR

Kebon Roek Market

AMPENAN

Bidy Tour

Police

Pelni

Museum Negeri Provinsi Nusa Tenggara Barat

Selaparang Airport

International Terminal

Domestic Terminal

JALAN ADI SUCIPTO

JALAN JEND SUDIRMAN

Immigration Office

Governor's Office

Rumah Sakit Umum

Perama

JALAN HOS COKRAMINOTO

JALAN PANCA MARGA

JALAN AIRLANGGA

JALAN UDAYANA

JALAN MAJAPAHIT

JALAN PANJI TILAR NEGARA

KAMASAN

MATARAM

RUNGKANG JANGKOK

Sayang Sayang Art Market

Lombok Handicraft Centre

CAKRANEGARA

Cakranegara Market

Slamet Riad

Puri Mayura

Pura Meru

Risa Sentra Medik Hospital

Lombok Pottery Centre

Kompleks MGM Plaza

JALAN SELAPARANG

JALAN TUMPANG SARI

JALAN PANCA USAHA

JALAN SRIWIJAYA

JALAN AA GEDE NGURAH

JALAN PEJANGGIK

JALAN BUNG KARNO

JALAN A. RAHMAN HAKIM

Kali Ancar

Kali Jangkok

Kali Ancar

Mataram Mall

Lingsar ▲ ⑤ & Lombok Pearls Collection ▲

Gunung Sari & Bangsal ▲

Senggigi ▲

Sekarbela ▶

Lembar ▶

RESTAURANTS ●
Aroma	1
Dirgahayu	2
Happy Vegetarian	4
Seafood Ikan Baru 99	3

ACCOMMODATION
Hotel Viktor 1 & 2	B
Lombok Raya	A

TRANSPORT ◎
Bemos to Bangsal	1 & 4
Bemos to Lembar	6
Bemos to Senggigi	2
Keboen Roek Bemo Terminal	3
Mandalika Terminal	5

N

1 km

0

6

LOMBOK AND THE GILI ISLANDS |

309

Bertais, on the eastern edge of the city, and is sometimes known as the Bertais terminal or even, confusingly, as the Sweta terminal because that's the suburb where it used to be located. As well as transport to destinations around Lombok, Mandalika also runs long-distance air-conditioned buses from and to major Indonesian cities, including Denpasar (Bali; 6–8hr; Rp250,000), Sumbawa Besar (6hr; Rp90,000) and Yogyakarta (Java; 22hr; Rp350,000).

For those catching a bemo out of Mataram **to Lembar** (for Sekotong or boats to Bali), there's a conveniently central pick-up point in Cakranegara, just south of the market on Jalan AA Gede Ngurah; bemos **for Bangsal** (for boats to the Gili Islands) pick up just around the corner, near Pura Meru on Jalan Tumpang Sari.

Arriving from **Senggigi**, you'll come into the **Kebon Roek terminal** in Ampenan. If travelling to Senggigi or on to Mangsit, there are frequent bemos throughout the day until about 6pm; pick them up on Jalan Saleh Sungkar, just north of the turn-off to the Kebon Roek terminal.

Information

The helpful regional **tourist office**, the Provincial Tourist Service for West Nusa Tenggara (Dinas Kabudayan Dan Pariwisata NTB; Mon–Thurs 7am–2pm, Fri 7–11am, Sat 7am–1pm; ☎0370/640471) is at Jl Langko 70, Ampenan.

City transport

Bright-yellow **city bemos** (Rp3000) ply numerous routes between the Kebon Roek and Mandalika terminals until late evening. Alternatively, reliable and clearly marked metered Blue Bird Lombok **taxis** (☎0370/627000) are plentiful; the initial pick-up charge is Rp4700.

Accommodation

Budget **accommodation** in Mataram is mostly rented "short time" and doesn't welcome tourists. A decent, tourist-friendly cheapie is *Hotel Viktor 1 & 2*, Jl Abimanyu 1, Cakranegara (☎0370/633830; fan ❶, a/c ❷), which has basic fan-cooled and air-conditioned rooms in two compounds across the lane from each other: *Viktor 1* is built losmen-style round a yard, while *Viktor 2* also has some upstairs rooms with balconies. Convenient for Mataram Mall, *Lombok Raya*, Jl Panca Usaha 11 (☎0370/632305, ⓦwww.lombokrayahotel.com; ❺) is a busy, mid-range place with 135 comfortable air-conditioned rooms overlooking an attractive pool and garden. There's wi-fi here, plus a spa, gym and travel agent.

The City

The **Museum Negeri Provinsi Nusa Tenggara Barat**, Jl Panji Tilar Negara 6, Ampenan (Tues–Thurs & Sun 8am–2pm, Fri 8–11am, Sat 8am–12.30pm, closed hols; Rp1000), focuses on the history, geology and culture of Lombok and Sumbawa and is worth a brief visit, even if English-language information is scant. Highlights include a scale model of Rinjani, collections of local textiles and sacred *kris* (daggers), and displays about the daily lives of Lombok's Sasak and Balinese people.

Otherwise, the main sight in the city is **Pura Meru** (donation; sarong and scarf available), also known as Pura Mayura, the largest Balinese temple on Lombok. Located on Jalan Selaparang in the Balinese neighbourhood of Cakranegara, it was built in 1720, during the period when the Balinese ruled west Lombok, in an attempt to unite the various Hindu factions on Lombok. The *candi bentar* (split gate) displaying scenes from the *Ramayana* is well worth lingering over. Across the road, the formal gardens and water features of **Puri Mayura** (Mayura Water Palace; daily 8am–6pm; entry by donation, plus Rp20,000 for optional guide) were built soon after, in 1744, but have been remodelled and are unremarkable.

Of Mataram's many **markets**, Kebon Roek in Ampenan is the most frantic, packed day and night with stalls selling food, household goods and all the necessities of daily life. The one in Cakranegara is slightly less hectic. The city's main modern shopping centre is **Mataram Mall**, where you'll find a department store, computer and phone shops, the Karisma **bookshop**, which stocks maps but nothing much in English, and, most usefully for anyone about to climb Rinjani, the Eiger **trekking outfitters** (second floor), which sells everything from walking boots to fleeces, at local prices.

The best one-stop craft centre is the **Sayang Sayang Art Market** (daily 9am–6pm), on Jalan Jend Sudirman, with stalls selling a big variety of handicrafts ranged around a car park. The **ikat** showroom and workshop Slamet Riady, at Jl Tanun 10, just off Jalan Hasanudin in Cakranegara (Sun–Fri 8am–6pm, Sat 8am–2pm; ☎0370/631196), produces high-quality weft *ikat* cloth very similar to that woven on Bali (see p.194) and you can also watch it being produced on site (except on Sundays).

For good-quality locally cultivated South Sea **pearls**, as well as imported freshwater pearls (see box above), follow the lead of domestic tourists, who flock to the Lombok Pearls Collection at Jl Achmad Yani 2 in Selagalas, just east of Cakranegara. For cheaper alternatives, try the suburb of Sekarbela, 2km south of Mataram, whose pearl shops (open Mon–Sat) line the main road west from the junction of Jalan Gajah Made and Jalan S Kaharudin.

Eating

After dark, a night market of **food stalls** lines Jalan Pejanggik, just east of Mataram Mall. During **Ramadan** many of the places listed below remain open during the day with a curtain at the window discreetly shielding diners. During the rest of the year, most places are open daily from around 10am to 9pm.

Aroma Jl Palapa I 2, Cakranegara. Delicious, packed Chinese restaurant where the decor is simple and the food is hot and fresh: try the fried squid with chilli sauce for Rp35,000.
Dirgahayu Jl Cilinaya 10. Local restaurant near Mataram Mall with a big Indonesian menu (take the dictionary). Excellent for cheap eats under Rp10,000.
Happy Vegetarian Food Beside the car park at Kompleks MGM Plaza, Jl AA Gede Ngurah.

Simple, cheap café that uses soy products instead of meat and fish in its vast range of typical Indonesian dishes such as *ayam bakso* ("chicken" soup), *bebek pelecing* ("duck" in chilli sauce) and *nasi rawon* ("black beef" soup). Mains from Rp10,000.
Seafood Ikan Baru 99 Jl Subak III 10, off Jl Panca Usaha. Grilled fish (*ikan bakar*) is the speciality at this popular spot. Fish is sold by weight: an *ons* is 200g.

Listings

Banks and exchange There are ATMs at all major banks, including BCA, Jl Pejanggik 67; BNI, Jl Langko 64; and Bank Danamon, Jl Pejanggik 117.

Consulates The closest consulates are on Bali (see p.59).

Dentist Dr Darmono, Jl Kebudayan 108, Mataram, speaks English (8am–noon & 5–9pm; ☏0370 6642385).

Hospital The best hospital is the private Risa Sentra Medik Hospital, close to Mataram Mall at Jl Pejanggik 115 (☏0370/625560 or 0370/632117). The public hospital, Rumah Sakit Umum, Jl Pejanggik 6, has a daily tourist clinic (9–11am; ☏0370/623498).

Immigration office Kantor Imigrasi, Jl Udayana 2, Mataram (Mon–Fri 8.30am–3pm; ☏0370/632520); visa extensions take much less time here than in Bali (see p.59).

Internet access In Mataram Mall.

Pelni ferries Advance tickets from the Pelni office, Jl Industri 1, Ampenan (Mon–Fri 9am–4pm, Sat 9am–noon; ☏0370/637212, ☲www.pelni.co.id), or on the day of departure from the port at Lembar (see opposite).

Recompression chamber Kantor Kesehatan Pelabuhan, Jl Adi Sucipto 13B, Ampenan (24hr hotline ☏0370/660 0333), but as there's no dive doctor here most dive centres prefer to use the one on Bali (see p.122).

Travel/tour agents Shuttle-bus, tourist-boat and long-distance-bus tickets to destinations on Lombok, Bali and beyond from Perama, Jl Pejanggik 66, Mataram (daily 8am–10pm; ☏0370/635928, ☲www.peramatour.com). Air tickets and tours from Bidy Tour, Jl Ragi Genep 17 (☏0370/632127, ☲www.bidytour-lombok.com).

Around Mataram

There are several enjoyable **excursions** from the city area: to the north, the road to Pemenang via Pusuk and its vast swathes of monkey-infested forest; to the south, the pottery centre of Banyumulek; to the east the gardens and temples of Narmada and Lingsar, and beyond that to the pretty countryside around Benang Stokel falls.

North via Gunung Sari and Pusuk Pass

Heading north out of Mataram on the Pemenang road, it's a couple of kilometres to **Gunung Sari**, the location of a lively morning market. From here the road is very scenic, twisting upwards through lush, towering forest to **Pusuk Pass**, then down again for 10km to the plains and the village of **Pemenang**, near Bangsal, the port for the Gili Islands (see p.338). Grey monkeys gather in groups along the roadside, and strategically located stalls sell bananas.

South to Banyumulek

The village of **BANYUMULEK**, about 7km south of Mataram, is one of the main **pottery** centres on the island, its access road filled with workshops and showrooms, including the recommended outlet Berkat Sabar (daily 8am–5pm). The range of designs is impressive – engraved, painted and plain, taking in everything from teacups to metre-high vases – and the pots come from all over Lombok as well as Banyumulek itself, though they're not especially cheap. Potters work on site and packing and shipping services are offered. Any Lembar-bound bemo from Mandalika terminal will drop you at the junction at **Rumak**, close to the enormous mosque, Masjid Jami' Asasuttaqwa, from where it's 1km west to the Banyumulek showrooms on foot or by cidomo.

East to Narmada and Pura Lingsar

In the market town of **NARMADA,** about 7km east of Mataram and served by frequent bemos from the Mandalika terminal, the gardens of **Taman Narmada** (daily 7.30am–5.30pm, Rp10,000 plus Rp20,000 for optional guide; swimming Sat–Thurs 7.30am–5.30pm, Rp10,000) are very popular with local families, especially at weekends. Built in 1805, they include a replica of Gunung Rinjani and its crater lake, made for the raja when he became too old to climb the real volcano to make his offering to the gods. More cynical commentators claim that he built the lake to lure local women to bathe while he watched from his pavilion. The grounds are extensive, and there's a public swimming pool and a Balinese temple, **Pura Kalasa**. The gardens are on the south side of the main Mataram–Labuhan Lombok highway, opposite the bemo terminal and daily market.

Pura Lingsar (daily 8am–6pm; admission by donation; optional guides Rp20,000), 5km northwest of Narmada, is used by Hindus as well as the Muslim Wetu Telu (see p.340) and is the site of one of Lombok's most enjoyable **festivals**. The temple was founded around 1714 and rebuilt in 1874; its highest, northernmost courtyard is the Hindu one, guarded by fierce monsters at the *candi bentar*, while the Wetu Telu area has a pond overlooked by a vivid statue of Wisnu, home to well-fed holy eels, which emerge for hard-boiled eggs brought by devotees. On the full moon of the seventh Sasak month (Nov or Dec), the local Hindu and Muslim communities cement their amicable co-existence and then ritualize their rivalries in a ceremony known as the **Perang Topat** or **Ketupat War**. Proceedings open with a procession, the presenting of offerings and prayers, and culminate in a good-humoured mock battle involving the raucous hurling of *ketupat* (packets of rice wrapped in leaves) and eggs at each other. Everyone participates, most wearing formal dress, and everyone gets splattered. Tourists are welcome to enjoy the spectacle. To get there, take a **bemo** from the Mandalika terminal to Narmada, then change on to a Lingsar bemo.

Benang Stokel Waterfall

If you're into waterfalls, or need an excuse for a very scenic drive through a landscape of rice terraces and tobacco fields that's reminiscent of Bali several decades ago (with added mosques), head for **Benang Stokel falls**, 21km northeast of Narmada. The trail to the falls is also the opening stretch of a challenging six-hour **hike** up to the crater rim of **Gunung Rinjani**, the least frequented of the routes up Lombok's majestic volcano (see p.343).

An easy ten-minute trail from the car park through light forest gets you to the unexceptional twin 10m-high cascades and bathing pool of **Benang Stokel** (Rp5000 plus compulsory guide), a hugely popular spot on Sundays, when it's busy with foodstalls. Continue along an undulating forest trail for another 45 minutes to reach the prettier, net-like spray of **Benang Kelambu falls**.

Road access to Benang Stokel is complicated and ill signed and may be best done with a local driver. Turn north off the main trans-island highway at **Pancordau**, 17km east of Mataram, and continue uphill via the village of Terutak (4km) to the village of **Aik Berik**, site of the falls car park, 11km from Pancordau.

Lembar

The main port for Bali is the huge natural harbour of **LEMBAR**, 22km south of Mataram. **Ferries** to and from Padang Bai operate round the clock (see p.211 for ferry details; if you're buying a ferry ticket for Bali, do so at the checkpoint booths, not from anyone else). There are also boats to Gili Nanggu (30min; Rp150,000/person). The town is industrial and swarms with traffic; there is no reason to linger.

The port has a reputation for **hassle**, with new arrivals being intimidated by transport touts loitering in the car park, so many tourists find it easier to pre-book **through-transport from Bali**, buying tickets that include the ferry and then a shuttle bus to Senggigi, Kuta or elsewhere. Perama and other shuttle-bus operators are allowed to wait for pre-booked guests in the port car park; **taxis**, however, whether pre-booked (phone Blue Bird Lombok Taksi on ☎0370/627000) or for hire, must wait at the rank 250m outside the port, near the *Tidar* hotel. A taxi to Senggigi should cost about Rp150,000, to Kuta about Rp200,000. The car-park **transport touts** quote Rp250,000 per car to Senggigi or Rp300,000 to Kuta. To ignore the touts you need to **exit** the port car park and walk 25m to the big "Keluar" (Exit) checkpoint. Once through the checkpoint it's 100m to a T-junction, where you turn right to reach the bemo rank 20m further on, and the taxi rank and *Tidar* hotel, beside a big archway, after another 100m. During daylight hours, public **bemos** run from the bemo rank to Mataram's Mandalika terminal (30min; Rp25,000) and Sekotong (1hr; Rp30,000). For other destinations in the southwest you'll probably have to charter: about Rp200,000 to Tawun or Rp350,000 to Bangko Bangko.

If you get stranded, there's basic **accommodation** and a small restaurant at *Tidar* (☎0878/6524 6460; ❶), just before the big archway on the main road, next to the taxi rank, 250m from the port. Staff are used to travellers arriving at all hours.

Sekotong and the southwest peninsula

Remote and beautiful, with an attractive shoreline and a scattering of picture-perfect white-sand islets just offshore, the **southwest peninsula** – often simply referred to as **Sekotong**, after one of the main settlements – is slowly beginning to take off as a tourist destination. The **snorkelling** is exceptional, with arguably the most pristine coral in Lombok, there's excellent **diving** and famously world-class **surfing** at Bangko Bangko's Desert Point. Accommodation is widely dispersed, and most visitors come simply for a day's snorkelling, but there are rooms for every budget and more in the pipeline. The main village centres are **Sekotong Tengah** and **Pelangan**, with **Tawun**, **Tembowong** and **Labuhan Poh** the easiest places to organize boats. Only a few of the islands (which are sometimes referred to as the "**Secret Islands**") are inhabited; there is tourist accommodation on **Gili Nanggu**, **Gili Gede** and **Gili Asahan**, and **Gili Sudak** has a restaurant.

It's 46km **from Lembar**, the port for ferries from Padang Bai in Bali, to Bangko Bangko at the tip of the peninsula. The route is served by public **bemos** from Lembar, but service is sporadic and many tourists end up having to charter; it's often less stressful, and sometimes cheaper, to pre-book **transport** via your

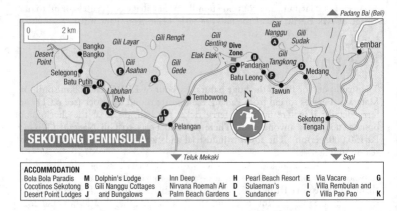

ACCOMMODATION								
Bola Bola Paradis	M	Dolphin's Lodge	F	Inn Deep	H	Pearl Beach Resort	E	Via Vacare	G
Cocotinos Sekotong	B	Gili Nanggu Cottages		Nirvana Roemah Air	D	Sulaeman's	I	Villa Rembulan and	
Desert Point Lodges	J	and Bungalows	A	Palm Beach Gardens	L	Sundancer	C	Villa Pao Pao	K

The Sekotong region used to be Lombok's poorest (along with Kuta), with all the problems that extreme deprivation brings, but its fortunes changed in 2008 following the discovery of **gold**. A mining company had found deposits but was scuppered by a bylaw that prohibited gold-mining on Lombok, so illegal freelancers immediately moved in, some with experience at mines in neighbouring Sumbawa but most novice chancers from the Sekotong area. An estimated three thousand people now mine for gold here, and the signs are everywhere: makeshift tarpaulin-sheeted camps dot the hillsides and every hamlet has its roadside rock-grinding machine. The rewards are enormous. Sekotong deposits are unusually rich and it's said that every 20kg sack of gold-bearing rock yields at least 0.5g of gold (worth around Rp150,000); some miners earn in a day up to fifty times what they'd make as a subsistence farmer. In the last few years, Sekotong's bamboo shacks have been transformed into good-sized concrete houses and many households now own a motorbike. But the cost is high: tunnels up to 30m deep are dug manually, miners breathe through pipes, and collapses are frequent, with reportedly an average of one death a day. The damage to the environment is also severe: hillsides are scalped of vegetation, with landslides a perpetual threat, and the use of mercury in the filtering process threatens to poison the water supply and decimate the fish population. The provincial government's response has been to amend its bylaw and take a stake in a professional mining company. Sekotong's fortunes look set to change again.

accommodation and then rent a motorbike locally. Senggigi tour operators offer **one-day boat-trips** to the islands. There are no international **ATMs** on the peninsula but some hotels will change money for you.

Sekotong Tengah to Tawun and Gili Nanggu

Heading south and west from Lembar, the main road winds inland through forested hills, via ricefields and coconut plantations and several small villages, before reaching **Sekotong Tengah**, one of the peninsula's principle settlements, 11km from Lembar and served by bemos from the port. A road runs 11km south from here to Sepi on the south coast. Continuing west to **MEDANG**, there's good diving nearby (see p.316) and unusual accommodation at *Nirvana Roemah Air* (T0370/646888, W www.floatingvilla.com; O), whose two bungalows float in the sea, on individual pontoons anchored offshore. They have cold-water bathrooms, fans and electricity – plus canoes and a telephone with which to communicate with the mainland; room service is an option. The shoreside **restaurant** makes a good refreshment stop. You can also rent a boat here (Rp100,000 return) to the sister café on Gili Sudak, which lies just offshore (see p.316).

The views of the islands become ever more enticing as you reach the harbour village and sweeping white-sand bay of **TAWUN** (also spelt Taun), 19km from Lembar. This is the usual place to organize boat rides and **snorkelling trips** out to the trio of **islands** visible from the shore: Gili Nanggu, Gili Tangkong and Gili Sudak. A day-trip taking in all three islands costs about Rp300,000 per boat (up to six people), plus Rp50,000 to rent a snorkel set; a transfer to Gili Nanggu is Rp125,000. Captain Rabiin speaks English (T0817/570 2031).

The three tiny islands are each encircled by white-sand beaches and are good for swimming. Lovely little **GILI NANGGU** (Rp5000 entry), a twenty-minute boat ride away, has excellent snorkelling, with lots of fish. It sees the most visitors, and suffers from a bit of a rubbish problem as a result. There are shady trees and lounging *berugaq* on the shore, as well as a restaurant and rudimentary thatched-hut **accommodation**, at *Gili Nanggu Cottages and Bungalows* (☏0370/623783, Ⓦwww.gilinanggu.com; ❸). You can also reach Gili Nanggu direct from Lembar (see p.313).

East of Gili Nanggu lies very quiet, uninhabited **Gili Tangkong**. East again, **Gili Sudak** has decent snorkelling at the reef just off its white-sand beach and a seafood **restaurant**.

Tawun to Elak Elak

Just 1.5km west of Tawun harbour, *Dolphin's Lodge* (☏0370/664 6444, Ⓦwww.lombok-cottages.com; ❺) sits right on the shore in the Balinese–Sasak village of **BATU LEONG**, offering three huge rooms in a couple of bamboo houses. Each has uninterrupted views of the three Gilis from their generous verandas, and come with DVD players, fans and cold-water bathrooms. The restaurant serves a small menu of Western and Indo dishes (from Rp25,000).

The southwest's most luxurious hotel, *Cocotinos Sekotong* (☏0819/3313 6089, Ⓦwww.cocotinos-sekotong.com; ❼), fronts its own 300m-long white-sand coral bay 1km west of Batu Leong. It's an attractive setup, with 28 cheerfully contemporary air-conditioned rooms and villas, all with DVD players and wi-fi. There's a sea-view pool, a spa, the Odyssea Divers dive centre (Ⓦwww.odysseadivers.com; two dives from Rp950,000) and boat trips for snorkelling.

Another kilometre brings you to **PANDANAN**, 23km from Lembar, where Dive Zone (☏0813/3954 4998, Ⓦwww.divezone-lombok.com), the longest-established **dive centre** in the area, is right on the beach; they charge from Rp750,000 for two dives (see box above for local dive info), can organize dive-and-stay packages and have accommodation on Gili Asahan (see p.318). Across the road is the blue-roofed white elephant of a resort development known as *Sundancer* (Ⓦwww.sundancerresort.com), still awaiting sufficient cash to open.

About 700m west of *Sundancer* (400m east of the Balai Budidaya Laut marine research complex), a dirt track snakes seawards, bringing you to the gorgeous sandy peninsula of **Elak Elak** (or Ela Ela), with great swimming and a sand spit at its northern tip that allows you to walk to miniature **Gili Genting** at low tide.

Tembowong and Gili Gede

Moving west again, **Tembowong**, 6km from *Sundancer* and about 12km from Tawun, provides access to **GILI GEDE**, the southwest's largest island, measuring about 4km from north to south. The island has half a dozen fishing hamlets around its coast but no paved roads and only a few motorbikes; walking round it takes about three hours. The shore is fringed with a mix of white-sand beaches and mangrove, offering fine views to the mainland hills and other nearby islands. The best **place to stay** is ☆ *Via Vacare* (☎0819/1590 4275, ⓦwww.viavacare .com; ❹), a beautifully designed and thoughtfully run retreat on the west coast with room notes that muse on "the art of doing nothing". The four huge bungalows all have sea views and there's also a backpackers' *berugaq* dorm with mattresses and nets (Rp60,000/person). The delicious meals are eaten communally and charged at Rp175,000 per person per day; electricity and running water are limited. All sorts of activities are offered, including snorkelling and visits to local healers; there's often yoga as well.

As for **transport** to the island, boatmen charge from Rp10,000 per person on the public service from Tembowong to Gili Gede, or Rp100,000 to charter the boat. To get to Tembowong it's about Rp200,000 by taxi from either Mataram or Lembar, or about Rp30,000 by public bemo from Lembar.

Pelangan

PELANGAN, 2km west of Tembowong, 33km from Lembar and 13km from Bangko Bangko, is the largest village in this part of the peninsula. The coast here is beautifully tranquil, with views to the nearby headland and across to Gili Gede, though in the wet season swimming's not so great, because of the rivers that empty into the bay.

Making the most of the setting are a couple of very nice **places to stay**. The calm, German-run *Palm Beach Gardens* (☎0818/0374 7553, ✉aniehof@web.de; ❶) is on the shore about 400m off the main road towards the west end of the village. Set beneath the coconut palms are five spotless and exceptionally good-value bungalows, all with sea views, fans and cold-water bathrooms; there is internet access, plus snorkel trips to nearby islands and diving with Dive Zone (see opposite). Booking is vital from May to September and December to January; phone ahead for transport from Lembar (about Rp150,000/chartered bemo).

Just 200m west along the coast, *Bola Bola Paradis* (☎0817/578 7355, ⓦwww .bolabolaparadis.com; ❹) has immaculate, idiosyncratic fan and cold-water rooms in two simple but well-thought-out octagonal buildings, plus three in the main building. Nearly all of them come with views over the neat seafront flower garden, though unfortunately they're close to quite a busy road. Boat trips are available. The attached ☆**restaurant** is pricey but excellent, cooking up a long and inventive menu that includes *sambal goreng* (a spicy stir-fry), *ayam taliwang* (chilli-fried Sasak chicken) and *fritto misto* (deep-fried seafood); mains start at Rp50,000.

West to Bangko Bangko

As more and more surfers head this way to take on the legendary Desert Point surf break at Bangko Bangko, an increasing number of places to stay are opening up along the 13km stretch of road between Pelangan and Bangko Bangko, at the end of the peninsula. The road skirts the dramatic, almost circular bay of **Labuhan Poh**, enclosed by forested hills and headlands, and takes in views of islands fringed with white sand. Accommodation is strung out along a 2.5km stretch of road around the village of **Batu Putih**, about 5km west of *Bola Bola*, less than 8km from Bangko Bangko. Just offshore is pretty little **Gili Asahan**, which has a tiny fishing village, a pearl farm and accommodation.

To get to Desert Point, drive west from *Sulaeman's* homestay in Batu Putih for 2km to Selegong village, where the sealed road ends, and continue 1km to an unsigned junction. The right fork takes you to the fishing village of **BANGKO**

BANGKO, 2.5km down the stony but passable track. Continue through the village to a wild beach with views of Nusa Penida. The left fork takes you via a much rougher 2km track to the **surf break** at **Desert Point**. From mid-May to September, and again in December, hundreds of surfers converge here from across the globe in search of its famously long barrels.

Accommodation and eating

Staff at every **place to stay** can arrange motorbike rental and snorkelling trips (Rp300,000/boat). Though not all have formal **restaurants**, they all provide meals on request. See the map on p.314 for accommodation locations.

Desert Point Lodges ✆0819/3676 7362, ⓦwww.desertpointlodges.com. Laidback place with four nice wood, thatch and bamboo *lumbung* in a flower garden next to *Villa Rembulan* and across from the beach. ❷

Inn Deep ✆0818/0629 9666, ⓦindoperfection .com. Efficient, friendly setup with five good-value bungalows, including one for families, and a restaurant. All rooms have a/c and DVD players and are by the shore, with fine views to Gili Asahan. ❹

Pearl Beach Resort ✆0813/3954 4998, ⓦwww .pearlbeach-resort.com. The only accommodation on Gili Asahan, this is a tiny resort and restaurant run by Dive Zone (see p.316). Shoreside bungalows have fans and hot water, and there's diving and

kayaking. Phone to reserve and organize a boat from Labuhan Poh. ❺

Sulaeman's ✆0817/578 7539. Simple, low-key homestay with eight rudimentary rooms, some sharing bathrooms. ❶

Villa Rembulan and Villa Pao Pao ✆0818/362788, ⓦwww.lombokvillas.co.uk. Some of the most luxurious accommodation on the peninsula, these twin properties, which sleep six and eight respectively, are across the road from the beach and have fabulous views. Both have vast, contemporary-styled a/c rooms, with kitchenette, DVD players and use of the pretty pool. Single rooms are sometimes available and there are a couple of cheaper bungalows further back. Bungalows ❸, villas ❼

Senggigi and around

Once Lombok's premier beach resort, **SENGGIGI** is these days in limbo, its greyish beaches trumped by the now easily accessible white-sand island idyll of Gili Trawangan, less than a couple of hours away, and its role as the closest resort to the airport soon to be eclipsed by Kuta, when the new airport eventually opens. As foreign tourists have looked elsewhere, **central Senggigi** seems to be focusing more on the domestic market, with a growing number of massage and karaoke joints along the broken pavements. It's not all bad news, however: there are some good hotels and restaurants in the central resort, and the outer beaches at **Batu Bolong** (a 10min walk south), and **Mangsit** and **Klui** (4–6km north) are genuinely appealing. The coastline is indisputably handsome, its 10km series of sandy, swimmable bays curving deeply between a sequence of dramatic headlands. And Senggigi does have the best tourist facilities on mainland Lombok: its many tour agencies and restaurants, plus its dive shops, souvenir shops and internet access continue to make it the most convenient base. Older, long-stay tourists in particular are drawn here for a few weeks in the sun, and an increasing number of expat villas are being built in the hills overlooking the coast.

The annual **Senggigi Festival** is well worth making the effort to get to, featuring several days of Lombok cultural performances, including classical dances, traditional stick fighting (*peresean*), costumed parades and music. It's usually, but not always, held in July, in Senggigi Square: check dates at ⓦwww .thelombokguide.com.

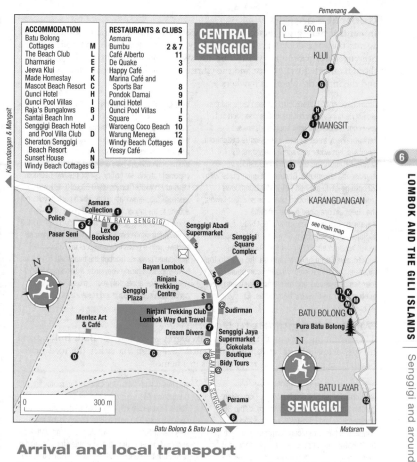

ACCOMMODATION
Batu Bolong Cottages	M
The Beach Club	L
Dharmarie	E
Jeeva Klui	F
Made Homestay	K
Mascot Beach Resort	C
Qunci Hotel	H
Qunci Pool Villas	I
Raja's Bungalows	B
Santai Beach Inn	J
Senggigi Beach Hotel and Pool Villa Club	D
Sheraton Senggigi Beach Resort	A
Sunset House	N
Windy Beach Cottages	G

RESTAURANTS & CLUBS
Asmara	1
Bumbu	2 & 7
Café Alberto	11
De Quake	3
Happy Café	6
Marina Café and Sports Bar	8
Pondok Damai	9
Qunci Hotel	H
Qunci Pool Villas	I
Square	5
Waroeng Coco Beach	10
Warung Menega	12
Windy Beach Cottages	G
Yessy Café	4

CENTRAL SENGGIGI

Arrival and local transport

Senggigi is less than 10km **from Selaparang Airport** (see p.308). For longer-distance travel from tourist centres in Bali (including Nusa Lembongan) and Lombok (including the Gili Islands), Perama **tourist shuttle buses** and boat/bus combinations are often the most economical option: see p.306 for travel to Lombok from Bali, and "Travel details" on p.355 for Lombok routes. Coming **from Mataram**, bemos depart at least every twenty minutes from the Keboen Roek terminal in Ampenan until about 6pm and run as far as Mangsit, so are also useful for travelling around the greater Senggigi area: central Senggigi to Mangsit should cost Rp3000. Metered Blue Bird Lombok **taxis** (☏0370/627000) are plentiful in Senggigi and can be flagged down or booked ahead; the 5km ride from Mangsit to central Senggigi should be about Rp15,000. **Rental cars and motorbikes** are widely available, as are cars with drivers (see p.322).

Accommodation

Good budget **accommodation** is hard to find, but there's at least one decent option in every area.

Central Senggigi

In **central Senggigi**, there's plenty happening, with restaurants, bars and tour agents on your doorstep. The two sandy bays, to the north and south of the *Senggigi Beach* promontory, are fine for swimming at all but the highest tides, though outside July, August and the Christmas holidays you may find it's just you and the indefatigable pearl hawkers.

Dharmarie ☎0370/693050. Eighteen large Indonesian-style bungalows, not in pristine condition but very comfortable and well appointed, are set beneath shady trees around an expansive beachfront lawn. A/c, hot water and some sea views. ❹
Mascot Beach Resort ☎0370/693365, ✉mascot@telkom.net. Central but quiet place with 22 cottage-style a/c and hot-water bungalows (some circular) set around spacious seafront lawns; the cheapest are close to the road. ❹
Raja's Bungalows ☎0812/373 4171, ✉Rajas22@yahoo.com. The only budget option worth recommending in central Senggigi is tucked away up a narrow path off the road to the mosque. Inside the small, walled compound the four fan bungalows are nicely furnished and have open-roofed cold-water bathrooms. ❷

Senggigi Beach Hotel and Pool Villa Club ☎0370/693210, ⓦwww.senggigibeach.aerowisata .com. Occupying an entire promontory, with access to two bays and extensive grounds that include a kids' play area, tennis courts, a decent pool and a spa, the rooms and cottages here are good value if not especially stylish; for luxury, opt for the two-bedroom villas at *Pool Villa Club* (☎0370/693210, ⓦwww .poolvillaclub.aerowisata.com), which each have direct access to the lagoon pool. Hotel ❻, pool villas ❽
Sheraton Senggigi Beach Resort ☎0370/693333, ⓦwww.sheraton.com/senggigi. A peaceful, upscale enclave with a great freeform pool and attractively manicured grounds fronting the beach. All 161 rooms have verandas facing seawards; there are also pool villas and one accessible room, plus a spa, dive centre and several bars and restaurants. ❽

South Senggigi: Batu Bolong

The swimming's good off the steeply raked grey-sand beach at **Batu Bolong** and it's just a ten-minute walk south of central Senggigi, via either the road or the beach (tide permitting), or two minutes in a bemo.

Batu Bolong Cottages ☎0370/693198, ✉bbcresort_lombok@yahoo.co.id. Occupying garden plots on both sides of the road, the 36 traditional, slightly old-fashioned fan and a/c bungalows here are nicely furnished but have fairly basic hot-water bathrooms; seaside ones cost more. Has a pool by the beach. Fan ❸, a/c ❹
The Beach Club ☎0370/693637, ⓦwww .thebeachclublombok.com. Four attractive bungalows in a beachside compound, each with traditional thatch-and-bamboo exteriors, and all mod cons inside (DVD, wi-fi, a/c and safety box) plus nice hot-water bathrooms. There's a pretty pool, too. The two "backpacker rooms" are small

and basic, with fans. Backpacker fan rooms ❸, a/c bungalows ❺
Made Homestay ☎0878/6561 8936, ✉ane_made @yahoo.com. The best budget option in the area, with half a dozen attractive losmen rooms, with fans and cold-water bathrooms, in a little strip across the road from the beach (and the *Café Alberto* pool, see p.323). Big discounts out of season. ❷
🏃 **Sunset House** ☎0370/692020, ⓦwww .sunsethouse-lombok.com. Enormous rooms with sea (and sunset) views, huge beds, spruce, contemporary decor, and all the trimmings – a/c, satellite TV, free wi-fi, big breakfasts and use of the generously sized beachside pool. ❺

North Senggigi: Mangsit and Klui

With just half a dozen beachfront hotels, a couple of tiny shops and a mosque, the beach is the focus at **Mangsit**, 4–5km north of central Senggigi; it has decent snorkelling at the northern end. Bemos shuttle into central Senggigi until 6pm, as do metered taxis. White-sand **Klui**, north over the headland from Mangsit, is very quiet.

Jeeva Klui Klui ☎0370/693035, ⓦwww.jeevaklui .com. The sole property on attractive white-sand Klui beach, this is a rather stylish modern boutique resort. Most of the "suites" have sea views through

their picture windows, and there's an infinity pool, wi-fi and fine views of Bali's Gunung Agung. ❼
Qunci Villas Mangsit ☎0370/693800, ⓦwww .quncivillas.com. Hugely popular design-conscious

beachfront hotel with two wings – *Qunci Hotel* and *Qunci Pool Villas* – all done out in cool, understated limestone and with original art on the walls. The pool villas are a little more upscale, with a luxurious pool, but both wings get rave reviews. A/c and wi-fi throughout. ❻

Santai Beach Inn Mangsit ☎0370/693038, ⓦwww.santaibeachinn.com. Excellent budget option. The very cheap *lumbung* rooms have tiny sleeping areas at the top of the ladder (and no door, but they're private enough) plus bathrooms downstairs. There are also more conventional double and triple thatched bungalows, some with hot water. There's wi-fi, and communal vegetarian/fish meals are served twice daily (not

included). The garden is by the sea but you have to walk 30m to get to the beach. *Lumbung* ❶, bungalows ❷

🏃 **Windy Beach Resort** Mangsit
☎0370/693191, ⓦwww.windybeach.com. Idyllically located on arguably the nicest stretch of beach in Senggigi – a 300m chunk of white-sand shoreline at the northern end of Mangsit – this is the perfect place to wind down undisturbed. The traditional-style bungalows are comfortable (hot water and wi-fi throughout) and set within an expansive tropical garden. There's a good pool, plus a kids' pool (Rp20,000 for non-residents), and decent snorkelling offshore. Significant discounts outside peak season. Fan ❺, a/c ❻

The resort and around

Senggigi's one sight is the small Balinese temple **Pura Batu Bolong**, which crowns a promontory at the southern end of Batu Bolong beach. It's built over an archway in the rock, the hole through which virgins were once supposedly sacrificed to appease the gods. Nowadays, when the tide is right, it offers access to Batu Layar beach and its famous fish restaurant (see p.323).

With your own transport, the spectacular **coastal road north** from central Senggigi to Pemenang (24km) makes a great day out, passing through small villages set behind sweeping, invariably empty, bays and stands of coconut palm. Wending up and over the steep headlands that separate the bays you get fine views of the Gili Islands – three tiny white-rimmed specks in a turquoise sea – and across to Gunung Agung on Bali. First of the beaches is **Karandangan**, with its charcoal-black sand, Sunday seafood warung, and a good restaurant (see p.323); **Mangsit** and **Klui** both have great beaches, with accommodation (see opposite); then there's Malimbu, the especially pretty whitish-sand **Nippah**, and Teluk Kodek and Teluk Nara (for fast boats to the Gilis and Bali, and with pearl farms offshore). There are occasional warung along the route, good for drinks and snacks, and there's nothing to stop you **swimming** off any of the lovely crescents of sand – outside of Sundays you'll likely be the only one in the water.

They don't mean to spoil your holiday

Walk along the beach or eat at a streetside restaurant in central Senggigi and you'll be approached by one or more of the local **hawkers** selling sarongs, pearls, T-shirts, paintings, more pearls, tours, transport and yet more pearls. (For more on Lombok pearls, see p.311.) It can be irritating, but it's worth bearing a few things in mind. Despite the tourist gloss, many people in Lombok are poor. Employment opportunities are few, not least because you need either a considerable amount of money, or well-placed connections, to secure many jobs, from government positions to jobs in hotels and restaurants. Family land is often insufficient to support all the people dependent on it and many end up becoming migrant workers in the Middle East, or even risking their lives mining for gold (see p.315). Working as a hawker in Senggigi is a way of trying to escape the cycle – a reality that admittedly is not the first thing that comes to mind when you're faced with the umpteenth request of the day to "just have a look please".

Pemenang marks the turn-off to Bangsal (for public and shuttle boats to the Gili Islands; see p.338.) A couple of kilometres beyond Pemenang you reach the beautiful beach at **Sire**, and its deluxe accommodation (see p.339).

Activities around Senggigi

There's no **diving** off Senggigi so all Senggigi dive centres ship their clients to Gili Trawangan or Gili Air for the day (about 1hr 15min away); a two-dive package costs $80. Reputable local **dive centres** include Blue Marlin (ⓦwww.bluemarlindive .com) at *Senggigi Beach Hotel* (ⓣ0370/693210) in central Senggigi and at *Holiday Resort Lombok* (ⓣ0370/693719) on Mangsit beach; and Dream Divers, on Jalan Raya Senggigi and at the *Sheraton Senggigi Beach Resort*, both in central Senggigi (ⓣ0370/693738, ⓦwww.dreamdivers.com). If you're on Lombok primarily for the diving, however, it's cheaper and more time-efficient to base yourself on the Gilis instead. Most dive centres will take accompanying **snorkellers** to Gili Trawangan or Gili Air for about $20 ($10 for under 10s) and may provide a dedicated snorkelling guide on request. A recommended alternative snorkelling destination is the reefs around tiny Gili Nanggu in southwest Lombok (see p.315), accessible by a two-hour boat ride from Senggigi; for this, Rinjani Trekking Centre on Jalan Raya (aka Kotasi Tour; ⓣ0819/0763 6172, ⓔbudisandra@yahoo.com) charges Rp600,000 for two people, including equipment.

Rinjani Trekking Club, on Jalan Raya (ⓣ0370/693202, ⓦwww.lombokdetours .com), do interesting-sounding overnight **kayak trips** to Gili Air; around Gili Nanggu, Gili Sudak and Gili Gede (both Rp1.5m/person, including tented accommodation and a co-pilot); and around Komodo. They are also a reputable agent for Rinjani **trekking** packages; numerous agents in Senggigi (with very similar names) sell trekking packages, but read our advice on p.342 before signing up. Nearby, Lombok Way Out Travel (ⓣ0370/666 9703, ⓦwww .lombok-wayout.com) organizes various Lombok **cycle trips**, from $18.

All agencies offer **tours** round Lombok – nearly everywhere on the island is accessible on a day-trip – but it's more fun to design your own by hiring a car and driver. A highly recommended local **driver/guide** is Made Minggir (ⓣ0819/9988 8910, ⓔmadetravel10@yahoo.com); expect to pay Rp400,000–600,000 per day.

Eating and nightlife

As you'd expect, **Central Senggigi** has the biggest concentration of restaurants, but **Batu Bolong**, with its candlelit tables and flaming torches on the beach, is the most atmospheric place to eat after dark. On Sundays local warung serve seafood from the sea-view shacks near Batu Bolong temple, as they do all along the beach at **Karandangan**, and every evening at sunset stalls sell barbecued sweetcorn on the headland just north of the *Sheraton Senggigi*.

Senggigi **nightlife** is mostly either restaurants with live music or karaoke places (not listed here) catering to male domestic tourists.

Except where stated, restaurants **open** daily from at least 11am to 9pm, or until about midnight if they have live music; during Ramadan all tourist places remain open. Where a phone number is given, the restaurant offers **free transport** within the Senggigi area.

Central Senggigi

🏃 Asmara Jl Raya ⓣ0370/693619, ⓦwww .asmara-group.com. This long-standing, family-friendly Senggigi favourite serves good Western and Indonesian dishes including *ayam taliwang* (Lombok fried chicken with chilli sauce),

Thai-style prawns, steaks with many sauces (from Rp150,000), home-made bread, and kids' meals. Has free wi-fi, a library and kids' toys. Mains from Rp40,000.

Bumbu Two branches, one on Jl Raya and another near the Pasar Seni. Hot, Thai-inspired curries are the

LOMBOK AND THE GILI ISLANDS | Senggigi and around

thing here, from classic red, green and *massaman* curries to inventive adaptations based around lemongrass, pineapple or peanuts. From Rp35,000.

De Quake Pasar Seni ⓦwww.dequake .com. Sophisticated beachside bar and restaurant serving refreshingly innovative Pan Asian cuisine – fish with ginger and caramel, Vietnamese chicken salad, lemongrass prawns – complemented by top strawberry margaritas and a "lounge food" menu that's just perfect at sunset-viewing time. There's free wi-fi and classy service too. Mains around Rp50,000.

Happy Café Jl Raya. Large, fun and very popular streetside restaurant known for its nightly live MOR music (from 9pm). Does half-litre jugs of Arak Attack cocktails (but, uniquely, no Bintang), as well as decent sushi and other Japanese food, plus Indo standards and pizza.

Marina Café and Sports Bar Jl Raya ⓦwww .marinasenggigi.com. Senggigi's main club has nightly live music, DJs and on-stage dancers and is very much a local scene (complete with ladyboys and beach boys), busiest on Saturdays. The adjacent Sports Bar shows big-screen sports and has free wi-fi and a pool table. Sports Bar 11am–2.30am; free. Club Sun–Thurs 10pm–1.30am, Fri 10.30pm–2am, Sat 8.30pm–3am; entry Sun–Fri Rp35,000, Sat Rp45,000 (includes one beer).

Square Jl Raya ⓣ0370/693688, ⓦwww .squarelombok.com. Fine dining and contemporary design make this *the* destination restaurant in Senggigi. Cuisine is Chinese, Indonesian and Western, with spicy tiger prawns, beef tenderloin, Norwegian salmon and fallen chocolate cake all on the menu. Also has imported wines and Cuban cigars, plus veggie and kids' menus. Mains from Rp60,000, gourmet set dinner Rp250,000.

Yessy Café Jl Raya ⓣ0370/693148. Cheap drinks and a big menu of good-value food, including Sasak favourites *ayam taliwang* (chilli-fried chicken) and vegetable *pelecing* (with chilli sauce) make this small place a popular spot. Mains from Rp30,000.

South Senggigi: Batu Bolong and Batu Layar

Café Alberto Batu Bolong ⓣ0370/693039, ⓦwww.cafealberto.com.

Sophisticated beachside restaurant with its own swimming pool, free wi-fi and fantastic sunset views. The Italian menu includes home-made seafood spaghetti, (small) wood-fired pizzas (evenings only), good bread and chocolate mousse; mains average Rp60,000. Phone for transport after 6pm, or flag down the shuttle van that circulates round central Senggigi from 6 to 9pm. Daily 8.30am–midnight.

Warung Menega Batu Layar beach, 3km south of central Senggigi. Unpretentious beach warung that does famously good seafood sold by the weight or in good-value set meals (from Rp90,000). Fresh lobster, prawns, crab, clams, snapper and barracuda are cooked on coconut-husk barbecues as at the seafood restaurants in Jimbaran, Bali. Daily noon–1am.

North Senggigi: Karandangan and Mangsit

Pondok Damai Mangsit. The seafront restaurant attached to the bungalows here sells well-priced barbecued fish every night.

Qunci Villas Mangsit. Happy hour two-for-one cocktails, comfortable loungers and the prospect of a dramatic sky draw almost everyone here at sunset. After dark the beautifully lit pool at *Qunci Pool Villas* makes an atmospheric setting for a seafood dinner, including deliciously garlicky spaghetti vongole, pan-fried sea bass and Asian moon scallops. The sister restaurant at *Qunci Hotel*, next door but one, serves Western and Indo food, with classics like *gado-gado* given a nouvelle twist. Mains from Rp70,000.

Waroeng Coco Beach Karandangan ⓣ0817/578 0055. A great place for Indonesian home-style cooking, especially vegetarian dishes. Highlights include *kare singkong* (tapioca leaf in coconut milk) and *terong tomat* (eggplant in deliciously spiced tomato sauce). Eat in classy *berugaq* on the edge of a coconut grove, just back from the black-sand beach. Free transport 6–10pm. Daily, noon–10pm.

Windy Beach Cottages Mangsit. Inexpensive Indonesian and European staples, from omelette and chips to *nasi campur* and excellent *gado-gado*. Mains from Rp25,000.

Shopping

Senggigi shops sell Lombok's greatest choice of **crafts**, although there isn't the variety that you'll find in Bali. Senggigi Abadi supermarket stocks necessities, postcards and snacks, but for pretty much everything else you're better off at the mall in Mataram.

Asmara Collection Jl Raya. Good-quality handicrafts, jewellery and textiles.

Ciokolata Boutique Jl Raya. Attractive designer cotton-print resortwear and swimwear.

Lex Bookshop Jl Raya. Secondhand books.

Mentez Art and Café Opposite *Senggigi Beach Hotel*. The gallery of prolific Javanese artist Bang, who paints abstract and figurative oils and acrylics on mostly Sasak and Balinese themes.

Pasar Seni Jl Raya. Tourist art market selling beachwear, sarongs, pearls and artefacts.

Sudirman Jl Raya. Long-established, reasonably priced outlet for Indonesian antiques.

Listings

ATMs There are several international Visa ATMs on Jl Raya Senggigi but none in Batu Bolong or Mangsit.

Doctor At the *Senggigi Beach Hotel* ☎0370/693210 (24hr). See p.312 for hospitals in Mataram.

Internet Wi-fi is available in many hotels and some restaurants and there are several internet centres along Jl Raya Senggigi.

Police In front of the Pasar Seni ☎0370/632733.

Tours and onward travel Perama (daily 7am–10pm; ☎0370/693007, ⓦwww.peramatour .com) are an excellent outlet for shuttle-bus tickets to destinations on Lombok and Bali, as well as for car and motorbike rental and tours to Komodo; they also operate a daily boat to the Gili Islands at 9.15am (45min; Rp200,000) and another to Nusa Lembongan and south Bali at 1pm. Countless other small transport operators offer shuttles to Gili Trawangan via Bangsal for about Rp70,000, to Kuta from Rp150,000 and Tetebatu from Rp175,000. Dream Divers can also arrange any tour, book accommodation on the Gilis and do boat transfers to the Gilis for $7.50/person. Airline tickets from Bidy Tour (☎0370/693521, ⓦwww .bidytour-lombok.com).

The Gili Islands

Fringed by dazzling white-sand beaches, limpid turquoise waters and reefs that teem with turtles and fish, the trio of tiny **Gili Islands** just off Lombok's northwest coast are strikingly beautiful and increasingly popular. With no motorized vehicles allowed on any of the islands (just horsecarts and bicycles), and swathes of the dusty interiors still taken up with coconut plantations and sandy tracks, these are as close as you can get to living the island dream without sacrificing the luxuries.

Gili Trawangan, the most developed of the three, has become Lombok's premier tourist destination and is fast eclipsing Bali's resorts as well, with its superior beaches, easy access from south Bali and mass of affordable yet quite sophisticated places to eat, drink and party. Families, honeymooners and backpackers are all well catered for, though ultra-cheap **accommodation** is nonexistent on any of the islands and prices everywhere soar from June to September and over Christmas; booking ahead is essential during these periods, when you'll be lucky to get the simplest room for under Rp300,000. Diminutive **Gili Meno**, next east from Gili Trawangan, is the smallest and quietest of the Gilis, with just a handful of places to stay and very low-key nightlife. East again, **Gili Air** falls somewhere in between, with plenty of restaurants and bars but a much larger population of islanders to balance out the tourist influx. Transport between the three islands is fast and easy.

All three Gili Islands – known collectively as Gili Indah ("Gili" actually, and tautologically, means "Island" in Sasak) – have only really been settled since the 1970s, mostly by Sasaks from mainland Lombok and Bugis fishermen from

Transport to and between the Gili Islands

Frequent boats run to Gili Trawangan **from Bali and Lombok**; for transport to Gili Meno and Gili Air you usually have to change on Gili Trawangan. Public and charter boats **between the Gilis** are plentiful. Though there is a jetty on Gili Trawangan, many boats dock in the shallows both here and on the other Gilis, so you'll probably get your feet wet.

From Bali
The fastest and most expensive way to get to Gili Trawangan from Bali is to take one of the many **fast-boat services**. Fast boats depart from several harbours around south and east Bali – **Benoa**, **Serangan**, **Sanur** and **Padang Bai** – but as tickets include transfers from hotels all over south Bali you don't need to base yourself at one of those ports. The sea crossing takes 1 hour 30 minutes to 2 hour in a fast boat, and all-inclusive tickets average Rp660,000; if you base yourself in **Padang Bai** you can sometimes get boat-only tickets for as little as Rp350,000 (see p.211). Tickets can be bought online or at any tour agent in any tourist centre; alternatively, there's a one-stop booking service at ⓦ www.gili-fastboat.com. Fast-boat companies include: Blue Water Express (ⓦ www.bwsbali.com), Gili Cat (ⓦ www.gilicat.com), Island Getaway (ⓦ www.island-getaway.com), Ocean Star (ⓦ www.gilifastboat.com), Scoot (ⓦ www.scootcruise.com) and Sea Marlin (ⓦ baliseamarlinexpress.com). There are also fast boats from **Nusa Lembongan** (see p.134) and **Amed** (see p.226).

A speedy alternative from Bali is to **fly** to Lombok's Selaparang Airport (30min; see p.308), then take a taxi to Bangsal (1hr; Rp115,000) and charter a boat to the Gilis (see below).

The cheaper option is to take one of the **slower boats from Padang Bai** (see p.211). Perama operates a daily slow boat between Padang Bai and all three Gili Islands (4–5hr; Rp300,000), with shuttle-bus connections across Bali. Cheaper still, but a lot more time-consuming, would be to take the public car ferry from Padang Bai to the west-Lombok port of Lembar (see p.313), then continue by bemos to Bangsal for the public boat to the Gilis (see below).

From mainland Lombok
On Lombok, the main port for the Gili Islands is **Bangsal**; this operates the cheapest and most frequent service to and from all three islands (Rp8000–10,000), but is famous for its hassle. You can also charter boats from Bangsal (Rp155,000–185,000/boat). See p.338 for full information about Bangsal.

The alternative is to use Perama's daily fast boat between **Senggigi** and the Gilis (Rp200,000; 45min; see opposite).

Between the Gili Islands
The "hopping island" boat service between all three Gili Islands does one circuit, Air–Meno–Trawangan–Meno–Air, in the morning (8.30–10am), and another in the afternoon (3–4.30pm), which makes day-trips straightforward; the islands are ten to twenty minutes apart. Fares are Rp20,000–25,000 and tickets are sold at each harbour.

This service is not, however, very usefully timed if you're arriving from Bali and need a transfer to Gili Air or Gili Meno (most fast boats from Bali only serve Gili Trawangan). If you don't want to wait for the afternoon hopping boat you'll have to **charter a boat** on to Gili Meno or Gili Air, which will cost around Rp250,000 per boat.

Sulawesi. Island dialect reflects these roots and all three islands are **Muslim**. Despite what disingenuous touts on Bali might tell you, however, the Gilis remain resolutely open to visitors during Ramadan, with just the nightlife being toned down. Note, though, that although local people are fairly used to seeing scantily clad Westerners, you should cover up when you move away from the beach.

There are no **police** on the islands, although Satgas (Beach Security) on Gili Trawangan has a role in tourist security: it's the job of the *kepala desa*, the headman who looks after Gili Air and Gili Meno, and the *kepala kampung* on Gili Trawangan, to deal with any problems. Ask at your accommodation, or one of the dive centres. If you need to make a police report (for insurance purposes, for example), go to the police on the mainland (at Tanjung or Mataram).

For reliable **Gili island information** on Bali contact Island Promotions, Shop 12, Poppies Lane 1, Kuta (℡0361/753241, Ⓦwww.gili-paradise.com; 9am–10pm). They can also book transport and accommodation and have a hotel booking site, Ⓦwww.gili-hotels.com.

Gili Trawangan

The largest and most built-up of the islands, with a permanent population of around nine hundred, **GILI TRAWANGAN** (Gili T) is enjoyably buzzy, and even congested in parts, yet still very laidback. Once a backpackers' party island, it now appeals to all ages and budgets, with private villas and boutique resorts at the top end and A-frame huts at the bottom. There are dozens of beachside restaurants and bars to choose from, and tour agents can organize everything from kayaking and horseriding to diving and snorkelling. Or you can simply go for the sybarite's option, lazing on the white-sand beaches by day, living it large at the party venues by night.

Arrival and orientation

Boats from Bali, mainland Lombok and the other Gilis (see p.325) dock either at the pier or at the harbour a few hundred metres further north. If you're staying on the east coast or in the village and can carry your luggage, it's about five minutes' walk from the pier to *Scallywags* or about thirty minutes up to *Alam Gili*. **Cidomo** (horsecarts) are the island taxis and meet all boats; they should charge Rp30,000 –50,000 to take you anywhere on the island.

The liveliest area to stay is the **east coast**, in particular the strip south of the harbour, known as **central**, which is wall-to-wall bungalows, restaurants and dive shops. The east coast north of the harbour is also built-up and has one of the loveliest beaches, which makes it busy with snorkellers and sunbathers during the day, though it's less popular after dark. The **north coast**, about twenty-five minutes' walk from the commercial centre, is, for the time being at least, a lot quieter, and places here have roomier grounds; the snorkelling's good but the beach is rocky and unswimmable at low tide. Head just a few metres inland from the east coast and you're in the **village**, dotted with corner shops between islanders' homes, a couple of mosques and the cheapest places to stay on the island. When everything else is booked out, this is the area to wander in search of a room.

Accommodation

There are no **hotels** right on the beach, and few offer real sea views, but none is more than a few minutes' walk away. Note that wherever you stay, especially along the east coast and in the village, **noise** is likely to be an issue, whether from the late-night bars or the mosques' early-morning calls to prayers. The ground-water on Gili T is brackish so **showers** are often salty; however, an increasing number of places now import fresh water.

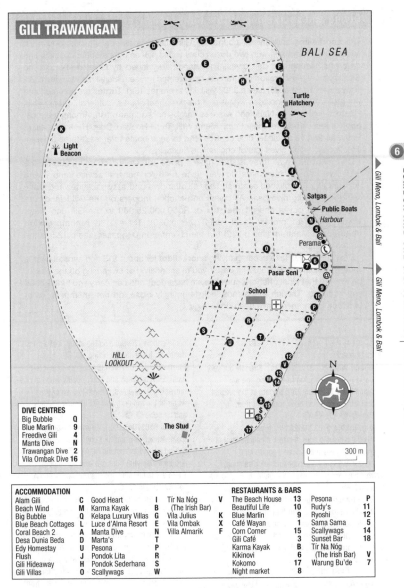

GILI TRAWANGAN

BALI SEA

Turtle Hatchery

Light Beacon

Satgas

Public Boats

Harbour

Perama

Pasar Seni

School

HILL LOOKOUT

The Stud

N

0   300 m

DIVE CENTRES

Big Bubble	Q
Blue Marlin	9
Freedive Gili	4
Manta Dive	N
Trawangan Dive	2
Vila Ombak Dive	16

ACCOMMODATION

Alam Gili	C	Good Heart	I
Beach Wind	M	Karma Kayak	B
Big Bubble	Q	Kelapa Luxury Villas	G
Blue Beach Cottages	L	Luce d'Alma Resort	E
Coral Beach 2	A	Manta Dive	N
Desa Dunia Beda	D	Marta's	T
Edy Homestay	U	Pesona	P
Flush	J	Pondok Lita	R
Gili Hideaway	H	Pondok Sederhana	S
Gili Villas	O	Scallywags	W
Tír Na Nóg (The Irish Bar)	V
Vila Julius	K
Vila Ombak	X
Villa Almarik	F

RESTAURANTS & BARS

The Beach House	13	Pesona	P
Beautiful Life	10	Rudy's	11
Blue Marlin	9	Ryoshi	12
Café Wayan	1	Sama Sama	5
Corn Corner	15	Scallywags	14
Gili Café	3	Sunset Bar	18
Karma Kayak	B	Tír Na Nóg
Kikinovi	6	(The Irish Bar)	V
Kokomo	17	Warung Bu'de	7
Night market	8

Despite the growing number of places to stay on Gili T, accommodation is at a premium, and most places charge wildly inflated **prices** during the peak periods (see box, p.329). Renting a private **villa** for a week or two is becoming increasingly popular: established options include *Kelapa Luxury Villas* (☎0812/375 6003, ⓦwww.kelapavillas.com) and *Gili Villas* (☎0812/375 5721, ⓦwww.gilivillas indonesia.com).

The **snorkelling** and **diving** around the Gili Islands is among the best and most accessible in Lombok, with two dozen sites within half an hour's boat ride, including drop-offs, slopes and drift dives. The islands are fringed by **coral reefs**, and the Biorock coral regeneration programme has created house reefs all the way down Gili Trawangan's east coast (see p.330); visibility averages 15m. **Turtles** are common and the prolific **fish** life includes white- and black-tip reef sharks, cuttlefish, moray eels, lobsters, manta rays, Napoleon wrasses and bumphead parrotfish. Among the most popular local **sites** are Shark Point, Meno Wall, Turtle Heaven, Deep Halik and Manta Point; as they're so close, dive centres tend to send boats to at least three different sites a day, which gives lots of choice and flexibility.

Dive centres on all three islands have a **price** agreement, charging $38 for the first dive, though standards do vary (see p.46 for general advice, and island accounts for established centres). They all offer dive-and-stay packages and many sell good-quality dive gear. All divers and snorkel trippers off the Gili Islands are requested to pay a one-off **reef tax** of Rp50,000/25,000 to the Gili Eco Trust, which works to protect local reefs (see p.330). There is a **recompression chamber** in Mataram (see p.312) but the chamber in Denpasar (see p.122) is the preferred option.

Dive companies take accompanying **snorkellers** for about $15 and snorkel gear is widely available for Rp25,000 a day. If you're snorkelling or swimming off the beach, be warned that local **offshore currents** are hazardous and can carry you further than you intended. Though the islands look temptingly close, do not attempt to swim between them; there have been drownings.

Central and the east coast

Beach Wind ☎0812/376 4347. Friendly but very basic place with facing rows of fan and a/c bungalows. There are DVD players in the priciest and table tennis and book rental out front. Fan ❸/❹, a/c ❹/❺

Big Bubble ☎0370/625020, ⓦwww .bigbubblediving.com. A dozen nicely decorated and generously proportioned good-value bungalows in a garden behind the dive shop, well back from the main thoroughfare. Fan ❸/❹, a/c ❹/❺

Blue Beach Cottages ☎0370/623538, ⓦwww .bluebeach.biz. Wood-and-thatch single-storey *lumbung*-style bungalows just across from a lovely stretch of beach. The best and priciest are at the front; some have a/c and hot water. Fan ❸/❺, a/c ❺/❻

Flush ☎0819/1725 1532, ⓔzalnulping@yahoo .com. A laidback and perfectly sited little place where two of the budget rooms have great verandas with views of the beach. Sturdier, slightly cheaper wooden bungalows are set further back. Hammocks and fans in every room. ❸/❻

Good Heart ☎0813/5350 9139, ⓔgoodheart _bungalows@yahoo.com. Attractive wood-and-palm bungalows with a/c, TV and hot water plus

some enticing *berugaq* on the shore, just across the track, for seafront chilling. ❺/❼

Manta Dive ☎0370/643649, ⓦwww.manta-dive .com. Eleven stylish and good-quality wooden rice-barn-style bungalows, all with hot water (fresh water at the top end) and a/c. Behind the dive shop and its pool. ❹/❻

Pesona ☎0370/623521, ⓦwww.pesonaresort .com. Attractively outfitted bungalows in a garden behind the Indian restaurant. All have DVD players and verandas with cushions and hammocks. There's a family villa and a streetside pool too. Fan ❹/❺, a/c ❺/❻

Scallywags ☎0370/645301, ⓦwww.scallywags resort.com. Exceptionally well designed little hotel where each of the ten rooms is fronted by its own tiny courtyard garden and comes with a/c, DVD player and comfortable, contemporary decor. Showers are solar-powered and a desalination system produces drinking water for the sinks. A good-sized pool and relaxed waterfront restaurant with free wi-fi (see p.331) complete the picture. ❻/❼

Tír Na Nóg (The Irish Bar) ☎0370/639463, ⓦwww.tirnanogbar.com. Right in the middle of the action, in a compact compound behind one of the island's main party bars. Rooms all have a/c, hot freshwater showers and safety boxes, with private gardens and TV in the deluxe ones. There's a small pool. Standard rooms ④/⑤, deluxe ⑤/⑥

Vila Ombak ☎0370/642336, ⊛www.hotelombak .com. With 115 rooms occupying a large chunk of the southern seafront, this upscale hotel is the largest on the island. Facilities include two pools, a spa, a dive shop and a clinic. Most accommodation is in contemporary concrete two-storey *lumbung* (some with downstairs bathrooms); all have a/c and hot freshwater showers. ⑦

Villa Almarik ☎0370/638520, ⊛www .almarik-lombok.com. More of a traditional hotel than most on the island, with 25 large, Bali-style cottages, all with a/c and hot freshwater showers, the brightest and most modern being the "superior", mid-priced ones. There's a big pool, a dive centre and sunloungers on the beach across the track. Rates are for half-board for two people. ⑦/⑧

The village and inland

Edy Homestay ☎0878/6562 4445, ⊛www .edyhomesty.co.cc. Good budget choice with neat, clean rooms, some designed in *lumbung* style, in a friendly compound in the village. A/c and hot water are available. Fan ②/④, a/c ③/⑥

Gili Hideaway ☎0812/374 4578, ⊛www .gilihideaway.com. Perfectly named, gorgeous little garden enclave, run as a home-away-from-home by a genial UK–Sasak couple. Accommodation (all with fans) is in two compounds and ranges from budget A-frame huts to thoughtfully outfitted superior bungalows. There's a pool, a lounging *berugaq*, books and games to borrow and home-made cakes. Huts ②/③, bungalows ④/⑤

Luce d'Alma Resort ☎0370/621777, ⊛www .lucedalmaresort.com. The enormous 80m saltwater pool is the star attraction at this luxurious, Italian-run little boutique hotel. Each of the elegant, wood-floored rooms opens onto the pool and all have wi-fi, living areas with DVD players and freshwater bathrooms with tubs. There's a gym and restaurant on site but you are 400m from the shore. ⑦/⑧

🏃 **Marta's** ☎0812/372 2777, ⊛www .martasgili.com. Run by a welcoming UK– Sasak couple, the great-quality two-storey rooms here have attractive wood floors and fretwork carving and all come with a/c and hot water; some can sleep families. Verandas with day beds look

onto the garden and pool and there's wi-fi. Book ahead and you'll be met off the boat. ⑤/⑥

Pondok Lita ☎0370/648607. Popular and clean budget choice in the village offering a handful of terraced rooms set around a small garden, with fans and cold-water bathrooms. ②/④

Pondok Sederhana ☎0813/3953 6047. Excellent-value budget losmen with a row of just four neat and super-clean, cold-water fan bungalows in a pretty, fenced garden towards the back of the village. ②/③

The north coast

Alam Gili ☎0370/630466, ⊛www.alamgili.com. Delightful wood-and-thatch bungalows, including one fabulous seaview room, in a quiet garden across from the beach and snorkel point. Most have fans, all have hot freshwater showers and there's a tiny pool. ⑤

Coral Beach 2 ☎0370/639946. One of the better options in a cluster of hastily built huts on Gili T's northeastern tip, just across from the snorkelling reef. Top of the range are the comfortable, thatched *lumbung* huts with a/c and fresh water, and there are cheaper fan bungalows too. Fan ②/④, a/c ④/⑥

🏃 **Desa Dunia Beda** ☎0370/641575, ⊛www.desaduniabeda.com. The most handsome hotel on Gili T is refashioned from salvaged 150-year-old Javanese *joglo* (grand) and *kampung* (village) homes: the enormous wooden bungalows come with antique and driftwood furniture, though only some have a/c and most have saltwater showers. There's a pool and you're steps from the shore. ⑥/⑦

Karma Kayak ☎0818/0364 0538, ⊛www .karmakayak.com. Run by two welcoming Dutch women (one a champion kayaker), this place has attractive, individually styled rooms, with wi-fi and hot freshwater showers. It's across from the beach, with loungers and beanbags on the sand, and kayaking trips are available (see p.330). ⑤/⑥

Vila Julius ☎0819/1603 4549, ⊛www.villajulius .com. Remote and peaceful, a 15min walk from other north-coast accommodation (or 25min from the east coast), this is a chic and popular hideaway of seven a/c rooms in a contemporary building that feels like a groovy seaside home. The deserted beach is a few steps out front, with dining tables on the sand, and there's a pool and wi-fi. ⑦

Since **room rates** on the Gili Islands often increase dramatically during the peak months of June to September, and over Christmas and New Year, we've given price codes for low/high seasons where relevant.

Around the island

A sandy track encircles the island and a tangle of paths crisscross it, with a few sections concreted. As the island is just 2.5km long by 1.75km wide you can **walk** round it in about four hours, or **cycle** it in less than two (pushing through the occasional stretches of deep sand); rental bikes are available all over from Rp25,000. Development is gradually encroaching inland, but there are still wide areas of dry scrub and coconut plantations. The 100m **hill** in the southwest is the compulsory expedition at sunset, with views of Gunung Agung on Bali.

The lush white sands, clear waters and plentiful fish around *Gili Café* towards the northern end of the east coast make this the most popular **beach**. The north- and west-coast beaches are a coral/sand mix and too rocky for comfortable swimming at low tide, but the **snorkelling** is good here, especially near *Coral Beach 2* and between *Alam Gili* and *Karma Kayak*, with regular visits from turtles. There are daily **glass-bottomed boat** snorkelling trips to sites around all three Gilis, with a stop for lunch on Gili Air (depart the harbour at 10.30am, return 3pm; Rp75,000/ person including mask and snorkel); many shops sell tickets, or you can buy them at the harbour. *Karma Kayak* (see p.329) offers guided **kayaking** trips to Gili Meno (Rp200,000/half-day).

Biorock and the Gili Eco Trust

Gili Trawangan has seen intense development in recent years and inevitably the escalating demand on island resources has come at a price. The **Gili Eco Trust** was established in 2002 to address the most pressing environmental and social issues, and to involve islanders, business owners, expats and tourists in a sustainable future for the island.

The Trust's most high-profile project to date has been the planting of **Biorock** installations to **regenerate the reef** around Gili T, counteracting degradation caused by anchor damage, fish-bombing and bleaching, and hindering erosion. Biorock frames are steel-grid structures that are fed a continual low-voltage electric current; the current causes the minerals in the seawater to crystallize into limestone, the building block of reefs, and coral then begins to grow along the steel bars at up to six times faster than normal, further stimulated by the grafting of live coral fragments. You can see for yourself how successful the programme has been by snorkelling and diving at the fifty-plus Biorock structures that now encircle the island (locations are mapped on signboards along the east coast). Local businesses supply the electricity, essentially growing their own house reefs, which attract huge quantities of fish. Biorock is also being used to promote coral growth off Pemuteran in northwest Bali (see p.296). It's possible to take a special dive course in Biorock and underwater conservation at a couple of Gili T's dive centres (see opposite). For more information on Biorock, see the websites of the Gili Eco Trust and the Global Coral Reef Alliance (Ⓦwww.globalcoral.org).

Biorock and the other work of the Gili Eco Trust is financed in part by a small, one-off **reef tax** that every diver and snorkel-tripper on Gili Trawangan is invited to pay (dive centres on Gili Air and Gili Meno have found this harder to implement). The Trust works alongside Satgas, the local island security organization. Another important initiative has been the forging of an agreement with fishermen that restricts fishing to designated zones and uses boat moorings. The Trust has also instigated improvements in rubbish collection and **recycling**, environmental education at island schools and the treatment of cidomo horses. A monthly **beach clean-up** is run in conjunction with the dive centres, offering a free dive to any tourist who participates (see opposite).

To find out more about the Gili Eco Trust, drop by the office at Big Bubble dive centre, or visit the website (Ⓦwww.giliecotrust.com).

There's **horseriding** around the island with The Stud (℡0878/6179 1565, ⓔrobbedelphine@yahoo.fr; from Rp300,000), and daily **yoga classes** at Freedive Gili (℡0878/6579 4884, ⓦwww.giliyoga.com; Rp90,000).

Dive centres

The **diving** around the Gilis is superlative, for more on which see the box on p.328. On the first Friday of every month all dive centres participate in the **beach clean-up** programme run by the Gili Eco Trust; help out and you'll get a free dive in return. The following dive operators are all well established.

Big Bubble ℡0370/625020, ⓦwww .bigbubblediving.com. Closely associated with the Gili Eco Trust and offers a *Padi* Biorock speciality.
Blue Marlin ℡0370/632424, ⓦwww.bluemarlin dive.com. Known for technical diving and tri-mix and rents out closed-circuit rebreathers.
Freedive Gili ℡0858/5718 7170, ⓦwww .freedivegili.com. Freediving specialist.

Manta Dive ℡0370/643649, ⓦwww.manta-dive .com. Offers both PADI and SSI courses.
Trawangan Dive ℡0370/649220, ⓦwww .trawangandive.com. Works with the Gili Eco Trust and can offer conservation specialities.
Vila Ombak Diving Academy ℡0370/638531, ⓦwww.gilidive.com. Provides all divers with a dive computer.

Eating

With a mass of **restaurants** to choose from, half the fun is wandering slowly down the main drag, trying to decide which to go for. Alternatively, from sunset onwards, head for the popular **night market** in front of the art market, where *kaki lima* hand-cart stalls serve up cheap and authentic food – *ayam bakso* (chicken soup), *nasi campur*, seafood and *nasi goreng* are all on offer, from Rp15,000 – which you can eat at the tables set out in front.

Central and the east coast

The Beach House A popular spot for nightly seafood barbecues, this beachside restaurant also serves lots of pasta dishes – lobster spaghetti, penne with salmon – as well as Balinese chicken, apple pie, a special kids' menu and plenty more. Most mains Rp30,000–65,000.
Gili Café The beanbag loungers under the casuarina trees are the big draw here, set out on a pretty stretch of beachfront, with views across to Gili Meno. Create your own sandwich from a good selection of cheeses and cold meats (from Rp40,000), or sip fresh strawberry juice between swims.
Kikinovi A vivacious grey-haired lady cooks up ten pots or so of cheap local food every lunchtime and sells it in the art market.
Kokomo ⓦwww.kokomogilit.com. Sophisticated fine dining on crisp white tablecloths beside the sea. Oysters are usually on the menu, along with imported scallops, Peking duck, crab ravioli, stuffed zucchini flowers and chocolate souffle. Mains from Rp65,000.
Pesona Excellent, surprisingly authentic Indian menu that includes tandoori dishes, kebabs, rogan josh, dopiaza, kofta, masala, biryani and dosas (from Rp55,000), plus shisha pipes with aromatic

tobacco to finish. There's seating by the shore plus low tables and cushions.
Ryoshi Very good, well-priced Japanese food at this local franchise of the Bali-wide chain. Sushi sets from Rp57,000, plus tuna carpaccio and *zaru soba* (chilled buckwheat noodles).
Scallywags Fantastic seafood barbecues in the evenings – buy the fish at market price and get potatoes and unlimited salad to go with it (from Rp73,000) – plus open sandwiches, innovative salads, good tapas platters and brownies with mint ice cream. Also has free wi-fi, comfy chairs and beachfront tables.
Warung Bu'de A favourite with expat divers, this small café charges from Rp15,000 for rice with servings of the day's stir-fries and curries. Shuts when the food runs out, so best for lunch.

The north coast

Café Wayan Great for bread, croissants, cinnamon rolls and death-by-chocolate cake (from Rp25,000). Also serves famously good prawns, plus salads, pizzas and pastas. Eat at tables on the beach in front of *Alam Gili*, on the north coast.
Karma Kayak Right on the beach, under the trees in front of a good snorkelling area on the north coast, this is a great place to chill out for a few

hours and is the prime spot for sunset viewing from May to mid-September. There are beanbags, loungers and tables on the sand (plus free wi-fi), and good tapas on the menu – calamari, vegetable tempura, patatas bravas, tapenade and baba ganoush among them (from Rp15,000).

Nightlife and entertainment

Gili T's famous **nightlife** chiefly revolves around three venues, which take it in turns to host the thrice-weekly all-night parties (every Mon, Wed & Fri from about 11pm), though there are plenty of alternatives throughout the week. The **drugs scene** of a few years ago has quietened down and doesn't dominate all island nightlife, though magic mushrooms are blatantly advertised – "Take you to bloody heaven and back, no transport necessary". You apparently don't always get the real thing, however, with reports of rotting vegetables and even bits of flipflop being used as substitutes. Be aware that penalties for the possession, use or trafficking of illegal drugs in Indonesia are severe (see p.57).

Several places screen **movies** every night, including open-air beachside *Corn Corner* at *Vila Ombak*, and *Beautiful Life*, which also has private booths where you can choose your own film. Viewing is free so long as you spend some money at the associated cafés.

Blue Marlin The big upstairs dancefloor above the dive centre is the Monday-night party venue. Has several bars and occasional theme nights.

Rudy's The Friday party venue, but rowdy till very late every night of the week.

Sama Sama Known for its really good live music, especially reggae, this bar's open late every night. Good atmosphere and good service.

Sunset Bar Follow the crowds heading south beyond *Vila Ombak* for one of Gili T's favourite sunset-viewing points, where a beach bar sells Bintang and plays music.

Tír Na Nóg (The Irish Bar) Perennially popular and lively beachside Irish bar with bottled Guinness, darts, movies and sports TV plus comfort food such as bangers and mash. There are nightly DJs from 10pm and it's the party venue every Wednesday, rated by many as the best of three.

Listings

Banks and exchange There are international ATMs in front of *Villa Ombak* and plenty of money-changers (rates are better on the mainland) but no banks. Dive companies offer advances on Visa and MasterCard, but you'll pay ten percent for this.

Clinic In the *Vila Ombak* complex (☏0370/642336 extn 716; 24hr; consultation Rp50,000). The nearest hospital is in Mataram (see p.312).

Internet At several dedicated centres along the main east-coast strip. Many hotels and some restaurants offer wi-fi.

Onward transport and tours Boats to Gili Meno, Gili Air, Lombok and Bali leave from either the pier or the nearby harbour; see p.325 for transport info.

Buy fast-boat tickets from agents, public-boat tickets from the Karya Behari office at the harbour, and shuttle bus/boat tickets to destinations on Lombok and Bali from Perama (☏0370/638514, ⓦwww.peramatour.com; daily 7am–10pm) or one of many other agents. Backpackers' liveaboard boat trips to Komodo are widely advertised and cost from Rp1.1m for three days. Rinjani treks can also be organized through Gili T agents; see p.342 for info.

Post There's a postal agent in the art market.

Shopping Stalls and shops along the east coast and in the small art market (*pasar seni*) sell daily neces-sities, beachwear, fashions and secondhand books.

Gili Meno

GILI MENO, 2km long and just over 1km wide, is the smallest and most tranquil of the islands, with a local population of just 350, plenty of space for solitary horizon-gazing and some gorgeous white-sand beaches. It takes a couple of hours to stroll around the island, with views across to Gili Air and Lombok from the east and Trawangan and Bali's Gunung Agung to the west. As on the other Gilis, there's no motorized transport, just a few cidomo (horsecarts); bicycles aren't widely available, but ask at your accommodation.

The **snorkelling** is good, especially between *Royal Reef Resort* and *Kontiki* on the east coast, as well as on the northwest at the Meno Wall, near *Diana Café,* and down at the disused Bounty jetty. Check locally for advice on currents (see also p.328). Snorkelling trips further afield cost Rp100,000 per person. For **diving**, consult Blue Marlin Dive (T 0370/639980, W www.blue marlindive.com); see also p.328.

You can **change money** in the harbour area, where Blue Marlin also does Visa cash advances. There's **internet** access at a couple of places here too, and several hotels on the island offer wi-fi. Buy **tickets** for the "hopping boat" at the harbour office and for fast boat connections from Gili T at harbourside outlets; see p.325 for routes. The Perama agent is the *Kontiki* hotel; other **shuttle-bus**

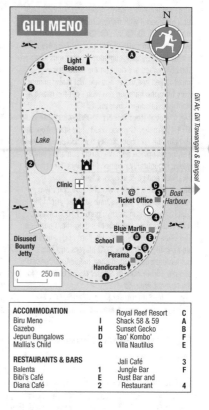

ACCOMMODATION		
Biru Meno	I	Royal Reef Resort
Gazebo	H	Shack 58 & 59
Jepun Bungalows	D	Sunset Gecko
Mallia's Child	G	Tao' Kombo'
		Villa Nautilus

RESTAURANTS & BARS		
Balenta	1	Jali Café
Bibi's Café	E	Jungle Bar
Diana Café	2	Rust Bar and Restaurant

(column 2 codes: Royal Reef Resort C; Shack 58 & 59 A; Sunset Gecko B; Tao' Kombo' F; Villa Nautilus E; Jali Café 3; Jungle Bar F; Rust Bar and Restaurant 4)

tickets are also widely advertised. Several places sell boat trips to Komodo (four days for Rp1.55m). Rust Shop sells basic necessities, including a few over-the-counter medicines; Sasak **handicrafts** and pots are sold at a stall between *Kontiki* and *Biru Meno*.

Accommodation

Accommodation on Meno is less flashy than on Trawangan: there's little air-conditioning and plenty of roughness around the edges, so things can feel quite rustic even though you're mostly paying above budget prices. This is part of Meno's charm but won't appeal to everyone. Prices fluctuate dramatically, so rates shown are for **low/high season**, where relevant; in high season (June–Sept and over Christmas) you definitely need to book ahead, which can be difficult as phone connections are unreliable – email is often a safer bet.

Biru Meno T 0813/3975 8968, W www .birumeno.com. Balinese-owned and designed bungalows, just back from the beach, a 10min walk from the harbour. All have large verandas, fans and cold-water bathrooms. ❹/❻
Gazebo T 0370/635795, W www.balibudgetinn andresidences.com. Attractive and very generously

sized fan and a/c coconut-wood bungalows (with brackish, cold-water bathrooms) set in a large, palm-shaded seafront garden. Fan ❹/❺, a/c ❻/❼
Jepun Bungalows T 0819/1739 4736, W www .jepunbungalows.com. Nine nicely outfitted rooms and *lumbung*-style bungalows in a garden, most

with wooden floors, glass doors and bamboo beds. All rooms come with freshwater showers and some have a/c. Fan ❸/❹, a/c ❹/❺

Mallia's Child ☎0878/6413 0719. The very simple beach-shack bungalows here, with fans and cold water, are right on the sand, enjoy unparalleled sea views and are just a few minutes' walk from the harbour. You won't get the island's warmest welcome, however. ❸/❹

🏕 **Royal Reef Resort** ☎0856/4691 7343, ✉rusligili@yahoo.co.id. Just steps from the harbour, the six good-quality bamboo bungalows at this friendly place all have partial sea and Lombok views, thoughtfully equipped interiors, fans, comfy verandas and wi-fi access. ❹/❺

Shack 58 and 59 ⓦwww.shack58.com. Two private villa-style homes, one just back from the beach, the other in its own garden 100m inland, both with private beachfront sitting-room gazebos. The villas, far from shack-like, are huge and very clean, with a/c, fridges, DVD players and chic garden bathrooms. Staff cook meals to order or it's about a 10min walk to *Sunset Gecko* or 20min to the harbour area. ❺

🏕 **The Sunset Gecko** ☎0813/5356 6774, ⓦwww.thesunsetgecko.com. An inspiring,

eco-conscious one-off, with strikingly innovative wood-and-bamboo architecture by the beach on the northwest coast, about a 30min walk from the harbour or Rp35,000 by cidomo. There are cheap single fan rooms in a house, and some A-frame bungalows (all sharing bathrooms), but the standouts are the two-room, two-storey bungalows with awesome sea views. Rooms ❶, A-frames ❷, bungalows ❺

Tao' Kombo' ☎0812/372 2174, ⓦwww.tao-kombo.com. Funky, inexpensive spot with wood-and-bamboo bungalows (with fans and fresh-water showers) set in a garden 200m behind the beach, plus a large bar and communal area. Also has two cheap backpackers' *berugaq* (open-sided sleeping platforms), with hanging bamboo screens for partial privacy but no walls or door, plus lockable luggage storage and a private bathroom. *Berugaq* ❶, bungalows ❸

🏕 **Villa Nautilus** ☎0370/642143, ⓦwww.villanautilus.com. Stylishly modern and light, these villas are the best on Meno, constructed with an abundance of natural materials and with glass doors opening on to the decks. All have a/c and hot water. ❻/❼

Eating and drinking

On the west coast, not far from the Meno Wall snorkelling reef, *Diana Café* is a fabulously chilled place to **eat**, drink and while away the day, with hammocks, cushions and fine views, plus a basic menu of drinks and Indonesian standards. Among other options, *Balenta*, further north, specializes in Sasak food (from Rp20,000); *Jali Café* does travellers' fare; *Bibi's Café*, attached to *Villa Nautilus*, serves excellent wood-fired pizzas (from Rp50,000); and *Rust* is one of several places doing nightly fresh-seafood barbecues, which you can eat in breezy *berugaq* pavilions on the beach. In the **evening**, *Rust* and *Jungle Bar* at *Tao' Kombo'* are the places to hang out, the latter with island musicians playing in high season.

Gili Air

Closest to the Lombok mainland, **GILI AIR** stretches about 1.5km in each direction and has the largest permanent population of the three islands (around 1500 people). Though tourism is important here, and increasingly so, village life and homes dominate the heart of the island, giving Gili Air a more Indonesian atmosphere than Gili Trawangan, while still being sociable and livelier than Gili Meno. Accommodation is spread around most of the coast but is concentrated in the southeast, which has the most popular beach and excellent snorkelling; ask locally about currents, which can be strong. Countless tracks, some of them paved, cross the interior and allow you to explore beyond the tourist perimeter into the many coconut plantations and *kampung* (villages) with their mosques, flower-filled gardens and grazing cows.

Arrival and information

Most **boats** arrive and depart from the harbour in the south (some fast boats drop passengers at *Scallywags*); see p.325 for details of routes from Bali, Lombok and the other Gilis. **Cidomo** (horsecarts) meet all boats, charging Rp50,000 to *Coconut*, for example.

You can buy boat **tickets** at the harbour office and **Perama** tickets from their office nearby, opposite *Villa Karang Hotel* (☎0370/637816 or 0818/0527 2735; ⓦwww.peramatour.com). There's no post office or ATM on the island but there are several **moneychangers** around the harbour and up the east coast – rates are poor. You'll find **internet access** next to Manta Dive and at Ozzy, which also sells wi-fi vouchers; *Scallywags* has free wi-fi. There is a limited **clinic** (7–9am & 5–7pm) but the closest hospital is in Mataram.

Accommodation

As **accommodation** prices rise dramatically during the July and August rush, and over Christmas, we give rates for **low season/high season** in the following listings. Book ahead during these periods. The cheapest rooms are inland, where a growing number of village homestays are opening.

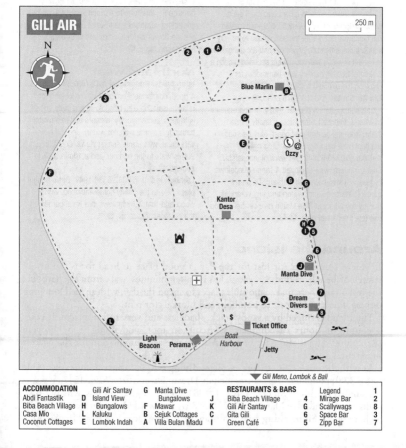

ACCOMMODATION					RESTAURANTS & BARS		Legend	1
Abdi Fantastik	D	Island View	Gita Gili	G	Manta Dive	G	Biba Beach Village	4	Mirage Bar	2
Biba Beach Village	H	Bungalows	F	Mawar	K	Gili Air Santay	G	Scallywags	8
Casa Mio	L	Kaluku	B	Sejuk Cottages	C	Gita Gili	6	Space Bar	3
Coconut Cottages	E	Lombok Indah	A	Villa Bulan Madu	I	Green Café	5	Zipp Bar	7

East and south

Abdi Fantastik A decent enough budget choice in a fine location on the east coast; the mainly wood-and-thatch bungalows are basic but have fans and sea views, and there are sitting areas overlooking the water. ❷/❹

Biba Beach Village ☎0819/1727 4648, ⓦbibabeach.com. Upscale Italian interpretation of the classic thatched-roof beach bungalow, with beach-chic furniture, nice bathrooms (some with hot water) and a communal sea-view lounging area. Fan ❸/❺, a/c ❹/❻

Casa Mio ☎0370/649330, ⓦwww.giliair.com. A burst of sophisticated creativity on the southwest coast, where the ample-sized thatched bungalows and rooms all have artsy decor, a/c and DVD players. There's an inviting chill-out lounge (with wi-fi) by the shore and reasonable snorkelling, though at low tide it's a long wade for a swim. A 5min walk from the harbour. ❻/❼

Coconut Cottages ☎0370/635365, ⓦwww.coconuts-giliair.com. You'll get a warm welcome at this lovely Scottish–Indonesian-run hideaway, 80m from the sea, whose eight very comfortable, differently styled fan and a/c bungalows (all with hot-water bathrooms) are secreted among a delightful tropical garden, with hammocks for enjoying the bird and butterfly life. ❹/❺

Gili Air Santay ☎0818/0375 8695, ⓦwww.giliair-santay.com. A popular spot with good-quality traditional thatched cottages in a shady garden 100m from the central east coast, plus *berugaq* on the beach for relaxing. Fan ❷/❸, a/c ❸/❺

Kaluku ☎0370/636421, ⓦwww.bluebeach.biz. Small, modern, well-equipped A-frame bungalows (a few with sea views), all with a/c, TV, pretty garden bathrooms (hot water) and tiny verandas. Run by the adjacent Blue Marlin dive centre, so you can use their small pool. ❹/❻

Manta Dive Bungalows ☎0813/5305 0462, ⓦwww.manta-dive-giliair.com. Quality, stylish bungalows, some of them Sasak-style cottages, behind the dive shop. All have a/c, hot water and safety boxes, some are connecting, and there's a small pool. ❹/❺

Mawar ☎0813/6225 3995. Good if basic budget choice a short walk from the harbour and the east-coast beach. All have fans and cold water as well as deep verandas with hammocks. ❶/❸

Sejuk Cottages ☎0370/636461, ⓦsejukcottages.com. Attractive, French-owned place 80m inland with a small but pretty pool. The variously styled bungalows include a family house and a couple of two-storey options with upstairs seating and sea views. Quality furnishings and optional a/c, hot water and DVD players add value. Fan ❸/❹, a/c ❺/❻

Villa Bulan Madu ☎0819/0733 0444, ⓦwww.bulan-madu.com. Luxuriously large villa-style cottages, each with a/c, freshwater bathrooms, kitchenette, French windows, all-but encircling verandas – and their own generous private flower garden, complete with *berugaq* and dining table. ❼

North and west

Island View Bungalows ☎0878/6524 4736. A good, comfortable option if you're looking for relative isolation. The bungalows are quite stylish, with fans, contemporary interiors and freshwater bathrooms (some with hot water), and the beach is very quiet, with prime sunset views. Count on a 20min walk to the harbour, and a 10min walk to *Legend*. ❸/❺

Lombok Indah ☎0852/5350 1947. Basic budget place next to the family home and shop, with wood-and-thatch bungalows in a floral garden on the northeast coast. ❷/❹

Around the island

If you're coming to Air just for the day, a good place to head for is the lovely stretch of **beach** around *Scallywags*, less than ten minutes' walk from the harbour; the restaurants here make enjoyable places to spend the day, with shaded lounging *berugaq*, fine views across to Lombok, and snorkels for rent.

The island is ringed by a sandy track, shadeless and very soft in places. It takes a couple of hours to complete a circuit on foot, and doing it by **bicycle** (Rp25,000/day) is also a lot of fun. Ask at your accommodation for the nearest bike rental outlet.

As with the other Gilis, there's excellent **diving** within twenty minutes' boat ride (see p.328); reputable dive centres include Dream Divers (☎0370/634547, ⓦwww.dreamdivers.com), Manta Dive (☎0813/5305 0462, ⓦwww.manta-dive-giliair.com) and Blue Marlin (☎0370/634387, ⓦwww.bluemarlindive.com), who all have pools. **Snorkelling** trips to distant reefs are widely advertised (Rp80,000).

Eating and drinking

The most popular places during the day are the **bars** and **restaurants** that line the east coast; all have mesmerizing views across the sea to the shifting cloudscapes around Gunung Rinjani.

East and south

Biba Beach Village Classy, authentic Italian food, including home-made ravioli, gnocchi and tagliatelle with many different sauces (from Rp40,000) and, from 7pm onwards, wood-fired pizzas and freshly baked focaccia. Tables under the shoreside trees and in *berugaq*.

Gili Air Santay The Thai food here (from Rp25,000) is recommended, with *pad thai*, *massaman* curry and *somtam* just a few of the classics on offer.

Gita Gili One of several beachside *berugaq* places doing "Gili Air food" such as *ikan parapek* (fish grilled with spicy sauce) and *olah olah sayur* (vegetables in coconut milk).

Green Café This vegetarian, Spanish-accented beachside-*berugaq* café is great for horizon-gazing. On the menu are chilled gazpacho, guacamole, patatas bravas and plenty of design-your-own salads (from Rp40,000).

Scallywags Like its sister operation on Gili T, this laidback beach café serves a lip-smackingly good menu of open and ciabatta sandwiches, salads, steaks and pies, plus fresh seafood

barbecues every night, and free wi-fi. Mains from Rp50,000.

Zipp Bar Popular with beach boys, expats and visitors, this is a fun place to spend the evening listening to mainstream dance music and working through the cocktail menu.

North and west

Legend Chilled north-coast bar and restaurant whose coral mobiles, *berugaq* seating and regulation Rasta accessories make it a nice, quiet spot to while away an afternoon. The food is great: hearty portions of Indo and Euro standards at cheap prices, including an especially good *nasi goreng* (Rp25,000), and there's schnitzel and chips and barbecued seafood too.

Mirage Bar There's good sunset-viewing at this north-coast bar, especially from June to August, with comfy by-the-sand chairs angled for the best panoramas. Known for its popular live jazz on Friday nights.

Space Bar ⓦ www.spacebar-gili-air.csmuc.de /home.html. Dayglo decor and occasional psytrance parties at this quite isolated north-coast beach bar.

North and east Lombok

The focus of any visit to **north Lombok** is **Gunung Rinjani**, Lombok's highest and most sacred volcano. Climbing the mountain is a popular though very challenging undertaking that takes a minimum of two days, but there are plenty of alternative attractions in the area, not least the dramatic mountain scenery, several waterfalls that can be accessed on short hikes, and a couple of traditional Sasak villages. It's perfectly possible to visit the Rinjani area on a day-trip from Senggigi, but if you're reliant on public transport you'll need to stay over – and you generally get the clearest views of the mountain in the early morning. There's accommodation in the villages at the start of the mountain trails, as well as some luxurious hotels on the beautiful **north-coast beaches**. Approaching Rinjani from the south, a couple of inviting villages in the foothills offer a chance to enjoy rural life, gentle treks and exhilarating mountain views. Much of **eastern** Lombok, immediately to Rinjani's east, looks and feels quite different from the lush volcanic uplands: densely populated towns line the corridor along the trans-Lombok highway from Mataram to the port at Labuhan Lombok (serving the neighbouring island of Sumbawa), and the land is either parched or used for tobacco farming.

The north-coast road

Gunung Rinjani is usually accessed via the **coast road** that runs north from Pemenang, near **Bangsal**, the harbour for boats to the Gili Islands. Lombok's two best hotels occupy beaches along here and there are a couple of waterfalls, a traditional Sasak village and Lombok's oldest mosque, all of which can be woven into a day-trip from Senggigi. The district capital of **Tanjung**, 14km up the road from Bengsal, has the region's only international **ATM**.

Bangsal and boats to the Gilis

Tiny **BANGSAL** is the port for public boats to the Gili Islands. Unfortunately, it has a reputation for **hassle**: keep your cool – the Gilis are worth it.

Bangsal is 25km north of Senggigi and 27.5km north of Mataram. Access is via the small town of **Pemenang**, on the main road. All **public transport** between Mataram and points around the north coast passes through Pemenang, some of it going almost via Selaparang Airport (see map, p.309); from Pemenang it's a 1.5km cidomo ride or a shadeless walk to the port. If you're coming **from Senggigi**, however, there's no bemo service so you'll either have to use the 7.30am shuttle-bus transport that's widely advertised (Rp70,000 including boat), or take a taxi.

Even if you're coming by taxi or shuttle bus you have to alight 500m before reaching the harbour, at **the Bangsal barrier** and car park; from here you can either walk or take a cidomo for Rp10,000. The **ticket office** (7.30am–6pm) for all boats to the islands is on the seafront, to your left once you get to the end of the road beyond the barrier; ignore other sellers and buy your ticket from this large, clearly signed building, which displays a printed price list covering public boats, shuttles and charters. Ideally, get your own bag onto and off the boats; if you can't, negotiate with the **porters** before you let them touch the bags – and be clear whether you're talking about rupiah, dollars, for one bag or for the whole lot.

Returning **to Bangsal from the Gilis**, you need to walk (or take a Rp10,000 cidomo) the 500m to the car park beside the barrier to either find your pre-booked shuttle bus connection or get a metered taxi; any tout who meets you directly off the boat will overcharge. There should be some Blue Bird Lombok **taxis** (T0370/627000) waiting in the car park but better still phone ahead and reserve one. A taxi to Selaparang Airport should cost less than Rp100,000, whereas a freelance tout may well charge you Rp200,000.

Bangsal boats to and from the Gili Islands

Public boats to Gili Air (20min; Rp8000), Gili Meno (30min; Rp9000) and Gili Trawangan (45min; Rp10,000) operate from Bangsal throughout the day, leaving when full between 8am and 5pm. If the quota of twenty passengers isn't met you can club together and pay the extra or **charter** a boat for up to twelve people (Rp155,000 –185,000/boat). The only public boat with a fixed departure time is the 2pm boat to Gili Meno, which costs Rp20,000 per person (minimum two).

Fixed-departure **shuttle boats** (20–45min; Rp26,000–28,000) leave Bangsal for all three islands at 9.15am and connect with a bus that leaves Senggigi at 7.30am. Returning **from the Gilis**, shuttle boats depart the islands about 8am and take you to Bangsal, where they're timed to connect with pre-booked through-transport to Mataram/Senggigi (Rp75,000 inclusive), Lembar (Rp125,000), Senaru (Rp195,000) and Kuta, Lombok (Rp200,000); this option avoids having to negotiate with transport touts at Bangsal.

There are a couple of restaurants by the barrier in Bangsal, a moneychanger and one **place to stay**, the *Taman Sari* (☎0812/3727 8070; fan ❸, a/c ❹), with clean fan and air-conditioned rooms opening onto a small garden.

Pantai Sire and Pantai Medana

The longest white-sand **beach** on Lombok, **Pantai Sire**, 6.5km north of Bangsal, is a blindingly beautiful two-kilometre strand of sand and coral, with ultra-calm waters, reasonable swimming at high tide (wear shoes to avoid sea urchins), lots of fish around the reefs about 100m offshore and fine sunrise views of Rinjani. Fronting the beach, the luxurious and idiosyncratic *Tugu* **hotel** (☎0370/612 0111, ⓦwww.tuguhotels.com; ❽) is a romantic getaway with low-lit private-pool suites and rooms that fuse colonial, village and Chinese aesthetic, and a huge infinity pool. The hotel's 🍴 *Kokok Pletok* **restaurant** serves an outstanding *pasar sate* feast (Rp175,000) of half a dozen different sates, sauces and home-style Lombok vegetable dishes that is not to be missed. The fairways of the nearby eighteen-hole Lombok Golf Kosaido Country Club (☎0370/640137; from $78) run down to the beach.

Visible across the bay from the *Tugu*, but on a different beach, **Pantai Medana**, 🍴 *The Oberoi* (☎0370/6138444, ⓦwww.oberoihotels.com; ❾) is Lombok's finest – and most expensive – **hotel**, and the winner of several prestigious awards. Indulgent without being fussy, its signature accommodation is in huge, beautifully appointed thatched villas, all with courtyard dining areas and many with private pools. Park-like palm-filled grounds edge the shore and there's a dive centre, generous pool and offshore reef.

Tiu Pupas and Gangga Falls

Beyond Pantai Medana, the coast road continues north, via **Tanjung**, the district capital of north Lombok; the region's only international (Visa) **ATM** is here, south of the post office. Beyond is the village of **Gondang**, the access point for **Tiu Pupas waterfall**, about 7km inland, via a very rough track. The falls are glorious, tumbling 40m down a semicircular, sheer rock face into a deep pool. In the dry season (May–Nov), however, the water reduces to a trickle. The trio of cascades at **Gangga waterfalls**, also known as **Selelos**, is about an hour's challenging trek beyond Tiu Pupas, through forest and ricefields and via the riverbed, bamboo bridges and a cave; guides will show you the way.

Segenter, Anyar and Bayan

Shortly before the coast road veers south towards Gunung Rinjani at Anyar, signs point inland and uphill to the traditional Sasak village of **SEGENTER**, a 2km drive off the main road through dry expanses of cashew plantation. The village is a favourite stop for tour buses on day-trips to Rinjani and you will be guided round it (donation expected). The traditional part of the village comprises a grid of very simple, mud-floored bamboo-and-thatch huts and the occasional open-sided *berugaq* (general-purpose hut). You'll be taken inside one of the houses to see the eating platform, stone hearth and the *inan bale*, a small house-within-a-house where newlyweds spend their first night, but which is otherwise used to store rice (see p.388).

If you're travelling to Senaru by public transport from Mataram or Pemenang, you'll need to change **bemos** at the market in the small town of **Anyar**, on the main road beyond the Segenter turn-off. Bemos to Senaru are most frequent in the morning so you may have to charter one (about Rp125,000), or hire an ojek (Rp20,000).

Followers of **Wetu Telu** – which translates as "three times", possibly referring to the number of daily prayer-times – adhere to the central tenets of Islam, such as belief in Allah as the one God and Muhammad as his prophet, but diverge significantly from the practices of orthodox Muslims, who, because they pray five times a day, are known as "Wetu Lima".

For the Wetu Telu, the older traditions of **ancestor worship and animism** persist and there are many similarities with Balinese Hindu beliefs and practices; both worship at Pura Lingsar, and Wetu Telu believe that **Gunung Rinjani** is the dwelling place of the ancestors and the Supreme God and make pilgrimages to the mountain. There are many Wetu Telu villages around Rinjani, including **Bayan**, whose ancient mosque is especially important (see below). Many Wetu Telu observe a three-day fast rather than the full month of **Ramadan**. The most important Wetu Telu rituals are **life-cycle ceremonies** associated with birth, death, marriage and circumcision, as well as rituals connected with agriculture and house-building. Their central annual festival is **Maulid**, Muhammad's birthday.

Throughout their history, the Wetu Telu have been subjected to varying degrees of pressure to conform to mainstream Islamic ideas. During the civil unrest in 1965 anyone less than scrupulously orthodox was in danger of being regarded as communist and there were attacks against the Wetu Telu. These days many Wetu Telu profess to follow orthodox Islam while also carrying out their Wetu Telu observances under the label of *adat*, customary practices.

Coming from Labuhan Lombok and the east, you'll change bemos in the village of **BAYAN**, 4km southeast of Anyar. Bayan is also the site of Lombok's oldest mosque, **Masjid Kuno Bayan Beleq**, located on the eastern edge of the village, 1km east of the junction with the road to Senaru. Said to date from before 1700, around the time when Islam probably first arrived on Lombok, the mosque is strikingly simple in design, constructed entirely from timber, woven bamboo and palm thatch, atop a foundation of stones. It's been renovated of course, but apparently in the original style. You can't go inside to see the mud floor and the bamboo torches, used to light the interior during the few festival days when the mosque is used, but you are free to walk around its exterior. This whole area, around the foothills of Gunung Rinjani and the sacred mountain itself, is a stronghold of the Wetu Telu branch of Islam (see box, above), and Masjid Kuno Bayan Beleq has a central role.

Continuing east from the mosque, you'll soon pass the turn-off for **Teres Genit** and its lovely accommodation at *Rinjani Mountain Garden* (see p.344). The main road winds 8km through the foothills of Gunung Rinjani, offering fine views of the volcano and soon giving way to the arid terrain of the east of Lombok. From the junction village of **Kokok Putih**, also known as Kalih Putih, buses run to the Sembalun valley, an alternative access-point for treks up Rinjani. The main road around the north coast continues for another 10km to Obel Obel and on to the east coast.

Gunung Rinjani and around

The **climb** up majestic, forested **GUNUNG RINJANI** (3726m), taking in the magnificent crater lake of **Danau Segara Anak**, is the most taxing and rewarding trek on either Bali or Lombok. Most climbs start from either **Senaru** or **Sembalun Lawang**, on the northern slopes. If you want to reach the

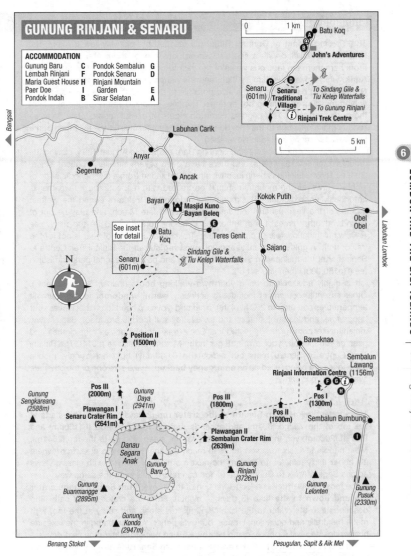

GUNUNG RINJANI & SENARU

ACCOMMODATION

Gunung Baru	C	Pondok Sembalun	G
Lembah Rinjani	F	Pondok Senaru	D
Maria Guest House	H	Rinjani Mountain	
Paer Doe	I	Garden	E
Pondok Indah	B	Sinar Selatan	A

0   1 km   Batu Koq

John's Adventures

Senaru (601m)   Senaru Traditional Village

To Sindang Gile & Tiu Kelep Waterfalls
To Gunung Rinjani
Rinjani Trek Centre

0   5 km

Bangsal

Labuhan Carik

Anyar

Segenter

Ancak

Bayan   Kokok Putih

Masjid Kuno Bayan Beleq

Batu Koq   Teres Genit   Obel Obel

See inset for detail

Senaru (601m)   Sindang Gile & Tiu Kelep Waterfalls   Sajang

N

Labuhan Lombok

Position II (1500m)

Bawaknao

Sembalun Lawang (1156m)

Rinjani Information Centre

Gunung Sengkareang (2588m)   Pos III (2000m)   Gunung Daya (2941m)   Pos III (1800m)   F G i
H
Pos I (1300m)

Plawangan I Senaru Crater Rim (2641m)   Pos II (1500m)   Sembalun Bumbung

Danau Segara Anak   Plawangan II Sembalun Crater Rim (2639m)   I

Gunung Baru

Gunung Buanmangge (2895m)   Gunung Rinjani (3726m)   Gunung Lelonten   Gunung Pusuk (2330m)

Gunung Kondo (2947m)

Benang Stokel   Pesugulan, Sapit & Aik Mel

summit, Sembalun Lawang is the best base. If you just want to see Danau Segara Anak from the crater rim, the easiest access is from Senaru. Other upland villages south of Rinjani, notably **Sapit** and **Tetebatu**, make pleasant rural bases with opportunities for gentle hikes as well as facilities for arranging Rinjani climbs.

Batu Koq and Senaru

The small, contiguous villages of **BATU KOQ** and **SENARU**, south of Bayan (about 86km from Mataram), are the main centre for Rinjani treks, full of

The 3726m **summit** of **Gunung Rinjani** is reached by relatively few trekkers; the majority are satisfied with a shorter, less arduous hike to the **crater rim** (2641m). From here there are fabulous views of the vast turquoise crater lake, **Danau Segara Anak**, which measures 8km by 6km, and the perfect, sometimes smoking, cone of **Gunung Baru** rising from it. It is also possible to descend to the lakeside and ease aching muscles in scalding **hot springs**. The lake is considered to be the abode of the gods, and Wetu Telu pilgrims come on nights of the full moon, while Balinese Hindus make offerings to the lake during the Pekelem festival (at the full moon of the fifth Balinese month, often in November).

Having lain dormant since 1906, Gunung Baru **erupted** in August 1994, closing the mountain for several weeks, and there have been several smaller eruptions since. Gunung Rinjani itself has been inactive since 1901, apart from a few periodic puffs of smoke. However, the mountain should be treated with respect, and its weather is notoriously unpredictable. The mountain is **closed to trekkers** during the wettest months of the year, usually from late December to late March, and may be out of bounds at other times if the authorities consider conditions to be too risky; see ⓦ www.rinjaninationalpark.com for details. Trekking at any time of year is not for the frail or unfit. A guide is essential and you must **register** at the Rinjani Trek Centre at Senaru or at the trailhead in Sembalun Lawang and pay the national park admission fee (Rp150,000) when you set off.

It is highly advisable to bring your own **walking boots** (trainers aren't suitable). Other essential equipment includes a seriously **warm, windproof jacket** (summit temperatures can drop to 2°C at night), a hat and gloves, a head torch that leaves your hands free, and loads of snacks and sweets (even if food is provided). See ⓦ www .rinjanimaster.com for a suggested list. Some trekking companies rent clothes and gear, or you can buy your own at Eiger in the Mataram Mall (see p.311). The Rinjani Trek Centre in Senaru rents out radios (Rp10,000/day) but, increasingly, mobile telephones are being relied on as **emergency backup**; make sure one or the other are available in your party.

Routes

The shortest trek is **from Senaru to the crater rim** (2 days, 1 night). This starts at the top of the village (601m) and ascends through forest to **Pos II** (1500m) and **Pos III** (2000m); you then leave the forest for the steep slog up to the rim (2641m). Most people take six to seven hours to reach the sheltered camp area, from where it's about thirty minutes to the rim the next morning for sunrise, with classic views across Segara Anak to Gunung Baru. You can return to Senaru the same way.

The most popular trek is a longer version of the above: **from Senaru to the crater rim and down to the lake** (3 days, 2 nights). From the crater rim, a path (2hr) descends into the crater to the lake (2050m). It is steep and scary at the top, with metal handrails and occasional ropes, but gets better. You can bathe in the lakeside hot springs and will probably camp nearby, walking back to Senaru the next day.

You can also combine **the lake and summit from Senaru** (4 days, 3 nights). From the lake, a different path (3hr; pretty steep but not as bad as previous descent) climbs to the rim on the Sembalun side and a site called **Plawangan II** (2639m), where everyone aiming for the summit overnights. From there it's an extraordinarily steep haul up to the summit of Rinjani (3726m; another 3–4hr, usually done for sunrise, then 3hr back down to Plawangan II). Trekkers usually descend via the shortest route, to Sembalun Lawang.

The **shortest route to the summit** is to climb **from Sembalun Lawang** (2 days, 1 night). It takes seven to eight hours from Sembalun Lawang (1156m) to Plawangan II and you attack the summit the next morning, before returning to Sembalun.

The most complete exploration of the mountain involves a round trip **from Sembalun Lawang to Senaru, via the summit and the lake** (4 days, 3 nights). This gets the most exhausting ascent over while you are fresh and enables you to soak tired muscles in the hot springs afterwards. Longer trips of up to six days, featuring caves around the lake as well as the summit, are also available.

Senaru and Sembalun Lawang are by far the most common trailheads, but recently a route up the southwestern flank has opened up, **from Benang Stokel**, the site of two well-known waterfalls about 28km northeast of Mataram (see p.313). This trail takes you up to the crater rim, via dense forest (6hr), and then down to the southern side of the lake (3hr), and is likely to be a lot quieter than the main routes. The return route is the same, unless you want to tackle the summit, in which case you need to arrange to get paddled across the lake to the Sembalun side.

Booking a trek

Agents in every tourist centre on Lombok, including Gili Trawangan and Senggigi, and even some on Bali, will offer to sell you a Rinjani trek, but choose wisely: this is a serious climb and there have been fatalities due to poor equipment (including lack of sufficiently warm gear) and reckless disregard for safety. You are likely to get the most authentic information from trek organizers based in the trailhead villages of **Senaru** and **Sembalun Lawang**, and from other trekkers.

The **Rinjani Trek Management Board** (RTMB; Ⓦ www.lombokrinjanitrek.org), which coordinates and licenses trekking facilities on the mountain, has established a ballpark pricing system that factors in the number of people in the group and the **level of service** – budget, standard or deluxe – required. In practice, there's plenty of competitive pricing going on, though corners are likely to be cut if you bargain too hard; insufficient food and unbearably thin sleeping bags are common complaints. Whatever your chosen service level, you should get a guide, porters, sleeping bags, tents, meals and water. If you opt for the budget service you should expect minimal food and water and shabby equipment; deluxe service, on the other hand, should get you air mattresses, bigger meals and toilet tents; there's a guide to these different levels of service at Ⓦ www.lombokdetours.com. Before you book, be sure to get specific details of exactly **what is included** in the price (transport, accommodation, precise list of equipment), how many people there will be in your group, what you'll be eating at each meal, and how many litres of water each trekker is allocated. **Prices** start at about Rp975,000 per person for the crater-rim trek from Senaru (2 days, 1 night), joining a budget group of up to ten people, or about Rp1,375,000 for the rim and lake (3 days, 2 nights). Doing the same routes in a group of two, with deluxe service, will cost around Rp1,850,000/2,350,000.

Senaru is by far the busiest trekking centre, with eighteen registered **trek organizers**. Organizers don't usually climb with you but employ guides and porters from the pool of three-hundred-plus local personnel registered with the RTMB. Many organizers are based at guesthouses, or you could try John's Adventures (Ⓣ0817/578 8018, Ⓦ www.rinjanimaster.com), which is long established and well known and is soon to open accommodation as well. The local RTMB office, the **Rinjani Trek Centre** (Ⓦ www.lombokrinjanitrek.org) at the Senaru trailhead can also help organize treks. **Sembalun Lawang** is much quieter and has far fewer trek organizers: try either *Maria* or *Lembah Rinjani* guesthouses (see p.345). A reputable Senggigi agent is Rinjani Trekking Club (Ⓣ0817/573 0415, Ⓦ www.lombokdetours .com); freelance guide Made Minggir (Ⓣ0819/9988 8910, Ⓔ madetravel10@yahoo .com) is also recommended.

guesthouses and trekking organizers. With cool temperatures and fine views of the mountain, they're also a pleasant destination in their own right.

Other than Rinjani itself, Senaru's main attractions are its waterfalls. The impressive 25m-high **Sindang Gile falls** (Rp20,000; also allows entry to Tiu Kelep falls) is reached via a twenty-minute hike along a path that begins just south of *Pondok Senaru* bungalows. Another hour's challenging uphill slog gets you to **Tiu Kelep** falls, where the water pours down in a double horseshoe. You should probably take a dip here; local belief is that you become a year younger every time you swim behind the falls. Guides are compulsory for Tiu Kelep (Rp60,000/group). Longer local treks such as the **Senaru Panorama Walk** (3hr; Rp150,000/person) take in the falls and are guided by women from the village; you'll probably get the best price if you arrange them through the Rinjani Trek Centre (see p.343).

Within a fenced compound a few metres from the Rinjani trailhead, at the end of the road and almost next door to the Rinjani Trek Centre, is Senaru's original **Sasak village** (entry by donation), whose residents still live in simple, traditional houses of bamboo and thatch, similar in design to those at Segenter (see p.339). A villager will show you round.

Arrival and information

Transport to Senaru is via Anyar or Bayan (see p.339 for details). Once here, John's Adventures (see box, p.343) has **exchange** facilities (and can arrange flights and fast-boat tickets to Gili Trawangan); some trek organizers will take Visa cards, but the nearest ATM is in Tanjung. There's **internet** access at *Sinar Selatan* bungalows and a **clinic** 100m uphill; Bayan has a small, local hospital.

If you're climbing Rinjani, you'll get information on the mountain at the **Rinjani Trek Centre**, at the trailhead at the southernmost limit of Senaru. It's run by the Rinjani Trek Management Board (see box, p.343) and displays maps of the mountain and background info.

Accommodation and eating

Accommodation, with one notable exception, is spread for several kilometres along the road through Batu Koq and Senaru. Places on the east of the road generally have the best views towards the mountain. Most are pretty basic, with cold-water bathrooms (some have squat toilets); all have small **restaurants** attached, and most can arrange local hikes and trekking guides and will store your stuff while you climb.

Gunung Baru ☎0819/0741 1211, ✉gunung baru-trekkingholiday@yahoo.com. Small setup not far from the start of the trail with five simple, tiled bungalows. ❶

Pondok Indah ☎0878/6543 3344. A row of nine perfectly acceptable bungalows set in a pleasant garden. ❶

Pondok Senaru ☎0818/0362 4129. The biggest place in the area, offering a range of decent bungalows, some with hot water, in a pretty garden with good views and easy access to the waterfalls. Has a large, panoramic restaurant too. Cold water ❸, hot water ❹

Rinjani Mountain Garden ☎0818/569730, ✉rinjanigarden@hotmail.de. A gorgeous, remote spot, designed and run by a German couple, with stylish recycled-wood bungalows, simple bamboo *pondok* huts with shared bathrooms (good single rates), and fully equipped tents erected on platforms. The garden has panoramic views and a freshwater swimming pool and there's excellent food. Access is via a very rough road to Teres Genit, 4km east of the old mosque in Bayan, so phone ahead for free Bayan pick-up. Senaru is an hour's walk away. Tent ❷, *pondok* ❸, bungalow ❹

Sinar Selatan ☎0818/540673, ✉jul.yadi @hotmail.com. Good-quality fan and a/c rooms, plus internet access. Fan ❶, a/c ❸

Sembalun Lawang and Sembalun Bumbung

Set in a high, flat-bottomed mountain valley filled with market gardens growing potatoes and chillies, **SEMBALUN LAWANG** is a very quiet village that's known chiefly as a trailhead for one of the main routes up Gunung Rinjani. There are several more gentle local **treks** as well: the leisurely Sembalun Village Walk to Sajang Waterfall (4hr; Rp117,000/person), the Sembalun Wildflowers Walk (includes an overnight camp; best May–Oct; Rp993,000), and the overnight jungle hike over Pegasingan Hill to Obel Obel on the north coast (Rp993,000). The area is also known for **handweaving**, and it's possible to visit local weavers. For all treks, ask at one of the village **guesthouses**. Longest established of these is *Lembah Rinjani* (T0818/0365 2511, Wsites.google.com/site/lembahrinjani; ❸), 200m along the Rinjani trail, which has a restaurant and clean rooms with verandas facing the mountain and can provide hot water in a bucket for bathing. Next door, *Pondok Sembalun* (T0819/1811 1163; ❷) has four simple, cold-water bungalows but no real views. *Maria Guest House* (T0852/3956 1340, Wwww .mariaguesthouse.com; ❷), across from the District Office on the main road, has reasonable rooms, with partial Rinjani views, and organizes treks. Sembalun is about 30km southeast of Senaru, via a steep 16km road from Kokok Putih, and about 16km north of Sapit on the other side of the mountains. It's about Rp200,000 to charter a **bemo** to or from Senaru, or Rp35,000 by ojek; Kokok Putih ojeks charge Rp20,000.

Continuing south towards Sapit, market gardens proliferate until the valley closes in. Some 4km south of Sembalun Lawang, the village of **SEMBALUN BUMBUNG** clusters round the mosque in the shadows of the surrounding mountains. You can stay here, at *Paer Doe* (T0819/1771 4514; ❷), a tiny, rudimentary **homestay** opposite the football field at the southern end of the village.

From Sembalun Bumbung, the mountain road winds for 15km across Gunung Pusuk to Pesugulan, the turn-off for Sapit; there's a fine valley viewpoint at the pass, then it's mostly forest, inhabited by grey macaques and rare ebony leaf monkeys. Rockfalls are common so the road is sometimes closed.

Sapit

Situated on the southern slopes of Gunung Pusuk, 10km south over the pass from Sembalun Bumbung, the small village of **SAPIT** makes a quiet retreat with views down to the east coast and over to Sumbawa. Tobacco-growing is the main industry round here, and Philip Morris the big employer; fields are dotted with red-brick drying towers. With two small **guesthouses** in the village (run by the same family), this is a good chance to get away from tourist crowds; staff will fill you in on **trails** to nearby waterfalls and natural swimming pools and can organize Rinjani treks. Both *Balelangga* (T0819/1737 3234, Wwww.balelangga.com; ❶), next to the mosque, and nearby *Hati Suci* (T0818/545655, Wwww.hatisuci.tk; ❶) have simple bungalows in lovely gardens with nice outlooks. Each has a small **restaurant**, and *Hati Suci* also has a table-tennis table. Sapit is 16km from Sembalun Lawang, served by a daily **bus**; there are also **bemos** from Aik Mel on the cross-island highway (17km), and a few from Pringgabaya (20km).

Tetebatu

Scenically situated on the southern slopes of Gunung Rinjani, 50km east of Mataram (11km north of the main cross-island highway), the little town of **TETEBATU** enjoys fine views of the mountain across terraced fields lush with rice in the rainy season and tobacco in the dry; tall, red-brick drying towers for the tobacco are visible at every turn. At an altitude of about 600m, the area is cool but not cold and makes an excellent base from which to appreciate small-town life and explore the centre of the island. You can also arrange ascents of Rinjani here (see p.342).

Arrival, information and local transport

Bemos and **buses** from Mataram will get you to Pomotong on the main road, from where it's about 10km to Tetebatu: either take a bemo to Kotaraja then an ojek, or an ojek all the way. Alternatively **Perama** offers shuttle transport from Mataram (Rp125,000; ⓦ www.peramatour.com).

There's currently no official **exchange** in Tetebatu, and the nearest ATM is in Masbagik, about 13km south. There's **internet** access 2km south of Tetebatu at the first intersection in Kotaraja.

It's easy to arrange **motorbike** rental (Rp60,000), motorbike taxis (Rp100,000/day) and **cars** with driver (Rp400,000/day). Maldy, 75m south of the T-junction, rents **bicycles** (Rp50,000/day), or ask at *Green Orry*.

Accommodation

Accommodation is generally very simple, with no fans and mostly cold-water bathrooms.

Green Orry ☎ 0812/372 4040. Lacks atmosphere or views but compensates with well-furnished, modern rooms and optional hot water. ❸
Hakiki ☎ 0818/0373 7407. Very bare-bones *lumbung*-style bungalows set in a garden encircled by paddyfields but quite isolated, about 1km from the centre. ❶
Pondok Bulan ☎ 03878/6592 3240. Tiny place

whose nice rooms have good bathrooms and rural views; posher versions are in the pipeline. ❷
🏃 **Pondok Tetebatu** ☎ 0818/0576 7153, ⓦ www.pondok-tetebatu.webs.com. With views of Rinjani from the pretty garden, thick mattresses, cheery decor and nice staff, the clean bungalows here are a great choice. Pricier rooms have hot water. ❷

The Town and around

Tiny Tetebatu has no sights of its own, though on a clear morning the views north to Rinjani are exhilarating. The main street has plenty of small *kios* to browse, mostly selling everyday necessities and fresh food.

The main local attraction is the **trek** through ricefields to the local monkey forest and **Jukut Waterfall** (entry Rp20,000), where the water streams down a towering jungle-clad rock face into a pool 20m below. Any guesthouse can organize this as a six-hour return trip: *Pondok Tetebatu* quotes Rp100,000 per person including ticket. With your own transport you can also travel by road to the falls car park (6km),

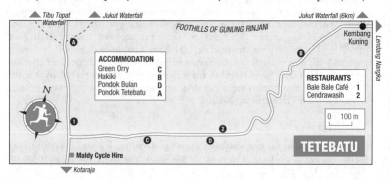

from where it's 1.5km on foot. The twin cascades of **Tibu Topat**, northwest of the village, are a pretty alternative, with a sunlit pool for swimming: the three-hour return trek through the fields costs Rp75,000 per person. Also to the northwest, **Joben waterfall**, or Otak Kokok Gading, is small and much less impressive.

With transport you can also explore the town of **Kotaraja**, about 5km south, which is known for its **blacksmiths** and for its traditional **stick fighting**, *peresean* (see p.383), held in August; and nearby **Loyok**, a centre for **bamboo basketware**.

Eating

During the day, the octagonal **restaurant** at *Cendrawasih* is a nice place to hang out, with cushion seating, views across fields to Rinjani, and a menu of travellers' dishes. After sunset, Tetebatu's main street is often in darkness, but it's worth venturing out for **food** at the *Bale Bale Café*, run by an English-speaking local character and his family; the Sasak menu is mostly vegetarian and includes *olah olah* (vegetables in coconut sauce), *berdegel* (corn fritters) and soups.

East Lombok

With an arid climate, sparse population and few facilities, **east Lombok** doesn't entice many visitors, although if you're heading to or from Sumbawa you'll pass through the port of **Labuhan Lombok**. The one reason to linger is the prospect of good snorkelling at the uninhabited islands off **Labuhan Pandan**.

Easiest access to east Lombok is via the busy **trans-Lombok highway** from Mataram, an almost continuously built-up 75km-long corridor whose urban sprawl is punctuated by huge mosques and feels a world away from the laidback south and west coasts and the sparsely inhabited Rinjani highlands. You can also get to the east from the north coast, via Obel Obel, and from Rinjani, via Sapit.

Masbagik and the Penakak potteries

You can't miss the principle mosque in **MASBAGIK**, Masjid Al-Jami Al-Akbar: it's on the main trans-Lombok highway, in the heart of this busy town, and is one of the largest in Lombok. Across the road is a BCA international **ATM** (the closest to Tetebatu and Sapit). Signed south off the highway, 1.5km east of the mosque, is the **pottery-producing** village of **PENAKAK**, whose road is lined with large and small outlets selling a vast array of pottery from all over Lombok.

Labuhan Lombok

LABUHAN LOMBOK, 75km east of Mataram, is the port for the island of Sumbawa but has little else of interest. **Buses** travel the length of the trans-Lombok highway from Mataram's Mandalika terminal to Labuhan Lombok; some continue to the **ferry terminal**, Pelabuhan Kayangan, which is 3.5km from the town centre. **Arriving** at the port from Sumbawa, it's Rp5000 by ojek to Labuhan Lombok's town centre and bus terminal for buses to Mataram; for Kuta you'll need to change first at Kopang, on the highway, then again at Praya. Alternatively, the private transport company Travel Kayangan runs cars from the port to Mataram, Senggigi and elsewhere, charging from Rp40,000 per person with seven people in the car, or Rp250,000 or more per car. If booked

Moving on to Sumbawa

The **ferry to Sumbawa** departs Labuhan Lombok round the clock (every 45min; Rp15,500, motorbike from Rp42,500, car with passengers from Rp322,000) and takes one and a half hours to reach Poto Tano on Sumbawa's northwest coast. Alternatively, you can book **long-distance bus** tickets from Mataram's Mandalika terminal through to destinations on Sumbawa (see p.308).

ahead, Perama shuttle buses will also do private transfers to Kuta, Tetebatu or Senggigi, quoting Rp500,000 per car for a maximum of four passengers (℡0370/693007, ⓦ www.peramatour.com).

If you need a **hotel**, try the very basic *Hotel Melati Lima Tiga*, Jl Kayangan 14 (❶), about 150m from the town centre on the road to the ferry terminal, opposite the market.

Pantai Pulo Lampu and the eastern islands

Beyond the radar of most foreign tourists, the isolated little beach of **Pantai Pulo Lampu**, 13km north of Labuhan Lombok, near the village of Transat, is popular with locals at weekends but otherwise very quiet. Its main attraction is access to the two groups of uninhabited **islands** just off the coast. The most southerly group – **Gili Lampu**, **Gili Kondo** and **Gili Bidara** – have sandy beaches as well as coral walls and attract plenty of fish. Further north, the larger islands of **Gili Sulat** and **Gili Lawang** are surrounded by coastal mangrove but have lots of coral.

The only **accommodation** is at *Pondok Gili Lampu* on Pantai Pulo Lamphu, (℡0819/1812 3389; ❶), which has basic wood-and-thatch bungalows in a garden behind the restaurant and beach. The enthusiastic, English-speaking manager arranges **boat trips** to the islands for snorkelling or fishing (from Rp300,000/boat for up to six people), and can organize a private "desert-island" camping trip (from Rp1,200,000 for two people all inclusive). **Bemos** from Labuhan Lombok will drop you on the main road for the 500m walk down to the bungalows.

South Lombok

The as yet largely undeveloped **south coast** of Lombok is extraordinarily beautiful, its mile upon mile of white-sand bays backed by wild, forested hills and washed by some of the most rewarding surf on the island. Low-key **Kuta** is the main tourist centre, centrally positioned for exploring the fabulous coastline to the west and east. **Inland**, there are worthwhile textile workshops at Sukarara, plus a couple of traditional Sasak villages at **Sade** and **Rembitan**.

Outside the peak periods of July, August and late December, Kuta and the south are remarkably quiet, but the region is set to become a lot more popular once the new **Lombok International Airport** finally opens, possibly by 2012 (see p.306); it's located 15km north of Kuta, 10km south of Praya and roads across the south have already seen a much-needed upgrade. In anticipation of a boom, land is also being snapped up all over the south, and plans for a huge resort development near Kuta are once again in the news.

Praya and around

The market town of **PRAYA**, 22km southeast of Mataram and 26km north of Kuta, is a transport hub for the south and will likely become even more important when the new airport opens, 10km south of town. Coming by **bus** from Mataram's Mandalika terminal, you'll have to change here for Kuta, and may have to change again at Sengkol, though some bemos go straight through. As the bus terminal is 3km northwest of the centre, most visitors bypass the town completely, but there are international **ATMs** (Kuta's nearest) on Jalan Jend Sudirman in the town centre. There's also a good **restaurant**, *Lesehan Asri*, a couple of blocks north, near the police and fire stations on Jalan Basuki Rachmad. Very popular with office workers, it serves delicious local food, including grilled fish and *kangkung pelecing*, for Rp25,000.

Sukarara

The village of **SUKARARA**, about 8km west of Praya, produces the widest range of textiles on Lombok, weaving highly coloured *songket* cloth on backstrap looms and *ikat* cloth on foot looms (see p.194). A sarong-and-scarf set can take up to five months to weave and designs are so numerous and complex that girls and boys start learning at the age of seven; young women must be skilled weavers in order to be considered marriageable. There are a number of **textile outlets** in Sukarara, and in the neighbouring village of Puyung, but worth singling out is Patuh Art Shop, 2km south of the junction with the main Praya road. It sells an enormous range produced by the local cooperative and on request will show you the weavers at work.

Sade and Rembitan traditional villages

North of Kuta on the Sengkol road are a couple of traditional **Sasak villages** that welcome tourists. Of the two, the northernmost, **REMBITAN** (suggested Rp10,000 donation and Rp10,000 for compulsory guide), 7km from Kuta, is the more authentic and the less grasping; with a good guide you'll learn a lot. As with other such villages in north Bali, the thirty homes here are simple, low-roofed windowless constructions, with mud and buffalo-dung floors, bamboo walls and thatched roofs (see p.388). Some have satellite TV but bathrooms are communal. Villagers farm soybeans and rice and weave cloth and make basketware, some of which is for sale.

The other traditional village is **SADE** (admission by donation), 1km south. It sees hordes of visitors, is more of a shopping and photo opportunity, and has a reputation for hassle.

Kuta and around

Located in the middle of Lombok's exhilaratingly untamed south coast, **KUTA** is the region's main tourist centre, set between rocky headlands amid swathes of sparsely inhabited wilderness punctuated by heart-stopping curves of soft white sand and turquoise water. Youthful, laidback and surferish, with much cheaper

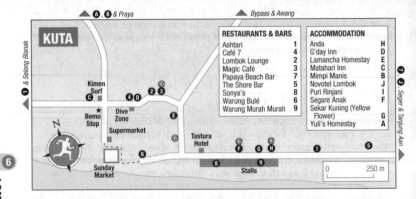

accommodation than Senggigi, Kuta is for the time being still strikingly low-key – not much more than a fishing village with surfers' accommodation, tourist restaurants and a few upscale alternatives. But real-estate agents are mushrooming and there is much talk of a building boom once the new international airport, a mere 15km to the north, is operational (see p.306). For years, shorefront land east of Kuta has been earmarked for a vast five-star resort; local resistance and inconclusive commitment from Middle Eastern investors has so far stalled the project but there's little doubt that the area won't remain undeveloped.

For the moment, however, there is plenty for all to enjoy and, apart from the Sunday **market**, the area is astonishingly quiet outside July and August. **Surfers** return year after year to pursue the perfect wave, most famously at **Gerupuk** and **Mawi**, and more remotely, at **Ekas**. **Kuta beach** itself is scruffy and unappealing – and some find its persistent hawkers wearying and even intimidating – but there are breathtakingly gorgeous white-sand bays nearby, notably **east** at **Tanjung Aan** and west at **Mawun**, both of which are good for swimming, though always ask locally about currents, which can be treacherous.

To access the beaches and get the best out of the area you need a **motorbike** – and strong nerves, as the roads, especially to the western beaches, are prone to atrocious potholes (upgrades are planned, however); alternatively, you can always hire someone to be the driver. Beach-shack **stalls** and other small shops sell basic necessities and transport services, and there's a small supermarket too.

Arrival and local transport

Kuta is 50km from Mataram and 26km south of Praya. Coming from the west you need to take a **bus** from Mataram's Mandalika terminal to Praya, and then change (see p.349). From east Lombok, bemos run to Praya via Kopang on the main trans-Lombok highway. **Shuttle buses** run to Kuta from the Gilis and Senggigi, and Perama (ⓦwww.peramatour.com) also operates services from Mataram (minimum two people; Rp125,000) and Lembar (minimum four; Rp125,000). *Segare Anak* (ⓣ0370/654846) is the local Perama agent.

Onward transport to destinations across Lombok, as well as to Bali, Sumbawa and Flores, is widely advertised in Kuta. Prices are set by the local transport co-op (minimum two people): Mataram/Selaparang airport or Lembar port Rp110,000; Senggigi Rp125,000; Bangsal Rp150,000; Gili Islands (including boat) Rp180,000; Kuta, Bali Rp200,000.

Motorbikes are available to rent everywhere from Rp40,000. **Bicycles** and **cars** are harder to come by: ask at *Mimpi Manis*.

Diving and snorkelling in south Lombok

The two areas for **diving** in the south are good at different times of year and are always very quiet; it's also possible to reach dive sites in the southwest, around Sekotong (see p.316).

Kuta sites are best from October to March and are good for novices. The area is known for its pelagics and (from December) its manta rays. At Gili Medas, in front of the *Novotel*, you'll encounter pygmy seahorses and manta rays, and Tanpa has plentiful coral. Mawun is the only real option for **snorkellers**.

Blongas, west of Selong Blanak, can be dived year-round but it's open ocean and is only for experienced divers with a minimum of fifty dives and Advanced certification. In August and September it's good for devil rays and hammerheads.

Accommodation

There's almost no on-the-beach **accommodation** and no real sea views but most places are an easy stroll from the water. Theft from rooms is an occasional problem: always lock your room and outside-bathroom door, including when you're asleep inside. Try to book ahead in July and August, when rooms can be hard to find.

Anda ☎0370/655049. Sixteen clean, tiled budget rooms in two different styles and sizes (the bigger ones are very spacious). Guests get an hour's free internet access per room per day. Fan ❷, a/c ❸

G'day Inn ☎0370/655342. Four simple, well-kept rooms with mosquito nets and attached cold-water bathrooms in a family compound. ❷

Lamancha Homestay ☎0370/655186. Run by a welcoming village family, there are seven rooms here: the simplest have bamboo walls and squat toilets; newer, pricier ones are more robust and nicely furnished. Basic rooms ❷, new rooms ❸

Matahari Inn ☎0370/655000. Friendly, mid-range hotel with over two-dozen good-quality, Bali-style rooms in buildings around a large garden compound with a swimming pool. Some have hot water and a/c, and the top-end villas are huge. Fan ❷, a/c ❹

Mimpi Manis ☎081/836 9950, ⓦwww.mimpimanis.com. A home-from-home run by a very hospitable Balinese–English family, this tiny, spotless homestay, about 2km north of the beach, is exceptionally good value. It offers one a/c and one fan room, plus a two-storey house, all with DVD players and safety boxes, plus internet access and motorbike, car and bicycle rental. Fan ❶, a/c ❷, house ❸

Novotel Lombok (Mandalika Resort) ☎0370/653333, ⓦwww.novotellombok.com. Kuta's top hotel is stunningly located on its own stretch of white-sand beach, a 15min walk from Seger beach, and 3km by road from central Kuta. It's designed like a thatch-roofed village of 101 tastefully decorated rooms; some have private pools, all have wi-fi. There's a large seafront pool (Rp50,000 for non-guests) and a spa, plus lots of activities. ❼

Puri Rinjani ☎0370/654849 A dozen clean, good-quality rooms in a big garden, some with hot water and a/c. Fan ❸, a/c ❺

Segare Anak ☎0370/654846. Long-established place with 23 rooms in many different styles and standards. Bottom-end options are very basic (with squat toilets) but some of the mid-priced ones are good quality and a few have a/c. Safe deposit boxes are available and there's wi-fi, a dinky pool and internet and travel services. Fan ❶, a/c ❸

Sekar Kuning (Yellow Flower) ☎0370/654856. A dozen well-maintained rooms with fans and cold-water bathrooms. The decor isn't fancy but rooms (in two-storey blocks) are a good size and some of the upstairs ones have partial sea views. ❸

Yuli's Homestay ☎0819/1710 0983, ⓦwww.yulishomestay.com. A strikingly modern homestay, 600m north of central Kuta, where the three large and sparklingly clean guest rooms – all with a/c and cold-water bathroom – are adjacent to the house of the charming New Zealand–Lombok owners. Guests have use of the pool and shady seating on the lawn. ❹

The resort

Screened in part by a line of beach-shack stalls and restaurants along the road that parallels it, Kuta's **beach** is no great shakes, so for a swim and a sunbathe you're better off heading up to the *Novotel* or west to Mawun.

Surfing is the main deal in Kuta and is possible year round. Selong Blanak is sandy and good for beginners, and novices can also usually surf Gerupuk; Mawi is a swell magnet. Several **surf shops**, including the long-established Kimen (T0370/655064, Wwww.kuta-lombok.net), repair and rent boards (Rp50,000/day) and offer lessons (Rp360,000/4hr) and trips (from Rp320,000 for up to two surfers to Gerupuk, Mawi or Are Goleng; Rp700,000 to Ekas; Rp1,500,000 to Bangko Bangko). They can also arrange surf-and-stay packages.

Mimpi Manis (T081/836 9950, Wwww.mimpimanis.com) runs half-day **fishing trips** ($100 for up to three people) and overnight **fishing camps** with nights spent on board or camping on remote beaches ($100/person/day all inclusive). Surfers are welcome to bring their boards.

Diving around south Lombok has the huge advantage of being extremely quiet (see p.351). Dive Zone (T0813/3954 4998, Wwww.divezone-lombok.com) charges from Rp750,000 for two dives all-inclusive and also does liveaboard trips to Komodo.

It's also possible to explore the area on horseback: guided **horseriding** costs from Rp400,000 (T0819/1599 9436, Wwww.horseridingkuta.canalblog.com).

Eating and drinking

Portions are large and prices generally reasonable at Kuta's **restaurants**, not least because of the surfers who return year after year. **Nightlife** mostly consists of a couple of local bands that play at one or other of the restaurant bars several nights a week.

Ashtari 3km west from central Kuta on the Mawun road. Occupying a spectacular panoramic hilltop position (on a steep, potholed road), with breathtaking views over the Kuta coastline to Tanjung Aan and beyond, this is a great place to spend a few hours, with a good vegetarian menu – including focaccia sandwiches and salads, juices and breakfasts – and an inviting chill-out zone. Mains from Rp20,000. Tues–Sun 8.30am–6pm.

Café 7 Good, hearty servings of pasta, plus pizzas, fairly cheap cocktails (Rp45,000) and often a nice relaxed buzz in the evening, with shisha pipes and regular live music.

Lombok Lounge Has a good reputation for seafood, including chilli crab. Also does tasty *fuyung hai* (sweet and sour Chinese omelettes) and better-than-average French fries. Mains from Rp25,000.

Magic Café Free wi-fi, squishy armchairs and a 6–7pm happy hour bring in the punters at sundown. There's also illy coffee, cakes and ice creams, plus tapas and more substantial dishes. Internet access is available in the adjacent real estate office, and there's occasional live music too.

Papaya Beach Bar Civilized seaside sundowners at the *Novotel Mandalika Resort*'s beachfront bar.

Nyale Festival

Celebrated on Lombok and the more distant islands of Sumba and Savu, this annual festival is all about the sea worm, *Eunice viridis*, known locally as **nyale**. The worms live attached to rocks in the ocean, but at roughly the same time every year, on the nineteenth day of the tenth Sasak month (Feb or March), they begin their sexual cycle and release brightly coloured male and female sexual parts, which rise to the surface ready for fertilization, turning the ocean into a seething mass of fluorescent spaghetti. The number of worms is believed to indicate the success of the next rice harvest and draws huge crowds to celebrate Bau Nyale, the **Nyale Festival**. Around a hundred thousand people travel to Kuta's Seger beach and other south-coast beaches to gather the worms – which are believed to be aphrodisiacs – and to enjoy traditional singing, dancing, poetry and a re-enactment of the Putri Mandalika **legend**. This tells how the beautiful Princess Mandalika, distraught because of the number of suitors who were fighting over her and loath to upset any of them and risk plunging her country into war, flung herself into the sea where her hair was changed into *nyale* sea worms.

The Shore Bar There's regular live music at this long-running two-storey bar–restaurant just across from the beach.

Sonya's Cheap seafront warung serving surfer-sized portions of all the standards, including all-day breakfasts. Mains from Rp10,000.

🏃 **Warung Bulé** A warung in a class of its own, and at deliciously good-value prices, run by a chef who cooked at the nearby *Novotel* for seven years. Sauces are exceptionally good and presentation is distinctly "nouvelle". Highlights include seafood *kemangi* – prawns, fish and squid in creamy basil sauce – *mahi-mahi* fillet with proper chips, and mushroom "cappuccino" soup. Many mains are just Rp45,000 and you get a bit of a sea view too.

Warung Murah Murah One of several simple seafront warung, this is a favourite for its eponymously cheap prices – juices for Rp7000 and mains around Rp13,000 – its surfers' breakfasts and its lemongrass chicken. Also does *nasi campur*, spring rolls and other Indo standards.

Listings

Airline tickets Book through *Segare Anak* (see p.351).

Clinic Lombok International Medical Service is a private clinic, 550m north of central Kuta on the Sade road (☎0370/655258 or 0818/353343). The nearest hospital is in Praya.

Exchange *Segare Anak* will sometimes change travellers' cheques and *Tastura Hotel* can sometimes do Visa cash advances; both nearly always have enough funds to change cash. The nearest international ATMs are in Praya.

Internet access Wi-fi and internet at *Magic Café* and *Segare Anak*; internet access also at *Anda* and south of *Lamancha Homestay*.

Phones Wartel at *Segare Anak*.

Police 500m north of central Kuta, near *Yuli's*.

Post *Segare Anak* is a postal agent; the nearest post office is in Sengkol.

West of Kuta

The coast **west of Kuta** has some of the loveliest beaches on Lombok. You'll need your own transport: motorbikes are more useful than cars for navigating the twisting and horrendously rough **road**. Don't ride the road after dark and do have enough petrol in your tank to cope with the steep inclines; there's no mobile signal between Kuta and Selong Blanak. Also be warned that there are occasional robberies of motorbikes on the road beyond Mawun: ask in Kuta and consider taking a local guide with you as driver or passenger. It's still mostly wilderness alongside the road, peppered with occasional hamlets and illegal gold-mining camps (see p.315); as you near Selong Blanak there are tobacco and ricefields too. All **beaches** are signed and all charge for parking (usually Rp5000 for cars, Rp5000/2500 for motorbikes). Except where stated they all have some **shade**, in *berugaq*, plus at least one tiny **stall** selling water, soft drinks and perhaps packet noodles. Except on Sundays and public holidays you'll rarely find more than half a dozen people on any of the beaches.

Are Goleng, Mawun and Mawi

The road west out of Kuta climbs for a couple of kilometres, passing the *Ashtari* **restaurant** (see opposite) and its panoramic vistas.

Some 7km out of Kuta a rough 2km-long dirt track heads to the coast and village of **ARE GOLENG**. The beach here is about 400m long and known for its excellent right-hand reef break, but a river empties into the bay and it's not one for sunbathers or sightseers.

The next beach west is the awesomely beautiful **Mawun**, 9km from Kuta, a semicircular bay of luxurious white sand and dazzling turquoise water, embraced by green headlands. It's usually calm and great for swimming and snorkelling, but has limited shade.

West again, the surf breaks at **Mawi** are some of the most famous, most challenging and busiest in the area. The beach is small, however, and not as pretty as many, and you wouldn't come here for swimming. The turn-off is about 12km from Kuta; the road to the beach is sealed for the first 2.5km then degenerates into a gnarly dirt track for the final 500m.

Selong Blanak and beyond

The magnificent beach at **SELONG BLANAK**, 15km from Kuta, is a vast sweep of empty white sand that stretches 2km west from the fishing village of the same name. Backed by green hills and framed by fine views of **Tomangomang** and **Serangan** beaches (both accessible by tracks), it offers excellent swimming and safe surfing for novices, who appreciate its sandy bottom. Making the most of the fabulous panoramas is the upmarket *Sempiak Villas* (T 0852/5321 3182, W www .sempiakvillas.com; ➏), a tiny boutique **hotel** of octagonal wooden villas set on a hillside overlooking the beach. The villas vary in size but all have air-conditioning, DVD players and kitchenettes, and there's a pool and restaurant. The hotel also runs *Laut Biru* **café** (daily 11am–5pm), just back from the shoreline, which serves home-made ice cream and cheesecake. More residential and holiday accommodation is on the cards in this area. **Access** to Selong Blanak is either from Kuta (via a road that was in terrible condition at the time of writing) or direct from Praya, 24km north, via Penujak.

West of Selong Blanak, the dilapidated road to the seaweed-farming village of Pengantap (18km) and on to **Sepi** (23km) was in mid-2011 about to be upgraded, though it may still require four-wheel-drive during the rainy season. From Sepi another road takes you 11km north to Sekotong Tengah (see p.315), but easiest access to **Blongas Bay**, 1km west, is by boat. Blongas offers challenging diving (see p.351) and isolated **accommodation** at *The Lodge @ Belongas Bay* (T 0370/645974, W www.thelodge-lombok.com; ➏).

The "road" marked on several maps west to Teluk Mekaki is a very rough track, more suited to a trail bike.

East of Kuta

A fifteen-minute walk from the *Novotel* beach takes you across the inlet and via the grassy-hummocked headland grazed by local cows to the white-sand beach of **Seger**. It's a popular surf spot, with a warung and some shade; currents permitting, it can also be good for swimming. In a different league, though, are the gloriously pretty twin white-sand crescents of **Tanjung Aan**, 6km from Kuta. The usually calm **Aan,** on the west side of the offshore outcrop, is perfect for swimming and (partially shaded) lounging; **Pedau,** to the east, has a **rip tide**. There's a drinks seller here, and usually a sarong hawker or two.

Beyond Tanjung Aan, the fishing village of **GERUPUK**, just under 8km from Kuta, sits on the western shores of Gumbang Bay. **Lobster** is the main source of income here, but with five famously good **surf breaks** within a fifteen-minute boat ride, surf-tourism is also important. There's no decent beach but the surf shops rent boards and arrange boats to the breaks (Rp70,000/person). **Accommodation** here is popular with Japanese surfers: *Edo Homestay* (T 0818/0371 0521; ➊) has five clean, tiled fan and cold-water rooms above its shoreside café and surf shop, across the road from the mosque. Next door, *Lakuen Hotel* (T 0878/6565 3232, W www.lakuen.net; ➏) has six enormous villa-style concrete *lumbung* on stilts, all with nice furnishings, air-conditioning, kitchenette and outdoor bathrooms, as well as use of the pool.

From Gerupuk, you can look across the huge bay to **BUMBANG** on the eastern shore and a rent a boat for snorkelling or to get to Ekas (Rp600,000 for a day-trip; 90min each way). At the remote southern end of fabulous gold-sand Bumbang beach,

Bumbangku Beach Cottages (☏0819/0735 5450, ⊚www.liriklomboktours.com; ❷) offers simple thatched bamboo **cottages** with attached *mandi* on the shorefront.

The thriving fishing village of **AWANG**, 16km east of Kuta, is worth the trip to see scenic **Awang Bay**, also known as **Ekas Bay**, with views east across to Ekas and south to the open sea. You can charter boats from Awang to Ekas, an easier option than tackling the rough roads (about Rp300,000 return). Access from Kuta to Awang is via a turn-off just before Tanjung Aan, though there's a better-quality road from Mujur east of Praya.

Ekas and the southeast peninsula

Lombok's isolated **southeast peninsula** is way off the beaten track. Travel isn't easy but the coastal views are startling, there's good surfing and some unique accommodation.

The road to the peninsula leaves the southern highway at **Sepapan** and is signposted to "Jerowaru, Tanjung Ringgit and *Heaven on the Planet*". The first village is **Jerowaru**, where the road splits – turn right at the southern end of the village, 4km from the highway. To continue south, turn left after another 1.5km at the Masjid Al-Muntaha mosque in the village of **Tutuk**. Carry on south for 5km to reach a major junction, signed straight on for **Tanjung Ringgit** – a very remote beach at Lombok's southeastern tip – and right to Ekas.

Follow the road to **EKAS** for 7.5km and a sign points you 2km down a steep, rutted track to *Heaven on the Planet* (☏0812/370 5393, ⊚www.heavenontheplanet .co.nz; ❼ full board). The only **accommodation** on the peninsula, this is a remote and popular clifftop hideaway, with a variety of chalets and villas above the white-sand beach, a swimming pool and surfing, windsurfing and diving facilities. Booking is essential and full-board rates include transport from elsewhere on Lombok. Irregular **bemos** link Ekas and the main road at Sepapan but the most comfortable way to get there is by **boat** from Awang.

Travel details

Buses and bemos

It's impossible to give the frequency with which bemos and public buses run: see Basics, p.30, for details. Journey times given are the minimum you can expect.

Bayan to: Mataram (Mandalika; 2hr 30min); Pemenang (2hr); Senaru (20min).
Kuta to: Praya (1hr); Sengkol (30min).
Labuhan Lombok to: Bayan (2hr); Kopang (for Praya; 1hr); Mataram (Mandalika; 2hr); Sembalun Lawang (2hr 30min).
Lembar to: Mataram (Mandalika; 30min); Sekotong (1hr); Tawun (2hr); Tembowong (2hr 30min).
Mataram (Ampenan) to: Senggigi (20min).
Mataram (Mandalika terminal) to: Bayan (for Gunung Rinjani; 2hr 30min); Labuhan Lombok (2hr); Lembar (30min); Pemenang (for the Gili Islands; 1hr); Pomotong (for Tetebatu; 1hr 15min); Praya (for Kuta; 30min).

Pemenang to: Bayan (2hr); Mataram (Mandalika; 1hr 30min).
Praya to: Kuta (1hr); Mataram (Mandalika; 30min).
Sapit to: Aik Mel (1hr); Pringgabaya (1hr); Sembalun Lawang (2–3hr).
Sembalun Lawang to: Aik Mel (2hr); Kokok Putih (1hr).
Senggigi to: Mataram (Ampenan; 20min).

Perama shuttle buses

Perama transport to Bali includes travel on their own boat.

Gili Islands: Candi Dasa (Bali; 2 daily; 8hr); Kuta, Bali/Ngurah Rai Airport (2 daily; 9hr 30min); Lovina (Bali; daily; 12hr); Padang Bai (Bali; 2 daily; 7hr); Sanur (Bali; 2 daily; 9hr); Ubud (Bali; 2 daily; 8hr).
Mataram to: Bangsal (daily; 2hr); Kuta, Lombok (2 daily; 2hr); Tetebatu (2 daily; 2hr).
Senggigi to: Candi Dasa (Bali; 2 daily; 6hr); Kuta, Bali/Ngurah Rai Airport (2 daily; 9hr); Kuta, Lombok

(2 daily; 2hr); Sanur (Bali; 2 daily; 8hr 30min); Tetebatu (2 daily; 2hr); Ubud (Bali; 2 daily; 8hr).

Boats

Boats depart at least once a day unless otherwise stated.

Bangsal to: Gili Air (20min); Gili Meno (30min); Gili Trawangan (45min).

Gili Air to: Bangsal (20min); Gili Meno (20min); Gili Trawangan (40min).

Gili Meno to: Bangsal (30min); Gili Air (20min); Gili Trawangan (20min).

Gili Trawangan to: Amed (Bali; 1hr 15min); Bangsal (45min); Gili Air (40min); Gili Meno (20min); Nusa Lembongan (Bali; 1hr 45min–3hr 15min); Padang Bai (Bali; 1hr 30min–4hr); Sanur (Bali; 2hr–3hr 45min); Senggigi (45min–2hr 30min).

Labuhan Lombok to: Poto Tano (Sumbawa; 1hr 30min).

Lembar to: Padang Bai (4hr).

Senggigi to: Gili Trawangan (45min–2hr 30min); Nusa Lembongan (Bali; 2hr 15min); Padang Bai (Bali; 5hr).

Teluk Kodek/Teluk Nara to: Benoa (Bali; 3hr); Nusa Lembongan (1hr 30min–3hr); Sanur (Bali; 4hr).

Planes

All flights depart at least once a day unless otherwise stated.

Selaparang Airport (Mataram) to: Denpasar (Bali; 30min); Jakarta (Java; 3hr); Labuanbajo (Flores; 3hr); Singapore (3 weekly; 2hr 35min); Sumbawa (35min); Surabaya (Java; 50min).

Contexts

Contexts

History

Two tiny islands, Bali and Lombok have been buffeted by powerful empires throughout history, and their fortunes have often been tied to those of their larger neighbours, Java and Sumbawa. More recently the islands have been subsumed in the fate of the vast Indonesian archipelago. Relations between Bali and Lombok have often been turbulent, and the origins of their present cultural, religious and economic differences are firmly rooted in past events.

Beginnings

Homo erectus, a distant ancestor of modern man, arrived in Indonesia around half a million years ago during the **ice ages**. At this time glaciers advanced from the polar regions and the levels of the oceans fell, exposing **land bridges** between the islands and the land masses of Southeast Asia and Australia. Homo erectus moved across these land bridges into and through Indonesia. The fossilized bones of "Java Man" from this period were found in Central Java and stone axes and adzes have been discovered on Bali.

Homo sapiens appeared around forty thousand years ago and were cave-dwelling hunter-gatherers whose rock paintings have been found in the far east of the archipelago. The **Neolithic** era, around 3000 BC, is marked by the appearance of more sophisticated stone tools, agricultural techniques and basic pottery. Remains from this period have been found at Cekik, in the far west of Bali.

From the seventh or eighth centuries BC, the **Bronze Age** spread south from southern China. Famed for bronze casting, decorated drums have been found throughout the Indonesian archipelago. The most famous example in Bali, and the largest drum found anywhere in Southeast Asia, is the **Moon of Pejeng**. It is nearly 2m wide and housed in a temple just east of Ubud. **Stone sarcophagi** from this period are on display in the Bali Museum in Denpasar and the Museum Arkeologi in Pejeng.

Early traders and empires

From at least 200 BC, **trade** was a feature of life across the archipelago. The earliest written records in Bali, metal inscriptions, or *prasasti*, dating from the ninth century AD, reveal significant Buddhist and Hindu influence from the Indian subcontinent, shown also by the statues, bronzes and rock-cut caves at Gunung Kawi and Goa Gajah.

The most famous event in early Balinese history occurred towards the end of the tenth century when a princess of East Java, Princess **Mahendratta**, married the Balinese king **Udayana**. Their marriage portrait is believed to be depicted in a stone in the Pura Tegeh Koripan near Kintamani. Their son, **Erlangga**, born around 991 AD, later brought the two realms together until his death in 1049.

In the following centuries, control of Bali was won by the Javanese and then wrested back by Balinese rulers. By 1300 Bali was being ruled domestically, by **King Bedaulu**, based in the Pejeng district, east of Ubud.

Little is known of the ancient history of **Lombok**, although it is known that the kingdom of Selaparang controlled an area in the east of the island for a period.

The Majapahit

One of the most significant dates in Balinese history is 1343 AD, when the island was colonized by **Gajah Mada**, the prime minister of the powerful Hindu

Majapahit kingdom of East Java. Establishing a court initially at Samprangan in eastern Bali and later moving to Gelgel, they introduced a caste system to the island and Balinese who did not accept this established their own villages. Their descendants, known as the **Bali Aga** or *Bali Mula*, the "original Balinese", still adhere to ancient traditions and live in separate villages, such as Tenganan near Candi Dasa and Trunyan on the shores of Danau Batur.

Throughout the fifteenth century, **Islam** gained influence on Java and when the Majapahit fell in 1515, many of its Hindu followers – priests, craftsmen, soldiers, nobles and artists – fled east to Bali, flooding the island with **Javanese cultural ideas** and reaffirming Hindu practices.

It is unclear why Islam did not spread to Bali, especially as it moved further east to Lombok, Sulawesi and Maluku. It could be that Islam spread along trade routes: with poor harbours and few resources, Bali was largely bypassed and the tide of Islam swept east, although there are small Muslim communities on the island.

An ancient text detailing the history of the Majapahit dynasty lists **Lombok** as part of its empire, and the villages in the Sembalun valley on the eastern flanks of Gunung Rinjani consider themselves directly descended from the Majapahit dynasty, claiming that the brother of a Majapahit raja is buried in the valley.

Bali's Golden Age

During the reign of **Batu Renggong**, who became king, or **dewa agung** (literally meaning "great god") in 1550 the Gelgel kingdom ruled an empire from Blambangan in Java in the west to Sumbawa in the east. This period coincided with a cultural renaissance in Bali and, as a result, is often referred to as the **Golden Age**. The Javanese Hindu priest **Nirartha** achieved a great following on Bali at this time.

Eventually, the glory faded and other kingdoms within Bali rose to prominence, most notably **Gianyar** under Dewa Manggis Kuning in the seventeenth century.

Foreigners and trade

Lacking the spices of the eastern isles, Bali appears not to have been in the mainstream of the archipelago's early trading history. The **Chinese** visited Bali, which they knew as Paoli or Rice Island, in the seventh century, but by this time trade had been established on nearby islands for a thousand years. Bali became known to **Europeans** at the end of the fifteenth century when Portuguese, Spanish and English explorers came in search of the lucrative Spice Islands. They marked Bali on their maps as Balle, Ilha Bale or Java Minor, but sailed on by.

The first documented contact between Europeans and the Balinese occurred in the sixteenth century. The **Portuguese**, having won the race for the Spice Islands, dispatched a ship from Malacca in 1588, aiming to construct a trading post on Bali. The ship hit a reef just off Bali and sank. The survivors were treated kindly by the *dewa agung* but not permitted to leave the island. Portuguese attempts at establishing contact were not repeated.

On February 9, 1597, four **Dutch** ships under the command of Commodore Cornelius Houtman anchored off Bali and three sailors landed at Kuta including Aernoudt Lintgens, whose report of his experiences is the first account by a Westerner of the island. The other two crew members were so entranced that they did not return to the ship.

The Dutch came again in 1601, when Cornelis Heemskerk arrived with a letter from the prince of Holland requesting **formal trade relations**, which the *dewa agung* accepted. The VOC, or **Dutch East India Company**, was formed in 1602, and its headquarters founded in Batavia (modern-day Jakarta) in 1619, from where the Dutch trading empire expanded as far as Sumatra, Borneo, Makassar and the Moluccas.

From then until the beginning of the nineteenth century, Bali was largely ignored by Europeans, as it produced little of interest to them. The exception was **slaves**, who were sold through Kuta to Dutch merchants from Batavia and French merchants from Mauritius.

The situation in Lombok

During the seventeenth century, the west of Lombok was invaded by the **Balinese** from Karangasem in the far east of Bali; the **Makassarese** of Sulawesi, who had conquered Sumbawa in 1618 also invaded eastern Lombok. The first major conflicts between these two outside powers occurred in 1677 when the Balinese, assisted by the indigenous **Sasak** aristocracy, defeated the Makassarese.

From the end of the seventeenth to the mid-nineteenth century, the Balinese struggled to secure control over Lombok. In 1775, **Gusti Wayan Tegah**, who had been placed on the throne by the raja of Karangasem, died, and disagreements over the succession resulted in four rival principalities in the west vying for control: Pagasangan, Pagutan, Mataram and Cakranegara. Meanwhile the Sasak aristocracy in the east of the island faced little interference in their affairs.

Eventually, in 1838, the raja of Mataram, **Ratu Agung K'tut**, triumphed over the other principalities and also brought the east of Lombok under his control. Astutely, he also provided four thousand troops to support the Dutch in their fight against Karangasem in eastern Bali. This ensured the defeat of the ruling dynasty in Karangasem, for which service the Dutch gave him the right to put his own nominee on the Karangasem throne.

Dutch incursions

By the mid-1830s, the Dutch interest in Bali had intensified. By that time Bali was ruled by a number of kingdoms, recognizable today as the regencies named after them; Badung, Bangli, Buleleng, Jembrana, Karangasem, Klungkung, Mengwi and Tabanan. The Danish trader **Mads Lange** had set up a trading post in Kuta supplying rice to British-held Singapore. The Dutch started trading with Bali, with the aim of gaining political control before the British. In 1839 they established an agent in Kuta with the agreement of the raja of Badung. In 1840, the Dutch envoy, **Huskus Koopman**, began a series of visits with the long-term aim of gaining Dutch sovereignty over the island.

The Dutch also wanted to abolish Balinese *tawan karang* or reef rights, which had been a long-term grievance. The Balinese had always asserted their right to goods salvaged from shipping wrecked on the island's reefs, much of which was Dutch. The plundering of the Dutch vessel *Overijssel*, wrecked on the Kuta reef on July 19, 1841, particularly outraged the Dutch.

By 1843 Koopman had made **treaties** with the kingdoms of Badung, Klungkung, Buleleng, Karangasem and Tabanan, agreeing to a Dutch trade monopoly. The rajas failed to realize that they had also given the Dutch sovereignty over their lands and surrendered reef rights. Following Koopman's retirement, a new commissioner arrived in 1844 to finalize the treaties, but it soon became apparent that there were huge differences in Dutch and Balinese understandings. Most kingdoms did ratify the treaties, but **Buleleng** and **Karangasem** stood firm. A further Dutch mission came the following year, including a military officer whose brief was to assess the Buleleng defences. At a meeting in Singaraja in May 1845, Gusti Ketut Jelantik, brother of the rajas of Buleleng and Karangasem, stated,

"Not by a mere scrap of paper shall any man become the master of another's lands. Rather let the *kris* decide."

Dutch military victory

On June 26, 1846, the **First Dutch Military Expedition** arrived off the Buleleng coast with 3500 men. On June 28, the military force landed and marched into Singaraja. The rajas of Buleleng and Karangasem eventually surrendered, agreeing to Dutch sovereignty and to paying costs for the victor's military expedition.

The Dutch departed, believing they had achieved their objectives, and left behind a small garrison until the compensation was paid. However, this fitted in with Jelantik's plan, and he continued to prepare for future battle. Meanwhile, nothing was paid to the Dutch, and ships that foundered continued to be plundered by the Balinese. On March 7, 1848, the governor-general of the Dutch East Indies sent ultimatums demanding compensation, payment of war debts, the destruction of defence works and the delivery of Jelantik to them. The ultimatums were ignored, and the **Second Dutch Military Expedition** arrived off the northern coast at Sangsit on June 8, 1848, with almost three thousand troops. Having quickly overcome the defences on the coast, the well-armed force marched towards **Jagaraga** where Jelantik had organized his army of around sixteen thousand, armed largely with *kris* and lances. The Dutch were eventually put to flight and around two hundred Dutch soldiers were killed or wounded. The Balinese suffered over two thousand casualties but on June 10, 1848, the Dutch sailed back to Batavia.

The following year, in the **Third Dutch Military Expedition**, the Dutch used almost their entire military force in the Indies to overcome the Balinese. Around seven thousand troops landed in Buleleng on April 4, 1849. Negotiations failed and on April 15, the Dutch attacked the fortress at Jagaraga and defeated the Balinese with the loss of only about thirty men to the Balinese thousands. Jelantik and the rajas of Buleleng and Karangasem fled east. With four thousand additional troops from Lombok, the Dutch attacked Karangasem first. On their arrival at the palace on May 20, the raja of Karangasem, Gusti Gde Ngurah Karangasem, along with his family and followers, all committed **puputan** (ritual suicide). The raja of Buleleng, accompanied by Jelantik, fled to the mountains of Seraya, where they were killed in further fighting.

Dutch troops then headed west towards Semarapura where the *dewa agung* signed an **agreement** on July 13, 1849. The Balinese recognized Dutch sovereignty and accepted that *tawan karang* was prohibited, and in return the Dutch agreed to leave the rajas to administer their kingdoms and not to base garrisons on the island. A feast on July 15 sealed the agreement.

The strengthening of the Dutch position

The Dutch regarded themselves as having sovereignty over the whole island but initially largely left the kingdoms of the south and the east alone, basing themselves in the north and placing Dutch controllers over the rajas of Buleleng and Jembrana.

From their administrative capital in **Singaraja**, the Dutch made some improvements to irrigation, planted coffee as a cash crop and outlawed slavery and the tradition of *suttee*, whereby widows would throw themselves on the funeral pyres of their dead husbands. They also quelled **local rebellions**, such as the 1864 uprising in the village of Banjar, close to modern-day Lovina.

Meanwhile, with the Dutch concentrated in the north, the kingdoms of Klungkung, Badung, Gianyar, Mengwi, Bangli and Tabanan in the south were weakened by internal conflicts and fighting with each other. The rajas increasingly turned to the Dutch for protection from their neighbours.

Rebellion and the Dutch in Lombok

In Lombok, meanwhile, Ratu Agung K'tut continued to rule. The **west** of the island was relatively harmonious, but in the **east** the frustrated Sasak aristocracy deeply resented their Balinese masters and there were failed rebellions in 1855 and 1871. In 1872, Ratu Agung K'tut was succeeded by his younger brother, **Ratu Agung Ngurah**.

The **rebellion of 1891** was more successful. For many years, Ratu Agung Ngurah had vied with the *dewa agung* of the Balinese kingdom of Klungkung over claims to the title of Supreme Ruler of Bali. In 1891 he decided to take action, but his demand for several thousand Sasak troops was met with resistance in **Praya**, and a local Sasak aristocrat was executed. On August 7, 1891, several thousand Sasaks surrounded and burned the palace of the Balinese district chief and rebellion spread quickly. By September 22, 1891, Balinese rule had been overthrown throughout East Lombok.

Hostilities between the Balinese and the Sasak aristocracy dragged on for years, gains being made and then lost, until 1894, when the Dutch army landed in West Lombok.

On the night of August 25, 1894, Balinese forces attacked the Dutch camp in the **Mayura Palace** at Cakranegara, where around nine hundred soldiers were camped. The Dutch escaped with heavy casualties, but they soon received reinforcements and, aided by the Sasaks from the east, proved too strong for the raja. Mataram was razed to the ground. Some members of the royal family surrendered while others committed *puputan*. The Dutch took control of the entire island, including the district of Karangasem on Bali, which had been under the raja's control.

Further confrontation in south Bali

The Dutch had wanted to emphasize their control of the **south of Bali** for many years, but it wasn't until the turn of the twentieth century that they made their move. On May 27, 1904, a schooner, the *Sri Kumala*, under Dutch protection, hit the reef just off Sanur. The owner complained to the Dutch Resident in Singaraja that copper and silver coins had been stolen from the ship. The Resident decreed a **blockade** of Badung and ordered that the raja of Badung, Gusti Gde Ngurah, should pay compensation.

The situation dragged on until July 1906, when the Dutch threatened military action. Dutch forces landed at Sanur, and by September 20, 1906, had advanced to **Badung** (modern-day Denpasar). Gusti Gde Ngurah realized defence was useless and arranged the traditional **puputan**. An eyewitness account from a Dutch observer, Dr van Weede, in his book *Indies Travel Memories*, describes the event:

The ruler and the princes with their followers, dressed in their glittering attire, with their krises girded on, of which the golden hilts were in the form of Buddha statues and studded with precious stones; all of them were dressed in red or black and their hair was carefully combed, moistened with fragrant oils. The women were wearing the best clothes and accessories that they had; most of them wore their hair loose and all had white cloaks. The prince had his palace burned down and had everything that was breakable destroyed.

When at nine o'clock it was reported to him that the enemy had penetrated Denpasar from the North, the tragic procession of 250 people started to move; each man and woman carried a kris or long lance, also the children who had the strength to do it, while the babies were carried in their arms. Thus they walked to the north along the wide road bordered by tall trees, meeting their destruction.

The prince walked in front, carried on the shoulders by his followers according to custom, and silently ... until all of a sudden, at a turning in the road, the dark line of our infantry was visible before them. Immediately a halt was commanded and Captain Schutstal ordered the interpreters to summon the arriving party to a halt with gestures and with words. However these summons were in vain, and in spite of the repeated warnings the Balinese went over to a trot.

Incessantly the Captain and the interpreters made signs, but it was in vain. Soon they had to realize that they had to do with people who wanted to die. They let them approach to a hundred paces, eighty, seventy paces, but now they went over to a double quick step with couched lances and raised krises, the prince always in front.

A longer delay would have been irresponsible in view of the safety of our men, and the first salvo was given; several killed men remained at the place. One of the first to fall was the ruler; and now one of the most horrible scenes one could imagine took place.

While those who were saved continued the attack, and the shooting on our part for self-defence remained necessary, one saw lightly wounded give the death-blow to the heavily wounded. Women held out their breasts to be killed or received the death blow between their shoulders, and those who did this were mowed down by our rifle fire, other men and women got up to continue the bloody work. Also suicides took place there on a big scale, and all seemed to yearn for their death: some women threw as a reward for the violent death which they desired from them gold coins to the soldiers, and stood straight up in front of them, pointing at their heart, as if they wanted to be hit there; if no shot was fired they killed themselves. Especially an old man was busily stepping over the corpses, and used his kris left and right until he was shot down. An old woman took his task and underwent the same fate, however, nothing helped. Always others got up to continue the work of destruction.

This scene was repeated later the same day at the palace of the prince of **Pemecutan**. Estimates of the number of people killed that day vary between four hundred and two thousand. Having defeated Badung, on September 27, the Dutch marched on to **Tabanan**, where the raja and crown prince surrendered and were imprisoned, where they both committed suicide rather than face exile.

The completion of Dutch control

On April 28, 1908, Dutch troops in **Semarapura** witnessed a scene similar to the Badung *puputan* two years earlier. Reports tell how the *dewa agung* stabbed his royal *kris* into the ground expecting its power to rent the ground asunder or bring torrential rain to destroy the enemy. Nothing happened and around two hundred members of the royal household committed suicide that day; the remainder were exiled.At this point the raja of **Bangli** realized a pretext would soon be found to attack him and, in October 1908, requested that his kingdom should have the same status as Gianyar and Karangasem and become a Dutch Protectorate. When this was approved in January 1909, the whole of the island of Bali came under **Dutch control**.

Colonial rule

The *puputan*s of 1906 and 1908 caused a stir in Europe and the United States and pressure was put on the Dutch to moderate their policies. They ruled with a philosophy they called the **Ethical Policy**, which they claimed upheld Balinese values. Traditional rulers remained as regents under the authority of the Dutch, although not all of the old royal families were amenable to this; in Buleleng, it was not until several generations after the Dutch conquest that an obliging member of the royal family could be found.

Under the Dutch, engineers, doctors and teachers were introduced to the colony and Bali was spared the less enlightened **agricultural policies** that had turned large parts of Java into plantations. Big businesses were discouraged from Bali, although the steamship line KPM began encouraging **tourism** on the island from 1924 onwards.

Lombok under the Dutch

The situation on **Lombok** deteriorated markedly following the Dutch victory in 1894, and brought the population to the point of starvation more than once. The Dutch were determined to rule profitably: they taxed the population harshly and introduced **compulsory labour** for projects such as road-building. In addition to land tax, there were **taxes** on income and on the slaughter of animals. These were initially payable in local currency, but eventually they were demanded in Netherlands Indies currency (NIC). The Chinese rice-exporters were one of the few groups on the island who traded in NIC, and increasing amounts of rice needed to be sold to raise money for taxes. Consequently, a high proportion of food grown on the island was exported, and local rice consumption dropped by a quarter. By 1934, it was estimated that a third of the population were **landless and destitute**.

World War II and independence

Following the bombing of the American Fleet in Pearl Harbour on December 7, 1941, Japan entered **World War II** and moved quickly through Asia. The **Japanese** fleet arrived off Sanur on February 18, 1942, were unopposed on their march to Denpasar and took control of Bali without a fight. Java and Sumatra had fallen by March 9.

The Japanese **occupation** was hard as the Dutch were expelled from the country but it showed the occupied islanders that the Dutch colonialists could be defeated. Throughout the war years, the idea of liberation grew and, on August 17, 1945, three days after the Japanese surrender, Indonesia made its **Declaration of Independence** in an announcement by President **Sukarno**. Some Balinese were strong supporters of independence but many were uncertain about joining a republic dominated by Muslim Java.

The fight for independence

Returning to their colony in March 1946 the **Dutch** faced ferocious fighting on Java. On Bali guerrilla forces, the most famous of which was led by **Gusti Ngurah Rai**, harried the Dutch relentlessly, despite suffering massive losses in a famous battle near Marga in Tabanan. Ngurah Rai is remembered as a hero: Bali's airport is named after him.

However, the Dutch were also under a different sort of attack. The US questioned the Dutch expenditure of Marshall Plan aid (money allocated to European countries for reconstruction after the war) on fighting to keep the Indies. Finally, in January 1949, the UN Security Council ordered the Dutch to negotiate. In December 1949, the United States of Indonesia was legally recognized, dissolving the following year to form the **Republic of Indonesia**, with Sukarno as president.

The Sukarno years

The early years of independence were not kind to Indonesia. The economic situation was disastrous as inflation, corruption and mismanagement ran riot. Martial rule was instituted and 1963 saw a catastrophic war against Malaya.

Although Sukarno's mother was Balinese, the Balinese felt neglected by the government in Jakarta, which, in turn, was suspicious of Balinese Hinduism. Sukarno visited his palace at Tampaksiring regularly, with a massive entourage that demanded to be fed, entertained and then sent away with gifts. During the 1960s, a groundswell of resentment against the government grew in Bali. The Balinese began to believe that a state of spiritual disharmony had been reached, and a huge purification ceremony, **Eka Dasa Rudra**, was held in 1963 against the backdrop of a rumbling Gunung Agung, which eventually erupted and laid waste to much of the east of the island.

Later events in Jakarta piled disaster upon disaster in Bali. In 1965 **Major-General Suharto** seized power after a mysterious attempted coup that was blamed on the communist party (PKI). It unleashed a bloodbath in the country with actual or suspected members of the PKI and their sympathizers the main targets, along with the Chinese population. At least half a million people were killed across Indonesia: an estimated hundred thousand on Bali and fifty thousand on Lombok. Around 200,000 were imprisoned, mostly without trial, more than half of them for ten years or more while their families were stigmatized well into the 1990s. Suharto officially became the second president of Indonesia in March 1968, a position he held for over thirty years.

Indonesia under Suharto

Suharto's **New Order** policy of attracting foreign investment, curbing inflation and re-entering the global economy was largely successful. It was helped enormously by Indonesia's massive **natural resources** of copper, tin, timber and oil. The **economic situation** of the country improved and the material prosperity of the average Indonesian rose.

However, the economic benefits came with a price as alongside this the government acquired almost complete control. **Political opposition** was crushed and the **media** silenced. Corruption was rife and the policy of transmigration, which moved landless people from Java to outlying islands, caused enormous ethnic strife. In every election from 1971 to 1997 the government party, Sekretariat Bersama Golongan Karya, known as **Golkar**, won the majority of seats in the House of Representatives and then re-elected Suharto as president.

The **economic crisis** of the late 1990s decimated the economies of Southeast Asia savaged Indonesia as well. Prices of imports (including food) rose sharply, and a series of riots in early 1998, centred on Java, targeted Chinese businesses – long the scapegoats of Indonesian unrest. Gradually, Indonesian anger turned against President Suharto and his family, who were seen to have been the biggest winners in the Indonesian economic success story.

Student rioting in May 1998 led to more widespread unrest and, eventually, to **Suharto's resignation** on May 21. He spent the ten years until his death on January 27, 2008, dodging corruption charges – in 2000 he was judged as unfit to stand trial. Transparency International, an international anti-corruption organization, estimates that he stole $15–35billion, possibly topping the worldwide list of corrupt politicians.

After Suharto

Following Suharto proved a tough job. The next two presidents, **B.J. Habibie** and **Abdurrahman Wahid**, lasted only short periods of time and on July 23, 2001 **Megawati Sukarnoputri** became president. Megawati – darling of the Balinese, to whom she is known simply as Mega – was regarded in Bali with something approaching fanaticism, based on the fact that her maternal grandmother (Sukarno's mother) was Balinese. Starting her presidency on a wave of optimism, she proved an ineffectual leader.

However, Indonesia hit the world headlines on **October 12, 2002**, when **bombs** planted in the heart of tourist Bali, at the *Sari Club* and *Paddy's Irish Bar* in Kuta, exploded, killing more than two hundred people, the majority of them tourists but with dozens of Indonesian victims also. A third bomb exploded outside the US consulate in Denpasar. The attacks were carried out by members of the Islamic militant organization Jemaah Islamiah (after hugely public and drawn-out trials, three men were executed in November 2008). Further bombings in Jakarta in 2003, 2004 and 2009 and Jimbaran and Kuta in 2005 emphasized to Indonesians and the wider world that fundamentalist forces represent an ongoing threat in the largest Muslim nation in the world.

Whatever Megawati's failings, she did lay the foundations for Indonesia's first-ever **direct presidential election** in 2004, in which 114 million voters across almost fourteen thousand islands voted her out of the job in favour of **Susilo Bambang Yudhoyono**, commonly known as **SBY**.

With 61 percent of the vote he was a popular winner and outside the country he received international approval for his peace deal with the Aceh separatists. He was re-elected again in 2009, again with a landslide victory, as Indonesia weathered the global financial crisis of 2008–09 far better than many of its neighbours and he promised continued attacks against corruption. However, the separatist struggle in West Papua is unresolved and inflation, unemployment, corruption, terrorism and nepotism are the concerns of every Indonesian – of whom more than thirteen percent live below the poverty line, with one estimate suggesting that almost half a million Balinese farmers are living in poverty.

Religion

Some ninety percent of Balinese are Hindus, with Islam the dominant minority faith, practised mostly in the west and north by migrants from Java. The reverse is true on Lombok, where around 85 percent of the population is Muslim, with Balinese Hinduism followed mainly in the west, by those of Balinese heritage.

Religious activity permeates almost every aspect of **Balinese** life. Every morning, tiny palm-leaf offerings are laid down for the gods and spirits who need 24-hour propitiation; in the afternoons, processions of men and women parade the streets en route to temple celebrations, towers of offertory fruit and rice cakes balanced on their heads.

While Islam is as pervasive on **Lombok** as Hinduism is on Bali, it has a much more austere presence. You'll hear the call to prayer five times a day, and streets are often deserted on Fridays around noon, when a large proportion of the population go to the mosque. Marriage and circumcision are celebrated, but the exuberant festivals of Balinese Hinduism have no Muslim equivalents.

Balinese Hinduism

Though it's not a proselytizing faith, **Balinese Hinduism** is a demanding one, which requires participation from every citizen. Despite certain obvious similarities, Balinese Hinduism differs dramatically from Indian and Nepalese Hinduism. Bali's is a blend of theories and practices borrowed from Hinduism and Buddhism, grafted onto the far stronger indigenous vision of a world that is populated by good and bad spirits.

Early influences

The **animism** of the Stone- and Bronze-Age Balinese probably differed very little from the beliefs of their twenty-first-century descendants, who worship sacred mountains and rivers and conduct elaborate rituals to ensure that the souls of their dead ancestors are kept sweet. In among these animist practices are elements borrowed from the **Mahayana Buddhism** that dominated much of Southeast Asia in the eighth century – certain Buddhist saints, for example, some of which are still visible at Goa Gajah, and a penchant for highly ornate imagery. The strongest influences arrived with the droves of **East Javanese Hindu priests** who fled Muslim invaders en masse in the early sixteenth century. High-caste, educated pillars of the Majapahit kingdom, these strict followers of the Hindu faith settled all over Bali and quickly set about formalizing the island's embryonic Hindu practices. Balinese Hinduism, or **agama Hindu** as it's usually termed, became the official religion, and the Majapahit priests have, ever since, been worshipped as the true Balinese ancestors.

As Bali's Hinduism gained strength, so its neighbouring islands turned towards Islam, and Bali is now a tiny Hindu enclave in an archipelago that contains the biggest Islamic population in the world. Hindu Bali's role within the predominantly Muslim Indonesian state has always been problematic. As part of its code of national law, or **pancasila**, the Jakarta administration requires that all Indonesian faiths be monotheistic and embrace just one God – a proviso that doesn't sit easily with either Hindu or animist tenets. The compromise decided on by Bali's Hindu

Council was to emphasize the role of the supreme deity, **Sanghyang Widi Wasa** (who manifests himself as the Hindu Trinity of Brahma, Siwa and Wisnu); this convinced the Ministry of Religion that Bali was essentially monotheistic, and in 1962 Balinese Hinduism was formally recognized by Jakarta.

The beliefs

At the root of *agama Hindu* lies the understanding that the world – both natural and supernatural – is composed of opposing forces. These can be defined as good and evil, positive and negative, pure and impure, order and disorder, gods and demons, or as a mixture of all these things, but must in any event be balanced. The desire to achieve **equilibrium** and harmony in all things dictates every spiritual activity. **Positive forces**, or *dharma*, are represented by the gods (*dewa* and *bhatara*), and need to be entertained and honoured with offerings, dances, beautiful artworks, fine earthly abodes (temples) and ministrations from devotees. The **malevolent forces**, *adharma*, which manifest themselves as earth demons (*bhuta*, *kala* and *leyak*) and cause sickness, death and volcanic eruptions, need to be neutralized with rites and special offerings.

To ensure that malevolent forces never take the upper hand, elaborate purification rituals are undertaken for the exorcism of spirits. Crucial to this is the notion of **ritual uncleanliness** (*sebel*), a state which can affect an individual (during a woman's period, for example, or after a serious illness), a family (after the death of a close relative, or if twins are born), or even a whole community (a plague of rats in the village ricefields, or a fire in village buildings). The whole island can even become *sebel*, and **island-wide exorcisms** are held every new year (Nyepi) to restore the spiritual health of Bali and all its people. The 2002 Kuta bombing caused the whole island to become ritually unclean, and as well as a huge purification ceremony at Ground Zero a month after the attack, exorcism rites were performed simultaneously across the island. Other regular, very elaborate island-cleansing rituals are performed every five, ten and twenty-five years, climaxing with the centennial *Eka Dasa Rudra* rite, which is held at the mother temple, Besakih. In addition, there are all sorts of **purification rituals** (*yadnya*) that Balinese must go through at various significant stages in their lives (see p.389).

The focus of every purification ritual is the ministering of **holy water** (*agama Hindu* is sometimes known as *agama tirta*, the religion of holy water). Ordinary well or tap water can be transformed into holy water by a *pedanda* (high priest), but water from certain sources is considered to be particularly sacred – the springs at Tirta Empul in Tampaksiring and on Gunung Agung, for example, and the water taken from the lakeside Pura Danu Batur.

As the main sources of these life-giving waters, Bali's three great **mountains** are also worshipped: the highest, and the holiest, of the three is Gunung Agung, site of Bali's most sacred mother temple, Besakih; Gunung Batur and Gunung Batukaru also hold great spiritual power. Ever since the Stone Age, the Balinese have regarded their mountains as being the realm of the deities, the sea as the abode of demons and giants, and the valleys in between as the natural province of the human world. From this concept comes the Balinese sense of direction and **spatial orientation**, whereby all things, such as temples, houses and villages, are aligned in relation to the mountains and the sea: **kaja** is the direction towards the mountains, upstream, and is the holiest direction; **kelod** is the downstream direction, the part that is closest to the sea and therefore impure.

Finally, there are the notions of karma, reincarnation, and the attaining of enlightenment. The aim of every Hindu is to attain **enlightenment** (*moksa*), which unites the individual and the divine, and brings liberation from the endless cycle of death and rebirth; it is only attainable by pure souls, and can take hundreds of lifetimes to attain. Hindus believe that everybody is **reincarnated** according to their **karma**, karma being a kind of account book that registers all the good and bad deeds performed in the past lives of a soul. Karma is closely bound up with caste and the notion that an individual should accept rather than challenge their destiny.

The gods

All Balinese **gods** are manifestations of the supreme being, **Sanghyang Widi Wasa**, a deity who is often only alluded to in abstract form by an empty throne-shrine, the *padmasana*, that stands in the holiest corner of every temple. Sanghyang Widi Wasa's three main aspects manifest themselves as the Hindu trinity: Brahma, Wisnu and Siwa.

Brahma is the Creator, represented by the colour red and often depicted riding on a bull. His consort is the goddess of learning, **Saraswati**, who rides a white goose. As the Preserver, **Wisnu** is associated with life-giving waters; he rides the *garuda* (half-man, half-bird) and is honoured by the colour black. Wisnu also has several avatars, including **Buddha** – a neat way of incorporating Buddhist elements into the Hindu faith.

Siwa, the Destroyer, or more accurately, the Dissolver, is associated with death and rebirth, with the temples of the dead and with the colour white. He is sometimes represented as a phallic pillar or lingam, and sometimes in the manifestation of **Surya**, the sun god. Siwa's consort is the terrifying goddess **Durga**, whose Balinese personality is the gruesome widow-witch **Rangda**, queen of the demons. The son of Siwa and Durga is the elephant-headed deity **Ganesh**, generally worshipped as the remover of obstacles.

Among the many lesser deities or *dewi* (*dewa* if male) are **Dewi Sri**, the goddess of rice, worshipped at tiny shrines in the paddyfields and celebrated at significant stages throughout the agricultural year; and **Dewi Danu** (more formally known as Ida Batara Dewi Ulun Danu), the goddess of the crater lakes – honoured with temples at lakes Bratan, Batur and Tamblingan, and so important to rice-growers as a source of vital irrigation that annual pilgrimages are made to all three temples.

The demons

Demons also come in a variety of manifestations. The forces of evil are personified by a cast of **bhuta** and **kala**, invisible goblins and ghosts who inhabit eerie, desolate places like the temples of the dead, cemeteries, moonless seashores and dark forests. Their purpose is to wreak havoc in the human world, causing horrible lingering illnesses and ruinous agricultural and economic disasters and entering villagers' minds and turning them insane. But they are not invincible and can be appeased with **offerings** just as the gods can – the difference being that the offerings for these demons consist mainly of dirty, unpleasant, unattractive and mouldy things, which are thrown on the ground, not placed respectfully on ledges and altars. Demons are notoriously greedy, too, and so the Balinese will often waste a dash of *arak* (rice liquor) on the ground before drinking, or drop a few grains of rice to the floor when eating.

Various other strategies are used to repel, confuse and banish the *bhuta* and *kala*. Most entrance gates to temples and households are guarded by fierce-looking statues and ugly demonic images designed to frighten off even the boldest demon. Many gateways are also blocked by a low brick wall, an **aling-aling**, as demons can only walk in straight lines, and so won't be able to zigzag around it. *Bhuta* and *kala* get particular pleasure from entering a person's body via their various orifices, so certain temples (especially in the north) have covered their walls in pornographic carvings, the theory being that the demons will have so much fun penetrating the carved simulation orifices on the outside walls that they won't bother to try their luck further inside the temple compound.

In addition to the unseen *bhuta* and *kala*, there are the **leyak**, or witches, who take highly visible and creepy forms, morphing into headless chickens, bald-headed giants, monkeys with rows of shiny gold teeth, fireballs and riderless motorbikes. *Leyak* can transform themselves effortlessly, and most assume the human form during the daytime, leading outwardly normal lives. Only at night do they release their dark spirits to wreak havoc on unsuspecting islanders, while their human shell remains innocently asleep in bed. Even in their human form, *leyak* cannot be killed with knives or poisons, but they can be controlled by harnessing the white magic practised by shamanic *balian* and priests.

The temples

The focus of every community's spiritual activity is the **temple**, or *pura*, a temporary abode for the gods that's open and unroofed to invite easy access between heaven and earth.

To outsiders, Balinese temples can seem confusing, even unimpressive: open-roofed compounds scattered with shrines and altars, built mainly of limestone and red brick, and with no paintings or treasures to focus on. But there are at least twenty thousand temples on the island and many do reward closer examination. Every structure within a temple complex is charged with great symbolic significance, often with entertaining legends attached, and many of the walls and gateways are carved with an ebullience of mythical figures, demonic spirits and even secular scenes. (Note that when **visiting a temple**, you must be appropriately dressed, even if there's no one else in the vicinity; see p.11 for details.)

The reason there are so many temples in Bali is that every *banjar* (neighbourhood) is obliged to build at least three. At the top of the village – the *kaja*, or holiest end – stands the **pura puseh**, the temple of origin, which is dedicated to the founders of the community. For everyday spiritual activities, villagers worship at the **pura desa**, the village temple, which always stands at the heart of the village. (In some communities, the *pura puseh* and the *pura desa* are combined within a single compound.) The trio is completed by the **pura dalem**, or temple of the dead, at the *kelod* (unclean) end of the village, which is usually dedicated either to Siwa, or to the widow-witch Rangda.

Bali also has nine directional temples, or **kayangan jagat**, which protect the entire island and all its people. They're located at strategic points across Bali, especially on high mountain slopes, rugged cliff faces and lakeside shores: Pura Ulun Danu Batur is on the shores of Danau Batur (north); Pura Pasar Agung on Gunung Agung (northeast); Pura Lempuyang Luhur on Gunung Lempuyang (east); Goa Lawah near Candi Dasa (southeast); Pura Masceti near Lebih (south); Pura Luhur Uluwatu on the Bukit (southwest); Pura Luhur Batukaru on Gunung Batukaru (west); Pura Ulun Danu Bratan on the shores of Danau Bratan (northwest); and Besakih on Gunung Agung (centre). The most important of these is **Besakih** – the mother temple – as it occupies the crucial position on Bali's holiest and highest mountain, Gunung Agung; the others are all of equal status, and islanders are expected to attend the anniversary celebrations (*odalan*) of the one situated closest to their home.

Temple layout

Whatever the size, status or particular function of a temple, it follows a prescribed layout. All Balinese temples are oriented *kaja–kelod*, and are designed around two or three courtyards, each section divided from the next by a low wall punctuated by a huge, and usually ornate, "split" gateway, the **candi bentar**.

In many temples, particularly in north Bali, the **outer courtyard** (*jaba*) and **middle courtyard** (*jaba tengah*) are merged into one. These courtyards represent the transition zone between the human and the divine worlds, containing thatched pavilions or **bale** (pronounced "ba-leh") for the preparation of offerings, as well as for cockfights and the less sacred dance performances (such as those for tourists). The **kulkul** or drum tower is also here, housing the wooden bell ("drum") used to summon villagers to meetings and festivals. Entry to the extremely sacred **inner courtyard**, *jeroan*, is via an imposing covered gateway, the three-doored **kori agung** or **paduraksa**, whose central door is kept locked, opened only for the deities at festival times. The *jeroan* houses all the **shrines**: the small, thatched, red-brick structures dedicated to a particular deity or ancestor are *gedong*; the distinctive, elegant pagoda-style towers with multi-tiered roofs thatched with thick black sugar-palm fibre are **meru**, after the sacred Hindu peak Mount Meru, home of the gods. A *meru* always has an odd number of roofs (three, five, seven, nine or eleven), the number indicating the status of the god to whom it is dedicated. All offerings are brought to the inner courtyard, the most sacred dances are performed within its confines, and prayers are held in front of the shrines. The *jeroan* is quite often out of bounds to the lay community and opened only during festivals.

Temple festivals

Aside from the daily propitiation of the household spirits, *agama Hindu* requires no regular act of collective worship, no daily mass or weekly service, and so, for much of the year, Bali's twenty thousand temples remain deserted, visited only by the village priest (*pemangku*) and perhaps the occasional curious tourist. But this all changes on the occasion of the temple's anniversary celebrations, or **odalan**, a three-day devotional extravaganza held at every temple either once every 210 days (every Balinese calendar year; see p.43 for an explanation of this) or once every 354–356 days (the *saka* year). With at least three temples in every community, any visitor who spends more than a week on the island will be certain to see some kind of festival. Most temples welcome tourists to the celebrations, provided they dress respectably (see p.48) and wear the temple sash, and that they don't walk in front of praying devotees.

The more important the temple, the more dramatic the *odalan* celebrations. But whatever the size, the purpose is always to invite the gods down to earth so that they can be entertained and pampered by as many displays of devotion as the community can afford. In the days before the *odalan*, the *pemangku* dresses the temple statues in **holy cloths**, either the spiritually charged black-and-white *kain poleng*, or a length of plain cloth in a symbolic colour. Meanwhile, the women of the community begin to construct their offering towers, or *banten*, and to cook ceremonial food.

Odalan are so important that everyone makes a huge effort to return to their home village for their own temple festival, even if they live and work far away; most employers will automatically give their Balinese staff time off to attend. **Celebrations** start in the afternoon, with a procession of ceremonially clad women carrying their offerings to the temple. Sometimes the gods will temporarily inhabit the body of one of the worshippers, sending him or her into a trance and conveying its message through gestures or words. Elsewhere in the temple compound, there might be a cockfight and some gamelan music, and sacred dances are often performed as well. After dark, a shadow play, *wayang kulit*, is often staged.

As well as the temple anniversary celebrations, there are numerous island-wide religious festivals, the most important of which are Nyepi and Galungan-Kuningan, described on p.43.

Cockfights

Because certain Hindu rituals require the shedding of fresh sacrificial blood to placate evil spirits, every temple's purification ceremony is prefaced by a **cockfight**, which attracts massive crowds and even larger bets. Providing you wear suitable temple dress and can stand the gore, tourists are quite welcome to attend.

Prize cocks can earn both their owners and the temple tidy sums of money – and plunge losing gamblers into debilitating debt – and you'll see men of all ages and incomes preening their birds in public. When not being pampered, the birds are kept in bell-shaped bamboo baskets, often in quite noisy public places such as by the roadside, to train them not to be scared or distracted when in the ring.

Fights generally take place in the temple's special cockfighting pavilion or *wantilan*. Complicated **rules** written on ancient manuscripts specify the days on which fights may take place, and describe the detailed classification system under which the birds are categorized. Before the fight, a lethal 11- to 15cm-long blade, or *taji*, is attached to the left ankle of each bird. This is considered a sacred weapon and cockfights are meant to be won and lost by skilful use of the *taji*, not just by brutish pecking. Fights last for a maximum of five rounds, and the winning bird is the cock who remains standing the longest – even if he drops dead soon after. The owner of the winning cock gets the body of the losing bird plus his opponent's share of the central fund.

Offerings

The simplest **offerings** are the ones laid out every day by the women of each house, and placed at the household shrine, at the entrance gate, and in any crannies thought to be of interest to *bhuta* and *kala*. These offerings, called **canang**, are tiny banana-leaf trays, pinned together with bamboo splinters and filled with a symbolic assortment of rice, fruit, flowers and incense. The flowers are always red or pink, to represent the Hindu god Brahma, and white for Siwa, with the green of the banana leaf symbolizing Wisnu. Though it's still common for women to make their own *canang*, an increasing number buy theirs at the market. Offerings for the gods are always placed in elevated positions, either on specially constructed altars or on functional shelves, but those meant for the demons are scattered on the ground. When the devotee places the gods' offering, she sprinkles holy water over it and wafts the incense smoke heavenwards. This sends the essence of the *canang* up to the appropriate god and ensures that he comes down immediately to enjoy it. Once the essence has been extracted, the *canang* loses its holiness and is left to rot.

In the run-up to festivals and celebrations, the women of each *banjar* band together to create great towers of fruit and rice cakes, tiny rice-dough figurines and banners woven from palm fronds. The most dramatic of these are the magnificent **banten**, built up around the trunk of a young banana tree, up to three metres high. *Banten* cannot be reused, but once they've done service at the temple they can be dismantled and eaten by the families who donated them.

On the occasion of major island-wide festivals, such as Galungan-Kuningan, or at the Balinese New Year, Nyepi, Bali's villages get decked out with special banners and ornamental poles, designed to attract the attention of the deities living on Gunung Agung and invite them onto the local streets. The banners, known as **lamak**, are amazing ornamental mats, often up to three metres long and woven in bold symbolic patterns from fresh green banana leaves. The most common design centres round the **cili** motif, a stylized female figure thought to represent the rice goddess Dewi Sri, with a body formed of simple geometric shapes and wearing a spiky headdress. Seven days before the great Galungan festival begins, special bamboo poles, or **penyor**, are erected along the streets of every village, each one bowed down with intricately woven garlands of dried flowers and palm leaves, which arch gracefully over the roadway. Attached to the *penyor* are symbolic leafy tassels, and offerings of dried paddy sheaves and coconut shells.

Lombok and Islam

Indonesia is the largest **Muslim** nation in the world, and almost ninety percent (around 202 million) of its population follow the faith. On Lombok, 85 percent of the islanders are Muslim, and most of the remainder are Balinese Hindus. A tiny minority of Lombok's Muslims adhere to **Wetu Telu** (see box, p.340) but as it is not officially recognized, numbers of followers are unknown.

On Lombok, you'll see that women dress modestly, but are not strictly veiled; the centre and east of the island are the most devout, but even here you'll see some women without head-coverings and relatively few with their entire body covered. The **mosque** is the centre of the Muslim faith, and prayers on Friday at noon pretty much empties the villages (see p.49 for etiquette required when visiting a mosque). Many new, extremely grand mosques are under construction throughout the island and driving around the interior you'll often be stopped by bucket-shakers asking for donations for mosque renovations. Thousands of islanders every year manage to afford the millions of rupiah needed for a pilgrimage to Mecca.

It is still unclear exactly how Islam came to Indonesia, but it seems likely that it spread along trade routes, probably via traders from Gujarat in India who had converted to Islam in the mid-thirteenth century, and by the sixteenth century it had reached Lombok. Traditionally, **the arrival of Islam** in Java is thought to have more exotic roots, brought by nine Islamic saints or *wali sangga*, one of whom is believed to be buried near Rembitan in the south of Lombok.

The most influential modern-day **Islamic social organization** on Lombok is Nahdlatul Wathan, which was founded in east Lombok by Guru Pancor in the 1930s. It now runs over seven hundred Islamic schools in Lombok and Sumbawa and has many adherents among government officials. Significantly, the current provincial governor, Zainul Majdi (popularly known as Guru Bajang, or "Young Teacher"), is Guru Pancor's grandson.

Traditional music and dance

M usic and dance play an essential part in daily Balinese life, and as a visitor you can't fail to experience them, either at a special tourist show, in rehearsal or at a temple festival. Ubud and its neighbouring villages have long had a reputation for their superb dance troupes and gamelan orchestras, and villagers now supplement their incomes by doing regular **shows** in the traditional settings of temple courtyards and village compounds. None is exactly authentic, as most comprise a medley of highlights from the more dramatic temple dances, but the quality is generally high and spectators are given English-language synopses. Ubud is also the place to take introductory lessons in the performing arts. To see wholly authentic performances you'll need to find out about imminent temple festivals or attend rehearsals, most of which take place in the local *banjar* after sundown; you'll probably be welcome to watch. There's a vibrant tradition of music and dance on Lombok, too, rarely witnessed by casual visitors to the island, since it's associated almost exclusively with religious practices.

Balinese performing arts

Traditionally, **Balinese** dancers and musicians have always learnt their craft from the experts in their village and by imitating other performers. Since the 1960s, however, arts students have also had the option of attending a government-run high school and college dedicated to the performing arts. The month-long Bali Arts Festival (Ⓦ www.baliartsfestival.com; see p.121), held every summer in Denpasar, showcases the best in the performing arts, staging both new and traditional works performed by professional arts graduates as well as village groups.

Balinese gamelan music

The national music of Bali is **gamelan**, a jangly clashing of syncopated sounds once described by the writer Miguel Covarrubias as being like "an oriental ultra-modern Bach fugue, an astounding combination of bells, machinery and thunder". The highly structured compositions are produced by a group of 25 or more musicians seated cross-legged on the ground at a variety of bronze percussion instruments – gongs, metallophones and cymbals – with a couple of optional wind and stringed instruments and two drums. All gamelan music is written for instruments tuned either to a five- or (less commonly) a seven-tone scale, and most is performed at an incredible speed: one study of a gamelan performance found that each instrumentalist played an average of seven notes per second.

"Gamelan" is the Javanese word for the bronze instruments, and the music probably came over from Java around the fourteenth century; the Balinese adapted it to suit their own personality, and now the sounds of the Javanese and Balinese gamelan are distinctive even to the untrained ear. Where Javanese gamelan music is restrained and rather courtly, Balinese is loud and flashy, boisterous and speedy, full of dramatic stops and starts. This modern Balinese style, known as **gong kebyar** (*gong* means orchestra, *kebyar* translates, aptly, as lightning flashes), has been around since the early 1900s, emerging at a time of great political upheaval on the island, when the status of Bali's royal houses was irreparably dented by Dutch colonial aggression. Until then, Bali's music had been as palace-oriented as Javanese gamelan, but in 1915 village musicians from north Bali gave a public performance in the new *kebyar* style, and the trend spread like wildfire across the island, with whole orchestras turning their instruments in to be melted down and recast in the new, more exuberant, timbres.

Gamelan orchestras are an essential part of village life. Every *banjar* that can afford to buy a set of instruments has its own *seka* or **music club**, and there are said to be 1500 active *gong kebyar* on the island. In most communities, the *seka* is open only to men (the all-female gamelan of Peliatan is a rare exception), but welcomes players between the ages of about 8 and 80. There's special *gong* music for every occasion – for sacred and secular dances, cremations, *odalan* festivities and *wayang kulit* shows – but players never learn from scores (in fact, few *gong* compositions are ever notated), preferring instead to have it drummed into them by repetitive practice. Whatever the occasion, *gong* players always dress up in the ceremonial uniform of their music club, and make appropriate blessings and ritual offerings to the deities. Like dancers, musicians are acutely conscious of their role as entertainers of the gods.

Although the *gong kebyar* is by far the most popular style of music and orchestra in Bali, there are over twenty different ensemble variations. The smallest is the four-piece **gender wayang**, which traditionally accompanies the *wayang kulit* shadow-play performances; the largest is the old-fashioned classical Javanese-style orchestra comprising fifty instruments, known as the **gamelan gong**. Most gamelan instruments are huge and far too heavy to be easily transported, so many *banjar* also possess a portable orchestra known as a **gamelan angklung**, designed around a set of miniature four-keyed metallophones, for playing in processions and at cremations or seashore ceremonies. There are also a few "bamboo orchestras", particularly in western Bali, where they're known as **gamelan joged bumbung** and **gamelan jegog**, composed entirely of bamboo instruments such as split bamboo tubes, marimbas and flutes.

Traditional dance-dramas of Bali

Most Balinese **dance-dramas** have evolved from **sacred rituals**, and are still performed at religious events, with full attention given to the devotional aspects. Before the show begins, a *pemangku* (village priest) sprinkles the players and the performance area with holy water, and many performances open with a Pendet, or welcome dance, intended for the gods. The exorcist Barong–Rangda dramas continue to play a vital function in the **spiritual practices** of every village, and the Baris dance re-enacts the traditional offering up of weapons by village warriors to the gods to invest them with supernatural power. Some of the more secular dance-dramas tell ancient and **legendary stories**, many of them adapted from the epic Hindu morality tales, the *Ramayana* and the *Mahabharata*, which came from India more than a thousand years ago. Others are based on **historical events**, embellishing the romances and battles of the royal courts of Java and Bali between the tenth and the fourteenth centuries.

There are few professional **dancers** in Bali; most performers don costumes and make-up only at festival times or for the regular tourist shows. Dancers learn by imitation and repetition and personal expression has no place, but the skilful execution of traditional moves is much admired, and trained dancers enjoy high status within the community.

Female dancers keep their feet firmly planted on the ground, their legs and hips encased in restrictive sarongs that give them a distinctive forward-angled posture. They express themselves through a vocabulary of controlled **angular movements** of the arms, wrists, fingers, neck and, most beguilingly, the eyes. Each pose and gesture derives from a movement observed in the natural rather than the human world. Thus, a certain type of flutter of the hand may be a bird in flight, a vigorous rotation of the forearms the shaking of water from an animal's coat. Dressed in pantaloons or hitched-up sarongs, the **male dancers** are much more energetic, emphasizing their manliness by opening shoulders and limbs outwards, keeping their knees bent and their heads high.

Most dramas are performed either within a temple compound, or in the outer courtyard of a noble family's palace. The **costumes and masks** give immediate clues to the identity of each character – and to the action that is to follow. Some dramas are performed in a combination of contemporary Bahasa Indonesia and the ancient literary Kawi language, while others stick to modern speech – perhaps with a few humorous English phrases thrown in for the tourists.

Baris

The **Baris** or **Warrior dance** is most commonly performed as a solo by a strutting young man who cuts an impressive figure in a gilded brocade cloak of ribboned pennants. He enacts a young warrior's preparation for battle, goading himself into courageous mood, trying out his martial skills, showing pride at his calling and then expressing a whole series of emotions – ferocity, passion, tenderness, rage – much of it through his eyes.

Barong–Rangda dramas

Featuring the most spectacular costumes of all the Balinese dances, the **Barong–Rangda dramas** are also among the most sacred and important. Essentially a dramatization of the eternal conflict between the forces of good and evil, the dramas take various forms but nearly always serve as ritualized exorcisms.

The mythical widow-witch character of **Rangda** represents the forces of evil, and her costume and mask present a frightening spectacle (see p.197 for Rangda's story). The **Barong** is much more lovable, a shaggy-haired creature with bug-eyes

The Mahabharata

Like its companion piece the *Ramayana*, the **Mahabharata** is an epic moral narrative of Hindu ethics that came to Indonesia from India in the eleventh century. Written during the fourth century AD by the Indian poet Vyasa, the original poem is phenomenally long, at over a hundred thousand verses. The **Balinese version** is translated into the ancient poetic language of Kawi and written on sacred *lontar* books kept in the Gedong Kirtya library at Singaraja. Its most famous episodes are known to every Balinese and reiterated in paintings, sculpted reliefs, *wayang kulit* dramas and dances.

At the heart of the story is the conflict between two rival branches of the same family, the Pandawas and the Korawas, all of them descendants of various unions between the deities and the mortals. The five **Pandawa brothers** represent the side of virtue, morality and noble purpose, though they each have their own foibles. The eldest is **Yudhisthira**, a calm and thoughtful leader with a passion for justice, whose one vice – an insatiable love of gambling – nonetheless manages to land the brothers in trouble. Then comes **Bhima**, a strong, courageous and hot-headed fighter, whose fiery temper and earthy manner make him especially appealing to the Balinese. The third brother, **Arjuna**, is the real hero; not only is he a brave warrior and an expert archer, but he's also handsome, high-minded and a great lover. Arjuna's two younger brothers, the expert horseman **Nakula** and the learned **Sahadeva**, are twins. Their rivals are their cousins the **Korawas**, who number a hundred in all, and are led by the eldest male **Durodhana**, a symbol of jealousy, deviousness and ignoble behaviour.

An early episode in the *Mahabharata* tells how the Pandawa boys are forced by the usurping Korawas to give up their rightful claim to the throne. Banished to the mountains for a minimum of thirteen years, the Pandawas grow up determined to regain what is theirs. Meanwhile, both families engage in countless adventures, confrontations with gods and demons, long journeys, seductions and practical jokes. A particular favourite is the exploit known as **Bhima Swarga**, in which Bhima is dispatched to Hell to rescue the souls of his dead father and stepmother. While there, he witnesses all sorts of horrible tortures and punishments, many of which are graphically depicted on the ceilings of Semarapura's Kerta Gosa. When Bhima returns to earth with the souls of his relatives, he's immediately sent off to Heaven in search of the holy water needed to smooth his dead parents' passage there. This episode is known as **Bhima Suci** and features the nine directional gods, as well as a dramatic battle between Bhima and his own godly (as opposed to earthly) father, Bayu.

Finally, a full-scale battle is declared between the two sets of cousins. On the eve of the battle, Arjuna suddenly becomes doubtful about the morality of fighting his own family, and confides as much to his friend and charioteer Krishna. Krishna, who is actually an avatar of the Hindu god Wisnu, then launches into a long theological lecture, in which he explains to Arjuna that the action is the all-important factor, not the result, and that because Arjuna is of the warrior caste, his duty is to fight, to act in a manner that's appropriate to his destiny. This episode of the *Mahabharata* is known as the **Bhagavad Gita**, and encapsulates the core Hindu philosophy of caste, and the notions of karma and destiny. Duly persuaded, Arjuna joins his brothers in battle, and at the end of eighteen bloody days the Pandawa brothers are victorious.

and a mischievous grin on his masked face, a cross between a pantomime horse and a Chinese dragon. The Barong Ket (lion) is his most common persona, but you might also see Barong Macan (tiger), Barong Bangkal (wild boar) and Barong Celeng (pig). All Rangda and Barong **masks** are invested with great sacred power and treated with extreme respect; when not in use, they're wrapped in sacred cloth and stored in the temple.

Barong–Rangda dramas can be self-contained, as in the Calonarang (see opposite), or they can be just one symbolic episode in the middle of a well-known story like the *Mahabharata*. Whatever the context, the format tends to be similar. Rangda is always called upon by a character who wants to cause harm (unrequited love is a common cause). She generally sends a minion to wage the first battles, and is then forced to appear herself when the opposition calls in the Barong, the defender of the good. In this final confrontation, the Barong enters first, occasionally joined by a monkey who teases him and plays tricks. Suddenly, Rangda appears, fingernails first, from behind the central gateway. Flashing her magic white cloth, she harasses the Barong, stalking him at every turn. When the Barong looks to be on his last legs, a group of village men rush in to his rescue, but are entranced by Rangda's magic and stab themselves instead of her. A priest quickly enters before any real injury is inflicted. The series of confrontations continues, and the drama ends in a typically Balinese stalemate: the forces of good and evil remain as strong and vital as ever, ready to clash again in the next bout.

The **Calonarang** is an embellished version of the Barong–Rangda conflict, grafted onto an ancient legend about the daughter of a witch queen whom no one will marry because they're scared of her mother. The witch queen Calonarang is a manifestation of Rangda who, furious at the lack of suitors for her daughter, demands that her followers wreak destruction in all the villages. This drama is acted out on a regular basis, whenever there are considered to be evil forces and impurities affecting the community, and sometimes the whole neighbourhood takes part, the men parading with hand-held *kulkul* drums and the women filing in to make offerings at the temple shrines.

There's also an unusual human version of the Barong, called **Barong Landung** ("Tall Barong"), which feature two huge puppets. The forbidding male puppet represents the malicious giant from Nusa Penida, Jero Gede; the far sweeter-looking female is the smiling Jero Luh. Together they act out a bawdy comic opera, which has exorcist purposes as well.

Kecak

Sometimes called the **Monkey dance** after the animals represented by the chorus, the **Kecak** gets its Balinese name from the hypnotic chattering sounds made by the a cappella choir. Chanting nothing more than "cak cak cak cak", the chorus of fifty or more men uses seven different rhythms to create the astonishing music that accompanies the drama. Bare-chested, and wearing lengths of black-and-white-check *kain poleng* cloth around their waists and a single red hibiscus behind the ear, the men sit cross-legged in five or six tight concentric circles, occasionally swaying or waving arms and clapping hands in unison. The **narrative** itself is taken from a core episode of the *Ramayana*, centring around the kidnap of Sita by the demon king Rawana, and is acted out in the middle of the chorus circle, with one or two narrators speaking for all the characters.

Although frequently attributed to the German artist and musician Walter Spies, the main creative force behind the Kecak was the famous Baris dancer **I Wayan Limbak**, who lived in Bedulu in Gianyar. In 1931 he developed the chants from the Sanghyang trance dances, in which the chorus chants the "cak cak cak cak" syncopation as part of the trance-inducing ritual, and created accompanying choreography to flesh out the episode from the *Ramayana*.

Legong

Undoubtedly the most refined of all the temple dances, the **Legong** is rather an acquired taste, characterized by the restrained, intricate weavings of arms, fingers, torsos and heads. It's always performed by three prepubescent girls who are bound tightly in sarongs and chest cloths of opulent green or pink, with gilded crowns filled with frangipani blossoms on their heads. The Legong is considered the acme

The Ramayana

Written in Sanskrit around the fourth century BC, the 24,000 verses that comprise the **Ramayana** have since fired the imaginations of writers, artists, dramatists and theologians right across Southeast Asia. Like the other great Hindu epic, the *Mahabharata*, the *Ramayana* has been translated into the classical Javanese Kawi language and transcribed on to sacred *lontar* texts.

It's essentially a morality tale, a dramatization of the eternal conflict between the forces of good (*dharma*) and the forces of evil (*adharma*). The forces of good are represented by Rama and his friends. **Rama**, the hero, is a refined and dutiful young man, handsome, strong and courageous, who also happens to be an avatar of the god Wisnu. Rama's wife, **Sita**, epitomizes the Hindu ideals of womanhood – virtue, fidelity and love – while Rama's brother, **Laksmana**, is a symbol of fraternal loyalty and youthful courage. The other important member of the Rama camp is **Hanuman**, the general of the monkey army, a wily and athletic ape who is unfailingly loyal to his allies. On the opposing side, the forces of evil are mainly represented by the demon king **Rawana**, a lustful and devious leader whose retainers are giants and devils.

The story begins with Rama, the eldest son of the king, being banished to the forests for thirteen years, having been cheated out of his rightful claim to the throne by a scheming stepmother. Sita and Laksmana accompany him, and together the trio have various encounters with sages, giants and seductresses.

The most crucial event in the epic is the **abduction of Sita** by Rawana, a crime that inspires the rather unwarlike Rama to wage battle against his enemy. A favourite subject for dances and carvings, the episode starts with Sita catching sight of a beautiful golden deer and imploring her husband Rama to catch it for her. The golden deer turns out to be a decoy planted by Rawana, and the demon king duly swoops down to abduct Sita as soon as Rama and Laksmana go off to chase the animal. The distraught Rama determines to get Sita back and, together with Laksmana, he sets off for Rawana's kingdom. En route he meets Hanuman, the monkey general, who agrees to sneak him into Sita's room at Rawana's palace and **give her Rama's ring** (another popular theme of pictures and dramas). Eventually, Rama, Laksmana, Hanuman and his monkey army all arrive at Rawana's palace and, following a big battle, Sita is rescued and Rawana done away with.

---

of Balinese femininity and Legong dancers have always enjoyed a special status in their village, a reputation that endures long after they retire at the onset of menstruation. In the past, many a Legong dancer has ended up as a raja's wife or, latterly, as an expatriate artist's muse.

The dance evolved from a highly sacred Sanghyang trance dance and takes several different forms. By far the most common is the **Legong Keraton** (Dance of the Court), based on a classical twelfth-century tale from Java. It tells the story of King Laksem, who is holding a princess, Rangkesari, captive against her will. Rescue is on the way in the form of Prince Daha, who plans to wage battle against King Laksem. The princess tries to dissuade the king from going to war, but he sets off anyway. As he leaves he is attacked by a raven, an extremely bad omen, after which he duly loses the battle and is killed.

The **performance** begins with a solo dance by a court lady, known as the *condong* (dressed in pink and gold). She picks up two fans from the ground in anticipation of the arrival of the two *legong* (literally "dancer"). Dressed identically in bright green and gold, the two Legong enact the story, adopting and swapping characters with no obvious distinction. The *condong* always returns as the raven, with pink wings attached to her costume. The final fatal battle is never shown on stage.

Sanghyang: trance dances

The state of **trance** lies at the heart of traditional Balinese dance. In order to maintain the health of the village, the gods are periodically invited down into the temple to help in the exorcism of evil and sickness-inducing spirits. The deities reveal themselves by possessing certain individuals, sometimes communicating through them with words, which may have to be interpreted by a priest, and sometimes taking over the whole physical being so that the medium is moved to dance or to perform astonishing physical feats. The chosen medium is put into a trance state through a combination of priestly chants and protective mantras, intoned exhortations by the a cappella choir, and great clouds of incense wafted heavenwards to attract the gods' attention. Trance dances are traditionally only performed when the village is suffering from a particularly serious bout of sickness or ill fortune – the versions that are reproduced at tourist shows have none of the spiritual dynamism of the real thing, though it is said that performers do sometimes slip into trance even then.

One of the most common trance dances is the **Sanghyang Dedari**, in which two young girls become possessed and perform a complicated duet with their eyes closed; though they have never learnt the steps, the girls usually perform in sync, sometimes for up to four hours. In the Sanghyang Dedari performed at tourist shows, however, the girls have almost certainly rehearsed the dance beforehand and probably do not enter a trance state at all. They wear the same tightly bound green and gold sarongs as the Legong dancers, and dance to the haunting backing vocals of an a cappella chorus of men and women.

In the **Sanghyang Jaran** (Horse Deity), one or more men are put into a trance state while the temple floor is littered with burning coconut husks. As they enter the trance, the men grab hold of wooden hobbyhorse sticks and then gallop frantically back and forth across the red-hot embers as if they were on real horses. The all-male Kecak chorus fuels the drama with excited a cappella crescendos until, finally, the exhausted hobbyhorse riders are awoken by the priest.

Topeng: mask dances

In the **Topeng** or **Mask dance**, the performer is possessed by the spirit of the mask (for more on which, see p.149). Before every entrance, the Topeng actor sprinkles holy water on his mask and recites a mantra. Women never participate in Topeng: female roles are played by men.

Topeng **storylines** usually centre around popular folk tales or well-known episodes from history, and the characters are immediately recognizable. One of the most popular is the **Topeng Tua**, a touching solo in which an elderly retired first-minister recalls his time in the king's service. His mask is fringed with straggly white hair and beard, and his gait is frail and wavering. Another favourite tourist Topeng is the **Frog Dance** – performed to the evocative music of the Balinese jew's-harp or *genggong* – which tells how a frog turns into a prince. In the **Jauk**, the soloist portrays a terrifying demon-king who leaps mischievously about the stage as if darting from behind trees and pouncing on unsuspecting villagers. His red or white mask has bulging eyes and a creepy smile and he flashes his foot-long finger-nails menacingly throughout.

Wayang kulit: shadow puppet shows

Wayang kulit or **shadow puppet shows** are typically staged as entertainment following weddings, cremations or temple *odalan*. The stories are often taken from the *Mahabharata*, but improvisation and topical jokes keep the art alive and a skilled and witty *dalang* (puppeteer), nearly always a man, can attract huge crowds and keep them entertained into the early hours. The performance takes place behind a white cloth screen illuminated by flaming torches and may star as many as sixty different **wayang** (puppets), which are always made from buffalo hide and mounted on a stick. (You can see the workshops of some well-known *dalang* in Sukawati, described on p.150.)

Amazingly, the **dalang** not only manipulates each of his many *wayang* himself, but speaks for each one of them as well, displaying an impressive memory for lines and an extraordinary range of different voices. At the same time he also conducts the special four-piece orchestra, the *gender wayang*. Not surprisingly, *dalang* are greatly revered and considered to have great spiritual power.

The torch-lit **screen** represents the world in microcosm: the puppets are the humans that inhabit it, the torch represents the sun, and the *dalang* acts as god. Puppets who represent good characters always appear to the right of the *dalang*, and those who are evil appear on his left. A leaf-shaped fan-like puppet, symbolizing the tree of life, marks centre stage and is used to indicate the end of a scene as well as to represent clouds, spirits and magical forces.

Lombok music and dance

Lombok has a rich heritage of music and dance. The indigenous Sasak traditions have been subject to many influences, both Hindu and Islamic, direct from Bali and Java, and through Buginese and Makassarese traders. The resulting melange of puppetry, poetry, song and dance is varied, but largely inaccessible to tourists. **Cultural shows** are all but nonexistent, except for during the annual **Senggigi Festival** (see p.318), but you may stumble across a wedding or other celebration on your travels.

Lombok's gamelan music

Lombok's traditional **gamelan** music is similar to Bali's, though some of the orchestras are different. The **gamelan gong Sasak** resembles the *gamelan gong*, but may be combined with the bamboo xylophones of the **gamelan grantang**. The **gamelan oncer** is also widely used, and accompanies the Gendang Beleq dance (see below).

Gamelan tawa-tawa and **barong tengkok** are used in processions at weddings and circumcision ceremonies. The usual gongs and drums are accompanied by eight sets of cymbals attached to decorated lances. The gamelan *barong tengkok* from central Lombok actually has gongs suspended within a Barong figure. **Gamelan rebana** consists of up to twenty different drums, which mimic the traditional sound of gamelan music, but without the use of bronze instruments. More unusual is the **gamelan klentang**, made up entirely of iron instruments. Other musical ensembles that are seen on the island include **kecimol** and **cilokaq**, consisting of an oboe (*preret*), flutes, lutes, violins and drums, and are often played to accompany Sasak poetry.

Lombok's performance and martial arts

In contrast to the huge academic interest in Balinese performing arts, Sasak **dances** have been studied far less.

Of the various **public dances**, the **Gendang Beleq** was traditionally used to send off soldiers heading into battle and to welcome them home again. It is performed to the distinctive rhythm of huge drums (*gendang*) and these days is staged to welcome VIPs. The **Batek Baris**, which is performed in Lingsar and elsewhere, has dancers wearing costumes mimicking Dutch army uniforms and carrying wooden rifles while they lead a procession to the sacred springs. At the Nyale Festival near Kuta the Putri Mandalika legend is re-enacted to large crowds (see p.352); the popular **Kemidi Rudat** retells the *Thousand and One Nights* stories, complete with colourful characters and clowns; the **Telek** is based on the tale of a princess who falls in love with a humble man; and the **Kayak Sando** (with masks) dramatizes the Panji stories from Java in which a prince undergoes numerous adventures while searching for his lost bride.

Local, village-based dances include the **Gandrung** of central Lombok, a demonstration of love performed by a solo female dancer who selects a man to join her, and the **Tandak Geroq**, staged in east Lombok to celebrate the end of the harvest. There are also **trance dances** such as the **Suling Dewa**, accompanied by flutes and song, which is particular to north Lombok and used to induce spirits to enter the local shaman and bless the village. The **Pepakon**, from east Lombok, causes the sick to become possessed so that their illness can be removed from them.

More a martial art than a performing art, but still a massive spectator draw, **peresean**, or **stick fighting**, involves two men attacking each other with long rattan canes, with only a goat-skin shield to defend themselves. The aim is to draw blood from the head – and it's all for real, as the injuries show. Every schoolboy learns the art of *peresean* and contests are staged between village teams. The best time to see a stickfight is on August 18, the day after Independence Day: Narmada, east of Mataram, and Kotaraja near Tetebatu are both famous centres. You can also see *peresean* at the Senggigi Festival (see p.318).

Modern Balinese music

The past decade has seen an explosion in the popularity of modern Balinese music – in Bali itself, throughout Indonesia, and even abroad. Uniquely in Indonesia, Balinese musicians no longer need to go to Jakarta to make their name, but can use Bali as a gateway to national and international recognition. More and more relatively small local bands are now playing overseas – including in Japan, Eastern Europe and Scandinavia – without first hitting the big time in the Indonesian capital.

There are two main genres of modern Balinese music: **Balinesia**, in which the Balinese artists sing in Indonesian, and **Balibali**, in which they sing in Balinese. Albums by musicians from both genres outsell their Western competition in Bali (though piracy has severely dented all markets), and concerts are often as well attended as those of the major national (mainly Javanese) bands. The cultural impact of this boom has been significant. Instead of feeling marginalized and crowded out by Java, Balinese youth now have a channel through which they can express themselves; they can at last voice their disappointment with the political elite and endemic corruption. There is also a renewed pride in the Balinese language, whose "cool" status has been given a big boost by artists singing in Balinese.

The growing **indie scene** actively encourages creativity, especially in the young (a big contrast with the repressively conformist years under Suharto's rule), and has opened people's eyes to the possibility of doing something different from the Balinese norm. This is reflected in the trend for all things rockabilly and punk, from independent clothing shops (*distros*) selling original fashion and music-related paraphernalia, to chopper-style motorbikes and low-rider pushbikes.

Meanwhile, the increasingly high-profile **OneDollarForMusic (ODFM) foundation** (Ⓦ www.onedollarformusic.com), funded by the Indonesian and Dutch governments, is supporting youth participation in Bali's music scene, and on Lombok as well, holding workshops at schools, training young musicians, staging regular concerts, and even releasing a compilation album of the bands they've mentored, *Young Sounds of Bali*.

Balinesia

Balinesia emerged in the mid-1980s with rock bands that favoured covers and drew large crowds. To be an AC/DC wannabe, to cover Gary Moore's songs, to shred guitar as fast as Rainbow's Ritchie Blackmore, was considered ultra cool.

But the Balinesia breakthrough came in 2003 when the first big Balinese band, punk-rock-styled **Superman Is Dead (SID)**, released their debut album, *Kuta Rock City,* with a major label, Sony Music Indonesia. They were the first Balinese band to make it big outside Bali and the first to record mostly in English (with about thirty percent of their songs in Indonesian). Having toured Australia, and participated in the legendary Warped Tour around the USA in 2009, they went on to break into the US Billboard chart.

Grunge band **Navicula** is the second-biggest Balinesia band on the island and the biggest grunge band in Indonesia. Their focus on social and environmental issues and flower-power fashion style has them tagged as new hippies.

Another star is virtuoso guitarist **Balawan** and his band, Batuan Ethnic Fusion. They skilfully combine jazz and Balinese music, using gamelan instruments, *kendang* (traditional drums) and bamboo flutes alongside guitars, modern drums and keyboards. Balawan is a master of finger-tapping and the only guitarist in Indonesia who plays a double-neck guitar with two independent hands (eight-finger touch style). He frequently performs overseas, mainly in Europe and Asia. Balawan is also involved in a Hindu/spiritual project called **Nyanyian Dharma**, in which he and other famous Balinese musicians sing in Sanskrit and promote peace and love around Indonesia and abroad.

One of Balawan's collaborators on Nyanyian Dharma is the increasingly famous world music singer **Ayu Laksmi**. She began as a "lady rocker" in the late 1980s but has since embraced jazz fusion. Her 2010 world music album, *Svara Semesta*, on which she sang in five languages – including Sanskrit, Kawi and Balinese – was a nationwide hit and rated as one of Indonesia's twenty best albums of the year.

Other notable local music artists include pioneer rockabillies **The Hydrant**, who have a significant fanbase in Bali and Java and are an exciting band to see live, with tours of Europe already under their belt. There's also the amazing trumpeter **Rio Sidik**, "psychobilly" band **Suicidal Sinatra** (mixing punk and rockabilly), punk collective Scared of Bums, electronic-rock outfit **Discotion Pill**, and extreme-metal group **Parau**. They are all massive in Bali and have enjoyed a similarly positive reception nationwide. Especially Rio, who, with his world music band **Saharadja**, has already travelled the world and can sometimes still be heard playing to capacity crowds in small local pubs in Kuta, Seminyak and Ubud.

Balibali

The **Balibali** phenomenon is unique in Indonesia: its artists sing exclusively in Balinese, and the music tends to be edgy and controversial. Its appeal is not as limited as you might expect, as there are tightknit Balinese communities also in Lombok, Kalimantan, Sumatra and Sulawesi. Interest in Balibali peaked between about 2003 and 2008, but its big-name artists still attract significant audiences.

Balibali began with folk-style bands of the 1960s and came of age in the mid-1980s, when several artists released pop–rock-style albums in Balinese and began writing more risqué lyrics, perhaps due to new Western influences. But the big shake-up came in 2003 when Lolot 'N Band released *Gumine Mangkin*. **Lolot**, the singer, was a complete original with his punk-rock attitude and confrontational Balinese lyrics, totally unlike the plaintive style common to the genre. He invented so-called alternative rock in Bali and pushed the boundaries with songs such as *Bangsat* (Bastard), a social protest anthem against the grasping Indonesian authorities: "Fuck, stop fighting/Look at the price of food commodities that are rising/Fuck, stop fighting/Look at the marginalized people, they are the victims".

Nanoe Biroe is another Balibali rock star, commanding a legion of fanatical fans known as "Beduda" who see him as a hero, or even a prophet. All over Bali, you'll come across young men wearing "President of Beduda" T-shirts, bearing a Nanoe version of the famous Che Guevara silhouette. "Beduda" is Balinese for dung beetle and so Nanoe has cleverly positioned himself as the leader of marginalized people.

But the biggest of them all today are **[XXX]**, Balibali's only hip-hop band. Their unique approach, rapping in Balinese, and great voices have made them the most enduring act. The island's top reggae artists are **Joni Agung & Double T**; their records go down well all over Bali and dreadlocked Joni is quite a local celebrity. Diva **Dek Ulik** is especially popular with Balinese women. Her debut album of 2005, *Rindu Ngantosang Janji*, sold over fifty thousand copies, a first for a Balinese female soloist.

Venues and festivals

The main live-music **venues** for Balinese bands are in Kuta and Denpasar, and are detailed in the relevant accounts. For gig **listings** check the free fortnightly English-language magazine *the beat* (Ⓦ www.beatmag.com), available throughout

Discography

Modern Balinese music is hard to find outside Indonesia, but within Bali the best sources are major **record-store** chains such as Disc Tarra, local records shops and *distros*. The following are the latest albums available from major local artists.

Punk rock/Alternative rock
Discotion Pill *Amphetamine* (Balinesia; lyrics mostly in English)
Lolot *Pejalan Idup* (Balibali)
Nanoe Biroe *M3tamorforia* (Balibali)
Painful by Kisses *The Curse of...* (Balinesia; some lyrics in English)
Superman Is Dead *Angels and the Outsiders* (Balinesia; some lyrics in English)
The Hydrant *Bali Bandidos* (Balinesia; a few lyrics in English)

Grunge/Metal
Navicula *Salto* (Balinesia; some lyrics in English)
Parau *Somatoform* (Balinesia; a few lyrics in English)

Jazz/World music
Ayu Laksmi *Svara Semesta* (Balinesia; some lyrics in English)
Riwin *My Sexy Life* (Balinesia; a few lyrics in English)

Reggae
Joni Agung & Double T *Melalung* (Balibali)

Hip-hop
[XXX] *Jingkrak Jingkrak* (Balibali)

Pop
Dek Ulik *Rindu Ngantosang Janji* (Balibali)

south Bali. You can also hear Balinesia and Balibali artists on the many dedicated local music radio stations.

Modern music **festivals** in Indonesia used to depend solely on corporate sponsorship but now get a little more support from regional government; check *the beat* for dates. Among the highlights are **Bali Jamfest**, a huge two-day event featuring every major Balinese artist, and **Soundrenaline**, a touring Indonesian version of Australia's "Big Day Out", which invites a lot of local bands to join in. The annual **Denpasar Festival**, held in downtown Denpasar (Dec 28–31), has a special stage presenting the best local bands, while **Kuta Karnival** (on Kuta Beach), is usually held in September (see p.44) and features a stimulating mix of Bali and national band line-ups.

Rudolf Dethu and Sarah Forbes

Village life and traditions

The majority of people on Bali and Lombok live in villages. People employed in the cities or tourist resorts may well commute and even those whose villages are far away still identify with them and return for particular festivals each year.

Balinese village layout

Orientation in Bali does not correspond to the compass points of north, south, east and west. The main directions are **kaja** (towards Gunung Agung, dwelling place of the gods) and **kelod** (away from the mountain). The other directions are *kangin* (from where the sun rises), and its opposite, *kauh* (where the sun sets).

All Balinese villages are oriented *kaja–kelod* and the locations of the three village temples, *pura dalem*, *pura puseh* and *pura desa* (see p.371), are determined on this axis.

House compounds

Each Balinese house compound is built within a confining wall. When a son of the family marries, his wife usually moves into his compound, so there are frequently several generations living together, each with their own sleeping quarters, but otherwise sharing the facilities. Most domestic activities take place outside or in the partial shelter of **bale**, raised platforms with a roof. The different structures of the compound are believed to reflect the human body: the family shrine (*Sanggah Kemulan*) is the head, the *bale* are the arms, the courtyard is the navel, the kitchen and rice barn are the legs and feet, and the rubbish tip, located along with the pig pens outside the *kelod* wall, is the anus. The Traditional Balinese House museum in Tabanan (see p.278) is a good example of a typical compound.

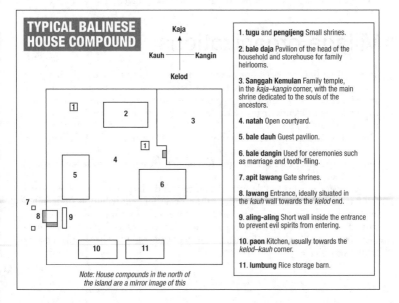

TYPICAL BALINESE HOUSE COMPOUND

Kaja ↑
Kauh — Kangin
Kelod

1. **tugu** and **pengijeng** Small shrines.

2. **bale daja** Pavilion of the head of the household and storehouse for family heirlooms.

3. **Sanggah Kemulan** Family temple, in the *kaja–kangin* corner, with the main shrine dedicated to the souls of the ancestors.

4. **natah** Open courtyard.

5. **bale dauh** Guest pavilion.

6. **bale dangin** Used for ceremonies such as marriage and tooth-filing.

7. **apit lawang** Gate shrines.

8. **lawang** Entrance, ideally situated in the *kauh* wall towards the *kelod* end.

9. **aling-aling** Short wall inside the entrance to prevent evil spirits from entering.

10. **paon** Kitchen, usually towards the *kelod–kauh* corner.

11. **lumbung** Rice storage barn.

Note: House compounds in the north of the island are a mirror image of this

Initially all prospective house-builders consult an expert in the Balinese calendar to choose auspicious days for buying land and beginning construction. The architect or master builder (*undagi*) follows rules laid down in ancient texts, taking a series of **measurements** from the body of the **head of the household** and using these to calculate the exact dimensions of the compound. Before building starts, offerings are placed in the foundations so that work will proceed smoothly. When the building work is finished, further ceremonies must take place before the compound can be occupied. The final ceremony is the **melaspas**, an inauguration ritual that "brings the building to life".

Sasak villages

Balinese people living on Lombok retain their traditional house compounds, as do the Bugis people, who have settled along Lombok's eastern and southern coasts and live in wooden houses constructed on tall piles. The indigenous **Sasak** people of Lombok also have their own architectural style.

Traditional Sasak villages, such as those at Segenter and Senaru in north Lombok, and Rembitan and Sade in south Lombok, are walled enclosures, with a gateway that is closed at night. **Houses** are made of bamboo with a thatch roof that slopes almost to the ground and floors of mud and dung; they may have none or only a few windows, with a veranda on at least one side. Traditionally, the cooking hearth and eating area are inside the house; a walled-off room, the *inan bale*, is used for storage but is also the place where newlyweds spend their first night.

The symbol of Lombok, the **lumbung rice barn**, with its bonnet-shaped roof, is a feature of only the south of the island. They are built in rows, on four piles, with a thatch roof and a single opening high up. A circular wooden disc, the *jelepreng*, on each post stops rats climbing up to the rice. Underneath each post, old Chinese coins (*kepeng*) are buried for good luck and protection.

Village organizations

The smallest unit of social organization in each Balinese village is the **banjar** or neighbourhood. Each adult male joins the local *banjar* when he marries; his wife and children are also members but only the adult men attend meetings. The largest *banjar* in Denpasar may have five hundred heads of household, the small rural ones just fifty.

Typically, the *banjar* meets monthly in the meeting house, the **bale banjar**, to discuss anything of relevance to the *banjar*, for example land issues, temple ceremonies or the gamelan orchestra. Although there is a head of the *banjar* (*kliang*), all decisions are reached by consensus.

The *banjar* has considerable authority. If residential land in the area is left vacant for a period of time, it will revert to the *banjar* for redistribution. If members neglect their duties, they can be fined or even expelled from the village. This is a particularly powerful threat among people where communal life is at the heart of their existence. Expulsion also means the loss of the right to burial and cremation within the village.

The subak

Much of the daily life of a village revolves around the *sawah*, or **ricefields**. The local organization controlling each irrigation system is the **subak**; these have existed on Bali since the ninth century, and are made up of all the farmers who use the water in that system. The maintenance of the irrigation system, along with complex planning that ensures every farmer gets adequate water, is coordinated by the *kliang subak*. Any *subak* with plans that have a wider impact or cause potential conflict with another *subak* – such as changing dry fields to wet – consults the regional water temples and, ultimately, the **Jero Gede**, chief priest of Pura Ulun Danu Batur, whose decision is final.

The **Subak Museum** on the outskirts of Tabanan (see p.278) is well worth a visit for more information on this unique aspect of Balinese life.

Balinese life-cycle celebrations

On **Bali**, rituals and ceremonies are carried out at important points in an individual's life for purification and to ensure the maintenance of sufficient spiritual energy for good health.

The first life-cycle ritual, **pegedong-gedongan**, takes place about six months after conception, when the fetus has a human form, and emphasizes the hope for a long, healthy life. Subsequent **birth rituals** focus on the placenta, which is buried inside a coconut wrapped in sacred white cloth near the gateway of the parents' household. A rock is placed over the spot to protect it, and regular offerings are made there.

Following the birth, the parents and child are regarded as unclean (*sebel*), and cannot participate in religious practices. For the mother and baby, this lasts 42 days; for the father, it lasts until the baby's umbilical cord drops off, when the **kepus pungsed** ritual is carried out. The cord is wrapped in cloth, placed in an offering shaped like a dove and suspended over the baby's bed, along with a small shrine dedicated to Sanghyang Panca Kumara, son of Siwa, who is invoked as the child's protector. There are further ceremonies at twelve and 42 days and then, after 105 days, it's **telubulan**, a large, elaborate ceremony at which the child is named, and may be given an amulet to guard against evil spirits.

The child's **first birthday**, *oton*, occurs after 210 days (a Balinese year in the *wuku* calendar; see p.43), and is the first occasion that the child is allowed contact with the ground, and may be accompanied by a ritual hair-cutting ceremony. The next ceremony, **maketus**, takes place when the child's milk teeth fall out. Sanghyang Panca Kumara, who has been protecting the child since birth, is relieved of his duties, and the child is now guarded by the family ancestors.

Tooth filing

The **tooth-filing ritual**, *mapandes*, which preferably takes place before marriage, is a huge celebration with guests, music and lavish offerings. It is considered vital, and the elderly, and even the dead, have been known to have their teeth filed if they have never had it done. The aim is to remove coarse behaviour from the person and rid them of lust, greed, anger, drunkenness, confusion and jealousy, in order that they will lead a better life and be assured a more favourable reincarnation. The upper canine teeth or fangs and the four teeth in between are filed down.

Marriage

There are two **marriage** options. The most correct is *mamadik*, when the marriage is agreed between the two sets of parents and a huge financial outlay for lavish ceremonies is involved. Much more common is *ngerorod* or *malaib* – elopement. The man and woman run off and spend the night together, not so secretly that nobody knows, but with sufficient subterfuge that the girl's parents can pretend outrage. The following morning the couple are married in a private ceremony. More elaborate rituals and a reception may be hosted later the same day by the boy's parents. The girl's parents will not be invited as there is supposed to be bad feeling between the two sides. However, three days later the two sets of parents meet at the *ketipat bantal* ceremony, and are reconciled.

Cremation

The ceremony that visitors to Bali are most likely to witness is **cremation** (*pengabenan* or *palebonan*). The Balinese believe that the soul inhabits a temporary receptacle, the body, during life on earth. After death, the body must be returned to the five elements of solid, liquid, energy, radiance and ether to ready the soul for reincarnation.

Following death, the body is usually buried, sometimes for years, while the **preparations** for the cremation are made. Poorer families often share in the cremation ceremonies of wealthier families as costs are crippling. The entire extended family and *banjar* is involved in preparations. Animals are slaughtered, holy water acquired and gamelan, dancers and puppet shows organized. An animal-shaped, highly decorated sarcophagus is built to hold the body. The cremation tower, representing the Balinese universe, supported by the turtle, Bedawang, and the two *naga*, Basuki and Anantaboga, is also built, with tiers similar to the roofs on the *meru* in temples. A *bale* at the base of the tiers houses an effigy of the dead person.

Accompanied by the bamboo **gamelan angklung**, the sarcophagus and cremation tower are carried to the cemetery and twirled around many times en route to ensure that the soul is confused and cannot return home to cause mischief for the family. At the cremation ground the sarcophagus and tower are burned and the ashes carried to the sea or to a stream that will carry them to the ocean. Further ceremonies are needed after three days and twelve days, finishing with the ritual of *nyagara-gunung*, when the family take offerings to important sea and mountain temples.

Traditional healers

Known as *balian* in Bali and *dukun* in Lombok, **traditional healers** are a vital adjunct to Western medicine on the islands. Illness is believed to stem from a lack of balance between the patient and the spirit world; for example, a patient may have paid insufficient respect to a god. There are many different kinds of *balian*, ranging from the most practical *balian tulang* (bonesetters), *balian manak* (midwives) and *balian apun* (masseurs), to the more spiritual, including *balian taksu*, mediums who enter a trance to communicate with the spirit world and *balian kebal*, who work with charms and spells, making love potions and magical amulets to protect the wearer against spiritual attack. *Balian* are also consulted to find out which ancestral souls have been reincarnated in the bodies of newborn babies, and which days are auspicious for certain events.

Sasak life-cycle ceremonies

Some of the ceremonies performed in Sasak communities on **Lombok** are associated with the more orthodox adherents to Islam, while others are associated only with Wetu Telu followers (for more on Wetu Telu, see box, p.340). The Wetu Telu **birth ceremony** of *adi kaka* is similar to the Balinese one involving the placenta. A few days after birth, the **naming ceremony** of *buang au* or *malang mali* takes place. A ritual **hair-cutting ceremony**, *ngurisang*, is also obligatory for a young child, although the age it takes place is variable.

The most important ceremony for a Muslim boy is his **circumcision** (*nyunatang*), which often takes place in the Muslim month of the Prophet Muhammad's birthday, accompanied by much ceremony and feasting.

There are three **marriage** options in Sasak culture: a marriage arranged by the families, one between cousins, or an elopement. Whichever occurs, the man's family pays a price (in cows, money, rice, betel nut, coconut, a white sarong and old Chinese coins) for the bride, who moves to their house. During the wedding ceremony, the couple are often carried on a sedan chair, and accompanied by a gamelan orchestra.

Under the laws of Islam, the dead are **buried**, rather than cremated. According to Wetu Telu custom, the dead are ritually washed and wrapped in a white sarong, carried to the cemetery and buried with the head towards Mecca. A death in the family sets in motion a whole cycle of rituals. The most important is **deena nitook**, seven days after the death, **nyatus** after a hundred days, and the final event, **nyiu**, a thousand days after death, when the grave is sprinkled with holy water, commemorative stones are placed on it and offerings such as toothbrushes and clothes are made to ensure the deceased is comfortable in heaven.

The impact of tourism

D
ebates about the **effects of tourism** on Bali and Lombok have been running for decades. In the 1920s and 1930s, soon after the first tourists arrived, some local commentators decried visitors who took photographs of bare-breasted Balinese women and damaged island roads with their motor cars. In fact **nostalgia** for a more peaceful Bali is even older; a Javanese mystic who visited Bali in 1500 complained that it was no longer quiet enough to practise meditation.

The history of tourism

Tourism in Bali effectively started in 1924 when KPM, the Royal Packet Navigation Company, established weekly **steamship services** connecting Bali with Batavia (Jakarta), Singapore, Semarang, Surabaya and Makassar, with visitors to Bali using the government rest-houses dotted around the island. Bali received 213 visitors that year, and the numbers, with a few blips, have continued to rise ever since; the island now receives more than two million foreign visitors annually plus more than three million Indonesian tourists, who are as fond of Bali as people from outside the country.

In 1928, KPM opened the first **hotel** on the island, the *Bali Hotel* in Denpasar; an air link to Surabaya was established in 1933; a daily ferry between Java and Gilimanuk was launched in 1934; and the airport at Tuban opened in 1938. By the 1930s several thousand tourists were visiting Bali each year, some of whom settled on the island. Artists, such as Walter Spies and Miguel Covarrubias, and anthropologists, including Margaret Mead and Gregory Bateson, focused on the artistic and religious aspects of Balinese life and, through their writing, painting, photography and film-making, enhanced the worldwide image of Bali as a paradise.

The Japanese occupation during World War II, followed by the struggle for independence, halted the tourist influx, but under President Sukarno and later President Suharto, the **promotion of tourism** became official government policy. The inauguration of **Ngurah Rai Airport** on August 1, 1969, marked the beginning of mass tourism; it is now the second-busiest airport in Indonesia, after Jakarta.

In 1972, the government-owned **Bali Tourist Development Corporation (BTDC)** was formed and built the resort of **Nusa Dua**, aimed at closeting high-spending tourists away from local people. However, the tourists didn't all stay hidden away. By the 1970s **Kuta** had become a surfer's mecca and local people in the small village turned their homes into small hotels. Not everyone was happy; due to their ragged clothes, the surfers were labelled as hippies, drug addicts and practitioners of free love and the negative impact of tourism on the island was contemplated fearfully.

There was also concern about the **over-commercialization** of arts and culture for tourist consumption. Dances, for example, were shortened and changed to suit tourist tastes; it was a rare visitor who could enjoy a five-hour performance. In the 1970s the annual Bali Arts Festival was inaugurated to encourage the Balinese to appreciate their own culture.

However, the advance of tourism continued. In 1971 about 60 percent of the island's income was derived from agriculture and around 33 percent from tourism. By 2000, agriculture contributed less than 20 percent and tourism over 62 percent.

Bali is one of the wealthiest of Indonesia's provinces and average income on the island exceeds that on neighbouring Java.

Brand Bali

Bali has an extremely high **global profile**. It is regularly voted one of the top island destinations in the world. The image of Bali as a **paradise** was sorely tested in 2002 and 2005 when the island was dragged into the apparent clash between radical Islam and the West. Without Bali's high profile and the global interest in the island, it is unlikely that the island would have held any interest for the bombers.

Following the Kuta bombing on October 12, 2002, the island emptied of tourists overnight. However, when it was discovered that the bombers were Muslims, the Hindu population of Bali made no moves against Muslim communities or individuals on the island. Many Balinese interpreted the bombing as an indication that the gods were angry and on November 15, 2002, a huge purification ceremony was carried out to resolve the problem. The annual commemoration service has always been an inter-faith service.

With an estimated eighty percent of the population relying on tourism for their living in some way or another, the economy nose-dived. By June 2003, a World Bank report estimated that the average Balinese income had dropped by forty percent. The fate of Lombok, inextricably linked to that of its more famous neighbour, mirrored Bali exactly. However, within a year there were signs of recovery aided by messages to the world that Bali was safe and needed tourists to return and support the island. When bombers struck again on October 1, 2005, in Kuta and Jimbaran, tourist arrivals plummeted again. Still, once again, Bali recovered and arrival numbers now far exceed those before the bombs.

Economy versus culture

Whatever the **economic benefits** to the island, in studies by Universitas Udayana (the University of Bali), some Balinese people described tourism as a tempest battering their coasts. Particular concerns related to tourism damaging **religion**; they condemned the desecration of temples by tourists and the fact that Balinese involved in the industry neglected their religious duties. One commentator noted, "Tourism is the fire that cooks your breakfast and the fire that burns down your house."

Even when tourism is thriving, the financial advantages are not evenly spread and there remain significant pockets of poverty on the island. Similarly, profits from multinational hotel chains flood out of the island to Jakarta and abroad. Equally concerning to many Balinese, the island is now a magnet for migrants from across Indonesia. Some people describe Kuta beach as *universitas pantai*, the beach university. Although many of the traders, from all across Indonesia, have no formal education, they end up as skilled, multilingual communicators with sales skills second to none and proceed to take jobs from the Balinese. A local phrase tells that, "… *the migrant sells beef balls to buy land, while the Balinese sells land to buy beef balls*". Some tourist businesses prefer to employ non-Balinese rather than cope with Balinese staff needing to take time off to attend religious ceremonies.

However, as families grow many people in Bali can no longer earn a living from agriculture; the tourist sector offers opportunities at all levels from chambermaids to managers, and Bali is now an exporter of skilled staff for the hospitality industry. Commentators have noted that the increased wealth of the Balinese is very often spent in highly traditional ways – in particular, on elaborate religious ceremonies.

Environmental concerns

Tourism also generates major **environmental concerns**. It is estimated that ten square kilometres of agricultural land are lost to tourist development every year. Rice cultivation, so prevalent in Bali, depends heavily on water; one five-star hotel room is estimated to consume 500 litres of water each day. Recent fears relate to the Balinese water table being polluted by salt water due to overuse and uncontrolled development.

Particular concerns have arisen about the effects of tourist developments on the island's **coral reefs**, global awareness of the environmental problems of **golf courses** is also growing and with thousands of new **vehicles** heading out onto the Balinese roads each month problems of noise and air pollution are increasingly apparent. The **rubbish** problem is visible for every visitor to see; in 2010 the provincial government announced plans to make Bali free from plastic waste by 2013.

In general, Balinese objections to tourist developments have failed to halt plans.

Social changes

Social change has inevitably followed the influx of tourism. Michel Picard, author of *Bali: Cultural Tourism and Touristic Culture*, suggests that Bali has now become a **"touristic culture"** whereby the Balinese have adopted the tourists' perceptions of themselves and their island as their own, and have "come to search for confirmation of their 'Balinese-ness' in the mirror held to them by the tourists".

There are also concerns about **HIV/AIDS** (more than 3000 cases are estimated on Bali, among the highest in Indonesia) and **drug addiction**. ECPAT (ⓦwww .ecpat.net), a global organization working to abolish the commercial sexual exploitation of children, has reported that Bali has a reputation as a **child sex tourism** destination and is also a major destination for trafficked girls and women.

However, many of the problems are those of any developing country and, while many articulate the negative side of tourism, many of the people in the villages are keen to develop tourist facilities that will bring visitors, and their money, to them. The Indonesian government agrees and Bali is hoping to attract 2.7 million foreign visitors in 2011 and each following year.

Responsible tourism organizations

Many organizations are working to raise awareness of the impact of tourism throughout the world, and encourage responsible travelling.

Ethical Traveler ⓦwww.ethicaltraveler.org

Global Anti-Golf Movement ⓦwww.antigolf.org/english.html

Indonesian Ecotourism Network ⓦwww.indecon.or.id

Responsible Travel ⓦwww.responsible-travel.org

Tourism Concern ⓦwww.tourismconcern.org.uk

The situation in Lombok

A trickle of tourists started arriving on **Lombok** in the 1980s and local people set up small losmen around Senggigi, the Gili Islands and, later, around Kuta. By 1989, there were over 120,000 visitors annually, and though the figures for 2010 were about 600,000, that's still less than a third of the number of visitors to Bali.

Lombok's fortunes are closely tied with those of Bali, and visitor numbers plummeted following the Bali bombings of 2002 and 2005. As on Bali, however, Lombok tourism has since revived. Indeed, one tiny, atypical corner – the island of **Gili Trawangan** – has boomed in recent years, raising widespread concern about the social and environmental sustainability of unregulated development on its tiny land mass. Islanders and expats are actively addressing this under the auspices of the impressive Gili Eco Trust (see p.330), and the island has become the subject of a surprising number of academic studies on island tourism.

To date the issue of sustainable tourism on "mainland" Lombok hasn't been so pressing, not least because there's been no strong **political appetite** for tourism on Lombok. Many Sasak people consider the gap between Muslim morals and those of their Western visitors to be unacceptably wide, while the tourist job market has been increasingly dominated by the better-qualified Balinese. Sasak people in particular, forced out of education due to poverty, have little chance of landing anything but the most menial work. However, the view at the top has now changed markedly: the current provincial governor of Nusa Tenggara Barat, Guru Bajang, is widely seen as pro tourism, to the point that 2012 is being energetically marketed as Visit Lombok and Sumbawa Year.

The 2012 campaign is closely linked to the planned opening of Lombok's new **international airport** near Kuta in south Lombok, a project that's been long delayed, stymied by local opposition and financial problems. The aim is to bring more direct international flights to Lombok – and more investment. It is the latter, of course, that concerns local people, not least because it has already led to the earmarking of a vast swathe of beachfront land around Kuta for what's billed as a luxury development, perhaps in the style of Bali's Nusa Dua. On the plus side, the airport project has resulted in the much-needed upgrading of roads across south Lombok and, if tourist development is carefully and inclusively managed, could boost the economy of one of Lombok's poorest regions.

Books

While plenty has been written on the culture, temples, and arts and crafts of Bali, there has been little coverage of Lombok. We have included publishers' details only for books that may be hard to find outside Indonesia. Ganesha (ⓦ www.ganeshabooksbali.com) in Ubud offers an online ordering service. Titles marked 🏃 are particularly recommended; "o/p" means out of print.

Travel

Elizabeth Gilbert *Eat, Pray, Love*. This insightful, funny journey of self-discovery, now a bestseller and a film, climaxes in Ubud with various life-changing encounters of the sensual and spiritual kind.

🏃 **William Ingram** *A Little Bit One o' Clock: Living with a Balinese Family*. Warm, funny, warts-and-all portrait of the author's life with an Ubud family in the 1990s. Both the author and his adoptive family still live in Ubud and are involved in the Threads of Life Textile Arts Center.

🏃 **Louise G. Koke** *Our Hotel in Bali* (o/p). The engaging true story of two young Americans who built the first hotel on Kuta beach, in 1936. Some of the book's photos are now displayed in Ubud's Neka Art Museum.

Adrian Vickers (ed) *Travelling to Bali: Four Hundred Years of Journeys* (o/p). One-stop anthology that includes accounts by early Dutch, Thai and British adventurers, as well as excerpts from writings by the expat community in the 1930s, and the musings of late twentieth-century visitors.

Culture, society and history

🏃 **Susan-Jane Beers** *Jamu: The Ancient Indonesian Art of Herbal Healing*. Fascinating look at the role of herbal medicine (*jamu*) in Indonesia.

Kathryn Bonella *Hotel K: The Shocking Inside Story of Bali's Most Notorious Jail*. Extraordinarily revealing exposé of Kerobokan Prison, the corrupt system that sustains it and the tourists and locals who end up doing time there.

🏃 **Miguel Covarrubias** *Island of Bali*. An early classic (first published in 1937) in which the Mexican artist and amateur anthropologist explores everything from the daily routines of his adopted village household to the philosophical significance of the island's arts, dramas and music.

🏃 **Dr A.A.M. Djelantik** *The Birthmark: Memoirs of a Balinese*

Prince (o/p). Fascinating, lively autobiography of the son of the last raja of Karangasem, who was born in east Bali in 1919, became Bali's most influential doctor, and lived through Dutch rule, World War II, the eruption of Gunung Agung and the communist killings.

🏃 **Fred B. Eiseman Jr** *Bali: Sekala and Niskala Vols 1 and 2*. Seminal, essential, wide-ranging anthologies of cultural and anthropological essays by an American expat.

David J. Fox *Once a Century: Pura Besakih and the Eka Dasa Rudra Festival* (Penerbit Sinar Harapan, Citra, Indonesia). Fabulous pictures and a readable text make this an excellent introduction to Besakih. Also includes accounts of the 1963 Eka Dasa Rudra festival and the eruption of Gunung Agung.

A.J. Bernet Kempers *Monumental Bali: Introduction to Balinese Archaeology and Guide to the Monuments*. A fairly highbrow analysis of Bali's oldest temples and ruins.

Gregor Krause *Bali 1912* (January Books, New Zealand). Reprinted edition of the original black-and-white photographs that inspired the first generation of arty expats to visit Bali. The pictures were taken by a young German doctor and give unrivalled insight into Balinese life in the early twentieth century.

Jeff Lewis and Belinda Lewis *Bali's Silent Crisis: Desire, Tragedy, and Transition*. Stimulating academic work that's especially interesting on the unresolved trauma of the 1965 massacres and Bali's troubled relationship with the greater Indonesian state.

Anna Mathews *Night of Purnama* (o/p). Moving description of village life focusing on events in the Iseh area in the 1960s, including the eruption of Gunung Agung. Written with affection and a keen realization of the gap between West and East.

Michel Picard *Bali: Cultural Tourism and Touristic Culture*. Fascinating, readable but ultimately depressing analysis of the effects of tourism upon the people of Bali.

Robert Pringle *A Short History of Bali*. An incisive history of Bali from the prehistorical era to the 2002 bomb, with focus on social, cultural and environmental developments.

K'tut Tantri *Revolt in Paradise*. The extraordinary, if embellished, story of British-born Muriel Pearson, who became an active member of the Indonesian independence movement between 1932 and 1947, for which she was tortured by the Japanese.

Adrian Vickers *Bali: A Paradise Created*. Detailed, intelligent and highly readable account of the outside world's perception of Bali, the development of tourism, and how events inside and outside the country have shaped the Balinese view of themselves as well as outsiders' view of them.

Art, crafts and music

Edward Frey *The Kris: Mystic Weapon of the Malay World*. Small but well-illustrated book outlining the history and making of the *kris*, along with some of the myths associated with this magical weapon.

John Gillow and Barry Dawson *Traditional Indonesian Textiles*. Beautifully photographed and accessible introduction to the *ikat* and batik fabrics of the archipelago; a handy guide if you're thinking of buying cloth in Bali or Lombok.

Brigitta Hauser-Schäublin, Marie-Louise Nabholz-Kartaschoff and Urs Ramseyer *Balinese Textiles*. Thorough and gloriously photographed survey of Balinese textiles and their role within contemporary society.

Garrett Kam *Perceptions of Paradise: Images of Bali in the Arts* (Yayasan Dharma Seni Neka Museum, Bali). Ostensibly a guide to Ubud's Neka Art Museum, this is actually one of the best introductions to Balinese art.

Jean McKinnon *Vessels of Life: Lombok Earthenware*. Exhaustive and fabulously photographed book about Sasak life, pottery techniques and the significance of the items they create in the lives of the women potters.

Idanna Pucci *Bhima Swarga: The Balinese Journey of the Soul*. Fabulously produced guide to the *Mahabharata* legends. Illustrated with glossy colour photographs and description of the stories.

Nathase Reichie *Bali: Art, Ritual and Performance*. Fabulous glossy catalogue accompanying the 2011 Bali exhibition at the Asian Art Museum of San Francisco. It centres on 130 gorgeous items and is supplemented with scholarly essays on all aspects of culture, art and ritual.

Anne Richter *Arts and Crafts of Indonesia* (o/p). General guide to the fabrics, carvings, jewellery and other folk arts of the archipelago, with some background on the practices involved.

Michael Tenzer *Balinese Music*. Well-pitched introduction to the gamelan.

Lifestyle

Gianni Francione and Luca Invernizzi Tettoni *Bali Modern: The Art of Tropical Living*. A celebration of modern Balinese architecture, from the tasteful to the ostentatious.

Rio Helmi and Barbara Walker *Bali Style*. Sumptuously photographed paean to all things Balinese, from bamboo furniture to elegant homes.

William Warren and Luca Invernizzi Tettoni *Balinese Gardens*. Gorgeously photographed exploration of the role of the garden in Balinese culture.

Made Wijaya and Isabella Ginanneschi *At Home in Bali*. The beautiful homes of Bali's beautiful (mainly expatriate) people.

Food and cookery

Heinz von Holzen *Street Foods of Bali*. The long-time Bali resident, chef and restauranteur provides a beautiful evocation of Balinese food including plenty of background information, pictures and recipes.

Janet de Neefe *Fragrant Rice*. The Australian co-founder of Ubud's *Casa Luna* restaurant paints an enticing picture of life with her Balinese husband and family, interweaving her observations with recipes for local dishes.

Travellers' guides

Dr Nick Jones *The Rough Guide to Travel Health*. Pretty much everything you need to know, in a pocket-sized format.

Natural history

John MacKinnon *Field Guide to the Birds of Borneo, Sumatra, Java and Bali*. The most comprehensive field guide of its kind.

David Pickell and Wally Siagian *Diving Bali: The Underwater Jewel of Southeast Asia*. Beautifully photographed and detailed account.

Fiction

🏃 **Nigel Barley** *Island of Demons*. Delightful, fictionalized account of the early expats in Bali told in the distinctive (imaginary) voice of Rudolf Bonnet, by turns sad, petulant, generous and tetchy, but never boring.

Vicki Baum *A Tale from Bali*. Occasionally moving, and always interesting, semi-factual historical novel based on the events leading up to the 1906 *puputan* in Denpasar.

🏃 **Diana Darling** *The Painted Alphabet*. Charming, sophisticated reworking of a traditional Balinese tale about young love, rivalry and the harnessing of supernatural power.

Garrett Kam *Midnight Shadows* (o/p). A teenage boy's life in 1960s Bali is turned upside down first by the devastating eruption of Gunung Agung and then by the vicious, divisive, anti-communist violence that swept the island.

Odyle Knight *Bali Moon: A Spiritual Odyssey* (o/p). Riveting tale of an Australian woman's deepening involvement with the Balinese spirit world through her romance with a young Balinese priest. Apparently based on true events.

Christopher J. Koch *The Year of Living Dangerously*. Set in Jakarta in the last year of President Sukarno's rule leading up to the 1965 takeover by Suharto and the subsequent violence, this story compellingly details ethnic, political and religious tensions that are still apparent in Indonesia today.

Putu Oka Sukanta *The Sweat of Pearls: Short Stories about Women of Bali* (o/p). Though all the stories were written by a man, the vignettes of village life are enlightening, and the author is a respected writer who spent many years in jail because of his political beliefs.

Language

Language

Language

On your travels through Bali and Lombok you'll hear a vibrant mix of languages; the national language of Indonesia, known locally as Bahasa Indonesia and in English as Indonesian, as well as the indigenous languages of Balinese and Sasak (on Lombok), which are just two of more than seven hundred native languages and dialects spoken throughout the Indonesian archipelago. In practical terms, Indonesian will help you to communicate effectively, and everyone on the islands is at least bilingual, but a few words of Balinese or Sasak used appropriately will get you an extra warm welcome.

Bahasa Indonesia

Until the 1920s, the lingua franca of government and commerce was Dutch, but the emerging independence movement adopted a form of Bahasa Malay as a unifying language and by the 1950s this had crystallized into **Bahasa Indonesia**, which is taught in every school and understood throughout Bali and Lombok.

Bahasa Indonesia is written in Roman script, has no tones and uses a fairly straightforward grammar – all of which makes it relatively easy for the visitor to get to grips with. There are several pocket-sized **phrasebooks** on the market, including one published by Rough Guides, and any number of apps. Among many downloadable **teach yourself** courses, you could try Talk Now DL Indonesian (Ⓦwww.eurotalk .com), or browse for a free alternative. A good **dictionary** is the *Tuttle Concise Indonesian Dictionary*. The best Indonesian language schools are in Denpasar and Ubud.

Grammar and pronunciation

For **grammar**, Bahasa Indonesia uses the same subject-verb-object word order as in English. The easiest way to make a question is simply to add a question mark and use a rising intonation. **Nouns** have no gender and don't require an article. To make a noun **plural** you usually just say the noun twice, eg *anak* (child), *anak-anak* (children). **Adjectives** always follow the noun. **Verbs** have no tenses: to indicate the past, prefix the verb with *sudah* (already) or *belum* (not yet); for the future, prefix the verb with *akan* (will).

Vowels and diphthongs	Consonants
a is a cross between father and cup	Most are pronounced as in English, with the following exceptions:
e as in along; or as in pay; or as in get; or sometimes omitted (eg selamat is pronounced "slamat")	c as in cheap
i as in boutique; or as in pit	g is always hard, as in girl
o as in hot; or as in cold	k is hard, as in English, except at the end of the word, when you should stop just short of pronouncing it. In written form, this is often indicated by an apostrophe; for example, beso' for besok.
u as in boot	
ai as in fine	
au as in how	

Useful words and phrases

Greetings and basic phrases

The all-purpose greeting is **Selamat** (derived from Arabic), which communicates general goodwill. If addressing a married woman, it's polite to use the respectful term **Ibu** or **Nyo-nya**; if addressing a married man use **Bapak**.

Good morning (5–11am)	Selamat pagi
Good day (11am–3pm)	Selamat siang
Good afternoon (3–7pm)	Selamat sore
Good evening (after 7pm)	Selamat malam
Good night	Selamat tidur
Goodbye	Selamat tinggal
See you later	Sampai jumpa lagi
Have a good trip	Selamat jalan
Welcome	Selamat datang
Enjoy your meal	Selamat makan
Cheers (toast)	Selamat minum
How are you?	Apa kabar?
I'm fine	Bagus/Kabar baik
Please (requesting)	tolong
Please (offering)	silakan
Thank you (very much)	Terima kasih (banyak)
You're welcome	Sama sama
Sorry/excuse me	Ma'af
Never mind/no worries	Tidak apa apa
What is your name?	Siapa nama anda?
My name is...	Nama saya...
Where are you from?	Dari mana?
I come from...	Saya dari...
Do you speak English?	Bisa bicara bahasa Inggris?
I don't understand	Saya tidak mengerti
Do you have...?	Ada...?
I want/would like...	Saya mau...
I don't want it/No thanks	Tidak mau
What is this/that?	Apa ini/itu?
another	satu lagi
beautiful	cantik
big/small	besar/kecil
boyfriend or girlfriend	pacar
clean/dirty	bersih/kotor
cold	dingin
expensive/inexpensive	mahal/murah
fast/slow	sepat/lambat

foreigner	turis
friend	teman
good/bad	bagus/buruk
hot (water/weather)	panas
hot (spicy)	pedas
how?	berapa?
hungry/thirsty	lapar/haus
ill/sick	sakit
married/single	kawin/bujang
men/women	laki-laki/perempuan or wanita
no (with noun)	bukan
not (with verb)	tidak (or tak)
open/closed	buka/tutup
tired	lelah
very much/a lot	banyak
what?	apa?
when?	kapan?
where?	dimana?
who?	siapa?
why?	mengapa?
yes	ya

Getting around

Where is the...?	Dimana...?
I'd like to go to the...	Saya mau pergi ke...
How far?	Berapa kilometre?
How long?	Berapa jam?
How much is the fare to...?	Berapa harga karcis ke...?
Where is this bemo going?	Kemana bemo pergi?
When will the bemo/bus leave?	Bila bemo/bis berangkut?
Where is this?	Dimana ini?
stop!	estop!
here	disini
right	kanan
left	kiri
straight on	terus
airport	lapangan terbang
bank	bank
beach	pantai
bemo/bus station	terminal
bicycle	sepeda
bus	bis

car	mobil
city/downtown	kota
to come/go	datang/pergi
to drive	mengendarai
entrance/exit	masuk/keluar
ferry	ferry
fuel (petrol)	bensin
horse cart	dokar/cidomo
hospital	rumah sakit
hotel	losmen
market	pasar
motorbike	sepeda motor
motorbike taxi	ojek
near/far	dekat/jauh
pharmacy	apotik
phone office	wartel/kantor telkom
police station	kantor polisi
post office	kantor pos
restaurant	restoran/rumah makan/warung
shop	toko
taxi	taksi
ticket	karcis
tourist office	kantor turis
village	desa
to walk	jalan kaki

Accommodation and shopping

How much is...?	Berapa harga...?
a single room	kamar untuk satu orang
a double room	kamar untuk dua orang
Do you have a cheaper room?	Ada kamar yang lebih murah?
Can I look at the room?	Boleh saya lihat kamar?
to sleep	tidur
to buy/sell	membeli/menjual
money	uang
is there...?	apakah ada...?
air-conditioning	ac
bathroom	kamar mandi
breakfast	makan pagi
fan	kipas
hot water	air panas
mosquito net	kelambu nyamuk
swimming pool	kolam renang
toilet	kamar kecil/wc (pronounced "waysay")

Numbers

0	nol
1	satu
2	dua
3	tiga
4	empat
5	lima
6	enam
7	tujuh
8	delapan
9	sembilan
10	sepuluh
11	sebelas
12, 13, 14, etc	duabelas, tigabelas, empatbelas
20	duapuluh
21, 22, 23, etc	duapuluh satu, duapuluh dua, duapuluh tiga
30, 40, 50, etc	tigapuluh, empatpuluh, limapuluh
100	seratus
200, 300, 400, etc	duaratus, tigaratus, empatratus
1000	seribu
2000, 3000, 4000, etc	duaribu
10,000	sepuluhribu
20,000, 30,000, 40,000, etc	dua puluhribu, tiag puluhribu, empat puluhribu
100,000	seratusribu
200,000, 300,000, 400,000, etc	dua ratusribu, tiga ratusribu, empat ratusribu
1,000,000	sejuta
2,000,000, 3,000,000, 4,000,000, etc	dua juta, tiga juta, empat juta

Time and days of the week

What time is it?	Jam berapa?
When does it open/close?	Kapan dia buka/tutup?
3.00	jam tiga
4.10	jam empat lewat sepuluh
4.45	jam lima kurang seperempat

6.30	jam setengah tujuh ("half to seven")	now	sekarang
... in the morning	... pagi	not yet	belum
... in the afternoon	... sore	never	tidak pernah
... in the evening	... malam	already	sudah
minute/hour	menit/jam	Monday	Hari Senin
day	hari	Tuesday	Hari Selasa
week	minggu	Wednesday	Hari Rabu
month	bulan	Thursday	Hari Kamis
year	tahun	Friday	Hari Jumaat
today/tomorrow	hari ini/besok	Saturday	Hari sabtu
yesterday	kemarin	Sunday	Hari Minggu

Menu reader

General terms

to eat	makan	plate	piring
breakfast	makan pagi	glass	gelas
lunch	makan siang	drink	minum
evening meal	makan malam	without ice, please	tolong tanpa es
menu	daftar makanan	without sugar, please	tolong tanpa gula
I am vegetarian	Saya seorang vegetaris	cold	dingin
I don't eat meat	Saya tidak makan daging	hot (temperature)	panas
		hot (spicy)	pedas
knife	pisau	sweet-and-sour	asam manis
fork	garpu	fried	goreng
spoon	sendok	delicious	enak
		I want to pay	Saya injin bayar

Meat, fish and basic foods

ayam	chicken	kecap asam	sour soy sauce
babi	pork	kecap manis	sweet soy sauce
bakmi	noodles	kepiting	crab
buah	fruit	nasi	rice
es	ice	petis	fish paste
garam	salt	sambal	hot chilli sauce
gula	sugar	sapi	beef
ikan	fish	soto	soup
itik	duck	telur	egg
jaja	rice cakes	tenggiri	king mackerel
kambing	goat	udang	prawn
kare	curry	udang karang	lobster

Everyday dishes

ayam goreng	fried chicken	nasi goreng	fried rice
bakmi goreng	fried noodles with vegetables and meat	nasi pecel	steamed green vegetables with spicy peanut sauce and rice
bakso	meat ball soup		
botok daging sapi	spicy minced beef with tofu, tempeh and coconut milk	nasi putih	plain boiled rice
		nasi sela	steamed rice and sweet potato
cap cai	mixed fried vegetables	pisang goreng	fried bananas
es campur	fruit salad and shredded ice	rijsttafel	Dutch/Indonesian spread of six to ten different meat, fish and vegetable dishes with rice
gado-gado	steamed vegetable with a spicy peanut sauce		
ikan bakar	grilled fish	rujak	hot, spiced fruit salad
ikan goreng	fried fish		
ikan pepes	spiced fish steamed in banana leaf	rujak petis	vegetable and fruit in spicy peanut and shrimp sauce
kangkung	water-spinach		
kelinci	rabbit	tahu goreng telur	tofu omelette
krupuk	rice or cassava crackers, usually flavoured with prawn	sate	meat or fish kebabs served with a spicy peanut sauce
lalapan	raw vegetables and sambal	sayur bening	soup with spinach and corn
lontong	steamed rice in a banana-leaf packet	sayur lodeh	vegetable and coconut-milk soup
lumpia	spring rolls	urap-urap/urap timum	vegetables with coconut and chilli
nasi campur	boiled rice served with small amounts of vegetable, meat, fish and sometimes egg		

Balinese specialities

ayam betutu	steamed chilli-chicken	megibung	Balinese rijsttafel
babi guling	roasted suckling pig	sate languan	ground fish, coconut, spices and sugar cooked on a bamboo stick
betutu bebek	smoked duck		
lawar	raw meat, blood and spices		

Sasak specialities

ayam taliwang	fried or grilled chicken served with a hot chilli sauce	cerorot	rice flour, palm sugar and coconut milk sweet, wrapped into a cone shape
beberuk	raw aubergine and chilli sauce		
		geroan ayam	chicken liver
		gule lemak	beef curry

hati	liver
kelor	vegetable soup
lapis	rice flour, coconut milk and sugar dessert, wrapped in banana leaves
olah olah	mixed vegetables and coconut cream
otak	brains
pangan	coconut milk and sugar dessert
paru	lungs

pelecing	chilli sauce
satay pusut	minced beef and coconut sate
sayur nangka	young jackfruit curry
sum-sum	bone marrow
tumbek	rice flour, coconut milk and palm sugar dessert, wrapped in coconut leaves
usus	intestines
wajik	sticky rice and palm-sugar sweet

Fruit

apel	apple
buah anggur	grapes
jeruk manis	orange
jeruk nipis	lemon
kelapa	coconut
mangga	mango

manggis	mangosteen
nanas	pineapple
nangka	jackfruit
pisang	banana
semangkha air	watermelon

Drinks

air jeruk	orange juice
air jeruk nipis	lemon juice
air minum	drinking water
arak	palm or rice spirit
bir	beer
brem	local rice beer

kopi	coffee
kopi bal	black coffee
kopi susu	white coffee
susu	milk
teh	tea
tuak	rice or palm wine

Bahasa Bali

The Balinese language, **Bahasa Bali**, has three main forms: High (*Ida*), Middle or Polite (*Ipun*) and Low (*Ia*). The form the speaker uses depends on the caste of the person he or she is addressing and on the context. If speaking to family or friends, or to a low-caste (Sudra) Balinese, you use **Low Balinese**; if addressing a superior or a stranger, you use **Middle or Polite Balinese**; if talking to someone from a high caste (Brahman, Satriya or Wesya) or discussing religious affairs, you use **High Balinese**. If the caste is not immediately apparent, then the speaker traditionally opens the conversation with the euphemistic question "Where do you sit?", in order to elicit an indication of caste. However, in the last couple of decades there's been a move to popularize the use of Polite or Middle Balinese, and disregard the caste factor. For more on castes and how to recognize them, see p.49.

Despite its numerous forms, Bahasa Bali is essentially a **spoken language**, with few official rules of grammar and hardly any textbooks or dictionaries. However, there's the *Tuttle Concise Balinese Dictionary*, available internationally. All phrases and questions given below are shown in the Middle or Polite form, unless otherwise stated.

Useful words and phrases

What is your name?	Sira pesengan ragane?	to go	lunga
Where are you going?	Lunga kija?	good	becik
Where have you been?	Kija busan?	house	jeroan
		husband	rabi
How are you?	Kenken kebara?	no	tan, nente
How are things?	Napa orti?	rice	pantu, beras, ajengan
(I'm/everything's) fine	Becik	to sleep	sirep sare
		small	alit
I am sick	Tiang gelem	wife	timpal, isteri
What is that?	Napi punika?	yes	inggih, patut
bad	corah	1	siki, diri
big	ageng	2	kalih
child	putra, putri	3	tiga
to come	rauh, dateng	4	pat
delicious	jaen	5	lima
to eat	ngajeng, nunas	6	nem, enem
family	panyaman, pasa metonan	7	pitu
		8	kutus
food	ajeng-ajengan, tetedan	9	sia
friend	switra	10	dasa

Sasak

The language of Lombok is **Sasak**, a purely oral language that varies quite a lot from one part of the island to another. However, even a few words of Sasak are likely to be greeted with delight. The following should get you started.

There's no Sasak equivalent to the Indonesian **greetings** *Selamat pagi* and the like. If you meet someone walking along the road, the enquiry "Where are you going?" serves this purpose even if the answer is blatantly obvious.

Useful words and phrases

Where are you going?	Ojok um bay?	big/small	belek/kodek
Just walking around	Lampat-lampat	brother/sister	semeton mama/ semeton nine
I'm going to Rinjani	Rinjani wah mo ojok um bay	child/grandchild	kanak/bai
Where is...?	Um bay tao...?	dark/light	peteng/tenang
How are you?	Berem bay khabar?	daughter/son	kanak nine/kanak mame
I'm fine	Bagus/solah		
And you?	Berem bay seeda?	delicious	maik
What are you doing?	Upa gowey de?	fast/slow	betjat/adeng-adeng
How many children do you have?	Pira kanak de?	friend	kantje
		frightened	takoot
See you (I'm going)	Yak la low	heavy/light	berat/ringan
No problem	Nday kambay kambay	hot	beneng
Go away!	Nyeri too!	hungry	lapar

husband/wife	semame/senine	2	dua
nothing	ndarak	3	telu
thirsty	goro	4	empat
tired	telah	5	lima
today	djelo sine	6	enam
tomorrow	djema	7	pitook
yesterday	sirutsin	8	baluk
none	ndarak	9	siwak
1	skek	10	sepulu

Glossary

adat Traditional law and custom.

alang-alang Tall, tough, sharp-edged Imperata cylindrical grass widely used for thatching roofs.

aling-aling Low, freestanding wall built directly behind a gateway to deter evil spirits.

Arjuna The most famous of the five heroic Pandawa brothers, stars of the epic Hindu tale, the *Mahabharata*.

bale Open-sided pavilion found in temples, family compounds and on roadsides, usually used as a resting place or shelter.

bale banjar Village **bale** used for meetings.

balian (or **dukun**) Traditional faith healer, herbalist or witch doctor.

banjar Neighbourhood. Also refers to the neighbourhood association or council to which all married men are obliged to belong; membership averages 100 to 500.

Barong Ket Mythical lion-like creature who represents the forces of good.

Barong Landung Ten-metre-high humanoid puppets used in temple rituals and dances.

bemo Local minibus transport.

berugaq The Sasak equivalent of a Balinese **bale**: an open-sided "resting" pavilion in family compounds and on roadsides and beaches.

Bhoma (or **Boma**) The son of the earth and repeller of evil spirits.

bhuta (and **kala**) Invisible demons and goblins, the personification of the forces of evil.

Calonarang Exorcist dance-drama featuring the widow-witch Rangda.

candi Monument erected as a memorial to an important person, also sometimes a shrine.

candi bentar Split gateway within a temple compound.

cidomo Horse-drawn cart used as a taxi on Lombok.

dalang Puppet master of *wayang kulit* shadow plays.

danau Lake.

desa Village.

dewa/dewi God/goddess.

Dewi Pertiwi Earth goddess.

Dewi Sri Rice goddess.

dokar Horse-drawn cart used as a taxi in a few Balinese towns.

dukun See **balian**.

dulang Wooden stand/pedestal used for offerings.

endek *Ikat* cloth in which the weft threads are dyed to the final pattern before being woven.

Erlangga (sometimes **Airlangga**) Eleventh-century king from East Java, son of the mythical widow-witch Rangda.

Galungan The most important Bali-wide holiday, held for ten days every 210 days in celebration of the triumph of good over evil.

gamelan Orchestra or music of bronze metallophones.

Ganesh Hindu elephant-headed deity, remover of obstacles and god of knowledge.

gang Lane or alley.

Garuda Mythical Hindu creature, half-man and half-bird, and the favoured vehicle of the god Wisnu.

gedong Building.

genggong Crude bamboo wind instrument, played like a jew's-harp.

geringsing Weaving technique and cloth, also known as double *ikat* because both the warp and the weft threads are dyed to the final design before being woven.

gunung Mountain.

Hanuman Monkey-god and chief of the monkey army in the *Ramayana* story; an ally of Rama's.

Ida Batara Dewi Ulun Danu (also just **Dewi Danu**) The goddess of the lakes in the centre of the island.

ikat Cloth in which the warp or weft threads, or both warp and weft threads, are tie-dyed to the final pattern before being woven: see also **endek** and **geringsing**.

jalan (**Jl**) Road.

jukung Traditional wooden fishing boat with outriggers.

kain poleng Black-and-white checked cloth used for religious purposes, symbolizing the harmonious balancing of good and evil forces.

kaja Crucial Balinese direction (opposite of **kelod**), which determines house and temple orientation; towards the mountains, upstream.

kala same as **bhuta**.

kantor pos General post office.

kantor telkom Government telephone office.

Kawi Ancient courtly language of Java.

kayangan jagat Highly sacred directional temple.

Kebo Iwa Mythical giant credited with building some of Bali's oldest monuments.

Kecak Spectacular dance-drama often referred to as the Monkey Dance.

kelod Crucial Balinese direction (opposite of **kaja**), which determines house and temple orientation; towards the sea, downstream.

kepeng Old Chinese coins with holes bored through the middle.

ketu Terracotta crown-shaped roof ornament.

kori agung See **paduraksa**.

kris Traditional-style dagger, with scalloped blade edges, of great symbolic and spiritual significance.

kulkul Bell-like drum made from a large, hollow log slit down the middle and suspended high up in a purpose-built tower in temples and other public places.

Kumakarma Brother of the demon king, Rawana, in the *Ramayana* story.

Kuningan The culmination day of the important ten-day Galungan festivities.

Legong Classical Balinese dance performed by two or three prepubescent girls.

leyak Witches who often assume disguises.

lontar Palm-leaf manuscripts on which all ancient texts were inscribed.

losmen Homestay or guesthouse.

lumbung Barn used for storing rice, raised high on stilts above a platform, and with a distinctive bonnet-shaped roof.

Mahabharata Lengthy Hindu epic describing the battles between representatives of good and evil, and focusing on the exploits of the Pandawa brothers.

mandi Traditional scoop-and-slosh method of showering, sometimes in open-roofed bathrooms.

meru Multi-tiered Hindu shrine with an odd number of thatched roofs (from one to eleven), which symbolizes the cosmic Mount Meru.

moksa Spiritual liberation for Hindus.

naga Mythological underwater deity, a cross between a snake and a dragon.

nusa Island.

odalan Individual temple festival held to mark the anniversary of the founding of every temple on Bali.

ojek Motorcycle taxi.

padmasana The empty throne that tops the shrine-tower, found in every temple and dedicated to the supreme god Sanghyang Widi Wasa.

paduraksa (or **kori agung**) Temple gateway to the inner sanctuary, like the **candi bentar**, but joined together rather than split.

pancasila The five principles of the Indonesian constitution: belief in one supreme god; the unity of the Indonesian nation; guided democracy; social justice and humanitarianism; and a civilized and prosperous society. Symbolized by an eagle bearing a five-part crest.

paras Soft, grey volcanic tuff used for carving.

pasar Market.

pasar seni Literally art market, usually sells fabrics and non-foodstuffs, and sometimes artefacts and souvenirs.

pawukon See wuku.

peci Black felt or velvet hat worn by Muslim men.

pedanda High priest of the Brahman caste.

pemangku Village priest.

perada Traditional gold, screen-printed material used for ceremonial garb and temple umbrellas.

prahu Traditional wooden fishing boat.

prasasti Ancient bronze inscriptions.

pulau Island.

puputan Suicidal fight to the death.

pura Hindu temple.

pura dalem Temple of the dead.

pura desa Village temple.

pura puseh Temple of origin.

puri Raja's palace, or the home of a wealthy nobleman.

Raksasa Mythical Hindu demon-giant with long teeth and a large club, often used to guard temple entrances.

Rama Hero of the Ramayana and an avatar of the god Wisnu.

Ramayana Hugely influential Hindu epic, essentially a morality tale of the battles between good and evil.

Rangda Legendary widow-witch who personifies evil and is most commonly depicted with huge fangs, a massive lolling tongue and pendulous breasts.

Rawana The demon king who represents the forces of evil (Rama's adversary in the Ramayana).

raya Main or principal ("Jalan Raya Ubud" is the main Ubud road).

saka Hindu calendar, which is divided into years made up of between 354 and 356 days; runs eighty years behind the Western Gregorian calendar.

Sanghyang Widi Wasa The supreme Hindu god; all other gods are a manifestation of him.

Saraswati Goddess of science, learning and literature.

sarong The anglicized generic term for any length of material wrapped around the lower body and worn by men and women.

sawah Ricefields.

sebel Ritually unclean.

shophouse Shuttered building with living space upstairs and shop space on ground floor.

Siwa (Shiva) Important Hindu deity; "The Destroyer" or, more accurately, "The Dissolver".

sok Square-lidded basket used for offerings or storage.

songket Silk brocades often woven with real gold or silver thread.

subak Irrigation committee or local farmers' council.

suttee Practice of widows choosing to burn themselves to death on their husbands' funeral pyres.

swastika Ancient Hindu and Buddhist symbol representing the wheel of the sun.

teluk Bay.

Topeng Masked dance-drama, performed with human masks.

tuak Rice or palm wine.

wantilan Large pavilion, usually used for cockfights and dance performances.

wartel Phone office.

warung Foodstall or tiny streetside restaurant.

wayang kulit Shadow-puppet play.

Wisnu (Vishnu) Important Hindu deity – "The Preserver". Usually shown with four arms, holding a disc, a conch, a lotus and a club, and often seated astride his vehicle, the Garuda.

wuku (or pawukon) Complex Balinese calendar system based on a 210-day lunar cycle.

Travel
store

Book Aid
International
www.bookaid.org

Books change lives

Poverty and illiteracy go hand in hand. But in sub-Saharan Africa, books are a luxury few can afford. Many children leave school functionally illiterate, and adults often fall back into illiteracy in adulthood due to a lack of available reading material.

Book Aid International knows that books change lives.

Every year we send over half a million books to partners in 12 countries in sub-Saharan Africa, to stock libraries in schools, refugee camps, prisons, universities and communities. Literally millions of readers have access to books and information that could teach them new skills – from keeping chickens to getting a degree in Business Studies or learning how to protect against HIV/AIDS.

What can you do?

Join our Reverse Book Club and with your donation of only £6 a month, we can send 36 books every year to some of the poorest countries in the world. For every two pounds extra you can give, we can send another book!

Support Book Aid International today!

Online. Go to our website at www.bookaid.org, and click on 'donate'

By telephone. Start a Direct Debit or give a donation on your card by calling us on 020 7733 3577

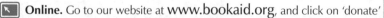

Book Aid International is a charity and a limited company registered in England and Wales.
Charity No. 313869 Company No. 880754   39-41 Coldharbour Lane, Camberwell, London SE5 9NR
T +44 (0)20 7733 3577   F +44 (0)20 7978 8006   E info@bookaid.org   www.bookaid.org

FAIR FARES from
NORTH SOUTH TRAVEL

Our great-value air fares cover the world, from Abuja to Zanzibar and from Zurich to Anchorage. North South Travel is a fund-raising travel agency, owned by the NST Development Trust.

ALL our profits go to development organisations.

Call 01245 608 291 (or +44 1245 608 291 if outside UK) to speak to a friendly advisor. Your money is safe (ATOL 5401). For more information, visit northsouthtravel.co.uk. Free Rough Guide of your choice for every booking over £500.

EVERY FLIGHT A FIGHT AGAINST POVERTY

Small print and
Index

A Rough Guide to Rough Guides

Published in 1982, the first Rough Guide – to Greece – was a student scheme that became a publishing phenomenon. Mark Ellingham, a recent graduate in English from Bristol University, had been travelling in Greece the previous summer and couldn't find the right guidebook. With a small group of friends he wrote his own guide, combining a highly contemporary, journalistic style with a thoroughly practical approach to travellers' needs.

The immediate success of the book spawned a series that rapidly covered dozens of destinations. And, in addition to impecunious backpackers, Rough Guides soon acquired a much broader and older readership that relished the guides' wit and inquisitiveness as much as their enthusiastic, critical approach and value-for-money ethos.

These days, Rough Guides include recommendations from shoestring to luxury and cover more than 200 destinations around the globe, including almost every country in the Americas and Europe, more than half of Africa and most of Asia and Australasia. Our ever-growing team of authors and photographers is spread all over the world, particularly in Europe, the US and Australia.

In the early 1990s, Rough Guides branched out of travel, with the publication of Rough Guides to World Music, Classical Music and the Internet. All three have become benchmark titles in their fields, spearheading the publication of a wide range of books under the Rough Guide name.

Including the travel series, Rough Guides now number more than 350 titles, covering: phrasebooks, waterproof maps, music guides from Opera to Heavy Metal, reference works as diverse as Conspiracy Theories and Shakespeare, and popular culture books from iPods to Poker. Rough Guides also produce a series of more than 120 World Music CDs in partnership with World Music Network.

Visit www.roughguides.com to see our latest publications.

Rough Guide credits

Text editor: Melissa Graham
Layout: Pradeep Thapliyal
Cartography: Rajesh Mishra
Picture editor: Rhiannon Furbear
Production: Rebecca Short
Proofreader: Amanda Jones
Cover design: Nicole Newman, Dan May
Photographer: Martin Richardson
Editorial: London Andy Turner, Keith Drew, Edward Aves, Alice Park, Lucy White, Jo Kirby, James Smart, Natasha Foges, James Rice, Emma Beatson, Emma Gibbs, Kathryn Lane, Monica Woods, Mani Ramaswamy, Harry Wilson, Alison Roberts, Lara Kavanagh, Eleanor Aldridge, Ian Blenkinsop, Charlotte Melville, Lorna North, Joe Staines, Matthew Milton, Tracy Hopkins; **Delhi** Madhavi Singh, Jalpreen Kaur Chhatwal, Dipika Dasgupta
Design & Pictures: London Scott Stickland, Dan May, Diana Jarvis, Mark Thomas,

Nicole Newman; **Delhi** Umesh Aggarwal, Ajay Verma, Jessica Subramanian, Ankur Guha, Sachin Tanwar, Anita Singh, Nikhil Agarwal, Sachin Gupta
Production: Liz Cherry, Louise Minihane, Erika Pepe
Cartography: London Ed Wright, Katie Lloyd-Jones; **Delhi** Rajesh Chhibber, Ashutosh Bharti, Animesh Pathak, Jasbir Sandhu, Swati Handoo, Deshpal Dabas, Lokamata Sahu
Marketing, Publicity & roughguides.com: Liz Statham
Digital Travel Publisher: Peter Buckley
Reference Director: Andrew Lockett
Operations Coordinator: Becky Doyle
Operations Assistant: Johanna Wurm
Publishing Director (Travel): Clare Currie
Commercial Manager: Gino Magnotta
Managing Director: John Duhigg

Publishing information

This seventh edition published October 2011 by
Rough Guides Ltd,
80 Strand, London WC2R 0RL
11, Community Centre, Panchsheel Park, New Delhi 110017, India
Distributed by the Penguin Group
Penguin Books Ltd,
80 Strand, London WC2R 0RL
Penguin Group (USA)
375 Hudson Street, NY 10014, USA
Penguin Group (Australia)
250 Camberwell Road, Camberwell, Victoria 3124, Australia
Penguin Group (NZ)
67 Apollo Drive, Mairangi Bay, Auckland 1310, New Zealand
Rough Guides is represented in Canada by Tourmaline Editions Inc. 662 King Street West, Suite 304, Toronto, Ontario M5V 1M7

Cover concept by Peter Dyer.

Typeset in Bembo and Helvetica to an original design by Henry Iles.

Printed in Singapore
© Lesley Reader and Lucy Ridout, 2011
Maps © Rough Guides
No part of this book may be reproduced in any form without permission from the publisher except for the quotation of brief passages in reviews.
432pp includes index
A catalogue record for this book is available from the British Library
ISBN: 978-1-40538-135-2
The publishers and authors have done their best to ensure the accuracy and currency of all the information in **The Rough Guide to Bali & Lombok**, however, they can accept no responsibility for any loss, injury, or inconvenience sustained by any traveller as a result of information or advice contained in the guide.
11 12 13 14 8   7   6   5   4   3   2   1

MIX
Paper from responsible sources
FSC
www.fsc.org   FSC™ C018179

Help us update

We've gone to a lot of effort to ensure that the seventh edition of **The Rough Guide to Bali & Lombok** is accurate and up-to-date. However, things change – places get "discovered", opening hours are notoriously fickle, restaurants and rooms raise prices or lower standards. If you feel we've got it wrong or left something out, we'd like to know, and if you can remember the address, the price, the hours, the phone number, so much the better.

Please send your comments with the subject line "**Rough Guide Bali & Lombok Update**" to ✉ mail@uk.roughguides.com. We'll credit all contributions and send a copy of the next edition (or any other Rough Guide if you prefer) for the very best emails.

Find more travel information, connect with fellow travellers and book your trip on ⑭ www.roughguides.com

Acknowledgements

From Lesley, many thanks to everyone who gave so generously of their time, knowledge and hospitality. Special thanks to Wayan Artana and Ketut, Marjan and Wayan, Amanda Spencer, Frank at Pro Surf, Else at Crystal Dive, Ted and Lillen Kruuse-Jensen and Linda vant Hoff. And, as always, to Yau Sang Man.

From Lucy, special thanks to: Barbara and Prihanto, Dewi and Hasan, Elaine and Kamil, Gemma and Made, Jo Green, I Gede Indra Juana Putra, Ketut Lagun, Made Minggir, Made Wijana, Ratu Putra Ratu, Tim and Reece.

Thanks, also, from both authors to Melissa Graham and the staff at Rough Guides.

Readers' letters

Thanks to all the readers who have taken the time to write in with comments and suggestions (and apologies if we've inadvertently omitted or misspelt anyone's name):

Hans-Dieter Amstutz, Steven Bland, Melvin Broekaart, James Bunning, Laura Chapman and Davy Goossens, Tatiana Cutts, Andrew Kirkman, Sarah Tibbatts, Gert-Jan Vernooij and Rosemarie Vos.

ROUGH
GUIDES

Photo credits

All photos © Rough Guides except the following:

Introduction
p.1 Girl in ricefields near Gunung Agung
© Lonely Planet/Superstock
p.6 Barong mask © Wolfgang Kaehler/Superstock
p.7 Fisherman casting his net in the sea
© imagebroker.net/Superstock
p.8 Outrigger boats on Sanur beach
© Robert Harding
p.9 Underwater shot of mola mola and divers
© Photononstop/Superstock
p.10 Munduk Moding Plantation © Munduk
Moding Plantation
p.12 Women carrying offerings © Peter Treanor/
Pictures Colour Library
p.13 Kuta beach © Peter Adams/AWL Images

Things not to miss
01 Gamelan musicians © Tibor Bognar/Alamy
06 Sunrise from Gunung Batur © imagebroker
.net/Superstock
08 Coral reef with fish, soft corals and diver
© Georgette Douwma/Getty Images
09 Traditional Kamasan painting © John
Banagan/Lonely Planet Images/Getty Images
10 Nusa Penida's south coast © Lesley Reader
12 Tanah Lot © FB-Fischer/Superstock
13 Crater lake inside Gunung Rinjani © Michele
Falzone/Getty Images
14 *Sardine* restaurant © Christopher Leggett/
Sardine restaurant
15 Gili Trawangan © Tom Bonaventure/Getty
Images
16 View from *Sari Organik* café, Ubud
© Sang Man
17 Sekumpul Falls © Lucy Ridout
18 *Ritual Flirtation Dance* by Dewa Putu Bedl
© Neka Art Museum
20 Canggu, west Bali © Lonely Planet Images/
Alamy
21 Surfer © Jason Childs/Getty Images
23 Fishermen coming ashore, Pemuteran
© Bill Bachman/Alamy
24 Amed © Lucy Ridout

25 Nusa Lembongan © Philippe Michel/
Superstock
27 Bola Bola, Sekotong © Lucy Ridout
28 Kecak dance © AFP/Getty Images
29 Sidemen © Lucy Ridout
30 South Lombok beach © Neil McAllister/Alamy

Crafts of Bali and Lombok colour section
Close-up of carved stone statue with flower
© Claire Leimbach/Robert Harding World
Imagery/Getty Images
Stonemason's shop near Ubud © Manfred Bail/
Superstock
Carving wood © FK Photo/Corbis
Woman selling batik cloth on beach © Bushnell/
Soifer/Getty Images
Batik detail © Michel Renaudeau/Superstock
Potter, village of Penujak, Lombok © Bruno
Morandi/Getty Images

Volcanoes and ricefields colour section
Temple ceremony at Besakih © Waterfall William/
Photolibrary
Gunung Rinjani and its crater lake © Erick Danzer
/Onasia
Trekking on Gunung Batur © Rob Henderson/
Photolibrary
Pura Ulun Danu Bratan © Peter Hendrie/Getty
Images
Balinese man in foreground working the terraces
© Richard Maschmeyer/Robert Harding

Black and whites
p.72 Surfboards, Kuta Beach © Neil Emmerson/
Robert Harding
p.144 Yoga in Ubud © Simon Marcus/Corbis
p.190 Rice terraces near Tirtagangga
© Hemis.fr/Superstock
p.270 Pura Luhur Batukaru © James London/
Alamy
p.302 Senggigi Beach © Travel Pix Collection/
AWL Images

SMALL PRINT

Index

Map entries are in colour.

I

INDEX

Map symbols

maps are listed in the full index using coloured text

– – – – –	Chapter division boundary		@	Internet access
———	Main road		(i)	Tourist information
═══════	Minor road		(C)	Telephone office
◄——	One-way street		$	International ATM/exchange
▬▬▬	Restricted access/ pedestrianized street		✉	Post office
			⊞	Hospital/clinic
= = =	Unpaved road		P	Parking
- - - - - -	Path		◉	Accommodation
⊞⊞⊞⊞⊞⊞⊞	Steps		▣	Restaurant/bar
———	River		🏊	Swimming
– – – –	Ferry route		🏄	Surf break
⊠—⊠	Gate		⋇	Diving/snorkelling area
) (	Bridge		⊙	Statue
▲	Mountain peak		⛨	Shelter
⌘	Crater		⛳	Golf course
～～	Reef		🌲	Balinese temple
⁂	Waterfall		🏯	Chinese temple
⋀⋀	Spring		🕌	Mosque
⬤	Cave		▬	Building
⬇	Viewpoint		▢	Market
⊤	Lighthouse		▬	Hotel compound
✈	Airport		⊞	Church
★	Bemo stop		▦	Park
◆	Point of interest		▭	Mangrove swamp
～	Boat		▨	Beach
⛽	Fuel station			

So now we've told you about the things not to miss, the best places to stay, the top restaurants, the liveliest bars and the most spectacular sights, it only seems fair to tell you about the best travel insurance around

WorldNomads.com
keep travelling safely

Recommended by Rough Guides